COLLECTED WORKS OF MAHATMA GANDHI

COLLECTED WORKS OF MAHATMA GANDHI

MOHANDAS KARAMCHAND GANDHI

Published by

FacsiMile Publisher
12 Pragati Market
Ashok Vihar, Ph-2
Delhi - 110052, India
Phone: 011-47034999
Email: www.facsimilepublishers.com
info@facsimilepublishers.com

Distribution Network
gyanbooks.com
India, USA, Canada, UK, Australia

ISBN: 978-93-6896-053-9 (PB)

First Published, 1927

2nd Impression 2025

Printed at: Gyan Press, Delhi.

COLLECTED WORKS OF MAHATMA GANDHI
Author: MOHANDAS KARAMCHAND GANDHI

THE COLLECTED WORKS OF MAHATMA GANDHI

XXXIV

(June - September 1927)

AT THE IMPERIAL DAIRY, BANGALORE

(Gandhiji and Malaviyaji with the pedigree cow, Jill)
Vide "Letter to William Smith", 25-6-1927, and Appendix I.

THE COLLECTED WORKS OF
MAHATMA GANDHI

XXXIV

(June - September 1927)

सत्यमेव जयते

THE PUBLICATIONS DIVISION
MINISTRY OF INFORMATION AND BROADCASTING
GOVERNMENT OF INDIA

PREFACE

This volume covers the three months from June 16 to September 15, 1927. Gandhiji had come down to Bangalore after his long stay in Nandi Hills and towards the end of June he began touring Mysore in easy stages. Well pleased with the progress as well as the friendly atmosphere of the State he said in his farewell speech at Bangalore, "More is expected of those who give much. I have found so much good in this State that I almost fancy that if you and the Maharaja together will it, you can make this State *Ramarajya*" (p. 417).

At the end of August he began a tour of Tamilnad, arrived at Madras on September 3 and proceeded south till he reached Mannargudi, East Tanjore, on September 15. In his numerous speeches he spoke as usual of khadi and charkha, of untouchability, of child widows and *Devadasis* and on the duty of municipalities to enforce sanitation. Often while addressing students, he talked about the imperative necessity of Hindus studying the *Gita*.

At the back of every word he uttered and every act he did, there was "a religious consciousness and a downright religious motive" (p. 450). But he recognized nothing as possessing spiritual or moral value "apart from work and action" (p. 451). And he recognized no religion which cannot be reduced to economic terms and no economics which cannot be "reduced to terms of religion or spirituality" (p. 452). In his brilliant tribute to the deep spirituality of C. R. Das, he says: "A time comes in the life of every Indian when mere political battle jars on him and . . . he seeks to base everything on spiritual, livingly moral foundations" (p. 500). Speaking at the Y.M.C.A., Cuddalore, on his own constant striving after perfection, he says: ". . . there is no distinction whatsoever between individual growth and corporate growth . . . The first condition therefore of individual growth is utmost humility." His advice then to students and young people wanting to serve the country and to do big things is: "First of all look after yourselves and make yourselves fairly good instruments of service." This process one has to start with a clean slate, i.e., a pure heart and this purity of the heart can only be achieved through what the Christians call a "new birth". The corresponding term in Hinduism is "to be twice born". This new birth

Gandhiji describes as an "inward change which is unmistakable. . . . It is a transformation of the heart . . . " (pp. 505-6). There is no conflict between *sadhana* and service. According to him, "the progress of the soul can best be achieved through the service of society. Service is the same as *yajna*" (p. 97). Whether it is karma, *bhakti* or *jnana*, Gandhiji is convinced "that the advancement of one promotes the advancement of all, and the fall of one implies the fall of all" (p. 334). Indeed Gandhiji derived spiritual sustenance from contact with fellow-workers. In a farewell speech at Bangalore he explains: "Man is both an individual and a social being. As an individual he may have his prayer during all the waking hours, but as a member of society he has to join in the congregational prayer. I for one may tell you that when I am alone I do have my prayer, but I do feel very lonely without a congregation to share the prayer with me" (p. 418).

All this was for the *sevaks*, not the masses. Poverty being the deep-seated disease and the sole obsession of the masses, he declared: "They will call you and me fiends if we talk about God to them. They know, if they know any God at all, a God of terror, vengeance, a pitiless tyrant" (pp. 453-4).

Hindu-Muslim dissensions weighed heavily on his mind though he spoke little about them. The silence was deliberate and a confession of humiliation which had gone "too deep for words" (p. 3). Though he had more confidence in the political acumen of Motilal Nehru and Jawaharlal Nehru, Gandhiji sponsored the election of Dr. M. A. Ansari as Congress President, because of his hope that he would help to achieve the miracle of Hindu-Muslim unity. In a frank and humorous letter, he counselled Dr. Ansari to tear to pieces his statement suggesting co-operation rather than non-co-operation by Congressmen in the Councils (pp. 304-5). When, however, the statement was published, Gandhiji wrote: "Consistently with your views about the necessity of communal unity, you may not now retire. But . . . I think it would be necessary for you to make a very brief statement making it clear that whilst you adhere to the opinion expressed in your statement, you will not seek to impose that view upon the Congress but that you will confine your own activity solely to the promotion of communal unity" (p. 403).

While in Madras, Gandhiji supported the free-lance agitation for the removal of the Neill statue. But he insisted that the art of satyagraha was to be learned from *Young India* and to be practised on the condition that success, if achieved, should go to the credit of the Congress but failure, if inevitable, should not be allowed to bring discredit to the Congress (p. 469). He claimed to be the keeper of the lighthouse called satyagraha in the otherwise uncharted sea of Indian politics (p. 173).

Those who were nearest to him were the most liable to be harshly criticized. Answering the charge that he was tender to the Christians and Muslims but not to the Hindus, he said that he had no fear of being misunderstood by his own people (p. 537). Not that he spared the Christian Missionaries who undermined instead of strengthening the faith of the people distorting the meaning of "the richest word, God" (p. 260). He advised Hindu reformers to carry on their mission "without cutting themselves off from Hindu society, bearing no malice and with perfect love of the Hindu religion" (p. 33). However, he was far from being a revivalist. While he objected to superficial Europeanization; he refused to believe that the only alternative was "a complete reversion to the ancient Aryan tradition" (p. 315). Not only Hindu society and Hindu religion itself had to change with changing circumstances, but the changes in Western society too when they are for the better should be recognized and made use of. "Wisdom is no monopoly of one continent or one race. . . . I gladly admit that a new power for good is slowly but surely arising in the West" (p. 316). Perhaps the most sustained example of this capacity for self-criticism is the conclusion of the "Drain Inspector's Report", a balanced review of Miss Mayo's malicious attack on the Indian people and on Indian culture. Though convinced that "her case is to perpetuate white domination in India on the plea of India's unfitness to rule herself" (p. 544) and while considering "the book to be unfit to be placed before Americans and Englishmen (for it can do no good to them)", Gandhiji certified that *Mother India* "is a book that every Indian can read with some degree of profit. . . . It is a good thing to see ourselves as others see us" (p. 546).

In an article on "Prohibition" he says, people drink if they are forlorn and uncared for. Those who take to drink "are no more vicious by nature than teetotallers are saints by nature" (p. 489).

As examples of his mastery of English, one may cite his appeal to caste Hindus to "come down from their insolent heights and brother the untouchable" (p. 452) and his reference to the poor sisters of Orissa who are in rags: "But they have not lost all sense of decency, but I assure you we have. We are naked in spite of our clothing, and they are clothed in spite of their nakedness" (p. 454).

Several letters deal with satyagraha within the family circle. To his grandson Kanti, who wished to see his father Harilal, his advice is: "Try to understand what your duty at the present moment is, and act with courage and determination in accordance with that duty. Consider, not what you would like to do, but what you should do. You may show this letter to anyone you may wish to consult" (p. 19).

Approving Raihana Tyabji's decision to give up a dress on which her mother had "lavished so much time and so much love", Gandhiji suggests that all those things would go to her younger sister when "mother is satisfied that you will never be likely to want them" (p. 28). At the same time, the daughter should recognize that when it comes to reducing an abstract right to concrete practice, even considerate and liberal-minded parents do interfere with the independence of their grown-up children. In such a situation the child should realize that some restraint on liberty is demoralizing and some is uplifting. "No restraint is demoralizing which one submits to, not out of fear, selfishness or the like, but out of consideration for, or affection for others" (p. 151). Writing to Kamala Das Gupta, he warns her that the Ashram, which she wishes to join, "is a place for toilers, those who believe in the necessity and the moral value of labouring with their hands and feet" (p. 263). Later he encourages her, saying, "If you are sincere about your desire to go to the Ashram and earnest and yet gentle in your effort, you will certainly bear down the opposition of your parents. Until you can secure the permission of your parents, you can mentally live the Ashram life" (p. 388). An interesting instance of such personal advice is that offered to Mirabehn on the question of segregation during monthly sickness. Using an argument derived from Morley's *On Compromise*, which Mahadev Desai had translated into Gujarati, and referring to St. Paul's advice to his congregation to abstain from meat "if meat offend thy brother", Gandhiji explains: "There are certain things not in themselves immoral which we do for the sake of others and there are certain other things which being in themselves immoral we will not and must not do for the sake of the whole world. If self-imposed segregation appears to you as immoral, you must not do it even to please me. If however there is nothing immoral in it, then you will do it for the sake of your neighbours whom you will rightly consider to be ignorant to that extent" (p. 400).

The series of letters to and about N. R. Malkani illustrate Gandhiji's concern for integrity in those whom he loved. Public events however grave did not shock him as much as a suspected breach of personal integrity. He declares: "Bardoli never disturbed my sleep; but Malkani does" (p. 195).

The letter to Santoji Maharaj is of high philosophical and autobiographical interest revealing as it does Gandhiji's personal and practical approach to the *Gita*. "I have somehow found something for myself by combining all the suggestions" derived from Shankara, Ramanuja, Madhva and others (p. 93). One should evolve one's code of conduct and regulate oneself in strict accordance with the code thus set up by oneself for oneself. Comparisons with "the average man" are totally wrong and "should never be held to justify sinning" (p. 198). That swaraj implies complete self-rule as well as freedom from other-rule is indicated by the recognition that "suicide becomes a duty" on certain occasions (p. 440). "Being moral requires that wherever there is a doubt, we should decide against our own interest" (p. 41).

While sentimentalists waste time and energy looking before and after, Gandhiji, the man of religion, recognizes the wisdom of "one step enough for me". The past and future are to be merged in the present and "the present means our duty at this moment. If we put all our strength into doing our duty, as we know it at this moment, we shall have made the highest human effort. Sorrow springs from dreaming of the future and from lamenting the past. Hence one who concerns himself with the present and does his duty has neither birth nor death" (p. 64). If this is karmayoga in a nutshell, it leads naturally to the attainment of *jnana*, for through the performance of *swadharma* one progressively realizes "the doctrine of oneness of life. . . Realization of the doctrine seems to be impossible unless we could reduce the 'I' in us to a complete cipher" p. (206). The non-violent worker is humbler than the mango tree that bends as it grows up and so becomes a cipher (p. 357). The humility is matched by courage and strength. "Anyone who has the strength to forget the 'I' in him and make himself a cipher can have a glimpse of this universal Soul. . ." (p. 93).

Instead of relying on light from the past, however glorious, the man of religion is content to bask and labour each day in that day's sunlight. To the missionaries who wanted to know how they might spread the glad tidings of the coming of Jesus and his death in redemption of the sins of humanity, Gandhiji replied, ". . . God did not bear the Cross only 1900 years ago, but He bears it today, and He dies and is resurrected from day to day. It would be poor comfort to the world if it had to depend upon a historical God who died 2,000 years ago. Do not then preach the God of history, but show Him as He lives today through you. . . . It is better to allow our lives to speak for us than our words" (pp. 261-2).

NOTE TO THE READER

In reproducing English material, every endeavour has been made to adhere strictly to the original. Obvious typographical errors have been corrected and words abbreviated in the text generally spelt out. Variant spellings of names have, however, been retained as in the original.

Matter in square brackets has been supplied by the Editors. Quoted passages, where these are in English, have been set up in small type and printed with an indent. Indirect reports of speeches and interviews, as also passages which are not by Gandhiji, have been set up in small type. In reports of speeches and interviews slight changes and omissions, where necessary, have been made in passages not attributed to Gandhiji.

While translating from Gujarati and Hindi, efforts have been made to achieve fidelity and also readability in English. Where English translations are available, they have been used with such changes as were necessary to bring them into conformity with the original.

The date of an item has been indicated at the top right-hand corner; if the original is undated, the inferred date is supplied within square brackets, the reasons being given where necessary. The date given at the end of an item alongside the source is that of publication. The writings are placed under the date of publication, except where they carry a date-line or where the date of writing has special significance and is ascertainable.

References to Volume I of this series are to the August 1958 edition. References to *An Autobiography* cite only the Part and Chapter, in view of the varying pagination in different editions.

In the source-line, the symbol S.N. stands for documents available in the Sabarmati Sangrahalaya, Ahmedabad; G.N. refers to those available in the Gandhi Smarak Nidhi and Sangrahalaya, New Delhi; C.W. denotes documents secured by the Collected Works of Mahatma Gandhi.

The Appendices provide background material relevant to the text. A list of sources and a chronology for the period covered by the volume are also provided at the end.

ACKNOWLEDGEMENTS

For material in this volume, we are indebted to the Sabarmati Ashram Preservation and Memorial Trust and Sangrahalaya, the Navajivan Trust and the Gujarat Vidyapith Granthalaya, Ahmedabad; the Gandhi Smarak Nidhi and Sangrahalaya and the National Archives of India, New Delhi; Smt. Radhabehn Choudhri, Calcutta; Shri Narayan Desai, Ahmedabad; Shri Valjibhai Desai, Poona; Shri Kanti Gandhi, Bombay; Smt. Lakshmibehn Khare, Ahmedabad; Smt. Mirabehn, Gaaden, Austria; Shri Parashuram Mehrotra, New Delhi; Shri Ramniklal Modi, Ahmedabad; Smt. Vasumati Pandit, Surat; Shri Mahesh Pattani, Bhavnagar; Smt. Gangabehn Vaidya, Bochasan; Shri S. R. Venkatraman, Servants of India Society, Madras; the Publishers of the books—*Bapuna Patro—Kusumbehn Desaine*, *Bapu—Maine Kya Dekha*, *Kya Samjha*, The Manuscript of Mahadev Desai's Diary; and the following newspapers and journals: *The Bombay Chronicle*, *Hindi Navajivan*, *The Hindu*, *Navajivan*, *The Tribune*, *Sabarmati* and *Young India*.

For research and reference facilities, we owe thanks to the All-India Congress Committee Library, the Indian Council of World Affairs Library, the Research and Reference Division of the Ministry of Information and Broadcasting and Shri Pyarelal Nayyar, New Delhi; and, for assistance in photo-printing documents to the Photo Division of the Ministry of Information and Broadcasting, New Delhi.

CONTENTS

1. LETTER TO GANGU

[After *June 15, 1927*][1]

CHI. GANGU,

Your letter. You write good Hindi. You will soon be avoiding the mistakes you now make.

You should bear no resentment even in your heart against Lakshmibehn for what she said. Doing the *Vatapooja*[2] was as much right for her as not doing it was for you. You have no faith in these things; therefore it would have been useless for you to join; it might have looked like weakness or even hypocrisy. We should have the same tolerance for other people's conduct and beliefs as we may expect from them towards our own.

You need not be unhappy if Chi. Maganlal did not give you the charkha. If you ask him he will surely tell you the reason. Even if we are not satisfied with the explanation, still we must not feel aggrieved. We must not hastily conclude that a person's attitude or act is all wrong just because he himself or the elders cannot give us a satisfactory explanation of it. Only by living in society can we learn to tolerate difference of opinion and the pairs of opposites such as happiness and unhappiness. And as you want to dedicate yourself to service and observe *brahmacharya*, you must fully acquire the qualities of forbearance and tolerance. Mirabehn thinks you need to improve your spinning, ginning, etc. In spinning the thread . . .[3]

Manibehn has been a *brahmacharini* till now, and proposes to remain one and she is making positive efforts towards it. The other has entered married life but is aware of the nobility of *brahmacharya* and endeavours to observe it herself. You must not suppress your feelings just because I write all this. Do write to me whatever you think. I shall try to point out the pitfalls ahead on your way. Take from this whatever you find acceptable and go ahead.

From a microfilm of the Hindi: S.N. 12324

[1] This letter appears to have been written after Gangu left Rewari Ashram for Sabarmati along with Mirabehn in 1927. The *Vatapooja* fell on June 15.

[2] Worship of the banyan tree by married women on the full moon day of *Jyaishtha.*

[3] As in the source

2. *HINDU-MUSLIM UNITY*

When the President of the Congress[1] wired that a unanimous resolution on the Hindu-Muslim question was reached by the All-India Congress Committee[2], I could not enthuse over the information. The wire told me enough about the contents of the resolution. When the President paid me a visit at Nandi[3], he asked me whether I would write on it. I told him I did not think I could write anything helpful. A few days after the visit I got a message from a friend. Its purport was: "You are responsible for the mischief that is going on in our midst. If you had not dragged the Hindus into the Khilafat agitation, the recent tragic events would not have happened. But you alone can now save us."

In translating the message I have softened the bitterness of the language of the original. It seems to me to call for a reiteration of my belief about Hindu-Muslim unity.

I do not repent of my part in the Khilafat agitation. It was a duty I discharged towards my Mussalman countrymen. The Hindus would have been wrong, if they had not helped their brethren in their distress. However ugly the present look of things may be, future generations of Mussalmans will recall with gratitude this great act of friendship on the part of Hindus. But the future apart, as I believe in the proverb that virtue is its own reward, I should always defend my action on the Khilafat question. I therefore received the friend's message of rebuke with perfect calmness.

But I wish I could fulfil his expectations and assist immediately and materially in bringing about peace. For I am just as strong a believer as ever in unity and the necessity for it. If it could be achieved by giving my life, I have the will to give it and I hope I have the strength for it. I should with the greatest joy undertake an indefinite fast, as I very nearly did at Delhi, in 1924,[4] if it would melt and change the stony hearts of Hindus

[1] S. Srinivasa Iyengar

[2] On May 15 and 16, 1927, at Bombay

[3] The reference is to Nandi Hills near Bangalore where Gandhiji was resting from April 19 to June 4 after he had fallen ill on March 26, 1927; *vide* Vol. XXXIII.

[4] From September 17 to October 8; *vide* Vol. XXV.

and Mussalmans. But I have no sign from God within to undertake the penance. If a penance is itself an act of purification, it has also to be preceded by an equal measure of initial purification. I am obviously not pure enough for that supreme penance.

If the reader does not see me now often refer to the question in these pages, it is because the sense of humiliation has gone too deep for words. It matters little to me whether the perpetrators of shameful deeds are Hindus or Mussalmans. It is enough to know that some of us are blaspheming a patient God and doing inhuman deeds in the sacred name of religion. I know too that neither assassination nor fratricidal acts can possibly save religion. Religion worth the name can only be saved by purity, humility and fearlessness of the uttermost type among its professors. It is the only *shuddhi*[1] and only propaganda.

Hence has the resolution of the All-India Congress Committee left me unmoved. For I know that we have not yet changed our hearts. We have not shed fear of one another. Any compromise that is unaccompanied by these two conditions must be a mere make-shift.

Moreover, I feel that any agreement between the component parts of the nation must be voluntary and must remain so for all time. It must not, if it is conceived in terms of swaraj, depend for its final ratification or enforcement upon a legal enactment. Ratification by our respective organizations must be held to be final and binding. Enforcement must depend upon the honour of the leaders of respective parties and ultimately, in the absence of reliance on non-violence, on the arbitrament of civil war fought decently or indecently as the case may be. It is a sign of weakness, not of fitness for swaraj to go to the foreign ruling power to arbitrate between us or to enforce the peace between us at the point of the bayonet.

If we the so-called leaders have no control over our fighting elements, our agreement must be held to be unreal and useless. Before we think of real swaraj, we must gain control over the masses. We must learn to behave ourselves. The agreement had no effect on Delhi, and to our eternal shame the Government has been the keeper of the peace on Bakr Id.

My creed of non-violence is an extremely active force. It has no room for cowardice or even weakness. There is hope for a violent man to be some day non-violent, but there is none for a coward. I have therefore said more than once in these pages

[1] Reconversion to Hinduism; literally, 'purification'

that if we do not know how to defend ourselves, our women and our places of worship by the force of suffering, i.e., non-violence, we must, if we are men, be at least able to defend all these by fighting. It is unmanly to ask or expect the Government to ensure the peace between rival parties or to defend our women against ourselves. And while we remain so unmanly it is hopeless to expect swaraj. In well-ordered societies, governments merely undertake the police work. But the recent elaborate preparations at Delhi or Lahore were no part of police work. Differences we shall always have. But we must learn to settle them all, whether religious or other, by arbitration. Before the rulers we must be able to present a united front and demonstrate to the world our capacity for regulating our own manners if we would have swaraj.

If, however, we have no leaders whom we can elect as arbitrators who would give wise and impartial decisions, or, if we are too unruly and barbarous to wait for and abide by decisions of arbitrators of our choice, we must fight till we are exhausted and come to our senses. The Government will no doubt always intervene, whether we will or no, either to keep the public peace or to preserve its own safety. But it will weaken us the least, if the rival factions will courageously and straightforwardly refrain from courting the protection or assistance of Government. Why should a murderer in such warfare be defended? Let him seek the gallows. Let breakers of places of worship come forth boldly and say, we have done this for the sake of religion, punish us if you like! Let those who kill innocent passers-by deliver themselves to the police and say, we have done it all for God's sake! All this may read heartless. But I have merely endeavoured to suggest a way that is straighter and less weak than the one we have hitherto adopted.

And if we cannot, after the manner of civilized men, resort to voluntary arbitration or, after the manner of brave barbarous races, fight out differences without seeking the intervention of British justice or bayonets, all we may expect to get in the shape of reforms is an increased agent's share in the bureaucratic Government; in other words, an increasing share in the exploitation of the dumb millions. Let us take care that any agreement we may come to does not reduce us to that unenviable condition.

Young India, 16-6-1927

3. NOTES

Sardar Kharak Singh

It must be a matter of joy to every patriot to find Sardar Kharak Singh once more free to take up national work outside the prison walls. By his indomitable will and refusal to bend himself to authority in order to gain his freedom he has risen in the estimation of his countrymen. May he have long years of service to the country in its fight for freedom.

Have I Boycotted Andhra?

When Deshabhakta Konda Venkatappayya saw me at Nandi and again at Bangalore, he told me that as Andhra was not on the tour list for the year, many Andhra friends had enquired of him whether I had boycotted Andhra. My old love of the Andhra people and the happy memories of my connection with them will not let me boycott Andhra, even if I wish to, though some of the Andhra workers do sometimes vex one into wishing to boycott the province till they set themselves right. They are fine men. They have got the patriotic spirit. But some of them are workers only so-called. They are all leaders and when everybody wants to lead there is nobody to serve, no one to obey and in the exercise of that false independence the people are neglected. I hope the workers to whom these remarks may apply will not say to themselves or to me that they are no worse than other provinces. It would be a wrong way of looking at the right thing. After all Andhra men and women who at one time gave promise of being the first in the field for real civil disobedience must not be satisfied with being as bad as the rest. Those who seek to compete for civil disobedience have to prove their capacity for exemplary obedience, restraint and discipline. Andhra, which might have easily been first in khadi and every one of its departments, has yet to come up to the mark. But I must not exhaust the whole of my battery of criticism. I must reserve it for my forthcoming visit, as I had never given up the idea of visiting Andhradesh. As a suitable month could not be set apart this year, the idea was to reserve Andhra for next year unless I could give it, as it was then thought, the first fortnight of December. God has however upset all my plan and the whole of the programme for the second half of this year has been dislocated. And if I am at all fit and well and there is no accident I would like to be in Andhradesh not for a few days but for a month or two next year. I have therefore told Konda Venkatappayya that if the people will still have me, I would like to visit Andhra early next year and combine rest with work. I must not be expected to rush through space and programmes as before. Let the workers also realize that I shall be devoting the stay in Andhra to khadi work alone.

Untouchability work is no doubt part of my being. But that work is largely included in khadi work. For, it is designed to level up those who occupy the lowest rung of the ladder with those who are at the top. It is the cotton thread which beginning in the humblest cottage of India and reaching the highest in the land can alone indissolubly bind the two and make them feel akin. I know that the Andhra workers are very ambitious. Let their ambition percolate down to the lowest stratum of society and all will be well.

A Welcome Step

A correspondent from Holakere in Mysore writes:

> I am highly glad to inform you that the people belonging to Lambani community of my taluk have completely abstained from drinking toddy and other liquors since a month and a half. It was in the Lambani Conference held in this town at the end of last April that they had taken an oath not to touch any liquor, prostrating themselves before the evening sun. Since then they have not swerved from their oath. If anyone of that community is seen near a toddy shop, he is strictly dealt with by the *Naik*, *Yajaman* and *Karabhan* of that hamlet. Their women carry to us every day the glad news, there are no broils at their hovel and that they lead a very peaceful life. This is an instance to show that your movement of purification had entered our State even before your entering it.

I congratulate the Lambani community upon the great step they have taken, and hope that they will not slide back like many who did so after the exultation of 1921 had subsided. Let me invite the attention of the leaders of the community to the case recorded in these pages[1] of the Raniparaj[2] people of whom those abstainers who took to the charkha as a means of occupying their time and attention not only had no hankering after liquor

[1] In *Young India*, 26-5-1927, under the title "Among Raniparaj People"

[2] Literally, 'hill-people' as renamed by Gandhiji; formerly known as Kaliparaj, which meant 'black people'.

but were able to double their savings. For, they not only saved what was spent upon the drink but they also added to their income by saving in the cost of clothing. It is the universal experience of temperance reformers that if the people who take pledges do not usefully occupy their time, the hankering returns and it becomes too strong to resist the temptation. I hope too that other villages will follow the example of Holakere and that when I am enabled to begin my tour in Mysore, I shall receive, side by side with glowing accounts which I have been promised of the progress of khadi, accounts also of eradication of the drink habit.

Young India, 16-6-1927

4. *RANIPARAJ INQUIRY COMMITTEE*

Sjt. Vallabhbhai Patel has lost no time in embarking upon the work of the Committee that was only recently appointed at the Raniparaj Conference[1]. The following extracts[2] from the interim report of the second tour of the Committee will be read with interest:

The Committee visited eighteen villages recording statements of witnesses from 47 villages in the Chikhli and Bulsar Talukas and is in the State of Bansda. It reflects credit upon the Bansda State that the Committee is able to give a glowing account of the interest that the Maharaja Saheb of Bansda is taking in his people. But all the good that is undoubtedly being done by His Highness to his people is really undone so long as he considers it necessary to derive an income from the drink traffic. No doubt the fact that the three neighbours adjacent to the Bansda territory, that is, the British, the Gaekwad and Dharampur have no prohibition makes it difficult for Bansda to carry out the policy of successful prohibition. But great things can not be done without great sacrifice and great measures. Bansda can not only lead the way by declaring out and out prohibition, but can then agitate for prohibition in the neighbouring States. The chief thing is to be prepared to sacrifice the drink revenue. An immediate beginning can be made by deciding not to use that revenue for any purpose, however laudable it may be, save for that of carrying on an in-

[1] Held on March 16, 1927; *vide* Vol. XXXIII.

[2] Not reproduced here

tensive anti-drink propaganda amongst the tribes given to drink. For, there is no doubt that any State that seriously wants its people to give up the evil habit cannot be satisfied merely with making it legally impossible to indulge in the evil habit, but to find out the cause of the habit and to educate the people to give it up. In the end, no State need suffer by depriving itself of the drink revenue. The inevitable outcome of any policy of prohibition carried out side by side with constructive work of the nature suggested by me must result in an ever increasing prosperity of the people and therefore of the State. India is the most promising country in the world for carrying out total prohibition for the simple reason that addiction to drink is not considered respectable or fashionable and is confined only to a certain class of people.

Young India, 16-6-1927

5. *LETTER TO SONJA SCHLESIN*

KUMARA PARK, BANGALORE,
June 16, 1927

DEAR MISS SCHLESIN[1],

Here is a letter from Dr. Jones[2] which perhaps you would like.

I hope you had my long letter[3], and I do hope also that you will make it a point to see Mr. Sastri[4]. When are you coming here? I wish you could also go to Phœnix and see Manilal and his wife.

Yours sincerely,

MISS SCHLESIN
POST BOX NO. 2284
JOHANNESBURG

From a photostat: S.N. 12360

[1] A Jewish girl who was Gandhiji's private secretary for many years in South Africa

[2] Stanley Jones

[3] Dated May 22, 1927; *vide* Vol. XXXIII.

[4] V. S. Srinivasa Sastri, Agent-General of India in South Africa

6. LETTER TO W. B. STOVER

ASHRAM, SABARMATI,[1]
June 16, 1927

DEAR FRIEND,

I thank you for your letter[2]. Your suggestion[3] is undoubtedly interesting. But I do not understand why you fall foul of the charkha which the millions can easily take up; whereas your suggestion requires technical knowledge and character at its back. Your friends of the West have made a god of literacy. I wonder what Jesus, whom you call the "Lord Christ", would say if he came in flesh and saw the people of the West crazy over a knowledge of letters, wealth and passing the best part of their time and life in seeking happiness from the external. Supposing that every person of education gave mechanically half an hour to teaching every untouchable, of what avail will it be to him or to the untouchables? And why are you so much enamoured of the material progress of Japan?[4] I do not know whether the material has gone side by side with the moral progress. I have no wish to judge the Japanese. I have not even the data for doing so even if I wished. But neither literacy nor wealth without the moral backing has any attraction for me. And do you know why I swear by the charkha? I do so because not merely the untouchables but millions of other people in India are starving because they have no work and because now they have even become too lazy to work. I am therefore presenting the charkha to the starving millions as there is no other simple productive work which can be presented to the millions; and I present it to the educated and the well-to-do people of India as an example for the rest.

I have the highest regard for my missionary friends, and that very regard makes me warn them in season and out of season

[1] Permanent address

[2] Dated May 2, 1927

[3] W. B. Stover had written: "I suggest that instead of the charkha every day, you set the example and put the challenge to all of educated India, to choose someone of illiterate India, and spend a half hour a day in teaching this illiterate person. I would suggest that the teacher and the one taught be of different castes. This idea carried to any great extent throughout the land would bring almost a revolution in the thinking of the people."

[4] Stover had written: "Japan has attained the highest literacy."

against misinterpreting the message of the Bible. You tell me, "you have taken the Lord Christ for your leader and guide. There is none better." You do not mind my correcting you. I regard Jesus as a human being like the rest of the teachers of the world. As such He was undoubtedly great. But I do not by any means regard him to have been the very best. The acknowledgment of the debt which I have so often repeated that I owe to the Sermon on the Mount should not be mistaken to mean an acknowledgment of the orthodox interpretation of the Bible, or the life of Jesus. I must not sail under false colours.

Your letter is sincere and I felt that I could not better reciprocate your sincerity than by putting before you frankly my position.

Yours sincerely,
M. K. GANDHI

W. B. STOVER, ESQ.
MOUNT MORRIS
ILLINOIS, U.S.A.

From a photostat: S.N. 12521

7. LETTER TO DR. M. S. KELKAR

KUMARA PARK, BANGALORE,
June 16, 1927

DEAR DOCTOR,

I see that the mental distance between you and me is really growing. I can sympathize neither your salic [*sic*] in astrology nor in black magic. They may both be substantial sciences; but they are sciences which I think we should avoid. As a matter of fact I do not attach so much value to things pertaining to the body as the wish to exhaust every available means for sustaining[1] the body or for keeping it in order as it has only a very limited importance in the scheme of life. I apply also equally limited means and therefore continually exclude those means which may seem to me to be of doubtful moral value. So then, if I err at all, I shall err on the right side. Excess care of the body and explorations into astrology—and what not—for the sake of that care-taking means going further away from his Maker, and seems

[1] The source has "subsisting".

like putting the shadow before the substance. I would not trouble you to travel with me.

Doctors here consider that 150 is normal blood-pressure for me and they have no misgivings whatsoever about my being able to resume moderate touring next month. I am certainly getting daily stronger physically.

Yours sincerely,

DR. M. S. KELKAR
C/o J. G. GADRE
NEW BHAT WADI
BOMBAY 4

From a photostat: S.N. 14157

8. LETTER TO A. A. PAUL

KUMARA PARK, BANGALORE,
June 16, 1927

DEAR FRIEND,

I have your letter and the pamphlet which I know I shall be interested to read.

I do not know when I shall be in Madras, I hardly think on the 23rd of July. But in any case I do not know whether I shall have gained sufficient strength during the year to conduct the retreat for hours' length as I was expected in the programme you had sent me before the breakdown in my health. The whole of the Southern tour is undergoing a radical transformation. I do not think Mr. Rajagopalachari has yet been able to reshape it.

Yours sincerely,

A. A. PAUL, ESQ.
7, MILLER ROAD
KILPAUK, MADRAS

From a microfilm: S.N. 14158

9. *LETTER TO MANECKBAI BAHADURJI*

KUMARA PARK, BANGALORE,
June 16, 1927

I have your letter. Do please continue to write giving me all the titbits of Panchgani, of your own beautiful nest, telling me all about the birds that come and go.

Bangalore is the finest and cleanest place I have seen as yet in India. I have no doubt, it too has its dark corners. But I have not seen them as yet. And I suppose I shall not be able to see them either, because I am taken for my walks only to beautiful places. And its climate at least at this time of the year is certainly glorious. It is cool and yet not too cold. Its flowers also are very beautiful and various.

Yours sincerely,

MRS. MANECKBAI BAHADURJI
OOMRA HALL
PANCHGANI

From a photostat: S.N. 14159

10. *LETTER TO A. RANGASWAMI IYENGAR*

KUMARA PARK, BANGALORE,
June 16, 1927

MY DEAR RANGASWAMI,

I have your letter enclosing extract from the Rev. Mr. Holmes' letter for which I thank you.

I have also your letter about the forthcoming special meeting of the All-India Congress Committee. I do not suppose you expect me to take any notice of this letter. I presume it is a multiplex copy sent *pro forma* to all the members of the Working Committee.

Yours sincerely,

SJT. A. RANGASWAMI IYENGAR
DESHBANDHU BUILDINGS
MOUNT ROAD
MADRAS

From a microfilm: S.N. 14160

11. LETTER TO R. B. GREGG

KUMARA PARK, BANGALORE,
June 16, 1927

MY DEAR GOVIND,

I have your letter. Of course I can agree with every word of what you have said about typewriters and typists. There is nothing inconsistent between your letter and my presentation. I simply told[1] you why there had been seeming indifference about getting the very best typists.

But the advertisement idea does not commend itself to me. We have so many limitations that people who know us will not care to apply, and if strangers in search of employment but not knowing what we are do apply, it would be a waste of time for them and us to trouble them. I am writing this from bitter experience. But I again entirely agree with you that there is certainly within limitations scope for educated Indians to find themselves in khadi work. And that process is gradually going on. There is much more that I can write on this subject. But it is unnecessary to tax you on details. I was long with my previous letter because I was anxious to discuss some principles.

I am entirely at one with you that Maganlalji should have all the assistance he needs and that whatever assistance we take should be of the best type available; and if I felt that advertising in the manner you suggest would do it, I should go in for it. And, in any case, Maganlal can certainly advertise. There is no principle at stake, nor is there any question of much expense.

I know that you never implied that there was anything wrong in handling human excreta and I also know that you yourself did the thing yourself in the Ashram. What I told you was that the untouchables themselves would feel as I suggested. That would be wrong I know. But I simply mentioned the difficulty. They will take up the kind of work you suggest only after some of us have done, and done it successfully.

I don't know whether it was your prompting or not, but I have got a new edition of Dr. Kellogg's book on diet. It is a big volume and it is lying in front of me. It is enough to make one giddy even to contemplate reading that volume especially

[1] In letter dated May 27, 1927; *vide* Vol. XXXIII.

when I have mortgaged every available minute for the work I have on hand and which I feel I must do. I shall therefore profit more by the correspondence lessons that you are giving me out of your experience on dieting than by reading the big book.

The new shorthand idea appeals to me. And if someone at the Ashram will go in for it, I would not mind spending the money. You will therefore press the suggestion on the people at the Ashram.

With love to you all,

Yours,

R. B. GREGG, ESQ.
C/o S. E. STOKES, ESQ.
KOTGARH
SIMLA HILLS

From a photostat: S.N. 14161

12. LETTER TO MIRZA M. ISMAIL

KUMARA PARK, BANGALORE,
June 16, 1927

DEAR FRIEND,

I esteem your letter enclosing copy of your address to the Mysore Representative Assembly. I shall go through the whole of it as soon as I get a few moments. But I have already gone through the portion kindly marked by you referring to the untouchables. It gave me great joy.

I had also your letter about the birthday greetings.

I hope to be able to visit Mysore before the 15th of next month and pay my respects to the Maharaja Saheb.

Yours sincerely,

MIRZA M. ISMAIL, ESQ.
'LAKE VIEW'
MYSORE

[PS.]

I now learn that the marking was done here.

M. K. G.

From a photostat: S.N. 14162

13. *LETTER TO DR. B. S. MOONJE*

KUMARA PARK, BANGALORE,
June 16, 1927

DEAR DR. MOONJE,

I am sincerely sorry for having given you offence. I was certainly not unbalanced when I wrote to you. I have really believed that it was part of your philosophy to beat an opponent in views with any stick that came your way. Indeed I can give you names of those who have valiantly defended that philosophy. But I shall not argue with you. If we meet, I shall give you chapter and verse for the belief I have held about you. But of course I like your energetic contradiction. For I can only like repudiation of a philosophy which I have considered to be morally indefensible and utterly false. Only my philosophy has room for holding in respect those who have a false philosophy but who do not know that it is false. You have quoted Jamnalalji in your support. I hardly think he will assist you. But I will preserve your letter and ask him about it.

Now for your question. I have certainly said that untouchability as practised today in Hinduism is the darkest blot on it. But that is different from saying that it is part of Hindu religion as you have made me say. For you will find in my writings an emphatic statement to the effect that untouchability is no part of Hindu religion, and that if it was, I should renounce Hinduism. Indeed, you will find in the cutting you have sent me the following sentence: "I find no authority whatsoever in Hinduism for treating any portion of the human family as untouchable." I have called it an excrescence.

Yours sincerely,

DR. B. S. MOONJE
NAGPUR CITY

From a photostat: S.N. 14616

14. LETTER TO KUVALAYANAND[1]

KUMARA PARK, BANGALORE
June 17, 1927

DEAR FRIEND,

I now understand all you say about the abdominal massage and massage of the heart. Of course it has been continued ever since I wrote to you. I simply wanted to clear what I did not understand. I have told you that in the physical application of these exercises, I propose to go by faith in you. Whilst I shall present my doubts to you so long as I do not understand your explanations, they shall be final for me.

I want to give the practice of these yogic exercises a full trial, if only because I regard them of all the methods of medical treatment to be the freest from danger.

After I wrote my letter[2] of the 8th, I took a forward step which I hope you would not consider hasty. On re-reading your notes, I saw that you expected me to go up to 30 degrees angle. So, after writing to you, I immediately broadened the angle but limited the duration to five minutes in accordance with the instructions. But I have my own doubts as to the angle being 30, because I have not yet secured an accurate measuring instrument. Not being satisfied with the raising of the cot, I looked about for a plank which I have now secured. The cot has a wooden surface. I spread on it not a mattress but a padded rug, and I take the *sarvangasan* on it with the help of the board. It is now infinitely better than the previous exercises. Mahadev has been measuring the thing, and he thinks that the angle at which I take it is nearer to 50 than 30. I am not satisfied that it is anything like 50. Be that as it may. I am feeling no discomfort. Today will be the 4th day, and the duration is only five minutes. Blood-pressure is taken every Sunday, and if I find that the pressure has at all gone up, I shall ascribe the rising to the angle and drop the exercise till I hear from you in reply to this. And I shall drop it, in any case, if you think that I have gone too far.

There is another passive exercise which I have been taking, not very regularly but fairly regularly, which I used to take when

[1] In reply to his letter dated June 14

[2] *Vide* Vol. XXXIII.

I was convalescing after dysentery and when I was physically much weaker than I am today. And it is to raise the legs at right angles to the trunk and keep them for two or three minutes there; that is for removing any fatigue there may be after the walk; and then, I have the legs in that straight condition bent as much as can be bent without any strain whatsoever towards the head, whilst the trunk is lying on the bed. This I take to strengthen the muscular exercise for the abdomen. I think I even mentioned to you that this was given to me by Dr. Kelkar whom, I understand, you know. And he has been writing to me to press that exercise on me. Both these things, keeping the legs straight and at right angles to the trunk and gently bending the legs towards the head seem to me to do good. There is no fatigue left and there is felt after the bending exercise a forward movement about the bowels.

I am still not taking tepid water and salt in the morning; for, the enema continues and I am now able to retain the water for half an hour. But I do take a tumbler full of water by the nose. Less than half of the quantity is spilt in the process of drinking through the nose. So I think about four ounces of cool water I take in this way just after the mouth wash.

The walking exercise in the morning and in the evening continues, 40 minutes each time. But the distance covered is greater than when I began after coming to Bangalore. It is nothing less than two miles every time.

I have not yet dared to go beyond two teaspoonfuls of melted butter. Milk has been increased, I think I told you, from 30 to 40 ounces and *bhakhari*[1] or oatmeal two ounces remain.

I enclose your original notes which you need not return because I shall remember the contents. You will please send me any further instructions you may think desirable.

Yours sincerely,

SRIMUT KUVALAYANANDJI
KUNJAVANA
LONAVLA

From a photostat: G.N. 5048; also S.N. 12596

[1] Thick cake prepared from wheat flour

15. LETTER TO KANTI GANDHI

BANGALORE,
Jeth Vad 2 [June 17, 1927]

CHI. KANTI,

I got your letter. You want my permission to go and see Chi. Harilal. A son need not seek his grandfather's permission to see his father. No one can stand in the way of a son's wishes. You have now come of age, and that is another reason why there should be no question of my giving you permission.

All I can do is to explain to you your responsibility, and this is my advice in regard to your seeing Chi. Harilal. I believe he is at present following a wrong path. He leads an immoral life. He has become an addict. He has forgotten his dharma, and, therefore, he is not fit to exercise his right as a father. I regard him as suffering from a kind of disease. His disease is not physical but spiritual, and spiritual disease is more dreadful than a physical ailment. It is not, therefore, your duty to go to him to comfort him; on the contrary, it is your duty to keep away from him. You, I and his friends and well-wishers should employ spiritual non-co-operation against him. If you have intended to go to him to reform him I regard your idea as worthy of support, and in that case I would facilitate your going. But just now it seems that you wish to go because of that letter. I feel, therefore, that your going to him will mean your encouraging him in his intention. Moreover, if you wish to go to him in order to reform him, you are not yet, from a practical point of view, fit and sufficiently mature to undertake such a task. From that point of view, you are yet a child. You are still studying. It is my desire, and also my effort to see that as you study, you should so develop your soul that you may acquire the power to do what I could not in regard to Harilal, and you should so impress him that the moment he sees you he would abjure his evil habits. I have been bringing up both you brothers with that aim in view. If you have the capacity, you will be able to benefit from such education. I would, therefore, advise you to write to Harilal and tell him firmly that until he gives up his addictions and his immoral life and is able to support you all, or until you are able by the power of your *tapascharya*[1] to awaken him from his slumber, you cannot go and see him. I do not, however, insist that you should forthwith accept my advice. So far, Harilal used to admit his weaknesses, and has been saying that he would try to shake them off; but now he has started writing letters against me in the papers. I have not seen those letters, but I know their purport. Harilal says that it is I who have forsaken my dharma, not he, and that I have been propagating the Buddhist faith. And he holds that such propaganda is harmful to people's welfare and, therefore, regards it as an evil. His rebellion, he says, is against that evil. And he intends to take you brothers away from under my undesirable influence at the first opportunity. As such are his views, you are likely to be assailed by doubts. If you have the slightest doubt whether my ideas are right or Harilal's, I think you should not be led away by my ideas. Hence this is my further advice to you that you should humbly consult the teachers under whom you have studied or those among the elders with whom you have come in contact in the Ashram and who command your confidence. Put all your problems before them and act as they advise. If you ask me to solve your problems, I too will help. The *Gita* which all of us study daily, which you have been learning by heart and trying to understand with great devotion, says that we should get our problems solved with the help of those whom we regard as our elders by earnestly questioning them with humility. We should have faith in them, accept what they say as true and act accordingly. I wish, and I advise you, that you should do what I have suggested. Do not reach a hasty decision. Do not act with childish immaturity. Try to understand what your duty at the present moment is, and act with courage and determination in accordance with that duty. Consider, not what you would like to do, but what you should do. You may show this letter to anyone you may wish to consult. I shall wait for your reply. Let me know how both of you are.

Blessings from

BAPU

From a copy of the Gujarati: C.W. 7703. Courtesy: Kanti Gandhi

[1] Self-suffering as moral discipline

16. *LETTER TO SATIS CHANDRA DAS GUPTA*

KUMARA PARK, BANGALORE,
June 18, 1927

DEAR SATIS BABU,

I have your letter. If you can at all bear the strain of travelling, the weather here should suit you remarkably for, it is superb at this time of the year. But you must not undergo any strain or risk. You should come only if the doctor advises.

I am glad everything is now being removed to Sodepur. Let the boys go to Wardha by all means. But the distance to Ahmedabad need not put them off, if they will be happier at Sabarmati, as perhaps they are likely to be. Wardha has not the convenience that Sabarmati in some respects has, especially when Jamnalalji is not there as he will not be now for some time.

With love to you all,

Yours,
BAPU

SJT. SATIS CHANDRA DAS GUPTA
HOME VILLA
GIRIDIH

From a photostat: G.N. 1574

17. *LETTER TO MANORAMA DEVI*

KUMARA PARK, BANGALORE,
June 18, 1927

DEAR FRIEND,

I have your pathetic letter. It is evident it is not written by yourself. As you seem to know some English you may write to me in your own English whatever you like; better still write in Bengali. I don't understand it myself, but I have Bengali assistants here permanently with me. And tell me what your age is; what you propose to do with your parents? Have you their consent to leave them? Are you keeping good health? Will you travel alone if permission is given to you to come to the Ashram? Do you know Sjt. Gopabandhu Das? And if you do, will you please see him and let him write to me? And even if you do not know him, will you make it a point to see him? He is well known in Orissa. He is President of the Congress Committee and he was at one time member of the Legislative Council. He is to be found either at Cuttack or at Puri. Who is your friend who has written the letter for you? I would like to help you. But before I know how I can help you, it is necessary for me to have all the particulars.

Yours sincerely,

SRIMATI MANORAMA DEVI
CHANDISAHI
CUTTACK (ORISSA)

From a photostat: S.N. 12578

18. LETTER TO FIROZA P. S. TALEYARKHAN

KUMARA PARK, BANGALORE,
June 18, 1927

Your note was received last night; but it was handed to me only just now. I am sorry you have been laid up. I was wondering why you had not come in as you had intended to do. Of course I shall be delighted to see you whenever you come. And do please bring Lady Banerjee with you. Of course you know the hour and you won't mind if there are other visitors sitting or coming in at the time. Then you could come any day without notice. But please do not strain yourself to come if you are at all unwell. I shan't misunderstand your not coming. We are both convalescing and, in any case, now that I know who you are there need be no formality whatsoever.

Yours sincerely,

SHRIMATI FIROZA P. S. TALEYARKHAN
3, RESIDENCY ROAD
BANGALORE

From a photostat: S.N. 14163

19. *LETTER TO PRINCIPAL, SANGLI INDUSTRIAL AND AGRICULTURAL SCHOOL*

KUMARA PARK, BANGALORE,
June 18, 1927

DEAR FRIEND,

I thank you for your very full letter. Only one further inquiry I would esteem it a favour if you would answer. Is there any difference in the ratio of nutrition between fertilized and sterile eggs? In your school, do you also teach cattle-breeding and dairying?

Yours sincerely,

THE PRINCIPAL
SANGLI INDUSTRIAL AND AGRICULTURAL SCHOOL
SANGLI

From a photostat: S.N. 14164

20. *QUARRELLING IN THE NAME OF RELIGION*

A gentleman has sent me newspaper cuttings regarding the dispute which occurred in Udaipur State between Shwetambars[1] and Digambars[2] and suggested that I should go through them and give my opinion about it. For one thing, in my present state of health I cannot spare enough time to read so many newspapers carefully, and, even if I had the necessary time and energy, it is not my practice to form an opinion on any matter—no one should, I believe—from what one reads in the papers. I, therefore, do not know which party is at fault, or more at fault. However, I shall express the thoughts which occurred to me after a fairly close reading of the cuttings.

The language of the writers indicates their partisan spirit. Each side blames the other and considers itself innocent.

I found no essential differences between this dispute and the writings about it, on the one hand, and the Hindu-Muslim quarrel and the writings about it on the other. There is more bitterness

[1] & [2] Sects of Jains

in the latter and the language of the writings is more venomous, but the difference is only one of degree.

The fact is that we have forgotten the very meaning of religion. Everyone fights to prove that his own view is the right one. There is no trace of any desire to understand what religion means, in what it consists, by what marks it can be recognized, and how it can be preserved.

We have a right to expect more wisdom from the Jains; they are votaries of *syadvada*[1] and claim themselves to be the only followers of the path of compassion. They should display tolerance; that is, be liberal towards others who hold different views. We should know that other people will be attached to what they regard as truth quite as much as we will to what we regard as truth. Even when we feel that our opponent is at fault, we should not get angry with him but should act towards him with charity.

As I read these articles, however, I felt that even in Jain homes and temples texts of *syadvada* and compassion merely decorate old books and have no other significance. I realize this in experience again and again. Where the doctrine of compassion is followed in action, it seems to be limited to feeding ants and preventing people from catching fish. I have also observed that if, in displaying compassion in this manner, cruelty is shown to human beings, that is regarded as dharma.

Raychandbhai often said that when Jainism was embraced by Vanias[2], it was interpreted in a Vania spirit, and knowledge and courage, which should be the signs of compassion, vanished almost completely; compassion became synonymous with cowardice and thus came to be despised.

Moreover, dharma and wealth are eternal enemies; but the Goddess Lakshmi took up her abode in Jain temples and the result was that religious issues, instead of being solved through *tapascharya*, came to be settled in courts of law through argument by lawyers. That is, those who could pay more could get a point of religious principle interpreted in their favour.

This picture may appear somewhat exaggerated, but it is not so. I know the Jains. I know them and the principles of their religion as intimately as I do Vaishnavism and Vaishnavas. Some in their anger believe me to be a Jain. Others in their love wish that I should become a Jain. Some Jains are pleased by my partiality for a few members of their community. I have learnt

[1] The doctrine of the plurality of truth

[2] Members of a community traditionally engaged in business and commerce

much from their books. My contact with many Jain friends has helped me much. All this has prompted me to write what I have done above and thereby awaken those Jains who love their religion.

Why should there be hatred between Shwetambars and Digambars ? Their religious principles are the same. The few differences which exist are easy enough to tolerate. They are such as can be resolved to the satisfaction of both parties, like the differences between the followers of the *advaita*[1] and the *dvaita*[2] doctrines.

There are numerous monks and nuns among Jains, and they have plenty of spare time. Why should they not engage themselves in real *tapascharya* ? Why should they not acquire the highest knowledge? Why should they not seek to impart to others the benefit of their experience?

Jain youths seem to be engrossed in earning wealth like their elders. Why should they not, though living the life of householders, become like *tapasvis*[3], generous-hearted and the very embodiment of the purest spirit of compassion?

I was asked to give my opinion about the Palitana[4] affairs, and now I am asked my opinion about the sorry dispute in Udaipur. The correspondents on this occasion, too, are young friends. This time I have given an opinion which probably they never expected. I do not distinguish between Hindus and Jains. I can establish the unity of Hinduism, that is, the Vedic doctrine, with Jainism, with the help of *syadvada* itself. For myself personally, I established long ago the unity of all religions with its help. The dispute between Shwetambars and Digambars cannot be settled through newspapers nor in a court of law. Both parties should atone for their errors and purify themselves, or one party should do that on behalf of both. Those who cannot do even this should stop talking about religion, be humble and keep silent.

[From Gujarati]

Navajivan, 19-6-1927

[1] Identity of the individual self with the universal Self

[2] Separateness of the individual self from the universal Self

[3] Those who practise *tapascharya*

[4] A Jain centre of pilgrimage in Saurashtra

21. *SWADESHI* v. *FOREIGN*

A friend from Kathiawar writes as follows:[1]

Many readers will immediately see the fallacies in this letter. Even so, since one often hears similar views expressed by others, it is necessary to explain again the meaning of swadeshi as clearly as one can. Moreover, we suffer a great deal through an abuse of the idea of swadeshi. If many of the activities which are being carried on in the name of swadeshi were stopped and the effort spent on true swadeshi, we should achieve our goal much earlier.

I am sure that I have become more and not less scrupulous in following the vow of swadeshi. I have been following it, as I had conceived it in 1920, and am following it even more scrupulously today. We may certainly accept a foreign needle, since it is a useful article and can be assimilated. By accepting it, we harm no industry or craft in the country and its acceptance, therefore, does not throw anyone out of employment. On the contrary, the needle provides work to hundreds, work which benefits the country. Foreign cloth may be good in quality, and cheaper, may even be offered free; even then, it should be rejected, for its acceptance has ruined crores of our countrymen. We had been producing cloth in our own villages, and have found no other work in place of that industry. We committed a great sin in abandoning it. Its abandonment resulted in starvation, and that led to an increase in disease, crime and immorality. If ever the time comes when the people of this country will have another, more honest occupation [than spinning and weaving] and when the cotton cannot be grown on the soil of this land or when the cultivators themselves will prefer to grow another, more profitable crop, then the vow of swadeshi cloth may serve no useful purpose. If future generations, reading the literature of this age, regard this vow as an immutable principle and even at that time apply the principle of swadeshi to cloth, they will show themselves foolish and will be acting like people who drown themselves in their ancestral well instead of swimming across it. My reason cannot conceive

[1] The letter is not translated here. The correspondent had criticized Gandhiji's view that foreign articles which could not be manufactured in India and which were useful should be readily accepted. For Gandhiji's views *vide* Vol. XXXIII, "The Cow and the Buffalo", 22-5-1927.

of such a time ever coming. Whether it comes or not, there can be no two opinions that in our present condition khadi is the purest form of swadeshi and we can even say that now there are no two opinions about it.

Raw materials worth crores of rupees are produced in this country and, thanks to our ignorance, lethargy and lack of invention, exported to foreign countries; the result is, as Shri Madhusudan Das has pointed out, that we remain ignorant like animals, our hands do not get the training which they ought to and our intellects do not develop as they should. As a consequence, living art has disappeared from our land and we are content to imitate the West. As long as we cannot make the machines required for utilizing the hide of dead cattle, worth nine crores, available in our country, I would be ready to import them from any part of the world and would still believe that I was scrupulously keeping the vow of swadeshi. I would believe that I would be only discrediting that vow by refusing, out of obstinacy, to import those machines. Similarly our country produces a great many things with medicinal properties, and those come back to us in the form of a variety of drugs or other articles. It is our duty to import any machines, and obtain any help, which will enable us to utilize these things in our own country.

Swadeshi is an eternal religious duty. The manner of following it may, and ought to, change from age to age. The principle of swadeshi is the soul and khadi is its body in this age and in this country. If in the course of time this body perishes, swadeshi will assume a new body but the soul dwelling in it will be the same. Swadeshi is service, and if we understand its nature we shall simultaneously benefit ourselves, our families, our country and the world. Swadeshi is not intended to serve self-interest but is pure altruism, and hence I call it a form of *yajna*. It certainly benefits ourselves, but there is no room in it for hatred of others. There can be no absolute duty of not importing anything at any time; only, we may not import anything which may harm the country. Nor can it be accepted as an absolute principle that everything that belongs to or is produced by one's own country is good. Anything, whether indigenous or foreign, which is good and serves our interest, should be readily accepted, and likewise anything, indigenous or foreign, which is bad and harmful should be rejected. The country produces a huge quantity of liquor, but all of it deserves to be shunned. There is no reason to believe that, if the whole country gives up drinking, those engaged in the liquor trade will be ruined. Their present business harms themselves and the country and they will not starve if they lose it; there will be other, better occupations which they can follow.

[From Gujarati]

Navajivan, 19-6-1927

22. *LETTER TO THE SECRETARY, A.I.S.A.*

KUMARA PARK, BANGALORE,
June 19, 1927

DEAR SIR,

With reference to the collections made in Benares, it is quite correct to state that they were all made for the Gandhi Ashram, Benares. They should therefore have the whole amount not as a loan but as a grant. It ought to appear in our books because the collection was responsibly made. It should be entered as earmarked for Gandhi Ashram, Benares, and there would be no need to get the sanction from the Council for the grant.

As to Laxmi Behn and Harjivan, my opinion is that the whole thing should be left to Rajendra Babu to manage, such help being given to him as he may require for facilitating the execution of his decision. This thing may be further discussed when we meet.

As to Gulbarga collection, I am conferring with Gangadharrao. But the position generally is this. Whilst it is convenient for us to know from which province collections have been received, all these collections are on behalf of the Association. If the idea is that the whole of the Maharashtra collections should be necessarily spent for Maharashtra, and that other provincial collections should be similarly treated, the doctrine is untenable. And I made it clear during the tour at all the places where the question was raised that whilst the places at which the amounts were collected will be borne in mind at the time of considering the allocation of funds, the Association could not undertake necessarily to spend funds in the place where they have been collected. It is therefore a matter of little importance what description is given to the entry of Gulbarga collections in our books. Theoretically, it is open to the Association to spend the whole of the Maharashtra collection, say in Orissa and *vice versa.* That it would be gross abuse of authority and that such abuse would break the Association is also true. But I mention this merely to illustrate my meaning and to show that so far as ledger entry is concerned, it is a matter of no moment where a particular collection comes from.

Yours sincerely,

THE SECRETARY
ALL-INDIA SPINNERS' ASSOCIATION
AHMEDABAD

From a microfilm: S.N. 19782

23. LETTER TO RAIHANA TYABJI

KUMARA PARK, BANGALORE,
June 19, 1927

MY DEAR RAIHANA,

I have your two letters. I am glad you have opened your heart to me. The very act of doing so often soothes one. Do not therefore apologize for writing at length and in whatsoever manner the spirit moves you. I am glad you have got the permission from mother for taking to simpler dress. I would like you to open out your heart to both father and mother as you have done to me. Never mind their laughing you out or smothering you with ridicule or putting you down even in anger. You will take it all in good part and with a smile on your lips. They have a right to do all those things. And when they recognize in you, in spite of ridicule, anger, etc., a seriousness and determination which shall not be moved, they will let you do what you like. How often have not young men and women built castles in the air only to be destroyed later. Why should you expect people to regard you as an exception? If you are an exception, you will stand ridicule, contempt and worse, and come out better through the ordeal. After all God *must* put us through the test.

I share your grief over your having to give up that dress on which mother has lavished so much time and so much love. But love is its own reward. And parents do not regret the trouble they have taken after things which their children outgrow. Let all those things of yours go to Sohaila when mother is satisfied that you will never be likely to want them.

Mira has left Rewari and before she migrates to Wardha for perfecting her Hindi, she has come to Bangalore where she will be for a few days.

I have not got the poetic language to describe the weather here, but it is really fine at this time of the year in Bangalore. Of course we have not the Himalayas here. But I suppose you know Bangalore better than I do. I am still progressing.

With love,

Yours,
BAPU

From a photostat: S.N. 9603

24. LETTER TO C. F. ANDREWS

KUMARA PARK, BANGALORE,
June 19, 1927

I have your brief letters. But I can read through them your grief as well as your victory over it. You are used to all kinds of charges and innuendoes. Sastri is now there. So after you have been there a month or so with him, I expect you will be returning. How I wish you were with me in Bangalore. You would have then been my door-keeper and enjoyed the glorious weather here. As it is Rajagopalachari and Gangadharrao are the gate-keepers. I see very little of them. They put in their appearance only to bring any visitors and take them out. I know nothing about their trials and their attempt to shield me. As Rajagopalachari himself has written in his latest story[1], "Illnesses of rich men or great men have a charm and romance all their own." One needs to be really a pauper to understand the chastening effects of illness. I am not going to give you any of the innumerable painful titbits from this end. You have enough of them all there. This is therefore merely to assure you that you are ever in my mind.

Yours sincerely,

From a photostat: S.N. 12362

[1] "The Blind Girl of Vellalapatti" in *Young India*, 23-6-1927

25. LETTER TO HARINDRANATH CHATTOPADHYAYA

KUMARA PARK, BANGALORE,
June 19, 1927

DEAR FRIEND,

Have you not unconsciously made a mistake and written to me when you should have written to the Poet? Or, have you really thought that I know the literary men and artists of Europe? If you have, it is then a case of distance lending enchantment to the scene. I have hardly any correspondence even with M. Romain Rolland. I do not think that I have written more than two letters to him. The European correspondents are all common readers of *Young India*. I do not even remember their names, and they will not be the persons whom you have in view. Now, please tell me what you will have me to do.

Yours sincerely,

H. CHATTOPADHYAYA, ESQ.
KODIALBAIL P.O.
MANGALORE

From a photostat: S.N. 12773

26. LETTER TO MOTILAL NEHRU[1]

KUMARA PARK, BANGALORE,
June 19, 1927

DEAR MOTILALJI,

I must still dictate, though this dictating is not to be regarded as any indication of weakness of body. I am simply literally following doctor's advice in order to store up energy for future use. Whether energy is being thereby stored or not remains to be known.

I have your telegram. If you could have braved the travelling through the hot parts, you would certainly have been amply rewarded and forgotten the heat of central India. I wonder whether chamber work could not be done outside Allahabad. Phe-

[1] In reply to his letter dated June 11

rozeshah used to drag clients after him. Of course it was cruel. I wonder whether for reasons of health you would not be justified in putting clients to the trouble of following you to a cool place.

Things, as they are shaping in the Congress, confirm the opinion that it is not yet time for Jawaharlal to shoulder the burden. He is too high-souled to stand the anarchy and hooliganism that seem to be growing in the Congress, and it would be cruel to expect him to evolve order all of a sudden out of chaos. I am confident, however, that the anarchy will spend itself before long and the hooligans will themselves want a disciplinarian. Jawaharlal will come in then. For the present, we should press Dr. Ansari to take the reins. He won't control the hooligans. He will let them have their way; but he may specialize in the Hindu-Muslim question and do something in the matter. It will be quite enough work for him in the coming year to solve the almost insoluble problem.

Yours sincerely,

From a photostat: S.N. 12867

27. *LETTER TO MATHURADAS*

BANGALORE,
Jeth Vad 5 [*June 20, 1927*][1]

BHAI MATHURADAS,

I have your letter. May your resolve to observe *brahmacharya* endure for ever and God give you the strength for it. Has this vow been taken with the willing consent of your wife? If it is, its observance will be easier.

Do not admit defeat about khadi; this work is a kind of *tapascharya.* We do not give up our faith in truth, or forsake its practice or its propagation, even if the whole world habitually speaks untruth; in this age and in the circumstances in which we are placed, we should act in the same manner in regard to khadi. What are you doing there now, and how do you carry on your work?

Blessings from
BAPU

From a photostat of the Gujarati: G.N. 3763

[1] Gandhiji was in Bangalore on this day in 1927.

28. LETTER TO MANILAL AND SUSHILA GANDHI

BANGALORE,
Jeth Vad 5 [June 20, 1927]

CHI. MANILAL AND SUSHILA,

I get your letters regularly. I feel happy. Whether the cause of this regularity is the regret I expressed in Bombay or the new broom in the form of Sushila is a question which only you two can answer. If my regret is the cause, may the memory of that regret remain fresh with you for ever, and if the new broom is the cause, let it never grow old.

My letter is late by a week. I will be more careful hereafter. Your regularity will keep me careful. When elders become old, the young can keep them vigilant. Perhaps you know that, had Gorakh[1] not proved stronger than Machchhendra, the latter would have fallen. If you do not know about this, ask me; I will explain the story in my next letter, and shall have a good subject to write upon.

I am very glad to hear that Sushila has put on weight. Has her deafness decreased somewhat? It is also good news she has started type-composing. She can become capable of managing a press. A girl of 17 or 18 can train herself in no time. The burden of household chores on her should not increase. For that, if you keep your food requirements simple as you used to do formerly, a great deal of time will be saved. Food should be cooked only once and that too should be very simple, so that the kitchen may not occupy all one's time. Manilal knows all this art, if, that is, he has not forgotten it. A woman is not born merely to cook meals. Since cooking must be done, both [husband and wife] should take a hand in it. If they do and work in a spirit of service, they can easily discover many ways of saving time.

You may take as much as you can digest from all this that I have written and leave the rest.

I shall certainly try to write a letter by every mail, but remember that the translation of the *Gita* which I have given you must also be counted among my letters. That translation is intended for people like you, and now it is being done at a faster rate.

[1] A disciple who saved his Guru Machchhendra, when the latter seemed to have yielded to the attraction of worldly life.

Let me know if you do not understand or like its language, so that I may be more careful and may revise that part which you find not easy to understand. This will help me as much as it will help you.

I am glad to know that you continue to read the *Gita*. You have sent your photograph to Ramdas. It does not seem that you have sent one here.

I shall respect your wish that no one else should read your letters, but they contain nothing private. Everyone naturally wants to hear news of you; if, therefore, you wish that no one should read your letters, you should from time to time write a letter to Chhaganlal which all people in the Ashram may read. All the same, I have respected your wishes and not passed on your letters to others.

Blessings from
BAPU

From a photostat of the Gujarati: G.N. 4721

29. LETTER TO LAKSHMIKANT

BANGALORE,
Jyaishtha Krishna 6 [*June 20, 1927*]

BHAI LAKSHMIKANTJI,

I got both your letters. I wanted to have a talk with *pujya* Malaviyaji and therefore could not reply to your previous letter immediately. I think you should not have written an open letter. The problem of caste-reform is very serious and difficult. It calls for great patience. Malaviyaji bears no ill will towards you. After having talked to him I am convinced that there was a difference between your way of working and his. *Pujya* Malaviyaji desires reform of Hindu society; he also wants the narrow caste restrictions to be liberalized but he believes that reforms cannot be effected just by the pioneering efforts of one man. But then he is making all possible efforts if only according to his own method. He would never think of annoying you.

Now here is my view. Whatever you did was right. Reformers should carry on their mission without cutting themselves off from Hindu society, bearing no malice and with perfect love of the Hindu religion, and while doing so, put up with all the hardships that might come in their way. Those who violate social conventions in the course of their activities must submit to the sanctions laid down by society and have a liberal attitude towards society while suffering them. This is what is called satyagraha. It is not for a social reformer to first disregard society's laws and then to feel sore about having to suffer punishment for this disregard. I hear if you go through some formal atonement you can be re-admitted to the caste. I am against submitting to such atonement. We atone for what we regard as sin. What you have done is no sin. It is therefore needless, even improper, to atone for it. But if you are not prepared to suffer excommunication you can return to your caste by going through the prescribed atonement. I was pained to see in your open letter a reference to Islam which looked like a threat. Every man follows his own faith not because he wants to oblige others but because he considers religion as the lifeline without which life appears impossible to him. If the tenets of Hinduism are to bring you *moksha,* there is no ground to revolt against it even if all the Hindus of this country were to oppose you.

From a microfilm of the Hindi: S.N. 12674

30. A LETTER

[Before *June 21, 1927*][1]

I have your letter. Books like the *Bhagavata* seem to have been written to meet the requirements of many different kinds of men. It is possible that immoral people will seek in it support for their immorality. If a man reads the *Bhagavata* with the desire to find God on every page of the work, any evil that may be present in his mind will disappear. The right course appears to be to give up reading a book which fills us with bad thoughts. The *Bhagavata* is not a historical work. It does not give an account of a historical Krishna. Krishna is the *atman* and the Gopis are the many senses. They are obedient servants of the self-controlled *atman* and dance before it as it wills.

[From Gujarati]

From the manuscript of Mahadev Desai's Diary. Courtesy: Narayan Desai

[1] The source has this letter before the entries for June 21, 1927.

31. LETTER TO ABBAS TYABJI

KUMARA PARK, BANGALORE,
June 21, 1927

MY DEAR BHRRRR,[1]

Better late than never. I have your letter at last. Why should marriage ceremonies cost so much time, trouble, money, and make even 70-year-young people look old for all the time and trouble taken over marriages of their children? What is there extraordinary in a marriage to elate parents and their children and almost make them mad with joy? Is it not an everyday occurrence like birth, youth, old age and death itself? They are all necessary changes attendant upon life. But of course all this is philosophy after the event. If I had a marriage in prospect, perhaps, I should write differently. But even if I intended to be married, there does not appear to be in existence a parent mad enough or sane enough to give me his girl in marriage. I can therefore safely deliver lectures to young people and old people who take pleasure in wasting their time and money over marriages. However I shall forgive all this extravagance, if Sohaila properly puts down her husband when he endeavours to restrain her freedom, and by sheer force of exemplary character breaks down the wretched *purdah* in Lucknow and the neighbourhood; and of course the propaganda of khaddar is the least I expect her to do.

I am still gathering strength and I am not likely to leave the South for another two months. It must therefore be some time before I shall have the pleasure of hugging you and touching your silvery beard and chatting on all matters important and unimportant. Raihana must be allowed to grow in her own way.

With love to you all,

Yours sincerely,
M. K. GANDHI

From a photostat: S.N. 9559

[1] This was a form of greeting used by Gandhiji and Abbas Tyabji for each other.

32. *LETTER TO DEBENDRA NATH MITRA*

KUMARA PARK, BANGALORE,
June 21, 1927

DEAR FRIEND,

I must apologize to you for entirely forgetting to give you my suggestions regarding agriculture. My impression is that unless improvements which are within the means of the poor are taken to their very farms as they were in South Africa, success will be slow. My recent studies more and more demonstrate to me the necessity of the State taking virtual control of all the cattle. It seems to me that unless the cattle problem is properly tackled, they will either be killed out mercilessly or we shall be. And while things are allowed to take their course, we are both being ground down. Destruction of uneconomic cattle, I hold to be impractical and criminal in our country. We must therefore take charge of the uneconomic cattle and find ways and means of supporting them as economically as possible, getting what return we can out of their manure and out of their hide, bone, etc., after they die. We should cease to allow a single calf to come into being except through proper bulls. Your farm should therefore, in my opinion, contain facilities for proper dairying and tanning and there should be series of experiments to find out the relative value of manure in connection with the feed of unused and unuseful cattle. I do not know whether you followed the series of articles that were published in *Young India* on the cattle problem. There are of course other things I might mention; but they require legislation and [are] therefore outside your jurisdiction and control.

Yours sincerely,

SJT. DEBENDRA NATH MITRA
GOVT. AGRICULTURAL FARM
FARIDPUR (EAST BENGAL)

From a microfilm: S.N. 12917

33. LETTER TO LAJPAT RAI

KUMARA PARK, BANGALORE,
June 21, 1927

DEAR LALAJI,

I do not know whether this letter will reach you. I simply passed on to you about the trust what I felt.[1] I know that you will do whatever is proper. I surely do not need any explanation.

I hope you are gaining strength day by day and taking rest without being concerned with the events that may be going on about you. I would like you to do what Asquith did in the midst of the War. He took, when his health threatened to break down, a fortnight's cruise in the Mediterranean and cut himself off from all communications. We may not afford to take any such cruise, but we can afford to retire unto ourselves untouched by the environment.

Yours sincerely,

LALA LAJPAT RAI
NATIONAL LIBERAL CLUB
WHITEHALL PLACE
LONDON S.W.1

From a photostat: S.N. 14166

34. LETTER TO VICTOR MOHAN JOSHI

KUMARA PARK, BANGALORE,
June 21, 1927

MY DEAR FRIEND,

Chhotalalji tells me you were grieved that I had not gone to Almora up to now. When you give me sufficient inducement about khadi work, you will find me taking my convalescence in Almora instead of Bangalore. Meanwhile, you have Prabhudas there, and whatever service may be rendered to him will be ren-

[1] *Vide* Vol. XXXIII, "Letter to Lajpat Rai", 1-5-1927.

dered to one who bids fair to become if he is spared by God a faithful servant of the nation.

Yours sincerely,

VICTOR MOHAN JOSHI
ALMORA

From a photostat: S.N. 14167

35. LETTER TO DR. BIDHAN CHANDRA ROY

KUMARA PARK, BANGALORE,
June 21, 1927

DEAR DR. BIDHAN,

I have your letter. I shall deal with the appeal[1] in the columns of *Young India*. I would suggest your going from door to door and making collections. There is really no other way. If I could at all come there, I should join you.

I cannot invite you and Basanti Devi to come here because I am still half-bedridden and not moving about. In the month of July the doctors expect that I shall be able to do a little travelling. But it won't enable me to put forth energy that I should have to if I invited you and took you from place to place. For that you will have to give me strength when I come to Bengal if I am ever enabled to do.

How is Basanti Devi getting on? She and Mona and Baby are all playing me false. Tell them I shall have my revenge one of these days. I am here at least up to the end of the month.

Yours sincerely,

DR. BIDHAN CHANDRA ROY
36, WELLINGTON STREET
CALCUTTA

From a photostat: S.N. 14168

[1] *Vide* "Chittaranjan Seva Sadan", 30-6-1927.

36. *LETTER TO VALJI G. DESAI*

KUMARA PARK, BANGALORE,
Jeth Vad 7 [*June 21, 1927*][1]

BHAISHRI VALJI,

I have just now received a telegram from Swami to the effect that your mother fell dead while she was walking with you. I can offer only felicitations on such a holy death. We should all pray for such a death. Her bodily presence with us was a source of support and comfort, and if we feel grieved for the loss of that feeling, our grief would be nothing but selfishness.

Vandemataram from
MOHANDAS

From Gujarati: C.W. 7392. Courtesy: Valjibhai Desai

37. *LETTER TO ASHRAM WOMEN*

Silence Day, Jeth Vad [*7, June 21, 1927*][2]

SISTERS,

Received your letter.

That I praised the bangles made of yarn does not mean that all of you should start wearing them. Such innovations will endure only if they proceed from the heart. And I wish that none of you should do anything merely for fear of not conforming.

Now I visit daily a milk-producing centre. It gives rise to various thoughts in my mind—one of which I shall put down here. Just as you have undertaken the work of the store, so also you can help to run these milk centres. Thousands of cattle perish daily owing to our ignorance and idleness. I find that this is work that can be done as easily by women as by men. The sturdy cowherd-women of Kathiawar appear before my mind's

[1] Gandhiji was in Bangalore on this date in 1927.

[2] The source has June 23, 1927, presumably the date of receipt. The source again has *Jeth Vad* 6 which, in 1927, was *kshaya*, not reckoned. *Jeth Vad* 7, June 21, 1927 was a Tuesday.

eyes. We are already farmers, weavers and sweepers; we need to be cowherds too.

Blessings from
BAPU

From a photostat of the Gujarati: G.N. 3654

38. LETTER TO J. P. BHANSALI

BANGALORE,
Jeth Vad 7 [June 21, 1927][1]

BHAISHRI BHANSALI,

I liked your letter very much because you had opened your heart in it. Manibehn has today given me the news that your seven-day fast is progressing well. A seven-day fast is child's play for you. I had not, therefore, felt worried over it at all. But I see an error in the argument you have advanced about the reason for the fast. The best thing is not to do a thing about doing which we have a doubt. If we have started doing a thing, and then we get a doubt about it, true expiation consists in abandoning it that very moment. Any other atonement which excludes this is useless. If your demand for a new house was wrong, you cannot atone for that error by means of a fast. If you see no error in that demand, atonement is not called for at all. If you have even the slightest doubt about having committed an error, to seek to cover it up by means of a fast amounts to committing a second error, because by undertaking a fast we banish the thought of error from our mind and we ought not to do this. Expiation such as fasting is a form of self-punishment and punishment can be only for a thing which we cannot undo. If we abuse someone or beat him, we cannot take back the abuse or the beating. We may, therefore, inflict on ourselves punishment like a fast; such punishment brings about self-purification, and also restrains us from making a similar mistake again. But suppose that we have stolen someone's money. At the time of doing so, we felt that there was nothing wrong in it but later on we got a doubt about what we had done and felt afraid lest we had done a wrong; then, at that very moment, we ought to return the money to the owner and thereafter, if we so wish, we may undergo self-punishment such as a fast. Returning the money is like returning

[1] From the reference to the addressee's seven-day fast

a loan and hence that does not amount even to punishment. You may perhaps argue why you should return the goods so long as you are not sure that stealing is bad, and tell yourself that you will return them when you decide that it is indeed bad. Many sins are, and have been committed in the world through such reasoning. Being moral requires that wherever there is a doubt, we should decide against our own interest. But we may go a step further and suppose that, so long as we have a doubt about stealing being wrong, we shall also have a doubt about the desirability of returning the money. Even then, in such circumstances a fast certainly is not a means of resolving such a doubt. On the contrary, the fast may prove an obstacle in our effort to discover the truth.

Here I have only analysed the ethical principle for your benefit. I myself have no doubt whatever in your case. You had a right to ask for a roomier house in a quiet part, for the inmates of the Ashram regard your living in the Ashram as conducive to its progress. The best place for the experiments which you have been making is the Ashram, and such experiments are an inseparable part of its life. Hence any facilities which you consider necessary for those experiments and which others accept as necessary should be provided to you if the financial condition of the Ashram permits them, and it is because this was the position that a house has been got ready for you. Moreover, if hereafter it is felt that such an arrangement ought not to have been made, you can move into another small house that may be vacant. On that score, too, we need have no fear. Moreover, Lilabehn may get more accustomed to the conditions there and come to like living in simplicity, and you may become so detached that the atmosphere round you will not affect you at all; then you yourself will decide to leave that house and ask for another. And if I see that you or Lilabehn has become weak, I shall not, as an elder and guardian, hesitate to speak to you about it. If I shrink from doing so, I shall fall from my dharma. Thus you are safe in every way. I could have explained all this in my reply to your very first letter. It even occurred to me to do so. But I did not think it advisable to do that and stop your fast abruptly. I was also afraid that I might shock you by advancing such an argument when you were about to start your fast. Hence I deferred writing this. Now you are in a position to appreciate my argument objectively, since the fast is now out of the way. There is a sound reason behind my plea. If you remain complacent because of the fast and believe that there is no reason now to feel doubtful about the propriety of having put up a new building, that would not be right. The truth is that it is our duty to feel doubtful about the propriety of every one of our indulgences, and it is complacency to feel no such doubt. If we do not feel doubtful in this manner, we shall never be able to practise complete renunciation. Hence this caution. I have also something to say about the other portions of your letter, but this is enough for the present. I shall attend to those portions when I have the time. The matter is certainly not urgent.

Please have no hesitation in writing to me whatever you wish.

M. K. GANDHI

From a photostat of the Gujarati: S.N. 12194

39. *LETTER TO SATAVALEKAR*

June 21, 1927

It is the common experience that *brahmacharya* is not essential for the conservation and development of bodily strength and so on. Hence there is the danger of overlooking the importance of *brahmacharya* in tracing the close association between *brahmacharya* and physical strength. We have fallen lower than the *asuri*[1] countries. The reason for it is that having fallen from our own position we are not able to attain another either. We are afraid of accommodating all that the *asuri* tradition implies, whereas we lack the strength to translate into action the *daivi*[2] traditions. It is for this reason that attempts are being made in the country today to bring in the *asuri* traditions—this is what I see everywhere. But these traditions simply cannot work. The people cannot digest them. And as they are lax in following the *daivi* tradition, they stand where they are. Hence I believe that since we follow the *daivi* tradition our acts must be pure and we must somehow save ourselves from copying the *asuri* tradition.

[From Hindi]

From the manuscript of Mahadev Desai's Diary. Courtesy: Narayan Desai

[1] Demoniac

[2] Divine

40. *LETTER TO DEVI WEST*

KUMARA PARK, BANGALORE,
June 22, 1927

MY DEAR DEVI,

I have your letter. I am getting better though I am still weak and convalescing at a cool place.

Yes. Manilal is still at Phœnix looking after *Indian Opinion.* His wife is now helping him. He tells me she has already learnt the compositor's work. She is a good girl and you would have liked her if you had seen her. Manilal is very devoted to her and both of them seem to be very happy. Manilal has all new men now on his staff.

Yes. Mirabai[1] is still with me. At the present moment, she is even at Bangalore where I am. She has come to be with me for a few days. Then she goes to a branch of the Ashram for perfecting her Hindi.

How do you occupy your time there? Devdas is with me, and Ramdas is at his post in a khadi workshop.

I am sorry you do not see *Young India.* I am now asking the manager to put you on the free list. Do you not get *Indian Opinion*? If you do not, you should write to Manilal without any hesitation to send you a copy. But if you would rather not write, I would do so gladly on hearing from you. You ought to have been getting both *Indian Opinion* and *Young India.* I should have myself enquired about the latter, but I took it for granted that you saw the paper.

With love,

Yours sincerely,
BHAI

MISS DEVI WEST
22, GEORGE STREET
LOUTH
LINCOLNSHIRE (ENGLAND)

From a photostat: S.N. 12506

[1] Mirabehn

41. LETTER TO H. HARCOURT

KUMARA PARK, BANGALORE,
June 22, 1927

DEAR FRIEND,

I wrote to you in my last letter[1] that I will send for the copy of your book[2] you had kindly sent me. I have now got it and having the leisure of a convalescent, I went through the book from end to end. I read it with interest. I liked your humorous touches especially with reference to the complainant who the accused said in his evidence had struck the latter's fist with his nose. I have remembered that joke well because you have unwittingly summed up my own belief. I have certainly run up my nose against many a fist, and have hitherto come out unhurt. I have found in my experience that when instead of putting up your nose for the man with the fist to play with, you try to ward off his play by holding it back, you really get the knock-out blow. But I must not try to present you my philosophy of life if the method I stand for can possibly be described by such a dignified word.

But I would say one word with reference to your estimate of me. I ask you to believe me when I assure you that I endeavoured to see myself in your looking-glass. But I have failed to recognize myself in it. I do not wonder at the picture you have drawn of me. I hope that I do not entertain any elongated notions about myself. But I cannot help expressing my grief that a man so sincere like you should have failed to study an honest movement which somehow or other caught the imagination of thousands upon thousands of men and women who had hitherto been left untouched, with more attention than you evidently felt called upon to give. Many English friends are now beginning to see that my movement was an honest attempt through non-co-operation to bring about hearty co-operation of equals, instead of an enforced and superficial co-operation between parties one of which regarded itself as superior to the other.

[1] *Vide* Vol. XXXIII, "Letter to H. Harcourt", 1-6-1927.

[2] *Sidelights on the Crisis in India* by H. Harcourt and Chhotu Ram; Harcourt was a member of the Indian Civil Service and Deputy Commissioner of Gurdaspur and Chhotu Ram was Minister for Agriculture in the Punjab Government.

I shall await your letter[1] telling me what your challenge was. And if I find it to be still capable of being taken up, and find myself equally capable of taking it up, you may depend upon me responding to it.

Yours sincerely,

H. HARCOURT, ESQ.
119, GIPSY HILL
LONDON S.E. 19

From a photostat: S.N. 12523

42. *LETTER TO G. K. DEVADHAR*

KUMARA PARK, BANGALORE,
June 22, 1927

MY DEAR DEVADHAR,

I thank you for your letter. I did read about your election in the papers. It was a foregone conclusion. I therefore did not send you my congratulations. And though in the opinion of the outside world, it is an honour conferred upon you, I know as well as you do that for you it is a matter of greater responsibility and greater opportunity for service. You call me a friend and supporter of the Society. I regard myself as something much more. I have never considered myself as anything but a member of the Society. Though I am not officially a member [and] am not taking any active part in its activities, [this] does not cause me the slightest worry. My abstention is my quota of service. When a member of a numerous family cannot see eye to eye with the rest although his heart is with them, he serves the family best by non-interference, always wishing that his head may be where his heart is so that he can render active service. Has it not been said that those also serve who wait and pray? You have therefore a right to command my service whenever you think that with my limitations it can be of any use to you.

I do not expect to be at Sabarmati before the end of August, for doctors here tell me I shall be able to do a certain amount of

[1] In his letter dated July 12 Harcourt wrote: "The challenge I referred to was yours and addressed to my countrymen in general. I tried to reply but I have no copy now" (S.N. 12531).

touring from next month, and if I can do so, I shall want to finish as far as I can the Southern tour that was mapped out and over which immense trouble was taken by Rajagopalachari and Gangadharrao Deshpande. If I must regard your headquarters as Poona, it is just as easy for you if not easier to come to Bangalore as to go to Sabarmati. And I am here till about 10th of July. You can come here therefore if you at all can and will. I shall always have my grievance against Mrs. Devadhar, for she is under promise to come to Sabarmati and stay there a few days, a promise she has never yet fulfilled.

With love,

Yours sincerely,
M. K. GANDHI

SJT. G. K. DEVADHAR
SERVANTS OF INDIA SOCIETY
POONA

From a photostat: S.N. 14169

43. LETTER TO G. D. BIRLA

KUMARA PARK, BANGALORE,
June 22, 1927

I have your letter from Geneva. I hope you have received all my previous letters including the last one which was in English. I see that you are observing things with your customary keenness. I hope however that you will form no hasty conclusions as so many of our superior men have often done. All is not gold that glitters. The converse of it is also equally true. All is not dirt that appears dirty. And how often do we not see the two co-existing, riches and poverty, virtue and vice, Jekyll and Hyde, God and Satan? The combination that you have described of wine-drinking, womanizing, etc., with physical strength, orderliness, common honesty and ardent patriotism is not to be denied. The fact seems to me to be that one virtue does not lead at any rate all at once to all the other virtues, and a particular quality ceases to be a virtue when it solidifies into a custom. Vegetarianism with us is really no virtue. We are vegetarians by custom. It would be a sacrifice for us a large majority of vegetarians to be otherwise. But vegetarianism in Europe will be a virtue. It would be an active force in the life of a European vegetarian, and if he is a seeker of truth that one reform will lead him to many others. Foreign visitors to India have remarked upon our general domestic happiness and family affection. This quality is part of our being. A father loves his children and children render willing obedience to parents without much effort on either side. People in Europe have found by experience that it is necessary for them to extend the family idea and regard the society to which they belong as a nation. Hence patriotism there is not a virtue which needs to be cultivated. Want of it would be noticed as a strange thing and would lead to excommunication of the type familiar in Europe. They have also understood the doctrine of honesty being the best policy and so up to a point, you will find that quality abundantly in evidence. With us patriotism has got to be cultivated. We have in practice not gone beyond family affection as a nation. But I shall not elaborate this point further as I must keep an appointment which I have put off to finish this letter.

It will be an agreeable surprise to me if you succeed in enlisting 500 paying subscribers for *Young India*. It would be further proof of European interest in what *Young India* stands for.

I am making steady progress. And doctors are of opinion that I should be able to resume touring on a moderate scale early next month.

Yours sincerely,

GHANSHYAMDAS BIRLA
C/O THOMAS COOK & SONS
LUDGATE HILL
LONDON

From a photostat: S.N. 14170

44. *LANCASHIRE BLOCK*

The long delay which took place in the publication of the Tariff Board report was almost a certain indication of the rejection of any recommendation for granting further protection to the great mill industry. The Government will not offend Japan by discriminating against it and favouring Lancashire. And it dare not displease Lancashire by applying it any protective duty. For Lancashire is the Government in substance; and to grant India effective protection against Lancashire would be almost like committing suicide.

This question of protection for the mill industry against Lancashire and other foreign competition is a question of life and death for India as it is supposedly one of life and death also for Lancashire. To realize the truth of this statement, one has merely to look at the table of imports. Imports from Lancashire are by far the largest of all the other imports, nearly half of all British imports. Lancashire has risen on the ashes of India's greatest cottage industry and it is sustained by the exploitation of the helpless millions of this land. The indigenous mill industry is really regarded as an interloper, and if it could be decently squashed in the interest of Lancashire, it would be suppressed without ceremony. The stupendous interest of Lancashire is allowed to override every moral consideration. The existence of that industry harms both Lancashire and India. It has reduced India to pauperism, and India's pauperism reduces Lancashire to moral bankruptcy.

The mill-owners of India will never be able to vindicate their position in the face of this almost insurmountable obstacle, unless they courageously make common cause with the people and force protection from the Government. It is the country's right. If a country has the right to determine the composition of its inhabitants, and to exclude those whom it considers to be detrimental to its existence, it has a greater right to determine the composition of the goods that it would permit to be imported within its borders and to exclude those that it may consider to be harmful to its population.

There can be no doubt that foreign cloth is the most harmful among all our imports. The mill industry may for a time flourish somehow, it may also show a temporary prosperity by various manipulations or by favourable accidents; but unless it secures effective protection against all foreign cloth, it is bound to go under sooner or later, and certainly much sooner than one expects. Some day or other there is bound to be a real sustained mass awakening, whether mad and undisciplined but organized in its own madness, or (as I hope), disciplined and organized non-violently. And when it comes the indigenous mill industry, unless it is recognized as their own by the masses, will perish in the flames that must overtake foreign cloth. It is time for the mill-owners to make common cause with khadi and wrest protection from an unwilling Government. There is room enough for years to come for both, if the province of each is now marked out and rigidly respected. It is then possible for them to prosper in spite of Government aloofness and even insidious opposition. But this presupposes intelligent sacrifice on the part of the mill-owners, a vital combination amongst them and an iron determination to carry through their programme.

I was glad to notice an authoritative repudiation of the rumour that a cut in the wages of the mill-hands was contemplated as a reply to the Government's decision. It would have been suicidal. What is wanted at this time is not antagonizing labour, but making common cause with labour and regarding mill-hands as much proprietors of the mills as the share-holders and agents. If the share-holders supply the capital, the labourers supply the muscle for the conversion of capital into cloth. A combination, therefore, between the mill-owners, the mill-hands and the masses would be an irresistible combination which the Government dare not ignore. Will the mill-owners have enough foresight, courage and patriotism for the task? The 1s. 6d. ratio, it was contended (with a great degree of force in the contention), was a hit against that great industry and a gift to Lancashire. The resolution on the Tariff Board report is another such hit and therefore another gift to Lancashire. I wonder whether this last hit will stir the mill-owners to right action. No petition, no resolution in the Legislative Assembly will be of any use unless it is backed by effective mass action, and, in my humble opinion, it is not possible to conceive of any milder mass action than I have ventured to suggest.

Young India, 23-6-1927

45. *NOTES*

The Forthcoming Tour

If the progress I am supposed to be making continues to the end of the month, Drs. Subbarao and Krishnaswami Rao who have been kindly attending on me tell me that I should be able to resume a moderate amount of touring taken in easy stages. In view, therefore, of the possible resumption, I would like the workers and all concerned to bear in mind that I shall not be able to sustain the strain to which I seemed to be equal up to the end of March. Processions and noises must be abandoned and people should be repeatedly warned against crowding round me shouting and touching my feet; nor may I be expected to visit institutions in the places to which I may be taken. One meeting and informal discussion with workers is about all I shall be able to manage per day. It is, I know, ungracious to use Chikballapur as my illustration to show how not to do it. The people of Chikballapur have been extraordinarily kind to me personally. A friend who noticed the exquisite attention paid to me at Nandi Hills by the representatives who used to come from Chikballapur from time to time to see that everything was supplied and in order, and who noticed the loving attention of the volunteers all drawn from representative families of Mysore, could not help remarking that it was a wonderful manifestation of selfless love that the people of Mysore exhibited, in that I had done nothing, specially for the people of Mysore, I had hardly even seen the country except for the flying visits to Bangalore. I could not help endorsing the spontaneous remark made by this friend. It was so true. The reception committee of Chikballapur left no stone unturned to anticipate my wants and supply them at considerable sacrifice of time and money. I would therefore gladly have avoided using Chikballapur for an unfavourable illustration.

But what happened there was so typical that I must not omit to mention it. Although there was to be no procession, and I was to be taken quickly and quietly to the place of the meeting[1] which was to be perfectly noiseless, the leaders and the people lost their heads when they saw my car, and though the sun was beating hot, Mr. Hamza Husain Saheb, who is the chairman of the general reception committee and who was escorting me, had to submit to the pain of seeing the hood taken off and the motor carried in procession at a snail's pace. Officiating Dewan and ex-Police Commissioner though he was, he knew that at this moment he was connected with a representative of India's paupers, and as such had meekly to submit to the risk of all the good that Nandi had done to his charge being undone. I pleaded with the leaders whom I had seen in Nandi and who were near the car to restrain the enthusiasm and quickly take the motor to the meeting place. "We shall soon reach it", was the only reply I could get. The meeting, too, was none too orderly, and on the top of that, though the majority of the audience did not understand English, the address was read to me in that language in spite of my repeated warning in these pages that it would be more in keeping with the surroundings, at least at meetings where poor people gather in thousands, to conduct proceedings in their mother tongue supplying me when necessary with a translation in Hindi.

[1] *Vide* Vol. XXXIII, "Speech at Chikballapur", 5-6-1927.

But this much must be said for Chikballapur. Its mistakes too were due to affection. I was told that they never had a popular meeting of this character before. They naturally did not wish to damp the enthusiasm of the people. They lost their heads themselves for the moment, being caught in the wave of enthusiasm, and for the Hindi translation possibly they had not a single person in Chikballapur knowing Hindi. But let the other local reception committees profit by the unavoidable mistakes of Chikballapur. Let them have previous rehearsals in checking their enthusiasm. Let them translate it into khadi purchases and hard work at the spinning-wheel. That would be an intelligent, profitable and national application of the energy created by the enthusiasm, and it would not only gladden their guest but will also strengthen his body, mind and soul.

Indecent Advertisements

Lying on my back and trying at times, in obedience to medical instructions, to take my mind off serious reading, I chance upon advertisement sheets of newspapers. They are sometimes painfully instructive. I see often in respectable papers advertisements of a lewd nature. The headings are deceptive. In one case, the heading was "Books Relating to Yoga". On looking at the contents of the advertisement, I discovered hardly one book out of ten having any reference to yoga; all the rest had reference to sex, suggesting that young men and women may indulge in sexual pleasures without coming to grief, promising to divulge secret remedies. I came upon worse things which I do not propose to copy in these pages. Hardly a newspaper is free from liquor advertisements, and advertisements regarding medicines designed to debase and corrupt youthful minds. The editors and the proprietors who are themselves known to be pure and opposed to drink, to smoking and such other evils, are at times found not to be averse to deriving an income from advertisements which are obviously intended to spread the evils which they shun. The argument sometimes advanced is that it is not possible to conduct a newspaper on any other condition. But is it necessary to conduct newspapers at any cost? Is the good that they do so great as to outweigh the evil that mischievous advertisements cause? We have a journalists' association. Is it not possible through it to cultivate a uniform code of morals among them and to create a public opinion that would make it impossible for a respectable journal to violate the prescribed code?

Young India, 23-6-1927

46. TELEGRAM TO RAMESHWARDAS PODDAR

BANGALORE,
June 23, 1927

RAMESHWARDAS
DHULIA

DIFFICULT PROVIDE FASTING TREATMENT FOR YOU AND MEDICAL TREATMENT FOR YOUR WIFE SAME PLACE. CAN YOU SEPARATE? WILL YOUR WIFE UNDERGO OPERATION IF NECESSARY BY MALE DOCTOR? SEND FULL REPLY BY POST.

BAPU

From a photostat: G.N. 739

47. LETTER TO HELENE HAUSSDING

KUMARA PARK, BANGALORE,
June 23, 1927

MY DEAR SPARROW,

I have your postcard. I am grieved to learn that you were still ailing at the time of writing. But I hope that by the time this reaches you, you will be at least just as healthy as I seem to have become. You must not prolong your sickness beyond certain limits and those limits have been crossed already.

For your edification, I send you a free rendering by Krishnadas of an article contributed by a fellow passenger of yours. I wonder if she has correctly reported the conversation ascribed to you.

The weather in Bangalore is extremely nice. I expect to be here yet for about 20 days by which time doctors expect I should be able to move about without difficulty.

Yours sincerely,

From a photostat: S.N. 12524

48. LETTER TO J. W. PETAVEL

KUMARA PARK, BANGALORE,
June 23, 1927

DEAR FRIEND,

I hope you duly received my previous letter[1]. You sent me your book at an opportune moment. Whilst I am convalescing, I have nothing to do but read what little I can and dictate a few letters and a few articles. I therefore took up your book with a view to learn the central fact of your programme, policy or teaching whatever it might be described as. I have just finished it and I am now dictating this letter. I am sorry to say that the book has not made any appeal to me. What is true in it, I began doing in 1909-10 when for the satyagrahis of the Transvaal a friend gave me the use of 1,100 acres of land which he and I called Tolstoy Farm. There we were doing exactly what you have suggested. Boys and their relatives everyone was expected to work, and boys had some tuition, plenty of work and plenty of play. If they were examined today some of them might perhaps say they would have preferred all play and no work, and the more modest ones might say they would have preferred more play and less work. But I was unable to advance any claim on behalf of that colony which you advance on behalf of yours. I wish that your claim could be sustained.

I very carefully studied the association's appeal to busy people. The picture suggested by your diagram No. 1 of the future, I fear, for a long time to come will remain a mere picture. c.d. may in course of time be magnified into C.D. But it will be absorbed as it is being absorbed now by A.B.

You have headed three chapters, "A Lesson from Switzerland", "Belgium" and "America". On going through the chapters, I find nothing of what these three countries are doing except a bare mention. I am not wiser about the Swiss method, no wiser about the Belgian or the American method. And your advice to copy the rapid locomotion of America, makes me giddy even to read it. I suppose, if you succeed (say) in converting Calcutta into a second New York with moving platforms and fourfold railways, etc., etc., and take me there to witness the marvellous perfor-

[1] Dated June 15, 1927; *vide* Vol. XXXIII.

mance, I should fall dead at the very sight of the thing. I have numerous, I was going to say innumerable, American friends. But they have all assured me that there is beneath the untold wealth of America, degradation, superstition and vice incarnate and the inequalities between A.B. and B.C. are enormous and that B.C. is being successfully exploited by A.B., in many cases B.C. not even knowing how. As I think of your chapter on America, I recall what Stead wrote many years ago, "If Christ Came to Chicago". And if my present informants have not misled me, what Stead wrote now nearly 40 years ago is truer today than when he wrote that biting article.

Of the Belgian and the Swiss examples I can say nothing; for, I know nothing. And you have given neither facts nor figures. Your book reminds me of what Ruskin wrote somewhere and which may be thus paraphrased: If men become machines and if bone and muscle could be removed from these machines, they could be flattened into bricks of a required size and these human bricks could then be consolidated into a majestic pyramid and made to do anything that the controller of these bricks desired. But unfortunately or fortunately you have to deal not with machines but with bony, intelligent muscle each having its own individuality and each pulling its own way. I wonder if your lineal cities, co-operative schemes, garden suburbs and transformed educational methods all drawn up with exactness and printed in beautiful type will change society in the manner you expect without devising some means of appealing to the soul within. I conclude with what I have said before to you: show some concrete example on a fairly large scale of successful policy so that a practical man like me may learn something.

Yours sincerely,

CAPTAIN J. W. PETAVEL, ESQ.
BAGH BAZAAR
CALCUTTA

From a photostat: S.N. 14171

49. *LETTER TO HARINDRANATH CHATTOPADHYAYA*

KUMARA PARK, BANGALORE
June 24, 1927

DEAR FRIEND,

I have your letter[1]. I send you the enclosed for what it may be worth.

You have tempted me with a bribe[2]. But a bribery being an unlawful thing, is always given in cash; whereas you have asked me to accept a credit note. However I rely upon cashing the note on presentation whether by me in person or by my successor in office as the representative of *Daridranarayana*.

Yours sincerely,

PS.

[All] letters pass through one or two hands before they [come] to me for signature. One of the . . .[3] me for letters of recommendation. As far as possible I avoid giving letters of recommendation to anybody. If there is any truth in the information given to me, I hope you will protect your and India's honour. I delayed the posting of the letter in order to find from the voice within what my course of duty was in the light of the information. This morning I felt I must send the letter with the enclosures and pass on to you the information in the hope that you would take it in the spirit in which it is offered and not think ill of the informant or me. The former has no malice against you.

May God be with us all.

M. K. GANDHI

From a photostat: S.N. 12773

[1] Dated June 22. The addressee had requested for a letter of introduction from Gandhiji for use in Europe.

[2] The addressee had promised that on his return when he founded the National Theatre, "the language of the plays shall be Hindi and that of the scenes or costumes, khaddar".

[3] The source is not legible here.

50. LETTER TO P. K. CHARLU

KUMARA PARK, BANGALORE,
June 24, 1927

DEAR FRIEND,

I have your letter, and also a copy of your journal. I have glanced through its pages. I am unable to congratulate you upon it. There is great deal of hasty ventures of this kind. I personally think that publication of magazines is being overdone and such overpublication can do no good to the nation. I fail to see from your magazine that you have a special message to give. What is really wanted at the present moment is silent and steady work. I am a believer in the proverb that example is better than precept. I wish indeed that I could even now wean you from proceeding further with your venture.

I had the privilege of meeting your father in 1896 when I was in Madras.

Yours sincerely,

SJT. P. K. CHARLU
EDITOR AND PUBLISHER
"DHARMA"
6, SUNKURAMA CHETTY STREET, G. T.
MADRAS

From a microfilm: S.N. 14172

51. LETTER TO P. RAJAGOPALA IYER

KUMARA PARK, BANGALORE,
June 24, 1927

MY DEAR RAJAGOPALAN,

I have read the report you have sent. It is good work you are doing. Do not try to do too much at a time, but go forward step by step, and never enter depth beyond your capacity, pecuniary, physical, mental and spiritual; your progress will then be even, substantial and never-failing. You should survey the villages that may be within five miles radius of your place and where the people are receptive, poor because they are idle part of the year, [and] present the charkha to them not by mere speech but by demonstration. Never offer a higher wage than the maximum fixed by the Spinners' Association, and if the people do not accept your message, do not worry, but do not give up hope. If your faith persists and your action corresponds to the faith, you will find a response sooner or later from the surrounding villages. I take it you are doing at your Ashram hand-ginning, carding and spinning and that nothing is being slurred over but everything done as perfectly as possible.

Please continue to send me a brief monthly report for my personal information. I do not propose to take any notice of it at the present moment in *Young India*. Let the institution take root.

Yours sincerely,

SJT. P. RAJAGOPALIER
PALAYUR
Via MUTHUPET

From a microfilm: S.N. 19783

52. *LETTER TO SAROJINI NAIDU*[1]

KUMARA PARK, BANGALORE,
June 25, 1927

MY DEAR MIRABAI,

I have your love letter. I hope Padmaja lying on a sofa was a case of a spoilt babe wanting to be fondled by her mother and not of sickness or fatigue. It is time for her to outgrow her illness and weakness and engage in some stern work and relieve us old people of the burden. Then you may talk of my right to take real rest.

If Dr. Ansari is not to lead us next year, we must find some other man or woman. There are many forces just now working against Motilalji. The burden will be too great for him to shoulder. I do not share the view that we must have a Hindu for the coming year. On the contrary, for the very purpose in view there is no other man than Dr. Ansari.[2] He alone can pilot a Hindu-Muslim pact through the Congress. His selection will command universal acceptance. Hindus will render him loyal obedience and the fact of the Congress being predominantly Hindu will not—cannot—be disputed by a Mussalman being in the Chair.

[1] President of the Congress in 1925

[2] *Vide* also "Letter to Motilal Nehru", 19-6-1927.

Think it over and if you have any doubt, wire your departure for Bangalore to discuss the question. I duly sent a wire today.

With love,

Yours,
"WIZARD"

SHRIMATI SAROJINI DEVI
TAJ MAHAL HOTEL
BOMBAY

From a photostat: S.N. 12868

53. *LETTER TO SHAH CHAMANLAL DUNGAJI*

KUMARA PARK, BANGALORE,
June 25, 1927

DEAR FRIEND,

I have your letter. I had already intended to deal in the pages of *Young India* with the question discussed by you. Do you want me to make public use of your letter and the facts contained in it, especially the fact that cows or bullocks are every day slaughtered for providing food for lions and tigers?

What is your authority for saying that I am against legislation altogether regarding cow-slaughter prohibition? I would like you to show me the statement ascribing to me the opinion which I have never held. What I have said and what I adhere to is that such legislation ought not to be embarked upon even in a Hindu State if an intelligent majority of the Mussalmans oppose it. I have also added that legislation alone will not save the cow. But I propose to deal with this subject fairly fully in the pages of *Young India*, which I expect you will see.[1]

If you are desirous of discussing the subject more fully with me, all the friends who are interested in the question may come any day at 4 p.m. except Monday. To avoid delay, I suggest your making an appointment beforehand so that I should be ready to talk to you precisely at the appointed time.

Yours sincerely,

SJT. SHAH CHAMANLAL DUNGAJI
PRESIDENT
SHRI GORAKSHAKA MANDALI
BANGALORE CITY

From a microfilm: S.N. 12918

[1] *Vide* "The Cow in Mysore", 7-7-1927.

54. LETTER TO WILLIAM SMITH

KUMARA PARK, BANGALORE,
June 25, 1927

DEAR MR. SMITH,

I have carefully gone through both your papers[1]. They are interesting and useful for a sceptic. I am a confirmed believer, but ill-equipped, ignorant man. I therefore want you to draw up for me and persons like me—of this there is a respectable number—a tangible business scheme which will enable the reader to immediately put it into practice, if he has skilled assistance and money. Could you therefore please give me such a scheme unembellished with argument? It would give plan and specifications, an estimate of the cost of plants, machinery, etc., and the probable working cost of and returns from the enterprise.

I have been thinking deeply over what you and your men so kindly showed me at the Imperial Dairy Institute.[2] I have several questions to ask. But for the present, I would like to say that in order to make the institution answer Indian requirements, it needs an addition of two things.

There seems to be no facility for studying methods of castration. The raising of the standard of the breed all over India seems to me to be impossible until the promiscuous herding of cows with bulls is done away with. Castration seems to be the only remedy. The indigenous method is hideously cruel.

Secondly, it seems to me that a dairy to satisfy Indian requirements has necessarily to become a tannery also. Countries of the West have found a short cut to economic success by killing cattle which they consider to be a burden. We in India have to deal with the economics of the cattle question subject to the limitation that cattle have to be supported even when they give inadequate or no return for their upkeep. Hence I feel that a dairy scheme, which does not provide for and against this necessary limitation, must be faulty from an economic standpoint. Whether the Imperial Institution can be expanded to cover these points

[1] "Dairies as an Indian Village Industry", dated January 3, 1927, and "The Need for a Village Dairy Factory System in India", dated June 10, 1927 (S.N. 12926)

[2] *Vide* Appendix I; also frontispiece.

or not, is not for me to say. But could you give me any guidance or recommend any literature on these points?

And generally what books will you suggest my studying in order to enable me the better to digest the information I have gathered during the few days' visit to the Dairy? If you have any literature in connection with the activities of the Imperial Dairy, and if it is saleable, I should like to buy it.

I cannot conclude this letter without thanking you for all the facilities you kindly gave me in connection with my visits to the Dairy.

Yours sincerely,

WILLIAM SMITH, ESQ.
IMPERIAL DAIRY EXPERT
BANGALORE

From a microfilm: S.N. 12927

55. *LETTER TO K. KELAPPAN*

KUMARA PARK, BANGALORE,
June 25, 1927

MY DEAR KELAPPAN,

I have been often thinking of you and wondering what you were doing. And now to my delight I have your letter. I cannot advise you how you should go about. If you cannot raise money in Kerala for the time being, I feel that money can be supplied if you can produce absolutely reliable workers who will be prepared to render service at a sacrifice. If you have such young men, prepare the list with qualifications and the scheme of work and then you can bring that scheme and discuss it with me. Ultimately of course it will have to be under the control of a board.

So far as a grant from the Municipality is concerned there will be no hesitation in accepting and even asking for it.

Yours sincerely,

From a microfilm: S.N. 14618

56. *"NAVAJIVAN"* IN DEVANAGARI SCRIPT

I draw the attention of readers to the following letter[1]:

I had received this letter as far back as in February. I had preserved it intending to publish it when I had time for it; then came my illness and there was more delay.

The correspondent's object is praiseworthy. I am of the view that all Indian languages should be written in the Devanagari script, and I do not except the Dravidian languages and Urdu from this. But I see difficulties in getting people to carry out this suggestion. So long as there is hostility between Hindus and Muslims, no Muslim will write Urdu in the Devanagari script. I am not suggesting that the Persian script should be given up, my idea is that common books in Urdu should be written in the Devanagari script. At present, however, even this is bound to remain a mere idea. But, without waiting for unity of hearts to be established between Hindus and Muslims, Gujarat, Bengal and other provinces can make a start if they wish to.

All good causes cannot be taken up by one person. Even if anyone tried to take them up, he would only render himself ridiculous. Someone else, therefore, should make this cause his own and devote all his time and energy to it.

However, readers of *Navajivan* can certainly prevail upon me to act upon one of the suggestions made by this correspondent. If a majority of them approve of *Navajivan* being printed in the Devanagari script, I would immediately discuss the matter with my co-workers. I do not have the courage to take the initiative about this without knowing readers' views. I attach greater importance to propagating my ideas about problems over which I have reflected for many years and which I regard as very urgent, than to the popularizing of a script. *Navajivan* has taken many risks in the past, but all of them were for the sake of fundamental principles. I would not take the risk of affecting the circulation of *Navajivan* for the sake of the Devanagari script.

Among readers of *Navajivan* there are many women, as also some Parsis and Muslims. I am afraid that all of them would find

[1] Not translated here. The correspondent had suggested that Gandhiji should advocate the adoption of Devanagari as the common script for languages of North India and himself publish the Gujarati *Navajivan* in that script.

it difficult, if not impossible, to read the Devanagari script. If my view is correct, I cannot print *Navajivan* in that script. Since popularizing this script is not my special field of work, I feel that I cannot take the risk of making a start in this regard. Even if the Gujarati *Navajivan* were published in the Devanagari script, the need for *Hindi Navajivan* would remain, for its readers cannot follow Gujarati.

But the correspondent's suggestion is worth being adopted and deserves the support of newspapers, etc. It is also worth ascertaining the views of *Navajivan*'s readers about it, and that is why I have published his letter. I would advise him not to rest content with writing the letter but, if he has the necessary time, to dedicate his life to propagation of his idea.

[From Gujarati]
Navajivan, 26-6-1927

57. *PHILANTHROPIC DOCTOR*

Antyajas First

I give below almost the whole of a letter which Shri Amritlal Sheth[1] has written to me describing how Doctor Lala Mathurdas visited Wadhwan and cured the eye diseases of hundreds of sufferers.

In former times, *vaids*[2] practised only for service. They got enough for their livelihood from what the rich paid them, but that was not looked upon as their fee. They believed that *vaids*' duty was to treat the patients for their diseases, and that God would provide for their livelihood. These days, like others the *vaids*, the *hakims*[3] and the doctors, all the three classes, by and large, practise to make money. But philanthropic doctors like Lala Mathurdas prove that all among them are not of that type.

The Arya Samaj has accepted the service of *Antyajas* as their special field of work; it is, therefore, not at all surprising that this good doctor felt very happy in serving them. The workers in Wadhwan deserve commendation for giving priority to *Antyajas*. As for Lala Mathurdas, what commendation can I offer him ? The

[1] A Congress worker of Saurashtra; founder-editor of *Janmabhumi*, a Gujarati daily published from Bombay. The letter is not translated here.

[2] Physicians practising the Ayurvedic system of medicine

[3] Physicians practising the Unani system of medicine

account given in the following letter proves that the satisfaction he felt in serving others is his best reward. I publish Shri Amritlal's letter in the hope that other doctors, *vaids* and *hakims* will follow this example of service.

[From Gujarati]

Navajivan, 26-6-1927

58. LETTER TO N. R. MALKANI

BANGALORE,
June 26, 1927

MY DEAR MALKANI,

Your letter[1] cuts me to the quick. I do not mind what happens to the Mahavidyalaya but I do mind what happens to a man. I had considered you to be good, strong and immovable under the greatest stress. You have been weighed and found wanting. This desertion in indecent haste is to me inexplicable. I am sorry also for Thadani[2]. He forgot the ordinary gentlemanly behaviour in his hurry to do good.

You may show this to him. May God help you and me.

Yours,
BAPU

From a photostat: G.N. 875 & S.N. 12599

59. LETTER TO ASHRAM WOMEN

Sunday Night, Jeth Vad 12 [*June 26, 1927*][3]

DEAR SISTERS,

Received your letter and the attendance book. Please do continue to send me the attendance book. I get to know many things from it.

I have been able to get a great deal of news from Manibehn. Whatever the odds, carry on the work in the store. We regard the

[1] Dated June 20, 1927. The addressee had intimated that he had joined the Sindh National College, Hyderabad (Sind), leaving the Gujarat Mahavidyalaya of the Gujarat Vidyapith, having sent his resignation to J. B. Kripalani, its Principal.

[2] N. V. Thadani, Principal, Sindh National College

[3] The year is inferred from the reference to the death of Valji Desai's mother.

Ashram as our family, and through it we try to learn to look upon our country and the whole world as one family. Therefore as in a family, so in the care of the store we should share one another's responsibilities.

Do not let my suggestions, like that for serving the cow, frighten you. I shall go on writing whatever occurs to me. Accept what you like, what is within your abilities, and do it when you have an opportunity.

Only the meritorious will meet with a death like that of Valjibhai's mother.

Blessed is the son, blessed the mother, and blessed the Ashram where such a death took place. I am also reminded of Vrajlalbhai's sacred death.

Blessings from
BAPU

From a photostat of the Gujarati: G.N. 3655

60. A LETTER

[Before *June 27, 1927*][1]

Just as it is useless to brood over the past, even so, it is useless to speculate about the future. "One step enough for me", says the voice of wisdom. What does it avail us to know the future? Or why not merge both the past and the future into the present? The present or the past does have a future. And when change confronts us from moment to moment, to think of some remote future is building castles in the air. And only a fool builds castles in the air. The present means our duty at this moment. If we put all our strength into doing our duty, as we know it at this moment, we shall have made the highest human effort. Sorrow springs from dreaming of the future and from lamenting the past. Hence one who concerns himself with the present and does his duty has neither birth nor death.

[From Gujarati]

From the manuscript of Mahadev Desai's Diary. Courtesy: Narayan Desai

[1] The source has this letter after the entries for June 21, and before those for June 27, 1927.

61. *LETTER TO TARA MODI*

BANGALORE,
Jeth Vad [*13, June 27, 1927*][1]

CHI. TARA,

I was very glad to read your letter. I refrained from writing to you merely in order to save you the trouble of reading my letter. But you are always before my mind's eye. I wish to see you strong and healthy in body and mind. Anyone who observes a difficult vow like yours in the prime of youth should never fall ill. But it may take ages to acquire such purity of heart. If one has holy merit acquired in previous births, one's heart will change the moment one wishes that it should change. We should try patiently till it does and not lose heart.

It is my firm faith and experience that one whose thoughts spontaneously and constantly flow towards the *atman* can never know sickness. My experience is very limited indeed, but one can judge the whole from a part.

For the present, continue the treatment which you are following and get well. Write to me everything you know about the person who is treating you, his experience, etc., etc. Do not be in a hurry to start walking; do as he directs you.

Write to me when you have the strength and inclination for it.

My health continues to improve. Manibehn and Chi. Keshu have come from the Ashram in connection with the Exhibition. It is likely that the others will come to[morrow.][2]

Blessings from
BAPU

From the Gujarati original: C.W. 1940. Courtesy: Ramniklal Modi

[1] From the manuscript of Mahadev Desai's Diary
[2] The source is not legible here.

62. LETTER TO DR. M. S. KELKAR

KUMARA PARK, BANGALORE,
June 28, 1927

MY DEAR DR.,

I have your letter. Of course when I refer to the increase of distance between us, it will only mean the distance in our methods of thinking, never in feeling. My regard for you cannot possibly be diminished no matter however much I may differ from you and your viewpoint. Of course I know that you are as much a seeker after Truth as I am. My impression is that you have your conclusions on very inadequate data, and to found a science upon your astrological observations, on what is now termed as black magic, you require overwhelming evidence of an absolutely unimpeachable character. So far as I know from discussions with you, I do not think you have such data for claiming finality about your conclusions or even [to] warrant preliminary inference. Do you not think that we have got to be far more exacting about things which men equally earnest as ourselves have rejected after trial?

Are you prepared for a fee to go to Dhulia and treat two patients, husband and wife?[1] And, if you are, please tell me what you would charge? The husband is suffering from habitual constipation and it seems to me to be a case for fasting. About the wife's disease I have not sufficient knowledge.

Yours sincerely,

From a photostat: S.N. 14174

[1] *Vide* "Telegram to Rameshwardas Poddar", 23-6-1927.

63. LETTER TO MRS. BLAIR

KUMARA PARK, BANGALORE,
June 28, 1927

DEAR MRS. BLAIR,

You are so good. Whenever there is [1], you never fail to send it to me. I hope that those who have given their names[2] will persist to the end. Of course it is quite the proper thing to spin wool in Darjeeling. The chief thing is to do hand-spinning. I expect you some day at the Ashram. Of course I am still convalescing, and have to do what little I can in the South.

Yours sincerely,

MRS. BLAIR
MALL VILLA 3
DARJEELING

From a microfilm: S.N. 14175

64. LETTER TO JAMINI BHUSHAN MITRA

KUMARA PARK, BANGALORE,
June 28, 1927

DEAR JAMINI BABU,

I have your letter. The policy of the Association is to discountenance the starting or manning of separate khadi organizations except for good grounds. Of course you might have sufficient reasons. But I do not know. In any case, it will be necessary for you to approach the Association through the Bengal Agent who, as you know, is Satis Babu. You have first of all to satisfy him. Lastly, perhaps you do not know that owing to my illness I have not been able to take an active interest in the proceedings of the Association. I would therefore suggest carrying on your further correspondence in this matter with the Secretary of the Association at Ahmedabad. Whenever there is any necessity, of course he does refer to me.

[1] The source has a blank here.

[2] To spin at least half an hour a day; *vide* "Notes", 7-7-1927, sub-heading, "Deshbandhu Day at Darjeeling".

I am forwarding your letter to Satis Babu in order that there may be no waste of time.

Yours sincerely,

SJT. JAMINI BHUSHAN MITRA
KHALISPUR ASHRAM
P.O.B. KHALISPUR
(KHULNA)

From a microfilm: S.N. 19784

65. *LETTER TO D. B. KALELKAR*

June 28, 1927

No matter what Chi. Shankar does, you should not feel sorry. How can the poor fellow help it? What should he do—keep pace with you, obey Kaki or be in tune with the wind that blows about him? Day by day, I find myself experiencing merely the bondage of human existence. Man has freedom only to attain *moksha*. In whatever else he does, he becomes more and more dependent on others. You can easily check up on this. Then you will not bother about Shankar and Kaki.

What wonder if Bal longs for Kaki's company? She alone is the medicine for him. If we decide not to take Kaki into the Ashram we should offer him his choice. He either stays with Kaki at Belgaum or wherever she would or in the Ashram with anyone we ask him to stay with. I have not yet decided that Kaki must come to the Ashram. I have had no reply as yet to my letter to her. I have been waiting for it a long while.

I welcome Gangubehn staying with you and coming in contact with Gangabehn and keeping it up. Gangubehn appears to be an absolutely innocent girl. I would like it very much if Gangabehn formed a separate group of the women in the Ashram. She should start it gradually and those who want to associate with her may do so. I like, as an ideal thing, even a married couple living apart in the Ashram. It appears difficult to implement the idea at present. But if we once accept an ideal, we can ultimately live up to it. Rather than discussing the ideal, at present, if only all the women who live scattered about come to live together and find it workable we shall have scored a great victory.

The path of non-violence is the most difficult of all. Truth is not a path, it is the goal. There is only one path—that of non-violence—to reach there, so how could it be easy? So far we have not yet attained non-violence in thought. When we see our duty clear as daylight, we sometimes lack the strength to carry it out. In view of this let us be as careful as possible in our thought and action and live happily. If what the *Gita* conveys is correct I get this same meaning out of it while translating it. . . .[1] Not to find fault in others is to see one's own. Those we see in others were once in us too and, in a sense, are still there. In the process of forgetting the difference of mine and thine, Surdas and others called themselves rogues[2] and so on.

[From Gujarati]

From the manuscript of Mahadev Desai's Diary. Courtesy: Narayan Desai

66. LETTER TO SURENDRA

BANGALORE,
Jeth Vad 14 [*June 28, 1927*][3]

CHI. SURENDRA,

I got your letter. I have written a long letter to Kaka Saheb. I do not understand why he worries. Lakshmidas has not so far sent me his new ideas about khadi propaganda. I have written to Kishorelal about *asana* exercises, and he will write to me after discussing the matter with Nathji. I should like you to send me your experiences of the institutions you visited. For instance, what did you see in Saswad? And in Supa? What did you notice elsewhere worthy of acceptance by us ? We wish, if we can, to accept whatever is good in others; we should, therefore, rejoice whenever we see something good and emulate it. If we happen to notice any shortcomings, we should tolerate them, since we too always expect the world to tolerate our shortcomings.

Blessings from
BAPU

From a photostat of the Gujarati: S.N. 9409

[1] As in the source
[2] *Mo sama kaun kutila khala kami*
[3] Gandhiji was in Bangalore on this date in 1927.

67. *LETTER TO NAJUKLAL N. CHOKSI*

BANGALORE,
June 28, 1927

BHAI NAJUKLAL,

I have your letter as also Chi. Moti's. Neither her elders nor you have been able to cure Moti of her lethargy. Let us now see whether her offspring succeeds in doing that. I hope you have recovered your health completely. It is some satisfaction to know that you have not been infected by Moti. I say this because the experience of the world is that when two persons live together one of them cannot but be influenced by the other. Hence either Moti will be infected by you—it is clear that she has not been—or you will be infected by her. I am all the time afraid that you will be infected by her. Write to me when the delivery is expected, and even otherwise write from time to time. For some time yet I shall remain hereabouts.

Blessings from
BAPU

BHAISHRI NAJUKLAL CHOKSI
SEVASHRAM
BROACH

From a photostat of the Gujarati: S.N. 12140

68. *LETTER TO RAJKISHORI MEHROTRA*

KUMARA PARK, BANGALORE,
June 28, 1927

CHI. RAJKISHORI,

I wrote two letters to you but got no reply. Now that I have your letter, I write this. Let me know how you are observing your vow. And how are the boys? How is your health? What have you been reading these days? Letters can be received at this address up to 10th July, after which they should be addressed to the Ashram.

Blessings from
BAPU

From the Hindi original: C.W. 6659. Courtesy: Parashuram Mehrotra

69. *LETTER TO BANARASIDAS CHATURVEDI*

BANGALORE,
June 28, 1927

BHAI BANARASIDASJI,

Your letter. I cannot understand why there was no reply at all from the Ashram. I am looking into it. It appears that I shall not be able to go to the Ashram for nearly two months. There would be nothing wrong if I happened to get your letter during my illness.

Yours,
MOHANDAS

From a photostat of the Hindi: G.N. 2572

70. *LETTER TO KUVALAYANAND*

KUMARA PARK, BANGALORE,
June 29, 1927

DEAR FRIEND,

I have your letter[1] for which I thank you. I am sorry to have to report to you that the blood-pressure taken on last Sunday week had been found to have risen from 150 to 160. The doctors could not make out why the increase had taken place. I then gave them an ocular demonstration of what I had been doing in the way of *sarvangasana*, as also *halasana*, as you have termed the practice I described to you. They urged me to stop the two practices for the time being.[2] I therefore stopped them. Otherwise too, as I said in my previous letter, I would have stopped *sarvangasana* if the pressure had gone up, till I had taken your advice. Last Sunday the blood-pressure was taken again, and it was found to have gone down by five degrees. I suppose, therefore, it is best for me to continue the suspension of the two practices for a while. In any event, they will remain suspended till I hear from you.

[1] Dated June 22, 1927

[2] In the draft (S.N. 14176), the words "for the time being" were put at the end of the next sentence.

Everything else continues as before, that is, walks, deep-breathing, the *shavasana* and the massage. I am able to take butter also without difficulty. It has been now increased to three teaspoons. I do not propose to go beyond this, unless you consider that it is necessary to increase the quantity. Milk stands at 30 ounces. I am now weighing the *bhakharis* I take, and the quantity I take weighs three ounces in a cooked condition. In view of the tendency of the system towards an increase in blood-pressure on the slightest provocation, do you want me to start *bhujangasana*? So far as physical strength is concerned, there is no difficulty about undertaking any of these practices. And personally I am unable to understand why some of these *asanas* should increase the blood-pressure, although they do not apparently affect the system otherwise. I suppose they do not increase blood-pressure in men enjoying normal health. It would be well if you could say which *asanas* are positively harmless, so far as blood-pressure is concerned.

Yours sincerely,
M. K. GANDHI

From a photostat: G.N. 5050

71. LETTER TO ALVI

June 29, 1927

I have your straightforward letter.[1] Of course, you have addressed it to the Editor but I shall not reply to it in *Navajivan* because the question you have raised is not likely to occur to many. I suspect from your letter that your study of the *Gita* is not deep enough. There is no difference between *nishkama karma*[2] and *tatastha karma*[3]. You take it for granted that a benevolent act is an unattached one. *But non-attachment and benevolence are two distinct qualities*. In this world one sees attachment in benevolence everywhere and hence numberless sins have been, are being and will be committed in the name of benevolence. The reason why the *Gita* is dear to me is that the divine author has seen this

[1] In which the correspondent had asked why Gandhiji had described his action in donating Badri's money for the cause of vegetarianism as neither unattached nor impartial.

[2] Desireless work

[3] Work done without attachment

distinction through experience and has in the course of his work endeavoured to explain it minutely and repeatedly in varying words and also in identical terms. It was certainly no selfish act on my part to have helped the vegetarian movement, but despite this fact I looked upon it as my own rather than God's; and where personal attachment develops there is no impartiality and no detachment. Today I clearly see my attachment and desire in having been emboldened to deploy my client's money for that work because I regarded that work as my own. Khadi work certainly is benevolent. Suppose I have some money belonging to you and of course I intend to return it to you. I may even be able to return it forthwith. Now if I am carrying on khadi work without personal attachment, I would never use your money. It should be my dharma to carry on the business of khadi only with the money specifically received for it. And as long as that work can be carried on without attachment and desire, I would not make use of any other money. Now you must have seen how in that case I lost my impartiality. Had I used my own money, there would have been no difficulty. Staying impartial does not mean withholding help. Where one feels one should help and if one has the capacity, one should certainly do so; one should not however press into service another's resources without his permission. And even in seeking such permission one ought to be discreet. I had the late Bhai Badri's permission though I do not regard it as such. He was not capable of thinking independently and giving his opinion. He had given his consent merely because of his faith in me. And that too in the distinct belief that I would never allow his money to be misused. Under such circumstances it was my dharma not to risk his money to the slightest extent. If you do not understand me after all this, do ask me for further clarification.

[From Gujarati]

From the manuscript of Mahadev Desai's Diary. Courtesy: Narayan Desai

72. *LETTER TO JAGMOHAN DAHYABHAI*

June 29, 1927

A healthy mother's milk contains all the elements that a child needs. Mother's milk is a complete food for the child. Hence there is absolutely no need to give it fruit juices. Sometimes we see such need because the mother is subject to passions and yields to temptations of the palate or may be she has a disease and therefore her milk is not quite wholesome and nourishing. I can therefore offer you only this advice: if the child keeps healthy and if you see his strength growing day by day, you need give it nothing besides milk but if you find it whining or growing thin or if mother's milk is not enough in quantity, you can certainly give it small quantities of orange or grape juice.

The sentence I have quoted from my book does not hold in the case of a child of two or three months. But when a child begins to sit, can exert itself sufficiently and when its gums have become strong, it should get used to green fruits in case it needs more than mother's milk. In short, we should first let it have milk and then start on fruits.

[From Gujarati]

From the manuscript of Mahadev Desai's Diary. Courtesy: Narayan Desai

73. *LETTER TO FULCHAND K. SHAH*

[After *June 29, 1927*][1]

I would advise you and Devchandbhai not to insist on running the administration of the Conference. And if both of you are interested in any other work in addition to the work of khadi, the *Antyajas*, national education, etc., or any other equally constructive activity, and if you are competent to take it up, do retain charge of the administration and do whatever is right. Speaking for myself, I have no interest at present in political activities apart from cow-protection and so on, nor do I find myself up to it. I therefore simply watch it from a distance. If someone says something about politics I discuss it a little with him. When I cannot

[1] The source has this letter after the entries for June 29, 1927.

avoid writing about it I scribble off something. In other respects I remain completely untouched.

[From Gujarati]

From the manuscript of Mahadev Desai's Diary. Courtesy: Narayan Desai

74. *OUR SHAME*

Sjt. S. D. Nadkarni is a clear writer, and has a very large heart for the so-called untouchables. I publish in another column, without any alteration, a letter[1] from him, in which he has poured out his feeling for the suppressed classes. And he has rightly used me as a peg, on which to hang his indictment of the touchables. Leaving aside, however, myself out of account, it seems to me that his deep feeling has overpowered the sense of logic which as a rule does not fail him. I venture to think, that terrible as the case for untouchables is, it had no place either in the discussions of the All-India Congress Committee at Bombay, or at the Unity Conference at Delhi, when only the question of Hindu-Muslim unity alone was on the anvil. It would have been just as logical to discuss at these meetings the question, say, of the woes of child widows, terrible as these are, as it would have been to handle the question of untouchability. But the slight illogicality of the letter must not be allowed to blur the very important question so forcibly presented by Sjt. Nadkarni. I entirely agree with him, that if there is no swaraj without Hindu-Muslim unity, much less is there swaraj without the removal of the shame of Hinduism, which untouchability certainly is. I am unconcerned with the question, what place untouchables will have in any political constitution that may be drawn up. Every one of the artificial props, that may be set up in the constitution, will be broken to bits, if we Hindus do not wish to play the game. The reasoning I have given against separate electorates and against separate treatment in the constitution is equally applicable in the case of untouchables. This removal of untouchability is not to be brought about by any legal enactment. It will only be brought about, when the Hindu conscience is roused to action, and of its own accord *removes* the shame. It is a duty the touchables owe to the untouchables.

[1] Dated May 28, 1927

> Let them not wait till the Suppressed Class Leagues and Touchable-Untouchable riots open their eyes to the needs of the most needy among us Indians.

This is a terrible sentence occurring in the concluding portion of the letter. It is impossible to deny the force behind it. It reminds me of the conversation that took place between the late Hari Narayan Apte and myself just before Gokhale died. It was at the Servants of India Society's quarters in Poona, that I was pleading for work amongst the so-called higher classes, rather than agitating amongst the suppressed classes after the fashion of some missionaries, and creating unrest among them. I was new to the work. I had not drunk deep of the ocean of miseries, in which the suppressed classes were being drowned, as the late Hari Narayan Apte had. In my philosophical prudence I asked this reformer, burning with the shame of the wrongs heaped upon the suppressed classes by the suppressing classes, whether he would incite suppressed classes against us. Instantly and indignantly came the reply:

> Certainly, if I could, I would make them rebel against us today, and wrest from us by force what we will not give them voluntarily and as a matter of duty.

Much progress has been achieved in the matter of this reform. But infinitely more remains to be done. Most reforms have been preceded by bloodshed. There seems to arrive a point, at which patience of the downtrodden is exhausted, and taking the law into their own hands and maddened with grief and rage they make short work of the tyrant, and in their turn repeat, on an opportunity occurring, all the mistakes of the tyrant. Though, therefore, I share now to the fullest extent, I hope, the indignation that filled Hari Narayan Apte, I must work in the hope that the so-called higher class Hindus will, whilst there is yet time, retrace their steps, and render to the suppressed classes the justice which has become long overdue, and in the further hope that, should the former not repent, the suppressed classes will know better than to rise in revolt against the wrongdoers. I must continue to work in the hope that they will vindicate themselves and their Hinduism by going through a process of conscious suffering and self-purification, and thus proving themselves superior Hindus to those who are today disgracing themselves and Hinduism before man and God. Every individual Hindu, who feels as Sjt. Nadkarni does for the untouchables, can meanwhile make common cause with them by himself or herself becoming untouchable by sharing their sorrows and their trials.

Young India, 30-6-1927

75. *CHITTARANJAN SEVA SADAN*

Dr. Bidhan Chandra Roy, the celebrated physician of Calcutta and one of the trustees of the All-Bengal Deshbandhu Memorial Trust, has issued an appeal for five lakhs of rupees for the Seva Sadan. It will be remembered that this institution is situated on the ground which Deshbandhu in his lifetime had made over to the trustees. The ground was partly encumbered. It was redeemed out of the memorial funds that were collected immediately after Deshbandhu's death, and for over a year, a well-equipped and well-managed hospital and a dispensary have been going on there. The total number of the cases treated at the outdoor during the year was 22,000, new cases being 7,023. The total number of in-door patients was 579 with only 23 beds. The trustees now propose to add 32 beds. There can be no doubt that the institution supplies a felt want, and that it needs expansion. Expansion means more money. Those, who revere the memory of Deshbandhu, and who appreciate the necessity of rendering aid to the ailing, will not lose time in responding to the appeal issued on behalf of the Board of Trustees. A full report of the institution, containing a certified account of income and expenditure, and an analysis of cases treated at the institution, accompanies the report, which can be had from Dr. Bidhan Chandra Roy, 148, Russa Road South, Calcutta. Subscriptions can be sent to the Secretary, Deshbandhu Memorial Trust, 36, Wellington Street, Calcutta, or to the account of Deshbandhu Memorial Trust, Central Bank of India, Limited, 100, Clive Street, Calcutta.

Young India, 30-6-1927

76. BANGALORE KHADI EXHIBITION

Sjts. C. Rajagopalachari and Gangadharrao Deshpande are making great preparations to make the forthcoming Khadi Exhibition at Bangalore a thorough success. They are aiming not at quantity but quality, and so they have purposely restricted the scope. It is to be therefore not an all-India, but a South India Exhibition. But they are inviting from all the provinces the assistance that may be necessary in order to complete the technical demonstration, and in order to make the Exhibition an instructive object-lesson. Those, therefore, who would learn all about the technique of khadi from hand-ginning to hand-weaving, and study the instruments used in the processes and to see them at work by skilled hands, will not fail to attend the Exhibition. It is a happy augury for the future of khadi in Mysore that the State has given a donation of Rs. 500/- towards the expenses of the Exhibition, and that the Director of Industries has become a member of the Exhibition Committee. Indeed the economic and the philanthropic side of khadi is so overwhelmingly important that it is a wonder that Rajas and Maharajas have not given the movement the support that it deserves. Everybody agrees that millions of villagers require a supplementary occupation. Scores of paper schemes are being hawked about the country for achieving village reconstruction. But not one scheme has the universal application that khadi has. And so far as I am aware, not one scheme is being tried on the scale that khadi is being tried. It is not a small achievement to be able to show that the khadi scheme is at work in at least 1,500 villages.

That khadi has a political side to it need not frighten a single person, even though he may be an official. Indeed many learned politicians laugh at khadi, when any political consequence is ascribed to it; and they would be right if the word 'political' was used in connection with khadi in the same sense that it is used in connection with Councils. Khadi has a political consequence precisely in the same sense that education has, co-operative schemes have, temperance reform has. It is impossible to avoid the political effect of any progressive measure that a nation may adopt. The Viceroy, and the Rajas, Maharajas and everybody must, if they are not traitors to the country, take an active part in promoting Hindu-Muslim unity, and yet nobody has ventured to laugh at the idea of Hindu-Muslim unity having a tremendous political consequence; nor have I known anybody keeping himself aloof from the movement for promoting that unity on the ground that it has a tremendous political consequence. Indeed the full success of khadi and therewith its political effect depend upon the support of all, politicians and non-politicians, the prince and the pauper, the zamindar and the ryot. Every attempt is therefore being made to keep khadi above political turmoil. It is not an emblem of revolt; but it is an emblem of self-assertion, self-reliance and determination to abolish artificial distinctions between rich and poor, between capital and labour, and establish a living bond between the two. I am hoping, therefore, that the forthcoming Exhibition will receive the solid support of all classes of people, including the numerous European settlements in the cantonment of Bangalore. That large population will be equally welcome with the rest. Indeed in my talks with the European friends, who have kindly visited me during my convalescence at Nandi and at Bangalore, I have not hesitated to present the message of khadi, that is the message of India's starving millions, for their acceptance.

One word to the fashionable people of Bangalore. I observe a teacher of Trichinopoly has been pleading for the adoption of a minimum in sartorial matters. I observed, also, that Sjt. Srinivasa Sastri the other day at a public meeting remarked upon what might almost be called the over-dress of the fashionable people of Bangalore. And I have noticed on the part of those who believe in khadi a timid hesitation to adopt it in the face of the Bangalore fashion. I plead for the necessary courage to set aside fashion, which can only be sustained at the expense of our starving neighbours. By all means let monied people have tasteful ornamentation, whether in dress or in other surroundings; but I do plead for an observance, as between themselves and their starving brethren, of a due sense of proportion, such as is always observed in well ordered society. India's minimum is a *langoti* requiring less than 1/6th of a square yard. Let our fashion have some correspondence to this minimum. Let not those, who would raise this minimum, and multiply India's wants in order to wake her up to action, think that they would achieve the end by first multiplying their own wants at the expense of the poor, and without in the same proportion enabling and inducing the latter to raise their standard of living. One universal and effective and immediate way to enable and induce these millions to raise their standard of living is for the fashionable middle class to adopt khadi, and thereby put a few coppers into their pockets. Many in Bangalore have given pecuniary contributions to khadi work. But this is not enough. Khadi cannot make real progress, unless there are people to wear it. I therefore ask the people of Bangalore and neighbouring districts not merely to visit the Exhibition, and give the movement pecuniary support, but also to identify themselves with the poor by adopting khadi for their dress.

Young India, 30-6-1927

77. *NOTES*

In Justice to Her Memory

The Modern Review[1] has a paragraph on what occurs in *The Story of My Experiments with Truth*, Chapter 19, Part III,[2] on Sister Nivedita. After quoting my remarks, *The Modern Review* has:

> The mention of "the splendour that surrounded her" without any other details conveys a wrong idea of Sister Nivedita's mode of living. The fact is, at the time when Mr. Gandhi saw her, she was the guest of Mrs. Ole Bull and Miss Josephine MacLeod at the American Consulate, and, as such, was not responsible for the "splendour". Her ascetic and very simple style of living in a tumbledown house in Bossepara Lane, Baghbazar, is well known to all her friends and acquaintances.
>
> We do not know whether Mr. Gokhale spoke to Mr. Gandhi in English and actually used the word "volatile" to describe her; for what has appeared in *Young India* is translated from the Gujarati *Navajivan*. But whoever may be responsible for the use of the word 'volatile' has wronged her memory. Sister Nivedita had her defects, as in fact even the greatest of mankind had and have, but volatile she was not in any sense of that word. As English is not our vernacular, we have consulted two dictionaries on our table to find out its exact meaning as applied to human beings. The Pocket Oxford Dictionary defines it to mean "of gay temperament, mercurial". In Webster's New International Dictionary the explanation given is, "light-hearted; airy; lively; hence, changeable; fickle". Sister Nivedita was a very serious-minded person, noted for her constancy and steadfast devotion to the cause of Hinduism and India.
>
> The reference to "her overflowing love for Hinduism" is quite just and accurate.

[1] Of July, 1927
[2] Published in *Young India*, April 14, 1927

I gladly reproduce this correction. For I never knew the fact, till I saw the note in *The Modern Review* that I had met the deceased not at her own place but at a guest's. The reader has to recognize my painful limitations. My reading is so poor that I have not read, much though I should like to have, the lives even of those who have contributed to the making of modern India. My only consolation is that the poverty of my reading is not due to any laziness on my part, but a life of ceaseless action and full of tempest from early youth left no time for much reading. Whether on the whole I have lost or gained thereby is to me a debatable question. But if it is a gain, it has been achieved in spite of myself. I can therefore claim no credit for it. And if in the story that I am writing from week to week,[1] I deal with men and women, I do so only in so far as such reference is necessary for showing the working of my mind, so far as I can, in my search for Truth. I am therefore leaving out innumerable instances in life, which would be certainly otherwise interesting, as also references to several men and women. And it will be unjust to those whom I am obliged to refer in the story and to me, if the reader concludes that the estimate that I may give about persons is my final statement or true in fact. Such references should be regarded merely as the impression left upon my mind at the time to which they may relate. I introduced Sister Nivedita, Swami Vivekananda, Maharshi Devendranath and others in the story simply to illustrate my desperate search, and to illustrate the point, that even then my political work in South Africa was an integral part of that search, which was never once subordinated to the political work. It has therefore given me pleasure to reproduce the paragraph in *The Modern Review* at the very first opportunity after reading it.

As to the use of the word "volatile", though the translation is not mine, I cannot dissociate myself from its use, because as a rule I revise these translations, and I remember having discussed the adjective with Mahadev Desai. We both had doubts about the use of the adjective being correct. The choice lay between volatile, violent and fanatical. The last two were considered to be too strong. Mahadev had chosen volatile and I passed it. But neither he nor I had the dictionary meaning in view.

[1] The reference is to Gandhiji's autobiography, chapters of which were being published in *Navajivan* from November 29, 1925 and in *Young India* from December 3, 1925.

What word Gokhale used I cannot recall. The word used in the original writing is *tej*. I have a full recollection of the conversation between Sister Nivedita and myself. But I do not propose to describe it. No fault in the translation or the original can possibly damage the memory of one who loved Hinduism and India so well. It will ever be cherished with gratefulness.

Young India, 30-6-1927

78. *KASHI VIDYAPITH*

The readers of *Young India* know that the Kashi Vidyapith is one of the very few national institutions still alive. I have much pleasure in publishing the following[1] sent to me by the Registrar of the Kashi Vidyapith.

Young India, 30-6-1927

79. *MESSAGE TO "FORWARD"*[2]

June 30, 1927

If we would be worthy of swaraj and of the sacrifice of Deshbandhu, we must show some tangible work of construction in terms of the nation. Khadi holds the field till something better and equally universal can displace it. And if khadi and the spinning-wheel be considered beneath dignity and notice, we stand in danger of being considered beneath notice by the Mother.

The Hindu, 1-7-1927

[1] Not reproduced here; it gave the date of reopening of the Vidyalaya, subjects taught, minimum qualifications for admission, etc.

[2] For its "Deshbandhu Number"

80. LETTER TO P. R. SUBRAMANIA SASTRI

KUMARA PARK, BANGALORE,
June 30, 1927

DEAR FRIEND,

Sjt. Rajagopalachariar has shown me your letter of the 29th instant. I am not yet fit enough to meet people for holding sustained discourse. Whilst therefore if you desire to come, you will be welcome any day between 4 and 5 p.m. I shall not be able to engage in any long conversation with you. If you have anything original to say, I would suggest your writing it as briefly as possible on one side of an ordinary note paper and sending it to me.

Yours sincerely,

SJT. P. R. SUBRAMANIA SASTRI
55, MALLESWARAM
BANGALORE

From a photostat: S.N. 14177

81. LETTER TO T. ADINARAYANA CHETTIAR[1]

KUMARA PARK, BANGALORE,
July 1, 1927

DEAR FRIEND,

It is a most dangerous thing to expect me to send replies by return post. It is by mere accident that I am able to deal with your letter immediately on receipt.

I do hope that you will be able to make further progress with the resolutions you refer to, namely, remarriage of virgin widows and post-puberty marriage. These two, I consider, to be elementary reforms and they are the least that Hindus owe to Hinduism and India and their womenfolk.

[1] This was sent as a message to the Arya Vaisya Conference which began at Salem on July 2.

I hope your conference will not forget the suppressed classes and the spinning-wheel.

Yours sincerely,

SJT. T. ADINARAYANA CHETTIAR
XIII ARYA VAISYA CONFERENCE
SALEM

From a microfilm: S.N. 14179

82. LETTER TO SAROJINI NAIDU

KUMARA PARK, BANGALORE,
July 1, 1927

I hope you got my letter. This is only to send you Andrews' cable[1]. I know that you are six inches taller, if such a thing may be said of a mere woman, for the triumph of the principle for which you stood up so bravely in South Africa. You have every reason to be proud.

Yours,
M. K. GANDHI

From a photostat: S.N. 12363

83. LETTER TO HARINDRANATH CHATTOPADHYAYA

KUMARA PARK, BANGALORE,
July 1, 1927

DEAR FRIEND,

I have your letter. I shall look forward to the end of June 1928.

As you have not told me anything about the lady you have in view, I can only give you general information. The Ashram is, you might almost say, a workshop. Men and women are engaged in doing some work or other, all activities centred round ginning, carding, spinning and weaving, and both men and women, boys and girls take their due share in these activities. There is, no doubt, literary training in a proper school conducted in the Ashram. But

[1] Dated June 25; it read: "Malan faithfully loyal towards settlement, rejected hostile amendments. Thank God worst strain over. Tell Sarojini."

vocational training is not sacrificed to literary training. One might almost therefore fancy that literary training is subordinated to the vocational. English is taught, it might almost be said, under compulsion. We don't encourage the teaching of English there, and the rule of first exacting a knowledge of Sanskrit and Hindi before going to English is more or less adhered to. If, therefore, this lady does not know Hindi, or wants to do everything through English, or is fond merely of literary pursuits, at the Ashram, she would be like fish out of water. Now if you want to know the details about the Ashram, you will please tell me and I shall pass on your letter to the proper quarters for reply.

Yours sincerely,

From a photostat: S.N. 12775

84. LETTER TO J. W. PETAVEL

KUMARA PARK, BANGALORE,
July 1, 1927

DEAR FRIEND,

I have your two letters. Isn't it funny that in spite of both of them being long, I find nothing there touching the direct question that I have put? Surely, it is the easiest thing possible for you to tell me what is Belgium doing, what is Switzerland doing? What are you *doing* as distinguished from writing?

I add another question. I have nearly 80 acres of ground on which we are nearly 200 souls, men and women and children, and therefore parents with their children. We are doing a little bit of agriculture and we are doing dairy work, etc. Tell me what we should do to fall under your scheme.

Yours sincerely,

From a photostat: S.N. 14178

85. LETTER TO B. F. BHARUCHA[1]

[Before *July 2, 1927*][2]

What will you see by going to Nagpur? It is not necessary for me to explain to you that a satyagrahi cannot break the Arms Act. From the outset, the meaning of civil disobedience has been violation of such laws as are opposed to *niti* (ethics), so that there can be violation of *jakati* laws (tariff or taxation laws). There cannot be violation of laws that forbid thefts. Similarly, the man who carries on a peaceful campaign cannot carry a sword or a rifle with the object of being arrested or with any other purpose. At Lucknow, where Maulana Mahomed Ali and I were going round, we found volunteers with naked swords and we made them give up their swords. At Bezwada Maulana Mahomed Ali and I made volunteers give up their big sticks, though no permit or licence was necessary to carry them.

The man who is out to die or to give up his life, how can he hold a sword ? Anything may happen after altering the aspect of the campaign, giving up the name of satyagraha or withdrawing the epithet *shanti*. But under cover of words such as *shanti*, satyagraha, etc., how could there be promulgation of *ashanti* or *asatya*? Ere this, I had seen your support to the Nagpur campaign and even then I felt pained. But it is hardly possible to correct even our friends immediately they err. I have written even this much because of your reference in your letter that you were proceeding to Nagpur to see what was going on there.

The Hindu, 4-7-1927

[1] This is part of a Gujarati letter the original of which is not available. *Vide* "Limitations of Satyagraha", 14-7-1927.

[2] This letter was read by the addressee at an emergent meeting of Nagpur Nagar Congress Committee held on July 2.

86. MESSAGE TO PEOPLE OF SOUTH INDIA

[*July 2, 1927*][1]

In a letter addressed to the men and women of South India, Mahatma Gandhi says:

It has been a matter of deep grief to me that owing to the collapse of my health, I was unable to enter upon the tour in South India on the appointed date. God willing, I hope to commence the tour some time in July though the original programme will have to be considerably modified and reduced. Meanwhile, however, I hope that those who have not yet taken to khadi will do so for the sake of the starving millions; for, whoever buys one yard of khadi puts the whole of the cost of it into the pockets of the poor people of this famine-stricken land, more than half of it going directly into the pockets of those to whom every pie means so much more money to buy the necessaries of life.

The Hindu, 2-7-1927

87. LETTER TO MOTILAL NEHRU[2]

KUMARA PARK, BANGALORE,
July 2, 1927

DEAR MOTILALJI,

So I can't have you in Bangalore, it appears. It will be cruel to have you follow me somewhere down South to melt there. But if you come even about the end of this month, I might be at some pleasant place in Mysore, because the whole of Mysore is Nature's favoured spot in India's plains.

About the time that Sarojini Devi wrote to you, she wrote to me also, and sent a peremptory telegram asking me to sup-

[1] Released on this date by the Associated Press of India from Bangalore

[2] In reply to his letter dated June 25. Motilal Nehru had written: "Your letter arrived just after I had posted my reply to Sarojini who was instigated by Jinnah and the Maharaja of Mahmudabad to offer the Crown to me in supersession of both Ansari and Jawahar."

port her request, and even to "issue orders". But I knew beforehand what you would say to the proposal kindly meant, but thoughtlessly made. I wrote to her almost in the same strain as you, and suggested that Dr. Ansari was the only possible president. I told her also that I did not at all believe that his occupancy of the presidential chair would in any way diminish the weight of any settlement arrived at by the Congress. In my opinion, if Dr. Ansari is chosen, a reasonable settlement has a better chance of being adopted by the Congress.

You did tell me about the appearance of *Tara*[1]. What with *Chand*[2] and *Tara,* there must be perpetual illumination in the house; and the appearance of *Suraj*[3] to support Chand and Tara is, let us hope, a question merely of time. I shall readily forgive Sarup for never thinking of writing to me if she brings up her Suns and Moons and Stars for the service of the Motherland. I hope both the mother and the baby are making steady progress.

I make my first appearance tomorrow to open a Khadi Exhibition which has been arranged in Bangalore in order to keep my chief warders Gangadharrao and Rajagopalachari occupied. They are doing a brisk trade in khadi and are not ashamed to exploit their prisoner's illness.

Yours sincerely,

From a photostat: S.N. 12598

88. LETTER TO VASUMATI PANDIT

BANGALORE,
Ashadh Shuddha 3 [July 2, 1927][4]

CHI. VASUMATI,

I got your letter. You have done well in going to the Ashram. Take good care of your health. Health permitting, help if you can in the work of the store which the women have taken upon themselves. My health is steadily improving. There is still room for improvement in your handwriting. It will improve if you write carefully and slowly for some time. Speed will come by and by. It is the same with this as with spinning. It is diffi-

[1] Second daughter of Sarup (Vijayalakshmi Pandit); literally, 'star'
[2] First daughter of Sarup; literally, 'moon'
[3] Literally, 'sun'
[4] Gandhiji was in Bangalore on this date in 1927.

cult to ensure strength in the yarn after first learning to spin fast; on the contrary, speed will increase of itself after one has learnt to spin strong yarn.

Blessings from
BAPU

From a photostat of the Gujarati: C.W. 587. Courtesy: Vasumati Pandit

89. LETTER TO SANTOJI MAHARAJ

BANGALORE,
Aso Sud 3 [July 2, 1927]

SHRI SANTOJI MAHARAJ,

I have carefully preserved your questions, and with God's grace I shall try to answer them now. I enclose the questions with this answer so that you may not have to take the trouble of recalling them and I may not have to copy them. I have numbered them serially, and there should be, therefore, no confusion.

1. Only he can interpret the *Gita* correctly who tries to follow its teaching in practice, and the correctness of the interpretation will be in proportion to his success in living according to the teaching. The *Gita* was not composed as a learned treatise. It may be a profound one, but in my view the realization of its profound quality depends on the depth of one's sincerity in putting its teaching into practice. I have read Lokamanya Tilak's and Shankaracharya's commentaries and tried to understand them as well as I could. I am not qualified to pronounce judgment on their learning. If we accept the point of view I have suggested, the question of expressing an opinion on their learning does not arise. The *Gita* is related to the Vedas and the Upanishads, for it gives the essence of both.

2. The *Gita* teaches that one should cultivate the state of *samatva*[1] and explains with every manner of argument the means of doing so, namely, *bhakti*[2] accompanied with *jnana*[3], that is, service of every living creature without thought of reward.

3. The godly heritage, according to the *Gita*, is that which helps one to attain self-realization. The sign of having acquired such heritage is the weakening of one's attachments and aversions, and

[1] Equanimity in all circumstances and equality towards all things

[2] Devotion

[3] Knowledge

the means of acquiring it is cultivation of *bhakti* for the Lord.

4. As far as I have been able to read and understand the teachings of our sacred writers of past times, I don't think there is any difference of view.

5. A Brahmin and a Bhangi[1] [let us suppose] are stung by a scorpion. I see that a *vaid* has arrived to help the former, and another has been sent for. The *vaid* simply does not look towards the Bhangi who has been crying for help. Both the *vaid* and the Brahmin hear his cries. If the Brahmin has learnt to regard all beings with an equal eye, he would ask the *vaid* to treat the Bhangi first. If I were the *vaid*, I would run to the Bhangi, suck out the poison from the wound and apply to him whatever other remedies I knew. Having done that, I would offer my service to the Brahmin, if he required it, and then attend to my other work. To cultivate an equal eye towards all beings means to serve all people in the world with equal regard.

6. It is not true at all that the Lord teaches in the *Gita* that one may kill one's kinsmen. When Arjuna got ready to fight for what he believed to be a just cause, and was overcome with ignorant attachment and weakness, through which he made a distinction between kinsmen and others, the Lord cured him of his attachment and weakness. We can only guess what reply Krishna would have given if Arjuna had protested and said that he did not wish to kill at all, whether his opponents were kinsmen or others. It is my humble view, however, that the *Gita* was not composed to give a direct answer to that question.

7. I have felt that there is a greater spirit of universality and liberalism in the *sanatana* Vedic dharma[2].

8. The question, which is the chief religious work, one can answer only for oneself. For me it is the *Gita*. One distinction at any rate among such works is based on the subject they deal with, namely, those which lay down codes of conduct and others which state and explain the nature of Godhead. If the question refers to anything more than this, I have not understood it.

9. The differences between the rules of conduct enjoined by the various religions will change from age to age, and as knowledge and the spirit of liberalism grow such differences will diminish.

10. I think this question is involved in question 9. But I shall

[1] Member of a caste traditionally associated with scavenging work

[2] The dharma based on the Vedic tradition

say this by way of further explanation. We should believe that the practices and modes of conduct which we find represented in the Koran, the Bible, the Vedas and other works were the best in those times and those lands. If our reason cannot accept them in this age, it is our dharma to change them or abandon them altogether. Only fundamental principles are immutable.

11. In acting towards other people and understanding their faiths one should follow the principle of regarding others as oneself.

12. I think it almost impossible to decide which out of the many interpretations of religious works represents undiluted truth. That is why the *Gita* has convincingly argued that *samanvaya*[1] is the best. God alone represents perfect truth. Imperfect man, therefore, should humbly believe that as one's truth is dear to one, so others' truths are bound to be dear to them. Hence everyone should follow his own path and others should not hinder him from doing so. People will then follow, of their own accord, that path which is found from experience to be the smoothest.

13. Till we come across a person of experience and of perfect purity in conduct, we should observe the rules of conduct and discipline enjoined in the religious work which we have accepted as our scripture, read it regularly, reflect over it and put its teachings into practice. Those who cannot do even this are ignorant people. Such of them as cannot observe purity in conduct have a protector only in God. I believe in the assurance given in the *Gita* that even people of this class are saved somehow. Words certainly have a meaning, but there are ebbs and floods in the meaning of words as if they had a life of their own.

14. As I understand the problem, without a belief in reincarnation it would be almost impossible to prove that the world is governed by justice. Moreover, one soul cannot have [full] experience of the world within the span of one life, which is but a moment in a vast cycle of time. I can practically say that I have direct proof every moment of the truth of the belief in reincarnation.

15. Virtue and sin exist in the same sense that light and darkness, happiness and suffering, truth and untruth, do. However, just as there is an unknowable and indescribable Reality beyond the categories of existence and non-existence, so also there is something beyond virtue and sin of which this body can have

[1] Synthesis

no experience. The descriptions given in Buddhist writings or in those of the Nyaya and the Sankhya schools of philosophy are not unalterable, but these too, can be understood and accepted from the respective viewpoints.

16. For the development of man's reasoning faculty, the right influences are certainly essential. To put it scientifically, every society solves the problem in every age for itself.

17. Violence means injuring a creature through bodily action or speech or in thought, with the intention of injuring it. Non-violence means not injuring any creature in this manner. The doctrine of non-violence propounded in Vedanta literature, as far as I have understood it, seems to me all right. But I cannot say myself whether I have understood the Vedanta teaching correctly, nor can I claim that my study of the Vedanta is deep.

18. For being able to observe *brahmacharya*, one must keep the mind, speech and body constantly engaged in morally pure activity. We can, therefore, say in a general way that a *brahmachari* should do the opposite of what householders given to the enjoyment of pleasures do. It is my experience that desires in the mind are closely connected with the kind of food one eats, but I know that such desires arise even when one's food is pure and small in quantity. We may, therefore, say that right food is a great help for the observance of *brahmacharya*, but that it is not all. The purest food is fruit, which has naturally ripened, eaten in solitude. I have no doubt about this at all. The chief thing is that, if the palate could be controlled, the observance of *brahmacharya* would become quite easy. We commit two errors in saying that knowledge has reference to the mind and food is connected with the body, which is a material object. The body of a living human being is not altogether inert. And the thing which we call mind and which learns from experience is as closely connected with the body as light is with the sun. A dead body is one from which the mind has gone; such a body does not eat or drink. Thus, it is the mind which eats through the body, and likewise it is through the body that really speaking it acquires knowledge.

19. The universal Soul in which all the souls exist is God. The living creature which does not know that universal Soul and looks upon itself as separate from other creatures is what we call *jiva*[1]. That universal Soul, though dwelling in all, is not directly expe-

[1] Individual soul

rienced; that is its beauty, its miracle, its *maya*[1]. The true end of human effort consists in crossing that *maya* and knowing that universal Soul, which is the one source of all. It is not a thing which can be experienced in a manner our reason can understand; how, then, can there be any means of experiencing it? But anyone who has the strength to forget the "I" in him and make himself a cipher can have a glimpse of this universal Soul, though he cannot help someone else to have it too. Such a person is so dazzled by the mere glimpse, and so utterly spell-bound, that he merges in it. He feels no desire and no need to describe his supreme bliss to anyone.

20. I have somehow found something for myself by combining all the suggestions made by the authors of Shastras. It is, therefore, quite difficult for me to say which path is acceptable. Shankara is dear to me, and so are Ramanuja, Madhva, Vallabha and others—I have relished delicacies from all, but have not been able to satisfy my hunger through what I got from any of them.

21. It may now be seen that the reply to this question is contained in the replies to the preceding questions. *Yajna*[2], *dana*[3], *tapas*[4], are obligatory duties, but that does not mean that the manner of performing them in this age should be the same as in ancient times. *Yajna*, *dana*, etc., are permanent principles. The social practices and the concrete forms through which they are put into practice may change from age to age and country to country. In my view, for example, the supreme *yajna* for this country and in this age is the spinning-wheel. The right gift which a seeker of *moksha* in this country and this age may make is to dedicate his all, body, intellect and possessions, to the service of the country. And, likewise, the right *tapas* for this country and this age consists in burning with agony at the suffering of countless untouchables and others who are starving for want of food or because of famines. Anyone who performs these three important duties certainly becomes purified and he may even have a vision of God's cosmic form which Arjuna had.[5]

22. *Saguna*[6], *nirguna*[7], etc., belong to the speech of human be-

[1] Mystery

[2] Sacrifice

[3] Gift-giving, charity

[4] Austerity

[5] *Vide* the *Bhagavad Gita*, XI

[6] With attributes

[7] Without attributes

ings trying to express their imperfect knowledge which is sheer ignorance. In truth God is beyond description. Even to call Him *nirguna* is an utterly vain attempt to describe Him. Since, however, He is a slave of His devotees, He can be described not with a thousand but with an infinite number of epithets, all of which can be applied to him from the point of view of the respective devotees, and it is His supreme mercy that He tolerates them all. There is no error, therefore, in saying that He exists as all bodies, all sense-organs and all other things. We may thus confess our inability to describe Him.

23. I wish to say in all humility that my fasts and other ordeals are inspired by the desire to see God face to face. I fast in order that, even if I go without food altogether, I may have a glimpse of God such as I have described in these answers. But one cannot force oneself to undertake a fast. One must have fitness even for a fast. I am constantly striving for such fitness. But it is possible that I may not acquire it in this life and may even die ingloriously.

This completes the list of your questions. If you have any other questions to ask besides these, do ask them. You will notice a certain positiveness in some or all of the answers. Please do not put it down to presumption or pride. If I did not write what I have done, I would be guilty of untruth, for it would mean concealing my real beliefs through false humility. If, therefore, you see impropriety in my positiveness, kindly forgive me for that.

The revered Malaviyaji Maharaj is here. I have discussions with him on all manner of religious issues. I will tell him of your desire too.

Yours,

MOHANDAS GANDHI

From a photostat of the Gujarati: S.N. 12323

90. *HONOURABLE LABOUR*

Cotton is produced in Viramgam, Lakhtar and other areas and, though the steam-engine has been introduced in these areas, it has not been possible to dispense with the human machine and therefore, extracting cotton from the pods and similar work is being done by men and women. This is work which cannot be done by one person, it must be taken up by a large number. If, therefore, the Machine Age comes to stay, machines for extracting cotton are bound to be introduced in these areas. At present, however, the work of extracting cotton from the pods is fortunately or unfortunately—according to one's point of view—done by men and women. I, therefore, put a few questions to a friend who does this work. He says in reply.[1]

If, fifty or sixty years ago, any person like me had put similar questions about spinning, he would have received literally the same reply as this; for at that time the spinning-wheel was a sign not of poverty but of culture and respectability, and the rich used to spin willingly as a matter of duty, just as they do now the work of extracting cotton from the pods and do not mind accepting money for it, though such work is a means of livelihood for the poor. As long as the rich had not given up spinning, the poor were safe and spinning did not disappear as an occupation. Such universal occupations are a duty as much as they are occupations, and they last only so long as the rich keep them up, for they offer no opportunities for making millions or for speculation. They remain alive only if the rich have regard for the welfare of society as a whole. When social concern ceases to be a motive, everyone strives to be a millionaire and looks for an occupation which may help him to be one. The *varnashrama*[2] dharma was conceived and accepted as part of Hinduism so that people may not yield to such wicked temptations which degrade them spiritually. This dharma now survives only in name and its real nature is forgotten. Everywhere we see only its distortions. A dharma which was conceived as a means of regulating occupations is now confined to restrictive practices about eating and marrying. How can I persuade people that in the revival of the spinning-wheel lies the revival of *varnashrama*, of pure dharma and, if I may say without being guilty of exaggeration, of dharma in its entirety?

[From Gujarati]

Navajivan, 3-7-1927

[1] Not translated here. The correspondent had explained that the work was regarded as honourable and was done by everyone, rich and poor.

[2] The division of society into four *varnas* or castes and of the individual's life into four *ashramas* or stages

91. THE DILEMMA OF A STUDENT

A simple-hearted student writes:

I have read your letter advising me to become a khadi-worker, with the greatest attention. I do want to take up some work which will enable me to serve the country. But I have yet to decide whether I should be a khadi-worker or take up another form of service. I have not yet felt that khadi work can be a means for inner progress. For the present, I spin just to do my duty to society, knowing as I do that spinning is necessary both for our economic amelioration and for the attainment of freedom. Eventually, of course, I will choose the work which satisfies me the most. For the moment, however, my aim is to acquire as much knowledge as possible and to prepare myself for service.

As for *brahmacharya,* what can I write about it? I can only pray to God to give me the strength to fulfil my desire to observe the vow of *brahmacharya.*

I do not understand why you give equal importance both to the acquisition of knowledge and craft-work in schools. I have felt that in trying to do both things at the same time we fail to do either of them well.

We do have to learn some craft. But would it not be better if it were taught after the intellectual part of our training is over? Spinning I do not regard as craft-work, but as a duty one owes to society. Everyone must therefore spin. But I feel that weaving, agriculture and carpentry may well be postponed till after the academic studies are over. Each of them is an independent subject of study complete in itself, and it would be enough if a year or more is allotted to it separately.

The way things are being attempted here harms both intellectual development and proficiency in craft-work. To do craft-work for three hours, to spin in spare time, and to study all those subjects which are taught in other schools, to do one's own reading, and then to take part with others in the necessary community chores—all this is indeed very difficult to do.

The amount of reading laid down for the boys cannot be lessened. It is necessary for them to learn all the subjects. How are we justified then in burdening the boys with extra work when they have to learn so many subjects besides doing their own reading? If they do not get enough time to fulfil even the assignments set to them, how can they be expected to do their own personal reading and thinking? I find that as teaching advances, it becomes ever more necessary to do extra-curricular reading and there is no time for it.

I have spoken of these difficulties to the teachers. There have also been discussions about it, but I am not satisfied. I think they have not sufficient appreciation of our difficulties. Will you please give the points I have raised some consideration and explain to me where I err?

There are two important points raised in this letter. The reader need not be told that it is a reply to my letter. I thought that instead of sending a private reply to the correspondent I had better discuss it in the *Navajivan* so that it may be of use to other students who have similar difficulties. I had therefore kept it pending these three months.

The distinction made here in inner progress and the service of society is also made by many others in India. I consider this distinction as due to an error of thought. I believe, and it is also my experience, that all that is against the progress of the soul is also against the true interest of society in general. The progress of the soul can best be achieved, according to me, through the service of society. Service is the same as *yajna*. Service which comes in the way of the progress of the soul is to be shunned and renounced.

There is a school of thought which says that service may also be rendered at times through lying. But everybody knows that lying degrades the soul and it makes it fall from its high state. Therefore, service through lying should never be thought of. Really speaking, the idea that lying can also serve as a means of service is just a delusion. Its result may seem beneficial to society for a while, but it can be proved that eventually it does more harm than good.

But, then, the charkha does good to society, to the world, and therefore to the soul also. This does not mean that a spinner can *ipso facto* realize the progress of the soul. He who spins for earning a few coppers gets only a few coppers. But he who spins with the object of realizing his soul may attain liberation through it. As has been said, he too becomes fit for liberation who offers water for the thirsty in the spirit of devotion. Of those who repeat the *Gayatri mantra* either for show or for money, the first falls while the other goes on farther than the fulfilment of his desire for money. Liberation is reached wherever the objective is of the highest and purest, and is backed by similar action.

In fact, the knowledge of Brahman, i.e., the Ultimate Reality, is necessary in order to know what is the highest objective and the highest action. To try to achieve proper fitness for khadi work with the object of the progress of the soul is no small matter. A khadi worker who wants also the progress of the soul must be free from all likes and dislikes. This covers almost all that needs to be said on this question. We have not yet had even a single khadi worker who would be content to receive just enough for his maintenance and settle down to work in unfavourable surroundings in a remote village far away from a railway station. I would expect such a worker to know Sanskrit and music, and have a fairly good knowledge of the essentials of all the important religions. He can put to good use those arts that he knows. But he can serve contentedly even if he knows nothing except the science of charkha.

In order to dispel the darkness and misery of age-long indolence, superstition, hunger and distrust, we need men of austerity who have got to the very door-step of liberation. Even a slight practice of this dharma wards off great calamity[1] and hence is easy. But its perfect implementation is as arduous as the austerities of a man thirsting for self-realization.

I do not mean to suggest that one should give up one's studies and devote oneself immediately to khadi work. I suggest that a student who has courage, strength and faith should take a vow from today onwards that he will become a khadi worker when he has finished his studies. If he makes this resolve one can consider that his service in the cause of khadi has already begun, because he will then choose whatever he decides to learn with the object of acquiring the necessary capacity for this particular type of work.

Let us now examine the second difficulty. The correspondent says:

> I do not understand why you give equal importance to the acquisition of knowledge and the learning of craft work at the same time.

I have been asked this question time and again ever since I returned to India, and I have always given the same answer to it, i.e., they must be given an equal importance. It used to be so in olden times. The student went to the teacher with a bundle of sacrificial sticks in his hands which indicated his readiness to work and his humility. The former consisted of fetching wood from the forest and water for the use of the guru. The student also learned something about agriculture, cow-keeping, etc.

Today this is not so, and that is one of the reasons why there is so much hunger, injustice and vice in the world. Literacy, i.e.,

[1] A reference to the *Bhagavad Gita*, II, 40

learning of books, acquisition of intellectual knowledge and useful manual work in various crafts are not different, though they may seem so. Efforts to separate them and break the link that binds them together results in the misuse of knowledge. The intellectual side of it is like the husband and manual labour like his wife. The bond between the two is indissoluble. Divorced from manual labour this husband is today acting like a libertine. He casts his evil eye here, there and everywhere and yet remains unsatisfied and in the end falls down tired and spent.

Indeed, if a comparison has to be made between the two, the first place will have to be given to manual work, for a child does not use his intelligence first but his hands and feet. Gradually, he learns to use his eyes and ears and begins to understand things only when he is four or five years of age. But this does not mean that with greater power of understanding he can neglect his body. If he does so he will destroy both the body and the mind. The intellect finds its expression in action by the body. Today the exercise of the body has come to be confined merely to gymnastics. Formerly this need was satisfied by useful labour. There is no suggestion that boys should not play games or take part in sports, etc. But there should not be any great need for games merely for health's sake. Rather, there should be rest and relaxation of both the body and the mind. There is no place for indolence in education. Whether learning a craft or acquiring knowledge of the three R's, education must always be interesting. If a boy gets bored either with reading and writing or craft work, the fault does not lie with him but with the method of education and the teacher.

While this letter was lying with me, I chanced to read a book about a new educational experiment being undertaken in England. An institution has been set up there which will start centres imparting literary education along with training in craft work. Among the list of the sponsors of this institution I find the names of almost all the eminent British educationists. Their aim is to change the present trend in education and impart to the children both literary education and training in crafts. More such centres will be started at places with plenty of open space around them so that arrangements could be made for their training in crafts. This will enable the boys to earn something while learning. The editor of the book says that this will probably lengthen the period of literary education, but he also states that it will do no harm; on the contrary, it will do good to the students. When a student starts to earn he realizes the value of money honestly earned and acquires respect for all forms of knowledge imparted to him.

I think the experiments that I carried out in South Africa confirm this view. To the extent that I could see how to carry them out and actually did carry them out they succeeded well.

Very little time is required to go over lessons or do extra-curricular reading if the method of teaching is good. Of course, students do need some time to do what they like—to read as they please or even to while it away in idleness. I learnt a while ago that this is what they call *shavasana* in the yogic science. *Shavasana* means to lie down like a corpse with the feet outstretched and with the body and mind completely relaxed and at ease. Of course, even here the repetition of Ramanama should go on with every breath, but it should not disturb one's rest. For a *brahmachari* every breath is but a repetition of the Lord's name.

But if what I say is correct how is it that this student and his other friends who are not untruthful or vain and who are ready to work hard to reach their goal do not experience its truth?

The tragedy with us is that all of us teachers have been born and have grown up in an age when the accent is on literary education, and training in crafts is very much neglected. And, yet, some of us have detected this fatal flaw. Efforts are being made to correct it, but it is not yet clear how the correction can be made. Besides, the little that we have understood we have not yet the power to implement. Those who can teach *Raghuvamsa* or *Ramayana* or Shakespeare have not either the training or the aptitude to teach carpentry or weaving. They have not the same knowledge of weaving as they have of *Raghuvamsa*; and when they have, they have not the same interest in it. No wonder that, on account of this imperfection in our teachers, we find it difficult to produce the right type of students—students who will be equally at home both in literary learning and in crafts and who will at the same time have character. Therefore, in this period of transition our imperfect and ill-equipped teachers and hard-working students must have both patience and faith. With faith one can cross the seas and storm even the most impregnable forts.

[From Gujarati]

Navajivan, 3-7-1927

92. *LETTER TO WILLIAM SMITH*

KUMARA PARK, BANGALORE,
July 3, 1927

DEAR MR. SMITH,

I thank you for your two letters and very carefully prepared notes and the Italian pamphlet illustrating the principle and use of castrating forceps.

I have now gone through your notes, and if you are free on Tuesday next at 4 p.m. I shall be delighted to see you.

Could I publish your valuable notes in the pages of *Young India* or make other public use of them?

Yours sincerely,

From a microfilm: S.N. 12919

93. *SPEECH AT OPENING OF KHADI EXHIBITION, BANGALORE*

July 3, 1927

FRIENDS,

You have extended to me a very great privilege by asking me to perform the opening ceremony at this function. It is a matter of great grief to me that I shall be unable to make my opening speech myself. You will agree with me that I ought not to take an undue advantage of the liberty given to me by Dr. Subba Rao and those medical friends who have been helping me. I want therefore to go as gently as possible and not to put an undue strain upon my constitution. I therefore reduced the few ideas that I have to present to you in connection with this Exhibition to writing. Mr. Tathachary will read a translation in the mother tongue of this province and then Mr. Rajagopalachari will read to you the English original. I am sorry that in this province you will not take the trouble of learning what is the lingua franca of India or should be. I have been obliged always, whenever I have come down to the South, to remark upon this deficiency. You have now a Hindi Prachar Office also in Bangalore and I do hope that at no distant time as I expect you will come up to Tamil Nadu and Andhra Desha in Hindi as in khadi and so make up your deficiency with reference to ignorance in Hindi. Had I seen in front of me only my Mussalman brethren I know that I could have spoken to them in Hindi. They are preserving the prestige of the lingua franca but the Hindus are lagging far behind in the South. I hope that you will run a close race with the Mussalman brethren in Mysore and make up your deficiency in Hindi. With these few words I shall call upon my friend to read the Kanarese translation.

After the reading of the Kanarese version of Mahatmaji's address was over, Mr. C. Rajagopalachari read in clear terms the following address of Gandhiji in English:

FRIENDS,

It is a matter of great pleasure to me to meet you in this lovely city and find in our midst our veteran leader, *Poojaniya* Pandit Madan Mohan Malaviyaji. Hindu tradition makes me always feel embarrassed to take a leading part in any function at which he is present. For ever since my return to our beloved country, I have looked up to him as to an elder brother. But what I feel to be a call of duty enables me somewhat to overcome the embarrassment.

On this my first permitted appearance on a public platform since my illness, let me thank His Highness the Maharaja of Mysore and its people for the great kindness and consideration shown to me during my prolonged convalescence. Your lavish hospitality has made illness itself attractive. But it has grieved me to observe, as I did in the appeal issued by my friends for enlisting your support for khadi, that they had endeavoured to exploit my illness by suggesting that if you all supported khadi by subscribing to funds and adopting it for your dress, my recovery would be quicker. I would ask you to dismiss this consideration from your minds altogether. If khadi makes no appeal to your reason and has no place in national economy, it must be suppressed in spite of my weakness for it. In great national causes, personal affections must be discounted as disturbing factors. And if I have become so soft as to become enervated for want of support for my whims and fancies, or may be, even follies, it is surely better for the nation that I should become and remain so ill as to be unfit for further mischief.

The Exhibition, which it will be my privilege presently to declare open, is a right and proper kind of appeal. It is carefully designed so as to give you an ocular demonstration of what khadi meant and what it has already achieved. If its careful study conquers your reason, but in spite of the conviction of your reason, you find yourselves too weak to translate its dictates into action, then, indeed, let your affection for me give you heart and courage to overcome your weakness. For I stand before you as a self-chosen representative of the dumb, semi-starved, because workless, millions of India whom the late Deshbandhu Chittaranjan Das appropriately called *Daridranarayana.* Every pice you contribute to the support of khadi, every yard of khadi you buy, means so much concrete sympathy shown by you for these millions.

Let me then summarize the conclusions of workers in the service of *Daridranarayana* which you may test for yourselves if you will patiently study the literature that you will find on the Exhibition stalls as also the results of khadi activity which you will find demonstrated at those stalls. The Prize Essay on Hand-spinning by Messrs S. V. Puntambekar and N. S. Varadachari traces for you the history of the ruin of the only national and universal cottage industry of India as also the possibilities of its revival. You will find it proved there that in this country there are millions of peasants who have no occupation for at least four months in the year, and that the only possible occupation for them in their own cottages is nothing but hand-spinning. Many good and well-intentioned people have suggested most ambitious and attractive schemes of village reorganization. But I make bold to say that not one of these schemes is at present in operation and that it is not possible to enforce any of them, at least during the lifetime of this generation; whereas, the spinning-wheel has been making its silent but slow progress throughout the length and breadth of India. Its revival dates from 1920 during which year, in spite of the forest of white caps one saw in the principal streets of cities, in reality there was not to be found khadi worth more than one lakh at the outside. But the carefully prepared report of the All-India Spinners' Association for the last year will show you that during the year 1926 alone over Rs. 23 lakhs worth of khadi was produced throughout India and that the sales amounted to Rs. 28 lakhs. Capital investment by the Association amounts to over Rs. 18 lakhs. Fifty-thousand spinners worked during the year under review for the production of this khadi. These spinners, before they took to hand-spinning, had not other earnings or occupation during the time that they gave to spinning. Their earnings have ranged from one pice to two annas per day according to the time they gave and the skill they put in it. The very fact that fifty thousand women were eager to do this work for what may appear to us to be a miserable wage should be sufficient workable demonstration that hand-spinning is not an uneconomic, profitless or unpractical proposition. In many instances women walk four miles to receive their cotton. Round hand-spinning as the centre have been built up many other occupations. Weavers, dhobis, dyers, printers and carders who had either died out or were dying out have found in the revival of hand-spinning a new hope. One new weaver and one new carder comes into being against ten spinners and their wages are anything between four annas and one and a half rupees per day. 1,500 villages are being thus served by an army of more or less educated workers whose salary ranges from Rs. 100 to Rs. 150 per month. Not less than 1,000 such young men and some young women find an honest livelihood in this national service. The spinners and other workers include Brahmins, Kshatriyas, Vaisyas, Sudras, the so-called untouchables, Mussalmans, Christians, Parsis, Sikhs, in fact every caste and creed. Besides the paid workers, there are several absolutely unpaid volunteers too engaged in this work of reconstruction. In Satis Chandra Das Gupta and Profulla Chandra Ghosh, Bengal has given to this service two of Acharya Ray's most brilliant pupils. Satis Chandra Das Gupta had built up Acharya Ray's chemical works. Profulla Chandra Ghosh had been assistant assayer in the Government Mint. Both left their lucrative posts to give themselves to khadi. Several distinguished lawyers, even doctors, some of whom you know personally, have given up their profession and taken to this work. And it is slowly dawning upon the merchant class that khadi is a service which does demand their mercantile ability. You will, perhaps, now understand why I have called this hand-spinning movement the greatest co-operative effort of modern times. And if six years' progress, insignificant as it may appear compared to the mighty result in view, is an indication of the future, God willing, at no distant time we shall find our villages, which at the present moment seem to be crumbling to ruins, becoming hives of honest and patient industry.

The Exhibition will enable you to understand all the processes that cotton goes through before it reaches you as khadi. For you will see ginning, carding, sliver-making, spinning and weaving demonstrated before you. You will see also the very simple tools and machinery which are being used for these processes. The charts will tell you the output of these little machines, most of which can be easily made in our villages.

I must not also omit to draw the attention of fashionable, artistic and moneyed members of my audience to the well-filled stall where you will see handsomely worked and embroidered fine khadi in the preparation of which nearly 400 girls in Bombay are earning anything between six annas and one and a half rupees per day. It is an organization conducted by Rashtriya Stri Sabha of Bombay, which, among other self-sacrificing ladies, includes the grand-daughters of the Grand Old Man of India, Dadabhai Naoroji, and a sister belonging to the great Petit family.

Madhusudan Das was a brilliant lawyer in Cuttack. The poverty of Orissa woke him from his dreams and he saw that necessary as work with plough and oxen in our fields was, we should soon be reduced to the status of the bovine species unless we added to our agriculture some industry which called forth the cunning of the hand, and he has himself become a finished artisan.

But I must not any longer stand between you and the feast for your eyes and intellect that has been prepared by the Exhibition Committee. May it enable you to appreciate the priceless value of khadi as a central fact in village organization and may it induce you to establish between yourselves and the poor villagers a living bond by sending those of you who have the leisure and the inclination to villages to deliver the message of the spinning-wheel, and all of you at least by adopting khadi for your dress and household use! In the work of God, as I venture to suggest it is, the harvest is indeed rich but the labourers are few. Every one of you can, if you will, add to the number.

I have much pleasure in declaring the Exhibition open, and I pray to God that He may bless the work, if it is commendable in His sight and the workers be found worthy.

This over amidst impressive silence, Mahatmaji spoke the following few words in conclusion:

FRIENDS,

I shall presently perform the opening ceremony by uncovering a model charkha prepared at the Industrial Shop of the Department of Industries in Mysore. Mr. Gangadharrao Deshpande, in his opening speech inviting me to perform the ceremony, drew your attention to the great help that is being rendered by the State and especially the Department of Industries to this movement. They have prepared many such charkhas. You will see in the Exhibition Court a variety of charkhas, old spinning-wheels, which are still to be found in a more or less dilapidated condition in Mysore and the evolution that a spinning-wheel has gone through during these six years. The charkha that I shall have the privilege of presently exposing to your view is by no means the best in the scale of evolution. But we thought it was in the fitness of things that an article made in Mysore should be first exposed to view.

Pandit Madan Mohan Malaviya will lead you to the Exhibition Court. He has kindly consented to do this work for me in order to spare me the strain of going through the Exhibition Court. He will also continue the present proceedings this evening at 5-30 when he will give you what his heart prompts him to give you on what he has seen in the Exhibition Court, and what he has gathered during these six years about khaddar and I do hope that you will all come and listen to the message that he might have to deliver to you. You will not attempt whilst he takes the leaders to the court to crowd round, otherwise it will not be really possible to study what is to be studied in the Exhibition. It is designed to be really a study for those who want to understand what this khadi movement stands for and what it has been able to do. It is not a mere ocular demonstration to be dismissed out of our minds, immediately we have gone out of the Exhibition Court. It is not a cinema. It is actually a nursery where a student, a lover of humanity, a lover of his own country may come and see things for himself. I invite sceptics to go there and pause not a few moments, but to go there and pause a few hours and I promise that he will find himself amply rewarded and possibly his scepticism also will be dismissed. I invite the candid critic also to go there and I have no doubt that he will find imperfections, he will find those charts not drawn in artistic fashion, but he will find heart put into those charts. They give you facts and figures which are compiled by students who want only to serve truth and nothing but the truth. You will find there always an understatement but not an overstatement. With these words I have much pleasure to uncover the charkha and I hope that you will all support this movement as it deserves.

Amidst great applause Mahatmaji then uncovered a charkha raised to the seat of Gandhiji by Mr. Deshpande.

The Hindu, 4-7-1927

94. *LETTER TO MIRABEHN*[1]

July 4, 1927

CHI. MIRA[2],

I had expected a letter from you today. But there is nothing as yet. There is just a slight chance of one more post. I hope you were not overcrowded in the train, that there was no difficulty at Guntakal. After you went there was a wire from Vallunjkar asking Mahadev to suggest your breaking journey at Golanad to see Kakasaheb, himself and Gangu. But you were gone and I did not think it worth while wiring in the hope (very distant) of catching you before you could leave Bombay.

How well you put it? You were parting but to come nearer. It was quite true. You did well in coming and equally well in leaving when you did.

Remember my parting words. You are not to kill yourself or ruin your health in trying to finish Hindi in two months. Let us hope that you will finish it. But it does not matter in the least if you cannot. Yours is but to try. Again do not take the vow to use only Hindi in Wardha unless you feel practically driven to it. Nothing hangs by it. You need not consider what I would like. In matters like this there should be no question of considering my opinion or wishes. After all it is a question of choosing the best way of *doing* Hindi. The way that suits you is the best for you and no other.

With love,

BAPU

[PS.]

The opening ceremony went off yesterday without any difficulty. I stood the strain well. The doctors came afterwards and they were satisfied to find no alteration in the pulse. I hope you left your constipation here.

B.

[1] In *Bapu's Letters to Mira*, Mirabehn explains: "I had now left Bhagavadbhakti Ashram, Rewari, and was spending a short time at Sabarmati after having been to see Bapu at Bangalore, and before going to Vinoba's Ashram at Wardha for continuing my Hindi studies."

[2] The superscription in this and other letters to Mirabehn is in Devanagari.

[PPS.]

Immediately after handing this for the post I got your expected beautiful letter[1]. It is perfectly intelligible. There are very few mistakes. Continue to write as often as you like.

B.

From the original: C.W. 5243. Courtesy: Mirabehn

95. LETTER TO MIRABEHN

Silence Day [July 4, 1927][2]

CHI. MIRA,

I have sent the Monday letter to Sabarmati. But if you leave for Wardha before getting it, you should not miss your Monday mail at Wardha either; hence this epistle.

I had expected your letter today but it has not come; it must tomorrow.

Blessings from
BAPU

[PS.]

Don't worry. The letter addressed to Sabarmati is in English.

[PPS.]

I have just had your Hindi letter. It is beautiful.

From the Hindi original: C.W. 5242. Courtesy: Mirabehn

96. LETTER TO ASHRAM WOMEN

Silence Day, Ashadh Sud 5[3] *[July 4, 1927]*

SISTERS,

I thought of you yesterday. Exhibitions and such other activities are really more the work of women than of men. No one was able to decorate his or her stall better than Mithubehn. It is just what one would expect; because all the twenty-four hours

[1] In Hindi

[2] From the postmark

[3] The source has Ashadh Sud 6, which is evidently a slip. The letter was written on the day following the opening of the Exhibition.

she keeps thinking how khadi can be made more lovely. Under her guidance, starting with a few, now about four hundred girls work on khadi and earn their livelihood, or wear only khadi spun by themselves.

Manibehn has been able to bring credit to herself and to the Exhibition by means of her carding bow.

As so many Ashram people have now arrived, the recitation of the *Gita* in the mornings has been started. Today Manibehn recited the fourth chapter. She had recited the first chapter too. Her intonation is good. Indeed all of you should learn to read the *Gita* in the proper way and understand its meaning. Just as a woman is not accomplished unless she is a good cook, so also a woman who does not know the *Gita* cannot be said to be accomplished.

Who is in charge of the store at present?

Blessings from
BAPU

From a photostat of the Gujarati: G.N. 3656

97. *LETTER TO J. B. PETIT*

KUMARA PARK, BANGALORE,
July 5, 1927

DEAR MR. PETIT,

The enclosed is a copy repeated at Bangalore of a cable[1] received from Andrews at Sabarmati. It speaks for itself. It will be a great calamity if Mr. Sastri's health breaks down, or if he has to undergo financial worries. Personally, I think that the Government of India will not be able to meet the special requirements in the present case. It would be wrong to set an awkward precedent, and yet, if Mr. Sastri's mission is to succeed, he must have ample funds enabling him to move from place to place and find decent accommodation. Future agents won't need triple accommodation. But Mr. Sastri has to break new ground and he has therefore to exploit not merely his official position for reducing

[1] Dated July 4. It read: "Sastri's health causing great anxiety. Financial worries superadded because allowances altogether insufficient. Cabled Viceroy Department. Sastri dislikes anything except constructive. Press notice suggesting absolute necessity ample allowances inform public. Probably necessary upkeep three houses. Hotels impossible. Watch my press cables."

the discordant elements to harmony but he has got to exploit his own special gifts to that end. His more solid work therefore will be extra-official. In order to be able to do this, he must have funds. South Africa like India is a place of distances. Between Cape Town and Durban it is nearly 1,400 miles by rail, and in each place he must have accommodation of his own. If he went to hotels, he would be inaccessible to the majority of the Indians who are poor.

I do not think we can state all these things in the press and make a public appeal for funds. The only legitimate thing therefore to do is for the Imperial Citizenship Association to place at Mr. Sastri's disposal a fairly large sum. No time should be lost. I have not a shadow of a doubt that such an expense would be a fair charge upon the funds of the I.C.A.

I suggest that Rs. 25,000/- may be at once transferred to him to be used as he may think necessary for his own personal convenience. He can be trusted to use the amount judiciously and to refund what he may not need.

For the sake of speedy despatch, I am sending a copy of this letter to the members of the Committee whom I know and who I think will be interested in the subject-matter.

Yours sincerely,

M. K. GANDHI

J. [B.] PETIT, ESQ.
IMPERIAL CITIZENSHIP ASSOCIATION
BOMBAY

From a photostat: S.N. 12365

98. LETTER TO JOSHI

KUMARA PARK, BANGALORE,
July 5, 1927

MY DEAR JOSHI,

I believe you are on the Committee of the Imperial Citizenship Association. The enclosed[1] speaks for itself. If you agree with the view I have set forth in the letter, you will please expedite business.

Yours sincerely,

From a photostat: S.N. 12365

99. LETTER TO K. S. NATARAJAN

KUMARA PARK, BANGALORE,
July 5, 1927

DEAR MR. NATARAJAN,

I enclose herewith a copy of my letter to Mr. Petit.[2] I do not need to add anything except to ask you please to expedite the despatch of funds, if you agree with the substance of my letter to Mr. Petit.

Yours sincerely,

K. S. NATARAJAN, ESQ.
"INDIAN SOCIAL REFORMER"
FORT
BOMBAY

From a photostat: S.N. 12365

100. LETTER TO SATIS CHANDRA DAS GUPTA

KUMARA PARK, BANGALORE,
July 5, 1927

DEAR SATIS BABU,

I have your two letters. Last was received only yesterday.

Your letter about the business of the Council was placed before the Council. Jamnalalji and Shankerlal will write to you fully. I have not attended any of the meetings except the first one which I simply opened without any remarks and retired. I think the Council has confirmed the original proposal to relieve

[1] &[2] *Vide* item 97 above.

me from all administrative work. I remain the president; but Jamnalalji becomes the officiating chairman of the Council. And I think that this is the best thing to do. This spares me the trouble of having to go into every detail of administration.

Your suggestion that the Council meeting should be held at different centres has been adopted.

No vital changes should be made in the constitution for five years according to the original intention. To change officers every year, and especially the secretaries, would be a dangerous thing. Secretaries should be helped by fresh suggestions. But as we are really a business house, administrative control should be continuous, if we are to make the house stable. And, personally, I think that it is impossible to get a secretary more energetic, more conscientious than Shankerlal.

Your letter about Hemprabha Devi's latest developments provides food for deep reflection. Let there be nothing done in a hurry.

The suggestion about maintenance is startling and I would like a long time in order that it may soak into me. We must meet before anything is done. Supposing that I am free from the Southern tour about the end of August or middle of September and go through it without any mishap, would you have me to undertake the Bengal tour in gentle stages? Please do not be anxious about me; for, I shall do nothing in haste and I shall watch myself as the tour progresses. Nobody wants to run avoidable risks. Both Rajagopalachari and Gangadharrao are taking elaborate precautions to avoid the slightest strain. Chikballapur was for them also a good lesson.

Yours sincerely,

From a microfilm: S.N. 19786

101. LETTER TO MANILAL AND SUSHILA GANDHI

Ashadh Sud 6 [July 5, 1927][1]

CHI. MANILAL AND SUSHILA,

I got your cable. You must have received my reply to it. You must have got my letters even before my reply to the cable. But I sent the cable as I thought that would make both of you happier, especially Sushila. If Manilal alone were there, I would not have spent money on a cable and would have rebuked him for wasting

[1] From the manuscript of Mahadev Desai's Diary

money on one. But considering that Sushila was in a foreign country, that she has never been abroad before now and that, therefore, she would be happy to hear from me, I thought it proper to send a cable. I am glad to know that both of you would like to receive letters from me, but at the same time I should like to make it clear that, if you do not receive one, you should not suppose that my failure to write was due to indifference or carelessness. It may be that I cannot find the time to write because of pressure of work, or that I miss writing because I do not remember the date on which the mail leaves. If I am ill, you will have somehow heard about it. But now I shall be more careful about writing.

Sushila should forget her attachment to her parental home. We ought always to remember our parents, but it is not possible to live for ever with them. A son cannot do so. How, then, is it possible for a daughter? Her home is with her husband. Sushila should, therefore, understand that her home is where Manilal is and learn to live like Savitri[1]. She should protect herself and also protect Manilal. In both of you maintaining simplicity, truthfulness, compassion and patriotism, despite the many temptations surrounding you, in your observing self-restraint as befits you and protecting each other's body and character lies the success of your marriage.

Sushila's physical strength does not seem to have increased in proportion to the increase in her weight. There is only one way of increasing it: that she should eat nothing but wholesome food, and only as much as can be digested, and take as much physical exercise in the open air as she can without getting exhausted, and that both of you should refrain, as much as possible, from sexual indulgence. I am a living example before you of how much even mental indulgence tells on the body. I failed to wake up for thirty years, and reap the fruits of that to this day. My body is comparatively good. I have, it may be said, suffered from very few illnesses. Still, I know that had I waked up earlier, my body would have been as strong as adamant. My capacity to serve would also have been far greater than it is. There was none to awaken me or to keep me vigilant. I am there to awaken you both and keep you on your guard. Learn from my experience.

I keep good health. As a khadi exhibition is on here these days and as there is to be a meeting of the Charkha Sangh, Jamna-

[1] Who wrested the soul of her husband back from the God of Death. The story is told in the *Mahabharata*.

lalji, Mithubehn, Jamnabehn, Maganlal, Keshu, Anasuyabehn, Shankerlal and others have come here. In a day or two the nest will be empty again.

You send your letters needlessly to Amreli. If you write the word 'personal' on your letters, no one will read them, but why do you wish that no one in the Ashram should read them? It would be all right if you wish that no one should read those letters of yours in which you consult me about your moral problems, but what can be there in ordinary letters that no one should read?

We all saw your photograph which Jamnalalji has received. The photograph which you have sent for me or Ba has not yet reached us. It must be on the way. Our time is wasted in inquiring about it without knowing to what address it was sent.

I hope you receive the translation of the *Gita* regularly.

Blessings from
BAPU

From a photostat of the Gujarati: G.N. 4724

102. LETTER TO MIRABEHN

KUMARA PARK, BANGALORE,
July 6, 1927

CHI. MIRA,

Your telegram is disturbing. No letters yet received. I shall anxiously await further news. May God keep you.

Yours,
BAPU

From the original: C.W. 5244. Courtesy: Mirabehn

103. LETTER TO A. FENNER BROCKWAY

KUMARA PARK, BANGALORE,
July 6, 1927

DEAR FRIEND,

I have your confidential letter of the 13th June last with the enclosures. I appreciate the honour you have done me by sending me your draft Bill, and I beg to tender my thanks to those members of the Independent Labour Party who have worked at the Bill.

I am however unable to give any effective advice or guidance as my work for the present lies in a different direction. I am devoting the whole of my energy to developing internal strength. I have therefore very little time left for studying the question what form the final constitution should take. I do not in any shape or form discount the importance of that question. But I know my own limitations, and so, as far as possible, I help the movement towards arriving at a suitable constitution by non-interference and sympathetic watch. But I take it that you have circulated the draft Bill among many other public men in India and invited their opinion. If at any time I feel that I can do any useful work in this connection, I shall not hesitate to correspond with you.

Yours sincerely,

A. FENNER BROCKWAY, ESQ.
14, GREAT GEORGE STREET
LONDON S.W. I

From a photostat: S.N. 12530

104. LETTER TO GIRIRAJ KISHORE

KUMARA PARK, BANGALORE,
July 6, 1927

MY DEAR GIRIRAJ,

I have your letter. I like your heart searching. There is always one danger in this process. A man who is not self-possessed becomes morose and imagines all kinds of things about himself. This is the state of a hypochondriac. Do you know what that word means in the medical world ? It means a person who imagines every disease to be in himself of which he reads a description. Whilst, therefore, it is the most proper thing to rid oneself of any weakness of which one is conscious there must be nothing imagined and there should be no brooding. Instead of saying to yourself, 'I am wretched, so evil and I shall never be good', the proper formula is, 'I will be good; for, God is good and merciful; He will make me good.' The first formula is weakening and the second is invigorating.

Your statement that an ideal cook is he who feels about the diners as a mother does for her children is perfect. It is of course difficult to feel like that; but by practice everything becomes easy. Be patient with everybody, return a kind answer to every enquiry and give up the last chapati and the last spoonful of dal, even though there may be nothing left for you and those who may be the last to dine being waiters. You may prepare something for yourself to satisfy hunger. This may mean additional time. Never mind it. And, therefore, cooks and waiters should never have any fixed appointments after the completion of kitchen work. There must always be a wide margin left for emergencies.

You must not regard yourself as unfit for the work. A man who wants to do work for society and in society, that is, in company with others, has to have practically the same qualities whether it is in the kitchen or in the sanitary yard or in the weaving-shed, and no man becomes a worthy human being unless he has gone through these purifying fires. I, therefore, want you to compose yourself completely, and find your satisfaction in your work, dealing with every emergency that may arise. I know that all this is easy enough to say. It is not so easy to practise. Nevertheless all our learning and everything we do has to be done in order to arrive at this equableness. I hope, therefore, you will never accept defeat.

Do please write to me whenever you like. Always try to cultivate a compact style. But if you cannot say what you want to, briefly, I do not mind even your long letters. But it will be a good practice for you after having written your long letter to reduce it to a quarter and see whether you cannot say the same thing in quarter length.

Yours sincerely,

GIRIRAJ KISHORE
ASHRAM
SABARMATI

From a photostat: S.N. 14180

105. LETTER TO JAIRAMDAS DAULATRAM

KUMARA PARK, BANGALORE,
July 6, 1927

MY DEAR JAIRAMDAS,

I need you badly if you can possibly spare yourself from Council work. Malaviyaji and I have been considering the advisability of establishing an All-India Anti-untouchability Association. Jamnalalji, Rajagopalachari, Shankerlal, Rajendra Babu and others think likewise. There is no man to take up the work so suitable like you. Jamnalalji thinks that I must press you to come out at any cost. I won't do that. But I thought I must place this proposition before you, and if the inner voice prompts you, then indeed I want you. But if you think that you can better utilize your abilities for the service of the country by being in the Council, I have nothing to say. Just think the matter over well and let me know. If you come to a firm opinion which you can transmit to me by wire, you may even wire.

Yours sincerely,

SJT. JAIRAMDAS DAULATRAM, M.L.C.
HYDERABAD (SIND)

From a microfilm: S.N. 14619

106. LETTER TO LILIAN EDGER

KUMARA PARK, BANGALORE,
July 6, 1927

DEAR FRIEND,

Krishnadas has handed your letter to me and the yarn sent with it. The yarn is not at all bad. It can of course be more even. I do not think that age is a bar. I know many as old as you who have taken to spinning and who have become very good spinners. No doubt it requires much patience in the beginning.

You have asked me whether the small quantities that you spin can be of any help to the poor. I say unhesitatingly, "Yes." This does not mean that the yarn you may be sending will be separately woven into khadi and sent to the poor. That is not what we are doing with the yarn contribution we are receiving. But what we are doing is to convert such yarn into khadi, and utilize the proceeds of the sale of that khadi for providing spinning and other ancillary work to the poor people. This is the very best help that can be rendered to them.

I quite agree with you that it is difficult for individuals to distribute their charity judiciously. The vast majority of street beggars are mere professional idlers when they are not much worse, and those who have money to spare do an ill-service to these beggars and to the country by giving them money, food or clothing. We have found by experience that we do no service by distributing amongst poor people khadi prepared from yarn contributions. The chief need is neither food nor clothing but work which they can do in their cottages. But where it becomes necessary to provide clothing side by side with work, we do not hesitate to do so. But that happens only in rare cases. The chief value, in my opinion, of any person spinning by way of sacrifice lies in the work itself, and in the promotion of the work atmosphere that is created in the country and in the promotion of a tangible feeling for the poorest in the land.

Now for your questions:

1. It is wrong to draw the thread and the twist. The thread must be drawn whilst the spindle is revolving rapidly round its own centre. This movement ensures the proper twist. Drawing of the yarn and the movement of the spindle go on simultaneously so that there is no difficulty about continuously drawing the thread with ease. And whilst the thread is being drawn the sliver is held fairly tight between the fingers so that the twist does not reach the thread up to the very end which is held between the fingers.

2. Wax has to be used occasionally for the *mal*, that is the chord that goes round the wheel and the spindle.

3. Oil has not to be used very often. The ordinary machine oil [can] serve the purpose. But in the absence of that, a drop of the ordinary cooking oil is quite serviceable. An occasional drop on the axle where it touches the uprights and on the holders which hold the spindle makes for smooth movement.

4. It will be better to wind off after an hour's spinning. Those who can spin very rapidly unwind every 20 minutes. When in unwinding the thread tangles, you know that the cone has not been made tight. If your yarn is well-twisted, you can wind it round the spindle each time fairly tight and the cone should feel hard to the touch and not at all soft.

5. When the chord breaks and if you cannot twist a chord out of your own yarn, you can use any bazaar twine of the diameter of your chord.

Lastly, if you will become a good spinner and if you will spin for sacrifice, it is really necessary for you to watch someone who spins well. Wherever you may be whether in Kashi or Darbhanga, there is no difficulty about your getting proper assistance.

Wishing you every success in your effort,

Yours sincerely,

MISS LILIAN EDGER
CARE OF POST MASTER
SRINAGAR (KASHMIR)

From a microfilm: S.N. 19785

107. LETTER TO SECRETARY, HINDI SAHITYA SAMMELAN

BANGALORE,
Ashadh Shukla 7 [*July 6, 1927*]

DEAR SIR,

I got your telegram yesterday. I hope you have my reply. You must have my earlier letter too. I am pained by your telegram. In my humble opinion, it was not decent to hold out a threat of legal action. I have said on several occasions and also reiterated in my letter that if you think the work accomplished here as the Sammelan's property, well, it can be settled by arbitration. I can understand that it will be your duty to go to a court of law if you hold that it would be in the interest of the Sammelan to obtain the court's verdict. If you deem it proper to go to the court, do not blame Pandit Harihar Sharma. Whatever changes in work have been brought about by him had my sanction. I have always thought that it was I who through the Sammelan conducted the work in the South. I always thought that by entrusting this work to the Sammelan I have only enhanced its prestige and that in case of a disagreement the Sammelan would not move to take charge of the work nor obstruct me from carrying it on according to my own plans. I still desire your co-operation in this work but if you think that the funds collected by Jamnalalji and those by Panditji in the South were all to be handed over to the Sammelan, I am sorry the matter can be decided only by arbitration or in a court of law.

Yours,

From a microfilm of the Hindi: S.N. 11817

108. A LETTER

[Before *July 7, 1927*][1]

Your questions are really very good but among the readers of *Young India* and *Navajivan* few would be eager for a casuistical enquiry into this question. I shall therefore rest content with answering you alone.

Sir Jagadish Chandra Bose's theory is not new. Our Shastras recognize the presence of life in plants as in human beings. Certainly therefore the statement that life lives on life is established by facts. And this is the one reason why the body is regarded as an appendage of the *atman* and its absence essential for the supreme state of the *atman*. Although all life must be embodied only through some sort of violence, the question still remains what form of life should comprise life's food. Human physiology as well as the experience of the wise shows that the right food for us is the fruit ripened on the tree and suchlike. The pure seeker will not use even fire. We may not reach this ideal state, yet it is our duty to strive for it as far as we can, and in this our endeavour meat-eating can have no place. [Feeding on] plant life should be the limit for us.

2. I can say from my own experience and that of others that there is absolutely no danger of tuberculosis and such other diseases resulting from vegetarian diet even in countries like England. Today thousands of Englishmen are vegetarians, [though] usually they do take eggs.

3. Vegetarian restaurants make use of egg and milk; they neither serve nor cook meat. They place eggs and milk in the same category and agree that it would be better to give up both as neither is a vegetable. This is my opinion too. Barring mother's milk during infancy man has no right to take milk. I shall say something about this in *Young India.* You will find it in the course of the autobiography. Till now it was my belief that every

[1] From the reference to the discussion about milk in the "Autobiography" (Pt. IV, Ch. VIII), which appeared in *Young India*, 7-7-1927

egg could be hatched. Now I learn from experts that a hen lays eggs even without mating and that such eggs cannot be hatched. These eggs are as much without life and therefore as unobjectionable as milk. Now I am wondering whether eggs may not have a place in a vegetarian diet since milk is included. But this much I do know that from the standpoint of *brahmacharya* eggs are to be eschewed as are many vegetables too. But this is a digression. Today I am considering eggs purely from the point of view of vegetarian diet.

I congratulate you on writing in Hindi.

Yours,

From a photostat of the Hindi: S.N. 12325

109. NOTES

Deshbandhu Day at Darjeeling

The reader will be glad to share the following with me from Mrs. Blair from Darjeeling:

> It may perhaps interest you to know that the Darjeeling Mahila Samiti held a meeting on June 15th in memory of the great patriot, the late Mr. C. R. Das, at which Shrimati Urmila Devi spoke. Her subject was the wearing of khadi and the obligation on those, who wished to help the poor of their country, to spin at least half an hour a day. On the following Wednesday, 22nd instant, nine of the members in the presence of Shrimati Urmila Devi promised to spin at least half an hour a day. Later on they may feel worthy to become members of the A.I.S.A.[1] At present they are going to spin wool in order to be able to give warm clothes in the winter to the Baby Clinic and the Hospital.[2]

It is a good thing that the ladies of Darjeeling observed the anniversary of Deshbandhu in the manner described by Mrs. Blair. I hope that the nine ladies who have given their names will persist in their effort. We have in this country a habit of making promises in a fit of enthusiasm, keeping them for a time, and then forgetting them altogether. I hope that these members will be steadfast enough to continue their sacrificial spinning so long as a single Indian has to starve for want of work in his or her own home. One knows the fashion of saying, 'If they have no

[1] All-India Spinners Association

[2] For Gandhiji's reply to Mrs. Blair, *vide* "Letter to Mrs. Blair", 28-6-1927.

work, why do they not emigrate, why do they not go to the tea plantations, why do they not go to the cities where labour is in demand, and earn as much as eight annas?' I have in these pages often demonstrated the falsity of this argument. Millions cannot leave their homes, even if they wish to. And it would be a calamity if they all did. Coal at the pit's mouth in Newcastle is probably to be had for nothing, or very little. But such cannot be the case in Bombay. If Bombay must use Newcastle coal, it has to pay for transport. Similarly work to be had in Bombay will be of no use to the millions, who cannot, will not and must not leave their cottages and fields. Work has got therefore to be transported to their cottages, and inversely as in the case of coal at Newcastle, the work transported to cottages is less paying than work in Bombay in terms of coin. But in terms of mental satisfaction, and grain or vegetable, the work obtained in the cottages is far more profitable than that obtainable in Bombay.

ADI KARNATAKAS

All the readers of *Young India* may not know who *Adi Karnatakas* are. They are the suppressed classes of Karnatak. Just as at the Raniparaj Conference, friends of the Raniparaj altered the name Kaliparaj to the more appropriate name Raniparaj, so the suppressed classes all over India have been not unnaturally taking for themselves names which have no bad odour about them. In this spirit the suppressed classes in Karnatak describe themselves as *Adi Karnatakas*. And so I notice under that heading two paragraphs in the address of the Dewan of Mysore to its Representative Assembly. One observes from these paragraphs, that

> exceptional facilities have been created for the education of the members of these classes, and methods have been adopted to suit their special circumstances. Among these methods are scholarships, exemptions from school fees, a free supply of clothes and school requisites, free hostels; and over and above the right of admission to all schools, 605 special schools have been provided for them. There are altogether 16,575 students of this class receiving tuition in Mysore.

An attempt is being made to organize a co-operative agricultural scheme with due provision of land, live-stock and direction.

The paragraphs end with the following suggestion:

> These people ought to be the strength of our strength. Shall we let them become our weakness? They have a rankling sense of wrong which only kindness can heal. The aim should be to "Hinduize" them more and more, for they belong to the Hindu community, and to

offer them every facility to remain within the fold. They will be a mighty accession to the strength of our body politic; if not, they will be an equally heavy subtraction from it. Alienated, they will introduce an additional element of heterogeneity which will further complicate the already difficult problems of administration. No possible means of amelioration should be neglected, and every friend of Hindu society, every lover of Mysore, should supplement the efforts of Government with all his strength.

This suggestion is a gentle warning both to the Christian missionary and the Mussalman missionary not to try to wean these suppressed classes from Hinduism, but if they at all wish to interfere, to act so that they may become better Hindus. If the suggestion is acted upon by the parties concerned, it will be a substantial contribution towards the attainment of real peace in the land.

Young India, 7-7-1927

110. THE COW IN MYSORE

I have received letters from Cow-protection Societies in Mysore, protesting against my letter[1] to the Mysore Cow-protection Committee appointed by the State. My letter was in answer to a questionnaire issued by that Committee. Extracts from that letter published in the Madras Press led the Cow-protection Societies in question to think that I was totally against legal prohibition of cow-slaughter under any circumstances whatsoever. I was surprised to receive these letters, and I wondered whether, in a moment of forgetfulness or inadvertence, I had ever said that there should never be any legislation against cow-slaughter. I therefore asked for a copy of my letter from the Cow-protection Committee, which they have kindly sent me. As the letter represents my considered opinion, and as it has been given some importance by the Committee and has caused misunderstanding among the public of Mysore interested in this very important question, I reproduce the whole of it below:[2]

Neither the discussion with the members of the several Cow-protection Societies, nor the correspondence before me warrants any alteration of the opinion expressed in this letter. The reader

[1] *Vide* Vol. XXXII, pp. 545-6.

[2] Not reproduced here

will observe that I have nowhere said that there should never be any legislation against cow-slaughter. But what I have said is that there should be no prohibition of cow-slaughter by legislation *without the consent of the intelligent majority of the subjects* adversely affected by it. Therefore, the Mysore State will be perfectly justified, and, indeed, bound to undertake legislation prohibiting cow-slaughter, if it has the consent of the intelligent majority of its Mussalman population. The members of the Cow-protection Societies that met me assured me that the relations between Hindus and Mussalmans in Mysore were cordial, and that a majority of Mussalmans in Mysore were as much in favour of legislative prohibition as Hindus, and I was glad to be assured by them that many Europeans, especially missionaries, were in favour of such prohibition. So far, therefore, as the question of legislation in Mysore is concerned, if the statements made to me are correct, the way is clear for legislative prohibition. But let me reiterate what I have pointed out in my letter, and what I have emphasized so often in these columns, namely, that legislative prohibition is the smallest part of any programme of cow-protection. The trend of the letters received by me, and the activity of most Cow-protection Societies, however, show, that they would be satisfied with mere legal prohibition. I wish to warn all such societies against staking their all on legislation. We have already too much of it in this law-ridden country. People seem to think that when a law is passed against any evil, it will die without any further effort. There never was a grosser self-deception. Legislation is intended and is effective against an ignorant or a small evil-minded minority; but no legislation which is opposed by an intelligent and organized public opinion, or under cover of religion by a fanatical minority, can ever succeed. The more I study the question of cow-protection, the stronger the conviction grows upon me, that protection of the cow and her progeny can be attained, only if there is continuous and sustained constructive effort along the lines suggested by me. There may be, probably there is, room for supplementing or amending the constructive programme sketched by me. But there is no room for doubting the absolute necessity of a vast constructive programme if India's cattle are to be saved from destruction. And the preservation of cattle really means also a step towards the preservation of the starving millions of India's men and women who have also been reduced to the condition of her cattle. The Indian States undoubtedly can in this as in many such matters give the lead to the rest of India. And among the States, probably, there is none better fitted, or better able, to make the right beginning than Mysore. It has, from all accounts received by me, a popular prince, an enlightened public opinion, no Hindu-Mussalman question, and a sympathetic Dewan. Mysore has also the Imperial Institute of Dairying and Animal Husbandry, and Mr. William Smith, the Imperial Dairy Expert, is himself stationed at Bangalore. The State has, therefore, all the materials necessary for evolving a constructive policy. Add to this the fact that Nature has endowed Mysore with a glorious climate. The title a Hindu king dearly cherishes is that of defender of the cow and the Brahmin. The cow means not merely the animal, the giver of milk and innumerable other things to India, but it means also the helpless, the downtrodden and the poor. Brahmin means the representative of divine knowledge and experience. But today, alas! Hindu princes are powerless, and in many cases even indifferent, if not unwilling, to ensure this full protection. Unless the States and the people co-operate with one another to control and regulate the breeding of cattle, the production of milk supply, and the disposal of dead cattle, for the benefit of the people as a whole, the cattle of India will be bred but to die an unnatural death at the hands of the butcher, notwithstanding all the legislation that may be passed against cow-slaughter. The ignorance of Nature's Law will be accepted as no excuse when men and women of India appear before the Throne of Judgment.

I was shocked to learn from the members of the Cow-protection Society that beef slaughtered in Bangalore and in Mysore was given to the animals in the State gardens, that beef was much cheaper than any other meat, and that the *Adi Karnatakas*, who claimed to be and were recognized as Hindus, and who knew the *Ramayana* and the *Mahabharata* as well as any other Hindu, were addicted to beef-eating. If all this is true, the better-placed Hindus are clearly to blame for such a state of things. If the *Adi Karnatakas* do not respect the sanctity of the cow, it is because they know no better. But what is to be said of the Hindus who have so criminally neglected their brethren as to omit to acquaint them with a fundamental truth of Hinduism?

Young India, 7-7-1927

111. WHAT IS A POLITICAL ASSOCIATION?

I read the following in *The Hindu* of the 25th June last:

> Under Rule 23 (1) of Government Servants' Conduct Rules, Government have, I understand, prohibited Government servants from subscribing to the Khadi Fund, which is in aid of the All-India Spinners' Association. The reasons for this prohibition are stated to be, (1) that it is an association, established with the consent of the All-India Congress Committee, as an integral part of the Congress organization, (2) that it declares itself prepared to receive and acknowledge yarn subscriptions for membership of the Congress and (3) that therefore it must be regarded as a political association.

If the information supplied by the special correspondent of *The Hindu* is correct, the ruling of the Madras Government appears to me to be a case of perverted judgment, and a gross interference with the private liberty of its servants. If it is intended merely as an attack upon khadi or the All-India Spinners' Association, I have no doubt that both will survive the shock. And if it is an invitation to the All-India Spinners' Association to sever its connection with the Congress, I should be extremely sorry if I discovered that the Association had done anything to deserve such an invitation. The Association is proud of its being an integral part of the Congress organization, and it will deem it an honour and a privilege to work under the Congress banner, so long as that venerable national institution regards it as worthy of its patronage. But if by merely owning the parentage and patronage of the Congress an institution becomes a political association, the interpretation would involve most awkward consequences, which I hope no self-respecting Government servant will tolerate.

There are many schools for suppressed class children run in several provinces under the Congress aegis, and with Congress funds, to which Government servants also have been known to contribute without any secrecy. Was it wrong for them to do so? And are schools for 'untouchables' political bodies, because they are run with Congress funds and by Congressmen? Provincial Congress Committees have been known to open famine relief funds, and invite subscriptions to which Government servants have subscribed. Was it a breach of Government Servants' Conduct Rules? These relief committees were and the suppressed class committees are integral parts of the Congress organization. Are they, therefore, political associations? The Congress may open hospitals as an integral part of the Congress organization and its activity. Will the hospitals therefore become political associations? Khadi is at the present moment an integral part of the Congress franchise. Is it a crime therefore for Government servants to wear it? Is it not possible for the Congress to have its political, its social, its moral, its economic, medical, sociological and such other departments, all integral parts of that organization, and yet wholly self-governing and wholly independent each of the others? Every Congressman regrets that the Congress, although among all the national bodies it is the most influential and the most important, is not yet able to command men and money enough to organize every department of national life. But as time goes on, and as it is able to draw to it men of the right stamp, as well as money, it will certainly touch every part of our national life. It would be ridiculous then to say that all its non-political activities became tainted with politics, and were therefore taboo to the Government servants. And if the Government dared to issue such a boycott, it would prove to be its own death warrant.

I am painfully conscious of the fact that the Congress is a long way off from attaining that height. But when it does, the Government will be absorbed by it, and there will be nobody to resent, resist, or interfere with the Congress influence. That the Government has been able—assuming that the information given in *The Hindu* is correct—to regard the All-India Spinners' Association as a political association, shows that the Congress influence is at a discount at the present moment, that the public voice is ineffective, and that therefore it is open for the Government to issue any ruling, no matter how insulting or how ridiculous it may be. I can only hope that there will be Government servants courageous enough to disregard this monstrous ruling and openly help the Spinners' Association which in spite of the Government order, I submit, is entirely a non-political body, and was in so many words intended by the Congress to be and to remain, for the reasons stated in the resolution which brought the Association into being. Here are the words of the resolution which is part of the constitution of the All-India Spinners' Association:

> Whereas the time has arrived for the establishment of an expert organization for the development of hand-spinning and khaddar, and whereas experience has shown that such development is not possible without a permanent organization, *unaffected and uncontrolled by politics, by political changes or political bodies*, an organization called the All-India

> Spinners' Association is hereby established with the consent of the All-India Congress Committee, as an integral part of the Congress organization, but *with independent existence and powers*.

Two things stand out unequivocal and emphatic in this preamble, namely, that it is unaffected and uncontrolled by politics, political changes, or political bodies, and that it has an independent existence and powers. How such an association could be called a political association, simply because it is an integral part of the Congress, and also because like a bank it has accepted the agency of the Congress for the collection of yarn subscription, passes comprehension. But acts of governments are often incomprehensible. It would have been more honest, if the reported action of the Madras Government had taken the form of a straight order to its servants to have nothing to do with the All-India Spinners' Association on the simple and intelligible ground, that it does not like the penetration of the charkha into the villages and the consequent progress of khadi and all that it means.

Young India, 7-7-1927

112. WORK BEFORE PINJRAPOLES

Sjt. Y. M. Parnerkar, whose services have been engaged on behalf of the All-India Cow-protection Association, has sent me notes of his impressions gathered from his visit to Kathiawar where he went in search of good cows. In the hope that his plea for the expansion of pinjrapoles into model dairies and cattle-breeding farms on a moderate scale and under skilled management will not fall upon deaf ears, I condense them below.

> One thing that strikes most a lover of cattle when he visits Kathiawar, the home of the well-known *Gir* animals, is the enormous number of charitable institutions, run as retiring places for disabled cattle, chiefly cows. They are known as pinjrapoles. When they were first started there was not the deep poverty that faces us today. It was then a matter of little importance, whether they were economically managed or not. But today the condition is altered. No such institution can now hope for long to stand well, unless it is put on a sound financial basis. The longevity of pinjrapoles could only be guaranteed if they became self-supporting. It was found that nearly eight lakhs of rupees per year were spent as recurring expenses only in Kathiawar on these institu-

tions. Yet it is difficult, if not impossible, to secure even a few good cows in a home for the best milk-producing cow in all India. This tract, once overflowing with milk, produces now hardly any pure and hygienic cow's milk. The once warlike race of Kathis is now deteriorating for want of proper nourishment, notwithstanding plentiful grazing facilities for cattle-breeding. Bullocks for agricultural labour are imported by the cultivators from outside. The buffalo is overpowering the cow in the production of milk and ghee, and so driving her off the stage. Time has come for the best brains of the country to take up this very important problem.

There can be no two opinions on the point that the duty of the *gosevak* does not end with merely saving the cow from the butcher's knife, but he has to stop the deterioration and try to raise the standard of milk production. It could be said that the surest way of saving the cow from going to the slaughter-house is to make it so expensive that the butcher cannot afford to purchase it. This could only be done, when the cow finds a good place among the paying heads in a dairyman's or a cattle-breeder's ledger. The productive power of an average Indian cow has gone down so low that it is difficult for a business man to take up the work. The problem has therefore to be handled on a religious or national basis.

The work can be accomplished by the existing pinjrapoles. They have capital, buildings, and above all, public sympathy. What is needed is good management and enterprise. When a pinjrapole maintains about 100 or 200 retired cattle, it can add a few good cows that will support themselves and leave a margin for the other heads. If the cows are well kept, regularly bred to good bulls, and the calves well cared for, during a short period these should become places where the dairyman can purchase his foundation stock, the agriculturist may get his draft cattle, the fancy cattle-keeper the use of a good bull, the needy man his sick animals well treated, the ignorant cow-owner guidance in the best way of maintaining his live-stock, and what is more important, all from the child in the cradle to the old man on the deathbed may get pure milk and its nourishing products at a moderate rate.

Young India, 7-7-1927

113. AGES-OLD PROBLEM

A sannyasi from Almora writes as follows:

> In replying to a correspondent, you have said in *Young India* of 14th April last that, even if you were attacked by a snake, you would not wish to kill it.[1] In my opinion, this would be improper; for in the first place, you would be thereby killing yourself, and secondly, by letting such a venomous reptile free, you would be instrumental in causing injury to others. Take another instance. If the owner of a house, in which a snake has entered, removed the snake without killing it from his house, it is sure to enter some other house and injure its inmates. Surely, the responsibility for the injury, it may be fatal, to the inmates of the other house, done by the snake that was let off, will be on the head of him who has under a false notion of pity let the snake off. There are many other reptiles, beasts and insects who injure human beings or spread disease. Surely, if the destruction of this life be considered *himsa*, then it is infinitely less than the destruction wrought by these creatures. Let it be granted that when a man kills for his own sake, it is *himsa*; but it cannot be when destruction is resorted to for the sake of saving many other precious lives. After all, the quality of an act is determined by the motive prompting it, and when the motive for destruction is the higher good, such destruction becomes a duty and ceases to be *himsa*. I would like you to answer this argument in the pages of *Young India*.

The Sannyasi's argument is ages old. There is no doubt that there is very considerable force in it. Had it not been so, destruction would not have gone on as it has from ancient times. Few men are wantonly wicked. The most heinous and the most cruel crimes of which history has record have been committed under cover of religion or equally other noble motive. But in my opinion, we are no better off for the destruction that has gone on even under the highest sanction, that is, of religion. No doubt destruction in some form or other of some life is inevitable. Life lives upon life. Hence only is the highest bliss attainable ascribed by seers to a state, in which life is possible without the necessity of a perishable case, for whose sustenance destruction becomes at all necessary. And it is possible for man whilst in the body to hope to attain that state, only if he confines himself to the least

[1] *Vide* Vol. XXXIII, pp. 233-4.

possible destruction, such as is caused in his taking of vegetable life. The freer he is, consciously and deliberately, from the necessity of living upon the destruction of other life, the nearer he is to Truth and God. That all mankind is not likely to accept what may appear to be an unattractive existence does not affect the validity of my argument. Men, who lead this life of utter selflessness and of pity for the meanest creature that lives, enable us to understand the power of God, and serve as leaven to lift up humanity, and light its path towards its goal. We have no right to destroy life that we cannot create. It seems to me to be atheistical to think that God has created some life only to be destroyed by man, either for his pleasure or for sustaining a body, which he knows, is after all doomed to death any moment. We do not know what part the many so-called noxious creatures play in the economy of Nature. We shall never know the laws of Nature by destruction. We have records of men, whose love has travelled beyond their kind, living in perfect safety even in the midst of ferocious beasts. There seems to be so much affinity between all life, that tigers, lions and snakes have refrained from harming men, who have shed all fear of them and will approach them as friends.

The argument that if I do not destroy a snake known to be venomous, he will cause the death of many men and women is deceptive. It is no part of my duty to set about seeking out all the venomous creatures and destroying them. Nor need I take it for granted, that if I do not destroy a snake I encounter, it is bound to bite the next passer-by. I must not be the judge between the snake and my neighbours. I have sufficiently discharged my duty to my neighbours if I do unto them as I would that they should do unto me, and if I do not expose them to any greater risk than I do myself, and if I do not better my own condition in any way whatsoever at their expense. I may not therefore leave the snake in my neighbour's compound as is very often done. The utmost I can do is to leave the reptile as much out of harm's way as possible, and warn my neighbours about its appearance in the neighbourhood and its disposal by me. I am aware that this is no comfort for my neighbours, nor any protection; but we are living in the midst of death, trying to grope our way to Truth. Perhaps it is as well that we are beset with danger at every point in our life; for, in spite of our knowledge of the danger and of our precarious existence, our indifference to the Source of all life is excelled only by our amazing arrogance.

I am not satisfied with the answer given to the sannyasi. His letter, which is written in Hindi, shows that my correspondent is himself a fellow seeker after Truth. Hence only have I felt the call to answer his query in public. My own position is pitiable. My intellect rebels against the destruction of any life in any shape whatsoever. But my heart is not strong enough to befriend those creatures which experience has shown are destructive. The language of convincing confidence, which comes from actual experience, fails me, and it will continue to be so, so long as I am cowardly enough to fear snakes, tigers and the like. I have entered upon the reply with the greatest diffidence. But I felt that it would be wrong not to declare my belief for fear of losing caste and being regarded as a dangerous animal myself. I was once so regarded by friends in South Africa. We were all sitting at a table, and discussion turned upon the very topic I have here discussed. They were English missionary friends. They did not mind my views about transmigration, cow-protection, vegetarianism, though they all appeared to be very crude to them. But they could not help betraying their disgust, which was written in their faces, when I said that I would not, if God gave me the courage, kill a snake,[1] even if I knew that not to kill would be certain death for me. Disgust was hidden by the suppressed laughter which accompanied, "O! You are a dangerous man then!"

Young India, 7-7-1927

114. LETTER TO B. F. BHARUCHA

[After *July 7, 1927*][2]

I have your letters. I shall now reply to them as far as I can; but for a completely satisfactory reply you must run down here, as you usually do. Take it that the replies I give are for your benefit only. If, however, you wire me asking for my permission to publish my replies, I am not going to decline it; just the same I should like to say that you have committed a blunder in publishing my last letter[3]. I had not written either to disturb the satyagrahis or to check them, but merely for your information and as a warning to you. When you solicited my permission, I thought you approved the substance of my letter and that you intended to stop the struggle and therefore you wanted to make use of my

[1] *Vide* also Vol. XXIX, pp. 202-3.

[2] The source has this letter after the entries for July 7, 1927.

[3] *Vide* "Letter to B. F. Bharucha", before 2-7-1927.

letter. Instead, you did just the opposite. If you had not understood my reply or if you did not approve of it there was absolutely no need to communicate it to the satyagrahis. I cannot understand how and why a rift was created among them. But it is no use crying over spilt milk.

Now that's all over. But I must say this: It is your duty and of other friends who regard the Nagpur struggle as a satyagraha to continue it. If you must have the sanction of the Congress, you must strongly refute my views and obtain its sanction. And know that I am not going to take it amiss if you do so. And if you obtain the sanction of the Congress I shall not be sorry; instead, I shall congratulate you. But let me strike a note of caution that before you do anything, make sure that you have correctly understood my views. The answers to your other questions are as follows:

1. It was not my duty to offer unsolicited criticism of the Nagpur satyagraha.
2. I did not think it proper to say anything beyond refuting what Awari[1] had written about my approval.
3. I do not understand on what matter I should have consulted Bhai Awari.
4. How do you hold me responsible for the resolutions that came up in the All-India Congress Committee? I had nothing to do with them. I do happen to be a member of the Working Committee, but my condition is that my presence should not be expected in any committee. If you ask me why I should agree to be on the Committee when I attend none of its meetings I must admit I have no defence or if I have any the President would be able to put it forward.
5. Now you will know that I had no hand in appointing Vallabhbhai; in fact the latter had told me that he had no idea of it. He could not disregard the Committee's insistence. Do you not yourself claim as much as Vallabhbhai does to understand my principles? But if I am to decide whose claim is stronger I can do so only at the time of my death, because how can I tell right today to what extent Vallabhbhai or you will be able to follow my ideas at some critical moment? But assuming that I myself were present at the Committee [meeting] and were against [the use of] arms, I would nevertheless find no inconsistency if I went to Nagpur at the Committee's insistence. I would go, explain my ideas and after having known the facts, make a report. If someone

[1] Manchersha Awari

can convince me that resorting to arms can come within the scope of satyagraha should I not let him do so ? How can one pronounce judgment without knowing the facts? Then if you would ask me why I wrote that letter to you, let me tell you that it is a common practice for friends to exchange ideas, that it is only rational to be willing to modify one's own ideas in the process, if possible. For instance today I do believe that God exists but I do not refuse to listen to the agnostics.

7. Won't you now agree that the answer to your seventh question is included in my answer to your sixth[1]? If you do not, then let me know so that I shall find time and answer it again.

8. I think this too is covered by my answers to the earlier questions.

9. When you say that the calm atmosphere necessary for satyagraha is not there, you make an observation applying to the whole of India. But there are a number of other conditions for satyagraha and when I talked of the general atmosphere in the country, you sought to limit your view to the local atmosphere. Here again you misunderstand my article[2].

10. If I tell the Congress President who has proffered help that a certain satyagraha is no satyagraha, although you are associated with it, what is there to be embarrassed about? Certainly you are no stranger to the well-known dictum: "There are as many ideas as there are heads."

11. I have a number of other ideas which the [Congress] President, Patel, Bharucha, Mahadev and Ba do not know and even I myself do not know. Do not therefore be unhappy when you come across some of my hitherto unknown ideas. And whatever regrets I felt on account of your support, I withdraw so that I may relieve you of yours.

12. I do want swaraj.

13. There is absolute need of self-protection.

14. For that my weapon is satyagraha. Because I realized the futility of weapons fashioned out of such gross material as wood, iron, electricity, etc., I invented the invisible substance of satyagraha and sought refuge in it. But that does not mean that everyone should have recourse to the same invisible weapon. Others may well obtain swaraj and defend it with arms.

In my scheme of swaraj there is a place for such weapons too, but it is of no use to me, as it cannot go with satyagraha.

[1] Answer to Question 6 is missing.

[2] *Vide* Vol. XXXIII, "Nagpur Satyagraha", 19-5-1927.

15. I think the answer to this question is covered by my answer to the fourteenth question.

16. The answer to this question too is practically covered by my answer to the fourteenth but, for the sake of clarity, I would say that those who do not understand satyagraha or in spite of their understanding it cannot digest it, will definitely take up material weapons and they have a right to do so. The State will have to provide training for it.

You ask to be excused for your long article. Now this is violence like the Western practice of deliberately committing an offence and then seeking to get out of it by formal apology. If you must apologize for writing a long letter, why write one at all? But you wrote it all the same and also apologized. We are at present under Western domination. Submitting to your violence, therefore, I forgive you because my satyagraha is none the worse for it. If you feel sorry you will not be excused; not only that but I shall have to launch satyagraha against you. If you can convey my message to Awari, send him word to eat, drink and be merry. His going to the jail has not pained me in the least. I regard him as a man of courage. But I also know that he is immature. There is no limit to his goodness as to his stubbornness. I put up with his lack of understanding and his haughtiness and praise his goodness, his courage and his patriotism.

[From Gujarati]

From the manuscript of Mahadev Desai's Diary. Courtesy: Narayan Desai

115. SPEECH TO ADI KARNATAKA BOYS, BANGALORE[1]

Before *July 8, 1927*

The students of the Bangalore State Hostel for *Adi Karnataka* Boys were brought over the other day to Kumara Park by Sjt. Shankarnarayan Rao . . . [Gandhiji was told:] "We have 145 boys now, but propose to take in more by cutting down Re. 1 monthly that is given them as pocket money. But the boys are opposed to the proposal." . . . Gandhiji who was requested to address a few words of advice immediately laid his finger thereon and said:

I was distressed, my boys, to find that you were forgetting your simple habits, and were reluctant to part with your pocket money for the sake of your brethren. I assure you that my father

[1] From Mahadev Desai's "Weekly Letter"

gave me no pocket money, and in no other part of India boys of the middle class are treated like you. But the State does not house and feed and educate you in order that you may learn idleness and forget simplicity and self-help. You must learn to wash your own clothes, cook your own food, and do all your work yourselves. And may I tell you? As I look at you I feel as though you were all foreigners. Can you tell me why?

The best amongst the students immediately answered: "Because we are wearing foreign cloth."

That is very good. Now there is no reason why you should not be wearing khadi, every one of you. I tell you I could give you for one-fourth the price much cleaner caps than you are wearing now. The circumstance that your superiors or your teachers do not wear khadi need not deter you. You will not drink liquor, or eat beef or carrion, because your parents or other *Adi Karnatakas* do so. You will on the contrary give up all these things, and insist on your Superintendent providing you with khadi clothes, telling him that in case they are dear you would gladly curtail part of your cloth rations. You must know that there are in the country millions of children who do not get the education that you get, who do not get not only the pocket money you get, but not even enough food that your pocket money could buy them. I want you for their sake to wear khadi and to learn to spin. Go to the Exhibition and see what it has to teach you.

Young India, 14-7-1927

116. LETTER TO MIRABEHN

July 8, 1927

CHI. MIRA,

I have your letters. There seems to be one missing still. Absence of further telegraphic news from you I take to mean good news.

Do stay as long as you wish and certainly till you are quite restored to health. Health must be kept.

With love,

BAPU

From the original: C.W. 5246. Courtesy: Mirabehn

117. SPEECH AT KHADI EXHIBITION, BANGALORE[1]

July 8, 1927

Distribution of prizes over, amidst an impressive silence, Mahatmaji spoke as follows:

FRIENDS,

Perhaps the best demonstration that you can all give of your interest in these proceedings is as soon as this function is over for you to proceed to the Exhibition Court and empty the stalls. Rajagopalachari read to you the figures of six days' sale with some degree of pride and satisfaction. I must confess to you that when I think of your own capacity, eight thousand rupees' purchase brings no satisfaction whatsoever to me. When in my imagination I picture to myself so many shops, cloth shops in Bangalore and when I look at the dresses that most men and women in Bangalore wear, eight thousand rupees seem to me to be a mere flea-bite. But khadi workers know their difficulties. They realize every moment of the progress of this movement how uphill the task is and so when compared to their experience of khadi exhibitions elsewhere, they find a little rise in the sale-barometer, they derive satisfaction. Such really is the kind of satisfaction that Rajagopalachari has derived. But I felt it would be wrong on my part if I did not draw the attention of you all who are living in this beautiful land to the work that lies before you, if you will do it.

Ours is not a city civilization and if there are any dreamers who think that some day or other we shall implant on our soil the city civilization of the West, being a dreamer of a type myself, I warn the dreamers against the slightest hope in our own generation and for some generations at least to come of such dreams being realized. Just think for one moment what our country is: 700,000 villages, in a vast continent, 1,900 miles long, 1,500 miles broad, and these villages even according to Western pandits handed down to us from times immemorial. America is a new continent. They have millions of acres of land lying absolutely fallow and a sparse population. There were no villages when the people from old England went to America, when Columbus went to America, not of the type you find here, and they brought into being a new civilization. It may be that it is the most per-

[1] At its closing ceremony; the Exhibition began on July 3.

fect of its kind for that soil, but what is good for the virgin soil of America need not, cannot, in my opinion is not, good for this ancient soil, watered by its mighty rivers, protected by the highest mountain peaks, and inhabited by people, the most conservative on the face of the globe, having traditions of their own, habits and customs which cannot be eradicated on the spur of the moment. Then I say that if you think that you will import the city civilization from the West and eradicate your villages you can do so on one condition, the condition of Chengizkhan, fabled in history. I do not know what Chengizkhan did or did not do. But if history gives [the truth] about him then I know that before you can implant the civilization from America onto this soil you will require at least several hundred Chengizkhans who will mercilessly kill off the villagers, pick out the sturdiest men and women whom these Chengizkhans can bend to their iron brutal will and use the human species as if they were so many brutes and beasts, then indeed such a dream can be realized. But if you want to keep your villages intact, if you want to assimilate the best that we may learn from the West, then indeed here is work enough for you, to men and women in Bangalore and Mysore and Karnataka, the Southern Peninsula and the few who have come from the North also.

I do not know whether you have been touched as I have been by the sight of these prize-winners who do not know the distinctions between Brahmin and non-Brahmin, Hindus and Mussalmans, rich and poor. They have also one thing in common, namely, the poverty of this land and those who belong to rich families have cast in their lot with those who are the poorest in front of us. I do not know whether you take the same interest, whether you have the same knowledge that you have of racing language. If in this assembly representing the poorest of India, if in spite of these you had prize-winners from the football ground, racing ground or the cricket field, I know what some of you will feel, I know how enthusiastic you will feel. But I do not know that you understand the language of spinners and carders. I do not know whether in spite of your having gone to the Exhibition you really understand the hidden meaning of these processes. If you do, then I know that you will have the same feeling that is welling up in my breast at this moment, when I feel impelled to speak out my mind to you in spite of my weak health.

At this stage Mahatmaji was visibly moved and there were tears in his eyes. He paused for a few minutes. . . .

I pray to God that He may give you strength and wisdom to understand the meaning of this Exhibition and this demonstration.

I have not many more words to say and you will forgive me if you find me breaking down in the midst of my delivery of the message to you. I am really too full of this thing and it is difficult in spite of the ability I too possess to control myself and to hide my feelings and speak to you purely the common language of reason. But sometimes emotion and sentiments overpower me and I wish God gave me the power that I daily yearn for to open out my heart to you so that you can read not the language that tongue can speak but the language that the heart can speak. May God bless you and may God bless the prize-winners and may He bless this function. I thank you all for attending.

The Hindu, 9-7-1927

118. LETTER TO MIRABEHN

July 9, 1927

CHI. MIRA,

I have your letter after the wire. You must have received my usual weekly letter. I sent also a postcard to Wardha but that was merely to tell you that I had sent the main letter to Sabarmati. I am glad you decided to stay on and to get the doctor's report. If we knew all the laws of nature or having known, had the power to obey them in thought, word and deed, we would be God Himself and not need to do anything at all. As it is, we hardly know the laws and have little power to obey them. Hence disease and all its effects. It is, therefore, enough for us to realize that every illness is but a breach of some unknown law of nature and to strive to know the laws and pray for power to obey. Heart prayer, therefore, whilst we are ill, is both work and medicine.

I went through another day's strain yesterday and stood it extremely well, better even than last Sunday. I am in no hurry to have your Hindi letters.

With love,

BAPU

From the original: C.W. 5247. Courtesy: Mirabehn

119. LETTER TO N. R. MALKANI

July 9, 1927

MY DEAR MALKANI,

Your letter. A broken bottle may somehow be held together but can it ever regain the quality of unbreakability that might have been ascribed to it by its owner? I have not yet got over the shock of your fall.[1] You do not know how I have sworn by you. You were among the very few of my unbreakables.

But I must bury the past. I shall try. Whether you should return to the Mahavidyalaya or not I do not know. Let Kripalani judge. The blow was so stunning that I did not think it fit to write to Kripalani or Nanabhai[2] nor have they said anything to me.

But it is quite clear that you may not now leave the Sind show without ample notice to Thadani. Your repentance is good and proper. Nothing however need be done in haste now. Please keep yourself in touch with me. Discuss your repentance with your wife and mother-in-law. Let them too realize what the return means.

I am here for some time yet.

Yours,
BAPU

From a photostat: G.N. 876

120. SPEECH AT AMATEUR DRAMATIC ASSOCIATION, MYSORE[3]

[July 9, 1927][4]

The week began with Gandhiji's attendance at the special dramatic performance—"Kabir"—organized by the Amateur Dramatic Association of Pandit Taranath. . . . The whole idea was to popularize Hindi and khadi. Whilst, therefore, Gandhiji summed up his criticism in just one phrase,—"Kabir in a modernized form",—he paid to all concerned a tribute of praise which

[1] *Vide* "Letter to N. R. Malkani", 26-6-1927.

[2] Nrisinhaprasad (Nanabhai) Kalidas Bhatt who was at the time the *Kulanayak* (Vice-Chancellor) of the Gujarat Vidyapith

[3] From Mahadev Desai's "Weekly Letter"

[4] According to Mahadev Desai's Diary

was well deserved. He thanked them for the threefold pleasure of "having given to the self-appointed representative of *Daridranarayana* a purse not to be counted", of listening in South India to "Hindi exquisitely pronounced and rendered" and of seeing the majority of actors dressed in khadi, and said:

The actors have realized the pain I feel when I do not see a single countryman of mine in khadi, be he a prince or a peasant, a lawyer, a doctor or a business man, be the person a man or woman, belonging to the highest or the lowest strata of society. I am hoping for a day when all will follow this common dharma of our motherland, and I hope that what has been acted will be translated into life by the actors and be a permanent part of them and us. I assure you that among the pleasant recollections that I shall carry with me, if God permits me to leave Karnataka alive, the memory of this evening will not be the least pleasant.

Young India, 21-7-1927

121. TWO SCALES

Writing about a girl, who had been married by her thoughtless parents while she was still a child and had never come to know her husband, and who had later become "a widow", I had expressed the view that I would not regard her as married at all, and that, apart from the question whether she should be regarded as married or not, it was the duty of her parents to get her married again.

Reading about this view in newspapers, a gentleman has written a long letter to me in Hindi to the following effect:

> The reasons which you advance to justify the remarriage of child-widows will also apply to other widows. Would you, then, encourage all widows to remarry? I would urge that we should prohibit even widowers from remarrying and should not in any case permit widows to remarry.

Men have committed through the ages a great many sins with the help of arguments such as these. I have come across meat-eaters who argue that, since man is obliged to eat meat in the region of the North Pole where the land is snow-bound all through the year, it is not sinful to eat meat in this country too, despite the heat here.

We easily find arguments to justify sinful practices. Widowers will not refrain from remarrying, but under cover of the argument that they should, we are urged to withhold justice from widows. Those who have made us unfit for swaraj now tell us: "You will get swaraj when you are fit for it." We who have suppressed and degraded the untouchables say: "Let them reform themselves and then mix with us."

Like a dishonest Vania, men keep two scales, one for buying and another for selling things with. They feel their own weaknesses, huge as hills, to be as small as mustard seed and regard the weaknesses of others, small like grains, to be as big as hills.

If men use reason, they will see that they have no right to suppress widows. Enforced widowhood is not virtue but sin. It covers up a disease which breaks out with the opportunity for contact with a man. If a grown-up woman who has become a widow does not even feel the desire to remarry, she deserves to be revered by the whole world, she is a pillar of dharma. But one who wishes to remarry and refrains from doing so out of fear of society or is restrained by law, has already remarried in thought. She deserves not reverence but compassion and should be free to remarry. In former times she was free. Following custom slavishly, so-called high-caste Hindus turned this voluntary dharma into a law and introduced coercion in dharma.

Justice required that, so long as widowers have the right to remarry, widows too should have it. Certain restrictions are necessary for the protection of society, but they should be the same for both men and women and should command the willing consent of all thinking women as of all thinking men.

We should not forget the difference between child-widows and other widows. It is the duty of parents and of society to get the former married again, but they have no such duty towards other widows. In their case, all that is necessary is to remove the present restraint enforced by custom or law. In other words, if such widows wish to remarry they should be free to do so.

The only restraint over the remarriage of grown-up widowers and widows can be that exercised by public opinion. That public opinion is now flowing in the opposite direction. Where, however, respect for dharma, discipline and self-control is widespread, very few men and women will violate them. As things are, people who respect them are exceptions rather than the rule. A rich old man of sixty feels no shame in marrying a girl of ten or twelve, the marriage being the third in his life, and society tolerates this. When on the other hand, a helpless widow of twenty wishes to remarry because she cannot observe self-control, despite her efforts, she is despised by society. This is not dharma but *adharma*[1].

It is useless and irrelevant to point to immorality and like evils prevailing in other countries as an argument against the removal of this coercion, this *adharma*. Even if all widows, from child-widows to widows of sixty, were as pure as the immaculate Sita, I would say that if any of them wanted to remarry nobody had the right to stop them from doing so. Society may plead with them with love, but it has no right to restrain them by force.

If we apply to others the yardstick which we use for ourselves, the world would be freed of the threefold suffering and dharma would prevail once again.

[From Gujarati]

Navajivan, 10-7-1927

122. A LETTER

KUMARA PARK, BANGALORE,
July 10, 1927

DEAR FRIEND,

I thank you for sending the copies of resolutions passed at the public meeting of the Mussalmans of the Ambala city on the first instant. In your letter you have specially invited my attention to Resolution No. 5 and requested immediate action. Perhaps you are unaware that I have recently gone through a very serious illness and that I am still lying on a convalescent bed and that I am under medical orders not to undertake much activity. I read no North Indian newspapers at all. The only paper I may be said to read is *The Hindu* of Madras, and I cast an occasional glance at a Bombay English daily. This gives me no information about what is in the Hindu papers. I have seen in these papers no offensive reference to the Prophet or Islam or the Muslims. If you have Press cuttings containing the references complained of in Resolution No. 5, I would thank you to send them if only as a loan if necessary. I shall undertake to study them and return them after perusal. I will certainly give my opinion upon them. So far as the judgment[2] in the *Rangila Rasul*[3] case is concerned, you

[1] The opposite of dharma

[2] *Vide* "Letter to M. Abdul Gani", 11-8-1927.

[3] An Urdu pamphlet

will permit me to say that the whole of the agitation in respect of it is unfortunate and unjustified. I do not seek to justify the judgment but all that is said against Justice Dilip Singh is in my opinion highly improper. If he has misread the law, as he well might have, the remedy is not a condemnation of the Judge as a man but the true remedy is to appeal against the judgment or if the law itself is defective to agitate for its amendment.

I am no defender of the author of *Rangila Rasul*. It may be a new thing to you. I had the opportunity of reading that pamphlet some years ago, and I commented upon it very severely in the columns of *Young India*.[1] Probably you do not know this fact. You may not also know that the author of *Rangila Rasul* is not the only misguided mischief-maker. I have seen Muslim writings just as offensive as *Rangila Rasul*. So far as I am aware there is nothing to choose between this class of writers, whether Hindu or Mussalman, and both are equally worthy of condemnation. But the remedy against this evil, so far as I am concerned, is not through a court of law, certainly not through violence, but through cultivation of healthy Hindu-Muslim opinion which will make the publication of sheets inflaming religious passions against one another an impossibility. But I am aware that my views are just now out of fashion. I, therefore, hold my silence so far as it is possible to do so. I could not ignore your letter, and delicate though my health is, I felt that I should send you a fairly full reply which I have done as lover of, and believer in, Hindu-Muslim unity and as your friend and brother if it is possible for you so to regard me. I have not written this letter for publication but it is written for you to share it with those who may wish to know my opinion and who desire to promote Hindu-Muslim unity. I have no desire to be drawn into a newspaper controversy or even into a profitless discussion by correspondence. If my letter makes no appeal to your reason I would urge you to dismiss it from your mind and throw it into the waste-paper basket. For your information I may tell you that I am no longer a Bar-at-Law. I am a poor scavenger and spinner.

Yours sincerely,
M. K. GANDHI

From a microfilm: S.N. 12384

[1] *Vide* Vol. XXIV, pp. 261 and 365-6; also Vol. XXXV.

123. LETTER TO J. B. KRIPALANI

KUMARA PARK, BANGALORE,
July 10, 1927

MY DEAR PROFESSOR,

I sent you a telegram yesterday in reply to your letter to Mahadev. I have purposely refrained hitherto from writing to you anything about Malkani. He wrote to me announcing his resignation.[1] It very nearly broke me to pieces. For, I regarded Malkani to be one of my unbreakables.[2] What would happen to the Vidyapith did not affect me but that a man had fallen shook me to the marrow. It is good that he has repented but you will be entirely justified in not taking him back. For his part, it would be another wrong if he left Thadani as unceremoniously as he left us. His wanting to be taken back, therefore, after three months or earlier if Thadani can spare him appears to me quite justified. That if he is truly repentant he must not remain at the Sind College permanently, I have no doubt. Nor must he feel hurt if he cannot be accepted by you. You will, therefore, come to a decision upon his letter solely from the point of view of the Mahavidyalaya. And if you think that the other professors would rather not have him I would not press for his reinstatement. It would embarrass him and it would put out the dissenting professors. If you therefore decide to have him, there should be a whole-hearted unanimity.

Yes. I have been getting some information about the new Vinayamandir. I was delighted to find so good an attendance. I did not expect that response. I hope that it would be a progressive success and that those who are responsible for its creation would never desert it, whether it continues to draw a large number of students or whether it declines.

I wish you would have a radical operation for piles if Dr. Dalal is now ready.

Kikibehn continues to favour me with a little letter from time to time.

[1] *Vide* "Letter to N. R. Malkani", 26-6-1927.
[2] *Vide* "Letter to N. R. Malkani", 9-7-1927.

You are not to expect me there before October as far as I can judge at present.

Yours sincerely,

ACHARYA KRIPALANI
GUJARAT VIDYAPITH

From a photostat: S.N. 12603

124. SPEECH AT ALL-KARNATAKA HINDI CONFERENCE, BANGALORE[1]

July 10, 1927

The All-Karnataka Hindi Sammelan held its session this afternoon at the Majestic Theatre before a vast concourse of people. . . . At about 3 p.m. Mahatmaji arrived and conducted the proceedings of the day. . . . He then distributed the diplomas to the successful candidates at the last Hindi examination, one of whom was a lady who had obtained a I Class. After distribution of prizes Mahatmaji, before speaking in Hindi, wanted to know how many would like the speech to be in English. The audience to a man raised their hands and Mahatmaji smiling next asked them by the same means to signify whether they wanted Kanarese translation to which also there was assent even from the ladies' gallery. He then spoke in Hindi and his speech was translated to the audience by Mr. Gangadharrao Deshpande. After dealing with the usefulness of the movement, Mahatmaji [said:][2]

India is divided into two parts today, and the portion north of the Vindhya has no heart relations with the southern portions. It is the duty of the South to learn the language of the North which is far larger. When I find it easy to travel from Sind to Bengal with the little bit of my knowledge of Hindi, it is impossible in these parts to get along without English. Unless you learn Hindi, you will not break through the Vindhya that stands between the South and the North. I do not want you to ignore your vernaculars—you may be as proud of them as I am of mine—but if we would be Indians and not merely Gujaratis, Bengalis, Tamilians or Karnatakas, we ought to learn Hindi. It is not difficult to learn. Those who have learnt it have not taken more than

[1] This was the first All-Karnataka Hindi Conference. It began on July 9 and ended on July 10. Gandhiji attended this Conference on the last day.

[2] This paragraph has been taken from *The Hindu*, 12-7-1927.

six months studying two hours a week. I appeal to you to devote that brief period to the service of the motherland.

Different from the question of a lingua franca is that of a common script. Whereas knowledge of Hindi enables you to come in contact with people of the North and send out your hearts to them, adoption on your part of Devanagari as the script for your vernaculars enables the people in the North to come in close contact with you.

Now is the question of funds. I am glad that South India has begun to contribute towards the expenses of the Prachar. But a yearly expenditure of Rs. 10,000 is necessary for the work, and I appeal to you to find that amount from South India.

Young India, 21-7-1927

125. LETTER TO MIRABEHN

[*July 10, 1927*][1]

CHI. MIRA,

I have your letter. You will follow the doctor's directions accurately. There need be no hurry about Wardha. You can do your Hindi just as well there. No Wardha until you feel quite free and secure. Dr. Harilal Desai is quite a sound man and very careful.

Do not strain yourself to write to me in Hindi. By all means do, whenever you feel like it. You will use the mosquito-net without any hesitation. Do not be in a hurry to move about quickly.

I had another meeting today, this time for Hindi. I stood it quite well.

With love,

BAPU

From the original: C.W. 5245. Courtesy: Mirabehn

[1] From the reference in the last paragraph to the Hindi Conference; *vide* the preceding item.

126. LETTER TO MIRABEHN

July 11, 1927

CHI. MIRA,

No letter from you today but there is your welcome telegram which is more than a letter because it gives me news todate. What an important part regularity of bowels plays in one's system? It is clear too that frequent fasting for purely health reasons is a desirable thing. But I do not need to emphasize the point with you.

My address up to 16th August is Bangalore. I shall be going out now and again for a day or two. But Bangalore is to be headquarters till the 16th August.

With love,

BAPU

From the original: C.W. 5248. Courtesy: Mirabehn

127. LETTER TO GOPALRAO

Silence Day, July 11, 1927

Your letter. You will, of course, have to consider what Kakasaheb says.

You want to enjoy the full bliss of *brahmacharya* immediately but this cannot be done. If you are content with forgoing marriage then do not marry. If not, make arrangements for getting married. You are no stranger to the difference between contentment and bliss.

The idea of merging into each other if you find an ideal wife is itself a great illusion. Many have been deluded by it and it will be no wonder if you too are lost. If you will escape it till the end, that would be a matter for wonder.

Having seen us all married people, if you are convinced that it is not worth while following suit—and convinced you ought to be—give up for the present the desire to taste the joy of *brahmacharya* and ponder over the joylessness of marriage, if you have observed it. Continue to think on this line—'God alone knows what bliss there is to be enjoyed in *brahmacharya*, but because there is no joy in marriage, I am not going to marry at all.'

Here is an argument on a lower level:

'I would not say I don't want to marry. Indeed, under certain circumstances I may marry. But today my country is in bondage; plight of the women is miserable. As I am engaged in this work, how can I marry? I must take this vow that until we attain the swaraj of my conception, I shall not marry even if Rambha[1] were to solicit me.' Try to think in this way if you can. Formulate your definition of swaraj. I suggest a simple one: 'The day when the spinning-wheel spreads throughout India and there is complete boycott of foreign cloth.' If you find this hard to work upon, write out one you like and vow not to marry until that is attained and put up a copy in your room where everyone can see it. Send one to Kakasaheb and one to me.

If you can do neither try this thought: 'I do have a desire to marry and it cannot be suppressed. But I will not marry a girl of my caste as I would not marry my own sister. I will insist on breaking the barriers of caste. The girl must know Sanskrit, Marathi, Hindi and Gujarati; she should not hanker after money; if her parents are alive we must have their consent. She must have absolute love of khadi; she must appreciate and have faith in my other ideals and love the untouchables, be strong of body and prepared to live in some remote village and be willing to honour the well-known discipline of *brahmacharya* in marriage.' If you cannot do even this, know that you will not be able to observe *brahmacharya* and therefore marry at the first opportunity. If you resolve to observe the above discipline, write down the vow and proceed as before.

But then what I have suggested to you is only the way of worshipping a Deity conceived with form and attributes. Observance of *brahmacharya* for the sake of attaining inviolate *brahmacharya* is like worshipping One without attributes. It is difficult for all of us.

I have pointed out to you the path that I myself took. I have just been tasting a droplet of the subtle bliss of *brahmacharya* from out of its physical advantages. My intellect has none the less realized its bliss but you should know all the same that I have not actually experienced it.

If anyone can truly describe what that bliss is, Vinoba, Surendranath and others, who, I believe, observe inviolate *brahmacharya*, may perhaps be able to. I could give you only a partial account of the [bliss of] *brahmacharya* which knows what sense-

[1] A celestial nymph

pleasures and marriage mean. Only the perfect can give a perfect account.

It is possible that you will not be satisfied by this too. If you would not find here the answer to your question you will now understand why it is so. Neither Kakasaheb nor I, in fact no one who has known married life, is competent to answer your question from personal experience. For these same reasons we, being embodied, are able to describe only partially the joy of *moksha*. Since there is no speech without a body, *moksha* is and will ever remain indescribable. Likewise, only an inviolate *brahmachari* can describe the path of pure *brahmacharya* or we should plod on in life, keeping in view the descriptions given by the Shastras.

[From Gujarati]

From the manuscript of Mahadev Desai's Diary. Courtesy: Narayan Desai

128. LETTER TO NAJUKLAL N. CHOKSI

BANGALORE,
Monday, July 11, 1927

BHAISHRI NAJUKLAL,

I got your postcard. God provides man with a means to learn from his fall. You two have it through the birth of a son, but Moti, if she wills, can so use it as to fulfil the true end of her life. You are, moreover, a teacher by vocation. I shall wait and see how you bring up the child born to you. Let Moti read this.

Blessings from
BAPU

[PS.]

Preserve this postcard.

From a photostat of the Gujarati: S.N. 12141

129. *LETTER TO RAIHANA TYABJI*

KUMARA PARK, BANGALORE,
July 12, 1927

MY DEAR RAIHANA,

In the abstract, there can be no doubt that you have a right to wear whatever you like and to see or be seen by any friends you like. But when it comes to reducing an abstract right to concrete practice, innumerable things present themselves for consideration. And my advice is that in everything you do, you should possess confidence enough to bear down all opposition and to be able to convince everybody around you of the justice of your action. Do you reason with mother with the same frankness that you show in your letters to me? But let me give a concrete suggestion. Do you permit me to discuss your letter with both father and mother? Can I send them your last letter? I destroy all your letters after replying. The last one I am preserving till I receive your answer. From what I know of them and the manner in which they have brought up their children, it seems to me that they are most considerate, liberal-minded parents and will not interfere with the independence of their grown-up children. Your recent letters have therefore been a surprise to me. I therefore say nothing further just now and await your reply.

Meanwhile I ask you not to worry about things over which you may have no control. If you cannot have your way about your dress or choice of friends or dealings with them, know that there are many in the same condition in which you are, and that there is no person on this earth who has really got the liberty to do what he or she likes. Some restraint on liberty is demoralizing and some is uplifting. No restraint is demoralizing which one submits to, not out of fear, selfishness or the like, but out of consideration for, or affection for others. I cannot conceive your yielding to fear under any circumstance whatsoever.

I heard some very fine music yesterday. It went on for full one hour whilst I was spinning. I thought of your voice the whole of that time, and fine as both were yesterday, I observed that yours was in no way inferior, and to me, it even appeared to be superior. But that may be due to my partiality for you. Anyway you have a voice that would certainly sing away others' cares. Invoke it for dispelling your own.

With love,

BAPU

MISS RAIHANA TYABJI
SOUTHWOOD
MUSSOORIE
U.P.

From a photostat: S.N. 9604

130. LETTER TO J. W. PETAVEL

KUMARA PARK, BANGALORE,
July 12, 1927

DEAR FRIEND,

I have carefully gone through the nine sides of your bank-note-size paper and I am not only none the wiser for it, but it has made confusion worse confounded. I do not yet know what Belgium and Switzerland are doing. I never told you[1] that the two colonies that I established in South Africa have failed. On the contrary, they succeeded as far as they went. I simply gave you the information in order to tell you that because those colonies succeeded to an extent, I could not draw the large deductions that you did from your untried plan.

For the Ashram, you have told me nothing new. And when you tell me that I must present something that will give in an hour what I promise in eight hours, we come to a standstill. I know no scheme that will give 300 millions of people two annas per hour. I have worked out your scheme to the best of my ability and it has failed me. Nor am I in a position to agree with you that it is possible to make something out of the modern craze for accumulation of wealth and destroying time and distance. Where, therefore, you see meeting-ground, I see absolutely none. Both your non-co-operation scheme and co-operation scheme appear to me to be unworkable and unintelligible. I cannot therefore give you room in the pages of *Young India*.

The certificates that you have secured from Sir Ashutosh and others make no impression upon me because I have always fought shy of certificates so much so that I destroyed what I used to hold myself. And as I feel that I have got the ability of testing schemes on their own merits, certificates are to me sometimes a hindrance and every time a superfluity.

[1] *Vide* "Letter to J. W. Petavel", 23-6-1927.

Before you can draw me to your scheme, two things are necessary. Show me something actually at work, and show me that it is capable of indefinite multiplication and yet producing the same results as I am doing for mine. I am showing my scheme at work in 1,500 villages and I can only wish that it was multiplied so as to reach 700 thousand and still the result will be constant. I want you to bear in mind that in corresponding with me you are corresponding with a practical man who has a horror of chimeras and who will not be dazzled by specious-looking things written or printed on paper.

Yours sincerely,

From a photostat: S.N. 14181

131. LETTER TO ASHRAM WOMEN

Silence Day, Ashadh Sud 13 [*July 12, 1927*][1]

SISTERS,

Received your letter.

Manibehn will tell you how many women took part in the Exhibition, and what they did. Here it is enough to say that one of them was expert in keeping accounts while some others were equally expert in selling khaddar. They have received silver and gold medals. A blind woman spun exceedingly well at the Exhibition. She was the centre of attraction for all. One of the women was first in spinning fine, strong yarn and won a gold medal. Manibehn upheld the good name of the Ashram. Her carding drew the attention of all.

There was a Hindi Sammelan here. Here also one of the women was first. Some of the women here are making very good efforts to learn Hindi.

All this awakening is proceeding beautifully in this State. I have already written to you how some of the women here sing sweet *bhajans* at evening prayers too. On Saturday one of them played the vina for me. She herself composes the *bhajans*. They say she is very skilful in playing the vina.

Blessings from
BAPU

From a photostat of the Gujarati: G.N. 3657

[1] The year is inferred from the reference to the Khadi Exhibition and the Hindi Sammelan held at Bangalore.

132. *SPEECH TO MYSORE STUDENTS, BANGALORE*

[*July 12, 1927*][1]

FRIENDS,

I thank God for being able to speak to you though in a low tone and for enabling me to speak to you in Hindi. You know perhaps that I speak with my friends in Hindi and in my own mother tongue Gujarati. I know however that in your schools and colleges and when you meet your friends and students you talk only in English. You have cultivated it as a habit and to me it appears it is a bad habit. I do not object to your learning English for the sake of acquiring knowledge or for the sake of earning your livelihood but I object to your giving so much importance to English and giving a low place to your national language, Hindi. I do not think it is right on your part to use in your conversation with your friends and relatives any other language than your national language or your mother tongue. Have love for your own language.

I have to make one request to my student friends. In the measure in which you learn English learn the national language and leave the glamour of the foreign tongue. I am grateful to you for this address presented to me in Hindi printed in Devanagari script. In order to serve our *Daridranarayana* in our land you have given me a purse and I am grateful to you all. You have all, in your love, collected so much for me but it is no wonder. Wherever I go I meet such sincere love and service from you students of India. That is your dharma, that is your duty. I ask why would you not help this fund? How much are you spending for your education and how many cities are there in the whole of Hindustan and how much money is being thrown away there? But do you know where those who live in cities get their money from? It is from the villages where there is only sorrow and where *Daridranarayana* lives. The money that you all spend for your education is all coming to you from your villages and you are being educated out of this sorrowful source. Twenty-five crores of rupees are going for the evils of the country as drink and can you who live in the cities, can you not give two pies for your poor

[1] From *Young India*, 21-7-1927 and *The Bombay Chronicle*, 13-7-1927

brothers and sisters in those villages? Let these two pies be your *prayaschitta*[1]. Today, I see you all in foreign clothes and caps. Our sisters there are all in foreign cloth. Do not say they are made in Mysore, do not forget that the yarn is made outside your own country. Let me say this to you today. Go to the khadi depots and buy the caps for four annas or five annas and discard these costly caps and buy khadi and wear. That would be a service truly rendered.

Today we have lost the real significance of the term *vidyarthi*[2]. In ancient days when all knew its meaning it stood for *brahmacharis* and *brahmacharinis* and it stood for *Brahmajnanam*[3]. It stood for *mukti*[4], our own *mukti*, the *mukti* or liberty for the country, for the liberty of the individual. Today I ask you how many of you are true *brahmacharis* and *brahmacharinis*? Do you know anything about the controlling of the senses and training of the mind in the true path of *bhakti* and service? Do you know what our forefathers were doing? If you really know the duties of true *brahmacharis*, if you are really *vidyarthis* in the real sense of the term, then there would not be the suffering in our land that we now see. Our ancient rishis[5], pious maulvis[6] and Christians have left us rich and precious treasures, to enjoy them and to become useful to others, whereby we must think of God every moment of our living life. We must leave off our coarse desires if we desire true *mukti*. I do not say that in youth you must all leave your amusements and pleasures and practise yoga, but I want that you recognize your duties, and do them as becomes real students and pupils of *Brahmajnanam*. The youths of today were not as the *brahmacharis* of old in health, they visit theatres, drink and eat wrong things and take pride in giving enjoyment to the senses. If your bodies are not strong your minds would also be affected and when your minds are affected you cannot have a knowledge of God and your duty. You cannot have the willpower to control yourself, you lose your vigour and energy and you become weak and slow. I have heard that some students take coffee as many as seven or eight times a day. I want my

[1] Expiation or atonement
[2] Student
[3] Knowledge of the Ultimate
[4] Freedom from phenomenal existence
[5] Sages
[6] Muslim scholars

young friends to remember I was also a student once. I ask them to answer me why they should not drink pure water or milk when they are thirsty and eat food when they are hungry? Why should they go on poisoning their bodies with all sorts of things ? I hope you will see the true significance of what I say to you today. Think of the ideal of *brahmacharya,* ponder over it in your wisdom and act upon it with conviction. In the *Bhagavad Gita* emphasis is laid on sacrifice; in the Koran and in the Bible it is the same; he who does not make any sacrifice is not really a man. Think of this term sacrifice and examine it in the present state of our country. I pray to God that He will give you strength and wisdom to understand the word sacrifice and make sacrifice yourselves. I pray to God that He may give you the wisdom to think of the poor of the country in the villages far away from the cities and towns that you are building in their blood and the sacrifice of their lives, on their miseries and the miseries of their families and children. Think of God for half an hour every day, spinning the charkha and weaving your cloth. Think of all these when you are thinking of God every day for half an hour. May He give you the wisdom to know how you can save the poor of your land. This is all I have to say to you today.

The Hindu, 13-7-1927

133. SPEECH AT INDIAN INSTITUTE OF SCIENCE, BANGALORE

[*July 12, 1927*][1]

I was wondering where do I come in? There is no place here for a rustic like me who has to stand speechless in awe and wonderment. I am not in a mood to say much. All I can say is that all these huge laboratories and electrical apparatus you see here are due to the labour—unwilling and forced—of millions. For Tata's thirty lakhs did not come from outside, nor does the Mysore contribution come from anywhere else but this *begar*[2] world. If we were to meet the villagers and to explain to them how we are utilizing their money on buildings and plants which will never benefit them, but might perhaps benefit their posterity, they will not understand it. They will turn a cold shoulder. But

[1] From *The Hindu,* 13-7-1927
[2] Forced labour

we never take them into our confidence, we take it as a matter of right, and forget that the rule of "no taxation without representation" applies to them too. If you will really apply it to them, and realize your responsibility to render them an account, you will see that there is another side to all these appointments. You will then find not a little but a big corner in your hearts for them, and if you will keep it in a good, nice condition, you will utilize your knowledge for the benefit of the millions on whose labour your education depends. I shall utilize the purse you have given me for *Daridranarayana.* The real *Daridranarayana* even I have not seen, but know only through my imagination. Even the spinners who will get this money are not the real *Daridranarayana* who live in remote corners of distant villages which have yet to be explored. I was told by your professor that the properties of some of the chemicals will take years of experiments to explore. But who will try to explore these villages? Just as some of the experiments in your laboratories go on for all the twenty-four hours, let the big corner in your heart remain perpetually warm for the benefit of the poor millions.

I expect far more from you than from the ordinary man in the street. Don't be satisfied with having given the little you have done, and say, 'We have done what we could, let us now play tennis and billiards.' I tell you, in the billiard room and on the tennis-court think of the big debt that is being piled against you from day to day. But beggars cannot be choosers. I thank you for what you have given me. Think of the prayer I have made and translate it into action. Don't be afraid of wearing the cloth the poor women make for you, don't be afraid of your employers showing you the door if you wear khadi. I would like you to be men, and stand up before the world firm in your convictions. Let your zeal for the dumb millions be not stifled in the search for wealth. I tell you, you can devise a far greater wireless instrument, which does not require external research, but internal—and all research will be useless if it is not allied to internal research—which can link your hearts with those of the millions. Unless all the discoveries that you make have the welfare of the poor as the end in view, all your workshops will be really no better than Satan's workshops, as Rajagopalachari said in a joke. Well I have given you enough food for thought, if you are in a reflective mood, as all research students ought to be.

In concluding, he [said that] they must keep the lamp of their love for the motherland and her children always bright, trim, and steady. And as they did that, so they deserved the knowledge and the advantage they were deriving from the Institute.[1]

Young India, 21-7-1927

134. MESSAGE TO "THE SEARCHLIGHT"[2]

July 13, 1927

Those who want a message from me must not be surprised to receive the same message again and again; for, I have nothing new. Let the editor, the proprietor and the staff of *The Searchlight* as also the readers do their quota of work for the millions, that is, let them wear nothing but khadi; let them exclude all foreign cloth from their use; let them give as much as they can towards khadi work; and let them spin at least for half an hour good, even and weavable yarn and make a present of it to the All-India Spinners' Association in the name of and on behalf of *Daridranarayana*. To know whether this message has at least been read by those concerned, I suggest their sending me contribution and telling me whether they have accepted and are acting in accordance with the message. If they do not appreciate the message, let them send me a postcard stating their objections and reasons.

M. K. GANDHI

From a photostat: S.N. 14182

135. LETTER TO MIRABEHN

July 13, 1927

CHI. MIRA,

Just as I am about to go to a place, I received your letter and wire. So you are off on Saturday. I note what you say about Gangu. God be with you.

Love,

BAPU

From the original: C.W. 5249. Courtesy: Mirabehn

[1] This paragraph is from *The Hindu*, 13-7-1927.

[2] For its anniversary number of July 15

136. LETTER TO J. Z. HODGE

As at the Ashram, Sabarmati,
July 13, 1927

DEAR MR. HODGE,

It was a delight to receive your letter[1] from Edinburgh and to find that my little friends had now become big friends and were getting on quite nicely.

When I receive the papers you refer to from Sir Daniel Hamilton, I will certainly study them with care and let him know my conclusions.

I am making fair progress. Please remember me to Mrs. Hodge.

Yours sincerely,

J. Z. Hodge, Esq.
C/o Nisbes
31, Warrender Park Terrace
Edinburgh

From a photostat: S.N. 12509

137. LETTER TO SHAPURJI SAKLATVALA

Kumara Park, Bangalore,
July 13, 1927

MY DEAR FRIEND,

I have your letter of the 16th June last through Bharucha. I understand and appreciate the viewpoint elaborated in your letter, and it would give me much pleasure if I can do anything whatsoever to assist you in coming to a settlement with the Tatas.[2] But I know my limitations and I would like you to recognize them.

[1] Dated June 1, 1927. Introducing Sir Daniel Hamilton, the addressee had requested Gandhiji to help him in spreading the co-operative movement in India.

[2] The reference is to "Saklatvala's forced resignation of his post in the Tata firm in London".

All I can do is to work through Panditji which I am doing.

Yours sincerely,

SHAPURJI SAKLATVALA, ESQ., M.P.
HOUSE OF COMMONS
LONDON S.W. 1

From a photostat: S.N. 12532

138. LETTER TO D. C. BOSE

KUMARA PARK, BANGALORE,
July 13, 1927

DEAR FRIEND,

I am ashamed that your letter of 30th June last year has remained undealt with by me throughout all this time. You however had acknowledgments from time to time. I am not disposed to blame my assistants in connection with the delay. Some of it was unavoidable and some could have been avoided but for the letter having been mislaid. I however understand that my reply will not yet be too late.

I should be inclined to agree with the advice received by you from an English friend and quoted at the end of your letter. If there was really no better way, there was certainly nothing wrong in your having written to me. For, part of my public work consists in sharing, where I cannot solve, difficulties such as you have mentioned. I can appreciate all you say about the good qualities of Englishmen and even add to what you have said in your letter. But in spite of the ample food I have received during the past seven years for reflection[1], my opinion of the system not only remains unaltered [but] has received further confirmation. And the Excise Department is among the blackest spots in the system. I could not therefore be reconciled to your being in it if I can in any way help you to be out of it. Your letter attracts me to you. I would like to have you in some of the departments of national service which I am more or less controlling. And if you can get some privilege leave, I would like you to overtake me wherever I may be so that I can see you face to face and discuss all the

[1] The addressee had written: "The failure of your movement with subsequent Hindu-Muslim tension . . . has no doubt given you sufficient food for reflection."

questions you have raised in your letter. I am in Mysore up to the 15th of August and my headquarters will be Bangalore till that time. I expect to be away from time to time from Bangalore, but within the Mysore State and therefore not more than a few hours' journey from Bangalore where the keeper of the house I am staying will direct you.

Meanwhile, I can answer one of your questions straightaway. If you have the real call from within you will be not only right but it will be your duty to resist all the pressure that can be brought to bear upon you for marriage. If you can control your carnal appetites, I have no doubt that the obligations which you feel you have towards the members of your family impose the restraint upon you.

If you intend to come and see me, please bear in mind that whilst it will be possible, all other conditions being satisfied, to find enough for the support of your family, you will have to be free to be posted wherever duty calls you and even to move about from place to place, and if you do not know Hindi, you will be expected to learn it.

Yours sincerely,

D. C. BOSE, ESQ.
55, CORNWALLIS STREET
CALCUTTA

From a photostat: S.N. 12601

139. LETTER TO S. RAMANATHAN

KUMARA PARK, BANGALORE,
July 13, 1927

MY DEAR RAMANATHAN,

Mr. Mahadeva Iyer of Shermadevi Gurukul is here. I never knew that you have anything to do with this Gurukul. But Mr. Mahadeva Iyer tells me that you are vitally interested in it. When V. V. S. Iyer was alive he wrote to me and spoke to me about the inter-dining controversy that was then going on. Mahadeva Iyer has briefly described to me the happenings after Iyer's death. Will you please let me know what connection you have with this Gurukul and what is now wanted by the party which Mahadeva Iyer describes as hostile to him or to the Gurukul?

I hope you have got over your fever.

Yours sincerely,

SJT. S. RAMANATHAN
ERODE

From a microfilm: S.N. 12930

140. LETTER TO MOTILAL NEHRU

KUMARA PARK, BANGALORE,
July 13, 1927

DEAR MOTILALJI,

Here is a characteristic letter from "Comrade" Saklatvala. The facsimile of the stamped letter he sends seems to make out a very strong moral claim for him. I do not need to say anything more; for, I know that whatever language he uses you will press his claim for all its worth.

I have another letter from Jawaharlal. There is nothing new in it.

Yours sincerely,

PANDIT MOTILAL NEHRU
'ANAND BHAWAN'
ALLAHABAD

From a photostat: S.N. 14183

141. A LETTER

Ashadh Shukla 14 [July 13, 1927][1]

Tulsidas has left nothing unsaid about the greatness of His name. The *Dwadasha mantra*,[2] the *Ashtakshara*[3], etc., bring peace to the victim of infatuation, and one should rely upon whatever *mantra* brings one peace. But for one who has never experienced peace and is in quest of it, Ramanama will certainly prove a *parasmani*[4]. God has been given a thousand names which only means that he can be called by any name and that his qualities are infi-

[1] The source places this along with the other letters belonging to 1927.

[2] *Om namo Bhagavate Vasudevaya*

[3] *Om namo Narayanaya*

[4] Philosopher's stone

nite. That is why God is also beyond nomenclature and free from attributes. But for us mortals the support of His name is absolutely essential to fall back upon and in this age even the ignorant and the illiterate can have recourse to an *Ekakshara mantra*[1] in the form of Ramanama. In fact, uttering Ramanama covers the *Ekakshara* and there is no difference between 'Om' and 'Rama'. But the value of reciting His name cannot be established by reasoning, it can only be experienced if one does it with faith.

MOHANDAS GANDHI

From a photostat of the Hindi: S.N. 12797

142. SPEECH AT MAHILA SAMAJ, BANGALORE[2]

July 13, 1927

Daridranarayana is insatiable and there is room enough in his belly for all the money and the ornaments you can give. The ornaments are your *streedhan* and you have a right to dispose it of as you like. Your real ornaments are your virtues, and you will be doing real service to the poorest of the land by disposing of part of your jewellery.

Young India, 21-7-1927

143. INTERVIEW TO MR. AND MRS. BJERRUM[3]

[Before *July 14, 1927*]

Among the new missionary friends is a Danish couple Mr. and Mrs. Bjerrum . . . Gandhiji was at his wheel when the friends came.

MR. BJERRUM: This is a new wheel different from the ones we saw at the Exhibition.

GANDHIJI: Yes, it is a travelling charkha. When you fold it, it looks like a medicine chest, and a medicine chest it is for our poor people.

After giving their pleasant impressions of the Exhibition, Mr. Bjerrum began to talk of the students of his college. "The dress of most of our students is Europeanized," he informed Gandhiji not without some sorrow.

[1] *Om*

[2] & [3] From Mahadev Desai's "Weekly Letter"

GANDHIJI: It is a great pity that Christianity should be mixed up with foreign dress and foreign ways of eating and drinking.

MRS. BJERRUM: It is indeed. But don't you think a change has already begun?

GANDHIJI: Well, a change in thought is certainly coming over, but not a corresponding change in conduct.

And with this he narrated some of his experiences with the friends of the Y.M.C.A. of Calcutta.

MR. BJERRUM: May we know what form in your opinion missionary work should take if the missionaries are to stay in India?

[GANDHIJI]: Yes. They have to alter their attitude. Today they tell people that there is no salvation for them except through the Bible and through Christianity. It is customary to decry other religions and to offer their own as the only one that can bring deliverance. That attitude should be radically changed. Let them appear before the people as they are, and try to rejoice in seeing Hindus become better Hindus and Mussalmans better Mussalmans. Let them start work at the bottom, let them enter into what is best in their life and offer nothing inconsistent with it. That will make their work far more efficacious, and what they will say and offer to the people will be appreciated without suspicion and hostility. In a word let them go to the people not as patrons, but as one of them, not to oblige them but to serve them and to work among them.

MR. BJERRUM: Thank you. We are going to Denmark next year and would like to take some message from you.

[GANDHIJI:] The external is always an expression of the internal, and if the people of Denmark would serve us, let them teach us their life-giving industry of co-operative dairy and cattle-breeding.

Young India, 14-7-1927

144. REFORM OF PINJRAPOLE

It has been my privilege during my convalescence at Bangalore to pay regular visits to the Imperial Animal Husbandry and Dairy Institute, and to take there, what may be called, regular lessons. Mr. William Smith, who is the Imperial Dairy Expert and Head of this Institute, and his assistants have most carefully shown me the working of the Institute and the different departments into which it is divided. I trust I shall make use of the knowledge thus gained in conducting the dairying experiment at the Satyagraha Ashram on behalf of the All-India Cow-protection Association. As a result of several discussions with Mr. Smith I asked him kindly to prepare for me notes on the working of pinjrapoles and on methods of cattle-improvement in our villages, which he very kindly and promptly undertook to do. I am already in possession of two valuable notes. I give below his note on pinjrapoles.

> Some of the existing pinjrapoles with more or less permanent and assured incomes are fairly well managed, and do provide a comfortable refuge for a certain number of cattle which have ceased to be economically useful in their old age. In many of these institutions it is however not an uncommon thing, when trade is bad and subscriptions are slow in coming in, to find cattle being kept in these places in a state of starvation which must mean great suffering to the animals and which eventually kills them. In cases like this instead of being a refuge for the animals the goshala becomes a cow-killing institution, the method of killing being a cruel death by starvation. In at least six cases have I seen the cattle in goshalas being starved to death. The first thing then to be done with the existing pinjrapoles is to see that they do not under any circumstances whatever admit to their shelters a larger number of animals than they can feed properly, house comfortably and take care of until they die a really natural death.
>
> All the larger pinjrapoles with an assured income, and which can command capital, should in my opinion be divided into three departments, the whole being managed by a trained dairy farm manager.
>
> 1. The refuge department where old and economically useless cattle excluding buffaloes should be comfortably fed and cared for until they die naturally.
>
> 2. A dairy department where all cows sent to the pinjrapole to escape slaughter and capable of breeding and all other cows capable of bearing calves and yielding milk should be fed, housed and milked as a

commercial dairy herd with careful milk-recording, and the milk sold to the best advantage. The very best class of stud bulls should be used in this herd and all calves carefully reared, males not good enough for issue as stud bulls to be castrated and those considered good enough for breeding either transferred to the stud department or issued to villages as breeding bulls. All female stock to be reared as milkers and breeders. When the home-bred progeny of this department gets too numerous for the pinjrapole to deal with, they could be sold to reputable Hindu owners on the distinct understanding that they are to be returned to the refuge department of the pinjrapole when too old to work or milk.

3. A stud department where the very best of the right class of breeding bulls should be kept as stud for the use of the breeders in the district. The service of these animals could be given free for all cows passed by the expert manager as suitable for breeding with the pinjrapoles stud animals and careful records of all servings kept. This department might also undertake the castration of all unsuitable animals in the district free of charge.

It is not necessary to take any specific steps to improve the quality of buffaloes. India cannot afford to keep any class of bovine which does not possess dual purpose qualities, i.e., milk in the case of the female and draught in the case of the male. Generally speaking the male buffalo is unsuitable for field or cart work, and consequently unless the males, except those required for stud purposes, are slaughtered at birth, they remain an incubus in the country. The majority of the people in India do not approve of the killing of any kind of animals, and in any case it is not an economic proposition to rear and kill these animals for beef, as the value of this class of meat in India is far below cost of production.

The buffalo exists and increases in India owing to the poor milking quality of the cows, and the aim of all cattle breeding propaganda ought to be to so increase the milk-yielding capacity of all classes of cows, that they will not only provide sufficient milk to rear a strong, healthy calf, but in addition to this give as much milk as pay the cost of their feed. If and when we attain to this standard there will be no need for the buffalo which will be automatically eliminated by economic forces. The existing conditions prevailing in many parts of India today, where a cultivator keeps two or three cows to rear bullocks from and one or two buffaloes to provide milk and ghee for his household, cannot continue. It is too costly and there is no reason whatever why the cows now kept for breeding should not in the future rear their calves and provide in addition all the milk and ghee required by the household. Our cattle have little or no beef value and we cannot afford to keep cows for draught cattle production and buffaloes for milk. The cow alone can and must do both duties. For these reasons the pinjrapole societies should confine themselves to caring for and improving the cow. Agriculture in India depends upon the efficiency of the cow as a bullock-producer not the buffalo; and the health of the people can be maintained and improved by the milk of the cow. In a sense the buffalo is an interloper introduced because of the poor milking qualities of the cow.

If all pinjrapoles employed really qualified men capable of managing the pinjrapoles on the foregoing lines, they could undoubtedly do a great work for India.

The reader will observe from the foregoing that Mr. Smith has written with a knowledge of the existing pinjrapoles. He told me that he had visited many of them. In his opinion the pinjrapoles should serve the purpose not merely of being a home for aged and otherwise disabled cattle, but also for protecting the cow, and educating the people in the art of such protection. To that end they must have a properly equipped model dairy and a stud department. I add to these conditions a tannery department. I discussed with Mr. Smith the question of adding tanneries. The idea appeared attractive to him, but being a specialist he naturally did not want to travel beyond his province. Mr. Smith's cautious remarks about the buffalo are worthy of attention. He has not, and he cannot be expected to have, the same feeling about animal slaughter, but he recognizes that in India any proposition suggesting slaughter of useless animals would be just as much out of place as a proposition for the destruction of aged and disabled parents would be anywhere. He has, therefore, endeavoured to enter into the Hindu feeling as much as possible, and suggested means of protection and conservation of cattle consistently with Indian traditions. I hope that managers of pinjrapoles will study the suggestions made in Mr. Smith's important note and make the necessary alterations in their management, which, I am certain, can be made with very little extra cost in the beginning, and with much profit in the end. I must deal in a future issue with the other material[1] Mr. Smith has kindly placed at my disposal.

Young India, 14-7-1927

[1] *Vide* "Village Cattle Improvement", 4-8-1927.

145. AN ALL-INDIA SCRIPT

A Gujarati correspondent wrote some time ago to *Navajivan* a letter advising that I should print *Navajivan* in Devanagari script, so as to give a practical demonstration of my belief in the necessity of there being one script for all India. Although it is my firm conviction that there should be one script for all the Indian languages, and that that script can only be Devanagari, I could not follow the correspondent's advice for the reasons stated in my note[1] in *Navajivan*, and which I need not reiterate here. But there is no doubt that we ought to seize the opportunity that the great national awakening gives us, of not merely popularizing the idea but of doing something concrete in that direction. The Hindu-Muslim madness no doubt stands in the way of a thorough reform. But before the acceptance of Devanagari script becomes a universal fact in India, Hindu India has got to be converted to the idea of one script for all the languages derived from Sanskrit and the Dravidian stock. At the present moment we have Bengali script in Bengal, Gurmukhi in the Punjab, Sindhi in Sind, Oriya in Utkal, Gujarati in Gujarat, Telugu in Andhradesha, Tamil in Tamilnad, Malayalam in Kerala, Kanarese in Karnatak, not to speak of Kaithi in Bihar and Modi in the Deccan. If all these scripts could be replaced by Devanagari for all practical and national purposes, it would mean a tremendous step forward. It will help to solidify Hindu India and bring the different provinces in closer touch. Anyone who has any knowledge of the different Indian languages and scripts knows to his cost what time it takes to master a new script. For the love of his country, no doubt, nothing is difficult, and time spent in mastering the different scripts, some of which are very beautiful, is in no way idly spent. But this spirit of abandon is not to be expected of millions. National leaders have to make things easy for them. Therefore, we must have an easily adaptable universal script for all India, and there is nothing so adaptable and readymade as Devanagari script. There is, or there used to be, an all-India organization for this very purpose. I do not know what its activities are at present. But if the work has to be done, either the original association should be strengthened, or a new one formed for this

[1] *Vide* "*Navajivan* in Devanagari Script", 26-6-1927.

purpose. The movement should in no way be confused with the spread of Hindi or Hindustani as the lingua franca. The latter work is going on very slowly, but steadily. Use of one script will facilitate the spread of one language. But the functions of the two run parallel only up to a point. Hindi or Hindustani is not designed to replace the provincial languages, but is intended to supplement them, and to be used for inter-provincial contact. And till the Hindu-Muslim tension lasts it takes the form either of Urdu written in the Persian script, and containing a preponderance of Persian or Arabic words, or Hindi written in Devanagari, and containing a preponderance of Sanskrit words. When the hearts of the two meet, the two forms of the same language will be fused together, and we shall have a resultant of the two, containing as many Sanskrit, Persian, Arabic or other words as may be necessary for its full growth and full expression.

But one script is undoubtedly designed to displace all the different scripts so as to render it easy for people belonging to different provinces to learn provincial languages. The best way of achieving the purpose is first to make the learning of Devanagari script compulsory at least for Hindus in all the schools, as it is in Gujarat, and secondly to print the important literature in different Indian languages in Devanagari script. Such effort has already been made to a certain extent. I have seen *Gitanjali* printed in Devanagari script. But the effort requires to be made on a large scale, and there should be propaganda carried on for the spread of such books. Though I know that it is out of fashion just now to suggest anything along constructive lines that may bring Hindus and Mussalmans together, I cannot help repeating what I have said in these columns and elsewhere, that Hindus must learn Urdu if they will come nearer their Mussalman brethren, and Mussalmans must learn Hindi if they will come nearer their Hindu brethren. Those who have faith in real unity between Hindus and Mussalmans need not be disconcerted by the present terrible expression of mutual hatred. Their faith, if it is of any value, must make them actively but unobtrusively perform, whenever possible, all acts of mutual toleration, affection and courtesy, and learning of one another's language is the least that one can do in that direction. Is it not better for Hindus to learn through the many ably-written Urdu books by devout Mussalmans what Mussalmans think of the Koran and the Prophet, and for Mussalmans to learn through equally well-written Hindi books by devout Hindus what Hindus think of the *Gita* and Krishna than that the respective parties should learn all the bad things that might have been said about their respective religious books and their inspirers through their ignorant or fanatical detractors?

Young India, 14-7-1927

146. LIMITATIONS OF SATYAGRAHA

An innocent paragraph, occurring in a letter[1] in reply to one covering other subjects, has led to what I venture to call a thoughtless misrepresentation of satyagraha and its author. The paragraph is part of a private letter written in Gujarati to Mr. Bharucha. It is no thesis on satyagraha, and like every letter it contains many things understood between the writer of the original letter and that of the reply. It was not meant for publication. But when Mr. Bharucha telegraphed asking for permission to publish the paragraph, I had no hesitation in wiring permission. It appears from the newspaper report before me that the speakers at the Nagpur meeting suggested that I should have explained at the time the Nagpur Satyagraha was launched out what I have explained in my letter to Mr. Bharucha. I must dissent from the view. Had Mr. Awari not ascribed to me endorsement of his campaign, I should not even have written the article I did in repudiation. Where I cannot help, it is my rule not to hinder by any unnecessary or uncalled for interference on my part. Instead, therefore, of giving an exhaustive opinion on what I then knew of Nagpur Satyagraha, I confined myself to a repudiation and an opinion on the general atmosphere of violence prevalent in the country. And I cannot help saying that it was an unlawful use to make of my private letter for suspending Nagpur Satyagraha, if those who were permitted to see the letter did not accept the reasoning contained in it. Moreover, when they decided to make public use of the letter, they owed it to me to have made clear to them the points which they could not understand, or which appeared to them to be inconsistent with my previous writings. They owed it to the enthusiastic young men in Nagpur neither to damp their zeal nor to disconcert them by hurling in their midst an opinion which the receivers did not understand and did not accept. For myself I do not consider it to be any part of my duty to express an opinion upon the many insane things that are going on in this country, for I am humble enough to recognize that what may appear to me to be insane need not appear so to

[1] *Vide* "Letter to B. F. Bharucha", before 2-7-1927.

those who are doing those acts, and may even be in reality an epitome of wisdom. Though, therefore, things are being done in the name of satyagraha in several places, I have not felt called upon to say one word about them. And I do suggest to the young men in Nagpur and to all concerned that they are not in any way bound to receive the permission of the Congress to offer satyagraha or any other resistance to any unjust act so long as they do not use the Congress name. And if they are really of opinion that the Nagpur Satyagraha was justified, that it was really satyagraha, it would amount to a desertion on the part of their commander and other comrades in jail not to immediately re-embark upon their campaign, unless they think with me that what they thought was satyagraha was not so in fact.

Having cleared the ground so far, let me now try to remove the confusion that the well-meaning friends who have undertaken to criticize the letter in question have created about satyagraha. I do maintain that the Arms Act could not be broken in terms of satyagraha in the way it was in Nagpur. Let it be remembered that the bone of contention between the "Republican Army" of Nagpur and the Government was not the Arms Act but the unjust and lawless detention of many patriotic young Bengalis. It was in every way wrong, therefore, to select the Arms Act for civil disobedience. Several speakers have read into my letter a meaning which I hold it does not bear and was never intended to bear. As long ago as 1917 or 1918, I said that amongst the many black deeds of the Government, disarmament was the blackest. And out-and-out believer in non-violence though I am, I hold that it is the right of any Indian who wishes to bear arms to do so under lawful permission. I do submit that an Arms Act is now and will ever be a necessity of good government. I do not believe in the inherent right of every citizen to possess as many arms as he chooses without a licence. On the contrary, I hold it to be absolutely necessary for good government that the State should have the authority to prohibit the holding of arms except under prescribed conditions. I can also conceive the possibility of satyagraha being offered against an unjust Arms Act or its unjust administration, as I can justify satyagraha against an unjust Act for preventing thefts or other crimes. But I do maintain that just as satyagraha cannot be offered against an unjust Crimes Act by committing the specific crimes, so can satyagraha not be offered against an unjust Arms Act by carrying arms.

Let us also appreciate the distinction between satyagraha and civil disobedience. All civil disobedience is a part or branch of satyagraha, but all satyagraha is not civil disobedience. And seeing that the Nagpur friends have suspended what they were pleased to call satyagraha or civil disobedience, let me suggest for their information and that of others how satyagraha can be legitimately offered with reference to the Bengal detenus. If they will not be angry with me or laugh at me, let me commence by saying that they can offer satyagraha by developing the power of the people through khadi, and through khadi achieving boycott of foreign cloth. They can offer satyagraha by becoming precursors of Hindu-Muslim unity, by allowing their heads to be broken whenever there is a quarrel between the two, and whilst there is no active quarrel in their parts by performing silent acts of service to those of the opposite faith to theirs. If such constructive methods are too flat for them, and if they will be satisfied by nothing less than civil disobedience in spite of the violence of thought, word and deed raging round us, I suggest the following prescription of individual civil disobedience, which even one man can offer, not indeed in the hope of securing immediate release of detenus, but certainly in the hope of the individual sacrifice ultimately eventuating in such release. Let a batch, or only one person, say from Nagpur, march on foot to the Government House in Calcutta, and if a march is irksome or impossible then let him, her, or them beg enough money for train fare from friends, and having reached Calcutta let only one satyagrahi march to the Government House and walk on to the point where he or she is stopped. There let him or her stop and demand the release of detenus or his or her own arrest. To preserve intact the civil nature of this disobedience the satyagrahi must be wholly unarmed, and in spite of insults, kicks or worse must meekly stand the ground, and be arrested without the slightest opposition. He may carry his own food in his pocket, a bottleful of water, take his *Gita*, the Koran, the Bible, the Zend Avesta or the *Granth Sahib*, as the case may be, and his *takli*. If there are many such real satyagrahis, they will certainly transform the atmosphere in an immensely short time, even as one gentle shower transforms the plains of India into a beautiful green carpet in one single day.

The question will legitimately be asked, 'If you really mean what you say, why don't you take the lead, never mind whether anyone follows you or not?' My answer is: I do not regard myself as pure enough to undertake such a heroic mission. I am trying every moment of my life to attain the requisite purity of thought, word and deed. As it is, I confess that I am swayed by many passions. Anger wells up in my breast when I see or hear about what

I consider to be misdeeds. All I can humbly claim for myself is that I can keep these passions and moods under fair subjection, and prevent them from gaining mastery over me. But the standard of purity that I want for any such heroic measure is not to have such passions at all and yet to hate the wrong. When I feel that I have become incapable even of thinking evil, and I hold it to be possible for every God-fearing man to attain that state, I shall wait for no man's advice, and even at the risk of being called the maddest of men, I shall not hesitate to knock at the Viceregal gate or go wherever God leads me, and demand what is due to this country which is being ground to dust today.

Meanwhile let no man mock at satyagraha. Let no man parody it. If it is at all possible, leave satyagraha alone, and the whole field is open for unchecked action. On a chartless sea in which there is no lighthouse a captain dares whither he wills. But a captain who knowing the existence of a lighthouse and its position, sails anyhow, or takes no precaution for knowing the lighthouse from deceiving stars, will be considered unfit for his post. If the reader can bear with me, let him understand that I claim to be the keeper of the lighthouse called satyagraha in the otherwise chartless sea of Indian politics. And, therefore, it is that I have suggested that those who make for satyagraha will do well to go to its keeper. But I know that I have no patent rights in satyagraha. I can, therefore, merely rely upon the indulgence of fellow-workers for recognition of my office.

Young India, 14-7-1927

147. THE GOOSE AND THE GANDER

TO THE EDITOR, "YOUNG INDIA"

DEAR SIR,

You affirm that swaraj is impossible without the removal of untouchability, even as it is impossible without Hindu-Muslim unity. I would link up the two impossibilities and say that Hindu-Muslim unity is impossible without the removal of untouchability—in other words, that Hindu-Muslim unity is impossible without Hindu unity. I hope you grant this proposition. Andrews is one of those who seem to have realized the truth of it.

But be that as it may, allow me to point out one little difficulty in your otherwise most helpful article entitled "Our Shame" in which you so generously notice my letter to you printed in the same issue (June 30th). If, because Hindu-Muslim unity is necessary for swaraj, special political provision is to be made for the Mussalmans, as was done by you in your scheme[1] published in *Young India* for 19-2-1925 or as is done in the latest communal Pact, viz., that of the A.I.C.C. which, be it noted, purports to be a general communal settlement, and not merely a Hindu-Muslim arrangement as you think—then why leave the suppressed class in the cold, when you grant that its unity with the rest of the nation is as necessary for swaraj as Hindu-Muslim unity? We leave the woes of our child-widows out of these schemes and pacts, because (1) these widows are not a community, (2) there is legislation to help them, and (3) most of us (rightly or wrongly) do not look upon the amelioration of their condition as the *sine qua non* of swaraj. If legal enactments are useless for Touchable-Untouchable unity, they must be equally so for Hindu-Muslim unity. But what do we find in actual practice? In the name of swaraj and Hindu-Muslim unity, the needs (real or supposed) of the most clamant but not the most needy community alone are attended to in our Acts, Pacts and Schemes. And that is excused on the plea that special provision for any community is a necessary evil.

Well, I say, if special provision is a necessary evil, tolerate it where it is most necessary, i.e., in the case of the suppressed class, who, as you have already recognized, have a much stronger case for special treatment than the Mussalmans, —and not merely where it is most vociferously demanded, as in the case of our Islamic countrymen. If communal representation is to be allowed in some form or other, in spite of its known evils, then allow it in all cases impartially, even at the risk of a *reductio ad absurdum*. Else mention no community at all in your scheme, but let equal opportunities for all *citizens* (and not communities), alike in the matter of education, the public services, and representation on elective bodies, be the guiding inviolable principle of your constitution.

I hope you will advise our Congress Executive to guide themselves along either of these two ways, the only logical ways as they appear to a humble student of and worker for his nation. For ourselves there is no question which of the two we would prefer. Have you not, at my instance, committed yourself to the latter, which I may call the Rational Nationalist way, in *Young India* for 20-8-1925, p. 292 ?[2] You have, and therefore I pray that you advise the Congress Committee who are charged with the drafting of a constitution for the future government of this country, and who have made a public appeal for suggestions towards it, not to go in for any unhealthy compromise between the oil and water of

[1] *Vide* Vol. XXVI, pp. 160-3.

[2] *Vide* Vol. XXVIII, pp. 93-4.

the two ways, but to stick to one of the two, preferably the latter. For Reason and Justice' sake avoid invidiousness, the original sin of the Pact of 1916.[1]

I am,

KARWAR (N. KANARA), *Yours, etc.,*

July 4, 1927 S. D. NADKARNI

I entirely agree with my correspondent that if there is a special provision in any future swaraj constitution in one case, there will have to be in every other similar case, whether there is clamour in connection with it or not. I have in my recent article on Hindu-Muslim unity[2] given my deliberate opinion against any legal enactment with reference to any understanding that might be arrived at between Hindus and Mussalmans. No special legislation without a change of heart can possibly bring about organic unity. And when there is a change of heart no such legislation can possibly be necessary. My effort which takes the form of prayer in our present helpless condition is mainly devoted to procuring that change of heart. And what is true of Hindu-Muslim unity is more true of the suppressed class. No protective legislation will help them unless the so-called higher class Hindus cleanse themselves, and are eager to do justice to the suppressed class. And when they have cleansed themselves no such legislation is necessary. At the present moment law enables them to use public schools and public wells, but the so-called high class Hindus successfully prevent their use by them. What, therefore, I would advise all fellow-reformers in this direction is to concentrate attention upon bettering in a concrete condition the lot of the suppressed class by providing schools, wells, and temples for them, and reformers themselves using all these in preference to those from which the suppressed classes may be excluded.

Young India, 14-7-1927

[1] Lucknow Pact, an agreement between leaders of the Congress and the Muslim League by which the Congress conceded separate Muslim electorates

[2] *Vide* "Hindu-Muslim Unity", 16-6-1927.

148. SPEECH IN REPLY TO MUNICIPAL ADDRESS, TUMKUR[1]

July 14, 1927

FRIENDS,

I thank you for this address but I wish it had not been presented to me in English. I see before me so many of my Mussalman and Hindu brothers and sisters and if you would have used either your own mother tongue or used the national language, Hindi, they would have heard and understood and I would have been pleased to receive that address. I hope you realize that it is they, the masses, that should understand the significance of all this. They must understand this and understand one another well. They are brothers and they are the right and left eye of our motherland. To make them understand we must use the language they understand very well.

I am pleased to see that many of you are clad in khadi. But I want you not only to wear khadi today for this function only but to continue to use it always, all your life and make your brothers and sisters in the villages also, when you go to them, use khadi. A khadi vastralaya is going to be opened here for you today. I want you all to go there and empty the depot. I am aware that our khadi work is increasing in your place. I pray to God that He may bless you with the strength and wisdom to continue that work. I hope you realize that you must all help in this cause for the sake of the poor of the country.

I want to speak to you one word today. I want to know how many amongst you who have gathered today are *Adi Karnatakas*?[2] Many of your brothers and sisters have not come here. To you and to those who have not come I will say this. Much is being done for the uplift of your community. In your Mysore Parliament (the Representative Assembly), the Dewan has dwelt upon this in his address. I am also glad to hear that His Highness takes a great interest in the cause of the downtrodden of your province. I feel for your position. We have to consider ourselves

[1] Gandhiji's speech in Hindi was rendered into Kanarese by Gangadharrao Deshpande.

[2] Some in the audience raised their hands.

Panchamas as *prayaschitta* for what we have done to a portion of our own brothers and sisters.

But I want to speak to you, the representatives or members of the *Adi Karnataka* community here. Wherever I go I have seen them in the grip of very bad habits, as eating the flesh of cow and mutton. They must know they belong to the great Hindu fold and that they must not eat cow's flesh. Many friends, many true and good men, in order to promote love and brotherliness among the communities of India have given up this habit. Hundreds of my friends, Mussalmans and Englishmen, have given up this habit. Many a high-placed Mussalman, I know, does not countenance the slaughter of cows. In your own State you have a society to protect cows and there is a movement to prevent their slaughter. I am glad your ruler is interested in this movement. In great numbers you have assembled here today but what is the number of cows that are living and how many are slaughtered? Mr. William Smith of the Dairy Farm in Bangalore has stated that there was much animal slaughter in Mysore State, it is much more than necessary. But I want to know why you do that at all?

We are an agricultural people and we are as a nation dependent upon our cattle from ancient times. When I was in the Nandi Hills my friends supplied me with good milk but I know the difficulty of good milk supply that is to be observed everywhere in our land. How many children there are in our land and can we say that we have enough good pure cow's milk for them all? In our own interest, in the interest of our country I want to appeal to them not to indulge in this habit of flesh-eating.

You have stated in your address that you are going to get water-supply and electricity.

Whilst I congratulate you on this, I may tell you that I expected you to give me assurances in other matters. Can you assure me that the children in the town will be ensured a liberal supply of clean and cheap milk? You have not told me that you have done all you can for cow-protection, short of legislation prohibiting it. You have told me that you have a population of 15,000, but you have omitted to give me the strength of your live-stock. There was a time in our land, when the wealth and prosperity of the people was measured by the number of children in the family and the head of cattle that it possessed. I assure you that you could have an ideal dairy here for much less than three lakhs you will spend on water works or even less than Rs. 50,000 that you will invest in electricity. For much less money you can have a dairy so as to make it possible for people to have milk as easily as water. Have you persuaded your *Panchamas* to give up beef and liquor? And what have you done for hygiene and sanitation? The West has come in for much blame from me, but its hygiene and sanitation are object-lessons for us. To me, the test of a people's knowledge of sanitation is the condition of their latrines, and I am told that the state of things here is scandalous. The most orthodox and learned amongst us do not scruple to infringe the laws of sanitation, though all scriptures say that every infringement of a law of health or hygiene or sanitation is a sin. I ask you to study this question deeply and to aim at being ideal scavengers. So long as you do not take the broom and the bucket in your hands, you cannot make your town and cities clean.[1]

Do you know what great advance in these matters the cities of the West have made? You must copy them and keep your own place clean and healthy if you want your citizens to have a clean and healthy life. I have gone to so many cities but I am not satisfied in this matter. You must all cultivate the habit of cleanliness and sanitation and you must all help to be scavengers of your town if you want to live without disease and dirt. . . .

Lastly I will say one word. For the poor of the country, I appeal to you to take to spinning at the charkha. Do not say you have no time. If you are rising from your bed at seven in the morning I request you, I beg of you to rise at five and give the two hours for spinning at the charkha.

Well, I tell you that the spinning-wheel I am placing before you is a symbol of industry, and lazy people cannot work it. Time is wealth, and the *Gita* says the Great Annihilator annihilates those who waste time.[2]

Two hours a day at the charkha would do a very great deal for the country and its poor millions. I have come to you today to ask this of you. I thank you all for this reception and address. May God bless you.

The Hindu, 18-7-1927

[1] & [2] These paragraphs have been taken from Mahadev Desai's "Weekly Letter" in *Young India*, 4-8-1927.

149. SPEECH AT PRANI DAYA SANGHA, TUMKUR[1]

July 14, 1927

FRIENDS,

I thank you for your address and purse. It also gives me pleasure to receive your address in your own mother tongue. You gave me an English translation of it but I have not read it. Instead, I have listened to the reading of your beautiful Kanarese and I understood much because, Kanarese, Tamil, Telugu and every other vernacular in the country are as sisters to our national language, Hindi. This morning in reply to your Municipal Address I have spoken at length on cow-protection and I hope and wish you will remember my appeal on behalf of the poor cows of our country. Perhaps you might know there is a big Sangha for the purpose in Belgaum and they have asked me to be its president. We have also a similar society at Sabarmati Ashram. The money you have given me today would go to that society for the protection of cows. But, I want you in Mysore to do in Mysore itself what we are doing there. You will have known of our work in the pages of *Young India* and *Navajivan.* I want you to do that work. You must do it here and you must all do it. For remember, friends, that whether it is khadi work or cow-protection work it is not going to be accomplished by one man alone. Also remember that in the protection of your cattle lies the wealth of your country. Cow is the mother of the land and if you understand the full significance of the term 'mother' you will realize the importance of cow-protection in the progress and welfare of our motherland. I thank you once more for your kindness.

The Hindu, 18-7-1927

[1] Gandhiji spoke in Hindi.

150. SPEECH AT MADDAGIRI[1]

July 15, 1927

FRIENDS,

In order to serve the poor of the country you have given me a purse and address for which I thank you all. You know that this service of the poor is very vast, the poor men—*Daridranarayana* has a big body, the biggest stomach. This *Daridranarayana* lives in the heart and the breath of the lowest and the poorest in the village huts. He lives far away from the towns, in the interior of your villages, he does not have even one single meal a day and yet you are raising your cities and towns from his money, from his toil and his earnings. You don't get money from outside, from foreign trade; you only send it outside by your trade. Do you know how much cotton trade is being carried on, and how much cotton is being grown here; its cost in Egypt for instance and its cost here? It has been said that when a country sends out its raw materials to a foreign country there is no improvement for that country. There is one way however for some improvement of this grinding poverty and that is by khadi work. You may not send out your cotton. You may spin it and weave it into cloth and wear it. I know it is for this purpose you have given me this purse but you could have given more. If I were well I would at this moment go amongst you with the charkha and appeal to you to spin along with me always. Some of you, many of you today have worn khadi. I am thankful that you have given some money to the poor weavers but I ask you if you are going to wear it always? If not your giving me this purse is of no value. If you are to help the poor, if you are to perform your dharma irrespective of caste or creed, if you think and hope that your motherland should prosper, if you think of God, then wearing khadi is your duty, it is your dharma. Will you do it?

In yesterday's meetings at Tumkur I have pleaded with my *Panchama* brethren not to take cow-flesh or eat any flesh whatsoever. I will not say further today to my *Panchama* brethren here. Do not eat cow's flesh, do not drink, live a clean and pure life without sin and disease. I am glad you have a hall called after Lokamanya Tilak. I hope you will remember the life of that great

[1] Gandhiji spoke in Hindi.

son of India, and act up to his principles. Friends, I thank you all.

The Hindu, 18-7-1927

151. SPEECH AT PUBLIC MEETING, TUMKUR[1]

July 16, 1927

FRIENDS,

I thank you for all your purses and addresses. Mr. Hamza Hussain suggested to me before I took seat that I should talk to you in English. But I am not going to follow that suggestion. There are so many here to whom if I speak in English it would be disrespectful, for how many of you have taught your ladies English? Or is it that you want to test me whether I know English? (Laughter) If so, I may tell you I demand fees and you will have to pay a very heavy fee for wanting to examine me. Perhaps you may say that the purse you have given me is a fee by itself. No. I know you have given me the purse because you want to serve the poor of the country not by actual food but by khadi work. You may not know how many poor people there are. Do you know how very big is the stomach of *Daridranarayana* of our land ? Whatever you give him is not enough. You may not know him but he lives far away in the villages, out of sight of your cities and towns; you do not know him because so many of you, so many of the ladies here have all come in foreign cloth. Do you know that every rupee's worth of Manchester cloth that you buy increases the *daridrya*[2] of our land ? When the people in the villages and huts are starving is it just that you should send away your wealth out of your land to distant Manchester? I want you all today to think well on this matter and I want you to feel this in your heart deeply. If you really feel the sense of grinding poverty of this land I want you to come to the conclusion that you ought not to go on wearing foreign cloth. Make a resolve today to do your bit by wearing khadi and by contributing your help to its cause, the cause of the poor. I may inform you with pleasure that when I appealed for help on behalf of this cause the ladies in the Mahila Seva Samaj at Bangalore threw away their jewels and ornaments. They knew that their chief ornament is their heart and that they are no true ornaments that adorn the body outside.

[1] Gandhiji spoke in Hindi.
[2] Poverty

Before I close, I want to say one word. I am very grateful to you all, particularly the Reception Committee of Tumkur who have made my stay here quite comfortable. I thank you once more for your excellent arrangements. The Headmaster of your High School told me they have started a poor boys' fund and that they have resolved to call it by my name. You know, my friends, I am very poor myself and so I am a relative to all the poor. If I could, I could put into that fund at least one single pie but I have not got a pie which I can call my own. What I eat, what I wear is all yours and long since my earning has been given up. So I cannot give the fund a pie of my own. I know however you can all give something to that fund. There are so many very poor students in our country. They all need your help. I hope you will all help the poor students of your place at least and make the fund a useful one. Do not spend out of it any sum for entertainment or other purposes but make it really serve the purpose for which it was started. I thank you once more and bid you good-bye.

The Hindu, 18-7-1927

152. LETTER TO MIRABEHN

KUMARA PARK, BANGALORE,
July 17, 1927

CHI. MIRA,

I have been away for two days, and there was no telegram yesterday. But I take it that as per your previous telegraphic information you left Sabarmati for Wardha yesterday.

The negative participle should always go with the verb, when the verb is to be negative and when the subject has to be qualified by a long phrase, the qualifying phrase should precede the subject. Hence your original sentence which read:
अब कोई नहीं बातचीत करनेके लिये अन्दर आयेंगे[1] should read as follows:

अब बातचीत करनेके लिये कोई अन्दर नहीं आयेंगे[2]!

Whilst you can say कोई सुधार[3], कुछ is better. कुछ means 'a little', कोई means 'someone'. But sometimes कोई is used in the place of कुछ. The safer thing, however, is to use कुछ whenever you mean a

[1] *Ab koi nahin batchit karneke liye andar aayenge.*

[2] *Ab batchit karneke liye koi andar nahin aayenge* meaning 'now no one will come in to talk.'

[3] *Koi sudhar* meaning 'a little improvement'

little or some. You cannot say कोई दूध; you must say कुछ दूध[1].

Do tell me for my information whatever improvement you would suggest about spinning, prayer, kitchen, etc. I would then be able to correct you if you have come to a hasty judgment; or if I accept your judgment, I might suggest the improvement.

One earns the right of fiercest criticism when one has convinced one's neighbours of one's affection for them and one's sound judgment, and when one is sure of not being in the slightest degree ruffled if one's judgment is not accepted or enforced. In other words, there should be love, faculty for clear perception and complete toleration to enable one to criticize.

You have used the word भावनात्मक in connection with Bhansali to mean 'emotional'. But here as emotional is used disparagingly, भावनात्मक will not do. You can say भावनात्मक for Andrews by way of compliment. The word perhaps you want to use for Bhansali is स्वप्नावस्थ meaning, living in the dreamland and missing the reality, or you mean soft-brained. He is a man of very lofty emotion. But I am getting concerned about him. More than one person has drawn my attention to his becoming over-emotional. If you have acquired any influence with him, do open up a brief correspondence and tactfully discuss him with himself. But you will do what you like. I do not want to add to your tasks.

Tomorrow I go to Mysore and return from Mysore on the 23rd. Here is a copy of my programme which will be carried out if my health permits it. But you should continue to send your letters to Bangalore. The difference would be only that of one day wherever I am. And as the programme is only tentative, it is better not to run any risk.

With love,

BAPU

From the original: C.W. 5250. Courtesy: Mirabehn

[1] *Kuchh doodh* meaning 'some milk'

153. LETTER TO A. I. KAJEE

AS AT THE ASHRAM, SABARMATI,
July 17, 1927

MY DEAR KAJEE,

I was delighted to receive your letter after a long absence. It is difficult to give you guidance from this distance over differences with the Transvaal. I am, however, hoping that Mr. Sastri's arrival has smoothed matters over.

As soon as I got the cablegram from Johannesburg, I sent a reply which I hope was duly received. Do please keep me informed of further developments.

I am glad that Manilal and his wife are happy and are both rendering national service.

Yours sincerely,

A. I. KAJEE, ESQ.
SOUTH AFRICAN INDIAN CONGRESS
175, GREY STREET
DURBAN
(NATAL)

From a photostat: S.N. 12361

154. LETTER TO VIJAYPAL SINGH

KUMARA PARK, BANGALORE,
July 17, 1927

DEAR FRIEND,

I have your letter. I mentioned almonds and grapes by way of example. Undoubtedly local fruits and nuts would be the best. But so far as the nutritive value is concerned, nothing is lost in taking the fruits sun-dried in other climates except, perhaps, the vitamins which can be easily supplied by adding fresh lemons. For we, poor people, groundnuts, coconut and the green which are to be had everywhere are perhaps an ideal diet. But I speak without any definite experience. I, therefore, dissuade people from being entirely guided by me in making dietetic experiment. But, if those who have independent experience and have some scientific training would conduct experiments in order to find physical and spiritual values of different fruits, they would no doubt render service in a field which is capable of limitless exploration.

In fasting for health's sake, copious draughts of water are necessary. I used salt and soda as neat water created nausea. For my fasts previous to the one in Delhi, I had nothing but water of which because of nausea, I was able to drink very little. I have a friend who only the other day fasted for full 40 days and drank fresh water only copiously, and he kept excellent health.

Yours sincerely,

SJT. VIJAYPAL SINGH, B.A., LL.B., M.L.C.
'PREM BHAWAN'
MEERUT

From a photostat : S.N. 14184

155. LETTER TO OTTAMA BHIKKHU

KUMARA PARK, BANGALORE,
July 17, 1927

DEAR FRIEND,

I have your letter for which I thank you. I wish that I could visit Burma. But if I keep up what little strength I have regained, it would be required for overtaking the interrupted programme during the year. I do not know what will be in store for me thereafter.

With reference to the secession of Burma from India, Burmese should certainly have my sympathy if they wished to secede. I would certainly not want them to sever their connection if they find it beneficial. At the present moment, I feel that India, in co-operation with the British, is exploiting Burma. That our cultures have a common origin has a strong appeal for me in favour of its absorption into India. But that absorption should come naturally and after both of us have become conscious of our strength. But I confess that I am speaking without much experience. I must, therefore, be content with a statement of the general principle that the benefit of Burma should be the sole consideration in deciding whether it should be an autonomous sovereign State or a province of India. I must not prejudice your case one way or the other by taking the matter up in *Young India.* That I can only do after visiting Burma if God provides that opportunity for me and studying the problem on the spot. I do not propose to publish your letter.

Yours sincerely,

OTTAMA BHIKKHU
MAHA BODHI SOCIETY
4-A, COLLEGE SQUARE
CALCUTTA

From a photostat: S.N. 14185

156. LETTER TO NARGIS CAPTAIN

KUMARA PARK, BANGALORE,
July 17, 1927

I have your letter. I wish I could go to Panchgani and see the little villages you describe. But that cannot be as I have already commenced gentle touring, and if it does not disturb my health, it will now continue practically to the end of the year. What I should like to do is of course that some of you sisters should take this responsibility of touring off my shoulders and do it yourselves. But since you will not do it, how can a poor lay man like me help going about begging from place to place?

Mithuben, Ratanben and Jamnaben are here, and they will be here for a few days longer. Mithuben has sold quite a lot of fashionable khadi.

I don't know which book you mean about me. Nobody to my knowledge has written inside of two or three months.

Yours sincerely,

From a photostat: S.N. 14186

157. *LETTER TO K. J. NARAYANAN NAMBUDRIPAD*

KUMARA PARK, BANGALORE,
July 17, 1927

DEAR FRIEND,

I have your letter. I suggest to you that our untouchability is not due to the distinction between rich and poor. But it seems to me to be due to the arrogance of those who are learned in booklore towards those who are not, and it has gone to the uttermost limit of calculated cruelty. I am both pained and surprised that you should defend what is perhaps the greatest wrong done under cover of religion.

Yours sincerely,

SJT. K. J. NARAYANAN NAMBUDRIPAD
VADAKKANCHERI P.O.
(COCHIN STATE)

From a microfilm: S.N. 14620

158. *SPEECH IN REPLY TO MUNICIPAL ADDRESS, BANGALORE*[1]

July 17, 1927

FRIENDS,

I thank you for the address you have given me on behalf of your Municipal Council. I am sorry I cannot speak loud enough so that every one of you might hear me. You have dwelt on what you are doing as members of the Municipal Council in your address. I am very much pleased with your work and I congratulate you on it. I must thank you for having introduced compulsory education in your city for your youths and I must also congratulate you for your having in your beautiful city such big roads and lights. It appears to me from what you have stated in your address that your municipal work is on right lines and that your record is one that would afford satisfaction to all. I might tell you the true germ of swaraj lies in municipal work, and I want you to recognize it.

[1] Gandhiji spoke in Hindi.

I have been amidst you for some time but because I could not go out on account of health, I could not personally find out your municipal work especially in regard to public health. But I take it, it is generally good. I have been told that your upper classes and middle classes are healthy. If so, I want to ask you a question. Have you got poor people in your city? If you have, I want to ask you as members of the Municipality whether you have kept their houses healthy and tidy? Do you take any interest in their lives and the way they are living and keeping their houses? In your address you have not told me of the state of your scavengers, nor have you informed me anything as to how you supply good milk to your children, the old and the sick of your town. You have many merchants and traders who pay you taxes but have you ascertained anything about them? Are they selling good flour and rations to the poor who come from the villages to purchase from them? Your market gets supplied with things from distant villages and you purchase them as you like but have you stopped to enquire of their conditions in their distant homes in the villages? I cannot gather anything from your address as to how many drunkards there are in your city and how many wanton sinners there are and what steps you have taken to prevent them from poisoning your city life. I want also to know what the state of your cows and cattle is and what you as a municipal body have been doing in this direction. Can you answer these questions? If so, I can talk to you still more. But if you cannot, I want you, I request you to consider all these questions and think of them always in your active municipal work.

I must say I am very grateful for your Municipality for giving a place to the charkha. To me, it seems that you are thinking of your poor. By this, I am sure you are aware that if you want to keep the land from getting poorer, if you want to help the poor sisters and brothers of your place, charkha is the only way. I feel truly grateful to you for this. I am also glad that you are supplying khadi to your employees. There are so many of you here today who know that if you have to help in the only way you could it is by purchasing khadi. Have some consideration for the poor, take the cloth they weave for you and let them be sure of their wages and your purchase. I pray to God that the city which gave me health may grow ever more in wealth. You have all given me of your love and I thank you all for this. May God bless you and your Municipality with a great future.

The Hindu, 18-7-1927

159. SPEECH TO LABOURERS, BANGALORE[1]

July 17, 1927

FRIENDS,

You have given me your addresses in the national language, Hindi, in the Mysore mother tongue, Kanarese, and also in Tamil and you have also given me a purse to serve the poor people of your country. I am deeply grateful to you all for this. Your offering for the cause of the poor does not bring to me any wonder because I have been a labourer myself for the past 35 years. Ever since I went to South Africa, I have known the woes of labour intimately. Having experienced some of them myself I also know that help in these matters seldom comes from outside. We must help ourselves and then only God will help us. That has been my experience. In South Africa when this burden of suffering was weighing heavily we found out that nobody could help us so well as we ourselves and we went on making our own efforts steadily and always on the right path. Then only relief came to us. In Ahmedabad also it was the same experience. The labourers did not set fire to property, they did not bully the employers, they harmed nobody and they went on fighting their cause in all just ways and right paths. They carried on in peace and suffering; they told their masters: "We are groaning under suffering, and you are happy, may you live more happily." This went home and truth triumphed.[2] This is the spirit of the silent and bold path of suffering; it is called 'satyagraha'. It means that you take your stand on truth and never swerve from the path of right in fighting your cause. It means success of truth, it means self-help. Remember that you must help yourselves. This path is open to every one of you, young and old.

You have stated in your address that conditions in your mills are more hard than in other mills. I do not know if it is true, but if it is, then I am sorry to hear of it. But I know one thing, and

[1] Of the Malleswaram Labour Union of the Maharaja Mills. Illustrating the case of a dismissed labourer, the address mentioned "the unfortunate position of labour in Mysore State, the indifference of Government and lack of public sympathy for labour movement in general". Gandhiji's speech in Hindi was rendered into Kanarese by Gangadharrao Deshpande.

[2] *Vide* Vol. XIV.

that is, your director is the son-in-law of my friend, Chandavarkar, and he would be very sympathetic to you. He invited me to the mills and agreed to any suggestions to be made. I sent Mr. Rajagopalachari who came to you and ascertained the matter. This was at the time of your strike. Since then I do not know what your state is but whatever it is, always remember that you must help yourselves in this and that you must learn to depend upon your own selves. I want to ask you if you can do so. You are quarrelling amongst yourselves, you do not make any co-operative and united effort, you have not all thought about bettering your conditions in real earnest, many of you waste your time. You do not feel that the sorrow of one of you is the sorrow of you all. You go to drink and you go to play cards or gamble. You should not do that if you have to better your conditions, if you have to help yourselves as men. You must be aware of all this. You have given me this purse and it is because you know there are millions who are much poorer than you, more hungry than you. You must know that you must help these poor souls. You must not forget that the cloth you produce in your own mills is not for you or for your people but for trade purposes. It is for the benefit of your masters and it is not for protecting the poor of your land, to help them get a morsel of food in the villages. You must wear khadi and help the poor men and women who weave it for you. It is you who must help them first, for the rich do not come as quickly. You must help them by wearing and purchasing khadi.

I know that the present troubles arise because the mill-owners and the shareholders consider they are one and that you workers are separate. It is only on the day they are going to consider that the workers also are one of them, that their interests are also the labourers' interests, on that day it is that this problem is going to be solved. When this recognition comes the mills would prosper for there would be no division of interests as between capital and labour. This day must come for that is dharma. But till that day comes it is your duty to go on fighting for your cause but fight for it as dharma and never swerve from the path of right and justice. Think well on what I have said to you today. Do not think there is any other path of bettering your condition or achieving success for your efforts. There is no other path than dharma or the path of righteousness. Never forget this. May God bless you all in your efforts with strength and success.

The Hindu, 18-7-1927

160. LETTER TO MIRABEHN

Half revised

July 18, 1927

CHI. MIRA,

I sent you a letter yesterday. I therefore do not want to say much today.

You have done well in explaining your position fully to Valunjkar and it is a correct position. You must be free to do the work that comes to your lot. Nor must Gangu hang on to your skirt. She must be taught to grow independently. But seeing that she wants to come under your influence you will handle her lovingly and give her what you can.

You will not experiment there with your health but eat what you need. Order the quantity of fruit you need as you used to at the Ashram and if anybody sends any fruit to you keep what *you* need and send the rest to the kitchen, i.e., Vinoba. Do not think that the others need it because you need it. You do not need the *jowari* that the others need. That fruit happens to be a delicacy as well as food is perhaps unfortunate. It is enough if we learn to take delicacies too as we would medicine in their proper measure and then we may harden our hearts and eat them although the others may not get them. The dangers surrounding this position are too patent to require mention. People have accommodated themselves to even vices under the plea of necessity. But we need not be afraid of such awkward consequences, if we would keep a ceaseless watch over ourselves. There are dangers every way we turn. But we must obey *our* fundamental natures be the cost what it may.

This has been a longer letter than I had wanted it to be.

With love,

BAPU

[PS.]

I am quite well.

From the original: C.W. 5251. Courtesy: Mirabehn

161. LETTER TO J. B. KRIPALANI

July 18, 1927

MY DEAR PROFESSOR,

Nanabhai tells me you have threatened to leave (almost?) if the Vidyapith does not take back Malkani. This attitude is wrong. You cannot manufacture charity by threats. And why would the Vidyapith be uncharitable if it cannot see its way to take Malkani back? Seeing that there is much opposition to his being taken back, it would be a mistake to press his reinstatement. Please revise your opinion.

In any event I have not seen the last of Malkani. I am carrying on correspondence with him and about him. For me Malkani's error is a national tragedy. His reinstatement is a most insignificant thing. How to put together the broken bits of Malkani and to find him again a man is the sole question with me. And I am giving the thing the best of myself.

With love,

BAPU

From a photostat: S.N. 12609

162. *LETTER TO J. B. PETIT*[1]

KUMARA PARK, BANGALORE,
July 19, 1927

DEAR MR. PETIT,

I thank you for your prompt attention to my letter[2] about Mr. Sastri. Of course, in my opinion, nothing has to be said against the Government. The point raised by you is, I think, debatable. What the service regulations come to is that no servant of the Crown should receive a single farthing from those whom he has to serve. But it seems to me that a Viceroy who, for example, may wish to do good to India beyond his province and receives aid from his friends and relatives in England will not be debarred from openly receiving such aid. I have no doubt whatsoever about the Government playing the game[3] in the matter of Mr. Sastri. The point of my letter went deeper. I hold that the Government may not go beyond a certain point. However, I do not wish to labour the point any further.

Yours sincerely,

JEHANGIR B. PETIT, ESQ.
PETIT BUILDING
359, HORNBY ROAD
FORT
BOMBAY

From a photostat: S.N. 12367

[1] In reply to his letter dated July 16 in which it was stated that "the [Imperial Citizenship] Association cannot finance Mr. Sastri". It also enclosed for Gandhiji's reference M. Habibullah's letter to J. B. Petit dated July 12, 1927. Habibullah had written: "There can, of course, be no question of any unofficial organization being required to assist the Government or their Agent financially. . . . He is to get a salary of £2,500 per annum which is exactly the amount given to a Cabinet Minister in South Africa, a sumptuary allowance of £500 per annum, a house which will be rented and furnished by Government, a car also purchased by Government—a maintenance allowance for the car of £200 per annum. For the house he will have to pay rent calculated at 10 per cent per annum of his salary, and 10 per cent per annum calculated on the capital outlay of the furniture for the use of the furniture. He will, so far as we are aware, have to pay no income tax . . . I am sure you will agree that these terms cannot be described as niggardly."

[2] Dated July 5, 1927

[3] There were proposals to increase the allowances.

163. LETTER TO N. V. THADANI

KUMARA PARK, BANGALORE,
July 19, 1927

MY DEAR THADANI,

I have your letter. You have entirely missed my point. I did not even know that your college was national merely in name. My complaint was not that Malkani went from a national college to a Government college. My complaint would have had the same force, if Malkani, instead of going from the Mahavidyalaya to a Government college, had deserted the Mahavidyalaya for a selfless expedition to the North Pole in search of knowledge, or say, had gone to Kashi Vidyapith or Bihar Vidyapith both of which are direct offspring of non-co-operation and with both of which I am more or less connected. And I should have considered the conduct of Sriprakash Babu and Rajendra Babu, respectively, as ungentlemanly if they had seduced Malkani behind the back of the authorities of the Mahavidyalaya as you have done. And I have felt it so keenly in this case because of my high opinion about Malkani. Many other professors deserted the Mahavidyalaya before Malkani. In their case, I felt nothing, because I had staked nothing on them. I do not know whether I have yet made my point clear. I know no distinction between Sind and Gujarat or any other province. If Malkani had been posted in Sind and was seduced by someone in Gujarat, I should have said and felt the same thing, again because of the personal factor that it was Malkani who had allowed himself to be seduced.

I do not underrate your difficulties; I do not underrate your cause; but what I feel is that you adopted a questionable method for achieving your purpose. You will not build up the morals of the Sindhi youth by undermining those of Malkani. Malkani standing at the helm of his sinking ship in Gujarat, himself starving, his wife and mother-in-law looking daggers at him, and his friends howling at him in indignation for his madness, would have been an ideal professor for your boys and a noble lesson for India. I wonder if I am still clear to you. Do not for one moment consider that the fact that it is Gujarat Mahavidyalaya that will come to grief that has weighed with me. My life has been a witness of many such institutions arising and falling with some of which I have myself been intimately connected. For me, their worth has consisted in their having thrown up heroes and thus finished their task. It may interest you to know that the Senate of the Vidyapith has been convulsed over Malkani's letter recalling his resignation. Many professors who were always more or less against Malkani offered strenuous opposition to Malkani's reinstatement. The question was referred to me and I sent in my opinion that Malkani could not be reinstated in the face of that opposition. It will be awkward for him as also for the professors and bad for the Mahavidyalaya. The question of the Mahavidyalaya therefore is settled so far as Malkani is concerned. But the question of Malkani himself still remains a running sore. I have already given my opinion that he cannot undo one wrong by doing another, and that therefore he may not now leave you in the lurch without your being able to replace him. But if you would know my opinion, it is decidedly this : that Malkani should not remain in your institution a minute longer than is absolutely necessary, that you should set about finding a substitute without the least delay, that you should set a time-limit for your search, and that after the expiry of the time-limit, whether you have found a substitute or not, Malkani should leave you and either do what he likes, or let me do with him what I like. I may inform you that I have not yet got over the shock. Bardoli never disturbed my sleep; but Malkani does. You will be entitled to say that I deserve no pity if I would depart from the lesson of the *Gita* by which I swear and have such unwarranted faith in men. I shall accept your judgment and plead in justification that I cannot surmount my fundamental nature all of a sudden. Please share this with Malkani.

Yours sincerely,

SJT. N. V. THADANI
HYDERABAD (SIND)

From a photostat: S.N. 12606

164. LETTER TO K. S. KARANTH

KUMARA PARK, BANGALORE,
July 19, 1927

DEAR FRIEND,

I have your letter and the medal. Here are the answers to your questions :

1. I do not think that there is any moral obligation for a man to take out an insurance policy for the sake of his creditors. But it is enough that he strains every nerve to pay his creditors while there is life in him. Of course, the great thing is never to incur debts on any account whatsoever. Having thus dealt with the ethics of insurance, I must warn you against throwing up your policy merely on the strength of my opinion. There is nothing wrong or sinful in your keeping up the insurance policy unless the consciousness of wrong comes upon you apart from my opinion. I would therefore dissuade you from hastily giving up the policy. There must be a definite living faith in God and complete reliance upon Him before one gives up what are generally regarded as legitimate things like insurance policy. Many other things should precede this sort of renunciation.

2. I think you were quite right in attending the marriage ceremony. It should be a warning against hasty promises.

3. I should draw a sharp distinction between *kirtans*[1] and theatricals. The question of theatricals is very serious, and as you seem to know all about the lives of actors, it may be as well for you to avoid the profession. But I am myself not on sure ground here. The theatre is as old as mankind. How far it has tended to make men better, I don't know. I have not studied its history. You must, therefore, not accept me as a guide. Either use your own judgment or go to those who can guide you with confidence and about whose purity of life you have no doubt. This covers the fourth question also.

5. In the male the sexual act is a giving up of vital energy every time. In the female that giving up process commences only with parturition.

6. M. Bureau does not refer to wet dreams at all. They are undoubtedly harmful. He merely refers to the conversion of the

[1] Devotional songs

excess of nutrition into seminal fluid in the male. But it requires to be husbanded and reserved for reproduction when the latter is desired, or transmutation into spiritual energy. This is my conviction. Whether M. Bureau means it or not, I can't say, because I have not the book with me at the time of answering.

So long as your friends know that any gift that they may make to you will go for some public purpose, there is no harm in accepting it if it pleases them better to serve the public cause by making gifts to their friends. There is, however, no doubt that it is best to dissuade friends from such practice.

Yours sincerely,

SJT. K. S. KARANTH
C/o G. N. POI, ESQ.
NIHALCHAND BUILDING
NEW QUEENS ROAD
GIRGAUM
BOMBAY

From a photostat: S.N. 14187

165. LETTER TO DR. M. S. KELKAR

KUMARA PARK, BANGALORE,
July 19, 1927

DEAR DOCTOR,

I thank you for your kind and thoughtful warning. I am simply going by the advice of the doctor here who constantly examines me. He is in charge of the Victoria Hospital and is reputed to be very clever and very careful. However, I am taking the tour in easy stages. But I quite agree with you that if I could bury myself in some seaside place, it would be better. However, your letter puts me further on my guard. I shall watch myself and not hesitate to still further restrain myself, if necessary.

I am keeping in touch with Uttam Chand, and I know that he is making fair progress and so also Kakasaheb. Their recovery will certainly be directly traceable to your treatment, and I am so glad that Gangabehn is also making steady progress.

Yours sincerely,

From a photostat: S.N. 14188

166. *LETTER TO SURAJ PRASAD MATHUR*

As at the Ashram, Sabarmati,
July 19, 1927

DEAR FRIEND,

I have your letter. My present life is no reaction of the past. Probably, my condemnation of my past life is an exaggeration. It should be remembered that the condemnation is according to the measure of standard I have evolved for myself. Life of perfect restraint had a fascination for me, even whilst I indulged myself with my wife. But though the spirit was willing the flesh was weak. I was able to control the flesh only by much patient effort, and God definitely helped me first by frequently sending me away from my wife and secondly by throwing circumstances in my way which made it necessary to restrain my lust even for the sake of meeting those circumstances. I do not think that I sinned against my wife more than the average man. But such comparisons are totally wrong and should never be held to justify sinning. Everyone must set up his code for himself and regulate his life in strictest accordance with it. After all, sin is a mental state. And, whilst a man who commits a particular sin will certainly receive his due punishment from Nature, if he is not conscious of that sin, he won't blame himself. But I being conscious of the same sin dare not justify myself and hold myself free from blame, because my ignorant brother commits it through ignorance, and therefore does not blame himself, and is probably not blamed by the society either. I think this covers all the points raised by you.

Yours sincerely,

Sjt. Suraj Prasad Mathur
Teacher, Sir Harcourt Butler High School
Helen Lodge
Simla

From a photostat: S.N. 14189

167. LETTER TO GANGADHAR SHASTRI JOSHI

KUMARA PARK, BANGALORE,
July 19, 1927

DEAR FRIEND,

I thank you for your letter and the pains you have taken to answer my questions. Do you claim cheapness, simplicity and efficacy for Ayurvedic medicine as we find it at present? After my own fashion, I have been interested in its success ever since 1891, and have even spent what little I was capable of and induced friends to spend on behalf of Ayurvedic physicians. But so far, I have found it to be neither cheap nor simple nor efficacious. Some of the prescriptions are most complicated. Ayurvedic physicians have been known to charge as much as men with medical degrees. I know Ayurvedic physicians who charge today even as much as Rs. 1,000 per day. The best of them are beyond the reach of the poor. And what I have also unfortunately found is that a very large number of patients have gone to the physicians with Western degrees after having found Ayurvedic treatment to be inefficacious. I am aware of the converse also having happened. But the scales seem to me to weigh in favour of Allopathy. My own desire has been and is now also to find Ayurveda practice successful, if only because I am probably fanatically vegetarian and because I have a horror of Allopathy for many reasons I need not go into. Even for simple home treatment, having studied something of both Ayurvedic and Allopathic drugs, I have been obliged to use Allopathic drugs instead of Ayurvedic. For instance, I have found nothing so efficacious as quinine for malaria or iodine for simple pains or Condy's fluid as a disinfectant. I must not, however, worry you with my own experience. If it is not troublesome, will you kindly illustrate in what way Ayurveda aims at purifying the whole system rather than affording only temporary relief? As time permits me, I shall go through the pamphlets you have kindly sent me. I shall also await the views from the friends to whom you have shown my letter. You will please write to me if you do not receive the relevant texts from Pandit Satavalekar.

Yours sincerely,

SJT. GANGADHAR SHASTRI JOSHIJI
9/2, SADASHIV PETH
POONA CITY

From a photostat: S.N. 14190

168. LETTER TO SATIS CHANDRA DAS GUPTA

KUMARA PARK, BANGALORE,
July 19, 1927

DEAR SATIS BABU,

Your letter arrived the same day as Dr. Ray who gave me doleful news about Pratishthan. He said that you were not at all fit for work, and that you were yet going back to Calcutta because your presence was needed at Sodepur. He added that Kshitish Babu was being over-worked. Knowing his pessimism, I have discounted the news he has given me. But I suppose the substance is true. You will, therefore, tell me all about the work there. But I want your assurance that, whatever may be the nature of the work, you are not going to put an undue strain upon yourself. Of course, you will laugh at this and retort "physician heal thyself". But I really believe that I do conserve my energy to the best of my ability. And, then, I have a solid wall of protection from so many sentinels. That I have not been able to avoid illnesses is a matter of humiliation for me. I should have been able to do so. But as I have said so often, I woke up too late in life to be able to have a disease-proof constitution. Up to the age of nearly 30, according to my notions of economy, I wasted myself whenever opportunity offered itself. The real building up began after that time, and then too, knowledge came in dribblets. This is only one though the main reason for breakdowns in my life. I want all co-workers to learn to avoid my mistakes. But of course all this is wretched philosophizing. You know what I want to say. Do not be anxious about khadi or the Pratishthan which is one and the same thing. Let us give the best of what we have, work in uttermost humility, and then say after the manner of Janaka, "What does it matter if khadi lives or perishes?"

With reference to the Bengal tour, you will not want me to

come to Bengal unless you are yourself able to bear the strain. Of course you will not discuss this thing publicly till you know how the present trial tour shapes. I must confess that I am not over-well or over-strong. But the doctor who is attending on me is a clever and a careful man, and he tells me that there is nothing wrong with blood-pressure or with anything else and that I am quite all right.

The Hindu-Muslim thing would be unbearable if I begin to think about it. But of whatever happens there, please keep me well-informed.

I have not written separately to Hemprabha Devi in order to conserve my energy. She is ever in my thoughts.

With love,

Yours,

From a microfilm: S.N. 19787

169. LETTER TO ASHRAM WOMEN

Silence Day, Ashadh Vad 5 [*July 19, 1927*][1]

SISTERS,

I have to write many letters today. But how can I miss writing to you?

I wish to hit two targets at one stroke. Now this is a rendering of an English saying which literally means to kill two birds with one stone. Such sayings come into vogue where violence is common in every walk of life. My rendering too is not faultless. But indeed we could hit a target without intending to hurt anyone.

My twofold purpose is to write my usual letter to you and to include in it my reply to Chi. Vasumati. She asks, "You say that women should know how to read the *Gita* as well as they should know how to roll chapatis. How is this possible? It will take a lot of time to learn."

It does indeed take time. But what can one not achieve with perseverance? A task can be accomplished if one devotes some time, if not a great deal, to it. It is difficult to learn cooking after you are grown up. Even then you can learn it with persistent efforts. If our women cannot pronounce Sanskrit well, the fault is not theirs. It is one's parents' fault, or if one is married

[1] The year is inferred from the reference to Karnatak.

it is the fault of one's husband or of his people. But what is the use of putting the blame on others? Let us see how we can remove the defect now. In the Ashram we look for our own defects and then try to remedy them. Of course we should not overdo learning to pronounce Sanskrit correctly. We should carry out our other duties in the Ashram, and while doing so, try also to improve our pronunciation as much as we can. The only point I wanted you to know was that in Karnatak many women pronounce Sanskrit more correctly than even men in Gujarat.

Blessings from
BAPU

From a photostat of the Gujarati: G.N. 3658

170. LETTER TO JETHALAL GANDHI

BANGALORE,
Ashadh Vad 5 [July 19, 1927][1]

BHAI JETHALAL,

I got your letter and the booklet about *snatakas*[2] which you have published. I could read the booklet only today. I can see that you have put great labour into it. The booklet is useful. I will find use for it in *Young India* and *Navajivan* too.

Blessings from
BAPU

[From Gujarati]
Sabarmati Snataka Vibhag, Book 6, No. 4, *Shishir*, 1984, p. 34

[1] Gandhiji was in Bangalore on this date in 1927.
[2] Graduates

171. *SPEECH TO STUDENTS, MYSORE*[1]

July 19, 1927

MR. PRINCIPAL, PROFESSORS, SISTERS AND FRIENDS,

You have honoured me with an address. You have likewise with a purse of Rs. 700 for the service of the *Daridranarayanas* of this land. I thank you sincerely for both. I am sorry I am not able to express to you here all that I feel, all that I want to say. I am not able to return in the least measure the overwhelming kindness that you have shown me in cities and villages alike. In a gathering like this, no student should ever be anxious that I should speak in English. Some of those present will not understand me if I speak in English. I have doubtless great attachment for English. If our object is to serve our motherland adequately, and if we desire that there should be greater affinity and harmony between the various classes, it is not to be achieved by spreading the knowledge of English. I have, therefore, a favour to ask of the students. That is also my message to them. They should cultivate a knowledge of Hindi, and devote themselves to the service of the motherland. My association with the students of our country dates back to 10 years, since my return to India. I know the hardships and the difficulties of the students. I have been seeing them every day. I also know their weak points. It has been my privilege to have a corner in their hearts. They have not hesitated to open their hearts to me, to tell me even what they had concealed from their parents. I do not know how I could bring them peace, or what message I could give them. I share in their sorrows, and I have been striving to alleviate their hardships. But in this world, we have to look only to God for help. None other could render any effectual help. There is no sin equal to that of disbelieving in Him, in denying Him. Amongst the students of today the spirit of atheism is gaining ground. I am deeply grieved that things should be so. Whenever I see Hindu students, I ask them to think of God, to pray, to repeat Ramanama. They ask me where is God, where is Rama and such other questions. When I see Mussalman youths and ask them to read the Koran, and to live the life enjoined therein, they also ask me similar

[1] Gandhiji's speech in Hindi was rendered into Kanarese by Gangadharrao Deshpande.

questions. The education which leads to the negation of God cannot make for the service of the country nor of humanity. In your address, you have referred to my service to my country. Whatever I have been doing is done with a sense of my duty to God. And this I consider to be the right thing. God is not seated in the skies, in the heavens, or elsewhere. He is enshrined in the heart of everyone—be he a Hindu, Mohammedan, Christian or Jew, man or woman.

I consider that real service of the country and of God consists in serving the poor humanity, whom Deshbandhu Das rightly designated the *Daridranarayana*. Such service however must be whole-hearted. When I see students, my heart goes out to them. If your hearts are not free from taint, neither the colleges, nor the libraries, nor this environment will avail you. His heart is pure who, seeing one in distress, will himself feel distressed. In our country, one-tenth of the population have not as much as one meal a day. Have our students any idea of this ? Having knowledge of this they are spending their time and money on cinemas, theatres, etc. Is this fair? Is this the way to serve the country? The education you are receiving in colleges is not for the poor of the country. Such education could serve its purpose only when it leads them to the service of the suffering millions. I therefore tell you that the real service of God consists in the service of humanity. For this end, wear khadi, and spin for half an hour a day. In your address you refer to my efforts to revive the charkha. If you merely praise me in the addresses, but do nothing yourselves to encourage spinning, it would be nothing short of fulsome flattery. I do not want to take more of your time. I have elsewhere spoken about the duties of students,[1] and you can read them. I always pray to God that He prosper you, the youth of India, that He speed you in the service of the country. God bless you all.

The Hindu, 21-7-1927

[1] *Vide* "Speech to Mysore Students, Bangalore", 12-7-1927.

172. LETTER TO MIRABEHN

As at Kumara Park, Bangalore,
July 20, 1927

CHI. MIRA,

I have your letter about prayer. The letter is beautiful. I like also the caution that you have uttered for yourself. Love means infinite patience, and exactly in the measure that we become impatient of our own weaknesses, we have to be patient with regard to the weaknesses of our neighbours. We easily enough see their weaknesses; but we have absolutely no knowledge of their striving to overcome them. However, I have forwarded your letter to the Ashram and asked Chhaganlal to read it to the Managing Board and see what can be done. One thing must not be overlooked. That the prayer meetings at the Ashram are not what they should be—full of fragrance and reality—is really due to my own shortcomings of which neither you nor anybody else can have any notion whatsoever. The value of prayer dawned upon me very late in life, and as I have a fair capacity for imposing discipline upon myself, I have by patient and painful striving been able now for some years to conform to the outward form. But do I conform to the spirit? My answer is: No. Whilst it is true that life would be insipid for me without the prayer, I am not absorbed in the message of the prayer at the prayer times. The mind wanders whither it would in spite of incessant striving. If I could but lose myself in the prayer like the great Ali, you will not have to make the complaint that you have rightly registered in your letter. You will not now wonder why I am patient with those who are slack even in attending to the external form. I therefore tremble to impose any iron rule upon the people. Knowing my own weakness, I sympathize with theirs, and hope that if I grow, they must grow with me. You will now understand more than ever what I have so often said to so many people: I must be measured not by what I appear personally, but by how I appear in the lives of the people at the Ashram. The Ashram, especially when I am withdrawn from it, is really the only infallible guide to a knowledge of me.

It is time for me now to keep an appointment.

With love,

Bapu

From the original: C.W. 5252. Courtesy: Mirabehn

173. LETTER TO LIES BURZAS[1]

AS AT THE ASHRAM, SABARMATI,
July 20, 1927

DEAR FRIEND,

I was pleased to receive your note through Sparrow[2].

The more I live the more real the doctrine of oneness of life becomes to me. But the difficulty of practising the doctrine is also growing with me instead of diminishing. Realization of the doctrine seems to be impossible unless we could reduce the 'I' in us to a complete cipher.

Yours sincerely,

From a photostat: S.N. 12525

174. LETTER TO HELENE HAUSSDING

KUMARA PARK, BANGALORE,
July 20, 1927

MY DEAR SPARROW,

I have your letter[3]. I see that you make a distinction between a letter and a postcard. I do not. But tell me why is a postcard not a letter except, of course, for the Postal Department. But seeing that we do not belong to that department, and that so far as we could we should as poor people use the cheapest method of exchanging our views, a postcard should be as good a letter if it could be made to contain all that you wish to say.

I must still continue to dictate my letters. Although I can be said to be a discharged patient, the memory of my being a patient is still very fresh and very definite.

Krishnadas has gone to Bihar in connection with A.I.S.A.'s work, as also to see his guru, and possibly his parents, and he will then go to the Ashram to finish the literary work that is weighing upon his head.

You ask me "if the diseases are due to our own transgressions, that transgression is to be laid at the door of a blind-born

[1] In reply to the addressee's letter dated June 23, 1927

[2] Helene Haussding

[3] Dated June 25, 1927

baby". I thought that being a Buddhist you believed in transmigration and previous existence just as fully as in the present. For me, I implicitly believe that we are a result of our past. I do not believe that every birth means the birth of a new soul. Birth and death to me, therefore, are almost interchangeable words and two modes of expressing the same state. If you will closely analyse the doctrine of transmigration, you will answer for yourself, also the question "why is the air laden with microbes?"

'Pearl'[1] and 'Lal' and others whom you know but casually, and whose names you won't be able to recall, much less to pronounce, are with me just now and will be for a few days longer. My headquarters still remain Bangalore and will remain so practically to the end of August.

I am forwarding your letter to Krishnadas. Here is a letter to the friend.

Yours,
M. K. GANDHI

From a photostat: S.N. 12526

175. LETTER TO JAWAHARLAL NEHRU

KUMARA PARK, BANGALORE,
July 20, 1927

MY DEAR JAWAHARLAL,

I have both your letters. Events have moved fairly fast between the dates of my letter and of the arrival of your letters. Sarojini Devi suggested under pressure from Mahmudabad[2] and Mr. Jinnah that I should press Father to accept the Presidential chair for the coming year. I totally dissented from her view and told her that Dr. Ansari was the only possible President, though even he will be able to do precious little.

Things are going from bad to worse, and it is quite plain that we have not yet drunk the last dregs. But I regard all this rising of the poison to the surface as a necessary process in national up-building. It is quite true that what was burrowing

[1] Not known. The addressee had written: "The knowledge of your love always gives him new strength to prune his plumage for new flights and fights. I am only echoing Pearl's thoughts, words . . ."

[2] The source has "Muhammadabad".

under the surface has now broken through the crust and allows itself to be seen by the naked eye.

I saw the other day in the daily press portraits of yourself, Kamala, Krishna and Indu, or was it you three without Indu, I now forget. You all seem to have grown fuller in the face and all over. I hope that the appearance coincides with the reality.

Though I am not yet physically quite strong, I have resumed the interrupted tour with considerable modifications and in gentle stages. I will not have resumed it but for the fact that collections were locked up and could not be freed unless I presented myself for receiving them.

Shankerlal and Anasuyabehn are just now with me in addition to the party mentioned by me in my previous letter.

From a photostat: S.N. 12611

176. LETTER TO G. D. BIRLA

As at Kumara Park, Bangalore,
July 20, 1927

I have not written to you for the last two mails, nor is there anything particular to say to you just now. But you will be glad to learn that for the first time during my 12 years in India after my return from South Africa, I had what may be called a fairly prolonged real contact with Pandit Malaviyaji. Instead of going to Ooty, he remained in Bangalore as long as it was possible for him to do in view of the Reserve Bank Committee meeting at Calcutta. Of course all the time we were under the same roof, and we had discussions on many things. We reached one definite conclusion, and it was that there should be, just like the All-India Spinners' Association, and All-India Cow-protection Association, a definite body called 'All-India Untouchability Association' brought into being with a definite constructive programme for the uplift of the suppressed classes. I have no time just now to discuss the outlines of the scheme. But I am now looking for an efficient secretary to believe in the work and who would give his whole heart to it to the exclusion practically of every other activity. A further stage will be reached as soon as I can find such a secretary.

Jamnalalji showed me your circular letter to friends. I see how your mind is working in that atmosphere. I would warn you against using the same scales and weights for two different materials. Eyes are well adapted for examining and inspecting a drawing-room furniture. Do they serve the same purpose for examining the furniture in the blue vault overhead?

I have resumed gentle touring. I do not know whether I have been wise in resuming it so early. But I am daily taking a measure of my capacity.

If Lalaji[1] is with you, please give him my love and tell him that there shall be a violent quarrel between him and me if he does not give himself full rest and return with full vigour for tackling the work that lies in front of him.

Yours,

From a photostat: S.N. 14192

177. *SPEECH AT HINDI BHASHA SEVA SAMAJ, MYSORE*[2]

July 20, 1927

After distributing the certificates to the successful students . . . Mahatmaji delivered his address in Hindi. The address was translated into Kannada by Desabhakta Gangadharrao sentence by sentence.

Mahatmaji observed that their President, Mr. M. Venkatakrishnaiya, was called by them all "the grand old man of Mysore". The expression "grand old man" was doubtless dear to him. But he would ask them to call Mr. Venkatakrishnaiya the aged grandfather of Mysore, *vriddhapitamaha*, as Mr. Gangadharrao called, or they might call him by any other better name in Hindi, Sanskrit or Kannada. The address they had presented him had a message behind it. It was that Hindi should become the common language of India, that the people living in India, of whatever community, should all become united as a nation. Today they had not a language which was the language of all their countrymen. Their hearts too were not united. There were differences between Brahmins and non-Brahmins, between Hindus and Mussalmans, and in the Hindu fold itself there were the untouchables who have been kept aloof, as though they were not part of it. Their hearts, instead of being united, had been drawn away from each other. The object of a common language for the whole country was to unite them all. When they were all thus united by this bond of a common language they would all understand the meaning of "grand old man". Let them imagine for a moment that they were living in the time of the Pandavas. If aged Bhishma came there, and they all said that the "grand old man" came, how ludicrous it would be.

[1] Lajpat Rai

[2] At its second Hindi convocation

They must ever remember Bhishma and his vows. Whenever they thought of Bhishma, every one of them would be thrilled with certain courage and heroic spirit, and everyone would be reminded of Bhishma's vows, and would receive an awakening. If they but put themselves in mind of Bhishma every morning, he was sure they would develop courage and heroism, so essential for national regeneration.

Mahatmaji expressed his gratification that in Mysore Hindi *prachar* had made such splendid progress. He thanked the *pracharaks* for giving tuition to as many as 700 pupils in the course of 11 months. Mr. Jamna Prasad did not desire that a gathering like the present should be called a convocation. He dreaded the use of the expression "convocation". For his own part, he did not see why it should not be called a "convocation". It meant simply a congregation and conversation. But through their association with English education, such an occasion had come to be regarded as some grand function. If they all made up their minds to spread Hindi, to learn Hindi themselves, and to show their sympathy, it would be a great thing, and this day would be remembered always.

In conclusion, Mahatmaji observed:

My appeal to you is that you should all give your mind to the spread of Hindi by providing the necessary funds and encouragement. You should not depend for funds from outside. There is no need for it. For this work, you must collect funds that may be necessary for one, two or more years. I believe it is possible to collect the funds needed at this gathering. I wish the progress would be greater in the future, and more abiding. To those who are the happy recipients of certificates I say, use the knowledge of Hindi for the service of the country. I thank you all for honouring me with the address, and for giving me the opportunity to participate in the function.

The Hindu, 22-7-1927

178. SPEECH IN REPLY TO ADDRESSES, MYSORE

July 20, 1927

Mahatmaji, in the course of his joint reply to the several addresses presented to him[1], said that their love for him was so great that to save his time and to afford him relief, they had arranged to present them all together. He was thankful to them for it. It pleased him to learn that His Highness's Government had shown their sympathy for the khaddar movement, and had agreed to the abolition of octroi on khadi imported into the city. All the addresses had alluded to the khadi and charkha movements. He was pleased to note that the people of Mysore liked khadi and the charkha, but his experience told him that he was not to be deceived by such praise as they showered in the addresses, for they had not gone far beyond the region of praise and entered the practical region.

He was delighted to see the beautiful city of Mysore with its palaces and mansions, its broad and well-kept roads, gardens and parks. This was one side of the view. When he considered the other side, the poor in the city and in the villages steeped in misery and pain, his heart was touched. He wished to see the day when the Maharajas in India and their advisers showed love and pity to the poor, who were grovelling in poverty and misery, so that the gulf between them, between the rich and the poor, may be bridged. It was not that he hated palaces and mansions, or gardens and parks. It was his desire to see that in India, the rich and the poor were united at heart. It was to bridge the gulf that was between them, it was to bring about contact between the rich and the poor that his efforts were directed these seven years. The gulf could not be bridged by such works as the Bhadravati Works and the gold mines of Kolar. The Bhadravati Works and the gold mines were doubtless necessary. The mines of contact between the rich and the poor was possible only by means of the hand-spun yarn. They might know that the bridge between Rishikesh and Gangotri called the Lakshmanjhula was constructed out of hand-spun yarn. Let none despise it. When once they worked at the charkha, they would see that it was what he represented it to be. He was overjoyed to learn that His Highness the Maharaja of Mysore also worked at the spinning-wheel and had thereby set an example to his people.

To the Kaniyars he said that he shared their grief. As long as Hindu society, observed Mahatmaji, kept even one Hindu outside its pale, he would

[1] By the Mysore City Municipal Council, the Mysore District Board, the Mysore Congress Committee, the Dattatreya Gorakshana Mandali, the Kaniyars and other citizens of Mysore. Gandhiji's reply in Hindi was rendered into Kanarese by Gangadharrao Deshpande.

also consider himself as a *Panchama*. He could not conceive of swaraj without the removal of the taint of untouchability.

He would, however, ask the Kaniyars why it was that they should think they were better than the *Panchamas*, and why they should desire to be included in the four *varnas*. His understanding of the Shastras told him that no one *varna* was superior to another. His impression was that the Brahmin was superior to the others when he maintained his own dharma, which was that of service. The Kshatriyas were likewise superior in their own dharma, of protecting the weak against the strong. There was no superiority by those of one *varna* preying upon those of the others. The Kaniyars should follow the example of Yudhishthira who, until his dog was allowed to enter *swarga*, would not enter it. Until the *Adi Karnatakas* also secured their proper place in Hindu society, they should not be anxious for their own rights. He was glad that the Kaniyars did not eat beef and drink intoxicating liquors.

As regards the question of temple-entry, Mahatmaji said that they had as much right to enter the temples as he himself or any other Hindu had. It grieved him to learn that the Kaniyars were kept out of temples. They had however to bear their difficulties patiently. Mahatmaji assured the Kaniyars that His Highness the Maharaja and the Government had been doing their utmost to improve the condition of the Kaniyars. One thing which they, along with other Hindus, ought to do was *tapascharya* and thereby attain *atma shuddhi*. The Hindu Shastras told them that even Brahma was able to undertake the task of creation by means of *tapascharya*. Parvati, the consort of Parameshwara, got him for her husband by *tapascharya*. The Kaniyars likewise could wrest all their rights by *tapascharya*.

In reply to the address of the Gorakshana Mandali, Mahatmaji said he was pleased to learn that in Mysore Hindus and Muslims were living in perfect amity and concord. It pleased him also to learn that the majority of the Muslims were also with the Hindus on the question of the prevention of cow-slaughter. He congratulated both the communities and wished that all the communities in India would follow the example of Mysore and maintain cordiality of relationship with each other. He had already stated his views on the question of legislation for cow-protection. In those States in which the majority of the Muslims were with the Hindus, the State, observed Mahatmaji, was justified in legislating for the prevention of cow-slaughter. So long as those who espoused the cause of cow-protection did no constructive work for preventing cow-slaughter, they could not be said doing any useful work. He had been trying to tell them why it should be done. As without knowledge *mukti* was not possible, so in the matter of cow-protection, mere blind devotion would not do. In his writings and speeches, he had discussed the question and they should all study them.

In conclusion, Mahatmaji thanked the various bodies for the addresses presented to him that day. He appealed to the ladies to buy khaddar and to show their interest in hand-spinning. The meeting terminated, as it had commenced, with national songs.

The Hindu, 25-7-1927

179. NOTES

The Late Sir Ganga Ram

The death of Sir Ganga Ram removes from our midst an able and practical agriculturist, a great philanthropist and a friend of the widow. Though advanced in years, Sir Ganga Ram had the energy of youth. His optimism was equal to the obstinacy with which he held on to his views. I had the privilege of coming in fair contact with him recently. And though we could not agree on several matters, I recognized in him a sincere reformer and a great worker. And although, with all the respect due to his age and experience, I expressed my dissent from many of his views with energy and insistence, his affection for me, whom he regarded comparatively to him as a young man of but yesterday, grew with my opposition to some of his extraordinary views on Indian poverty. He was so eager for long discussions with me, and so hopeful of weaning me from the error of my ways, that he offered to take me to England at his own expense, and promised to drive all the nonsense out of my head. Though I could not accept the offer which he had seriously meant, I wrote to him on the eve of his departure, promising to see him and undertaking to convert him to the creed of the spinning-wheel, which he thought was fit only to be burnt as firewood. The reader may well imagine my grief therefore over the news of his sudden death. But it is a death which we could all wish to have. For he went to England not on a pleasure trip, but on what he considered to be a peremptory duty. He has therefore died in harness. India has every reason to be proud of having a man like Sir Ganga Ram as one of her distinguished sons. I tender both my congratulations and condolences to the family of the deceased reformer.

Congress President for 1928

The election of Dr. Ansari as President of the National Assembly for the coming year is a foregone conclusion. There is no one on the national horizon to challenge the election. Dr. Ansari is as good an Indian as he is a Mussalman. He has been never suspected of fanaticism. He has been continuously Joint

Secretary of the Congress for years. His recent efforts to promote union are well known. And as a matter of fact, had I not stood in the way at Belgaum, Shrimati Sarojini Devi at Cawnpore and Sjt. Srinivasa Iyengar at Gauhati, Dr. Ansari would have been elected on any of these occasions. For his name was on everybody's lips when these elections took place. But special reasons postponed Dr. Ansari's claim, and it now seems that fates had conspired to postpone the election so that he might come in when he was most wanted. If any possible scheme of Hindu-Muslim unity is to be found acceptable to both the parties, Dr. Ansari undoubtedly is the man to pilot such a scheme through the Congress. I respectfully dissent from the view that in a Congress which is predominantly Hindu, a Hindu should be the President, so that such a scheme might be claimed to have whole-hearted acceptance by the Hindus. On the contrary, nothing can be more auspicious for the inauguration of such a scheme than that, in spite of the poisonous atmosphere prevailing in the country, a national association containing a preponderating majority of Hindus should unanimously and whole-heartedly elect a Mussalman as its President. That fact by itself would be an earnest of the Hindu desire for such unity. And of all the Mussalman nationalists, there is no Mussalman more respected than Dr. Ansari by the Mussalmans in general. It is, therefore, in my opinion, in every way desirable, that Dr. Ansari should guide the National Congress during the coming year. For it is not merely the passing of a scheme that is wanted, but a proper working of it is, perhaps, more necessary than its acceptance by the two parties. And assuming that a scheme acceptable to both is passed, ceaseless watch will be required during the coming year as to its operation. Dr. Ansari is the most fitted for this work. I hope, therefore, that all the provinces will unanimously recommend Dr. Ansari's name for the highest honour that is in the gift of the National Assembly.

KHADI IN UDAIPUR

Some time ago the daily Press published the news that khadi workers in Bijolia were arrested and that the manager of the khadi organization there was required to give an undertaking that he would give notice to the authorities of any person coming to him. On receiving this information Sheth Jamnalalji proceeded to Udaipur to ascertain the true situation. Having seen the authorities in Udaipur and then having gone to Bijolia, Jamnalalji came to Bangalore for attending the meeting of the Council of the

All-India Spinners' Association, and the South India Khadi Exhibition. During the Bangalore visit, he told me that it was quite true that two khadi workers had been arrested in Bijolia, and that they were arrested not for doing khadi work, but under the suspicion that they were meddling with the politics of the State. The authorities assured Jamnalalji that they not only did not wish to interfere with khadi work, but that they welcomed khadi workers, and that they were even prepared to give khadi work substantial help under well-defined conditions. Jamnalalji then saw the local authorities in Bijolia, and it has now been arranged, that no undertaking is to be taken from the khadi workers, it being understood between Jamnalalji and the local authorities, that the khadi workers will not directly or indirectly take part in or interfere with the politics of the State, and that they will confine themselves merely to the organization of the people for khadi production and sales. Jamnalalji had no hesitation in giving the undertaking for the simple reason that it has been the uniform and invariable practice of the Charkha Sangh to confine its work in the Indian States purely to khadi work.

Young India, 21-7-1927

180. STARVING MUNICIPAL BOARDS

The brief address, that Sjt. Vallabhbhai Patel delivered before the First Conference held in Gujarat of its Municipalities and Local Boards, is worthy of study by everyone interested in the efficient working of Municipalities, Local Boards and District Boards. It is packed with facts as startling as they are disturbing. On the one hand, he says, the responsibilities of these bodies have been increased by conferring on them larger rights, and on the other, the means of discharging those responsibilities have been somehow or other curtailed. Himself being President of one of the first class Municipalities of India, he has a long record of municipal service behind him. Even the Government have been obliged to give his administration of Ahmedabad Municipality unstinted and unmixed praise. He has slaved for his Municipality as few persons have done. Like Phirozeshah Mehta, having accepted the chair, he has held the work of his office to be far more important for him than any other national work, no matter how urgent or greater in extent it might be. Having made the choice of his dharma, he has preferred it, even though a superior has often called for the exercise of his singular abilities and powers of application. His address, therefore, needs to be studied carefully by everyone concerned. He backs his assertions with concrete facts which anybody may challenge. He thinks that the 157 Municipalities of the Bombay Presidency are economically in straightened circumstances. In some cases, he says, the salaries of municipal teachers are in arrears. Their incomes are really inadequate for the work before them. Their sanitary measures have to be held in abeyance for want of funds. Compulsory education schemes are shelved for similar reasons. He adduces in support of many of his statements his own painful experience, and he severely criticizes the Government's niggardly policy in connection with Municipalities.

The President is as unsparing of the citizens as he is of the Government. He exclaims:

> Citizens of our cities regulate their lives as if they were living not in cities but in villages, and therefore, many houses have no sanitary accommodation or receptacle reserved for collection of rubbish. They do not hesitate to keep their cattle anyhow, though living in crowded quarters. Shepherds bring their droves of cattle and plant them in the midst of cities with the greatest unconcern. Generally speaking, people are indifferent about observing simple rules of health and sanitation. They neither know how to observe them for themselves or for the sake of their neighbours. It is common experience to see them shoving rubbish on to their neighbour's yards. They do not hesitate to throw from their heights rubbish or water on to the streets heedless of the passers-by. They would spit anywhere, they would perform their natural functions anywhere. The condition of villages is no better. Rubbish-heaps meet your gaze on approaching them. Village ponds become stinking cess-pools, and soaking dirt near village wells is a common feature.

Sjt. Vallabhbhai Patel says, and most people would agree with him, "that it would be criminal to look to the Government for help in such matters".

I suppose that he has purposely refrained from touching in his address upon the petty intrigues that go on in Municipalities, and make the work of the real worker and reformer almost an impossibility. Some of the foremost workers tried, but to meet severe disappointment. Pandit Jawaharlal Nehru in Allahabad, Babu Rajendra Prasad in Patna found intrigue to be too trying for them. Deshbandhu Chittaranjan Das strove manfully against heavy odds, and the responsibility nearly crushed him. The fact is that the municipal voter has not yet become alive to a sense of his civic responsibility. He does not regard himself as in any way responsible for the well-being of all the citizens. Our educational system is not designed to give an object-lesson in corporate responsibility. Municipal councillors therefore need feel responsible to no one.

In the heyday of Non-co-operation, I ventured to suggest that if the people had really developed a sense of civic responsibility, three-fourths of the municipal work could be done without Government's assistance or patronage. I showed by taking facts and figures of municipal work in Mehmadabad, that the citizens could manage their municipal work with half the cost without having a statutory Municipality. And I showed too that a statutory Municipality became a necessity only when the councillors had no co-operation from the people, or when they wished to force their reform schemes down the throats of unwilling citizens. They needed in a small place like Mehmadabad no elaborate machinery to light their streets, to clean their latrines, and their roads, and to manage their schools, and there could be no question of police, if the citizens were all good and pure, or if they had a citizen-guard for guarding peaceful citizens against thieves, loafers or hooligans. Those men who are real servants of the people, would become municipal councillors for the sake of service and not for the sake of gaining fame or engaging in intrigues and finding employment for their needy friends or relatives. What is wanted, therefore, is zealous education of the people on the part of workers, not merely by means of speeches, but through silent social service rendered without the slightest expectation of reward, even in the shape of thanks, but on the contrary, with every expectation of receiving the execration and worse of a public enraged over any attempt to make it give up its superstitions or insanitary habits. I know of a poor sanitary inspector, who was very nearly lynched for his zeal in impartially getting hold of all the culprits who with criminal indifference dirtied the streets of the town, whose sanitation the poor man was paid to guard.

Young India, 21-7-1927

181. 'G' WARD D. C. C. KHADI BHANDAR

Sjt. M. N. Padweker of 'G' Ward District Congress Committee, Bombay, draws my attention to the omission from the list of khadi bhandars published in these columns of this bhandar. I hasten to rectify the unintended omission. Such omissions are bound to occur whilst the All-India Spinners' Association is trying to secure an exhaustive list of khadi bhandars within its knowledge.

In his letter, the writer says:

> The shop was about to be closed for want of good sales; but the energetic efforts of some of the workers, who took up hawking khadi on Sundays and holidays, the only days they could spare being employed for their maintenance on week days, have saved it. In Bombay, this is the only shop which endeavours to take khadi to every door; and the workers are quite confident that in the near future this bhandar will have taken the message of khadi to every house in the city and suburbs.

I wish the workers every success.

Young India, 21-7-1927

182. LETTER TO MIRABEHN

MYSORE,
July 21, 1927

CHI. MIRA,

I have your letter. I shall try to secure Shanti's room for you if it is at all possible.

With love,

BAPU

From the original: C.W. 5253. Courtesy: Mirabehn

183. LETTER TO S. V. KAUJALGI

As at Kumara Park, Bangalore,
July 21, 1927

Dear Friend,

I have your letter. Owing to the touring, I have not been able to overtake it. I have shown it to Gangadharrao, and I see that though you are both servants of the country, you are temperamentally so hopelessly different or seem so to me.

I have not resumed the tour with full confidence. I simply felt that what little strength I had gathered might be carefully used for finishing in a mild form the programme that had already been mapped out and for realizing the khadi collections. The tour was undertaken also purely in the interest of khadi. I had neither the desire nor the capacity for doing general propaganda work in the existing state of the country. For me, khadi is my propaganda. For, if that one thing can be shown to be a thorough success, everything else will follow. My idea is that we must have at least one constructive item made a demonstrable success on a wide scale. As it is, the people seem to have lost confidence in themselves, and have made up their minds that they can succeed in no constructive effort.

Gangadharrao is a wholehogger like myself for khadi. I would, therefore, let him take me to those parts which may be promising either for khadi production, or for sale, or for collections for khadi. I would therefore not ask you to join me in the tour, but would expect you to give Gangadharrao or khadi work such help as you can by way of writing to friends in the places I may visit.

Mysore will take me up to the end of August, and if I feel at all strong enough, I shall do the Tamil Districts after. For Karnatak, I am not likely therefore to be ready, if at all this year, before the middle of October. But I should know definitely only after the Mysore tour is finished. I am asking everywhere for reduction of the programme to a minimum and avoidance of places which can be avoided.

Yours sincerely,

Sjt. S. V. Kaujalgi
Bijapur

From a photostat: S.N. 12612

184. LETTER TO Y. M. PARNERKAR

MYSORE,
July 21, 1927

DEAR PARNERKAR,

I have secured the forms that are kept in the Palace Diary at Mysore for some guidance to us. I enclose them herewith.

I had a chat with Maganlal to the effect that we should have an accurate record of all the observations that we may make. These forms may help you to draw up something necessary. Of course I would like our forms to be kept in Hindi or Gujarati.

Yours sincerely,

Encl. 1

From a microfilm: S.N. 12920

185. LETTER TO K. P. PADMANABHA IYER

AS AT KUMARA PARK, BANGALORE,
July 21, 1927

DEAR FRIEND,

I have your letter. Do you recommend the diet mentioned in your letter on the strength of extensive experiences and experiments? And, if you do, I would like you to give me an idea of the experiments you have made. Have you considered the real values of banana and tender coconut-milk? Is it not a fact that banana and coconut contain little or no proteid; whereas, milk contains comparatively a fair amount of proteid? And is it not also a fact that coconut fat is less digestible because less assimilable than animal fat, that is, ghee? Could you recommend coconut-milk in the place of cow's milk for babies?

Yours sincerely,

SJT. K. P. PADMANABHA IYER
SUB ASST. SURGEON
A. E. DISPENSARY
PUDUKKOTTAI
Via TUTICORIN

From a photostat: S.N. 14193

186. SPEECH TO ADI KARNATAKAS, MYSORE

[*July 21, 1927*][1]

I am both happy and unhappy to meet you. I am happy because I have had occasion to purify myself by having met you, but I am unhappy that for health and other reasons I have to reconcile myself to staying in palaces, although I know full well the miserable conditions in which you live. Truth or God whose votary I am tells me every moment that my place is not in palaces but among you. But this may be a temporary fit of desire for renunciation. It may be that the moment I leave these surroundings I will forget you and your cottages, but it is also possible, and let me hope that a day will come, when God will give me the strength to do the thing I prize so much. Today I have just come to assure you that there is an ever-increasing band of workers interested in and striving for your welfare. I congratulate the Brahmin lady who has dedicated herself to your service. It is my firm faith that in the near future Hinduism will be purged of the stain of untouchability. There is no one high or low in the sight of God, and he who considers himself superior to another is described by the Shastras as foolish. But so far as you are concerned, I am quite sure that your salvation is in your hands. How can you, being Hindus, whose duty it is to protect the cow, eat beef and carrion? It is because it is cheap, I am told. Well, nothing is cheap that holds religion cheap, nothing is dear that holds religion dear. I tell you I find it difficult to persuade the orthodox to mix with you, for they tell me, that you are given to beef-eating, liquor and the like. If you will therefore cleanse yourselves you will make work easy for me. Don't retort that the touchables are no better. They are no better, I know, but they may not listen through their pride, you need not imitate them. You have to raise yourselves. You therefore have to purify yourselves. And if you do, no power on earth can stop your onward march.

Young India, 4-8-1927

[1] From a report in *The Hindu*, 25-7-1927

187. LETTER TO KUSUMBEHN DESAI

BANGALORE,
Ashadh Vad 8, Samvat 1983, July 22, 1927

CHI. KUSUM,

About Haribhai what shall I write to you? You are not alone in your loss. Many others share the grief. But one must bear one's grief. Everyone departs at the appointed time. We too shall do that. I need not have written even this to you, for Bhai Najuklal tells me that you have shown great courage. And that befits one who has been trained by Haribhai, because you were more his pupil than his wife.[1]

What do you wish to do now? I do not know if your parents are alive. Let me know your position. If you wish to live in the Ashram, let me know that too. Write to me without any reservations.

Blessings from
BAPU

[From Gujarati]
Bapuna Patro—Kusumbehn Desaine, p. 3

188. LETTER TO NAJUKLAL N. CHOKSI

[*July 22, 1927*]

BHAISHRI NAJUKLAL,

I got your letter. Before that, I had received Dr. Chandulal's telegram and had sent a reply to it. It must have been received there.

Please hand over the enclosed letter[2] to Chi. Kusum. Let me know all the facts about her. I hope Chi. Moti and the child keep well.

Blessings from
BAPU

From a photostat of the Gujarati: S.N. 12140-A

[1] *Vide* also "Death of a Satyagrahi", 7-8-1927.
[2] *Vide* the preceding item.

189. LETTER TO RAMESHWARDAS PODDAR

Ashadh Vad 10 [July 23, 1927][1]

BHAI RAMESHWARDAS,

Your letter. I am writing to Nanasaheb Deo. The venture just undertaken is highly commendable. Nanasaheb will write to me if any help from Vinoba or Kakasaheb is needed for this work.

Keep Ramanama firm in your heart.

Blessings from

BAPU

From a photostat of the Hindi: G.N. 184

190. SPEECH AT FAREWELL MEETING, MYSORE

July 23, 1927

In the course of his speech, Mahatmaji thanked the citizens of Mysore for their contribution and proceeded to observe that their leading citizen, Sowcar D. Banumaiya, had given Rs. 1,501 and to him he had given his word that his contribution would be used only for the poor in this State. It was his desire and that of his co-workers that whatever was collected in Mysore should if possible be spent in Mysore. It was however the usual thing, where there was not an adequate number of the poor, or where there was no scope for encouraging the manufacture of khadi, to spend the amount collected in another part of the country, where poverty was acute, and where they could not raise any fund. For example, in Utkal Province, where the people were extremely poor and miserable, and where consequently they could not raise any fund, funds raised elsewhere had to be spent on khadi work and thereby for feeding the poor of Utkal.

Bombay and Cutch had subscribed large sums, but not a pie could be spent in Bombay. All that was collected there was spent elsewhere. He had collected lakhs of rupees from his Marwari friends in Marwar, but they were not spent there.

They must bear in mind one thing, that South India and North India are not separate, and that in South India, Andhra, Tamilnad and Karnataka

[1] *Vide* Vol. XXXIII, "Letter to Rameshwardas Poddar", before 5-6-1927 and 12-6-1927.

are not separate. They should never think that there is no sort of connection or relationship between these, or between North India and South India. They should all make effort for the prosperity of Karnataka. It was not merely for Karnataka, but for the progress and prosperity of the whole country.

As regards the sums raised in the town, and especially that one on the way to Krishnarajasagara, viz., Rs. 51 given at the Tuberculosis Sanatorium, he saw the patients there and they had left a deep impression on his mind. To use Pandit Malaviyaji's expression, their gift was *suddha* cowrie given with a pure heart. He had no idea they would offer him anything, and when such pure gift came up [of] its own accord there was a heavy responsibility on those entrusted with it. That was not the only *suddha* cowrie he had received. He had been daily praying to God that not a pie should be mis-spent, that every pie may be utilized for the cause. The accounts may be examined not merely by the donors, but by the public, and mistakes and mishandling pointed out. If they slept away, if they gave no thought to it, those that handled the fund today might die, and there would be none to look to its administration or to carry on the work.

In India there were many institutions, many charitable institutions existing for promoting dharma. The funds of not a few of these were used for personal ends. If the public knew their responsibility such things should be impossible. Mahatmaji appealed to one and all to see that the amount raised for the cause of the charkha was properly spent. In order, however, to ensure the success of the undertaking, they needed men who had a conscience and a sense of their duty and responsibility.[1]

There is no lack of efficiency among the people of Karnataka. You have a distinguished engineer[2], you have distinguished musicians, you have a distinguished artist[3], and many others that I could name in various other spheres. I want you now to produce a distinguished spinning expert. You have three khadi shops here. I wish you had need for them and even more, but today I know, and this meeting is an eloquent proof of it, that there is no need for three shops. Even many of you who are sympathetically inclined towards khadi are not wearing it. Have therefore instead of those three, one efficient khadi shop and organize it properly. There are many institutions where the charkha has been introduced. I was told that His Highness' bodyguards were spinning, but I also know how inefficiently this work is going on. In all those institutions and for the bodyguards you must engage a spinning expert. Bad yarn, like bad music, is good for nothing.

[1] This and the preceding paragraphs are from *The Hindu*, 25-7-1927.

[2] Dr. M. Vishveshvarayya

[3] Venkatappa

I would like to assure those who would serve *Daridranarayana* that there is music, art, economy and joy in the spinning-wheel. I have seen quite a number of institutions in Mysore—the Princess Krishnarajamanni Sanatorium where I expected nothing, but where the patients insisted on my receiving their genuine token of love for the poor millions; the home for the blind and the mute of which the blind inmates have entertained me to soulful music these two days; the home for the destitute and the infirm as also your school for *Adi Karnataka* boys. These are proofs of the Maharaja's humanitarian spirit, but I may tell you that you have to extend it still further. The blind and the infirm have, thanks to our charitable instincts, not to go without food. But there are millions of our villagers, who cannot go out to beg, who solely depend on a fraction of an acre of land each, and who have often to go without food. We are responsible for their starvation and their poverty. In Mysore which is the home of humanitarian and philanthropic institutions I would urge you to have some provision for the toiling, starving millions.

You are doubly fortunate. You have a glorious climate and wonderful natural scenery, and you have a ruler, who from all accounts is good and benevolent and always thinking of the welfare of his people. In a State like this there should not be a single beggar or a single man suffering from starvation and impoverishment. I saw the Krishnarajasagara dam today and was delighted to see that wonderful engineering feat of Sir M. Vishveshvarayya, the second I am told of its kind in the world. In a home of such great enterprises I beg of you to make some provision for *Daridranarayana*. I thank you for the love you have showered on me, and I pray that I may be worthy of it.

Young India, 11-8-1927

191. LETTER TO N. R. MALKANI

KUMARA PARK, BANGALORE,
July 24, 1927

MY DEAR MALKANI,

I have your beautiful letter. Let nothing be done in a hurry. I wrote four days ago at length to Thadani and asked him to share the letter with you.[1]

Gujarat Vidyalaya at present is out of the question. But if you will place yourself in my hands, of course, I have many uses for you. But that is neither here nor there. Discuss everything firmly and calmly with everyone who has the slightest influence over you and then see where you stand. You know what lasting association with me means. Though you may never have to mount the gallows, you must be prepared to mount them as you would mount a throne or a professorial chair.

Thadani did not understand my previous letter at all, or my letters to you. I do not know how my last letter to him will fare.

Yours sincerely,
BAPU

From a photostat: G.N. 877; also S.N. 12616

192. LETTER TO N. R. MALKANI

July 24, 1927

MY DEAR MALKANI,

I have your letter which I was daily expecting.

I understand your situation. You must finish the contract with Thadani first. You have now taken up Sindhi Sahitya Sabha and of course you could not possibly refrain from the flood relief service. When you are free from these obligations you should write to me. Let there be no haste this time. You should discuss the thing fully with your wife and mother-in-law. If while you are testing yourself, you feel more attracted to any work there rather than being at my beck and call, you shall be absolved. If you come back to me, you should do so because you cannot

[1] *Vide* "Letter to N. V. Thadani", 19-7-1927.

do otherwise. After all you will give a good account of yourself wherever you are. Only I had my eye on you as one of the 'chosen few'. But that is not a forced growth. Being in that state must give the greatest satisfaction to the soul. I would therefore like you to test yourself through and through before you return to me. It won't be a bed of roses. Though I have many plans, I do not know where I should put you, even if you came to me today. All I know is that I should put you where there is the greatest heat.

You may share this letter with as many friends as you like.

I am sorry for Thadani. I know that he won't misunderstand me long. My bitter language was not from anger but from love.

Please ask Jairamdas if he is in need of funds. Have you many workers for the flood relief? I see that where we have not enough true workers, funds are useless.

With love,

Yours,
BAPU

From a photostat: G.N. 873

193. LETTER TO RAIHANA TYABJI

KUMARA PARK, BANGALORE,
July 24, 1927

MY DEAR RAIHANA,

I have your letter. As you think that the matters between you and Mother are fixed up, I am not writing to her or to Father, but look to you to smooth your way, which you will do if you know your own mind and adhere to it with firmness though with greatest gentleness.

We are not bound to patronize any industry whatsoever. But when in satisfying our vital wants we are bound to patronize some industry, we naturally patronize that which supports our neighbours who need our help most. This answers your question.

With love,

Yours sincerely,
BAPU

From a photostat: S.N. 9605

194. LETTER TO K. T. CHAKRAVARTI

KUMARA PARK, BANGALORE,
July 24, 1927

DEAR FRIEND,

I have your letter of the 11th instant. I hope that "your prayer to lead me to true light" will be answered.

What passage in *Young India* made you think that I considered the treatment I received from the Congress in 1901 was "beggarly"? Anyway I certainly did not expect nor had any right to expect better treatment than I received from everyone. I do not recall the introduction you refer to, but I have referred elsewhere to the fatherly treatment I received from Surendranath Banerjea. Sir Dinsha Wacha had a perfect right to stop me as he did.[1] It would be intolerable if every youngster, because he has rendered some slight service, claimed the privileges which old and tried servants of the nation should have. Gokhale's name you will find repeatedly mentioned in these chapters for the simple reason that he singled me out for his special attention, not because I think that I deserved it or because he alone gave me my due when others failed. Can you not see that I have endeavoured to show in the chapters that the connection between Gokhale and myself was spontaneous even as it is between husband and wife? It would be a sorrowful thing for the world if a woman, because she happens to attract a particular person and not others, were to consider that she has been slighted by the others and her merit recognized only by one man. Can you not see that these things illustrate the mysterious working of nature, and that these affections can only be somewhat accounted for by the doctrine of previous birth and previous connection?

Yours sincerely,

K. T. CHAKRAVARTI
CHITTAGONG

From a photostat: S.N. 12615

[1] *Vide An Autobiography*, Pt. III, Ch. XV.

195. A LETTER

KUMARA PARK, BANGALORE,
July 24, 1927

DEAR FRIEND,

I have your letter. I am certainly sorry that General Dyer is suffering from paralysis. I do not think that his paralysis has any necessary connection with his action in Jallianwala Bagh. Have you considered the implications of such beliefs? After all people whom we consider to be good and pure have also been known to have suffered from serious diseases. My own case is in point. My dysentery, appendicitis and this time a mild attack of paralysis must have been known to you. I should be very sorry if some good Englishmen were to think that these diseases were due to my fierce opposition as it must appear in their estimation to the English Government. Though I believe that every disease is a direct result of some transgression of Nature's laws either in this birth or the previous, we have got no data to know invariably the transgressions which led to these diseases.

Yours sincerely,

From a photostat: S.N. 14194

196. LETTER TO KHURSHID

KUMARA PARK, BANGALORE,
July 24, 1927

This one line to acknowledge your letter. I was thinking why I have not heard from any of you. How I wish you were with me during this trip because this is a most beautiful country. There is much art here to be seen, and very fine music.

You will tell me what happens ultimately about your getting a post as a music teacher in an Indian State.

I am keeping good health.

Yours sincerely,

MISS KHURSHID
NEPEAN SEA ROAD
BOMBAY

From a photostat: S.N. 14195

197. LETTER TO KUVALAYANAND

KUMARA PARK, BANGALORE,
July 24, 1927

DEAR FRIEND,

I have your letter. I am taking all the care I can of the body and the tour is taken as gently as possible. I quite agree with you that if I had not moved at all, perhaps, it would have been better. But as the doctor here encouraged me, I felt that I had no right to postpone the tour. After all one has got to take risks in this life and know . . .[1] a body which must perish one day. And, if any mishap occurs, I shall certainly not blame the yogic exercises in the slightest degree but I shall blame myself for having tried an experiment which was fraught with some danger.

The exercises continue as before. Do please come whenever you can.

Yours sincerely,

From a photostat: S.N. 14196

198. LETTER TO SUNDER LAL MATHUR

KUMARA PARK, BANGALORE,
July 24, 1927

DEAR FRIEND,

I have your letter. Any clean earth, black or red, but clay will do. The mud poultice should be taken at least for seven days continuously and if it does good, you may continue it till you feel that you have had enough. For dyspepsia, a complete fast with copious draughts of water is a fine thing even while earth bandages continue. And if you have the fast, you should clean the bowels once a day by means of enema.

Yours sincerely,

SJT. SUNDER LAL MATHUR, B.A., LL.B.
Vakil
PIRGHAIB
MORADABAD (U.P.)

From a photostat: S.N. 14197

[1] The source has a blank here.

199. LETTER TO J. W. PETAVEL

KUMARA PARK, BANGALORE,
July 24, 1927

DEAR FRIEND,

I have your letter. I shan't get tired of you, because it is not an easy thing to tire me out; but soon you will have to give me up as a bad case. For even your latest letter does not give me the bread I want.

Which is the brilliant successful model colony referred to in your article? I wish I could persuade you to write less and do more. I have told you what I am doing at Sabarmati. It seems to me to be along the lines suggested by you without the American . . .[1] which is your ideal but not mine. You seem to me to build on insufficient data. For instance, what is the use of your telling me that Germans grow 70,000 grains out of one grain, whereas, we in India grow 70 out of one. For, what applies to Germany does not apply to India and will not for generations to come. I wish too that I could cure you of the habit of stringing together all the distinguished names you can think of, without regard to the relevancy of such stringing. Will you not, like a scientist, appeal to cold reason testing every fact for yourself and enabling the reader to test your tests? Surely you should by this time know that authorities are not required in support of sound propositions except by way of some little stimulation, and they are worse than useless when they are invoked in aid of propositions of doubtful value.

If I was the editor-in-chief of your magazine, nine-tenth of what I read in the specimens you sent me I should score out, and I would require you to rewrite fortifying it with concrete facts, and then I would perhaps still further condense it. Just think what a saving of time it would mean for the busy reader and saving of expense in printer's ink, compositors' and proof-readers' salaries, etc., and the matter thus printed would pass muster even in scientific scale and if it was seasonable, it would sell like hot cakes.

Yours sincerely,

From a photostat: S.N. 14198

[1] The source has a blank here.

200. SPEECH AT CIVIC AND SOCIAL PROGRESS ASSOCIATION, BANGALORE[1]

July 24, 1927

FRIENDS,

I have heard of the work of your Association and I am very much pleased. You have today given me an opportunity to learn of your activities and I am gratified to find that one of the prominent among them is the effort that you are making towards the betterment of your *Adi Karnatakas* here. Though one of the chief ways of achieving the progress of your city is by means of an association such as yours, I can tell you, there is no other *punya karma*[2] than this work of uplifting your own brothers and sisters known as *Adi Karnatakas*. But as you yourselves have stated in your address, you have done much in this direction, but much more, very much more remains to be done. You know fully well, the work would never be complete, would never be perfect so long as there is a temple in this land which shuts out your *Adi Karnataka* brother, and so long as there is one person amongst you who would not allow the *Adi Karnataka* to approach him as a brother.

Of course you know the condition of the poor *Adi Karnataka* and you also know that it is not part of the Hindu dharma to eat the flesh of the cow. On the other hand protection of the cow is enjoined on all by the Hindu dharma. And you who know of this, have you taught this to your brethren in the villages? Ignorance of this Hindu dharma had bred evil habits amongst them who are also Hindus, but they must be made to understand that you are really anxious to help them better their lives according to Hindu dharma. You must all open out your hearts to make them understand that. You must do your duty by them if you are true members of the society to which you belong.

Do not think that you have only one duty, the duty to your country to perform. There is also the duty to society and these two are interdependent. You cannot perform the one and neglect the other. You cannot hold them as apart from each other. You will realize that in the uplift of your brethren, in the reform

[1] Gandhiji's speech in Hindi was rendered into Kanarese by Gangadharrao Deshpande.

[2] Meritorious deed

of your social evils, in making your society a real force in the country and in establishing communal harmony, perfect and long-lasting friendship between Hindus and Mussalmans—in all these lies also your duty to country. Thus you will realize that both duties are one for you and if you are to serve your country you must also serve the society to which you belong.

Having realized this you will have to turn your attention to the crying evils of early-marriage system. Do not call it dharma or a thing supported by Shastras that you can marry a little girl fondling on the knee, that it could be straightway married and asked to become a housewife. And yet, I have known many of my friends, learned lawyers and doctors, educated and enlightened men marry girls before they were thirteen. (Laughter) Friends, it is no laughing matter, it is a matter for shame and tears. I tell you, there is no sadder evil in our society than this. You must think of this seriously and not with laughter. Our youth must resolve that they would not marry girls before they are fifteen. It is they who must help in this task of reform. You must all help in this cause, both young and old.

You have doubtless heard of the great name of Ganga Ram[1]. This great man has done great things in the Punjab by his engineering skill, as your great man, Sir Vishveshvarayya has done here in Mysore. But greater than all these is the work he has done for the cause of widow remarriage. Like that you must also do your bit to help in this cause of the widow. But I ask who is a widow? A widow is a person held in high veneration amongst us but can you say that widowhood has come to a girl of 14 and 15 because she has lost her husband? If a parent, due to poverty or other causes, married his girl of 13 who loses her husband next year or immediately, can you say that she is a widow and that she has to suffer all the miseries of life ever after? Day after day this question has been arresting our attention very vitally and we cannot ignore it or afford to remain indifferent. Do not perpetuate suffering. When you men have got the right to marry again, why do you deny it to your ladies? You must recognize that you have got to restore this right and I ask, will you do this and serve your society most truly?

One last word. I have known that societies like yours confine their activities to the cities. This must not be. You must extend your work beyond your cities, to the villages and hamlets. I ask

[1] *Vide* p. 213.

you to remember this. May God bless your society and its noble efforts.

The Hindu, 25-7-1927

201. LETTER TO MIRABEHN

July 25, 1927

CHI. MIRA,

I have your long letter but none too long for the matters covered by it.

You will guard yourself against the scorpions. Earth should be kept always ready at hand in a receptacle and often exposed to the sun. You should use plenty of it and whenever possible let it directly touch the skin if it is not bruised. It may be renewed every few hours if the pain persists.

Now about the monthly sickness. You perhaps know that observing seclusion is not compulsory at the Ashram. But I am not sure as to what should be exactly done. The women have really to help. For they alone can say what is needed. The untouchability is, I fancy, really due to man's inability to curb his beastly lust. Untouchability merely as to the act probably did not serve the purpose but when it was complete and became a religious observance, perhaps it came to be respected by man. I wonder how man behaves in the West during this sickness and also how the Mussalman behaves in such circumstances. For the time being you should continue your search and read some literature bearing on it if there is any. If you can correspond with some of your people in the matter, do. And now that you are about this, I shall try to gather what information I can.

I understand what you say about the prayers, etc. I shall wait.

The strain of Mysore was quite bearable.

With love,

BAPU

From the original: C.W. 5254. Courtesy: Mirabehn

202. LETTER TO ASHRAM WOMEN

Silence Day, Ashadh Vad 12 [July 25, 1927][1]

SISTERS,

I wish to devote this letter to the subject of attendance at classes. I find great irregularity in your attendance. In the Ashram, social life and lessons in social service begin with these women's classes. Therefore, just as we do not give up taking our daily food except when we are ill or because of some extraordinary circumstance, so also we may be absent from the classes only for unavoidable reasons. You have taken a vow to attend the classes regularly. Then how can you break that vow? As the body can be sustained only by observing the rules of bodily health, an institution or society can be sustained only by observing social rules. Will you not, therefore, promise me that you will not absent yourselves except for reasons which no one can question?

Blessings from

BAPU

From a photostat of the Gujarati: G.N. 3659

203. LETTER TO VASUMATI PANDIT

Silence Day [July 25, 1927][2]

CHI. VASUMATI,

I have received your two letters. Study as much as you like, but take good care of your health.

I think you intend to call on Haribhai's widow, Chi. Kusum. If you do so, find out what her condition is. I have written a letter to her.[3] What is her wish? Are her parents alive? How old is she, and what is her financial condition ? Is she self-controlled or overcome with grief? If you know the background to her marriage, let me know it. If not, try to learn it. I had intended

[1] The year is inferred from the reference to Gandhiji's examining the Ashram women's attendance register.

[2] From the reference to Haribhai's demise

[3] *Vide* "Letter to Kusumbehn Desai", 22-7-1927.

to know about it from Haribhai himself, but he is gone.

Blessings from
BAPU

From a photostat of the Gujarati: C.W. 616. Courtesy: Vasumati Pandit

204. LETTER TO KUNVARJI PAREKH

Silence Day [July 25, 1927][1]

CHI. KUNVARJI,

I write this postcard only to tell you that I think of you every day. I get no time to [write]. Ramdas gives me news about you. I hope your mind is at peace.

Blessings from
BAPU

From a photostat of the Gujarati S.N. 9703

205. LETTER TO M. CHENGIAH CHETTY[2]

KUMARA PARK, BANGALORE,
July 26, 1927

DEAR FRIEND,

Sjt. Rajagopalachariar has shown me your letter. I thank you for the warning about the management of Khadi Funds. I do not know what happened to the Khilafat Funds, except that the banker with whom the funds were placed failed. But I may state that I never had anything to do with the management of the Khilafat Fund. For the Khadi Funds, I am certainly responsible. There is a Council of the All-India Spinners' Association which is entrusted with these Funds and their management. Seth Jamnalal Bajaj who is a very well-known merchant of long standing and a director of several important concerns is the treasurer of the Association. Sjt. Shankerlal Banker who is the son of late Ghelabhai Banker of the Bank of Bombay is the Secretary. The moneys are kept in well-known banks. Proper books of account are kept and

[1] From the S.N. Register

[2] In reply to his letter dated July 21 in which the addressee had asked "if any committee had been appointed to manage the Khadi Funds". He had also criticized Gandhiji's views on *streedhan*.

they are audited by chartered accountants from time to time. There are inspectors appointed to inspect the accounts of subordinate organizations. Everything that is humanly possible to safeguard the Funds and their proper distribution is being done.

I enclose herewith a copy of the printed report published by the All-India Spinners' Association in which you will find the audited accounts also. If, after perusal of the report or even before, you have any suggestions to make for further safeguarding the Funds, I shall be thankful to receive them.

With reference to my appeal[1] at the Mahila Samaj for ornaments and calling them *streedhan*, I do hold very strong views. Ever since I have been in India, and even in South Africa, I have not hesitated to induce sisters both Indian and European to part with their jewellery. As long ago as 1906, I remember the late Surendranath Banerjea having also appealed to the ladies at Lahore, and I remember too that ornaments were showered upon him. I do not feel that in my appeal I am doing anything out of the way. Indeed yours is the first note of dissent I have yet had. In fact, many well-to-do friends have been glad of my appeal, and some of them even took me to their homes when I was appealing on behalf of the Tilak Swaraj Fund and asked me to appeal to their womenfolk to part with their ornaments, their intention being to wean the latter from a craving for hoarding and wearing costly jewels. I have been often publicly thanked for having succeeded to some slight extent in introducing simplicity in the households of the rich people of the land. Never has any pressure been brought to bear upon the sisters. In every case where wives have parted with their jewellery, I have presumed the co-operation of their husbands. I have never accepted from little girls anything unless their parents or guardians were consenting parties. Nevertheless, I have believed that it is wrong on the part of husbands to arrogate to themselves the right of dictating what their wives shall or shall not do with their jewellery. It is the one thing which is in their exclusive possession, and I think that they should have the freest right to dispose of them how they will. But this is my own personal opinion and has nothing to do with what has actually happened in practice.

Do you think that because some people, who in their enthusiasm parted with their foreign cloth and allowed them to be burnt, now repent, I should also repent with them for

[1] *Vide* "Speech at Mahila Samaj, Bangalore", 13-7-1927.

having asked them to do what they did in a moment of lucidity and what it was their sacred duty to have done. If you do, I must again respectfully dissent from you. I had not only no compunction when I made an appeal for burning of foreign cloth, very costly in many instances, but I have not the slightest trace of repentance in me for having got the response I did. I always look forward to[1] that act of burning as one of the many sacred acts I have been privileged by God to be party to.

Yours sincerely,

SJT. M. CHENGIAH CHETTY
CHAMARAJPET
BANGALORE CITY

From a microfilm: S.N. 12618

206. LETTER TO RAJKISHORI MEHROTRA

BANGALORE,
July 26, 1927

CHI. RAJKISHORI,

Your postcard. Keep up this practice of writing. What are you reading these days? What is your daily routine? How is your health? I am in Bangalore up to August. I am recouping strength.

Blessings from
BAPU

From the Hindi original: C.W. 4963. Courtesy: Parashuram Mehrotra

207. LETTER TO JETHALAL JOSHI

BANGALORE,
Ashadh Krishna 13 [*July 26, 1927*]

BHAI JETHALALJI,

Your letter. I see no harm—in fact there would be advantage—in chanting the *Gayatri mantra* while plying the *takli*, especially when there is sacrificial spinning, i.e., as gesture of sympathy for the poor.

[1] Perhaps a slip for "I always look back on"

Your wife should visit her father's place clad in khadi only and if her parents urge her to give up khadi, she should gently convince them. Her parents' displeasure, she should bear with calm. If she has neither this courage nor the strength to bear her parents' displeasure she should, as long as it might be necessary in order to please them, wear whatever clothes they give her.

You need not take the vow of having only one meal a day. It is wrong and also harmful to eat at one time a quantity equal to two meals. Of course one should give up the evening meal and eat sparingly at the other meals.

Let me know what your present occupation is and also what else you are equipped to do, your educational qualifications and so on. Perhaps you can get good milk from the Ashram. Make enquiries there. Milk from the Ashram cannot be delivered at your residence.

Yours,
MOHANDAS

From a photostat of the Hindi: G.N. 1355

208. A LETTER

July 26, 1927

Your letter.

If your wife has fallen, I would hold you too responsible for it. You were separated from her. The girl would not have been keen on marrying you nor would she have consented to your separation. If she could not live without sex and went astray, why blame her? When a man errs, his wife puts up with it with suppressed anger. If the son which your wife has borne is not yours, you can sever your relationship with her. But I feel you must yourself support the woman. If she abandons you or chooses to live with the other man, you have to bear it. You are not obliged to live with your wife out of a sense of shame. If you intend to live with her, pitying her for falling because you had gone away, that too would not be regarded as immoral. But you can take this step only when the woman has repented for her action and she is going to be happy in your company. If, however, she has become absolutely depraved, it is your duty to abandon her.

[From Gujarati]

From the manuscript of Mahadev Desai's Diary. Courtesy: Narayan Desai

209. *SPEECH AT UNITED THEOLOGICAL COLLEGE, BANGALORE*[1]

[*July 26, 1927*][2]

The first desideratum was a knowledge of Hindi for those who aspired to be ministers to the masses of the country. I confess that it is the fault of the previous generation who committed us to the medium of English. But you must break the barrier, if you would reach the masses beyond the Vindhya range. As regards the service that can be or should be rendered by you, I don't think I need speak much, for you have made my task easy by endorsing my mission of the spinning-wheel. You have mentioned the depressed classes, but there is a vast mass of men who are more depressed than the so-called depressed classes, and who constitute the real India. The vast network of railways touches but a fringe of these masses, and if you will travel somewhat outside the railway beat you will visualize them. These railway lines running north to south and east to west are arteries which drain away the wealth of the masses—Lord Salisbury used the word "bleed"—and no return is made to them. We in the cities become partners in the blood-sucking process, which phrase, however bad it may be, truly depicts the state of things. I have known something of this class. I have brooded over their wants, and if I was a painter I could draw a picture of them with their blank eyes, without a spark or lustre or life in them. How are we to minister to them? Tolstoy gave the picturesque phrase, "Let us get off the shoulders of our neighbours." If everyone performs that single operation he would have rendered all service God requires of him. It is a startling proposition, and as you are in a place where you are learning the art of ministry, you must work it out. Build up the premises one on another and see what you arrive at. If you discover any other method than I have suggested of getting off the backs of those poor people, let me know. I am a learner myself, I have no axe to grind, and wherever I see a truth, I take it up and try to act up to it.

[1] From Mahadev Desai's article "Talks with Missionaries". The motto of the college, "Go ye not to be ministered unto, but to minister unto other people", served as the text of the talk.

[2] From Mahadev Desai's "Weekly Letter"

A missionary friend from America wrote to me suggesting literary education for the masses instead of the charkha[1]. Well, I felt sorry for him, especially because he had written the letter from the fulness of his heart. I do not think even Jesus knew much of letters, and if the early Christians cultivated literary knowledge, it was in order to perform their ministry better. But I suppose there is no passage in the New Testament in which there is even the slightest emphasis placed on mere literary education as the first condition for people to come to their own. Not that I discount literacy. It is a question of emphasis. It is like a good thing misplaced just like matter which is misplaced becomes dirt. And whenever I see wrong emphasis being placed on a good thing, my soul rises up against it. Before a child has knowledge of letters, it must be fed and clothed and taught the art of feeding itself. I do not want it to be spoon-fed, but self-reliant. Let our children first know the use of their hands and feet. So I say the first condition is to take to them the message of the spinning-wheel.

I did not like the expression "patronizing khadi" used by you. It has a bad odour. Will you become patrons or servants? So long as khadi is patronized it will be a fad or fashion, but when it becomes a passion it will be the symbol of service. The moment you begin to use khadi, you begin to serve. During my 35 years' constant contact with the poor I have found the art of service incredibly simple. It is not learnt in colleges and schools. The spirit of service can be learnt anywhere. Again here it is a question of emphasis. The art itself is as simple as the process whereby Saul became Paul[2]. The change came over him with a flash, and immediately there is a change of heart in you, you become ministers. May God help to clear this for you.

Young India, 11-8-1927

[1] *Vide* "Letter to W. B. Stover", 16-6-1927.

[2] New Testament, *The Acts*, ix

210. *SPEECH AT MYTHIC SOCIETY, BANGALORE*

July 26, 1927

FRIENDS,

I do not know whether you can all hear me. I am sorry I cannot raise my voice. I thank you sincerely for your address and garlands and for having brought me to this Temple of Peace. I must confess I feel like a fish out of water, for I have long been out of touch, that touch with literature which this Society rightly expects. For one long unbroken period of 35 years my lot has been cast in less peaceful spheres which have kept me out of all literary studies, much as I should have valued it. Except for the short time that I was in prison, I had no other time to turn to literature. I have seen your journal and I congratulate you on your work. You have stated you are interested in research work and I see that your research work has been thorough-going.[1]

I suggest that some one of you should make researches to find out what led to the curse of untouchability to descend upon this land. I wish that the learned men of Mysore, amongst whom there are some of the finest scholars, could find out authorities to show that untouchability could be no part of the Hindu religion, and that our remote ancestors through whom we received the inspiration of the Vedas and who gave us the rich heritage of the Upanishads never believed in untouchability, even as I don't, and that it is merely a vicious excrescence upon Hinduism. And I tell you that if you can do so, among the many services you have already rendered this will not be by any means the least. Workers like myself say on their own authority that this thing is no part of Hinduism. I am no scholar and have not read the Shastras in the original, but my Hindu soul rises up in revolt against such an abomination. However, I look to you scholars and research students to arm workers like myself with authoritative declarations that would command the attention of the pundits, and to furnish workers with evidence so forceful and masterly as would dissolve the orthodox opposition. It should be the proud privilege of your Society to furnish workers with authoritative texts which they could not get anywhere else, and fortify them in their work.

Young India, 18-8-1927

[1] This paragraph has been taken from *The Hindu*, 27-7-1927.

211. LETTER TO J. P. BHANSALI

[After *July 26, 1927*][1]

I have your letter intended for *Young India*. At first I laughed over it and dictated a brief note on it and sent it to be typed for *Young India*. But today I woke up to find myself sorry at the thought of your letter and my laughter disappeared because I see in it a lack of restraint and understanding. I cannot now recall your expressing a difference of opinion with me. I know there were discussions between us but I had thought that in the end you were convinced. But if that is not so, the certificate you grant me in your letter is out of place, and your letter suggests that the mental weakness you mention has been with me from the moment we knew each other. The publicity you have given to my mental weakness does not pain me. But I am hurt because you kept your knowledge of it from me till today and because I see that some matters have been twisted in your letter. Moreover, a telegram from Ahmedabad today says that many activities are at a standstill because of unusually heavy rain and if *Young India* cannot come out this time the matter already sent is enough to fill the next issue. Nature has, therefore, provided me with enough respite to await your reply. Where you blame me for scribbling away in haste, I do not see even a trace of hurry, but since your letter has hurt me I do feel that I should be in no hurry to write about it. I understand from your last letter that you did not, as usual, hasten to meet me because of your mother's illness. I want you therefore to call on me if her condition has improved. If you feel that you are not likely to misunderstand me at any point, I do not think you need see me. Write to me if you hold the latter view or send me a telegram, so that I shall certainly publish your letter.

[From Gujarati]

From the manuscript of Mahadev Desai's Diary. Courtesy: Narayan Desai

[1] The source has this letter after the entries for July 26, 1927.

212. LETTER TO J. P. BHANSALI

[*July 27, 1927*][1]

Your letter (or ultimatum?) to hand. My letter appears to have crossed yours. I urge you not to act in haste. You do not think you are in a hurry because you are impatient to start your fast. However, I do feel that you are in too great a hurry. If you accept the moral position at any rate that when you take such a step you should do so in my presence, please withdraw your ultimatum. I have received three strong letters urging me to dissuade you from undertaking this fast. One is from Bhai Kishorelal, another from Ramniklal and the third from Mirabehn. Mirabehn met you after a long interval, became very sad on seeing you and found your countenance "queer". She found even your talk "queer" and felt that you had become extremely "emotional". All these words in quotes are hers. The letter was in Hindi but she had used the English words in it. I suggested to her that she write to you directly.[2] I have received her reply also and she says that she dare not go to that extent lest she should hurt you. In spite of my reporting all these three opinions, if I were near you and you could persuade me, I would grant you permission to undertake the fast and also bless you. But since I am so far away, I must also let these three letters make their impact on my mind. Your letter appears to contradict your own earlier letter because you were till now hoping for my permission, and I presumed that you would not undertake the fast if you do not have it. But in your last letter you say nothing about my permission, you no more expect it but seek my blessings. If you are hoping for my permission, I shall not be able to grant it. How could I permit what I do not consider right? Personally I think even if you have my permission for your course of action, both you and I must obtain the permission of the Managing Committee. If there is anyone who can be free to do such things after obtaining such permission, it is perhaps myself because, being the founder of the Ashram and initiator of the new and vital experiments in satyagraha, I may be expected to have such privilege, but I do have some doubt in this regard too. Even I should not have the right to

[1] *Vide* the succeeding item.

[2] *Vide* "Letter to Mirabehn", 17-7-1927.

take any steps that might harm the institution once it has been founded. I was mindful of this also when I had undertaken the seven days' fast. And even about that, there was some talk.

I have indulged in so much autobiography in order to make you see your duty. I am one of those who believe that there is a place for a fast like yours in certain situations. But I see clearly from this distance that yours is not such a situation and how can I bless a thing which I regard as improper? Hence if you would be persistent I can only say that I shall bear with your persistence and acquiesce in the inevitable unwillingly and painfully. Before you take any step, discuss the matter with the Managing Committee with a calm mind and also with those whom you regard as your personal friends. Consider your duty towards Lilabehn; if she consents to your step, I would not value her consent; but if she opposes, I would value it greatly because you have sheltered her. If you can and will withdraw your ultimatum and give me an assurance that without my permission you will never embark on a fast, I am ready, at present through correspondence and personally if necessary and when an occasion offers, to discuss the ethics of fasting and whatever points you have raised in your earlier letter. I wish our friends and the Managing Committee to read this letter and you should give it to them for reading. May God help you.

[From Gujarati]

From the manuscript of Mahadev Desai's Diary. Courtesy: Narayan Desai

213. LETTER TO MIRABEHN

KUMARA PARK, BANGALORE,
July 27, 1927

CHI. MIRA,

I have your letter. Of course you know that Wardha is but a branch of Sabarmati. But Wardha has to specialize for discipline and Vinoba is developing it without troubling me and without being hampered by me. Nor has Wardha the same changes to face or new experiments to make as Sabarmati has. And then Sabarmati has no one mind uncontrolled by outside force to change it as Wardha has. But for all practical purposes, Sabarmati and Wardha must be considered as one and indivisible.

But now your mind must be freed for the next two months from even having to think of these places. Your sole concern during these precious two months is to concentrate on your work and on your health.

I have an ultimatum from Bhansali that he proposes to commence his long fast as from the 6th of August. I have warned him against it and implored him not to undertake it at least till I have gone to the Ashram and had an opportunity of discussing the thing with him. The letter goes today. I have mentioned your opinion also about his proposed fast and about his appearance. I hope he will listen to my entreaty.

What food are you taking daily?

With love,

BAPU

SRIMATI MIRABAI
SATYAGRAHASHRAM
WARDHA

From the original: C.W. 5255. Courtesy: Mirabehn

214. LETTER TO FRANCISCA STANDENATH[1]

AS AT THE ASHRAM, SABARMATI,
July 27, 1927

MY DEAR FRIEND,

I have your letter. I am glad you have come in such close touch with the friends[2] to whom I gave an introduction note for you. I have regarded them as among the best of the wealthy people of my acquaintance.

From your letter I suspect that you regard cotton-spinning as the only spinning. But it is not so. Wool-spinning is also important, though nothing like cotton-spinning, for the simple reason that millions live on the plains and hardly require woollen clothing. By all means do cotton-spinning when you can; but why not wool-spinning in the absence of cotton-spinning. And then the woollen yarn may be woven for your own use. You must know that I myself do use hand-spun wool without the slightest compunction. Even as I am dictating this letter, I have covered myself with a woollen blanket, hand-spun of course. It is fairly cold where I am recuperating. I am asking Swami Anand to send you some hand-spun wool, and I am also asking him to

[1] In reply to her letter dated July 26
[2] Ranchhodlal Amritlal Thaker and Bhogilal Thaker

send you a blanket piece which you can either use as a blanket or for making blouses, etc. It won't be smooth to the touch, but then you won't need to wear it next to the skin.

I note that you are persevering in your study of Sanskrit and other languages.

Whenever you can spare some money, you should both come to India, if only for a season and see things for yourself. You will then perhaps get a true perspective and probably be enabled to modify some of the exaggerated notions you might have about India in general and the Ashram and myself in particular. I am anxious that you should know things as they are, or at least as they appear to you at close quarters and not as they seem to you from a distance.

Yours sincerely,

From a photostat: S.N. 12527

215. LETTER TO TARINI PRASAD SINHA

AS AT THE ASHRAM, SABARMATI,
July 27, 1927

DEAR FRIEND,

I have your letter. I am asking *Young India* office to send the *Manchester Guardian* copy of *Young India* to Mr. Dickes personally.

As to the suggested change, I have not yet felt the force of Mr. Dickes' remarks.[1] With me it is a matter of "experiments with truth". But not knowing the use of English words so well as an Englishman, I would like Mr. Dickes, if he can find time, to explain more fully his reasoning.

As to what Mr. Dickes calls the "God stunt", I can only say in all humility that it is a precious fact with me much truer than the fact that I am writing to you.

Will you please pass this letter on to Mr. Dickes?

Yours sincerely,

From a photostat: S.N. 12529

[1] The addressee had passed on to Gandhiji a suggestion of E. W. Dickes that the title of *The Story of My Experiments with Truth* be changed into "The Story of My Schooling with Truth".

216. *LETTER TO SHAPURJI SAKLATVALA*

AS AT THE ASHRAM, SABARMATI,
July 27, 1927

DEAR FRIEND,

I have your letter. I should love to respond, as I know you would like me to, to your earnest call; but I see that we look at things differently. Pray do not think that my labour work unlike khaddar work is merely confined to Ahmedabad. If labour elsewhere will accept my guidance, I would certainly organize it all over. But I am content with guiding Ahmedabad and hope that if Ahmedabad proves successful, it will be copied by the whole of India.

There is no analogy between the khaddar movement and the labour movement. If khaddar like labour were conducted by several distinct organizations, probably I would be compelled to restrict my activities to those organizations only that would listen to me. I have no magical power for bringing labour organization out of disorganization. The organic touch with labour all over India I have because wherever I go labour flocks round me. But that touch is not strong enough to enable me to organize it after my own fashion. I give you my assurance that the moment I feel that I can usefully come in, I shall not hesitate to offer my services to the all-India organization.

About the Khaddar Fund, I can only say you have written without knowledge. Even law will prevent me from using the Khaddar Fund for any other than the advertised purpose even if my conscience becomes elastic enough to permit me to use it otherwise.

I read the other day in the papers that you had a slight operation performed on you and that you were already on the road to recovery. I hope that you have now fully recovered.

I wrote to you only the other day about your own personal affairs which shall not escape my attention.

Yours sincerely,

From a photostat: S.N. 12533

217. *LETTER TO C. V. VAIDYA*

KUMARA PARK, BANGALORE,
July 27, 1927

DEAR MR. VAIDYA,

I must thank you for your delightful letter with its humorous touches. I am not sending it to Pandit Satavalekar, but drinking in the facts, or what is a better term, your opinions—for are not facts stated but opinions,— all for myself.

In the course of my practice, I have so often envied the poor judges who, if they were honest, I knew, must have been hard put to it for coming to a just decision. And in spite of knowing this thing, I have become a self-constituted judge and much trying on account of my ignorance of the originals to know the correct interpretation or practice of the Vedas or practice of our remote forefathers. Of course I don't go so far remote as to the monkeys as Darwin would have as our remote ancestors. And I am safe from destruction in the midst of the war of opposite opinions by my sane belief that it is our right irrespective of the interpretation of the written Vedas or the practice of our ancestors to regulate our practice in the light of modern research and the behest of our own conscience.

Yours sincerely,

SJT. C. V. VAIDYA
POONA CITY

From a microfilm: S.N. 12621

218. LETTER TO S. RAMANATHAN

KUMARA PARK, BANGALORE,
July 27, 1927

MY DEAR RAMANATHAN,

I have both your letters. I hope you are now completely restored.

Mr. Mahadeva Iyer has been coming to me since my return from Mysore almost every day, and I have been giving a few minutes daily to him. If I find anything useful to say, I shall write to you again.

Yours sincerely,

SJT. S. RAMANATHAN
A. I. S. A.
ERODE

From a microfilm: S.N. 12933

219. LETTER TO NARGIS CAPTAIN

KUMARA PARK, BANGALORE,
July 27, 1927

I know why you have not written to me all these long long days. But all the same I have got to write to you. I saw your letters both to Jamnabehn and Mithubehn. I had long chats with the latter, and I see that whilst she is most lovable and a woman having immense capacity for work and service, she has an awful temper and a highly suspicious nature. She has developed, what seems to me to be utterly groundless, suspicion of Yashwantprasad whom she has come to regard as her determined enemy. This makes it practically impossible for Jamnabehn to work with her. On the whole, therefore, it seems to me that it would be better to leave her alone in the development of fashionable khadi which she has made her speciality and to which she gives the whole of her time. After all her accounts are perfect in the sense that every penny received and spent is accounted for. The account-keeping is not in the orthodox style. That I suppose is now being done. The accounts can also be regularly audited. And so long as she does that, there is no reason why her work should not be treated as an independent branch of the Stree Sabha. You may all still hold yourselves ready for services whenever she wants them. I say you all because Mithubehn does not want interference from anybody except when she requires it. I sympathize with her in this attitude because with her highly suspicious nature of which she has no knowledge, she cannot take up any other attitude if she is to work in peace. I endeavoured to show her that Yeshwantprasad had no axe to grind and that he was interested in her work because Jamnabehn was in it, and every one of you appreciated his help. But I could not remove her suspicion. On the contrary, she reiterated it and said that like hers my eyes would in course of time be opened to Yeshwantprasad's intriguing nature as she called it. This is unfortunate. But we have to make the best of it. Unfortunately the women of India have not before now worked in an organized fashion. It will therefore be some time before they can do so. As a matter of fact even the men of India are not yet able to run many successful organizations without friction and without mutual suspicion. I do not want you to overtax yourself about this matter. But if you can send for Mithubehn and others and, seeing that they accept you as their commander-in-chief, pull them all by the ear and make them work together, it would be very nice.

I see that since your return home, you have not kept first class health. But you must really be strong. I shan't be satisfied till you have gone to Kashmir. Though I have never seen it, I have heard a lot about it. It is highly likely that the bracing air of Kashmir will suit you admirably.

Do write to me and tell me all about your health. How I wish you could have come here. The weather is really superb and quite cool for us, but of course it may not be for you.

MRS. NARGIS CAPTAIN
OOMRA HALL
PANCHGANI

From a photostat: S.N. 14199

220. *LETTER TO S. V. KAUJALGI*

KUMARA PARK, BANGALORE,
July 27, 1927

DEAR FRIEND,

I see my letter has hurt you. But I do not know what else I could have done in the circumstances. The verse you have quoted is perfect. As a woman I should feel pride in nestling myself in the bosom of my husband. As a creeper I should be faithful to the immovable tree which lies near me and affords me protection and feel pride in circling myself round it. And as a leader or president of the Spinners' Association I should be false to my trust if I do not depend upon those co-workers whom I ever find near me and ready to do the work entrusted to them. Is it not the essential condition of the very existence of the three named by the poet in the verse quoted by you? Come near me, woo me and I shall be a faithful wife. Be like an immovable tree near me, and I shall circle round you. Merge yourself in khadi work and lead me by the nose. But if you will not occupy any of the three positions, then I shall accept you with quiet resignation as a candid critic offering explanations to the Press. You shall still remain a friend and fellow-worker, and I shall demand from you such quota of service as, in my opinion, you can render.

Yours sincerely,

From a microfilm: S.N. 19790

221. *LETTER TO PRABHAVATI*

BANGALORE,
Ashadh Krishna 14 [*July 27, 1927*][1]

CHI. PRABHAVATI,

Your letter. Let me know what is being arranged for you. I had always held that you could never fall ill. And now I learn from your letter that you too have fallen ill. What was it? I am

[1] Gandhiji was in Bangalore on this date in 1927.

keeping well. These days I also do a bit of touring but Bangalore will remain my headquarters till the end of August.

Blessings from
BAPU

From a photostat of the Hindi: G.N. 3320

222. LETTER TO T. PARAMASIVA IYER

KUMARA PARK, BANGALORE,
July 29, 1927

DEAR FRIEND,

I thank you for your letter and warning. But I am none the wiser for your letter. I shall try to read what you have written about Bhadravati.

What however briefly is your objection to Krishnarajasagara? What do you think can be the motive prompting him to falsehoods, etc., which you ascribe to Sir M. Vishveshvarayya? Everything I have heard about his character is entirely in his favour. Outside Karnatak he is known as a very patriotic man. Personally I am totally opposed to him in his ambition for Americanizing India. Nor do I share his dream about supplying electric power to every village in India. But this fundamental difference does not blind me to his great abilities and his great services. I would therefore require positive unchallengeable proof to dislodge him from the position he occupies in my estimation.

Yours sincerely,

SJT. T. PARAMASIVA IYER
RETIRED JUDGE
'THE WHITE HOUSE'
BANGALORE CITY

From a microfilm: S.N. 12623

223. LETTER TO S. D. NADKARNI

KUMARA PARK, BANGALORE,
July 29, 1927

DEAR FRIEND,

I do not propose to publish your letter suggesting the adoption of Devanagari as the all-India script. I have denied myself the pleasure of publishing a similar and more elaborate letter from

Kakasaheb Kalelkar because it would merely lead to confusion. The reform of Devanagari, however desirable it may be, is a side issue. If we can but induce leaders of thought to adopt Devanagari as a common script its reform wherever necessary is bound to come.

Personally I like your suggestion for dropping the horizontal caps as I would call them. Kakasaheb goes one better and suggests the Gujarati script which is really re-formed Nagari. But I have suppressed Kakasaheb's proposal because it would simply lead to an interminable controversy and take the mind of thinking India away from the main issue. Whilst I believe that the re-formation of Devanagari in some shape or other is necessary, I am only indifferent to it at present. It would be a tremendous saving of national energy and a move on the part of different linguistic provinces towards one another to adopt one script however imperfect it may be.

For your information I give you the reason for not printing *Navajivan* in Devanagari. *Navajivan* has its own work cut out. In order to make good its message it has submitted to a curtailment of its subscription list. You may not know that at one time it and *Young India* had each nearly 30,000 subscribers. But today it has come down to less than 7,000. I do not mind its coming to zero for enforcement of the mission for which the papers were brought into being. Adoption of Devanagari was not part of that mission. I have a large number of women readers and Parsis and Mussalmans who can struggle even through Gujarati type with some labour. They find it difficult even to understand the moderate number of Sanskrit words that have got to be used in editing *Navajivan*. If I adopt Devanagari all these would be helpless and give up *Navajivan* and me in sheer disgust. Amongst what may be called the upper ten, I have, I fear, very few readers of *Navajivan*.

Yours sincerely,

SJT. S. D. NADKARNI
KARWAR
(N. KANARA)

From a photostat: S.N. 12625

224. *LETTER TO T. R. MAHADEVA IYER*

KUMARA PARK, BANGALORE,
July 29, 1927

DEAR FRIEND,

In my opinion you will be justified and you are bound after due notice to the public and especially to the donors to hand over the Gurukula property both movable and immovable to those who have declared themselves the committee of management, if the committee will not agree to arbitration.

The answers I have given to your questions are not to be considered as legal opinion in any sense. They are merely answers that common sense has dictated to me. And though I have no objection whatsoever to your publishing the answers, I would much rather that they were not, because I have no desire to be drawn into a public controversy over any of the answers.

Yours sincerely,

SJT. T. R. MAHADEVA IYER
TAMIL GURUKULA
SHERMADEVI

From a microfilm: S.N. 12935

225. LETTER TO T. T. SHARMAN

KUMARA PARK, BANGALORE,
July 29, 1927

DEAR FRIEND,

I have your letter together with a copy of your Weekly. It seems to me to be perfectly useless for me to send anything for your paper and I cannot read it and therefore know nothing of its contents. I do not remember ever to have written anything for any paper whose policy and principles I did not know and whose conductors were equally unfamiliar to me. I hope you will therefore please excuse me, and I am sure in my present state of health you will not want me to have a friend to translate for me your paper and give so much of my time to it.

Yours sincerely,

SJT. T. T. SHARMAN
EDITOR
"VISVAKARNATAKA"
BANGALORE CITY

From a microfilm: S.N. 14201

226. LETTER TO N. SANKARA AIYER

KUMARA PARK, BANGALORE,
July 29, 1927

DEAR FRIEND,

I thank you for the extract from Tchehov story and the information about mill khaddar. I know that several mills are openly selling what is called mill khaddar. I am working through the khaddar organizations to minimize the effect of this deception.

Yours sincerely,

SJT. N. SANKARA AIYER
14, PATKAR'S BUILDING
BANDRA,
BOMBAY NO. 20

From a microfilm: S.N. 19791

227. *LETTER TO RADHA SUNDER DAS*

KUMARA PARK, BANGALORE,
July 29, 1927

DEAR FRIEND,

I have your letter. I am sorry that your application has not been favourably received. But you must be neither despondent nor enraged against those who have rejected your application. These things must always happen. And it would be wrong to suppose that because our applications are not accepted injustice has been done. Please keep me informed of your progress and movements.

Yours sincerely,

SJT. RADHA SUNDER DAS
SURI P.O.
BIRBHOOM DISTRICT

From a microfilm: S.N 19792

228. *LETTER TO H. G. PATHAK*

KUMARA PARK, BANGALORE,
July 29, 1927

MY DEAR HARIBHAU,

I have your letter. No apology is needed for not writing in Hindi. But I shall certainly be glad at the end of six months from now to find you writing in Hindi.

I did not take part in any of the proceedings of the A.I.S.A. Council meeting here. Nor had I seen the resolution of which you have sent me a copy. I have promised Jamnalalji and other members of the Council faithfully not to intervene in anything that they may do except when they ask me.

Whatever you think is not proper in the resolution I would like you to write to Jamnalalji or to Mr. Banker. But I quite agree with you that the workers ought not to be hampered by unnecessary restrictions. I do not think there is any desire on the part of the Council to put any obstruction in the way of the young men.

With reference to the Rs. 2,500 loan I did not understand that it was to be used for buying the *Gandhi Shikshanamala* but that it was to be used for paying off Mr. Kanitkar's debts and that the books were to [be] held as security for the amount of the loan. Nor did I contemplate that if there were any profits made from the sale of the books they were to go to A.I.S.A. So far as I recollect our conversation I did not contemplate making any profits. But if there were any, they should go towards the upkeep of the *Swarajya* which after all is as much Mr. Kanitkar's concern as any other. You may make use of this letter in your communication with Jamnalalji, and if necessary, the resolution will be altered accordingly at the next meeting of the Council. But, even as the resolution stands, I do not think that for your purposes it needs any alteration.

Instead of calling the copies "a security", they have called the transaction "a sale" which in effect is one and the same thing, and the question of profits is a very distant hope.

The pronote required should of course be sent without delay by you even if you wish for any alterations in the resolution.

I do not think that the charge against the Council of lukewarmness towards Maharashtra is correct. That you have to suffer is true and that perhaps makes workers sensitive and makes them expect from the Council what it really cannot do. But the suffering will only make you all the fitter for service if the suffering does not weaken the principles of the sufferers.

Regarding Lokamanya's reminiscences you are asking me to put an extra tax upon the very limited energy that I have got and which I require for my present work. Nothing that I may write can possibly remove the impression that might have been created with reference to my attitude towards Lokamanya or his life-work. That can only be removed by my uniformly correct conduct, and the question of conduct can only be determined after my death. If, therefore, I write anything at all I should certainly not do so in the hope of the reward that you hold out before me.

About the unemployment, I don't know what I can do from here beyond saying that you should send all the likely names to the Technical Department. Personally I think that every willing worker can be accommodated in the Khadi Service. But I cannot give that faith to all the co-workers. And for such practical work, therefore, it is best for the present to treat me as dead. If I come to life again and plunge into practical work, you will certainly come to me. But, for the present, you have to go to Mr. Banker. Frame a policy and then see whether many can be accommodated. Do not give up the hope or the work on behalf of the unemployed fit men because you can no longer rely upon me.

About the co-operation with mill-owners, it is really for them to co-operate with us. Our co-operation therefore just now consists in cheapening khadi, making it stronger and in helping the mill-owners to get all the Government aid they can.

Have I made myself clear? I shall make note of Annapurnabai's *vrat*[1]. Please write to Mr. Banker for a formal receipt of your policy.

I shall look forward to Mr. Joglekar's pocket looms.

Yours sincerely,

SJT. H. G. PATHAK
283, SADASHIV PETH
POONA CITY

From a microfilm: S.N. 19793

229. LETTER TO KUSUMBEHN DESAI

BANGALORE,
July 29, 1927

CHI. KUSUM,

I had been waiting for your letter. Chi. Vasumati had given me some information. Now your letter completes the picture.

I cannot think of any better arrangement than that you should take charge of Haribhai's pupils and they should look after you. But whether you can take up this work, you alone know best. I see that you were as much Haribhai's pupil as his wife. You and your well-wishers will know only by experience how far your mind has become trained. We do not always understand our mind.

I see from the letters of Chi. Vasumati and Bhai Chhaganlal Joshi that your marriage was largely your own choice. It was your own strong wish that you should marry Haribhai. You can show in many ways that your choice was worthy. A girl who selects as her husband a man who is much older than herself marries not his body but its master. Haribhai's body has passed away. But he himself is still with you, and will remain with you as long as you wish.

Ask me anything you wish to. I shall be here in Bangalore till the end of this month.

Blessings from
BAPU

[From Gujarati]
Bapuna Patro—Kusumbehn Desaine, p. 4

[1] Vow

230. DISCUSSION WITH MISSIONARIES[1]

[*July 29, 1927*][2]

Gandhiji opened the discussion by claiming himself to be a friend of the missionaries, ever since his close contact with them in South Africa.

Though I have been a friend, I have always been a critic, not from any desire to be critical, but because I have felt that I would be a better friend if I opened out my heart, even at the risk of wounding their feelings. They never allowed me to think that they felt hurt, they certainly never resented my criticism.

Then he referred to his first speech before the missionaries in India on swadeshi, since which twelve years had rolled away and with them much of the mists also.

The first distinction I would like to make, after these prefatory remarks, between your missionary work and mine, is that while I am strengthening the faith of the people, you are undermining it. Your work, I have always held, will be all the richer, if you accept as settled facts the faiths of the people you come to serve—faiths which, however crude, are valuable to them. And in order to appreciate what I say, it becomes perhaps necessary to re-read the message of the Bible in terms of what is happening around us. The world is the same, but the spirit ever broadens intensively and extensively, and it might be that many things in the Bible will have to be re-interpreted in the light of discoveries—not of modern science—but in the spiritual world in the shape of direct experiences common to all faiths. The fundamental verses of St. John do require to be re-read and re-interpreted. I have come to feel that like us human beings words have their evolution from stage to stage in the contents they hold. For instance the contents of the richest word—God—are not the same to every one of us. They will vary with the experience of each. They will mean one thing to the Santhal and another to his next door neighbour Ravindranath Tagore. The *sanatani* may reject my interpretation of God and Hinduism. But God Himself is a long-suffering God who puts up with any amount of abuse and misinterpretations. If we were to put the spiritual experiences together we would find a resultant which would answer the crav-

[1] From Mahadev Desai's article, "Talks with Missionaries"

[2] From Mahadev Desai's "Weekly Letter"

ings of human nature. Christianity is 1,900 years old, Islam is 1,300 years old, who knows the possibility of either? I have not read the Vedas in the original, but have tried to assimilate their spirit and have not hesitated to say that though the Vedas may be 13,000 years old—or even a million years old, as they well may be, for the word of God is as old as God Himself—even the Vedas must be interpreted in the light of our experience. The powers of God should not be limited by the limitations of our understanding. To you who have come to teach India, I therefore say, you cannot give without taking. If you have come to give rich treasures of experiences, open your hearts out to receive the treasures of this land, and you will not be disappointed, neither will you have misread the message of the Bible.

Interesting questions and answers followed, which I summarize below:

Q. What then are we doing? Are we doing the right thing?

A. You are trying to do the right thing in the wrong way. I want you to complement the faith of the people instead of undermining it. As the Dewan of Mysore said in his address to the Assembly, the *Adi Karnatakas* should be made better Hindus, as they belong to Hinduism. I would similarly say to you, make us better Hindus, i.e., better men or women. Why should a man, even if he becomes a Christian, be torn from his surroundings? Whilst a boy I heard it being said, that to become a Christian was to have a brandy bottle in one hand and beef in the other. Things are better now, but it is not unusual to find Christianity synonymous with denationalization and Europeanization. Must we give up our simplicity, to become better people? Do not lay the axe at our simplicity.

There are not only two issues before us, viz., to serve and to teach, there is a third issue, viz., evangelizing, declaring the glad tidings of the coming of Jesus and his death in redemption for our sins. What is the right way of giving the good news? We need not undermine the faith but we may make people lose their faith in lesser things.

That lands me into the region of interpretation. Whilst I must not enter into it, I may suggest that God did not bear the Cross only 1,900 years ago, but He bears it today, and He dies and is resurrected from day to day. It would be poor comfort to the world if it had to depend upon a historical God who died 2,000 years ago. Do not then preach the God of history, but show Him as He lives today through you. In South Africa I met a number of friends, and read a number of books—Pearson, Parker and Butler—all giving their own interpretations, and I said to myself I must not bother myself with these conflicting interpretations. It is better to allow our lives to speak for us than our words. C.F. Andrews never preaches. He is incessantly doing his work. He finds enough work and stays where he finds it and takes no credit for bearing the Cross. I have the honour to know hundreds of honest Christians, but I have not known one better than Andrews.

But what about animistic beliefs? Should they not be corrected?

Well, we have been working amongst the so-called 'untouchables' and backward classes, and we have never bothered ourselves with their beliefs, animistic or otherwise. Superstitions and undesirable things go as soon as we begin to live the correct life. I concern myself not with their belief but with asking them to do the right thing. As soon as they do it, their belief rights itself.

You speak of simplicity. But what are we to do in this age of motor-cars? You could not have come here without a motor-car!

Well, a motor-car is not a necessity. I certainly did not need it to come here. If God wants you to be useful he should find the means to make you useful. Motor-cars do not mean the sum of our spiritual experience. There was no motor-car in Jesus' or Mahomed's time, and yet they did not need them for their work. I do not hold them to be essential for real progress. We need to be humble. And humility and simplicity are not mere outward expressions. When Paul speaks of humility he means heart-humility. A true Christian has little need to speak. He goes about his Father's business. May I cite my own case? Speeches were the least part of my work in South Africa. Most of the 16,000 people who rose like one man and joined me had not even seen me, much less heard me speak.

How can we help condemning if we feel that our Christian truth is the only reality?

That brings me to the duty of tolerance. If you cannot feel that the other faith is as true as yours, you should feel at least that the men are as true as you. The intolerance of the Christian missionaries does not, I am glad to say, take the ugly shape it used to take some years ago. Think of the caricature of Hinduism, which one finds in so many publications of the Christian Literature Society. A lady wrote to me the other day saying that unless I embraced Christianity all my work would be nothing worth. And of course that Christianity must mean what she understands as such! Well, all I can say is that it is a wrong attitude.

Young India, 11-8-1927

231. LETTER TO KAMALA DAS GUPTA

KUMARA PARK, BANGALORE,
July 30, 1927

MY DEAR FRIEND,

I hope you will not mind my dictating what is a reply to a personal letter.

You are not the only girl with the difficulties mentioned by you. But if you have patience, perseverance in your ideals and humility, you will have no difficulty in conquering your parents' pressure. For, after all, they have to go by the ordinary experience and the ordinary experience is that both young men and young women have often entertained lofty ideas in moments of enthusiasm which they are not able to carry out to the end. I myself know many such instances. Parents are therefore cautious and chary of taking seriously their children's lofty ideals. If your parents insist upon your marriage how could they permit you to go to the Sabarmati Ashram? And then I must warn you against drawing a flattering picture of the Ashram. It is a place for toilers, those who believe in the necessity and the moral value of labouring with their hands and feet. Then English is rarely spoken there. A knowledge of Hindi is an absolute necessity.

I know the standard of Bethune College girls. If you have learnt to consider what is provided in that college and what the girls provide themselves with there to be your necessaries, you are hardly likely to be satisfied with the simplicity of the Ashram life. But in spite of my warning, if you still feel drawn to the Ashram and your parents permit you, I shall send your name to the Managing Board.

In your next letter please give me some more particulars about you. Give me your age, the occupation of your father and such other things that you think I should know.

Yours sincerely,

SHRIMATI KAMALA DAS GUPTA
1, AKHIL MISTRY LANE
CALCUTTA

From a microfilm: S.N. 12626

232. *LETTER TO DR. B. S. MOONJE*

KUMARA PARK, BANGALORE,
July 30, 1927

DEAR DR. MOONJE,

I was relieved to have your letter giving a full description of your accident. Thank God that the injury received is not permanent. What a miraculous escape you all had!

Please tell your grandson that his singular escape without injury should mean great things for the country and that he must from now prepare to dedicate his life for the service of the country with the fullest determination to do better than his grandfather and his old contemporaries like myself.

Yours sincerely,

From a photostat: S.N. 14202

233. *LETTER TO E. S. PATWARDHAN*

KUMARA PARK, BANGALORE,
July 30, 1927

DEAR FRIEND,

Owing to my illness and movement I have not been able to overtake your letter for a long time for which please excuse me. Had I been up and doing as I used to before the collapse, I should have done something regarding your difficulty. But now I am really powerless. As you know I have given up practically all administrative work. I am simply attending to the correspondence, editing and absolutely necessary touring in slow stages. Jamnalalji is the officiating Chairman of the Association and I would like you to approach him and convince him.

I did discuss the whole of your affairs with him before the collapse. Though he was here recently for the meeting of the Council of the Association, I took no part in the proceedings of the meeting and discussed no administrative measures with Jamnalalji. I had indeed hoped to study the Vidyalaya and your difficulties much more than before. But my incapacitation upset this as well as other similar plans. I hope you will therefore forgive me.

The enclosure will be sent on Monday by registered post.

Yours sincerely,

SJT. EKNATH SRIPAD PATWARDHAN
PRAMUKH
TILAK MAHAVIDYALAYA
MAHAL, NAGPUR

From a microfilm: S.N. 19794

234. LETTER TO V. V. DASTANE

KUMARA PARK, BANGALORE,
July 30, 1927

MY DEAR DASTANE,

I have your letter. I am sorry that I did not see you. If I was what I was before the collapse I would certainly not have turned away a single aspirant for khadi service merely on the ground of want of accommodation. But Jamnalalji and Shankerlal must manage according to their abilities and their self-confidence. You must discuss the pros and cons with them. I shall do likewise but my doing will be in a leisurely fashion. Of course you must not suffer any loss of confidence if it is at all possible. But if we are really helpless, we must not pretend to be brave. Above all we must be true.

Yours sincerely,

SJT. V. V. DASTANE
A.I.S.A. (MAHARASHTRA BRANCH)
PIMPARALA P.O.

From a microfilm: S.N. 19795

235. *SPEECH AT CHAMARAJENDRA SANSKRIT PATHASHALA, BANGALORE*

July 30, 1927

I appreciate the honour you have done me in giving me a Sanskrit address. I hold that every Hindu boy and girl must acquire a knowledge of Sanskrit, and that every Hindu should have enough knowledge of Sanskrit to be able to express himself in that language whenever an occasion arises.

I was pained to hear that there were pundits in the Mysore State who fought shy of teaching Sanskrit to Sudras and *Panchamas*. I do not know how far the contention that the Sudras have no right to learn Sanskrit and hence to read the Vedas is supported by the authority of scriptures, but as a *sanatani* Hindu I am firmly of opinion that even if there is any authority we must not kill the spirit of our religion by a literal interpretation of the texts. Words have, like man himself, an evolution, and even a Vedic text must be rejected if it is repugnant to reason and contrary to experience. Thus so far as I understand the Shastras I think that there is no authority in them for untouchability as we understand it today, and my experience of the so-called untouchables in different parts of India has shown me that man to man the 'untouchable' is in no way inferior to his 'touchable' brother either intellectually or morally. I know suppressed class people who are leading as clean and moral lives as any one of us, and I have seen *Adi Karnataka* boys who read and recite Sanskrit verses as well as any of the Brahmin boys and girls here. I am grateful therefore that you should have thought fit to invite a man of such radical views in your midst, and even to vote an address to him, and to approve of those views in the address. I am glad to see so many Brahmins plying their *taklis*, but I want you not to confine yourselves to making your sacred threads out of the yarn. The *yajnopavits*[1] of course will continue to be of *takli* yarn, but you will make your clothes also from that yarn or charkha yarn. I tell you I was pained to see boys and girls dressed in foreign clothes reciting verses from the scriptures. To say the least, it struck me to be incongruous. The external is in no way the essence of religion, but the external oft proclaims the

[1] Sacred thread worn by the Hindus

internal, and whenever therefore I go to a Sanskrit college or an institution where Aryan culture is taught, I look forward to being reminded of the simple and sacred surroundings of our ancient *rishis*. I am sorry that you have not fulfilled my expectation, and I appeal to the teachers and the parents of these children to make the children true representatives of ancient culture.

Young India, 18-8-1927

236. NATURE'S 'WRATH'

Nature never acts in anger. Its laws work unfailingly, like good clock. No changes ever occur in them. In fact Nature has not even reserved the right to change them, nor does it need to do so. Nature is perfect, and her laws too are perfect.

But we do not know these laws and, therefore, when they surprise us by their working we describe them as Nature's wrath. She has just shown such wrath against Gujarat. How can I, staying in far-away Bangalore, form a true idea of this miniature *pralaya*[1]? My only means of knowing its magnitude are the reports appearing in newspapers and one wire from Vallabhbhai and another from the Ashram.

God alone knows whether this flood is a punishment for some sins of ours or some event which, on certain conditions being fulfilled, may give us some needed benefit. We would do well to regard it as a punishment for our sins. There is not only no great difference between moral sins and economic sins, but on the contrary the two kinds of sins are closely related. Among the three classes of sins, telling lies, dirtying the river-water and raising an opium or tobacco crop in the fields in place of wheat there is only a difference of degree, none of kind. It is not true that one who tells a lie suffers spiritually but he who dirties the water does not, or that the soul of him who raises an opium crop prospers. As our discrimination improves, we understand the nature of our sins better.

If, however, we wait doing nothing till we know our sins better and take no steps to relieve the people's losses which we see with our naked eyes, we would be reckoned fools.

Vallabhbhai has started a fund on behalf of the Provincial

[1] The universal flood which is believed to end a cycle of creation. Gandhiji here refers to the unprecedented floods in Gujarat in July 1927.

Committee[1], and Manilal Kothari[2] is going round to meet people to collect contributions to it. There was a telegram from him to say that philanthropic rich men have already contributed Rs. 30,000. Let people contribute as much as they can. Though it avails little to try to mend a rent in the sky,[3] if everyone helps to the best of his ability the people cannot but feel cheered by the sympathy thus shown. The Committee will try to reach as many people as it can. As yet, it is not even likely to have an idea of how many people have suffered, or how much they have suffered and in what manner. Some details, which I do not know at the moment of writing this (on August 1) will have become known by the time this appears in print. On knowing them, those who have paid nothing as yet should pay something and so contribute to this essential relief-work.

[From Gujarati]
Navajivan, 7-8-1927

237. LETTER TO MIRABEHN

August 1 [*1927*]

CHI. MIRA,

I have your beautifully written Hindi letter. Your time-table seems to be crowded. There is no breathing time between different periods. I suppose it is the same with all. It is quite capable of execution, if one concentrates and does not fuss or waste in idle thought or talk.

You know the plight of Gujarat. Rain has done very great damage and the Ashram too has come in for its due share. I have a telegram too that Kantilal who was keeping accounts was drowned in the river. It appears to be a case of suicide. I have no definite particulars yet.

I shall be absent from Bangalore for four days from tomorrow, returning Friday evening.

No more this time.

With love,

BAPU

From the original: C.W. 5256. Courtesy: Mirabehn

[1] Gujarat Provincial Congress Committee

[2] A Congress worker of Saurashtra who worked for many years as Secretary of the Gujarat Provincial Congress Committee

[3] A Gujarati saying

238. *LETTER TO V. S. SRINIVASA SASTRI*

BANGALORE,
August 1, 1927

MY DEAR BROTHER,

I was thankful for your first letter from South Africa. The hopeful note cheers me.

The Transvaal, I see, is causing you some anxiety. But I have every hope that the people there will ultimately listen to you.

I notice your appeal for social workers. You won't get many from this end. I know Devadhar contemplates sending or even taking a batch. But my own feeling is that it is essentially work for local volunteers. But whether it is done by local volunteers or workers imported from here, the work is worth doing and has got to be done. The Government of India, the Natal Government and the planters are not a little to blame for the mischief. The tone having been once set, it is tremendously difficult to set another all of a sudden. All strength to your elbow.

Do please keep your health.

Andrews cabled about your expenses.[1] I am not going to weary you with what was done here. But I am informed that you will have all the assistance you need. I personally feel quite at ease. It is not the style of living that is going to count in your case, it is your internal strength that is going to count and is counting already.

I am keeping well and am likely to be in the South practically to the end of October. I shall not be leaving Mysore before the end of the month.

With love,

Yours,
M. K. GANDHI

From the original: C.W. 9229. Courtesy: S. R. Venkataraman

[1] *Vide* "Letter to J. B. Petit", 5-7-1927.

239. LETTER TO SECRETARY, HINDI SAHITYA SAMMELAN

BANGALORE,
August 1, 1927

DEAR MR. SECRETARY,

A copy of your letter to Pandit Harihar Sharma, dated *Shravan Krishna* 10[1], has been sent to me. Sharmaji has gone to Rameshwaram.

Some time ago[2] I wrote to you in reply to your telegram and letter but having had no response from you I presume you did not get my reply.

In case that reply has not reached you let me repeat what I said in it. Whatever changes have come about in the Madras Hindi Prachar Office have been publicly approved by me. Sharmaji is not at all responsible for them. You will certainly not look upon Sharmaji as your paid employee. Our differences over the ownership of the office is an old story. I had made clear this point to you also in Wardha. If you deem it proper, this dispute can be settled by arbitration. If you think resorting to arbitration would not be in the interest of the Sammelan, you can take whatever legal action you will against me alone.

Yours,

From a microfilm of the Hindi: S.N. 12777

240. LETTER TO RAMDAS GANDHI

Silence Day, August 1, 1927

CHI. RAMDAS,

I have read your letter to Devdas. Write to me whatever you notice about Kanti and Rasik, but I don't want you to worry about it. We should not worry about a task which has not fallen to our lot even if it is urgent or personal. This is what the *Gita* and our dharma teach us. Either one should regard nothing as personal or only that which is with one on hand and devote one-

[1] Corresponding to July 23, 1927, according to the Vikram calendar followed in North India

[2] On July 6, 1927

self to it. One should not worry even about one's own father if he is far away and should have faith in God that He is the protector of all and He employs whomever He wishes as His instrument. This rule holds good even when one's father is close by and someone else is engaged in attending on him and one has some other work to do. What applies to the father also applies to a brother, a nephew, the wife, a son and others. You are in the Ashram only to learn your job and to pick up whatever you can from its atmosphere. While doing so you may see or hear many other things. But your duty requires you only to pass on this information to some responsible person. It is only in this way that we can live in peace in society. We cannot afford to sit in judgment upon the world.

You have good experience of the Divine wrath there.[1] Write to me about it. Let me know all about your health too.

Blessings from
BAPU

[From Gujarati]

From the manuscript of Mahadev Desai's Diary. Courtesy: Narayan Desai

241. LETTER TO ASHRAM WOMEN

Shravan Sud 4 [*August 1, 1927*]

SISTERS,

This time the post has been irregular. The mail due on Monday was received here only yesterday. I hope none of you was frightened on account of the torrential rains and the flood. Such calamities occur only to test whether we have learnt the lessons of life. What would it matter if the Ashram or for that matter Ahmedabad itself was washed away by the flood in spite of our best efforts? The wonder is that so much has remained safe in spite of such torrential floods. But after all, who knows whether we gain more by saving or by losing? It may be that what has been saved has really been lost and what has been lost has really been saved. But everyone likes to be saved, and we are thankful to God when we are saved. Actually, one should thank God for everything that happens. That is what is meant by *samatva*.

[1] Torrential rains; *vide* the succeeding item.

But think of the loss of Kantilal.[1] How can we bear this grief? That also we must bear however difficult it is. One's intellect works in accordance with one's karma. If it is true that Kantilal has committed suicide, I can guess the reason, I think. But we need not worry about the reason. We should make up our minds that we ourselves will never commit suicide. The kind of people who commit suicide either worry too much about the world, or try to hide their faults from the world. We should never pretend to be what we are not, or try to do what is clearly beyond us.

Blessings from
BAPU

From a photostat of the Gujarati: G.N. 3660

242. *SPEECH TO LAMBANIS, ARSIKERE JUNCTION*[2]

August 2, 1927

You must all wear khaddar; it is made by your people, and the cost goes to feed them. You must all completely give up drinking and flesh-eating. Also you must listen to me and follow my words, if you are really true in your love and affection for me. You must understand that when once a girl is married among your community, she must not be taken away again by someone of you and remarried according to your pernicious old custom. This is against all Hindu dharma.

Turning to the Lambani women, Gandhiji said they must not unnecessarily burden themselves with heavy ornaments as they were now doing.

The Hindu, 5-8-1927

[1] *Vide* "Letter to Mirabehn", 1-8-1927.

[2] At the station yard, in reply to the welcome address in Lambani presented on behalf of the Mysore Provincial Lambani Sangh

243. LETTER TO C. V. VAIDYA[1]

KUMARA PARK, BANGALORE,
August 3, 1927

DEAR MR. VAIDYA,

I highly appreciate your letter. I know that you have the instinct of the judge and had been a judge in Gwalior for a long time. But your letter has whetted my curiosity, and I must make time to study your volumes. Are they in Marathi or in English? You must pardon my gross ignorance even of our good authors of whom I have long known you to be one. But fate has never left me any time for doing this kind of reading.

Are the authorities in favour of your conclusion—that our forefathers in the Vedic times ate beef—collected in those volumes?

Yours sincerely,

SJT. C. V. VAIDYA
SADASHIV PETH
POONA CITY

From a photostat: S.N. 12629

244. LETTER TO DR. GURUDAS ROY

KUMARA PARK, BANGALORE,
August 3, 1927

DEAR FRIEND,

I have your letter. I am perfectly confident that you can do without any European clothing in England and Scotland provided that you take sufficient stock of hand-spun woollen clothing. It may be found a little more costly if you go in for very fine Kashmir woollen hand-spun. You may not know that Pandit Motilalji when he was preparing to go to Europe as a member of the Skeen Committee[2] had an entirely hand-spun outfit including his cardigan jackets. You can get very warm and very cheap hand-spun Nepali blankets.

As to the quantity, it is very difficult for me to prescribe. But if I were you, I should take half a dozen blankets. I presume

[1] In reply to his letter of July 3, 1927 (S.N. 12627)

[2] Appointed with Sir Andrew Skeen as president to investigate the question of establishment of an Indian Sandhurst

you will wear trousers. You can get suitable woollen stuff for trousers, etc. I suggest your consulting Satis Babu of Khadi Pratishthan, and if he cannot furnish you with an outfit, I know that the Khadi Bhandar of Bombay can, because that Bhandar has provided many England-going Indians with proper outfits. Khadi Pratishthan's address you know—170, Bow Bazaar Street, Calcutta. The address of the Khadi Bhandar is Princess Street, Bombay. All your underclothings may well be cotton khadi.

Yours sincerely,

DR. GURUDAS ROY
BALAGARH P.O.
HOOGHLY DISTRICT
BENGAL

From a photostat S.N. 14205

245. LETTER TO V. V. DASTANE

KUMARA PARK, BANGALORE,
August 3, 1927

MY DEAR DASTANE,

I have your letter. I like the idea of Malaviyaji touring Maharashtra in the interest of khadi. But I do not want you to trouble him just now. He is himself in a weak state of health, and we must not be party to putting any strain upon it. Then again the workers do not now need the stimulation of further awakening and spectacular meetings. You have hardly yet time to consolidate the energy set free during my tour. You have to build up and put on a solid basis all the different centres that have been brought into existence. Watch the work in the different centres and put Pimparala itself on a solid foundation. All this means that you should be free from having to organize any big tours at present. And, thirdly, if Professor Kale, the *Kesari* people and others who have hitherto stood aside from khadi are inclined to view it with favour, let that sentiment silently grow. It does not need any encouragement from you or me; but it is bound to be encouraged by any solid achievement we may show in the shape of larger production, regular silent improvement in quality, reduction in prices and steady employment of young men. You must learn not to live on stimulants. Do you not agree?

Yours sincerely,

From a microfilm: S.N. 19796

246. LETTER TO A. RANGASWAMY IYENGAR

KUMARA PARK, BANGALORE,
August 3, 1927

MY DEAR RANGASWAMY,

I do not know whether you want any reply from me to your circular letter about the Nagpur Satyagraha. But if you do, I can think of adding nothing to my recent article[1] in *Young India*. If, beyond what is contained in that article, any further information is required, or if the Committee has any further questions to ask me, I shall gladly answer them. But this letter need not be part of the record if my opinion can for my own sake be dispensed with.

Yours sincerely,

From a photostat: S.N. 14206

247. LETTER TO R. B. GREGG

KUMARA PARK, BANGALORE
August 3, 1927

MY DEAR GOVIND,

I have your letter. I am dictating this during my tour which I am taking in very slow stages without putting any undue strain upon my health which seems to be steadily getting better.

I shall look forward to a typed copy of your work and I shall certainly go through it and let you have my opinion on it and suggestions if there are any to make.

You certainly do not need to explain to me why you could not pay for the proposed operation. I can easily arrange for it. But why do you want to postpone it till December? Is it not better to spare yourself from Kotgarh for a fortnight or so and get the operation done now or as soon as I can get an appointment from Dr. Dalal? I shall write to him after hearing from you.

Yours sincerely,

From a photostat: S.N. 14208

[1] *Vide* Vol. XXXIII, "Nagpur Satyagraha", 19-5-1927.

248. LETTER TO KRISHNADAS

HASSAN,
August 3, 1927

MY DEAR KRISHNADAS,

I had your letter that you left on leaving Bangalore. There was nothing in it that needed a reply. I have now seen your letter to Subbiah and was delighted to hear that you were successful in Muzaffarpur. In the letter you left, you promised to write again from Darbhanga. That letter has still not arrived. I am anxious to know that you are keeping quite well and fit and to know all about Guruji's health.

This I am dictating from Hassan where we arrived yesterday evening. We reach Bangalore again on the 5th instant and resume tour on the 9th, still confining it to Mysore. I shall not leave Bangalore finally before the end of the month. But you will know if there is any change.

You must have heard all about the awful rains in Gujarat. The Ashram also came in for a bit of loss. Poor Kantilal who was keeping books in the Ashram was drowned. It seems to have been a case of suicide; but I am still awaiting full particulars.

Yours sincerely,

SJT. KRISHNADAS
CARE OF SJT. SATIS CHANDRA MUKERJEE
LAL BAGH
DARBHANGA
BIHAR

From a photostat: S.N. 14204

249. LETTER TO SHANKER

HASSAN,
August 3, 1927

MY DEAR SHANKER,

I have your postcard. I see you have already made yourself quite at home there. You will cover yourself well if you find it very cold there. The climate however is very bracing and is bound to agree with you.

Do write to me regularly.

Yours sincerely,

SJT. SHANKER
C/o MATHURADAS TRIKUMJI
PANCHGANI CASTLE
PANCHGANI

From a microfilm: S.N. 14207

250. LETTER TO SECRETARY, JUBILEE COMMITTEE

HASSAN,
August 3, 1927

DEAR FRIEND,

I am much obliged to you for the invitation to the Maharaja Silver Jubilee Commemoration[1]. I hope that the function will be worthy of the occasion.

Yours faithfully,

THE SECRETARY
JUBILEE COMMITTEE
BANGALORE CITY

From a microfilm: S.N. 14209

[1] On August 8, 1927

251. *SPEECH AT TOWN HALL, HASSAN*[1]

August 3, 1927

FRIENDS,

You have given me addresses of welcome and you have given me a purse, and I thank you for the same. I am also pleased to hear of your khadi work and your invitation to open your Khaddar Co-operative Society. I must also thank you for your work in the uplift of the *Adi Karnatakas*. In doing so, let me remind you that this great work cannot be fully accomplished merely by the establishment of a school, etc. You must do the work in your heart. You must get rid of the untouchability-feeling from your thoughts. You must know that there is no sanction in the Shastras for such thinking. When you get that feeling of brotherliness, when you get that oneness of feeling between you all, Hindus and Mussalmans, and both sexes, when you get that feeling by using khadi, every one of you, then only our condition, and the condition of our country is going to improve and not until then. That is the force of khadi and, in establishing your Khadi Co-operative Society, you must all co-operate in this great task. That task is to give food to the starving poor of your place, for, when you take khaddar and make others purchase it, the weavers who wove and the spinners who spun are sure of their wages and of their food. Are you going to help this cause?

I am appealing to you for your help. I once more express my satisfaction at your efforts to establish an institute for the *Adi Karnatakas* on the lines of the Tuskegee Institute of Booker T. Washington. Friends, now, the need is for many such institutions all over the country. The names of General Armstrong and Booker T. Washington are very great names of service and sacrifice; I want you to understand and realize the amount of their work. I want our educated friends to realize this. I want them also to realize that when they are propagating intellectual culture, they must also inculcate the principle of dignity of labour as is done in those institutions. Please remember this. I thank you all for your reception.

The Hindu, 5-8-1927

[1] In reply to welcome addresses presented by the District Board and Hassan Municipality

252. EXHIBITION SALES

Sjt. Sitaram Shastri wires:

> Cloth exhibited Andhra branch stall, Bangalore Exhibition, worth Rs. 4,085; sales—retail Rs. 1,705, wholesale Rs. 1,516.

Masulipatam Satyanarayana informs:

> Exhibition Stall: Cloth worth Rs. 3,051; sales—retail Rs. 980, wholesale Rs. 966.

That means 80 per cent, and 63 per cent, of the stock, which is indeed very good.

Young India, 4-8-1927

253. INDIAN SHIPPING

The ceremony performed by Sjt. Vithalbhai Patel at the launching of *Jalabala*, the Scindia Steam Navigation Company's new ship, does not evoke any feeling of national pride or rejoicing. It only serves as a reminder of our fallen state. What is the addition of one little ship to our microscopic fleet? The sadness of the reminder is heightened by the fact that our mercantile fleet may at any moment be turned into a fleet warring against our own liberty or against that of nations with which India has no quarrel and with whose aspirations India may even have every sympathy, as for instance, China. There is nothing to prevent the Government from commandeering any one of the ships belonging to the swadeshi companies for carrying soldiers to punish China for daring to fight for liberty. There is no wonder, therefore, that Vithalbhai Patel, who in spite of his being the Speaker of the Legislative Assembly cannot cease to be an ardent nationalist, recalled the history of the calculated destruction of India's mercantile marine. He pointed out to his audience that "there was a time when first-rate vessels built, owned, manned and managed by Indians used to carry the rich products of India to distant lands." "A combination of circumstances," which the speaker did not think it worth while to mention, "made it extremely difficult for Indians to pursue it, killed that industry outright, and subsequently made it extremely difficult for Indians to revive their past glory." Sjt. Vithalbhai went on: "It is again interesting to note that shipping companies were started during the last 50 years in India, but they were all wiped out of existence by the rate war and other methods, about which the less said the better."

But even as a patient derives comfort, if anything gives him a little hope and a little energy, and the whole family joins him rejoicing over the acquisition of slight unexpected strength, so did Vithalbhai Patel derive joy and hope from the launching of this new enterprise of the Scindia Steam Navigation Company. Let us hope that *Jalabala* will be a precursor of many other steamers and that in the near future it would be possible to revive the old ship-building trade of India, and for some patriot to perform the ceremony of launching an Indian-built ship on Indian waters free of the fear of its being used for warring against ourselves or any other nation and free also from the greed of exploitation of any other country.

Young India, 4-8-1927

254. CULTURAL SPINNING

An English friend sends me a cutting from the *Scotsman* of 21st April. It is entitled "Value of Rhythm". It is an account of a spinning demonstration at the Easter Conference held at Edinburgh under the auspices of the Institute of Handicraft Teachers. Dr. John Gunn presided at the meeting. The lecture demonstration was given by Mr. William Kirkness F.S.A. (Scot). I quote below verbatim the interesting report[1] from the *Scotsman*:

Young India, 4-8-1927

255. VILLAGE CATTLE IMPROVEMENT

This week I give Mr. W. Smith's note[2] on a co-operative scheme for the improvement of village cattle. The pinjrapole scheme published in the issue of July 7th[3] is capable of being enforced almost immediately, because the machinery is ready and only requires supplementary improvement, whereas the proposed scheme for the villages outside the ghee-producing tract and

[1] Not reproduced here. The lecturer spoke highly of the value of spinning in the education of temperamental children.

[2] Not reproduced here

[3] By Y. M. Parnerkar; *vide* "Work before Pinjrapoles", 7-7-1927

remote from cities is comparatively difficult of operation. But real improvement has to begin from these numerous villages, which, on account of economic pressure and the ignorance of people in cattle-breeding, helplessly become centres for slaughter-houses to draw upon. If a careful student were to study the movement of cattle that find themselves in the numerous slaughter-houses of India, he will find that agents who know no principle save that of making money as fast as possible and anyhow purchase cattle from these remote villages for the slaughter-houses. A *gosevak* is not easily made, certainly never for the wishing. He has to study his art as much as an engineer or a lawyer or a doctor, and has to take more pains than any of them. Mr. Smith's scheme should, therefore, be studied by those who desire the welfare of cattle and of Indian villages, with a view to putting it into operation in select villages. There is nothing sacrosanct about the scheme. It serves as a model for one who knows nothing about cattle-breeding or co-operative schemes. Nor need a non-co-operator be frightened of it, because of the mention of Government co-operative department. There is no such thing as national non-co-operation at the present moment. When it was in vogue, it did not touch all Government departments. There were non-co-operators who did not taboo co-operative societies, and I know several today who call themselves non-co-operators although they belong to active co-operative organizations. But a *gosevak* who does not wish to take advantage of a statutory co-operative society may still utilize the scheme. Indeed I do not know that on the whole it would not be better to do without seeking the shelter of a statutory society. He may take the advice of the co-operative department if it will whole-heartedly give it to him, and may also make use of studs if any are available. The chief thing is to make a beginning in the matter of the education of villagers in cattle improvement. The proposed scheme is a help in that direction. Mr. Smith promises a double increase in the value of cattle and the yield of milk if the scheme is properly worked.

Young India, 4-8-1927

256. *HELP GUJARAT*

Proud Gujarat is laid low and she who has hitherto filled the beggar's bowl is now obliged to take the bowl herself. I have had up to now nothing to go by except the newspaper reports. Though Sjt. Vallabhbhai Patel was preparing me for the worst through his private wires he was unable to give details. I give below his telegram just received on my return from Hassan:[1]

> Most part of Gujarat North of Narmada and Kathiawar devastated. People rendered homeless. Cattle and belongings washed away. Total damage in crores. Loss of life small except in Baroda. Kheda district is worst with 100 inches of rain. Borsad still isolated. Piteous appeals for help coming from all parts of Gujarat and Kathiawar. Public meeting was held on August 2nd, Relief Committees formed. Three lakhs for food relief Ahmedabad district and ten lakhs for advancing loans reconstruction of houses to be raised. Provincial relief to be separately conducted under Prantik Samiti. Relief centres have been opened under Amritlal Thakkar, Lakshmidas Purushottam and Narahari Parikh respectively at Anand, Nadiad and Mehmedabad. Maganlal Gandhi will reach Borsad and establish communications. Other centres are also being reached and relief operations started. Amritlal Sheth is trying to reach areas of Kathiawar and is organizing relief. The immediate problem is one of saving life by the timely supply of foodstuffs. Local resources are inadequate. Pray issue a general appeal to all India for succour without delay.

Sjt. Fulchand Shah sends a detailed wire from Nadiad about Kheda. Dr. Chandulal of Broach sends an angry wire asking me what I intend doing towards the relief of the distress in Gujarat. I have been dumbstruck by the newspaper reports. Those who know anything of the devastating floods in the South can somewhat realize what a howling wilderness parts of Gujarat must have become. Kheda owes its fertility to the industry of its resourceful farmers. It is no joke for them to find the whole of their crops washed away and their fields stinking with the stench of the carcasses of their valuable and splendid cattle.

I know that no human effort can possibly make up for the loss of crores' worth of crops, cattle and belongings, together with rich manure washed away into the ocean, but human sympathy can do much to relieve the mental agony of the people who

[1] Gandhiji returned from Hassan on 4th evening.

have lost their all. I do hope that all who see this appeal and who can will send their mite towards relief.

Sjt. Patel is a seasoned soldier and has no other occupation than that of service. He has got an efficient agency of workers under him. Donors need, therefore, have no fear of wasteful expense or misappropriation. Properly audited accounts will be published, and all sums received will be acknowledged in the columns of *Young India* and if necessary *Navajivan*. Relief work will be done by him in collaboration with other agencies that may be brought into being. The chief thing is to send help. Let the donor choose his favourite and most trusted agency, but let him make sure that he sends not the least but the most he can.

Young India, 11-8-1927

257. LETTER TO H. HARCOURT[1]

AS AT THE ASHRAM, SABARMATI,
August 4, 1927

DEAR FRIEND,

I thank you for your warm letter. You may not know that I expressed before the trying judge the same sentiments that you express, namely, that my viewpoint not being accepted, the Government was bound to arrest and imprison me.[2] The challenge to Government to do either the one or the other was for me the only honourable course, and, in my opinion, the only alternative to violent rebellion on the part of those who rightly or wrongly feel oppressed. But the largest part of my life has been devoted and is still being devoted to finding points of contact rather than difference. But experience has abundantly proved to me that to every honest man there come in his life occasions for parting of ways which I have termed "Non-co-operation".

Yours sincerely,

H. HARCOURT, ESQ.
119, GIPSY HILL
LONDON S.E. 19

From a photostat: S.N. 12535

[1] In reply to the addressee's letter dated July 12, 1927

[2] *Vide* Vol. XXIII, p. 115.

258. *LETTER TO G. A. PATKAR*

As at the Ashram, Sabarmati,
August 4, 1927

DEAR FRIEND,

I have your letter. Your idea of starting a fund is praiseworthy; but I am afraid it will not work. It is not a small thing for one who draws a salary of Rs. 50 to save Rs. 5 out of it every month, and I have found even amongst those who can afford, very few steadily paying. Nor, when the capital required is collected in the manner you suggest, is it an easy thing to start industries. The starting of industries requires more than mere capital. And, thirdly, my own time which owing to my failing health is limited is entirely absorbed by the industry of khadi, and if your friends would be content to pay their quota to this national industry, I shall be pleased to receive it, but not for any other industry.

Yours sincerely,

Sjt. G. A. Patkar
Bombay

From a photostat: S.N. 14211

259. *LETTER TO SWAMI*

[After *August 4, 1927*][1]

Your two letters. One is about relieving you and the other about the floods in Gujarat.

I do not know and I believe that your request to be relieved has nothing to do with your quarrel with Kaka[2]. If I have to grant you the discharge, I cannot do it until I go over there, because I must, as is my practice, first get to know the main persons there. Only then could I know what to do. I would know nothing about Bhai Mohanlal. If you have full confidence, I have no objection to your shouldering the responsibility of the work while taking up the other job and moving wherever you like.

[1] From the reference to heavy floods in Gujarat and to Vallabhbhai's appeal published in *Young India* of this date

[2] D. B. Kalelkar

If the responsibility is not yours, I can be carefree only when I come to know Bhai Mohanlal and put him in charge or appoint someone else as superintendent. I think neither course is possible at the moment. Even the trust matter is uncertain at present.

Since you are coming here in connection with your work, we shall discuss the matter further then. Kaka is all right. I had gone out on tour for three days but did not take Kaka with me. You may rest assured from my side about Kaka because I am not the one to coerce. I shall try to give full weight to the idea suggested by you if you come and explain it to me; if you do not come at all I shall try to put it across to the extent I have understood it. If you are suggesting that I have no right to direct Kaka, I will not accept that view. I sensed some such hint in your letter. I cannot quite agree with the meaning you seem to attach to friendship. I too had interpreted it somewhat like that in my nonage. If my assumption that you put a similar interpretation on it is correct, I also know that it is contrary to dharma. I have written somewhere in *Navajivan* itself that in this world there can be no friend except God and that we are all bullocks together; in that some are more close to each other, some less so. But then I have digressed into a new subject. In short, it is enough if I could satisfy you by being as agreeable as I could.

Now my view about the collection from Malabar is that it should not be used in Gujarat. I think it would be upright to act as if the amount had been spent up when the time-limit of the notice I had issued expired. That it has not been spent up is mere chance. That we act differently when pressed by circumstances and through weakness is another thing. I merely give my opinion. But if you or Vallabhbhai do not approve of that view, please do correct me. There is no place for delicacy[1] in such matters, and certainly none among us.

Now about my going over there. While reading your letter I felt I should start soon. Not even three quarters of an hour has passed after reading it, but the swoon is over now. I am no longer fit to travel. I know my body well enough. I still have enough strength to be left alone to think and do my work, but the ability to talk to a group, to guide and to explain things to a succession of people coming to me, to humour them, to get angry with them and to get work out of them has all but left me. After all it may possibly return. At present the ability to lie down and sleep is on the increase. In this condition, I think

[1] The source has this in English.

it is not possible for me to go over there, sit in the Ashram and rally volunteers. Moreover, I believe one cannot do work without running around and I never had the knack of taking work from new people while sitting in one place without moving about. If we cannot get volunteers in response to Vallabhbhai's appeal[1], we had better realize our limitations. If more funds come in, let them remain unused; we may offer them to those others who could do better work than we; on the other hand if we know that we still command respect enough to collect more money but not the strength to rally workers we should sit quiet, not squander our influence by asking for funds. You may not be aware that everyone in Malabar had surplus money left with him not because of lack of volunteers but because when everything is uprooted people work in a different way and do not even think of the losses. There is no power in the world which would meet the wants of crores of people. All of us can therefore do only some patchwork. And I think we ought to do that. While doing so if we can ensure that the rogues and thieves do not get at the money or that the protectors do not become looters, we shall have acquitted ourselves as well as taking a dip in the Ganga.[2] Such floods suggest that what we say in our childhood is *veda vakya*[3]—this is God's play with bat and ball. One day there is sure to come a flood bigger than the present one. Even then some will survive who will not brood over the dead but will be able to laugh and multiply the race. Do not deduce from this that I wish to say that it would not matter if we became cruel or if we did nothing. Absolutely not. However, I must say we need not take upon ourselves the responsibility for all this destruction. But we needs must make our contribution to the extent possible to relieving the misery arising from this destruction and rest content. I do not at all approve of the argument that at this time we should organize an army of volunteers and awaken Gujarat once again. When the time comes, and the understanding is there and if it has been decreed that we become the instruments, anything may or may not happen now, Gujarat will wake up and so will the whole of India. But this is for me a matter of faith more or less. It is out of place here even to think of it. We should not shirk doing whatever we can in regard to this emergency.

[1] Published in *Young India*, 4-8-1927

[2] A Gujarati proverb meaning the highest achievement

[3] Scriptural utterance

I can think of nothing more.

[From Gujarati]

From the manuscript of Mahadev Desai's Diary. Courtesy: Narayan Desai

260. LETTER TO MIRABEHN

KUMARA PARK, BANGALORE,
August 5, 1927

CHI. MIRA,

I have your letter. I understand and do not mind the distinction you draw between Wardha and Sabarmati. I am glad you have written to Bhansali. There is nothing further about the Ashram beyond what I wrote to you.

The learning of Hindi must not be a strain upon you. You must not do it as a task. Immediately it gets on your nerves, you must let it go. I have told you that I have infinite patience and I shall certainly not take you to task if you can't finish your programme in two months' time. The work must give you pleasure, and it must be left off as soon as it fatigues you.

If I knew what work is to be given to you as soon as you go to the Ashram, I would certainly tell you; but I do not know it myself. I quite agree with your argument against teaching English, and I shall certainly avoid giving that work. So far as I can see at present, it will be some work to be done in company. For, I want you to be accustomed to different temperaments and working under circumstances no matter how adverse they may be. But if you have any choice, by no means tell me. My own habit is never to tax myself about things which I need not decide at the moment. But if you will begin to think of it from now, by all means do, and discuss with me through your letters. In no case would I have given you anything without first consulting you. I shall certainly want to know your choice whether now or after you have gone to the Ashram.

It is quite right your not having written to the Rao Saheb until you had the inspiration. There is no hurry, and so long as the proper language does not come you need not write at all.

I just returned from touring this morning to find your letter. The touring will be resumed on the 9th instant. Then probably I shall be away for nearly 10 days. But it would be safer to send your letters to Bangalore. I said Bangalore City before, but I find that Bangalore brings your letters two hours earlier. Kumara Park is not served from the City office but from the Central office.

With love,

SRIMATI MIRABAI
WARDHA

From the original: C.W. 5258. Courtesy: Mirabehn

261. TELEGRAM TO MIRABEHN

[*August*] 5 [*1927*][1]

MIRABAI
SATYAGRAHA ASHRAM
WARDHA

LETTER DULY POSTED.[2] ALL WELL. LOVE.

BAPU

From the original: C.W. 5257. Courtesy: Mirabehn

262. LETTER TO MAHARAJA OF MYSORE

BANGALORE,
August 5 [*1927*][3]

DEAR FRIEND,

Next Monday[4] will be perhaps next to your coronation the happiest day in your life. In what manner should I send you my felicitations? Not by mere words of good wishes however well meant they may be. But I feel that I could not as a true friend do less than suggest your doing for your poorest subjects what you seem so successfully to have done for the middle class, the town-dwellers. You may not be able to do anything striking so soon as Monday next. But is it impossible to do away with the drink traffic? It is ruining the people.

It has been a matter of deep joy to me to learn wherever I have gone nothing but praise of your benevolence and purity.

[1] From the postmark

[2] *Vide* the preceding item.

[3] Gandhiji was in Bangalore on this date in 1927

[4] August 8, 1927 was the 25th anniversary of the Maharaja's coronation. A formal message, *vide* the succeeding item, also appeared in the Press.

The drink curse under a rule so good appears to be so out of tune.

But I must not turn what is meant the heart-wish of a friend into a lecture. May you be long spared to give happiness to your people and to make yours a model State in every sense of the term.

I shall pray on Monday for a due fulfilment of all your noblest wishes.

I am,
Your Highness's

[PS.]

Pray do not feel bound to acknowledge this note.

THE MAHARAJA OF MYSORE

From a photostat: S.N. 12630

263. MESSAGE ON SILVER JUBILEE

[August 5, 1927][1]

It has been a most agreeable thing for me to find that no one has ever had a word to say against the Maharaja Saheb. I have almost wondered whether the friends round me have conspired to keep all evil reports from me. May all the good I have heard of the Maharaja be and for ever remain wholly true. I join the people of Mysore in wishing His Highness many a long year of useful service to the State and its people.

From a photostat S.N. 12630

264. ANSWERS TO QUESTIONS BY MOOLCHAND AGRAWAL

[August 5, 1927][2]

[Q.] 1. Do you believe in the distinct existence of Trinity—Nature, Soul and God?

[A.] I do believe but the word "distinct" sticks in the throat, for though the three are separate in name they are one in substance.

2. Whether soul is one or numerous? Has it entirely its separate existence or is it a portion of the Great *Atman*—God?

[1] Presumably written on the same date as the preceding item

[2] *Vide* the succeeding item.

Souls seem to be many; but underneath the seeming variety, there is an essential oneness.

3. If it is a particle [of God] it ought to be all-knowing, quite free from all evils and should possess all the qualities of God, as a particle of fire, water or gold possesses all the talents of the whole from which it is separated.

In its essence the soul is free from all evil, but torn from its source it partakes of evil and all other limitations even as a drop of water torn from its source and found as part of a dirty pool seems for the time being to partake of the pool's dirt.

4. We often see that a man does evil deeds. Whence that evil comes?

We should be satisfied to know that there is evil in the world and that it has got to be avoided. If we knew its origin we should be God Almighty. But at the present we are in the unfortunate position of that drop of water in the dirty pool, and whilst we are doers of evil deeds, we must suffer the consequences thereof.

5. In the world we see different men. Those who work and do right deeds are gifted; those who do wrong or bad deeds are punished and have to suffer. This is all in accordance with the theory of karma. When one suffers —as a peasant or a labourer in India does at present, he suffers through his own past deeds, that is the Will of God. Why should we interfere in the Will of God by helping him so that he may not suffer?

If the Indian peasant was isolated and was seated on some mountain top, we shall not be perhaps responsible for his state. But seeing that he is part of the same society that we are, we cannot divest ourselves of responsibility for his state even as that drop of water in the pool cannot. Why God suffers this evil to exist, I am thankful to feel that He alone knows.

6. Instead of devoting our energies for the good of *others* should we not devote our energies in acquiring knowledge or earning money for ourselves or at the most for our relatives and neighbours and that too because they may help us in time of need?

Precisely for the reason that we may help our relatives, must we help all others whom in our ignorance we refuse to recognize as relatives. We are like the drop of water. It enjoys even that dirty existence by the help of its neighbours at the farthest end; for, its near neighbours have to depend upon theirs and so on to the end.

7. Yourself as well as others define "swarajya" as control over the self, reformation, betterment or improvement of the *self*, and also it is evident, that if

one controls and improves or reforms himself, the society or the nation will be reformed by itself as the *nation* is a composition of *individuals*.

It is a correct statement; self-rule is home-rule.

From a photostat: G.N. 765

265. LETTER TO MOOLCHAND AGRAWAL

BANGALORE,
Shravan Shukla 8 [*August 5, 1927*][1]

BHAI MOOLCHANDJI,

I do not think it necessary to answer your queries[2] in *Young India*. Ask me any other questions if you want to.

Yours,
MOHANDAS

From a photostat of the Hindi: G.N. 765

266. LETTER TO W. LUTOSTAWSKI

AS AT THE ASHRAM, SABARMATI,
August 6, 1927

DEAR FRIEND,

You will now see my reply to your questions in *Young India*,[3] and if you have any further questions, please do not hesitate to ask.

I like your three rules about preservation of health. The two I understand thoroughly. For, I myself don't believe in worry and always try to snatch moments for sleep and possess a fair capacity for going off to sleep almost at will. Fasting too I understand. But I do not do as you seem to have been doing. You say you fast for 10 or 15 days before each voyage. This requires explanation. 10 or 15 is a very vague number. For, 10 days or 15 days make a great difference for a fasting man, at least such is my experience. And what is this fasting? Do you take nothing during the fast except water, not fruit, not milk? Have you record of your weight before and after fast? How often have you taken these fasts? What is your weight now, and what is the meaning of each voyage? What is its duration? Do you fast,

[1] Gandhiji was in Bangalore on this date in 1927.
[2] *Vide* the preceding item.
[3] *Vide* "Unity in Variety", 11-8-1927.

for instance, if you have to be at sea for one day only? You say you take one meal about midday at a time of intense activity. What does that meal consist of? And, do you take no fruit, no milk, no other drink except water either in the morning or in the evening? Then, again you say you fast only when you have too much weight. Do you then say that you have always too much weight before each voyage? And why do you ever have too much weight if you are a spare eater as you evidently seem to be? When you are not intensely active, how many meals do you take?

Then you say that you use at least 20 quarts of water to clear your bowels every day, until the water is returned clean and transparent and this you do when you have too much weight. What do you mean by use of water? Is it enema, or do you drink 20 quarts, even whilst you are taking your one meal per day? If you drink it, do you work it out through the kidneys or through the bowels? The experience of myself and all my friends who have fasted for long lengths of time is that when we have fasted the water has to pass through the kidneys, never through the bowels unless we have taken the enema. As you may know I am deeply interested in all experiments in fasting and dietetics whether merely for health or spiritual growth.

Yours sincerely,

PROF. W. LUTOSTAWSKI
JAGIELLONSKA 7 m. 2, WILNO
(POLAND)

From a photostat: S.N. 12513

267. TELEGRAM TO JAMNALAL BAJAJ

[On or after *August 6, 1927*][1]

JAMNALALJI
SATYAGRAHASHRAM
SABARMATI

CONSIDER YOUR ATTENDANCE HINDI SAMMELAN MEETING ALLAHABAD FOURTEENTH INSTANT ABSOLUTELY NECESSARY. YOU SHOULD CANVASS OTHER MEMBERS.

BAPU

From a photostat: S.N. 15172

[1] From a note in Gujarati in the source, it is evident that this was sent at the same time as the following two telegrams.

268. TELEGRAM TO SAROJINI NAIDU[1]

[On or after *August 6, 1927*]

SAROJINIDEVI
TAJMAHAL

AM CONSTANT COMMUNICATION VALLABHBHAI. CONSULTING HIM ABOUT NECESSITY MY PRESENCE.

GANDHI

From a photostat: S.N. 15173

269. TELEGRAM TO VALLABHBHAI PATEL

[On or after *August 6, 1927*]

VALLABHBHAI

SAROJINI DEVI SAYS I SHOULD GO THERE FOR MORAL SUCCOUR. IS MY PRESENCE ABSOLUTELY NECESSARY? AM STILL USELESS FOR ACTIVE WORK OR LONG DISCUSSIONS CONFERENCES.

BAPU

From a photostat: S.N. 15173 A

270. DEATH OF A SATYAGRAHI

Perhaps all readers of *Navajivan* may not be familiar with the name of Shri Harilal Maneklal Desai. He died a few days ago in Broach. A friend who lived with him says in a letter that his face was lit up with an expression of joy till the very end.

Shri Harilal resigned from the Baroda High School at the time of the Non-co-operation movement. He was the French teacher there. From then until his death he retained unwavering faith in non-co-operation. He strove to the best of his ability to follow truth as he understood it, and so I called him a satyagrahi. His humility was an ornament to his love of truth. He toured

[1] In reply to her telegram received on August 6, 1927, which read: "Dear Bapu even risking your health do visit Gujarat. Your presence essential. Give moral succour and solace in terrible distress. All friends join me this request."

with me for a while in the early days of the Non-co-operation movement and I was struck at that time by his clean method of work, his thoroughness and alertness. During those days it was he who replied to many of the letters I received, and helped me in other ways. During that period of my association with him, I could see that he took great pains to understand satyagraha and non-co-operation. He started khadi work in Kapadwanj by his unaided efforts and made a success of it. During the last years of his life, he helped the Broach Education Society and did whatever teaching work came his way. Among the names which I have mentally noted of those who can be relied upon to plunge into a civil disobedience movement if such an auspicious occasion arises, Haribhai's was one. Cruel fate has now erased that name. A satyagrahi, however, does not feel sorry even for this. A satyagrahi friend helps even in death as much as he does when alive. "To live on in death" is the great *mantra* which inspires his life.

[From Gujarati]

Navajivan, 7-8-1927

271. LETTER TO MIRABEHN

August 7, 1927

CHI. MIRA,

I must be very brief this time, for I have much writing in front of me. The Gujarat floods and visitors occupy my time.

I have discussed with Kakasaheb what Valunjker told you. Kakasaheb says he never intended to give the impression that with Valunjker he was ready and willing to establish an ashram for women and do educational work among them. He loves that work but does not consider himself to be yet ready for it.

With love,

BAPU

[PS.]

Later—I have your letter. The Monday letter was duly posted. May it be that you have inferred from the date of the letter that it was not Monday's? This passes as a Monday letter. The date you will see is Sunday's, because it was written last night as nowadays I often do after taking silence. This I do to avoid continuous strain on Mondays. Of course you must not read so as to strain your eyes.

BAPU

From the original: C.W. 5259. Courtesy: Mirabehn

272. *LETTER TO GULZAR MOHAMAD 'AQUIL'*

KUMARA PARK, BANGALORE,
August 7, 1927

DEAR FRIEND,

I have your letter and I am glad you have written to me.

I am indeed aware of the unfortunate controversy over the book *Rangila Rasul*. You may not know that probably long before you knew the book or its contents, it came into my hands and I denounced it in strong language in the columns of *Young India*. This happened three years ago. I have not the *Young India* file before me. But the book is not a recent publication. If you are not a regular reader of *Young India* I shall be glad to ask the manager to send you the reference.

I have taken no part in the present controversy because I think that the Mussalman agitation is almost altogether wrong. Their denunciation of the judge[1] is uncalled for. Agitation for an amendment of the law is absolutely proper. But whether there is agitation or not the Government will be bound to strengthen the law.

So far as the merits are concerned, there are at least an equal number of equally scurrilous anti-Hindu writings as anti-Islamic. All this has been stated by me in clear language in the pages of *Young India*.

I do not read all the newspapers. The Hindu-edited newspapers have not appeared to me to have vigorously or at all supported the action of the author of *Rangila Rasul* or in any other way been disrespectful to the Prophet. I shall thank you to let me have the newspapers you have in mind. Or, if you will give me the number and names of the newspapers, I shall send for them myself.

I am sorry to know that you think that the communal taint has affected me. So far as I know myself, I can give my assurance that I am the same to my Mussalman brethren that I was in

[1] Justice Dilip Singh; *vide* also "A Letter", 10-7-1927.

1920, and it is my constant prayer to God that I may be and remain the same up to the end of my life.

Yours sincerely,
M. K. GANDHI

GULZAR MOHAMAD 'AQUIL', ESQ.
HATI GATE
BATALA (DISTRICT GURUDASPUR)
PUNJAB

From a microfilm: S.N. 12385

273. LETTER TO WILLIAM SMITH

KUMARA PARK, BANGALORE,
August 7, 1927

DEAR MR. SMITH,

I thank you for your letter about the Italian method of castration enclosing a letter from the Superintendent, Imperial Cattle-breeding Farm, Karnal.

I shall see if I can prepare something for you that may be fit for publication. But I hope you will not mind delay; for, as you know I have not much time at my disposal. But I am asking the manager to let me have accurate details and figures.

Yours sincerely,

From a microfilm: S.N. 12921

274. LETTER TO Y. M. PARNERKAR

KUMARA PARK, BANGALORE,
August 7, 1927

MY DEAR PARNERKAR,

I enclose herewith two letters for your file and note. When you can get the time I would like you to give me notes containing the information enabling me to prepare the article of the kind Mr. William Smith wants.

I hope that you are now thoroughly acclimatized and that both of you are keeping well and fit.

Yours sincerely,

SJT. PARNERKAR
DAIRY
ASHRAM
SABARMATI

From a microfilm: S.N. 12922

275. LETTER TO SATIS CHANDRA DAS GUPTA

KUMARA PARK, BANGALORE,
August 7, 1927

DEAR SATIS BABU,

I have your letter. You must take only that service from Dr. Ray which he can freely give from his heart. Khadi has ultimately to stand on its own merits and legs. It is well if we can get real co-operation from our great men. But it must be well also if we do not. We must rely upon the eternal truth that nothing on this earth that is intrinsically sound and is represented by a living force can possibly die.

Your difficulties I can understand well. And if I had a bagful of coins I could send them to you by express parcel in order to relieve your pecuniary distress; but I have not much hope of getting anything either. What I am able to collect in these parts will have to be used for development here. Therefore the only way to give pecuniary help to Bengal is for me to go to Bengal when you are ready and tour to collect.

This year is to go without, and the programme here will have to be carried over to next year, almost up to the end of March with an interval of a fortnight at the Ashram for Ramdas' marriage. I therefore want you to become accustomed to think that you must manage our business, as it may now be called, with what capital we have. Therefore, I would like you, Kshitish Babu and others who are associated with you to confer together and evolve a programme which will save you from all worry and trouble. Once we recognize our limitations we shall cease to fret.

From your letter, I gather that there will be no office in Calcutta proper and that all your work would be done as from Sodepur. Will there be a store in Calcutta, or not even that? Personally, I would not mind if you thought that there should be no store in Calcutta, that is to say, that there should be none if it was not self-supporting.

I am still keeping fit. I shall be in and about Bangalore up to the 28th of this month, if there is no peremptory call from Gujarat owing to the floods. Pressure is being put upon me to go there. But till Vallabhbhai wants me, I shall resist the pressure. For I know that I can do nothing by my mere presence if I cannot do active work.

Yours,

BABU SATIS CHANDRA DAS GUPTA
KHADI PRATISHTHAN
SODEPUR

From a microfilm: S.N. 19797

276. LETTER TO ASHRAM WOMEN

Silence Day [August 8, 1927][1]

SISTERS,

Today I must be brief, I lack both time and subject.

I have been forgetting to answer your inquiries about Manibehn's return. Most probably she will leave soon after the 20th and, stopping at Poona and Bombay for a day each, she will go to Broach and from there to the Ashram.

We are having a difficult time at the Ashram at present. All of you should continue to be brave. Our responsibilities are very great. If we always have Rama in our hearts, no harm can ever befall us.

Kakasaheb who is here is keeping well.

Blessings from
BAPU

From a photostat of the Gujarati: G.N. 3662

277. LETTER TO J. B. PETIT

KUMARA PARK, BANGALORE,
August 9, 1927

DEAR MR. PETIT,

You will forgive me for troubling you once more. Probably Andrews has cabled to you that he is returning on the 20th instant. I see that the Corporation has voted an address. I have suggested in my article in *Young India*[2] that it should be made the occasion of a public demonstration on a wide scale. For, not

[1] From the reference to lack of time; *vide* also "Letter to Mirabehn", 7-8-1927.

[2] *Vide* "Welcome Good Samaritan", 11-8-1927.

only does Andrews deserve all the honour that we can show to him but the occasion will bear a political significance in South Africa and will strengthen Mr. Sastri's hands if the presentation of the address becomes not a humdrum function but an enthusiastic popular demonstration.

The main purpose of this letter is to suggest that the Imperial Citizenship Association should present him with a solid purse to be utilized by him for educational and kindred work in South Africa. You might have seen Mr. Sastri's appeal for social. . . .[1] All this is in conjunction with Mr. Andrews. No doubt our people in South Africa must find the means; but both their capacity and will are limited. Anything sent from here will encourage the workers there and strengthen Mr. Sastri's hands. And the reason why I suggest the presentation of the purse in a public manner to Mr. Andrews is that its demonstrative value may be emphasized. Indeed, in my articles I have even suggested the Corporation instead of giving a costly casket should vote a purse, that is of course if it is permissible under its rules.

I am sending a copy of this letter to Mr. Natarajan.

Yours sincerely,
M. K. GANDHI

From a photostat: S.N. 12369

278. LETTER TO K. S. NATARAJAN

KUMARA PARK, BANGALORE,
August 9, 1927

DEAR MR. NATARAJAN,

I enclose herewith a copy of my letter to Mr. Petit for your consideration. The letter speaks for itself.

Yours sincerely,
M. K. GANDHI

SJT. K. S. NATARAJAN
BOMBAY

From a photostat: S.N. 12369

[1] The source has a blank here.

279. LETTER TO KONDA VENKATAPPAYYA

KUMARA PARK, BANGALORE,
August 9, 1927

DEAR FRIEND,

I have your letter. Mahadev has not been able to place before me the papers you refer to as yet; for, he has found me too busy.

The inks I shall test and let you know my impression.

How is your daughter getting on both in health and studies? She must some day come to the Ashram.

Yours sincerely,

SJT. KONDA VENKATAPPAYYAGARU
GUNTUR

From a microfilm: S.N. 14212

280. LETTER TO E. S. PATWARDHAN

KUMARA PARK, BANGALORE,
August 9, 1927

DEAR FRIEND,

I have your letter. I am sending it to Sheth Jamnalalji and asking him to go into the matter carefully and do whatever he thinks just and possible. Beyond that I must not influence him.

Yours sincerely,
M. K. GANDHI

E. S. PATWARDHAN, ESQ.
PRESIDENT
TILAK VIDYALAYA
NAGPUR

From a microfilm: S.N. 14215

281. *LETTER TO JAMINI BHUSHAN MITRA*

KUMARA PARK, BANGALORE,
August 9, 1927

DEAR JAMINI BABU,

I have your letter. I appreciate the confidence you repose in me. But the attitude you have adopted is wrong. Even if I was well, I should be powerless to do anything single-handed. But I am still more powerless seeing that I could take no part in the administrative work. Surely, you and Satis Babu know each other much better than you and I. And if you cannot convince Satis Babu, how shall I be able to help? But if you think that Satis Babu is prejudiced against you, you should have self-confidence enough to be able to convince the Secretary of the Association and the members of the Council other than Satis Babu of his prejudice. I can give you this assurance that Mr. Shankerlal Banker in the first instance and the other members of the Council in the second will consider all you might have to say quite impartially and independently of Satis Babu. There is also Dr. Ray and he will surely listen to you as much as to Satis Babu. For I know what affection he has for you. For my own part I must also add that Satis Babu will not do any conscious injustice to you. As a matter of fact, he wrote to me a kind letter about you and nothing will please me better than to find that you have met Satis Babu and become satisfied that he has no prejudice against you. After all he has no ends of his own to serve by putting obstacles in your way. He has exchanged a life of ease, comfort and honour for one of deprivation, pains, sorrows and self-effacement. If I am wrong you may correct me. It grieves me that self-sacrificing workers cannot hold together and work away for a cause which is common to them all.

Yours sincerely,

SJT. JAMINI BHUSHAN MITRA
KHALISPUR ASHRAM
P.O. BALIKHOLA
KHALISPUR
KHULNA (BENGAL)

From a microfilm: S.N. 19798

282. LETTER TO SWAMI

August 9, 1927

Your latest telegram.[1] I have sent a reply by wire which you must have received. Your telegram and your letter are full of your love and your sorrow. I expect nothing else of you.

It is my duty to restrain excess of love. I could not see from the figures you sent me that we are at the moment in a position to produce Rs. 25,000. I understand that at present we can somehow balance the two sides.

But if we have a saving of Rs. 25,000, does it not prove that we must be making a huge profit somewhere or that we do not pay enough to our workers?

It may or may not be as you say. None the less I do feel that if we have the capacity to make this donation it could be done only anonymously. If our small institution could make such a large donation, it would have an impact on others and this may arouse jealousy, obviously it could not be emulated. Generally, a donation is announced so that others may follow suit. Else it is merely showing off.

For us being in good shape means not being able to give away anything at all. I see from your report that the tenements of our workers are in a state of disrepair. If our resources permit we should utilize what we can spare for repairing their houses so that they would not be a burden on the public funds. I would regard that as our substantial contribution.

No one here has understood fully the meaning of your telegram. If you thought that the workers, etc., would accept minimum wages and pay up the remainder as monthly instalments, I would suggest that as they save up progressively, those savings should be utilized for the benefit of the Dheds and the Bhangis and something permanent can thus be achieved. I believe all will receive the help urgently needed and they will find their feet. If we have earned our money honestly, I wish you to make the purest use of it.

[1] Suggesting that Rs. 25,000 be set apart for flood relief by *Navajivan* and offering to defer his retirement for two years so that the institution need not suffer financially

But you may, if you like, treat all this as needless fuss. I might have scribbled a lot without knowing things. You are free to do anything in consultation with Vallabhbhai, Jamnalalji and others and I shall approve of whatever you do. I shall be quite content if you regarded the above ideas as emotional outburst of one of the press workers and treat them accordingly.

It may be that you would be bound for two years; but I like that.

Whatever I send you now is sent only after being shown to Kaka. And that will be the case hereafter. Take it that he has approved, what he has not objected to.

Had I not had on my hand today grave matters beyond my capacity, I would have written much more.

[From Gujarati]

From the manuscript of Mahadev Desai's Diary. Courtesy: Narayan Desai

283. *AN APPEAL*

BANGALORE,
August 10, 1927

FRIENDS,

This is addressed to the Gujarati-speaking Hindus, Mussalmans, Parsis and Christians if any. The other citizens will have the opportunity of subscribing to a fund which I am hoping will be soon started.

This appeal is in connection with the heavy floods of Gujarat the like of which have not occurred within living memory. I hope therefore that all Gujaratis, men and women, will contribute to this fund as much as they can. The funds will be sent to Sjt. Vallabhbhai Patel, the President of the Ahmedabad Municipality and of the Gujarat Provincial Congress Committee.

The appeal is being taken up by Messrs Chimanlal Bhogilal Desai, Raojibhai Patel and Chhotalal Kothari. Every subscriber is[1] requested to give his or her name against the sum subscribed so as to facilitate accurate publication of the list in the pages of *Young India* or *Navajivan*.

[1] End of page 2. In the photostat volume, two pages (numbered 3 and 4) are interpolated after page 2 and the original page 3 has been renumbered 5. But these two pages, which seem to be part of another appeal, are reproduced below.

[PAGES 3 & 4]

to organize relief in times of distress. Let those Gujaratis who are not wanted for work in Gujarat or who can be spared turn their attention to the places where help may be most needed. The distress of Gujarat must not blind the Gujaratis to the need of the other provinces. The present distress must be utilized to make us less provincial and more national. We must feel one with the least and the remotest of the thirty crores of God's creatures who inhabit this land.

M.K.G.

From a photostat: S.N. 12797

284. LETTER TO DR. M. A. ANSARI

KUMARA PARK, BANGALORE,
August 10, 1927

DEAR DR. ANSARI,

I have your bomb-shell. I had as long chats with Panditji over it as it was possible for us both to have. Your draft statement does not shock me. The atmosphere about us is so debilitating and irresponsive that the tallest of us becomes dazed for the moment. The suffocation has clearly overtaken you. It is no fault of yours. And as I could say to Khwaja in spite of his going back upon his brilliant professions that I could love him, so I can literally say of you in spite of what is admittedly a lapse. I say "admittedly" because you still believe in Non-co-operation, but the situation demands, in your opinion, a different conduct and you deceive yourself into the belief that the different conduct would hasten Non-co-operation. I don't believe it. But I can't impart my belief or unbelief to you. You must act up to whatever is natural for you.

But I have this suggestion. Keep those views to yourself. You are in no way called upon to publish them. For, if I am no politician, you are still less. When swaraj is established, you won't want to belong to the diplomatic service, nor to the military. You would fight shy of the law department. You would be content, if you are placed in charge of the medical service and given a free purse for all your researches, intelligent or otherwise, even as I would aspire after nothing more serious or important than the spinning department, if hand-spinning has not become universal by that time. The law, diplomacy, military and the rest, we shall leave to Motilalji and company; and if Panditji thinks that Shaukat Ali would be good company, he may throw at him the military departments.

If my reading is correct, you and I, but you more than I, will not be expected to contribute to the discussion over Assembly and Councils programme, constitution making and what not or better still, what rot. I, therefore, think that you will commit no crime against God or Indian humanity, if you announce to the world that you have no opinion on these matters which must be left to specialists and politicians. I am sure you have not made the mistake of supposing that I have sponsored your election[1] because I considered you to be a brilliant political thinker or anything near that state. The country has acclaimed your election with one voice because you are a true and good Mussalman, you are a lover of your country, there is no camouflage in you, you know your limitations, you keep your head about you, but because above all, Hindu-Muslim unity is a passion with you, and you entertain ideas about it which you would gladly share with your country and which you are impatient to share with it, and enforce them even if it be at the point of the bayonet. Your election is a demonstration, in spite of the madness raging round us, that the country is thirsting for domestic peace, and that it is sick over dishonesty, fraud, immorality and violence committed in the sacred name of religion. I therefore ask you to tear your statement to pieces. Keep that opinion to yourself, accept the election with grace, dignity and thankfulness, and announce that you have no political policy of your own to place before the country, that so far as that is concerned, you will take up a strictly judicial and impartial attitude and act merely as a chairman of meetings guiding deliberations, keeping order and enforcing decisions of majorities, that you have accepted the election with the sole intention of guiding the country during your year of office, by all the power at your command, to domestic peace. For, you owe it to the country as a Mussalman and a staunch nationalist to vindicate the religion of the Prophet and the honour of the country by giving all the talents you have for securing a domestic peace honourable to all parties. Nobody expects more of you. And, if you meddle in anything else, you will be travelling outside your province.

[1] For the Congress presidentship

I have not telegraphed to you; for, I thought I would save a few rupees of the poor spinners. That I have left to Panditji who is better able to patronize the telegraph department. You made him your carrier, and I give myself the same honour by letting him carry my reply. And in the face of this reply, you dare not refuse the crown of thorns that is offered to you by a grateful country, and you dare not publish your statement, however precious your views are. If you wish to place them before a few friends gathered together in a drawing-room enjoying hookah, you may certainly enliven the company with your views. But beyond the four walls of such a drawing-room, your views may not travel.

This letter gives you sufficient indication of my health and ill-health. Health you may gather from the length of the letter and the views expressed therein. Ill-health you are entirely to infer from the fact that much against my will I have been obliged to dictate what is purely a personal and affectionate letter of an old friend.

You need not apologize for not coming. If I find myself on the brink of the precipice, I shall not hesitate to telegraph for you, nor, if I undertake a fast more prolonged than 21 days. And I know that whatever your engagement may be, you will leave them to see a friend patient if only to say good-bye to him or to wean him from his mad fasting career. Meanwhile by all means continue to make your thousand per day on condition that a certain respectable percentage of your ill-gotten gains is reserved for the poor spinners, if only by way of penance.

May I expect a reassuring telegram from you?

When you meet Hakimji, please warn him against forgetting me altogether.

Yours sincerely,

Dr. M. A. Ansari
No. 1, Daryaganj
Delhi

From a photostat: S.N. 12870

285. *LETTER TO T. R. MAHADEVA IYER*

KUMARA PARK, BANGALORE,
August 10, 1927

DEAR FRIEND,

You must excuse me for not being able to write to you earlier. I waited purposely for one or two days as Dr. Varadarajulu was coming. I have now discussed the situation with him also. He tells me that the people in the Malay Peninsula are also with the Committee and he really thinks that I need not bother myself about the matter as in course of time the possession of the property was bound to revert to the Committee. My own opinion is that where there is a large number of people who want to observe caste restrictions, they should be able to send their children to the gurukul with the option to them to feed them separately. But if the majority of those who are in power do not favour the view and wish to have a rigid rule excluding all who wish to observe caste restrictions you should gracefully and instantaneously give up possession. If what Dr. Varadarajulu says is true, namely, that you have no effective opinion behind you, it appears to me to be useless to go to arbitration. If you will give up possession at once, you are at liberty to use this letter in order to justify your step.

Yours sincerely,

SJT. T. R. MAHADEVA IYER
NO. 1, KRISHNAMACHARI ROAD
NUNGUMBAKKAM
CATHEDRAL P.O.
MADRAS

From a microfilm: S.N. 12936-A

286. LETTER TO S. SRINIVASA IYENGAR

KUMARA PARK, BANGALORE,
August 10, 1927

DEAR FRIEND,

We had a fine family gathering yesterday—three Brahmins against two non-Brahmins or in modern language three co-operators against two non-co-operators, myself being in each case in a minority. But strangely enough, the party forgot differences of opinion and differences of *varna* and came to the unanimous opinion that you should be advised, asked and pressed to send a nice little love letter to Mr. R. K. Shunmugam Chetty asking him to see you at once for a personal chat. This decision was taken because we felt that you being a Brahmin, President of the Congress, and a leader of the Swaraj Party had an advantage over the poor non-Brahmin member of the Party, and we also felt, apart of course from Mr. Chetty, that you will honour our decision without any ado, in spite of a certain amount of delicacy about sending any such letter.

I do not need to give you the contents of the discussion; for, you will have them all from Mr. Satyamurti, and you will not expect a fellow-patient to enter into any explanation or discussion. If Panditji who is in better health and in the best of spirits wishes to inflict upon you an explanation and a discussion instead of issuing orders as chief of the Swaraj Party and ex-President of the Congress, he may do so. For my part, I shall simply expect you to write the love letter in your best style and with the diplomatic reserve of the English diplomat.

I was disturbed when I saw a brief paragraph about your illness. Your telegram reassured me, and I hope that this will find you fit enough to undertake the fatiguing journey in front of you.

Yours sincerely,

SJT. S. SRINIVASA IYENGAR
MYLAPORE
MADRAS

From a photostat: S.N. 14213

287. LETTER TO VALJI G. DESAI

BANGALORE,
Shravan Shuddha 12 [August 10, 1927][1]

BHAISHRI VALJI,

In our circle you are the only student of the Vedas. Today I am sending you an issue of *Vaidik Dharma*. Go through it carefully and let me have your opinion about it. Is the view correct that in Vedic times respectable people did not favour eating meat, and especially beef, and that animals were not killed in sacrifices? If you think that it is, what have you to say about the contrary view expressed by Shri Vaidya[2]?

I should like to have from you regular news about the dairy, the tannery, etc.

I hope you are keeping good health.

Vandemataram from
MOHANDAS

From a photostat of the Gujarati: C.W. 7393. Courtesy: Valjibhai Desai

288. LETTER TO CHHAGANLAL JOSHI

Wednesday, August 10, 1927

BHAISHRI CHHAGANLAL,

I cannot make out from your letter whether Purushottam has left his job or not. You will be truly able to influence your pupils only when you all give your spare time to manual work and handicrafts and the pupils realize that you enjoy doing it. If you say you do not get time, I shall retort that you do not find time because you have no real interest in it. I can certainly understand that our students too wish to earn money. The fact remains that we ourselves do not face poverty and are not labourers in the true sense. Again, it is not that accumulation of property is distasteful to all of us. We can only say that it should be so and that we are trying to make it so. How can the students rise above this position? Hence, before the students stop dreaming of

[1] Gandhiji was in Bangalore on this date in 1927.
[2] C. V. Vaidya, Sanskrit scholar and Indologist

the future, the Ashram ought to make great headway. Indeed the fact is that though, comparatively, our sacrifices and efforts appear illustrious actually both are as good as nothing. It may be that we are not to blame for it and that circumstances are responsible for it. But we must not on that account ignore it.

I have discussed your letter with Kakasaheb today. Whenever we get time, we do engage in such discussions. Since Kaka will write more about this, I shall not. I shall concede this much that as long as Kakasaheb is the Vice-president of the managing committee, the moral responsibility will be his. Therefore, although far away, you have a right to obtain his opinion. We are both considering whether Kaka will be able to do his duty of pronouncing an opinion. But Swami, who in this matter enjoys authority over both of us, is far away. We must also consider what he thinks.

Blessings from
BAPU

[From Gujarati]

From the manuscript of Mahadev Desai's Diary. Courtesy: Narayan Desai

289. *ANOTHER KHADI BHANDAR*

The Honorary Secretary of the Khaddar Co-operative Society Limited of Shimoga writes to say that among the khadi bhandars of Karnatak should be included the khadi bhandar run by this Society at Shimoga. The bhandar was only recently opened. I gladly mention this bhandar. But I warn all the new ventures that they must be run on business lines and by those who know something of the techniques of khadi sales. Not everyone can run a khadi bhandar successfully, not even everyone who has been in charge of a cloth shop. A manager of a khadi bhandar should know the different varieties of khadi, and should know how to distinguish between genuine khadi and imitations. He should also know the art of presenting khadi to the public in an inviting manner, and above all, he has to be scrupulously honest. I invite other bhandars like the Shimoga Bhandar to send in their names with full particulars to the Secretary, All-India Spinners' Association, Ahmedabad.

Young India, 11-8-1927

290. *INDIAN SETTLERS IN SOUTH AFRICA*

India's first Ambassador has not allowed the grass to grow under his feet. He is busily sowing seeds of true union by a seasonable word now addressed to the Europeans and now to the Indian settlers, and he seems to be having fair success with both. Europeans gracefully acknowledge his splendid worth and exquisite impartiality. Indians gratefully recognize the immense strength of character which backs every word that this great son of India utters.

He has now appealed to them to produce an army of social workers in the cause of public health and sanitation. Let us hope that his appeal will not fall upon deaf ears, and that well-to-do and educated Indians will respond as zealously as they did when C. F. Andrews appealed to them for assistance for the scavenging work he did during the outbreak of smallpox in Durban some months ago. Agent though he is of the Government, if Reuter's report is correct, Sjt. Sastri did not spare it over its criminal indifference about the sanitary and social welfare of the indentured Indians. For the neglect of sanitation amongst the indentured Indians, three parties are really responsible—the Government of India, the employers, and the Local Government. If the Government of India had insisted upon a minimum standard, and if the employers had taken a human interest in the employees and the Local Government had considered the indentured Indians as future citizens of South Africa, they would have learnt, during their five years' indenture, habits of modern sanitation. For during the five years of indenture they had to live like soldiers in barracks and they could have been made to conform to any reasonable sanitary regulations that might have been framed, even as they were made to conform to labour regulations which were often even harsh and severe. But this is past history. There is no more indentured emigration now.

The question is now to make of the existing Indian population model citizens, and if the Government and the Indian settlers co-operate, it is not at all impossible to set a better tone, and create a healthy Indian public opinion that would not tolerate any insanitation or ugliness. Let the Indian settlers do their part of forming sanitation brigades, cleaning up latrines and streets and instructing ignorant people in the elementary laws of sanitation, even as they did in 1897 in Durban. Sjt. Sastri's work will be fruitless unless he is willingly, intelligently and whole-heartedly helped by the Indian settlers. They must conform to the wholesome maxim of law that those who seek justice or equity must come with clean hands. Let the settlers be clean in body, mind and soul, and thus make the best use of the golden opportunity they have of having an Ambassador who has got the ability to serve them and who has in a remarkable measure the ear of the European inhabitants of South Africa.

Young India, 11-8-1927

291. THE HAVOC IN GUJARAT

The destruction wrought by the heavy floods in Gujarat appears to be of an unprecedented character. The meagre accounts I have seen in the Press supplemented by two telegrams from Vallabhbhai Patel and one from the Ashram gave me but a faint idea of the enormous damage done by the flood. I am handicapped, too, as I am writing this in an out-of-the-way place in Mysore where newspapers reach very late. When communications are thoroughly established, the total extent of the damage done will probably be found to be much heavier than the estimates made by responsible workers. Benevolent and wealthy gentlemen of Bombay and Gujarat have been as prompt in their work of mercy as Nature has been furious in her work of destruction. Sjt. Vallabhbhai Patel has already issued an appeal. I hope that there will be a liberal response to the appeal. A private telegram tells me that Sir Purushottamdas Thakordas has also, as is his wont on such occasions, started relief work. On occasions of such calamities when deepest emotions are stirred, many relief agencies are brought into being to render help. They must be all welcome. Not one agency can hope to overtake the whole work of relief over such a vast area. However, it will be the duty of several agencies to co-operate with one another, so as to avoid overlapping and so as to make every rupee go to the longest length and every grain of wheat find its way to the neediest hands. Let those whom God has blessed with ability to give remember the proverb: "He gives twice who gives the quickest."

Young India, 11-8-1927

292. *WELCOME GOOD SAMARITAN*

Someone gave C. F. Andrews the affectionate title of Dinabandhu. It certainly fits him. His overpowering ambition in life is to be friend of those in need, and the way he helps is by utter self-effacement. It is fitting therefore that the first city in India should have voted an address to be presented on his return which takes place on the 20th instant. I have no doubt that the address will be worthy of the occasion. But in the abundance of their affection let the members of the Corporation not forget, that Dinabandhu Andrews is not a monied man. He has almost literally nowhere to lay his hand on. He has no cupboard, no treasure chest, no house of his own. For his very few belongings he needs a caretaker. He never keeps anything for himself. Anybody may take away his box with its contents. When in South Africa, Pearson and I used to despair of him ever taking care of himself or things which could be called his own. To present him with a rich casket or any casket at all would be a cruelty to him.

But if the Corporation would spend any money it would be proper to vote a purse for him to be used for his life mission. He appreciates affection. But he is never so awkward as when he receives thanks and honours and wonders why he should be thanked or honoured at all. But however awkward he may feel, let the honour to be done to him be not a hole-and-corner affair. For whilst it is undoubtedly due to him for his magnificent work in South Africa, it will also serve the purpose of reciprocating the goodwill that has been created in South Africa, and would be a demonstration of the fact, that in his work he carried with him the weight of opinion of all India, and that he was no less an ambassador for India than Sjt. Sastri.

Young India, 11-8-1927

293. *UNITY IN VARIETY*

The Polish professor[1] whose earnest questions I endeavoured to answer a few months back, having read my answer[2], sends me the following further questions:

> 1. Men are not equal. Do you also admit that there is a vast inequality between nations?
>
> 2. If this is true, do you think that representative elective bodies, called parliaments, which have brought Europe to the Great War, are really suitable for India?
>
> 3. Do you think that India may become one nation in a similar sense as Italy or France?
>
> 4. Is it right to suppose that the future of Asia depends on this unification of India, which alone could overrule the materialistic tendencies of Japan and China?
>
> 5. Is this not the real alternative for Asia, either superficial Europeanization as in Japan, or going back to ancient Aryan tradition which seems to be the rule for great Indian masters?
>
> 6. Has this recalling of original Aryan tradition also an importance for Europe?
>
> 7. Do you not see in European civilization, with all its faults, a new power which goes beyond all Hindu experience?
>
> 8. Is there, in all India, a single little town, like many French little towns, in which everybody is really free to follow his aspirations, all people are well-to-do, all have a very high level of education and sociability, and representatives of opposite tendencies meet in friendly intercourse? I know such towns in France and also in England. I wonder whether such a thing exists in India.

My correspondent has stated only a half-truth when he says, "Men are not equal". The other half is that they are equal. For, though they are not all of the same age, the same height, the same skin, and the same intellect, these inequalities are temporary and superficial, the soul that is hidden beneath this earthy crust is one and the same for all men and women belonging to all climes. It would therefore be, perhaps, more accurate to say, that there is a real and substantial unity in all the variety that we see around us. The word "Inequality" has a bad odour about

[1] W. Lutostawski

[2] *Vide* Vol. XXXIII, pp. 245-7.

it, and it has led to arrogance and inhumanities, both in the East and the West. What is true about men is also true about nations, which are but groups of men. The false and rigid doctrine of inequality has led to the insolent exploitation of the nations of Asia and Africa. Who knows that the present ability of the West to prey upon the East is a sign of Western superiority and Eastern inferiority? I know that the East meekly, and all too hastily, submits to this pernicious doctrine, and then makes an ineffectual attempt to imitate the West. There is, after all, a world of truth in the poetic statement, "Things are not what they seem".

The second question does not seem to follow from the first. And seeing that I reject the doctrine of inequality in the sense used by the writer, I am unable to admit that the representative elective bodies are really unsuitable for India. But for the reasons, which I have stated in the *Indian Home Rule* and which in the main I have found no occasion during the past 20 years to revise, I should be extremely sorry, if India entirely copies the Western model. Representative elective bodies were not unknown to India before the European advent. But the contents of the words "representation" and "election" were, so far as I can see, far different from the European.

In my opinion, India is today one nation, even as Italy or France is; and this I maintain in spite of a vivid and painful knowledge of the fact, that Hindus and Mussalmans are murdering one another, that Brahmins and non-Brahmins are preparing for a similar battle, and that both Brahmins and non-Brahmins exclude from their purview the classes which both have left no stone unturned to suppress. But I have known similar quarrels in families and in other nations. It has often seemed to me that a family connection is necessary to establish a good ground for a quarrel. But it flatters me to be able heartily to endorse the proposition that the future of Asia depends upon a proper and demonstrable unification of India.

I do not, however, think that the alternative to superficial Europeanization consists in a complete reversion to the ancient Aryan tradition. I hold with that great thinker, the late Justice Ranade, that there is no such thing as a literal complete revival of ancient tradition possible, even if it were desirable. In the first place, no one knows authoritatively what the ancient Aryan tradition was or is. It is difficult to state unerringly the period which can be described as the "Golden Age" and then to give a categorical description of that age. And I am humble enough to admit that there is much that we can profitably assimilate from the West. Wisdom is no monopoly of one continent or one race. My resistance to Western civilization is really a resistance to its indiscriminate and thoughtless imitation based on the assumption that Asiatics are fit only to copy everything that comes from the West. I do believe that if India has patience enough to go through the fire of suffering and to resist any unlawful encroachment upon its own civilization which, imperfect though it undoubtedly is, has hitherto stood the ravages of time, she can make a lasting contribution to the peace and solid progress of the world.

I gladly admit that a new power for good is slowly but surely arising in the West. Whether it will transcend all Hindu experience or not, I do not know. But I should welcome every fresh contribution to the enrichment of humanity, no matter where it comes from.

Lastly, I am unable to say anything about the glowing tribute that the learned professor pays to the self-contained French and English little towns. I know so little about English towns, and still less about the French. I own I have my doubts. But I know that if the professor could stand the almost forbidden exterior of Indian villages, I would undertake to take him to some of them where he would see a culture of a high order, and though he will miss the literary polish he will not miss the human heart and the human touch, and where, if he can accommodate himself to the strange Indian ways about exclusive eating and drinking, he will see amazing tolerance of opposite ideas and friendliest intercourse of the mind and the soul. Let me also remind the professor that the English and the French prosperity and amenities which such prosperity brings depend upon, what I must again repeat and what I would gladly avoid if I could, namely, exploitation.

Young India, 11-8-1927

294. 'HUMANIZING WAR'

I extract the following interesting paragraphs from an article headed "War" in the March number of the *Brotherhood*:

> Last time the women and children were only starved—it was done by a process cunningly disguised as "economic pressure"—but next time they are to be gassed to death. Aeroplanes will drop penetrating poisons which will exterminate civil population—Edison says that it should not be difficult to dispose of London's millions in three hours. In every civilized country the chemists are at work searching for some particularly deadly poisons. In England, says *Truth*, our Government is busy experimenting with improvements in poison gas and killing animals at the rate of two a day in the process. It obtained in one year 689 cats, guinea pigs, goats, mice, monkeys, rabbits and rats, and killed 618 of them with poison gas in search of improvements.
>
> Some idea of the horrors of the next war may be gathered from the fact that the range of guns has been doubled since the Armistice[1], and that machine guns are now available which fire 1,500 shots a minute. An automatic cannon will fire one and a quarter pound shells at the rate of 120 a minute, and there is a sixteen-inch gun which hurls a missile weighing more than a ton for a distance of twenty-seven miles. The Chemical Warfare Service in America has discovered a liquid three drops of which applied to any part of the skin will cause a man's death. One aeroplane, carrying two tons of this liquid, could kill the whole population over miles of territory. General Swinton, of the British Army, says: The great future weapon of war will be deadly germs. We have since the war discovered and developed germs which, dropped down upon cities and armies, will slaughter a nation in a day.
>
> If anyone is ever in danger of becoming unduly optimistic, let him remember that we spent in 1924 forty millions in education, a hundred and twenty one millions on armaments, and three hundred and sixteen millions on drink. The business of scientific killing is very expensive, and I am told that enough nitrogen was thrown away in one small and indecisive battle in France to save India from a famine. The great world powers are still pouring out an incredible amount of their treasure upon armaments, although history so plainly teaches that increasing armaments do nothing but increase the likelihood of wars. Peace-loving America voted eighty-five million dollars for aviation expansion in a few

[1] Of 1918

minutes, and no one took the slightest notice of this forward movement in the race for armaments. The irony of the situation is, that while Great Britain is spending nearly twice as much money on armaments today as she spent in 1913, the victorious nations have relieved Germany of the burden of such expenditure, so that, in competing with her in industry and commerce they work under a severe handicap of their own creation.

I add to this the following from the *Lancet* (June 18, 1927):

> Since the arrival of the British troops, there have been many cases of influenza and pneumonia, but the question of venereal disease has been the most clamant one, and in spite of every possible precaution the number of those affected has steadily increased. . . . Numbers of prostitutes from North and South have flocked to Shanghai, most of them being Chinese (60 per cent), Russians (30 per cent), and Japanese (5 per cent). The majority of the brothels are in the French Concession and in Chinese districts bordering on municipal roads. The high venereal rate has given the Command much concern, and no stone is left unturned in the effort to lower it.

And yet there are intelligent men who talk, and gullible men who subscribe to the talk, of the "humanizing influence" of war!

Young India, 11-8-1927

295. *WHEN SCIENCE AND ART ARE REAL*

A friend sends me an extract from Anton Tchehov's stories which is worth reproducing. The extract runs as follows:

> I have a very definite opinion on this subject, I assure you. To my mind, all these schools, dispensaries, libraries, medical relief societies, under present conditions, only serve to aggravate the bondage of the people. The peasants are fettered by a great chain, and you do not break the chain, but only add fresh links to it.
>
> What matters is, not that Anna died in childbirth, but that all these Annas, Mavras, Pelageas toil from early morning till dark, fall ill from working beyond their strength, all their lives tremble for their sick and hungry children, all their lives are being doctored, and in dread of death and disease, fade and grow old early and die in filth and stench.
>
> Their children begin the same story over again as soon as they grow up, and so it goes on for hundreds of years, and millions of men live worse than beasts—in continual terror, for a mere crust of bread. The whole horror of their position lies in their never having time to think of their image and semblance. Cold, hunger, animal terror, a

burden of toil, like avalanches of snow, block for them every way to spiritual activity—that is, to what distinguishes a man from the brutes and what is the only thing which makes life worth living.

You go to their help with hospitals and schools, but you do not free them from their fetters by that. On the contrary, you bind them in closer bonds, as by introducing new prejudices, you increase the number of their wants, to say nothing of the fact that they have got to pay Zemstvo for blisters and books and so toil harder than ever.

Yes, I am against medicine. It would be necessary only for the study of diseases as natural phenomena, and not for the cure of them. If one must cure, it should not be diseases, but the cause of them. Remove the principal cause, —physical labour —and then there will be no disease.

I do not believe in a science that cures disease. When science and art are real, they aim not at temporary and private ends, but at eternal and universal —they seek for truth and the meaning of life, they seek for God, for the Soul, and when they are tied down to the needs and evils of the day, to dispensaries and libraries, they only complicate and hamper life.

Scientific men, writers, artists are hard at work. Thanks to them, the conveniences of life are multiplied from day to day. Our physical demands increase, yet truth is still a long way off, and man still remains the most rapacious and dirty animal; everything is tending to the degeneration of the majority of mankind and the loss for ever of fitness for life.

I have not read the original story, but I suppose physical labour which the author refers to as the principal cause of diseases is not wholesome farm labour or any such labour, but the grinding toil which for the sake of eking a miserable livelihood the peasants of his experience must have been obliged to undergo. It would be interesting to know the original Russian word which has been rendered by the translator as "physical labour".

The most telling passage in the extract is perhaps that which distinguishes real science and art from the ephemeral. Who can deny that much that passes for science and art today destroys the soul instead of uplifting it and instead of evoking the best in us panders to our basest passions?

Young India, 11-8-1927

296. *TEST OF FIDELITY*

A study of the chart of membership of the All-India Spinners' Association discloses a painful fact. Out of 1,980 members of the A Class, 1,255 have been found to be unsteady in their fidelity to their promise regularly to send their yarn quota. Let no one think that if it was an insignificant monetary contribution rather than that of self-spun yarn, the result would have been very different. Somehow or other people are neglectful in the performance of self-imposed duties, whose breach does not carry with it an immediate punitive consequence. But unless a nation contains a large enough number of men and women who would carry out their voluntary obligations, although their breach may not entail any felt punishment, it can make slow progress. Forfeiture of rights of membership of an organization which carries with it no pecuniary or other earthly loss is lightly regarded by the members, and some even consider that by belonging to such an institution they confer on it a patronage which should be treasured by the institution in question. But I warn the members, if there are any, against harbouring such notions about the All-India Spinners' Association. To belong to the Association should be considered a rare privilege, because by contributing half an hour's free and intelligent labour capable of being easily performed by any ordinary man, woman or child, a member becomes a partaker in the tremendous aggregate effect of the contributions. I would therefore urge the defaulting members to be as punctual in sending their quota as they would be in keeping the time for catching their train or attending their offices. Let them remember that apart from the intrinsic value of spinning, there is no less value in cultivating regularly a daily remembrance of the condition of the dumb millions and a daily concentration over drawing an even strong thread as much for themselves as for the rest of the 300 millions of India. I understand that each one of the members has been sent a reminder. Let the defaulters please realize that each reminder costs at least half an anna over and above the salaries of men employed in attending to the writing and despatch of reminder cards. It has been suggested that some postpone sending their quota till several months' contributions are collected, so as to save postage. The saving of postage is a proper consideration. But those who would save postage should send their contributions in advance. To spin 12,000 yards in a month's time is not a very great strain as must be abundantly clear to every reader of these pages. And if after having sent one lot in advance, the spinners continue to give 30 minutes regularly to the wheel, they will never be in arrears, and they will never feel the strain of the work, no matter how busy they may be otherwise. And if punishment has any appeal to them, let them remember that at the end of the first five years of the existence of the All-India Spinners' Association, it will descend surely and swiftly upon them, when the time comes for revising the constitution and conferring further privileges upon members.

Young India, 11-8-1927

297. NOTES

True Sacrifice

Two young men only the other day presented themselves before me and placed into my hands Rs. 10 being the commission they had earned in terms of the rules of the All-India Spinners' Association for hawking khadi. They were entitled to keep this money themselves. But they did not wish to retain this commission; for they felt the force of the argument that there were millions who were much worse off than themselves. The young men went away promising to bring me more such refunds.

Whilst I mention this instance in appreciation of the self-sacrifice of these young men, no khadi-hawker is to infer from it that he is also expected to refund his commission, in other words, that every khadi-hawker is expected to hawk without any charge. I know that it is not possible for everyone to do so, and khadi work requires as many honest, industrious and intelligent hawkers as can be had. To recommend for all the standard that the two young men have chosen for themselves would be to restrict the number of khadi-hawkers, whereas the object is to attract as many young men for the work as possible.

After all the commission to be had out of khadi sales is not much and is not easily earned because it is not possible to command sales of khadi simply by[1] exhibiting it for sale. I know that hawkers have to go from door to door often even without any response whatsoever, and seeing that the commission is given only on actual sales, khadi-hawking means earning one's bread by the

[1] The source has "for".

sweat of one's brow. Let the example of these young men therefore spur those who are doing nothing for khadi to some effort, and let the example result in adding to the number of hawkers without their being expected to refund their hard-earned commission. There are no doubt many young men and young women who have plenty of leisure and do not need any pecuniary reward. They may follow the example of these young men and offer their services for hawking. Let would-be khadi-hawkers however understand that they cannot get khadi to hawk unless they are able to produce certificates of character, and are able to furnish security for the amount of khadi they may receive for sale.

Fatigue Test in Spinning

Satish Babu who after prolonged convalescence has returned to the Pratishthan works at Sodepur writes:

> One of the spinners here was encouraged to sit for continuous spinning. He worked one day whole time for carding and making slivers. He was ready with the slivers at night, and sat for spinning from 9 p.m. to 7 p.m. the next day. He took three hours' respite, two hours for sleeping and one hour for eating, etc. In 19 active hours he spun 10,500 yards of 18 counts yarn including reeling. He may show better record in future.

It would be interesting to know the test of the strength and the evenness of this great quantity of yarn spun in 19 out of 22 consecutive hours.

Virtue of Testing Yarn

Ever since the introduction of the system of testing self-spun yarn received by the All-India Spinners' Association there has been steady improvement in its quality. Following are some of the very striking results obtained:

Name		Count	Strength	Evenness
Sjt. V. K. Vishvanathan, Kerala				
	Before test	26	31	83
	After test	32	95	81
Shri S. M. Padmavatibai, Shimoga				
	Before test	16	20	91
	After test	25	80	89
Dr. M. Venkatrao, Gadag				
	Before test	21	40	92
	After test	19	79	88
Sjt. Motilal Roy, Chandranagar				
	Before test	39	47	92
	After test	33	78	95

Sjt. Dayaljibhai Shivji, Gujarat

Before test	14	23	71
After test	20	74	93

The following are some names in whose case the test has been found to be uniformly good, the yarn being any day equal to the strongest mill yarn:

Name	Count	Strength	Evenness
Shri Gangabai Kunte, Bombay	30	98	93
Sjt. Ishvarlal Patel, Bombay	15	92	93
Dr. A. P. Kothari, Bombay	22	96	86
Sjt. Jogendra Chatterjea, Sodepur	30	96	92
Shri. Lakshmibai Gokhale, Bombay	33	95	84
Sjt. Govindbhai B. Patel (Juvenile)	15	87	93
Vithal Liladhar (Juvenile)	11	80	88

Mill 'Khaddar'

A friend writes:

> I know you have several times alluded to what is mistakenly called 'mill khaddar', but apparently the mill-owners are still unable to resist the temptation of the name. The worst offender in this respect is . . . who openly quotes and advertises mill khaddar. This is for your information, and what action you may like to take in preserving the purity attached to the name khaddar.

What the correspondent says is unfortunately but too true. And I have been painfully aware of it. I had hoped that the mill-owners would give up the undesirable practice. But it was hoping against hope. Wherever I have gone people have drawn my attention to this unpatriotic conduct on the part of some mill-owners. The only comfort I have derived from the usurpation by the mill-owners of the name 'khaddar' is, that it is proof of the popularity of khaddar among the masses upon whose ignorance the mill-owners are playing. For I know that wherever the buyers have discovered the deception, they have cursed themselves and the mill-owners. The only remedy against this deception is for the buyers to beware, and for khadi lovers to educate the people so as to enable them to distinguish between real khaddar and its imitation.

Hand-spinning in Almora

A correspondent sends me an interesting report of the progress that hand-spinning of wool has made in the schools conducted by the District Board of Almora. The following should prove both interesting and instructive to those who believe in the introduction of *takli* spinning in municipal schools:[1]

> The elections of 1925 to the Almora District Board returned the Swarajists in a majority. Since then the Swarajist members have in various ways tried to give a national stamp to the institution particularly its educational side. The most important work in that direction has been the introduction of national songs, national sentiments, khadi uniform and wool-spinning into the village schools.
>
> The village teachers of a number of District Board schools purchased wool at their own cost and thus spinning came into being. The Board, seeing the popularity of these voluntary and spontaneous efforts, constituted a spinning and weaving sub-committee and granted Rs. 3,000 at the beginning of 1926 for purchasing wool to be spun at District Board schools in the district. Some nineteen maunds of wool was purchased and distributed throughout the district in village schools. . . . The boys everywhere welcomed the *takli* or *katua*, and the village schoolmasters did their best to make wool-spinning successful. . . . The Board deserves congratulations for giving this support, in spite of the opposition of conservatives. . . . The Board has ordered spinning classes to be held after school hours as the curriculum has no provision for this type of education. In order to enthuse the masses and to encourage the village students, several *katua dangals* (spinning matches) have been arranged at different centres of the district during fairs. Prizes (including khadi, khadi caps, national flags and national books) have been awarded to the best spinners. This feature has been very much appreciated by the people and has been of great educative and demonstrative value. Seeing the spinning of young schoolboys, the villages have been conscience-stricken and at many places the long-forgotten art of spinning is undergoing a revival. The villagers at several places have established their own looms to weave their hand-spun wool-yarn. So the spinning in schools is touching the masses as well. . . .
>
> Our experiments in wool-spinning convinced us that there was nothing better than *katua* or *takli* for wool-spinning—simple, light, inexpensive and practical. So *katua* or *takli* is reigning supreme in the Board's schools as well. A small boy can make his own *katua* without any trouble or expense and play it at any time or any place whenever or wherever he likes. . . .

If this experiment is continued and spinning is properly supervised, it can not only become self-supporting but be even profitable. For if hand-weaving is not also done by the boys, spun wool should find a ready market; or it can be woven on behalf

[1] Only excerpts are reproduced here.

of the Board or the school concerned, and the woven stuff either used by the boys themselves or sold in the open market.

Young India, 11-8-1927

298. *WORTHY OF EMULATION*

Shrimati Annapurnabai Ghare who contributed during the last *chaturmas* one lakh yards of yarn to the All-India Spinners' Association has again taken the same vow as last year, and is religiously at the wheel every day for fulfilling it. This means 833 yards per day for four months. If she is an average spinner, she would have to give to her *yajna* at least three hours per day to be able to spin good yarn. Will the other sisters copy the example? The *yajna* no doubt requires faith in the wheel and love for the unseen millions.

Young India, 11-8-1927

299. *LETTER TO M. ABDUL GANI*

AS AT BANGALORE,
August 11, 1927

DEAR FRIEND,

I have your letter for which I thank you. Probably before you knew even the existence of *Rangila Rasul*, I wrote very strongly against it in the pages of *Young India*. This was 3 years ago. I have taken no part in the present controversy because I do not approve of the tremendous agitation that has been got up after the judgment in the *Rangila Rasul* case. I think that the attack upon the judge is unfortunate. He may have committed an error of judgment, but surely has betrayed no prejudice. I understand he condemned the pamphlet in unmeasured terms. He simply thought that the law itself was not enough to bring the author of the pamphlet under its purview. The agitation for altering the law is sound, but the alteration will take place with or without agitation if the law is found to be defective.

Yours sincerely,
M. K. GANDHI

M. ABDUL GANI
KURNOOL

From a photostat: S.N. 12386-A

300. LETTER TO A. BAQUI

As at Bangalore,
August 11, 1927

MY DEAR FRIEND,

I am glad you have written to me about the *Rangila Rasul* agitation. Yours is the fourth letter of its kind. The *Rangila Rasul* pamphlet I saw nearly three years ago, and it gave me deep pain. I expressed it all in the pages of *Young India.* The agitation that is going on at present has appeared to me to be altogether unjustified and quite on wrong lines. If I wrote at all, I should have to write in condemnation of the agitation, although I should reiterate the opinion about the pamphlet itself. The attack against the judge is very unfortunate. I could not associate myself with a demand for his resignation or a demand for the release of the writers who insulted the judge. The only part of the agitation that is in my opinion correct is the demand for alteration of the law, if it is inadequate for the punishment of offenders against the religious sentiments of any class of people. But that agitation does not require all the bitterness that has been imported into it. Even without a whirlwind agitation, the Government is bound to set the law right if it is defective.

The correspondents mentioned by me have written to me to say that the Hindu Press has associated itself with the degrading sentiments of the *Rangila Rasul.* I have never seen such writing in any of the Hindu-edited papers that I get and read here. I have asked these correspondents to refer me to the writings mentioned by them.[1] But I have had no acknowledgment from them Have you seen any such writings mentioned by them? If so, please pass them on to me. I should certainly like to take some action on them.

I hope the College is doing well.

Yours sincerely,
M. K. Gandhi

A. Baqui, Esq.
Koath P.O.
District Shahabad (Bihar Province)

From a microfilm: S.N. 12387-A

[1] *Vide* "A Letter", 10-7-1927, and "Letter to Gulzar Mohamad 'Aquil' ", 7-8-1927.

301. LETTER TO HELENE HAUSSDING

As at Bangalore,
August 11, 1927

MY DEAR SPARROW,

I have your letter. You agitate yourself unnecessarily over the translation that was sent to you. Surely you have humour enough to take all such stuff lightly. I merely passed it on to you so that you might see what is written by your fellow-passenger about you. Why should we take notice of such writings especially when strangers write? So far as I am concerned, your repudiation is quite enough. I am not going to send your repudiation to the Press. I don't suppose that anybody now remembers the writing.

Are you now perfectly all right? I am doing a little bit of touring now and feel quite fit though not yet as strong as before the collapse. Krishnadas has just gone on Association's business to Bengal and incidentally to see his Guruji as also his parents. I am forwarding your letter to him which I know will delight him.

I want your assurance that you will never worry about it. All the nasty things that may be said about you need not worry you; for, after all the chief thing with which we should be concerned is to know what the inner voice tells us about ourselves.

With love,

Yours sincerely,
Bapu

From a photostat: S.N. 12511

302. LETTER TO T. PARAMESWARA IYER

AS AT BANGALORE,
August 11, 1927

DEAR FRIEND,

I was trying to make time to reply to your letter undated enclosing papers about Bhadravati and Krishnarajasagar, and now I have got your second letter sending me more cuttings. But that was not what I wanted. I wanted you to give me, if you could spare the time, a very brief note containing unchallengeable facts and figures which a busy man like me could go through easily and act upon.[1] I should have another breakdown if I attempted to study the papers you have sent.

I have read the article you had referred me to in your very first letter. It did not carry conviction and it did not appear to me to have been written dispassionately.

The quotation from Mr. Sastri's letter seems to me to be irrelevant. Whilst he congratulates you upon your sustained interest in the welfare of the State even after retirement, he is silent as to his own opinion on the Bhadravati works.

I do not return to Bangalore before the 21st instant. If I could find a little time I would be glad to make your acquaintance. Will it be too much for me to suggest that on my return, you should try to see me, and if I am not busy when you come, I shall certainly be delighted to meet you.

Yours sincerely,

SJT. T. PARAMESWARA IYER
RETIRED JUDGE
WHITE HOUSE
CHAMARAJPET
BANGALORE CITY

From a microfilm: S.N. 12631

[1] *Vide* "Letter to T. Paramasiva Iyer", 29-7-1927. Though the addressee's name is spelt differently in the two letters, it is evident from the contents that they are addressed to the same person.

303. LETTER TO KRISHNADAS

DAVANGERE,
August 11, 1927

MY DEAR KRISHNADAS,

I now understand what you have done about Ram Binode. I think the whole arrangement is quite satisfactory. But apart from my own opinion, it pleases me to know that both you and Rajendra Babu are satisfied with Ram Binode's conduct and that you have no suspicions about his honesty.

I take it that you will have seen Suresh Babu, probably visited Comilla, and I would like you if you have not the thing in mind to go to Sodepur and visit the works and see Satis Babu and Hemprabha Devi in particular so as to enable you to tell me from a personal visit how they are looking and how far Sodepur has progressed. You may also discuss with Suresh Babu and Satis Babu the opinion cited by you in your letter about khaddar. There is no doubt that middle men do get something. There is nothing wrong in it. But there is no doubt too that the spinning and weaving wages go direct into the pockets of the artisans whom we have in mind.

We are today in Davangere and we shall be away for 10 days in this district, reaching Bangalore on the 21st instant. Mysore State will be finally left on the 28th instant.

From a photostat: S.N. 14216

304. LETTER TO JAYANTI

August 11, 1927

CHI. JAYANTI,

Your letter. The flood has disturbed all time[-schedules]; so it is not possible that my blessings would reach you on your birthday itself. But take it that they have reached you on that very day. May you live long and become a pure worker and may your exalted hopes bear fruit! One thing you and all other pupils should do is to make your handwriting beautiful like pearls. This can be done easily. Just as singing out of tune is not music, so too bad handwriting is no writing. I am not competent to proffer this advice because I know that my own handwriting is no good. But just as a drowning man's warning not to go to a particular spot is heeded by the wise, I hope all of you wise pupils will take this warning from me. Words must be written separately. There must be some space between the lines. A line ought to run straight and every letter must be delineated as an artist draws a picture.

Now about the *Ramayana*. I would certainly pay more respect to Tulsi's *Ramayana* as a religious work. Valmiki's may excel in art, but I have not the slightest doubt that Tulsidas is richer in devotional spirit. Moreover, at present Valmiki's *Ramayana* is available in Sanskrit only. I have so far come across no Gujarati translation which re-creates the interest of the original. You must know that neither of the works is historical. True, Valmiki has portrayed a few historical men and women, but these are not clearly defined. I firmly believe that one cannot infer historical facts from them. But in the case of Tulsidas the question of historicity does not arise. We might say that he adapted Valmiki to suit his own age, but while doing so, having come under the spell of *bhakti*, he took such liberties as he wished to and thereby he has done no harm but only done good to Hindu society. With the passage of time men and women of divine glory become gods and goddesses and are ultimately worshipped as such. This will always happen and that is right. A man being embodied can never worship God in any other form. It being so, whatever Tulsidas writes about Lord Ramachandra are only his own feelings. Tulsidas has portrayed God as beyond description, as inapprehensible by mere sense-organs and as also beyond attributes. If therefore we cannot swallow the killing of Vali, we should leave aside that passage or believe that while depicting it Tulsidas acted only in conformity with the beliefs of his own age and could not transcend them. As man progresses, his idea of God necessarily becomes subtle and pure, inevitably so. Therefore, we should regard the *Ramayana* rather as a devotional work than a historical record and while we read its fiction part we should ignore whatever we find contrary to morality. Tulsidas himself describes his work *Ramacharitamanasa* as full of faults. He gives a different reason for it but that he has regarded it as not without fault should suffice for us. Moreover, in his well-known verse beginning, "God created the world full of animate and inanimate objects with good qualities as well as bad", Tulsidas has taught us the art of looking at things. Since all human action is partly good and partly bad, we should, like the proverbial swan[1], take in the essence in the form of good qualities and leave alone the defects that spoil it. This is the golden rule that should apply to the reading of all books. We should humbly ask the teacher what we do not understand and we should leave aside what nevertheless we fail to understand; we should however never let our reason be clouded or our mind be corrupted. Whatever appears contrary to truth, non-violence and so on, should be rejected as unauthoritative although it may have been printed in an avowedly scriptural work.

Although this letter is written for you alone, regard it as meant for all of you and let them read it; and let the seniors too read it. For, I do not remember having written my thoughts on the *Ramayana* so clearly and concisely anywhere else, though I have explained them often here and there.

[From Gujarati]

From the manuscript of Mahadev Desai's Diary. Courtesy: Narayan Desai

305. LETTER TO RAMDAS GANDHI

August 11, 1927

You have no reason at all to be anxious on account of Kantilal. You must have known of the step I have taken. I have already written to you that you should never worry about a matter which does not concern you. A further hint we can read in yet another verse: "therefore what is unavoidable thou shouldst not regret".[2]

You will find this verse in the second chapter. It means, you should not grieve over that which you cannot control. Thus the Lord assuaged Arjuna's grief. Generally, we act contrary to this. We weep when someone passes away. We are plunged in sorrow if our house is burnt to ashes; the flood almost robbed us of our sense, but death, fire, floods, etc., are inescapable. What is the use of grieving over them? But this statement does not mean that we should become hard-hearted. We should undertake such remedies as we can to put out a fire, to retrieve the loss caused by floods and to save the dying, but we should not let those events affect us in any other way. Now I have to take it that you can-

[1] Which is supposed to separate and drink the milk from a mixture of milk and water

[2] *Bhagavad Gita*, II. 27

not come here and that is right; but come when you are free and feel like it. Just come to me wherever I might happen to be.

[From Gujarati]

From the manuscript of Mahadev Desai's Diary. Courtesy: Narayan Desai

306. LETTER TO VASUMATI PANDIT

DAVANGERE,
Shravan Sud 13 [*August 11, 1927*][1]

CHI. VASUMATI,

I got your letter only yesterday—that is, after seven days. I am glad that you sent me information about Chi. Kusum. If you come to know anything more, let me hear. I have of course written a letter to Kusum.[2] I have not so far received a reply to it. All of you must have been put on your mettle at the time of the floods. I was glad to hear this time that you maintain good health. Keep it up.

Blessings from
BAPU

From the Gujarati original: C.W. 586. Courtesy: Vasumati Pandit

307. LETTER TO V. S. SRINIVASA SASTRI

AS AT BANGALORE,
August 12, 1927

I do not know that you would want to know Mr. Andrews' opinion about your work. But he has thought it worth while to spend money on cabling the following to me:—

> Sastri's success unprecedented. Governor-General admirably supporting, also Ministers and officials.

It is difficult to trust Andrews with any monies for telegraphic charges, and yet I cannot summon sufficient courage to swear at him for this cable news. I am not going to make use of it for the Press. I never had any doubt about your success. All I want to be sure of is your health.

[1] Gandhiji was in Davangere on this date.

[2] *Vide* "Letter to Kusumbehn Desai", 29-7-1927.

I see you are already telling the public that your term of office will not go beyond one year. Anyway I have your assurance that you will not run away even for the Commission if your presence is indispensable there at the end of the year which is fast spinning away its course.

There was too a good letter from Miss Schlesin from which I was tempted to quote, but I restricted the temptation and destroyed the letter. Ere this reaches you, if she kept her promise, she must have seen you.

Yours sincerely,
M. K. GANDHI

THE RT. HON. V. S. SRINIVASA SASTRI
AGENT-GENERAL
SOUTH AFRICA
DURBAN

From a photostat: S.N. 12370

308. LETTER TO BAL KALELKAR

August 12, 1927

It is not enough merely to say that you do not like Kakasaheb turning a recluse. When I wrote to you that one's son attaining the age of 16 becomes one's friend, I also meant that you had acquired the capacity to think independently and one who thinks independently should be able to give strong reasons for one's opinions whether to convince himself or others. He must give reasons why he likes one thing and does not like another. Having developed such faculty from their very childhood some men have become great such as the sage Dayananda, Chaitanya, Ramakrishna Paramahamsa and other historic figures. Let us leave aside Hinduism and consider sannyasa independently. Sannyasa is a mental state and it is reflected in a man's actions. But if another man imitates these actions without the mental state, that will not be sannyasa. In this way, we all and the entire world have, to some small extent, to live a life of sannyasa and those who don't do so writhe in triple agony[1]. Sannyasa means abandonment of worldly pleasures. Complete abandonment constitutes complete sannyasa. Even a householder has always to observe

[1] Due respectively to nature, fate and spiritual causes

some restraint or other. He who does not has to suffer; he becomes a burden to the earth and falls a prey to diseases of many kinds. Thus we can see that restraint or renunciation should grow with our progress in life and it is man's duty to develop restraint as much as he can. If you accept the above argument that restraint is a good thing, you will have to grant that for doing a good thing a husband need not seek his wife's consent or *vice versa*. There is only one way of maintaining the sanctity of the marital tie, namely, husband and wife should both be willing partners in sensual pleasures. One who wants to progress abstaining from sensual pleasures should have the right to do so. Else there will be no progress in the householder's order, and this would halt the advancement of the whole world. Will you not, at least now, admit that Kakasaheb has a right to practise this kind of sannyasa? That renunciation will not harm Kaki or anyone else but actually it will be in her own interest. I believe that the religion of non-violence springs from the fact that the advancement of one promotes the advancement of all, and the fall of one implies the fall of all. We have therefore been enjoined to show compassion to every living being. If Kaki or you, through ignorance or infatuation, halt Kakasaheb's inclination towards sannyasa, it will harm, rather than benefit, you, him and society. After realizing the need for renunciation and attaining the strength for it, if Kakasaheb still holds himself back to please Kaki or you, he would be stifling his humanity. Would you let that happen? Please ponder over what I have written to you and then write to me whatever occurs to you.

I have to examine one more idea which you have expressed in your letter. You seem to differentiate between devotion to father and devotion to mother, but actually both are one. And a son may not discriminate between them. But the devotion of a wise son cannot be blind. Suppose a father is a drunkard, the mother is a woman of restraint and the father asks the son to help him with drinks. The mother entreats the son not to give such help. The son submits to his mother and does not help his father. Such a son has discharged his duty of being devoted to his mother and his father, though in doing so he hurts his father. This example does not point to the difference between the two devotions but explains the nature of intelligent devotion. This same argument would now apply to you. If Kakasaheb practises mental renunciation, it will promote the well-being of all of you. Kaki does not like this because of her ignorance and infatuation.

If you accept that Kakasaheb's renunciation is right, your devotion to your parents would tell you to help Kakasaheb and to entreat Kaki to agree to his resolve and even if she does not consent you should agree and have faith that ultimately Kaki too will appreciate this duty.

I can understand your desire to live with Kaki, but it is a delusion. In your letter you have already approved of *brahmacharyashrama* or sannyasa during the student days. In the olden times pupils used to leave their parents' homes and stay with their preceptors. In the Ashram we try to bring back that state; you should help in this effort. One must learn to live with contentment and restraint while one's parents are away. I admit that the teachers do not yet have so much restraint, so much knowledge and so much love that pupils could easily forget their parents, but you know that we want to revive a thing that is dead. The teachers are trying hard and intelligent pupils ought generously to help them in their endeavours. Wherever the teachers are not able to fill the place of parents you should bear with them and cultivate patience. If even a few among you begin to do so, we shall be able to improve the Ashram.

Write to me always with the same frankness with which you wrote your first letter. True modesty consists in laying open one's heart before one's elders without reserve. We may make our language sweet and polite but if we try to repress our thoughts and hide them, we may commit a serious fault. Besides that would not be modesty at all.

[From Gujarati]

From the manuscript of Mahadev Desai's Diary. Courtesy: Narayan Desai

309. *SPEECH AT PUBLIC MEETING, DAVANGERE*[1]

August 12, 1927

Gandhiji said that khadi would in part rebuild the villages that were destroyed by modern industrialism and that it was the duty of prosperous merchants in cotton centres to help towards the revival of spinning. The khadi movement stood for even distribution of the good things of the world. Khadi represented *dharmik* political economy, whereas industrialism was *rakshasik* or Satanic economics. For it stood for the accumulation of wealth in the hands of the few.

I am going to do my best to prevent this Satanic economics from destroying us. I want all of you—Hindus, Mussalmans, Parsis, Christians, and all—to help me in this work.

He dealt with cow-protection in which the people of Davangere were keenly interested and for which they had an efficient organization called the Prani Daya Sangha. He said that well-conducted dairies and good tanneries for hides of dead cattle were absolutely necessary for true cow-protection in India.

We should not depend as Hindus for carrying out the dharma of cow-protection on compelling the Mussalmans to co-operate with us. We should be able to stand on our own legs and save the cattle. If we did not sell by reason of poverty and ignorance our cattle for slaughter, we can do more than by any such compulsion. The co-operation of the Mussalmans should be secured by love.

Dealing with the municipal address Gandhiji said that no programme of sanitation can succeed unless young and old, boys and girls were taught how to use and keep the latrines clean.

The Hindu, 15-8-1927

[1] In reply to welcome addresses presented by the local Municipality and the citizens

310. SPEECH TO ADI KARNATAKAS, DAVANGERE[1]

August 12, 1927

All these professions are noble, and I wish you to flourish in them. Playing on your pipes you can produce tunes which carry men nearer to God. The weavers' and the shoemakers' professions are as essential for your livelihood as for India, and I propose to address a few remarks to both. I ask the weavers to eschew foreign and even mill yarn. Ever since the growth of the mill industry in India, the handloom weavers are daily diminishing in numbers so that today their number is scarcely half of what it was some years ago. The objective of the mill industry is to monopolize all the weaving if possible and in consequence to rob the hand-weaver of his occupation. That was what industrialism did in Europe, but whereas the unemployed hand-weavers and hand-spinners found other employment there, they found none here and were reduced to destitution. I want you therefore to specialize in your profession, especially in weaving hand-spun yarn, and make your wives and children self-spinners so that you will have a colony of self-contained families.

I come to the shoemakers now. Here too as with the weavers there are things you may do and may not do. Just as the weaver may not touch foreign or mill yarn, the shoemakers must refuse to handle hide of slaughtered animals, and have hides of dead cattle cleaned and tanned by them. If it can be any encouragement to you, I may tell you that I have once done the shoemaker's work and can do it even today, and in our Ashram we have a tannery which takes charge of dead cattle's hides, tans them and sells them to shoemakers. I could provide you with such leather if you want. I want you to be not only shoemakers and earn your livelihood, but to be cow-protectors and earn merit. Being Hindus we should all hold the cow dear, and I want you to join me in the noble work of cow-protection. But how am I to make you understand this? Being Hindus you deny Hinduism every day.

I want you to take His Highness the Maharaja's Jubilee message to heart. A portion of it is distinctly addressed to you.

[1] From Mahadev Desai's "Weekly Letter". In their address the *Adi Karnatakas* had said that they were mostly pipers, weavers, and shoemakers.

Whilst a spirit of brotherhood should prevail as between the citizens of the State, His Highness emphasized:

> I pray that a similar spirit may extend itself to the dumb creation, and that we may see animals, and especially those we hold sacred, treated with ever increasing consideration for feelings which they cannot express.

Let us realize all the implications of that pregnant prayer. It is not so much an exhortation addressed to those who abstain from meat and beef, as to those like you who have no regard for the cow. It is equally intended for the Mussalmans and Christians, and if you feel anything like grateful to His Highness for his benevolent rule, I want you to abjure cow-slaughter and beef.

Young India, 25-8-1927

311. LETTER TO J. P. BHANSALI

Saturday, August 13, 1927

BHAISHRI BHANSALI,

I got your letter. You must have got my telegram. I have a letter from Shri Chhaganlal Joshi. I gather from it that my letter made you unhappy and a little angry. Recall what you had written earlier to me. You had actually welcomed my criticism and my opinion and the fact that I had not sent you the former during your fast had hurt you. In your letter to Mirabehn you say that you want to realize God through renunciation, *samadhi*[1], etc. "Never is this steadiness of mind destroyed by excessive possessions or fear of calamities." This is the state you should cultivate. If someone vents his anger upon you and calls you an ignorant fool, even then you should forgive him. But this merely by way of preface.

My aim in writing this letter is to tell you that you should preserve calm while this question is being settled. You should understand that the managing committee, too, wishes to come to a decision on moral issues. That does not necessarily mean that you should leave the Ashram if it does not give its consent to your intended fast. I certainly cannot guess what decision the managing committee will arrive at. I do not at all insist that it should do what I wish that it should. I shall forward your letters to it. Take no decision in haste.

[1] Yogic trance

You say in your letter to Mirabehn that your letter to me was not an ultimatum. While handing it over to me, Mahadev at any rate told me that it was an ultimatum. On going through it, I too read an ultimatum in it. Do not read too much in the word "ultimatum". It only means a firm decision. In your letter you have really asked for my blessings, not for my permission. But now stick to your decision that you will take the next step after seeing me. I believe that we shall be carrying on this correspondence now to reach a decision on a moral issue.[1]

Blessings from
BAPU

From a photostat of the Gujarati: S.N. 12962

312. SPEECH AT HARIHAR[2]

August 13, 1927

It is said that if God made man in His image, man made God in his own, and it is no wonder that what we see in our temples, at the present day, are lifeless images of us, lifeless devotees. If we would make them living images of God, we must transform our lives, we must end our communal squabbles, and we must befriend the suppressed, and live pure lives. Hari is the Protector in the Hindu Trinity, and Hara is the Destroyer. When God finds that the rich oppress the poor, instead of taking them under their protecting wings, He then assumes His fearful aspect of Hara, and deals destruction all round. When the rich and the poor identify themselves with one another, then will Hari and Hara unite, and it is my ambition to establish a real living image of Harihareshwara by presenting a charkha to the country. The charkha is the symbol of sacrifice, and sacrifice is essential for the establishment of the image of the deity.

Young India, 25-8-1927

[1] *Vide* also letters dated after July 26 and July 27 to the addressee and "Letter to Mirabehn", 27-7-1927.

[2] From Mahadev Desai's "Weekly Letter". The venue was opposite Harihareshwara temple.

313. TO VOLUNTEERS

A calamity such as that which has befallen Gujarat can be put to good or bad use. From such terrible floods godfearing men learn humility, simplicity, compassion and similar virtues. They realize that one would do well, in this transitory world, to live with as much self-denial and self-control as one can. The wicked go out stealing at such times, rob people and indulge their evil propensities in all manner of ways.

Very often money given for help is also misused. A large number of volunteers is required for distributing relief over a large area. If they are greedy, they pocket the money which is entrusted to them. It would be foolish to expect Gujarat to be completely free from such malpractices. But it can certainly be expected of volunteers that they will have no greedy thoughts and, working wholly in a spirit of service, will win credit for themselves.

Volunteers are subject to weaknesses of another kind. They do not steal like thieves; but they feel some pride in being volunteers and, though in fact they are servants of the people, expect service from others as if they were their benefactors. They look after themselves before they help others and get angry with people who do not carry out their instructions promptly. I hope that every volunteer will keep himself free from such weaknesses.

The volunteers should know that even the poor are contributing, at some personal sacrifice, towards the fund which is being collected. I am certain that we shall not be short of money. If, however, the money is not properly used, all our work will have been wasted.

Moreover, we should also guard against the danger of the really poor getting nothing and the assertive getting a lion's share. I have already had heartening reports of instances of persons not accepting help though they were in real difficulty, but I know from my previous experience that there are always people who will grab at whatever help is offered. It is as necessary that we do not, out of false compassion or fear or weakness, give to people who do not need help as that we should see at any cost that help reaches those who really need it.

At a time of such terrible calamity, one becomes very generous and is inclined to give help to anyone who asks for it. I do not think that such undiscriminating help really benefits the people.

The common rule is that everyone should bear the hardships which befall him. If all of us shoulder our own burdens, we would find very few in this world who are really helpless. But large numbers become a burden on others in various ways: they enjoy a greater share than is theirs by right, and that is why we see a great number of helpless and poor people in the world. Hence in a situation like the present one actual help and in the largest quantity has to be given only for a few days, and that consists in providing food and clothing for some time to those who need them. Afterwards, what is necessary is to help everyone to find a means of livelihood; there should be no need, by and large, of giving money to those who are sound in limbs.

After the *mahapralaya* a new creation comes into being. This flood may not be that, but it is of the same kind. If, therefore, the volunteers can take up reform work, if they have knowledge and patience, they can even create a new world. They can persuade people to sacrifice, as in a *yajna*, their baneful habits and can spread new ideas about building houses. The villages which have been completely ruined should be reconstructed according to a plan instead of being rebuilt somehow. Villages which suffer from frequent floods should be shifted and rebuilt on new sites. This work, however, cannot be accomplished by one person. It requires the services, by way of advice and active work, of leading social workers, of men and women of wisdom. It also requires the sincere co-operation of the administration.

My appeal, however, is addressed to Vallabhbhai and to bodies of workers of his type. More it is beyond my capacity to suggest at present.

[From Gujarati]

Navajivan, 14-8-1927

314. LETTER TO MIRABEHN

SHIMOGA,
August 14, 1927

CHI. MIRA,

I have your letter. Today is Sunday, and I am at an out-of-the-way place called Shimoga, where I have to pass four more nights visiting surrounding places during these days. I will have left this place by the time this reaches you. I hope now the riddle of the missing letter has been solved. I now know that even if I write the Monday letter on Sunday night after taking the silence, I should mark it Monday. But I want you to shed this anxiety about my letters. If they come, it is well. But it should be well also if they do not come, when you have the assurance that if anything untoward happens to me, you would be bound to know it by wire. That the contents of one letter may be lost or delayed in transmission need cause no worry, because I should remember and be able to reproduce anything of importance.

The Gujarat work is evidently being done in a most orderly manner. Of course if you had been there, you would have thrown yourself in the fray, but those also are as good as having thrown themselves in the fray who stand watchful at their post however remote it may be from the scene of a calamity.

What you describe of Vinoba is just like him. But my sympathy is with the orthodox resisters. This monthly untouchability is an old custom not altogether harmful, certainly not altogether superstitious. And it is difficult to draw distinctions between married and unmarried women in such matters. I have looked upon the restriction as a check upon man's lust. The confinement of the sick woman to a wretched miserable room, rags for dress, etc., is horrible, barbarous and can have no justification. But the sentiment of segregation during the monthly sickness should not be violently disturbed. I want you, therefore, to see the other side and not merely barely tolerate the attitude of people like Mogheji, but regard it with due respect as you would have them to regard your own opposite attitude. I am therefore hoping that Vinoba has been managing the thing gently and that he has not carried the orthodox inmates with him by sheer force of affection without producing a genuine conviction. And, even if they have willingly withdrawn their opposition, I would advise you to put a voluntary restraint upon yourself during the monthly sickness. You may share this letter with Vinoba if you like so that he may understand my argument. Remember that my own opinion is the same as yours. My only plea is for respectful and intelligent toleration, and remember also that when you tolerate in this manner, you do not "suppress" yourself. Self-suppression comes and is necessary where blind superstition has to be tolerated. It should not be "revolting" to you to accept such untouchability. On the contrary, you should impose it on yourself or accept it with grace and cheerfulness without thinking that the orthodox party is in any way unreasonable.

Now about future work: I accept your description of yourself as being illiterate. But I do not want you to remain so for ever. It should be not too late to do much to remove illiteracy. I should be satisfied if you could develop a taste for removing illiteracy, and to this end, you may take up a decent little grammar book and master it through and through. Similarly, for arithmetic. You should take up a very simple arithmetic book. If you think that constitutionally you will be unfit for both or either, I will say nothing and in any case I do not propose this addition during these two months which are fast running out, but I should like you to take these up later if they can be taken up as recreations.

To start with work in the kitchen will certainly be very nice, if only in order to discipline yourself in controlling your temper and suiting yourself to all kinds of people. In practice, we have found kitchen work to be the most trying of all.

I know that you have brought me boundless love. Everything else without it would have been perfectly useless, and with it everything needful will be easy. But I am not going to speculate about the work. When you have finished your course there, I know that the way will be open both before you and me with sufficient clearness.

Bhansali has sent me copy of his reply to you. Do keep up the correspondence.

With love,

BAPU

[PS.]

This is Sunday. Monday's letter will be separate.

From the original: C.W. 5260. Courtesy: Mirabehn

315. LETTER TO C. F. ANDREWS

August 14, 1927

MY DEAR CHARLIE,

At last you have come after working wonders in South Africa. I hope you have brought with you fair health.

I am writing this in an out-of-the-way place in Mysore. Here is my time-table. You will probably want to come to me at once. If you leave Bombay on 21st you can reach Bangalore on 23rd morning *via* Guntakal. You could of course overtake me at the places mentioned for 24, 25, 26. They are no distance from Bangalore.

I had your cable about Gujarat. Well, it seems to have been a divine purification. For, all the accounts I have received go to show that the people in the deluge area have risen to the occasion. But as yet it is too late to say what permanent effect it is going to have.

More when we meet.

With love from us all—Ba, Mahadev, Rajagopalachari, Gangadharrao, Devdas, Kaka, etc., etc.

MOHAN

From a photostat: S.N. 12371

316. LETTER TO A. I. KAJEE

AS AT THE ASHRAM, SABARMATI,
August 14, 1927

MY DEAR KAJEE,

I continue to receive your useful letters. I am delighted that you are so happy over Sastriji's activities there. I am only hoping that the community will make the rightest use of him. I know that the community will not get another opportunity of redressing its grievances.

The judgment[1] of the Natal provincial division of the Supreme Court does not cause me any surprise. A dealer's licence has

[1] The reference is to the case of a Pathan, trading as "Empire Furniture Manufacturing Co.", *versus* the Durban Corporation in appeal against the refu-

always been distinguished from a manufacturer's licence. For instance a carpenter surely must be able to sell furniture of his own making without the necessity of the dealer's licence. If he is required to take out a licence, it will then be an artisan's licence.

Yours sincerely,
M. K. GANDHI

A. I. KAJEE, ESQ.
SOUTH AFRICAN INDIAN CONGRESS
175, GREY STREET, DURBAN (NATAL)

From a photostat: S.N. 12372

317. *LETTER TO SONJA SCHLESIN*

AS AT THE ASHRAM, SABARMATI,
August 14, 1927

DEAR MISS SCHLESIN,

I have your letter of 24th June. Herewith receipt for £21 s. 10. If you still remember your Gujarati, you will make out the Gujarati writing.

The cause of my illness so far as I can see it is the very terrific strain I put upon the body and the brain, addressing numerous meetings almost every day and motoring from place to place. The day[1] on which the breakdown occurred was one of very high tension, and little rest on the previous night. This is also the doctor's diagnosis. I feel however that I should have been able to prevent it. And if I had taken a complete fast on the day of the tension, I might have avoided it. As it was, I had put myself on half diet during those days.

The first volume of what you call the autobiography will be sent to you. The history of passive resistance struggle was published three years ago, but the English translation is not available. It is being published by Mr. Ganesan in quarterly instalments in his magazine *Current Thought.* It would be ultimately published, I expect, in book-form. But it will take time. You can have the Gujarati copy if you will make up your Gujarati.

---

sal to renew his licence. The court had held that they had the right to interfere only in matters of retail or wholesale dealers and as this was a case of manufacturing licence they could not intervene.

[1] March 26, 1927; *vide* Vol. XXXIII, pp. 194-5.

My food at present is 30 ounces goat's milk with honey and any fruit that is available and generally home-made bread like Jewish passover cake unleavened. I take no nuts. Diet is restricted to five articles, that is to say, milk, grapes, oranges and bread will count as four articles, and if I add figs it will be the fifth.

I never knew that you had £150. I thought you had only £40. I shall await your impressions of the visit to Manilal and his wife.

I shall see your handiwork when Mr. Andrews returns and if he has not given it away or lost it. Whether you could get over the shock of your having me described as with one garment or not, your surmise was quite correct that a poor man could not consistently possess a tray such as you have described. You have unconsciously altered the sense of my letter by mere atrocious reading. For, I did not suggest as you make me suggest that I could identify myself with the poor by merely wearing one garment. But I do say that even that little thing is something. To understand the logic of such a step is probably expecting too much of you now. For, there was a time when you appreciated my change of dress I adopted in Durban for almost identical considerations. I look forward to your description of your visit to Mr. Sastri.

I quite agree with you that, if we are to do anything, our womenfolk should have the same facilities that men have for education, etc. And you will be interested to know that at the Ashram here we have over 40 women of all ages excluding little girls. They have a special class every day, and in my opinion they are making very wonderful progress. The utmost freedom is enjoyed by them at the Ashram.

Yours sincerely,

Enclosure

From a photostat: S.N. 12373

318. LETTER TO S. GANESAN

As at Bangalore,
August 14, 1927

MY DEAR GANESAN,

I have your two letters. Krishnadas is just now in Bihar. I am asking him to let you have the revised manuscript. I am glad that you seem to have tided over your difficulties.

I note the announcement with reference to your publishing scheme. It seems to read all right.

I hope that you will on no account embark on any speculative venture. Let everything be deliberate and well-calculated.

I understand that you have already published Mahadev's writings. But you do not seem to have sent any copy here.

I suggest your removing from your advertisement the reference to giving the Ashram 25 % of profits.

Yours sincerely,

Sjt. S. Ganesan
18, Pycrofts Road
Triplicane
Madras

From a microfilm: S.N. 19799

319. LETTER TO KRISHNADAS

Shimoga,
August 14, 1927

MY DEAR KRISHNADAS,

Here are two letters from Ganesan. You may now send him the revised manuscript he wants. I understand that he has already published Mahadev's writings which he had announced though he had not sent a copy here as yet.

Yours sincerely,

Sjt. Krishnadas
110, Hazra Road
Calcutta

From a microfilm: S.N. 19800

320. LETTER TO A. A. PAUL

SHIMOGA,
August 14, 1927

DEAR FRIEND,

I have your letter with enclosures. I am writing this from Shimoga though you may send your reply, if any, addressed to Bangalore which will be my headquarters till the 29th instant.

I like your scheme for inter-religious fellowship. I have not been able to read it with sufficient attention to be able to offer any useful criticism. The first reading of it appeals to me.

I shall be at your disposal when I am in Madras for all the time that Sjt. Rajagopalachariar may be able to spare for you and during that time we can discuss the scheme. You would also then have made some further advances as you will have held your committee meeting on the 22nd.

As I had finished dictating this letter, I got your letter of the 11th instant. I am glad that international fellowship is well on its way to formation in Poona. I know Professor Wadia well through correspondence.

Yours sincerely,

From a photostat: S.N. 19801

321. LETTER TO M. F. KHAN

As at Bangalore,
August 14, 1927

DEAR FRIEND,

I have now found time to read your dialogue "What the little ones can do". It shows where your heart lies. But, whilst I do not regard myself to be a judge of art, as a journalist, I can say that the dialogue does not make interesting reading. There is no plot about it.

The verses quoted by you are interesting, and I might be able to make use of them. Please give me the name of the author.

Yours sincerely,

M. F. Khan, Esq.
Palam Road
Frazer Town
Bangalore

From a microfilm: S.N. 19802

322. LETTER TO DEVCHAND PAREKH

Shimoga,
August 14, 1927

I have replied to your telegrams. I have got your letters too. I can understand your importunity, but I am convinced I must not leave my present station. Personally I believe my going over there[1] would do some harm instead of doing any good. I can visualize the one loss resulting from Vallabhbhai putting aside his own powers and I can imagine others too. Even if I go over, we cannot collect all the funds, as you seem to think we can. Nor should we overdo our attempts to accomplish this task at this time. Marwaris should work through him alone who commands your confidence and I would regard that as proper. Confidence is certainly based on honesty and fitness too. They would not credit either me or you all who are my companions

[1] Gujarat

with as much ability as they expect in a businessman—and why should they? Bhai Amritlal is doing his work separately, and he has himself gained the confidence of certain people by dint of his ability and service. They would give him funds as long as he does something and I would regard that as right. You should adopt the same attitude in the case of the Hind Sevak Samaj. Our duty is to serve wherever we can reach easily.

You write that if I were to engage you on relief work you will get engrossed in it and discontinue the Conference work. I do not like this line of thought. How absurd that you would take up a job if I ask you to, else you would hold the Conference! At such a moment if you say that you must hold the Conference, you ought to do so—whatever I may think or in whatever other work I may wish to engage you—and when you wish to serve, why should you wait for signal from me? Why don't you join Bhai Amritlal's group? Or if he cannot cover the whole of Kathiawar, why do you not cover the remaining part? Of course, you can have the funds from Vallabhbhai after submitting your scheme to him; you can have it also from the Hind Sevak Samaj. It is Vallabhbhai's duty to cover those parts which are not served by others. If the satyagrahis, that is, Fulchand's army, wait for my orders, it will hurt me deeply and I shall regard them as unfit to launch satyagraha. How can those who miss opportunities of service launch satyagraha, that is civil disobedience? The fitness to go to jail should be backed by a proof of services rendered and self-purification. My permission and my authority relate to the launching of civil disobedience. I would not restrain anyone from offering satyagraha in the form of service or self-purification.

I have nothing to say about the Conference.

[From Gujarati]

From the manuscript of Mahadev Desai's Diary. Courtesy: Narayan Desai

323. LETTER TO MANILAL AND SUSHILA GANDHI

August 14, 1927

CHI. MANILAL AND SUSHILA,

Your letters still arrive after many wanderings.

I should get faithful account of Sastri's visit, but have not received one so far.

Sushila has asked a question about social service. Any work which we do for people's welfare and with sincere motives is social service. If in your family life you merely aim at enjoyment and do not think of society, that will be serving self-interest; if, on the other hand, you adopt simplicity for the sake of society, take care not to set a bad example to others and, when buying anything, consider whether it is morally right or wrong to do so, then that is social service. Going further, if your aim in helping in the press work is merely to save money, that is service of self. If, however, your aim is to learn that work and spend the money saved by your work for some public purpose, if it is that you should bring out the paper even at the cost of hardship to yourself, that is social service. Go a step further still; if, finding that your neighbour is ill, you sacrifice your comforts in order to nurse him and learn nursing work, that is social service. From these examples you can think of any number of others and extend the field of social service within the limits of your capacity. If, tired of India, Manilal lives in South Africa to enjoy the pleasures which that country offers, that is selfishness. If, believing that the paper conducted by his father was good and that his country stood to gain by his continuing to run it, he lives and forces you to live in exile without the aim of amassing wealth, he is rendering a great social service and you, too, are making a contribution to it.

Today we have come to a far-off place in Mysore State. About sixty miles from here is a waterfall like the Inanda Falls, but much bigger than that, which we are all going to see tomorrow. Devdas has stayed back in Bangalore. He will arrive here this evening with others. We shall remain here and collect contributions for about four days and then return to Bangalore. At the end of this month, we shall cross the boundary of Mysore State and enter Tamilnad.

My health continues to improve. I do not think we shall get back to the Ashram by the end of December. We positively wish to return in January, since *Vasantapanchami*[1] falls at the end of that month and Ramdas's wedding has been fixed for that day. Whether Nimu turns out to be as wise as Sushila and gives Ramdas a life-companion exactly like yours and makes him a prisoner is still to be seen. Nimu of course is wise, but are there not degrees even of wisdom? How much distance is there between you two and who is better of the two, only the future will tell. For myself, I wish that both of you should reach the summit and that all the four of you should strengthen one another's moral character and stand foremost in the *yajna* of service. Ramdas has gone out to help in flood relief work.

Blessings from
BAPU

From a photostat of the Gujarati: G.N. 4725

324. SPEECH AT SHIMOGA[2]

August 14, 1927

There is sympathy, there is the suitable atmosphere, there is faith. What I now want is expert knowledge to fructify that faith. I know it from experience that where knowledge has not been combined with faith, faith has quickly evaporated, and glorious beginnings have ended in smoke. I want you, lawyers and businessmen, to bring to bear all the expert knowledge, that you do in your own departments, also in the new department that you are favouring. Study the economics and master the technique of spinning, and build up with the aid of experts in the various branches of cloth-production an organization equal to the splendid administrative machinery that the State has brought into being.

Young India, 25-8-1927

[1] The traditional beginning of the vernal season

[2] In reply to the addresses presented by the local Municipality and the citizens at a meeting held in the Jubilee Grove

325. LETTER TO MIRABEHN

Monday, August 15, 1927

CHI. MIRA,

So you have the missing letter at last. Poor Mahadev![1]

You must not damage your eyes even for the sake of Hindi. What you need most however is conversation without restraint. Make your own dictionary as you proceed. Or annotate your printed dictionary. But of course I do not consider the London specialist's to be the last word about your eyes. Often the simplest remedies escape the specialist and he comes to the conclusion that as no alteration in the lens will answer, nothing else will. However, this can wait. When you return to the Ashram, you should let Haribhai examine you. He is reputed to be a good man for eye defects.

Your letter to Bhansali was not too strong. I liked its style.

If my letter of yesterday was not clear, you will of course write.

With love,

BAPU

From the original: C.W. 5261. Courtesy: Mirabehn

326. LETTER TO ASHRAM WOMEN

Silence Day [August 15, 1927][2]

SISTERS,

Received your letter. Today we are in a place far off from Bangalore. It is less cold, but more green here. It is somewhat like Amboli.

Although I appear to be at work here, my thoughts hover round the Ashram and Gujarat. This is not a virtue, but a defect, since it shows undue attachment. What more could I have done had I been in the Ashram? How can I help Gujarat? And yet

[1] Mahadev Desai had inadvertently addressed the letter to Sabarmati instead of to Wardha. Explaining this, in his letter to Mirabehn, dated September 12, he had written: "So many letters addressed to the Sabarmati Ashram the same day, and one only to Wardha!"

[2] Gandhiji was in Shimoga, "far off from Bangalore", on this date.

my soul is restless. You should guard yourselves against such attachment. But remember the conditions in which non-attachment is possible. He alone can remain untouched who is always absorbed in the performance of his duties. The stone may be indifferent, but we regard it as insentient. We on the contrary are sentient. It is only when we remain indifferent to our environment, because of complete absorption in our immediate duties, that we may be held to have succeeded in life. Such steadiness of mind does not come about suddenly. I have explained to you my own defects clearly, so that you may learn to avoid them.

My language today is slightly difficult. If a word or an idea is difficult to grasp, you must make an extra effort to understand it.

Blessings from
BAPU

From a photostat of the Gujarati: G.N. 3661

327. LETTER TO MANIBEHN PATEL

Silence Day, 1927[1]

I had your card but not the promised letter. What type of work are you doing in Matar and who are your co-workers? Maintain your peace of mind, no matter what work you do.

I wrote to your uncle[2] that Manibehn would come to him when he had learnt to ply the *takli* while sitting in his chair. He wrote in reply to say that Manibehn was a crank. I sent a rejoinder that, being a crank herself, she lived in company with another crank.

What is the name given to Yashoda's[3] son?

Blessings from
BAPU

CHI. MANIBEHN PATEL
MATAR

[From Gujarati]

Bapuna Patro—Manibehn Patelne, p. 53

[1] The precise dates of this and the following letter are not ascertainable. But from the reference to the addressee's work in Matar, to Yashoda's son (born in May 1927) and to V. J. Patel who had "gone there with high hopes of being useful", it is presumed that they belong to the period when there were floods in Gujarat. They are, therefore, placed on the Silence Day after "The Havoc in Gujarat", 11-8-1927.

[2] Vithalbhai J. Patel

[3] Dahyabhai V. Patel's wife

328. LETTER TO MANIBEHN PATEL

Silence Day, 1927

CHI. MANI,

Your letter. Keep a record of your experiences of life in villages for future use. Never be impatient, despondent or uneasy. I have many questions to ask you but not now; I shall ask you when we meet or when your present task is finished. Write to me regularly. Do preserve your health.

I hope you met uncle.[1] He has gone there with high hopes of being useful. May these be realized.

Blessings from

BAPU

[From Gujarati]

Bapuna Patro—Manibehn Patelne, p. 64

329. LETTER TO CHHAGANLAL JOSHI

SHIMOGA,

Shravan Krishna 2 [*August 15, 1927*][2]

BHAISHRI CHHAGANLAL JOSHI,

I send you Shri Bhansali's letters along with this. You must have seen my telegram and letter[3] to him. You and others in the Committee should read these letters carefully and think over them. After doing so, hand them back to Shri Bhansali. The letter addressed to me, you may either file in the office or return to me.

Think over this matter quite impersonally. I believe that Shri Bhansali will keep the promise, given to me in a letter which he wrote before this, that he would await my return there; nevertheless, we must consider this thing for the future. My opinion is that we should not permit Shri Bhansali to fast, and that, if he fasts despite this, we can put up with it. We tolerate many things in the Ashram, but would not permit them if our permission was sought.

[1] Vithalbhai J. Patel; he was then Speaker of the Central Legislative Council. He came over to Nadiad when the province was ravaged by floods, and undertook an extensive tour of the flood-stricken areas.

[2] Gandhiji was in Shimoga on this date in 1927.

[3] Dated August 13, 1927

There are also many things for which we would not give permission and which we would not tolerate. We should think in which category to place this idea of a fast. All of you should consider the point and do what you think proper. I cannot guide you from here, because in order to express an opinion it is necessary that I must talk things over with Bhai Bhansali and let the effect of the talk sink into my mind. Moreover, before you decide anything you should hold talks with Shri Bhansali in private and also in the presence of the Committee. Try to know the deepest thoughts of Lilabehn, and write to me if you like. There is no need for the slightest hurry to take a decision in this matter. If Shri Bhansali cannot keep his promise in the present letter and if, since I have suggested a reference to the Committee, you let me hear from you after a talk with the Committee and if he asks for the Committee's decision before my return, you will have to give it. But it is necessary in any case that he look to the convenience of the Committee. I also believe that we cannot decide this matter without consulting the absent members of the Committee too. This is so because, on the one hand, dharma suggests that even if we are not able to keep pace with an aspirant for *moksha* and a seeker after knowledge like Bhansali and we disapprove of a step contemplated by him, we should let him proceed, that is to say, we must keep him in the Ashram; on the other hand, dharma tells us that it is perhaps our obligation not to tolerate his proposed step in the Ashram even if we consider it not as immoral but merely as thoughtless and dangerous. We have thus to discover the point of balance between social conformity and individual freedom, and we cannot do this in a hurry. Explain our difficulties to Shri Bhansali and request him to respect our honest efforts, if for no other reason, at least in order that he may then more easily have the vision for which he is so eager. Keep me informed about this from time to time and, if necessary, even send me a telegram.

If Lala Mohanlal of Lahore is there and if he has been quietly and honestly doing physical work, let him do so and live there till I arrive. But this is my opinion only. Having observed his behaviour or having regard to the other arrangements in the Ashram, if you think that you cannot keep him, ask him to leave. Give him the accompanying letter.

Blessings from
BAPU

From a photostat of the Gujarati: S.N. 12965

330. LETTER TO BALKRISHNA

August 15, 1927

CHI. BALKRISHNA,

I cannot help writing to you today.

I do not like to interfere much in your course of thinking or way of work because you arrange your thoughts with great care. But very often the experience of elders helps even one who arranges one's thoughts carefully. I sometimes get into an argument with you with a view to helping you. I think we needs must stay in society in order to build up our character and we have even to bear with our leaders' temper. New principles do not come up every day before a philosopher; but conflicts of duty do crop up every day—ponder over the difference between the two. It is when duties conflict that a soldier obeys his general and he puts his own reason aside. The intelligence of one who always indulges in its exercise obstructs his self-realization. When a leader is not deliberately immoral, it is non-violence to submit to his intelligence. Non-violence is humbler than even a mango tree. It is said that a mango tree bends as it grows up. When non-violence grows fully, it acts like a cipher. Instead of attempting to prove its own point, non-violence lets everyone else prove his. Hence it has been sung: "When non-violence is established, in its vicinity all hatred is given up."[1] Who can hate a cipher and how?

You will lose nothing by subordinating yourself to Maganlal. Both yourself and Maganlal will benefit by submitting to his mistaken orders, whatever they be, because we have in doing so accepted a principle. Your subordinating yourself to him will be a means of correcting his error. I have experienced this thing myself many times. I have corrected the errors of my associates by subordinating myself to them and who knows how many errors of mine my associates daily correct by subordinating themselves to me? But what if they were to analyse my errors before me every day and annoy me? If that were so, where would they and I be today?

[1] *Yogasutra* by Patanjali

Think deeply over this letter. Do not again come back impatiently running to me. I wish and I pray that you may have peace.

[From Gujarati]

From the manuscript of Mahadev Desai's Diary. Courtesy: Narayan Desai

331. LETTER TO RAMDAS GANDHI

August 15, 1927

These smaller floods come to warn us. There will surely be the final deluge. None need doubt it. The magic of this illusory world makes a man forget all his sorrows. This is doubtless an advantage but that man wins who, mindful of the deluge and persuaded of the transience not only of himself but of the world, lives his life in a detached way. To gain this mastery constitutes man's highest achievement. Truly speaking, all of us are condemned to death the moment we are born, and yet why do we all—the young, the old and the children—drown ourselves in sensual pleasures? It is obvious that we do revel in them, but we should always ask ourselves the above question; at the time of such floods, we should ask it with all the more earnestness. Then, one day, the answer will spring from within. The intellect provides the answer even today: "Oh man, give up all trace of passion." But as long as the call does not come from the heart, the poor intellect is ineffectual.

[From Gujarati]

From the manuscript of Mahadev Desai's Diary. Courtesy: Narayan Desai

332. *LETTER TO DEVESHWAR SIDDHANTALANKAR*

AS AT BANGALORE,
August 16, 1927

DEAR FRIEND,

I thank you for your long letter and the reprint of your articles. I shall try to find time for re-reading the articles.

I shall appreciate your English writing. I do not know whether I stated in my previous letter[1] that the English I wanted not for myself but for circulation amongst Mussalman and other friends, who claim to know the Koran and Islam intimately. My own reading I don't regard as in any way deep or learned. It was purely for my own satisfaction.

You seem to think that the *dasyus* do not give the same meaning in the Vedic times that the word Kaffir does in Islam. Not to go back to historical times, I would like you to look at the history that is being enacted in our midst. Do not thousands of Hindus regard Mussalmans as enemies to be converted or destroyed because they are Mussalmans? Do not many cultured Indians hate the British people as wicked? If somebody wrote a learned treatise today describing the relations between ourselves and the British and had not a boundless spirit of charity, would he not describe the British as *dasyus* or *atatayis* fit only to be destroyed at sight, and if that treatise [should] survive some periodic upheaval and afterwards become religious literature, posterity is likely to indulge in the same error that we do and say that those *atatayis* and *dasyus* of these times were not political exploiters but were wicked people as you now interpret the term wicked people, or would you say even now that the British as a people are really wicked? Or take another instance: I know as the author of non-co-operation that many so-called non-co-operators hated co-operators as if they were wicked monsters and if the former had been allowed, they would have drawn these poor co-operators and certainly would have made short work of them. Supposing that some very learned non-co-operator of the type I described wrote a treatise, he would of course describe co-operators as wicked men. Would you accept that verdict or take to a free fight like the one that took place between Shwetambars and Digambars, first cousins

[1] *Vide* Vol. XXXIII, pp. 357-9.

as they might be called. Was not each wicked in the sight of the other? The fact is that immediately you accept the doctrine of slaying people whom you consider to be wicked, you really surrender the whole case and come under the same category as the writer or the writings on the Koran. I do not need to cite any history in support of what I am saying but I can supplement it if necessary.

I have considered you to be an honest seeker. I have contrary opinions to what you have given about Nanak Dev and Kabir. But this is after all a small matter. If I do reach your pamphlet, I shall gladly give you illustrative passages where I thought your translation was not just.

It is curious that Professor Sahgal did not write the Hindi letter which I certainly received. I knew the name from the letter. Yet unfortunately that letter I destroyed after replying. The only possible mistake is that somebody else might have written on his paper and in his name. But this is merely nothing and by the way I pass it on to you as a piece of information.

Yours sincerely,

From a microfilm: S.N. 12388

333. *THE GUJARAT FLOODS*[1]

Good if True

On reading the reports of flood relief operations as well as Swami Anand's article in *Navajivan*[2] I hesitated, and still hesitate, to believe in the examples there given of the people's heroism, solidarity and humanity, as false praise, exaggeration and self-deception are the order of the day in the country. But I have no reason to disbelieve these reports. Exaggeration, untruth and the like are studiously eschewed in *Navajivan.* The Swami knows this ever since the paper was started, and indeed it is this policy of the paper which induces him to interest himself in and work for it.

Therefore so long as I have not any reason to consider the *Navajivan* reports as erroneous, I must take them to be true. And I tender my congratulations to Gujarat and the Gujaratis. For a

[1] Translated by Valjibhai G. Desai from the Gujarati which, however, was published in *Navajivan*, 21-8-1927

[2] Dated August 7, 1927. *Vide* "Notes", 25-8-1927, sub-title "Too Good to Be True".

moment one is almost tempted to welcome a disaster which has been the occasion for the people to display such virtues.

Catastrophes and calamities will now and then overtake the country. Wealth may be in our possession today and be lost tomorrow. We construct houses and make farms and gardens, and when these are destroyed, we can remake them. The distress will soon be forgotten.

But what if Gujarat along with the distress also forgets the virtues which she has realized in herself on the present occasion? We are everywhere familiar with momentary fits of heroism and renunciation. If Gujarat's present heroism proves to be only a temporary fit, the lesson of the floods will have been lost upon her. Let the Gujaratis, men as well as women, beware.

Let us convert the virtues of courage, patience and humanity in us, of which we have had a sudden glimpse, into a possession for ever. Hindus and Mussalmans embraced one another as brothers. The higher classes sheltered and succoured the suppressed like blood-brothers. If we now give up these relations as only suited for the days of adversity, our last state will be worse than the first, and we will have passed in vain through this calamity, which is really the throes of a new birth. And such calamities there will be, so long as we have not experienced a true rebirth.

Gujarat's doings on this occasion amount in my view to pure swaraj. If the virtues now manifested by the people become a permanent feature of their daily life, Gujarat may be said to have acquired the fitness for, as well as the power to win, swaraj.

The havoc worked by the floods was of a most unprecedented character; before which even Dyerism pales into insignificance. Dyer killed or wounded a thousand or twelve hundred men. No one can tell the heavy toll of life exacted of the immense property destroyed by the floods. But we did not abuse the floods. We practised satyagraha against them. We purified ourselves. We did constructive work. We achieved Hindu-Muslim unity. We removed untouchability. We became self-reliant. We placed our all at the disposal of our brothers and sisters. We did not wait for a leader. Instead of falling back before the enemy, we bravely faced him, and set to work as if nothing had happened. If we had feared the floods, if we had wasted precious time in abusing them, if we had engaged in violent struggle with them, we would only have multiplied our troubles.

All honour to Gujarat for the proof she has given of her greatness.

But What about Me?

But has a Gujarati, who is away from the scene of danger and of achievement, the right thus to bestow praise and tender congratulations ?

I received three wires and a letter asking me to come and lead the relief operations in Gujarat. The letter was Swami Anand's and the wires were from Sarojini Devi, Chandulal, whom I mistook for Dr. Chandulal, and Devchand Parekh.

But I did not give myself to anxiety. I was fully confident of Gujarat's self-reliance, I had not the shadow of a doubt that monetary help would be forthcoming in an adequate measure. I whole-heartedly trusted Vallabhbhai to do the needful. I was in touch with him by wire. I wired to him informing him of the insistent calls I had received and asking him to let me know if he thought my presence necessary. Vallabhbhai at once wired me in reply, that though the distress of the people was beyond words, it was not advisable for me to come over to Gujarat in the present state of my health; that my effort to make Gujarat self-reliant and the organization I had helped to set up therein had achieved more for her than my presence would have done; that people there would be, who would misinterpret my absence but it could not be helped; and that I must continue to rest without worrying over my absence from Gujarat.

I have not related this history in defence of myself. A servant of the people never needs to offer defence. Again I do not think my health is so delicate, that I could not come over. My health is certainly delicate. Physically I am not today equal to even a tithe of the strain which I successfully stood during the days of the Kheda Satyagraha[1]. The brain is nearly useless and is easily fagged. I have still to keep to my bed. But when there breaks out a fire, even a person who is ill must at risk to himself take a bucket of water and do his bit if he can. Even if he can only sit himself and issue orders to others, he must attend the place in a stretcher and help to extinguish the conflagration.

But I propose to point a moral from these events and to put co-workers on their guard. In Gujarat we have obeyed an unwritten law that when once a task has been entrusted to a worker, others should not seek to have a hand in it unless the worker in charge wishes or permits it; that the workers in charge of various branches of activity should be trusted but fearlessly re-

[1] *Vide* Vol. XIV.

moved in case they betray their trust. Our leader in Gujarat is Vallabhbhai. I may pass as an elder, but so far as work in Gujarat is concerned, I must bow to Vallabhbhai's rulings. It is only by a strict observance of this rule that we have been enabled to do whatever stands to our credit in Gujarat. We have thus subjected ourselves to discipline, conserved our energies and carried out an efficient division of labour.

But even independently of Vallabhbhai's instructions, I was of opinion that my presence was not needed in Gujarat. I have implicit confidence in Vallabhbhai's ability to serve the country. He has been my co-worker ever since the Kheda struggle. The self-sacrifice of none of us is greater than his. He has often placed before Gujarat the ripe fruits of his intelligence. He has previous experience of such relief work. In view of all this I fail to see what I myself could possibly have done more than he has.

Again if I came over to Gujarat specifically for this, Vallabhbhai according to his temperament would expect a lead from me, and would resign his liberty of action in my presence. On occasions like the present I should consider this to be nothing short of a misfortune. If I ran up there and began to meddle with this, that and the other thing, new as I would be to the work, I should only make an exhibition of ignorant vanity.

And I am not here enjoying a holiday. According to my lights I am pretty fully occupied in grappling with the fatal disease which is eating into the vitals not only of Gujarat but of India as a whole, a disease which is beyond all comparison very much more powerful and insidious than a week's deluge. It would not only be not meritorious but on the other hand a clear breach of duty on my part to give up this work for something else that is more tempting. We have the charge often levelled against us that we are apt to lose our heads in times of danger. To the extent that this is true, we must get rid of this shortcoming.

None of us, especially no leader should allow himself to disobey the inner voice in the face of pressure from outside. Any leader who succumbs in this way forfeits his right of leadership. There is much truth in the homely Gujarati proverb that "the person concerned can see things in the earthen pot and his neighbour cannot see them even in a mirror". I have not been able to see that it was my duty on the present occasion to run up to Gujarat.

The insistent calls I have received are evidence of a wrong attachment which we must surmount at all costs. I am nothing but a mere lump of earth in the hands of the Potter. Truth and Love

—ahimsa—is the only thing that counts. Where this is present, everything rights itself in the end. This is a law to which there is no exception. It would be very bad indeed that Gujarat or India should look up to me and sit with folded hands. Let her worship Truth and Love, look up to that divine couple, employ servants like myself so long as they tread the straight and narrow path and check them when they swerve from it.

If I had come over to Gujarat, perhaps she would not have done what she has done and is still doing.

Invalided leaders or public servants should give up the hankering after active leadership or service. There is no place for a sick man in these operations for relief, which require only such persons as are able-bodied, can run up from place to place, and have the power of enduring hunger and thirst, heat and cold. Those who do not reach this standard would only act as a drag on a quickly marching army.

Finally, a servant of the people should never fear or give way to bitterness if he finds himself a victim of misunderstanding, whether unintentional or wilful. The acts of men who have come out to serve or lead have always been misunderstood since the beginning of the world and none can help it. To put up with these misrepresentations and to stick to one's guns come what might—this is the essence of the gift of leadership. Misunderstandings have been my lot ever since I entered public life, and I have got inured to them.

In short, let Gujarat ever be, as it has been on the present occasion, self-reliant and self-helpful and proceed from achievement to achievement. Men like myself will come and go, but let Gujarat go on forever.

To Co-workers

A few words more to co-workers.

1. I take it that none of the workers will allow their pride to come in the way of their heartily co-operating with their compatriots.

2. Anyone who works for name and fame on an occasion like this incurs sin.

3. There should be the fullest co-operation between the various agencies at work.

4. Where Government offers help on our own terms we should freely accept it, as it does not involve any breach of the principle of non-co-operation. But all hair-splitting is out of place where the question is one of serving the people and serving them

in time and to the fullest extent possible. If the money in the hand of the Government is available for *good use*, we should unhesitatingly ask for it and accept it.

5. Let us not forget that organizations are meant for the service of the people, and not the people for the service of the organizations.

6. I see that there are three agencies at work, the Provincial Congress Committee under Vallabhbhai, the Saurashtra Sevasamiti under Amritlal Sheth and the Servants of India Society under Sjt. Devadhar. Possibly there are others. But in any case we must prevent any overlapping and insure the closest co-operation among the agencies. Workers who have not still reported themselves should join the centre of work which is nearest to them or which they like best. Anyone who remains aloof either from angularity or from pride will dig his own grave. The people will fail to benefit by his services and will think lightly of him.

7. It would be really terrible if anyone in disregard of existing organizations tries to start a fresh one. Seeing that time lost can never be regained, everyone should take his place at the point which he can reach the soonest.

Young India, 18-8-1927

334. BACKWARD CLASSES

Our woes are numerous. We have suppressed classes and we have also backward classes. The distinction between the two is that the suppressed classes as a rule include only the so-called "untouchables", whereas, the backward classes refer to those who are mentally and morally behind the other classes. I have made the acquaintance of one such class in Mysore. They are the Lambanis. Since the Belgaum Congress[1] one of them who has received a fair education has been exerting himself for their uplift. They had even a Conference last year and the State contributed a small sum towards its expenses. These appear originally to have come from Gujarat. They are otherwise recognized as gypsies. Their dialect corresponds to Gujarati. The address[2] which they gave me whilst I was passing Arsikere on my way to Hassan was written in Devanagari. The majority of the words in it were

[1] Of 1924

[2] *Vide* "Speech to Lambanis, Arsikere Junction", 2-8-1927.

Gujarati. The curious student will see the specimens from the address reproduced in *Navajivan*. He will not fail to notice even the Gujarati grammar in the language of the address. The customs of these people I find described as follows in the address of the President of the Conference:

> I am told that the Lambanis are otherwise known as Vanjaris; and that they were the grain-carriers of India when it had no good roads and railways; they worship to this day their queen Durga, a wealthy Lambani lady of the 13th century, who brought grain from Nepal, China and Burma, and saved many lives in a continuous famine that raged for twelve years in India; their chief God is Balaji and Goddess Tulaja Bhavani, and their principal feast is *Gokulashtami*, the day of the birth of Shri Krishna. They long respected cows and Brahmins, and to this day they abjure animal food and liquor at death dinners; they cremate the married dead and bury the unmarried. They were as a rule a robust and well-built class, and peaceful and well-behaved.
>
> But, alas! their carrying trade has practically ceased since the opening of roads and railways. Some of them now deal in cattle; some have settled as husbandmen, a few live by driving carts, a few others spin coarse hem *tag* and sell grass and fuel and work as labourers; some are under police surveillance, some are reputed to be robbers, cattle-lifters, kidnappers of women and children, manufacturers of false coin and distillers of illicit liquor. But these sinners can be reclaimed and should be reclaimed.

I understand that workers in their midst are now carrying on propaganda to combat the evil customs. Like all backward classes the Lambani womenfolk are heavily laden with cheap and tawdry ornaments devoid of all art. Like the Raniparaj, the reform amongst these people has gone side by side with the introduction of the spinning-wheel. The yarn which they presented to me of their own spinning was fairly good and fine. These Lambanis number roughly 45,740 in Mysore State alone, and there are many also in British Karnatak. There is work here for many a reformer.

Young India, 18-8-1927

335. LETTER TO N. R. MALKANI

BHADRAVATI,
August 18, 1927

MY DEAR MALKANI,

I expect that you received my letters[1]. I should like to have your reply.

Yours sincerely,
BAPU

Reply to:

C/o Sjt. S. Srinivasa Iyengar,
Amjad Bagh,
Luz, Mylapore,
Madras.

From a photostat: G.N. 879

336. SPEECH AT BHADRAVATI[2]

August 18, 1927

Your kind invitation, your purse and the iron casket remind me very strongly of my visit to Jamshedpur. But one thing that strikes me most here is that the whole undertaking is from top to bottom a self-contained one. The originator is a Mysorean, the staff and labourers are mostly Mysorean, at any rate entirely South Indians. That is a thing of which you and India may well be proud. You have given the lie to the statement made in some quarters that India has intellect but no practical genius. I hope and pray that the Iron Works may grow and add to the prosperity of the State from day to day. In a country rich in mineral resources we have a place for such undertakings and it is our duty to use these resources for the welfare of the people. I am sorry Sir M. Vishveshwarayya is not here, but his telegram of cordial welcome shows that his spirit is here.

[1] Of July 9 and 24

[2] From Mahadev Desai's "Weekly Letter"

A word now to you workers here, just as I did to those at Jamshedpur. There is as I have said need for your undertaking, but there is greater need for the work for which you have given your purse. Undertakings such as yours are necessary for the middle class and the rich, but you may not afford to neglect the helpless poor. There are two ways in which you can help—by contributing money for khadi, and by wearing it yourselves. Just as your works would have to stop if there was no market for iron, even so the khadi movement would be unprogressive if you did not wear the product of the poor man's labour. I appeal to the capitalist not to neglect the poor, whilst he may go on with his undertaking. In conclusion I hope that the relations between the officials and the workmen are sweet and friendly, and that care is taken to keep the liquor house and the gambling den miles away from your quarters.

Young India, 1-9-1927

337. APPEAL TO TAMIL NADU

August 19, 1927[1]

God willing, I expect to enter upon the long-deferred tour in Tamil Nadu in the beginning of September. Had there been no programme already fixed, I would have prolonged the rest and not undertaken any touring. But under Dr. Subbarao's advice, I took the risk of trying gentle touring in Mysore and though I am by no means as strong as I felt five months ago, the result of the tour in Mysore emboldens me to take up the Tamil Nadu tour.

But it will be impossible to keep to the original programme which was both intensive and extensive. It is necessary now to reduce the engagements in each place to the minimum as also the number of places to be visited. I have therefore asked Mr. Rajagopalachariar to confine the tour to principal centres in the hope that the neighbouring places that may have been omitted will bring their purses and send as many villagers as possible to the centres to be visited. It is a matter of no small grief to me that I cannot personally deliver the message of the wheel at all the places that had been fixed. But I can only do what is humanly possible. Indeed, if it was possible, I should love to visit every

[1] Released from Chikmagalur on this date

one of the seven hundred thousand villages of the motherland. But I have humility enough to recognize my very grave limitations and be content with what little God permits me to do.

I seek the co-operation, however, of all the lovers of khadi in order that its life-giving message can reach the remotest village. I hope that those who have the means will give, for and in the name of *Daridranarayana*, the most that they can, so that the organization which is slowly but surely growing in our villages and the revival the spinning-wheel has brought about may not die a lingering death.

I appeal to the Reception Committees in the places which are to be visited to cut down all unnecessary items, especially those of show, and also reduce the demonstrative expenditure to a minimum. Let every pie that the Committee may have to spend on ceremonial be saved and gained for the cause of the voiceless millions.

The Hindu, 19-8-1927

338. LETTER TO S. D. NADKARNI

As at Bangalore,
August 19, 1927

DEAR FRIEND,

I have your letter with very carefully written articles on untouchability. I had expected them to be up to your usual standard. I gave them for type-copying at once so that I could send the typed copies for any correction that you may want to make. But before sending them I had intended to read the articles, which I have now done, and whilst, as I have said, they are very carefully written, they are neither original nor as closely reasoned as I have known your writings to be. I haven't the time to give you a detailed criticism; but I would just point out the defect in your definition, which, in any case, seems to me to be ponderous.

Untouchability is no 'avoidance' but it is being untouchable on account of certain characteristics of birth. In the other paragraphs you have not kept close to the sub-heading which from the opening paragraphs one expects to be accurate and exclusive.

In the second article the texts do not seem to disprove untouchability, but seem to attack an excessive observance of it. If you will deal with the Shastras, it is really necessary to enter upon a deeper examination. When did the idea of untouchability arise and what is its extent? I wonder if you have read Pandit Satavalekar's treatise on this subject. In a way it is fairly exhaustive.

If you will write for *Young India* on this subject in a learned way, I would like you to study it more carefully, if you have the time, and produce something original, or write something popular and original ridiculing the extravagance of the practice as it obtains today—extravagance both in the manner and the extent of its application, even assuming that there is a warrant for untouchability in Hinduism pure and undefiled. I return your articles.

Yours sincerely,

From a microfilm: S.N. 12632

339. *LETTER TO K. P. PADMANABHA IYER*

AS AT BANGALORE,
August 19, 1927

DEAR FRIEND,

I have your letter. You have told me nothing new. My question was simple, whether you had made any experiments yourself, and, if so, with what result.[1] You have instead of answering that question given me a thesis of which I was not in need. People write to me giving me advice on all sorts of matters of which they have no personal knowledge. I had thought that you had perhaps some knowledge, being a qualified man.

I have read almost all the Western books on food reform. They are good only up to a point. Many of the observations have to be taken with the greatest caution, because of our different habits of life. The results obtained by experiments under Western conditions will not be the results necessarily to be obtained here. And then, I have also noticed that the experiments are not in every case faithfully described. Many data are omitted. The majority of us whether in the medical line or any other do not take a scientific interest in our professions, our only concern being to make money or somehow to get on in life. Hence is there an utter dearth of original research work.

Being unable now to make experiments myself, I would gladly receive aid from the experience of others. But it must be real experience and not book knowledge.

[1] *Vide* "Letter to K. P. Padmanabha Iyer", 21-7-1927.

Perhaps the typed matter is your only copy, and I therefore return it to you.

Yours sincerely,

From a microfilm: S.N. 12633

340. LETTER TO T. W. KALANI

AS AT BANGALORE,
August 19, 1927

DEAR FRIEND,

I have your letter. You should omit all novel-reading, and you should repeat Ramanama. Learn *Bhagavad Gita* if possible in the original. Take a cold bath every day. Sleep out in the open air. You should retire to bed early and get up early in the morning at 4 o'clock and pray to God that He may give you strength to resist all evil thoughts. Do not brood over discharges when they occur. Find out each time the reason, and avoid the reason next time. Tell your father of the disease and tell him that it is perfectly useless for you to go to London till you have conquered these discharges and your thoughts.

Before you think of perfecting your English I would advise you to take up Hindi and Sanskrit and when you have got your mastery over both, you may certainly proceed further with your English.

Yours sincerely,

T. W. KALANI
OLD SUKKUR
(SINDH)

From a microfilm: S.N. 19775

341. LETTER TO N. SETHURAMAN

As at the Ashram, Sabarmati,
August 19, 1927

DEAR FRIEND,

I have your letter. I do not think that a husband has any right to impose his own views on his wife or a parent on his grown-up children. But he is not obliged to provide things for them in which he himself does not believe. But if his wife has her own private means as she well may either from gifts given by the husband or his parents or the money she might have brought from her own parents, she has a perfect right to make what use she likes of these monies. So far as children of tender age are concerned, I am unable to say by way of general rule as to who should regulate their lives in the event of difference between husband and wife. Probably it is a matter of mutual accommodation. Finally it is the law of love that should govern relations in a family life and no hard and fast rules can really be laid down for mutual conduct. What may be perfectly justified in one case may not be wholly justifiable in every other case apparently similar.

Yours sincerely,

Sjt. N. Sethuraman
Thirukkannangudi
Kivalur. S.I. Rly.

From a photostat: S.N. 19803

342. A LETTER

As at the Ashram, Sabarmati,
August 19, 1927

DEAR FRIEND,

I have your letter. All my sympathies are with you. Your last state is simply due to excessive self-abuse. The vital fluid is evidently now passed even without stimulation. My advice to you is not to go to your wife at all at least for one year and not till you have acquired mastery of yourself, whether it is inside of the year or even beyond. You must not hesitate to tell your parents the reason for your abstention. When they understand how you have weakened yourself and become diseased, if they are at all wise, they will know the reason and trouble you no more in your attempt to rebuild your constitution. You must learn cooking for yourself, so that you may regulate your diet. Give up cycling. Walk to your college, seek the company only of good boys. Do not be in a hurry to pass your examination. Take your own time. Retire to bed early, and at that time of retiring, think good thoughts and pray to God for help with an implicit faith that there is a high power ruling our destination and responsive to our innermost cravings for betterment. Take gentle walks before retiring to bed, but without overfatiguing yourself. Jump out of the bed as soon as you are awake no matter when, and do not go to bed again before the next bed time unless you feel so giddy that you must sleep, in which case you will take as much sleep as may be necessary. Repeat the practice from night to night till you have won long sweet undisturbed sleep from 9 to 4. At 4 o'clock you will get up, have your mouth washed, and even a full bath if you can get your bowels to move at that time and are not too weak to have the bath so early, and then read the *Bhagavad Gita* or any other religious book or simply utter Ramanama for half an hour or at least for five minutes if you cannot concentrate longer and for five minutes you will [pray][1], whether with or without concentration, always trying to concentrate. After this religious practice, you will take at least half an hour's walk out in the open. And then a cup full of fresh milk, boiled without sugar and you may have some fresh fruit if it is available, otherwise twenty dried raisins. Wash the raisins and chew them well. You will take no other food till 10 o'clock or 12 o'clock or whatever the time is when you may take a little chapati and some clean boiled vegetable without salt and nothing more. In the evening, before dark the same quantity of milk as in the morning and chapati with or without vegetable. If you don't take vegetable, you may take raisins or fresh fruit. If you do not know how to make chapati, you must learn it. Any green vegetable can be taken. Not starchy ones if possible. But when you cannot get green stuff, you may have potatoes or any other starchy vegetable and add to it fresh lemon's juice. Don't take any sugar or condiments. Keep your bowels in good order. And at the time of retiring at night take an earth bandage.

You may read with profit, perhaps, my *Guide to Health* and the booklet *Self-Restraint* v. *Self-Indulgence*.

[1] The source has "have".

If you have discharges either in night or in the day time you must immediately have a cold hip-bath. On no account must you practise self-abuse. On the approach of the least sensation, you must get up and walk briskly keeping your fist closed so tight as if you were about to hit anybody. Sit at the spinning-wheel for half an hour at least concentrating yourself on your work to God and do the spinning in a proper humble sacrificial spirit. It will compose you. Make a fixed determination to re-build yourself and undo the past. Do not brood over the past and forget it and do not feel dejected if you have discharges, but resolutely refuse to be party to those discharges. Keep your mind ever occupied with nobler things and away from yourself.

Yours sincerely,

R.B.T.
BENARES

From a photostat: S.N. 19804

343. LETTER TO B. GOPALACHAR

CHIKMAGALUR,
August 19, 1927

DEAR FRIEND,

Here are the answers to your questions:

1. In my opinion State aid should not be asked and should not be given except on the following conditions:

Every school in which the head master is or teachers are prepared to learn carding and spinning and submit to an examination should receive Rs. 5 per month as an increase in the existing salary of the head master or the teacher in question, provided that he guarantees manufacture of five *tolas* of yarn of at least 6 counts per boy or girl per month, the increase to be drawn only upon certificates by the inspector of the required amount of yarn and a capital expense of annas four per boy or girl for spinning outfit.

Note: Unless some such provision is made, my experience is that expense incurred over the introduction of hand-spinning in schools becomes a mere waste. And it would be wrong to introduce spinning in schools unless there is a staff of qualified inspectors and itinerant teachers for teaching these school-masters, and, if necessary, in the preliminary stages even the boys and girls.

2. Spinning should be made compulsory only in such primary and middle schools where the majority of municipal or local board voters consent. Compulsion would be useless where there is no public opinion in favour of hand-spinning.
3. The unfortunate experience just now is that boys take to spinning more quickly than girls. Therefore, I would make no distinction, and it is wrong to introduce the idea amongst boys and girls that spinning is essentially meant for girls and not for boys. It is to be treated as a national duty and it is to be prized for its cultural advantages so far as the boys and girls are concerned.
4. The question of cotton-growing tracts is irrelevant to the consideration of introducing spinning in schools and cotton trees (that is, the *devkapas* variety) can be planted anywhere.
5. As I do not know the incidence of the education cess in Mysore, I am unable to answer the question.
6. Public sympathy and support can only be obtained by propaganda on behalf of the Industrial Department just as was done and is still being done in the matter of co-operation. Hand-spinning is really the greatest aid to co-operation.
7. As there are weaving sheds in the *Adi Karnataka* work-shops conducted by the Government, all yarn manufactured in the schools should be sent to these sheds for weaving and a stipulated price should be paid by these institutions to the schools manufacturing yarn.

If you are serious about this matter and are convinced as to the absolute necessity of spinning becoming universal, you should give some attention to the study of the technique of hand-spinning, which you can easily do in a month's time if you devote a whole month to it, or in three months' time if you devote at least one hour per day before taking up questions. Merely putting questions in the Assembly and throwing the blame or the burden upon the Government is to damage the cause. For, after all the Government can only respond to the atmosphere around it. And Government after all is what the people make it. It has no power or capacity apart from the people.

Yours sincerely,

SJT. B. GOPALACHAR
R. A. MEMBER
TIRTHAHALLI
SHIMOGA DISTRICT

From a microfilm: S.N. 19805

344. LETTER TO VASUMATI PANDIT

Shravan Vad 8 [August 20, 1927][1]

CHI. VASUMATI,

I have your letter. How old is Haribhai's widowed sister and how well educated? How about her constitution? Please let me have these and other facts about her. There was a letter from Kusum from Broach. She appears to be calm. Why did you have to stop studying with the help of Shri Mrityunjaya?

Did you not begin studying Gujarati some time ago? How much Gujarati does Uttamchand's wife know? We should not undertake a task beyond our capacity.

I should like to have the daily diary completed for the remaining period. What I get from it, I do not get from the letters.

I am all right. Our Mysore tour will end on the 29th.

Blessings from
BAPU

From the Gujarati original: C.W. 592. Courtesy: Vasumati Pandit

345. REMARKS IN BELUR TEMPLE VISITORS' BOOK

August 20, 1927

I was thankful to be able to visit this glory of Indian architecture (sculpture?). I wish the temple could be thrown open to the so-called untouchables on precisely the same terms as to other Hindus.

The Hindu, 22-8-1927

[1] The year is inferred from the reference to the end of the Mysore tour.

346. SPEECH AT BELUR TEMPLE[1]

August 20, 1927

Who would not be drawn to this wonderful temple of Indian art? But a representative of *Daridranarayana* like myself may not indulge in that feast of eyes. All my time and my energy are consecrated to the service of the poor, and I confess that I should not have come to this place if Keshavdas had not promised a purse of Rs. 500.

Young India, 1-9-1927

347. SPEECH AT PUBLIC MEETING, ARSIKERE[2]

August 20, 1927

We do not know what Shri Krishna's life means for us, we do not read the *Gita*, we make no attempt to teach it to our children. The *Gita* is such a transcendental book that men of every creed, age and clime may read it with respect, and find in it the principles of their respective religions. If we thought of Krishna on every Janmashtami day and read the *Gita* and resolved to follow its teachings, we should not be in our present sorry plight. Shri Krishna served the people all his life; he was a real servant of the people. He could have led the hosts at Kurukshetra, but he preferred to be Arjuna's charioteer. His whole life was one unbroken *Gita* of karma. He refused proud Duryodhana's sweets and preferred humble Vidura's spinach. As a child he was a cowherd and we still know him by the name of Gopala. But we, his worshippers, have neglected the cow today; the *Adi Karnatakas* slaughter cows and eat beef, and our infants and invalids have to go without cow's milk. Krishna knew no sleep or idleness. He kept sleepless vigil of the world, we, his posterity, have become indolent and forgotten the use of our hands. In *Bhagavad Gita* Lord Krishna has shown the path of *bhakti*—which means the path of karma. Lokamanya Tilak has shown that whether we desire to be *bhaktas*, or *jnanis*, karma is the only way, but that karma should not be for self but for others.

[1] From Mahadev Desai's "Weekly Letter"

[2] From Mahadev Desai's "Weekly Letter". The meeting was held at the Travellers' Bungalow.

Action for one's own self binds, action for the sake of others delivers from bondage. What can be the altruistic action which can be universally done, by Hindus, Mussalmans, Christians, by men, women and children? I have tried to demonstrate that spinning alone is that sacrificial act, for that alone can make us do something in God's name, something for the poorest, something that can infuse activity in their idle limbs. Lord Krishna has also taught that to be a true *bhakta* we should make no difference between a Brahmin and a scavenger. If that is true, there can be no place for untouchability in Hinduism. If you are still hugging that superstition, you can cleanse yourself by getting rid of it on this the sacred day of Krishna's birth. He who swears by the *Gita* may know no distinction between Hindu and Mussalman for Lord Krishna has declared that he who adores God in a true spirit by whatsoever name adores Him. The path of *bhakti*, karma, love as expounded in the *Gita*, leaves no room for the despising of man by man.

Young India, 1-9-1927

348. LETTER TO MIRABEHN

August 21, 1927

CHI. MIRA,

I have your letters. The longest Mysore tour is finished and next week I commence the Tamil land. The address will now be Madras. Mahadev will give it[1]. I leave for Madras on 30th morning. The post will be received here up to 29th instant.

I am not surprised at your fight with the devils. For us imperfect people this constant duelling is our only test and spur to action. So long as these fellows do not get the better of us in the end, all is well. Of course, I want to know you and see you as you are and only then will you be what you ought to be.

You shall certainly not stay there a day beyond the stipulated time and then the Hindi will have to take care of itself. But even during the remaining period, I do not want you to get sick over it. I would not mind even if you threw away every Hindi book and simply picked up what was possible without an effort. There should be no violence about this Hindi learning. Of course I

[1] C/o S. Srinivasa Iyengar, Amjad Bagh, Mylapore, Madras

would like you not to forget your Urdu writing. But in all these things let there be no overstraining.

Yes, Vinoba is an extraordinary man. His weeping is an intense longing to be with the Maker. Do cultivate him as much as you can, draw him out when you can. You may not have opportunity of coming in close contact with him again. Ask him any questions you like.

About Gangu you may not worry. It is quite enough that you are still allowed by her to guide her. It does appear to me that she should live altogether apart from Valunjkar and stand on her own legs.

With love,

BAPU

From the original: C.W. 5263. Courtesy: Mirabehn

349. LETTER TO JAMNADAS

BANGALORE,
Silence Day [*August 22, 1927*][1]

CHI. JAMNADAS,

I got your letter. It is good that you wrote. I rather wish that you should write. Perhaps I can give you some peace of mind by replying to your letters.

I even understand your reasoning. I can now prescribe for you only one medicine: having placed before me all difficulties and shortcomings, you should have faith in me and cheerfully submit to my orders. If you see any error or defect in them, you should let the sin of that or the responsibility for that rest on my head. A soldier who knows his duty carries out scrupulously his general's orders, even when he sees the latter's error. He who has faith in his leader sees no error in him even when the world sees one. The first attitude is acquired by practice, the second is the fruit of *tapascharya* done in this or a previous life. In the first, it is reason which is active in the second the heart.

I wrote about you to Nanabhai last week itself. The problem of money will be solved. If there are delays, bear them as inevitable. Have a frank talk with Nanabhai and do what he advises you. This is my order at the moment.

[1] From the reference to the end of Gandhiji's Mysore tour; *vide* also the succeeding item.

Come here whenever you wish to. Ask for money from the Ashram. Don't forget to take care of your health.

Blessings from
BAPU

[PS.]

I shall be in Bangalore till the end of this month.

From the Gujarati original: C.W. 8595. Courtesy: Radhabehn Choudhri

350. LETTER TO ASHRAM WOMEN

Silence Day [*August 22, 1927*]

SISTERS,

We returned here yesterday after completing our longest tour in Mysore. I am to leave Mysore by the end of this week, i.e., on Tuesday, the 30th instant. So letters which can reach me later than Monday should be addressed to Madras. I do not know our exact address at Madras.

It is very good that you are going to contribute to the Flood Relief Fund by doing such work as sewing. Get the women labourers at the Ashram also to co-operate in this work. I do not mean that they should sew. But if they like, they can contribute a day's wages. It will be enough for the present if you get to know them on this pretext. If they are not willing, they need give nothing. If we realize even now that we have so far failed to enter into their life your contacts with them will increase in the future. We have to develop in ourselves the quality which enables us to look upon all as equals, as laid down in the *Gita*.

Blessings from
BAPU

From a photostat of the Gujarati: G.N. 3663

351. *LETTER TO CHHAGANLAL JOSHI*

August 22, 1927

I have both your letters. As Kaka has gone to see the gold mines today, I could not show them to him. He will write to you as soon as he returns and thereafter he or I shall return the letters to you. Mahadev will write to you in addition to this, if necessary.

It was right that you wrote to me. It would have hurt me had you not written to me. I destroyed that letter as it was not worth preserving. My idea in destroying it was that the fewer the people who read it the better it would be.

I already knew the first part of what you wrote. That is to say, I knew the matter up to Maganlal's fast[1]. What was news to me was the breach of pledges by both even after the fast as also the experience of Ramdas. Indeed that has aroused my suspicion but my opinion is not based on it. It is based solely on the frequent violation of truthfulness. Even if one who commits such a breach is good in other respects, the Ashram which lays stress on *satya* cannot accommodate him. Moreover, the Ashram provides maintenance to a great extent. It is not our duty nor do we have the right to extend that maintenance to one who cannot serve the Ashram. The reason for this decision is therefore only the proved faults of Chi. Kashi in telling lies. But it is only if all of you can come to the same decision calmly that you should give effect to my advice. I am and am not in a hurry. I am not because in these matters we must act with full circumspection. I am in a hurry to the extent that once a decision is taken it is *adharma* to delay putting it into effect.

The Managing Committee ought certainly to read and understand this letter. It may, if it wants to, ask me anything. Certainly get from me whatever you need to in order to reach a decision.

[From Gujarati]

From the manuscript of Mahadev Desai's Diary. Courtesy: Narayan Desai

[1] *Vide* "Letter to Balwantrai Mehta", after 2-9-1927.

352. LETTER TO CHHAGANLAL JOSHI

August 22, 1927

I write this separately for your convenience.

It is regrettable that you and Maganlal have not yet made it up with each other but I also see that it is inevitable. Since all of you have taken a clear pledge twice, neither of you can leave the place and be separated from each other. Neither you nor anyone else can sever the bond of marriage or spiritual relationship which has come to be formed between you. This is a moral issue. That a man can free himself from all bonds by abandoning morality is, however, a different matter.

That being so, we have to consider just how your relations can become cordial. We are all married people. We should consider how husband and wife behave with each other and should order our conduct accordingly. You should meet Maganlal's angry red eyes with calm affection and *vice versa*. If such mutual give-and-take is not possible, do as Ba did[1]. When I opened the door for Ba, she asked me to pause and think and made me feel ashamed of myself and although she was ready to go out, she retracted her steps. Keep on repeating, "We can never be separated" like Govardhanbhai's[2] Kumud[3]. Thereafter, God alone knows how He will dispose of whichever of you is Pramadadhana[4], whether through death or otherwise. He stages a new play every day, so that He does not have to draw upon Govardhanbhai. Have faith in Him.

[From Gujarati]

From the manuscript of Mahadev Desai's Diary. Courtesy: Narayan Desai.

[1] *Vide An Autobiography*, Pt. IV, Ch. X.

[2] Govardhanram Madhavram Tripathi, author of *Sarasvatichandra*, a Gujarati novel

[3] Heroine of *Sarasvatichandra*

[4] Another character from *Sarasvatichandra* to whom Kumud was married

353. LETTER TO GANGABEHN

August 22, 1927

I have your letter; Kakasaheb too read to me the one you wrote to him. I can understand your wish to tour with me and at the same time serve Kakasaheb, but I shall not encourage you in it.

1. Kakasaheb ought not to stand in need of so much service and Chandrashankar should make up for your absence. If that is not possible Kakasaheb should become too dependent.

2. If Ba needs the services of anyone, she should go to the Ashram. If one who serves me needs to be served by someone else such a one's service will not be service at all and I must give up such service.

3. Instead of benefiting by tours you would only suffer harm. With me one has to move from place to place, no studies will therefore be possible. It will be good indeed if I have with me some woman attendant, but she should have completed her studies. I see if Manibehn too remains longer, she would stand to lose. Her studies have already suffered. Deep in her heart she desired to stay. She is yet a child. As she had come here on business, she was allowed to stay.

You should of course be engrossed in your studies. When Kakasaheb gets settled, you may certainly stay with him, serve him and learn from him.

Now you should give up your reserve and learn reading and writing from anyone who can teach and offers to do it.

Self-knowledge can be had only from saints. Reading and writing should be learnt from wherever it is available. Hence give up your idea that you will learn only if a certain person will teach you. A girl full of passion would certainly entertain such an idea. You cannot have it at all. But I do understand that you feel shy of disclosing your ignorance. You should certainly shed such shyness. As Rasik knows Sanskrit well, why should I not learn it from him? And to us all other boys should be like Rasik.

[From Gujarati]

From the manuscript of Mahadev Desai's Diary. Courtesy: Narayan Desai

354. LETTER TO ANANDIBAI

August 22, 1927

CHI. ANANDIBAI,

Women must learn as part of elementary education at least their own mother tongue, Hindi if it is not their mother tongue, enough Sanskrit to be able to understand the drift of the *Bhagavad Gita*, elementary arithmetic, elementary composition, elementary music and child-care. Along with this, I think they should know well the processes up to the weaving from cotton. When a woman receives this education she should have an environment that will shape her character and enable her to see clearly the evils in society and to avoid them. I have not mentioned religious education separately as it is acquired by practice and would be covered by general reading. Truly speaking, it is a part of the elevating company of a teacher. This is about girls. The education of a widow or a married woman is of course a different matter.

[From Gujarati]

From the manuscript of Mahadev Desai's Diary. Courtesy: Narayan Desai

355. LETTER TO SHARDA[1]

Shravan Vad 10, August 22, 1927

CHI. SHARDA,

I have your letter. Life is full of difficulties. If we can, like the weaver, patiently unravel tangled yarn, only then can we weave the pattern of our life properly.

You should know that if the Managing Committee or Maganlal refuses to accommodate your brother in the Ashram that is after full deliberation and you should remain calm and not get angry with any of them. The Ashram is not an institution for correcting the delinquent, but is one for giving good people education for service and for preparing a field for service. The Ashramites will be committing a sin if they believe that they are perfect;

[1] The addressee had complained to Gandhiji that the Ashram would not admit her brother who had been turned out of the house by their father.

"good" only means those who are like them. They would not admit people who fail when measured by that yardstick. If we would turn the Ashram into a home for the disabled, it must have an altogether different set-up. You yourself can imagine this position. And once it is turned into a home for the disabled, which disabled person may not be admitted to it? A little thought will convince you that we shall not then be able to start and run dairies, tanneries, etc., but the whole pattern will have to change. Remember one thing. You have abandoned those family relationships which run counter to other larger relationships. Your father and your brother are a father and a brother to the same extent as those of comparable age in the Ashram or outside. Towards these you will have the same attitude as towards your own father or brother. Knowing this you should not grieve because your brother cannot join the Ashram. Will your brother be willing to go to some orphanage? Would he go to the Bardoli Ashram? I am not sure whether he will be admitted there, but as Bhai Jugatram is conducting a number of experiments there, he may perhaps fit into them. But even if by chance Bhai Jugatram keeps him, there will be the question of his maintenance. Will your father pay it? Consider the whole question calmly and objectively and write to me without reserve.

[From Gujarati]

From the manuscript of Mahadev Desai's Diary. Courtesy: Narayan Desai

356. *FAREWELL MESSAGE TO STUDENTS*

[After *August 22, 1927*][1]

I am not going to be satisfied with the students' performance merely by their donations to khadi, etc., no matter how great they are. I want them for the country body and soul. That would be some, not much, return for what they are receiving.

From the manuscript of Mahadev Desai's Diary. Courtesy: Narayan Desai

[1] The source has this after the entries for August 22.

357. LETTER TO KUVALAYANAND

KUMARA PARK, BANGALORE,
August 23 1927

DEAR FRIEND,

My stay in Mysore comes to an end on the 29th. I leave for Tamil Nadu on the 30th, and for some time my headquarters will be Madras (Sjt. S. Srinivasa Iyengar, Amjad Bagh, Luz, Mylapore, Madras).

But this is written to send under your care Punjabhai, a worker in the Ashram. He has been suffering for some time from indefinable abdominal pains. You will hear from him the whole of the history of his case. Punjabhai is an abstemious man, will go through any rigour. I have considered his case to be specially adapted for yogic treatment. I, therefore, commend him to your attention.

Punjabhai does not know anybody in the place. If he can be accommodated at your Ashram, that would be ideal; but if he cannot, you will perhaps be able to tell him where he could stay. He must be a paying patient, because he has some means of his own and does not wish to become a burden upon anybody. At the Ashram also he pays for his own expenses. There need be therefore no hesitation about taking your charges.

I am keeping my strength and doing the tour without feeling the strain.

Yours sincerely,
M. K. GANDHI

From a photostat: G.N. 5052

358. *LETTER TO T. R. KRISHNASWAMI IYER*

KUMARA PARK, BANGALORE,
August 23, 1927

MY DEAR KRISHNASWAMI,

I have your letter. I am sorry to have to tell you that I have not yet tried the oils for the simple reason that I have been away, and I don't want to carry the bottles about with me and doctor myself on the journey.

The idea of cotton cultivation is good. But it has to be conceived not in the interest of the buyers of cotton for the foreign market or even for the mills, but for the convenience of the spinners. Therefore cultivation has to be distributed. It cannot therefore be considered as a revenue measure. Thus then cotton has to be grown on particular portions of every holding just as indigo was grown on 3/20th of every holding in Champaran. It was a magnificent thing, only it was designed solely for the planter. And then you have to find out what variety should be grown, how tree-cotton would fare and so on. If, therefore, you will interest yourself in this, you have to study the whole of the question of cotton cultivation in all its phases. Such experiments have been made at the Ashram, and you may know further on the subject by correspondence with the Director of the Technical Department of the All-India Spinners' Association, Sabarmati.

Yours sincerely,
M. K. GANDHI

SJT. T. R. KRISHNASWAMIER,
SABARI ASHRAM
OLVAKOT

From a photostat: G.N. 6832

359. *LETTER TO KAMALA DAS GUPTA*

KUMARA PARK, BANGALORE,
August 23, 1927

DEAR FRIEND,

I have your letter. I know that many girls are now tending towards simplicity. But what I felt was that the Ashram life might be considered too simple. Let me however make my meaning clear. I do not by any means consider simplicity as synonymous with shabbiness, shoddiness or slovenliness; nor need a devotee of simplicity be devoid of a sense of taste or decency. What I have found is that the simplest things are the neatest possible and this neatness that comes from simplicity can be the common heritage of all mankind instead of the manufactured taste which has become the exclusive property of the monied few.

If you are sincere about your desire to go to the Ashram and earnest and yet gentle in your effort, you will certainly bear down the opposition of your parents. Until you can secure the permission of your parents, you can mentally live the Ashram life.

And why do you say that there is no way for Indian girls for leading a simple and pure life? Just think of the millions of the poor girls. They can't afford to look elegant even for getting suitable matches; nor is it true that here in India all the girls are bound to marry. But the fact is that the vast majority want to marry, and in middle class society to which we belong, the fashion is to think that girls are born only to marry. But I know that there are many girls who are now trying to remain unmarried. They have their parents' co-operation also. But it is a hard struggle in which they are engaged.

What made you think that I was stopping the writing of the autobiography? It is continuing.

I am in Bangalore up to the 29th instant. My address after will be: Care of Sjt. S. Srinivasa Iyengar, Amjad Bagh, Luz, Mylapore, Madras.

I would like you to see Sjt. Satis Chandra Das Gupta and his wife Srimati Hemprabhadevi of Khadi Pratishthan at Sodepur. They both know the Ashram. They have lived there for some time. They will tell you all about it. You must not be in a hurry even though your parents may leave you free to go to the Ashram.

Yours sincerely,

From a microfilm: S.N. 12634-A

360. LETTER TO T. R. MAHADEVA IYER

KUMARA PARK, BANGALORE,
August 23, 1927

DEAR FRIEND,

Herewith a copy of a letter received by me. I think that you should give up possession now without any ado whatsoever.

Please let me know your decision so that I may write to them.

Yours sincerely,

From a microfilm: S.N. 12938

361. LETTER TO KRISHNADAS

KUMARA PARK, BANGALORE,
August 23, 1927

MY DEAR KRISHNADAS,

I have your letter. I have sent you a telegram in order to save you suspense. There is a moral undertaking to give the English manuscript[1] to Ganesan. He should therefore have it. But the terms are quite proper. I shall discuss them with him and deliver the manuscript after coming to terms. I shall vary them if necessary for his accommodation.

You have still the Bengali manuscript. So you will have to fix up something there.

We leave here on the 30th morning for Vellore.

Yours sincerely,

From a microfilm: S.N. 19771

[1] Of *Seven Months with Gandhi*

362. LETTER TO DR. SATYAPAL

KUMARA PARK, BANGALORE,
August 23, 1927

DEAR DR. SATYAPAL,

I have your letter. I understand what you say, but I do not appreciate your attitude towards Lalaji. There are many matters on which I do not agree with him, but his sincerity, his love of the country are undeniable. His self-sacrifice and unbroken record of service entitle him to our respect and affection and make him indispensable for any public work in the Punjab. You may know that even in the heyday of Non-co-operation, I used to say this very thing and used to tell co-workers that without Lalaji, I could and would do nothing in the Punjab and that my business was to convert Lalaji and that the Punjabis had a right to defer to Lalaji rather than accept the views of one like myself who was comparatively a stranger to them. If I were you therefore, I should go again and again to him and strive with him but not strive against him.

Yours sincerely,

From a photostat: S.N. 19774

363. LETTER TO MANIBEHN PATEL

[After *August 23, 1927*][1]

CHI. MANI,

I have your letter. Over a remark of mine, Mahadev showed me your letter without waiting for your permission to do so.[2] No one should expect Mahadev to keep any secrets from me. It is beyond his power. Once we form a habit it becomes beyond our power to do something different. This conformity is worthy of being cultivated in regard to a good habit. One who meditates with a pure mind on non-violence ultimately becomes unable to commit violence, not physically but psychologically.

[1] The source has this after the entries for August 23.

[2] Mahadev Desai had read to Gandhiji a long letter written to him by the addressee regarding her embarrassment in living in the Ashram.

Thought is itself the root of action. If there is no thought, there can be no action.

What if our separation has hurt me and still hurts me as much as it hurts you? You chose *shreyas*[1]. And so did I. Therein alone lies your good and mine and everyone else's. It should be the end of all education to make *shreyas* also desired. Hence if you believe that living in the Ashram will benefit you, learn to like it. In this cheat neither yourself nor me. When you come to like to live only in the Ashram, know that I shall be fully prepared to put you in another place. You should write to me without reserve. It may be that I may not understand or that in reply I may lecture you. One should learn to put up with one's elders' lecturing.

Blessings from
BAPU

[From Gujarati]

From the manuscript of Mahadev Desai's Diary. Courtesy: Narayan Desai

364. LETTER TO A GUJARATI STUDENT

[After *August 23, 1927*][2]

It is quite proper that fasting has been extolled among us. But what kind of fasting is it? There is a religious dictum to the effect that the man who starves his body but leaves his mind uncontrolled is a hypocrite. We have ultimately to control the mind even in fasting. Fasting or not fasting is the same thing for a man who has conquered his mind. But conquest of the mind is so difficult. We can control the mind only by repeatedly controlling the body. My salutation to those who adopt this discipline of fasting and do so for self-purification.

[From Gujarati]

From the manuscript of Mahadev Desai's Diary. Courtesy: Narayan Desai

[1] The better (as against the more pleasant)

[2] The source has this after the entries for August 23.

365. *TELEGRAM TO MOTILAL NEHRU*[1]

[*August 24, 1927*]

PANDIT MOTILAL NEHRU
ALLAHABAD

YOUR WIRE. ANSARI'S STATEMENT UNFORTUNATE. BEING INTERIOR MYSORE HAVE BEEN WITHOUT TOUCH PAPERS. IF ANSARI SPONTANEOUSLY RETIRES SITUATION WILL CERTAINLY EASE. AM NOT SURE WHETHER I SHOULD ISSUE STATEMENT[2]. RETURNING BANGALORE TOMORROW MORNING.

GANDHI

From a photostat: S.N. 12873

366. *SPEECH AT KRISHNAGIRI*[3]

August 24, 1927

MR. CHAIRMAN AND FRIENDS,

I have to thank you for the address you have presented to me; also for the two purses. You have asked me to perform the unveiling of the portrait of the late Deshbandhu Chittaranjan Das. I thank you for the honour you have done me by asking to perform the ceremony and I do so with the greatest pleasure. I hope that his life and work will be an inspiration for us all. It can be said of him that he gave his life for the sake of his country, and he himself lived and died for it. This is not a meeting in which I can speak to you at length. There is too much noise and it will be cruelty on my part to inflict a speech on you. It does me a great deal of good and gives me a good deal of pleasure to see so many smiling faces about me. But when I see in those faces what you and I will never see, the faces which have not even the ability to smile, my heart sinks within me; and when we contemplate God residing in those people without smiling faces, we recognize in him *Daridranarayana*. It is for the sake of *Daridranarayana* that you have given these purses and so

[1] In reply to his telegram of August 23; *vide* Appendix II.

[2] *Vide* "Letter to Dr. M. A. Ansari", 26-8-1927.

[3] In reply to addresses by the Union Board, the citizens and the co-operative society

far as I have been able to see and think there is the conviction growing upon me that the only way you can render service to *Daridranarayana* is through the spinning-wheel. We are suffering from the chronic disease which can be called want of work and the only work you can find for the millions in the seven lakhs of villages is the spinning-wheel. But even the spinning-wheel has no force and no application unless you and I can make up our minds to discard all foreign cloth. You have done well in being exceedingly brief in your address. My faith in the other items of the constructive national programme is just as firm as in khadi. I know that the horizon before us is very black. But in spite of that horizon being black, there is hope. I reiterate my faith in the possibility and necessity of Hindu-Muslim unity. I reiterate also my belief that unless we Hindus rid ourselves of the curse of untouchability Hinduism will be waning.

I consider that total prohibition is the sacred duty of the State. In my opinion it is long overdue. If there is any country in the world which is immediately ripe for total prohibition, it is undoubtedly India; and if all of you unitedly demand total prohibition, prohibition can come without the slightest difficulty.

I was glad to receive this address from the co-operative society. May I humbly suggest to the co-operative society that their work, good as it is, is wholly incomplete and excludes the necessity of the population, unless they include the spinning-wheel and khadi in their programme. I am also glad that students have collected a small purse separately. They have done so at almost every place I visited. It gives me hope, because I regard their purse as an earnest of their determination to serve the poorest of their countrymen; and let me tell them from my experience that service to the country would be impossible unless they lead pure and abstemious lives.

I am glad to see so many sisters at this meeting. May I remind the men about me of the duty we owe to our sisters? We have been guilty of gross indifference, to put it mildly, towards our sisters. If we desire true national regeneration, we will have to reconsider many of our ideas about the status of women. Child marriage and child widowhood, wherever existing and in whatever form, are great evils in society. Surely it is a matter entirely resting within ourselves, and we shall have to answer both before God and the world if we do not wake up betimes and reform our own lives. In this vast assembly, I know everybody has not contributed to the purse. I want for this work every pie that can be willingly and intelligently given to me. I want the poorest, man and woman, boy and girl, to give whatever they can for the purse. As I have said in the beginning, let us know that there are men and women poorer than we are. I would earnestly ask you to preserve complete silence while the volunteers go about collecting money. Those only should give who believe in the message of the spinning-wheel. But those who do not want to give, may remain in their places till collections are over. May God bless all those who are here and also those in whose name we propose to work.

The Hindu, 27-8-1927

367. STUDENTS AND THE "GITA"

The other day, in the course of a conversation, a missionary friend asked me, if India was really a spiritually advanced country, why it was that he found only a few students having any knowledge of their own religion, even of the *Bhagavad Gita.* In support of the statement, the friend who is himself an educationist told me that he had made it a point to ask the students he met whether they had any knowledge of their religion or of the *Bhagavad Gita.* A vast majority of them were found to be innocent of any such knowledge.

I do not propose to take up at the present moment the inference that because certain students had no knowledge of their own religion, India was not a spiritually advanced country, beyond saying that the ignorance on the part of the students of religious books did not necessarily mean absence of all religious life or want of spirituality among the people to which the students belonged. But there is no doubt that the vast majority of students who pass through the Government educational institutions are devoid of any religious instruction. The remark of the missionary had reference to the Mysore students, and I was somewhat pained to observe that even the students of Mysore had no religious instruction in the State schools. I know that there is a school of thought which believes in only secular instruction being given in public schools. I know also that in a country like India, where there are most religions of the world represented and where there are so many denominations in the same religion, there must be difficulty about making provision for religious instruction. But if India is not to declare spiritual bankruptcy, religious instruction of its youth must be held to be at least as necessary as secular instruction. It is true that knowledge of religious books is no equivalent of that of religion. But if we cannot have religion we must be satisfied with providing our boys and girls with what is next best. And whether there is such instruction given in the schools or not, grown-up students must cultivate the art of self-help about matters religious as about other. They may start their own class just as they have their debating and now spinners' clubs.

Addressing the Collegiate High School students at Shimoga, I found upon enquiry at the meeting that out of a hundred or more Hindu boys, there were hardly eight who had read the *Bhagavad Gita.* None raised his hand in answer to the question, whether of the few who had read the *Gita* there was any who understood it. Out of five or six Mussalman boys all raised their hands as having read the Koran. But only one could say that he knew its meaning. The *Gita* is, in my opinion, a very easy book to understand. It does present some fundamental problems which are no doubt difficult of solution. But the general trend of the *Gita* is in my opinion unmistakable. It is accepted by all Hindu sects as authoritative. It is free from any form of dogma. In a short compass it gives a complete reasoned moral code. It satisfies both the intellect and the heart. It is thus both philosophical and devotional. Its appeal is universal. The language is incredibly simple. But I nevertheless think that there should be an authoritative version in each vernacular, and the translations should be so prepared as to avoid technicalities and in a manner that would make the teaching of the *Gita* intelligible to the average man. The suggestion is not intended in any way to supplement the original. For I reiterate my opinion that every Hindu boy and girl should know Sanskrit. But for a long time to come, there will be millions without any knowledge of Sanskrit. It would be suicidal to keep them deprived of the teachings of the *Bhagavad Gita* because they do not know Sanskrit.

Young India, 25-8-1927

368. NOTES

Insolent Reminders

The trial of two young men in Madras, one a Hindu aged about 30 and the other a Mussalman aged 25, on a charge of having attempted to disfigure a statue in Mount Road, Madras, of General Neill of the Mutiny fame, has a deep significance. Their attempt reminds one of the abortive effort made in Lahore during the heyday of Non-co-operation to have the Lawrence statue, or at least the highly offensive inscription "the pen or the sword", removed. The Lahore attempt was on the part of the general populace. The Madras attempt was confined to two young men who went about their work with quiet determination and without any fuss. The following statement made by the accused according to *The Hindu* report will be read with great interest:

> The first accused stated that he was born in Tinnevelly but lived in Madura. He knew what kind of punishment he would get before doing this act. They were prepared to undergo anything for this. From his study of history he knew that Neill had done much harm to the country, and thought that his statue should not be there, and he (the accused) determined to destroy it. They had brought the hammer and the axe as they came from their place. They did not bring the hammer and axe for this particular purpose. After coming to Madras they went round the city for sight-seeing in the course of which they saw the statue. They remembered his history and so attempted to destroy it this morning. But the statue was neither bronze nor marble as they thought. As it was copper only some parts broke. After that the sergeant took them to the police station. For that offence they were prepared to take any punishment His Worship might think fit to impose.

Asked as to whether they pleaded guilty, they said that they were guilty "if they were bound by the law of the Government", but in their own opinion they "do not feel guilty".

It is impossible to withhold sympathy from these brave young men, alike for the motive which prompted the act and for the dignity with which they approached their trial. The report before me adds that the accused were unrepresented and did not even cross-examine the prosecution witnesses. There seems to be no doubt that as national consciousness grows, the resentment over the insolent reminders, which such statues are, of abused British prowess and British barbarity will grow in strength.

A wise Government, however powerful it may be, will remove every such offensive reminder, and not goad infuriated public opinion into acts, which, however regrettable and reprehensible they may be in themselves, will be held justifiable as a fitting answer to the criminal indifference to legitimate national sentiment. And every abortion of attempts to remove these running sores only adds to the bitterness, and widens the gulf that separates us and the British. Surely the Municipality of Madras which owns the statue should remove it.

Too Good to Be True

Swami Anand has collected, in the issue of *Navajivan* of 7th August 1927, information about the heroic deeds of people all over Gujarat. In the sketches are given instances of Hindus and Mussalmans helping one another as if they had never quarrelled, also of the suppressed and the suppressors living together under the same roof and sharing the same food, people saving one another at great personal risk. Whilst I was reading the sketches I was wondering if they could be all true. Then I remembered that it was *Navajivan* I was reading, and unauthenticated stories were inadmissible in its columns, and that Swami himself was, if it was possible, more careful than I about admitting anything doubtful. The sketches show from Bhavnagar to Broach—a wide enough area of distress—stories of unexampled self-help, self-reliance and mutual help. As Swami well remarks, for the moment the "people exhibited every quality that makes a nation great and self-governing". There was no fear, no panic, but grim determination to battle with death. If the account is true,—I must still be cautious—it reflects the highest credit on all concerned. All were leaders and all were led. It was a spontaneous organization that came into being on the advent of distress.

The thing for the leaders to see to is, whether the lessons of the mighty deluge can be made permanent. Will the Hindu-Muslim friendship outlast the immediate need? Will the yoke of the suppressed be lifted for ever? Will the self be used to subserve the benefit of all in everyday transactions? Will the pre-deluge avarice remain under check in the face of the charity that is freely flowing Gujarat-ward? Will the stewards in charge of relief funds resist the temptation to steal or misappropriate trust funds? Will there be no feigning of distress and no needless applications for relief?

The answers to these and many such questions can only be satisfactorily given, if the many leaders who are now operating will be good as gold. That would mean real change of heart and real penitence and purification. It is said that there is always, after a deluge of any magnitude, a reformation of life among the survivors. It may be that, extensive as the calamity was, it may not be classed as a real deluge warranting a sweeping reformation. Mankind is notoriously too dense to read the signs that God sends from time to time. We require drums to be beaten into our ears, before we would wake from our trance and hear the warning and *see* that to lose oneself in all is the only way to find oneself. Will Gujarat show enough advance to regard the recent floods as an all-sufficing warning to us to write a new and brilliant chapter in the history of this afflicted land of ours? Posterity will have every reason to distrust the contemporary accounts of heroism, self-reliance and mutual help, if the people of Gujarat are unable to show any lasting and demonstrable reformation.

Young India, 25-8-1927

369. *THE LAW OF CONTINENCE*

A friend sends me relevant extracts from *The Science of a New Life* by Dr. Cowen. I have not read the book. But the advice contained in the extracts[1] is certainly sound. I have omitted from the extracts certain paragraphs about food which are not of much value to the Indian reader. Let no one desirous of leading a pure and chaste life think that the practice of it is not worth pursuing because the expected result is not attained in a moment. And let no one expect perfection of body after successful practice of continence even for a long time. The majority of us who endeavour to follow the rules laid down for observing continence labour under three handicaps. We have inherited imperfect bodies and weak wills from our parents, and by an incorrect life we find ourselves to have further debilitated both our bodies and wills. When a writing advocating purity of life attracts us, we begin the reformation. Such reformation is never too late. But we must not expect the results described in such writings; for those results are to be expected only from a strictly regulated life from early youth. And the third handicap we labour under is that in spite of the exercise of all the artificial and outward restraint we find ourselves unable to restrain and regularize our thoughts. And let every aspi-

[1] Not reproduced here

rant after a pure life take from me that an impure thought is often as powerful in undermining the body as an impure act. Control over thought is a long, painful and laborious process. But I am convinced that no time, no labour and no pain is too much for the glorious result to be reached. The purity of thought is possible only with a faith in God bordering on definite experience.

Young India, 25-8-1927

370. THE BLIND SPINNERS

On reading an account of the blind spinner at the recently held Khadi Exhibition in Bangalore, a correspondent has sent me the following beautiful lines by Helen Hunt Jackson:

Like a blind spinner in the sun
I tread my day;
I know that all the threads will run
The appointed way;
I know each day will bring its task
And, being blind, no more I ask.

I do not know the use or name
Of what I spin;
I only know that someone came
And laid within
My hand the thread and said, 'Sir you
Are blind, but one thing you can do.'

Sometimes the threads so rough and fast
And tangled fly,
I know wild storms are sweeping past,
And fear that I
Shall fall, but dare not fly to find
A safer place, since I am blind.

I know not why, but I am sure
That tint and place,
In some great fabric to endure
Past time and race,
My threads will have; so from the first,
Though blind, I never felt accurst.

What a transformation there would be in our country, if all who can—who cannot? —will spin with the faith of the blind spinner. Can we not feel that every thread we spin will have place "in some great fabric to endure"?

Young India, 25-8-1927

371. LETTER TO MIRABEHN

KUMARA PARK, BANGALORE,
August 26, 1927

CHI. MIRA,

I have your letters. Pray do not worry about the possibility of my straining myself to write to you. When I write I do so because I must, and what I must do always gives me pleasure in the doing. When I become an instrument so pure and sensitive that it would react and respond to every circumstance around it, I shall cease to write or speak and yet my thoughts will work their way to the hearts of those who need my guidance or assistance. But till that time is reached, I must make use of the less reliable and imperfect instrument of the pen and the tongue.

I still feel that you have unnecessarily excited yourself over the segregation. Why do you call it compulsory? For you it would be an act of purest love on your part. You know 14 Romans. There Paul, himself not a vegetarian, says to his congregation, "If meat offend thy brother abstain from it." I am quoting from memory,[1] therefore the words may not be the same, but the substance is the same. You will segregate yourself not because you feel yourself impure in any sense of the term, but you will do so for the sake of your neighbours and for the sake of those women who believe in segregation from a right motive. I do not know that I have made my meaning sufficiently clear. The whole point is this. There are certain things not in themselves immoral which we do for the sake of others and there are certain other things which being in themselves immoral we will not and must not do for the sake of the whole world. If self-imposed segregation appears to you as immoral, you must not do it even to please me. If however there is nothing immoral in it, then you will do it for the sake of your neighbours whom you will rightly consider to be ignorant to that extent. In the theory of it I am wholly at one with you. For a virgin, there should be no segregation whatsoever. Monthly sickness is no sickness for her. And while it comes, she

[1] The reference is to *I Corinthians*, viii. 13: "Wherefore, if meat make my brother to offend, I will eat no flesh, while the world standeth, lest I make my brother to offend."

takes note of it and changes her occupation but not her mentality. And even for married women after the necessity for precaution is understood by them, ceremonial segregation should have no meaning. I think I told you that so far as I am concerned, I never respected the rule even with reference to Ba herself. And when I began to see things clearer, I never felt the call to have the rule observed. Radha and Rukhi certainly and all the other girls so far as I am aware do not observe it. Amina does not. Gomatibehn does and everybody respects her wishes even to the extent that when the women who do not observe it for themselves have the monthly sickness, they do not go near Gomatibehn. If then self-segregation appears to you to be a task, you need not observe it. But if you do not, you should observe it as a pleasurable duty for the sake of others and in any case, it is not now a matter of any practical value so far as you are concerned; for, your next sickness probably does not come in Wardha at all. Or if it does, it is a question only of once whilst you are there. At Sabarmati nobody will want you to observe it. Amina does not observe it for anybody including Gomatibehn, nor is she expected to, much less will you be expected to observe it, even for Gomatibehn when she is there. So far as I know she has herself never asked anybody to observe it for her and in her presence. She is satisfied with the observance of it for herself. If the matter is still not clear you must continue to write and meanwhile to act as may seem proper to you.

Now about grammar and arithmetic. I understand and appreciate all you say. But, for the work in hand, a knowledge of figures and grammar as a science and as an aid to a knowledge of languages are necessary. You will therefore do both to the extent that you can tackle without feeling giddy. If you find that it is impossible for you to take kindly to simple arithmetic and comparative grammar, we must do without it.

Andrews is coming here tomorrow. You must have known he arrived last week. If you have not already written to him, do please write now. Here is the further programme. But you will send your letters Care Sjt. S. Srinivasa Iyengar, Amjad Bagh, Luz, Mylapore, Madras, till I ask you to do otherwise.

I was weighed on Tuesday and my weight was lbs. 113½. This is really very good. Up to now I have fared quite all right. It remains to be seen now how I shall take the Madras climate. It is almost like Bombay, a trifle hotter, but just as moist.

With love,

BAPU

[Encl.]

TAMIL NADU TOUR PROGRAMME

August

Stay in Bangalore up to 29th

30th Leave for Vellore in the morning

September

1st Gudiyatham

2nd Ami

3-9th Madras (Sjt. S. Srinivasa Iyengar, Luz, Mylapore)

10-12th Cuddalore

13th Chidambaram

14th Mayavaram

15th Mannargudi

16th Tanjore

17th to 20th Trichinopoly

21st Pudukkottah

22-27th Karaikudi and Chettinad

28-30th Madura including Tirumangalam on 30th

From the original: C.W. 5264. Courtesy: Mirabehn

372. LETTER TO DR. M. A. ANSARI

KUMARA PARK, BANGALORE,
August 26, 1927

DEAR DR. ANSARI,

I had your telegram. I hope you got my reply. Your published statement[1] is certainly an improvement on the original. But I cannot help thinking that it would have been better if you could have stayed your hand. But I fully recognize that you had no business to do so when the inner voice told you otherwise.

After having waited all these days, I felt that I should write just a brief thing for *Young India*. I send you a copy of the statement. If you think that I should not publish it, please wire. This letter should be in your hands at the latest on Monday. If I receive a wire from you disapproving of the statement, I shall cancel it. If the letter does not reach you before Tuesday, please wire direct to the Manager, *Young India* Office, Ahmedabad, asking him to withhold publication of the note. I am instructing the Manager not to publish the note if a countermanding wire is received from you. So much regarding the publication of my opinion[2].

[1] According to Ansari's letter of August 12, he had "asked the Councillors to unite and to confess to themselves that they are co-operating in the Councils and not non-co-operating" (S.N. 12872).

[2] This was not published.

Whether the note is published or not, I feel that the suggestion made in it is the only proper course for you to adopt, unless of course, you feel strongly that those who enter the Councils must take up office and otherwise adopt the policy adumbrated in your statement, and that if you accept the Presidentship, you must actively work to that end. I recognize that you cannot take up an impartial attitude, if you must become an avowed propagandist of your own policy.

Three or four days ago when I had a long telegram from Motilalji, I thought that in view of your statement, spontaneous retirement on your part was perhaps the best way of dealing with the difficult situation that had arisen.[1] But I now feel that consistently with your views about the necessity of communal unity, you may not now retire. But I feel equally that if you are to make a Herculean effort for bringing about unity, you have to forget Council politics, adopt an attitude of absolute neutrality and act merely as an impartial chairman regulating proceedings of the Congress, All India Congress Committee, and the Working Committee, but not guiding or shaping the political programme and if you accept my suggestion, I think it would be necessary for you to make a very brief statement making it clear that whilst you adhere to the opinion expressed in your statement, you will not seek to impose that view upon the Congress but that you will confine your own activity solely to the promotion of communal unity.

Yours sincerely,

DR. M. A. ANSARI
1, DARYAGANJ, DELHI

From a photostat: S.N. 12874

[1] *Vide* "Telegram to Motilal Nehru", 24-8-1927.

373. LETTER TO MOTILAL NEHRU

KUMARA PARK, BANGALORE,
August 26, 1927

DEAR MOTILALJI,

I had your letter as also your telegram. To the latter I sent a reply[1] from Krishnagiri which I hope was duly received. Having been in the interior of Mysore and continuously touring, I am considerably in arrears.

I have at last decided to issue a small note on Dr. Ansari's statement. Having championed his election, I thought that I could not observe absolute silence. I shall watch the movement of the barometer and wherever I can do anything or write anything to purpose, I shall not hesitate.

So far I am not inclined to favour Jawaharlal's election, that is, assuming that Dr. Ansari retires. It is highly probable that he will take up the attitude suggested by you and me and merely become an impartial chairman. Nothing more will then remain to be done. If, however, a fresh election does become necessary, I shall watch events and Reuter's cable will inform you of the result. Please however send me your address in London so that I may write or cable in case of need. But I want you to leave India with a light heart, as I know you will do without any coaxing from me. Evidently we have not yet reached the freezing point.

I am fixed up in the South almost for the rest of the year. I send you herewith a copy of my programme up to the end of September though it will be safer probably to use the Sabarmati address from where telegrams are quickly repeated and letters as quickly redirected.

I hope you will have a nice time in Europe and return in time with Jawaharlal before the Congress week. You will please ask Indu whether she ever thinks of her old Indian friends and among them a frequent visitor to Anand Bhawan who would drink nothing but goat's milk and will eat all the choicest fruits leaving none even for little children.

Yours sincerely,

PANDIT MOTILAL NEHRU
ALLAHABAD

[1] *Vide* "Telegram to Motilal Nehru", 24-8-1927.

[PS.]

I am enclosing copy of my *Young India* notes. I have sent a copy to Dr. Ansari too for approval.

M. K. G.

From a photostat: S.N. 12875

374. PROBLEM OF CHILDREN OF MIXED UNIONS

An Indian living in the city of Mabuki in French Africa has written a painful letter, the substance of which is as follows:

> There is a very large number of children of mixed unions in this country. Both Hindus and Muslims are responsible for their birth. Coming here for trade, they live with any Negro women whom they choose. They do not look after the children which are born to these women. The children grow up somehow. When the traders who contract such unions return to India, they leave behind these women and their issue, making no provision even for their maintenance. When a person like me tries to look after their maintenance and wishes to establish an institution for that purpose, no one helps him. Will you not kindly tell us what is my duty and that of other Indians like me towards these children of mixed unions? Do you believe that by supporting children born of sin we only encourage sin and, therefore, we owe no duty towards them? If you do, consider this: These children will certainly get someone or other to look after them; God will not let them perish helplessly. If that is so, will they not grow up to be our enemies, and if they do, can anyone blame them? Can it not be said, rather, that those who bring such progeny into the world and leave it uncared for, bring into existence the instruments of their own and their community's destruction?

I have with my own eyes seen in Delagoa Bay and other cities the conditions described by this correspondent, and I have heard still more from clients and friends. There is no doubt that it is a painful state of affairs. Muslim friends display human feeling in such matters. Hindus become extremely hard-hearted in the name or under the pretext of religion. Muslims do not seem to consider it morally wrong to live with women professing other faiths than their own. Hindus look upon such unions as morally wrong and still form them. Thus they are not afraid of gratifying their desires but shrink from accepting responsibility for the consequences. They feel it pollution to have to live with their own progeny, so that in the end they hand over the children either to Muslims or to Christians or, likely enough, just run away without entrusting them to anyone or leaving a single pie for their maintenance. The Negroes of Africa are simple-minded and ignorant and, therefore, do not know what their rights are. This state will certainly not last for ever. Some of them are bound to get education; they will then fight with hatred in their hearts, tell the poor women of their rights, incite their children to fight for legitimate or illegitimate causes and, though they themselves observe no distinction between morality and immorality, will have the sympathy of the world on their side in their fight illustrating the law that, no matter how strong a person is, he will sooner or later meet his match.

There are many straightforward ways of preventing such a situation from arising. The best course, certainly, is that a trader who cannot observe self-control should take his wife with him. If he goes alone and forms a union with a Negro woman, he should behave decently, treat her with love and accept the responsibility of providing for the children which may be born to her. He should understand that, under the law, he is bound to provide for the maintenance both of the woman and her children. But a lustful and shameless man has no thought of right and wrong and no sense of what is due to others; he lives like a man bereft of his senses, intoxicated with lust. How is he, therefore, likely even to read such articles? Even if he reads them, he will certainly not heed them. Hence social reformers like this correspondent should consider what their duty is. I am afraid society will have no choice but to shoulder the burden of the consequences of sin so long as there are wicked men and women in it, just as it eagerly reaps the benefit of the virtue of virtuous men and women. There is no man or woman who is completely free from sin; we are all a band of sinners. But society condones the sins of those who observe a certain decency in their conduct and regards them as virtuous people, whereas it looks upon those who cross the bounds of that decency as wicked. Thus society's definitions of the wicked and the virtuous are dictated by practical considerations. In God's court, however, all of us will be treated as sinners and will be punished in accordance with the nature of our sins.

Being in such a sorrowful plight, society must shoulder the burden of children of mixed unions. Accordingly, reformers living in Africa have two courses open to them: one which seeks the help of courts and another which is independent of such help.

They have a right to adopt both. The second course consists in a reformer seeking the help of other like-minded citizens and, without raising disputes about religion, establishing an institution to look after such progeny. If the fathers of the children desire to take charge of them and bring them up in their own faiths and if they are ready to pay the institution the expenses incurred on the children up to the day of their removal, the children should be handed over to them. Whenever the parents can be contacted, they should be requested to pay for the maintenance of the children and, if they refuse to pay though they have the means with which to pay, due legal steps should be taken against them. Side by side with this, efforts should also be made to bring about moral reform. If anyone who lives with a Negro woman is married and has a wife living in India, he should be persuaded to call her to Africa. But the friend who has written the letter says:

> Our countrymen do not wish to start any such institution. In my view, 75 per cent of the money earned in this land comes from immoral sources and, therefore, it is not spent on worthy causes. It is wasted in drinking or paying doctors' bills or Government taxes, or in all three ways.

Even if this is a true picture of the state of affairs, I advise this friend to work patiently and quietly.

[From Gujarati]

Navajivan, 28-8-1927

375. WHO MAY TAKE 'DIKSHA'[1]

In the Jawra State there is a married woman of the Oswal community named Gulabbai. She has got a pamphlet printed in Hindi and has distributed copies of it to people. It seems from it that her husband, who is still young, has left his house with the intention of taking *diksha*, and written as follows to his sixteen-year-old wife:

> The desire to take *diksha* has grown upon me during the past two years or so. I have been trying my best to obtain the permission of family members. Even after coming here, I wrote five or six letters, but I have not received the permission. Now I have decided to take *diksha* on my own responsibility.

This young man has a mother who is sixty years of age. In reply to my request for more particulars, the gentleman who

[1] Initiation; vow of asceticism

sent me this pamphlet has given the following information. I translate the letter, which is in Hindi, into Gujarati:

> Gulabbai has had ordinary education. She can read and write Hindi. A friend drafted for her the pamphlet which expresses her feelings as she described them to him, and she has got it printed. She herself went to the press, accompanied by her brother, and got it printed. The husband can read and write Hindi fairly well. Financially the family's condition is difficult. No one has given him *diksha* so far.

I hope that no one will give *diksha* to this young man, and also that he himself will realize his duty. A Buddha or a Shankaracharya may take *diksha* at a young age, and his action will be admired by the people. If, however, every young man decides to follow the example of these great men, instead of shedding lustre on dharma and themselves they will disgrace both. When people take *diksha* in these days, we see nothing but cowardice in their action, and this is why even sadhus, instead of being men of light and power, are a majority of them weak and ignorant like us. Taking *diksha* is an act of courage, and it is the result either of very holy influences on a person in his or her previous life or of wisdom born of experience in this life. A man who decides to take *diksha* without thinking of what will happen to his old mother and young wife should be so disinterested towards the world that the people round him cannot but see and understand his detachment. It does not seem that this young man who desires to take *diksha* is equipped for it in any such manner.

However, young men who feel very eager to take *diksha*, why should they not expand the meaning of the term *diksha*? In these times, we see few people who observe even the householder's dharma properly. It requires no small measure of courage to live, while being a householder, as if one had taken *diksha*. The real test lies in living so. I know many who have taken *diksha*; they frankly admit that they have not overcome sloth nor subdued the five senses. By taking *diksha*, these people have only acquired better means of meeting their needs of food and clothing. To live with one's family in poverty and meet its needs contentedly and preserving one's purity, following truth, looking upon all women other than one's wife as either a mother or a sister, to be moderate even in enjoying conjugal pleasure, to study scriptures and other holy books and to serve the country to the best of one's ability —this is *diksha* of no mean order. *Diksha* means self-dedication. This is not achieved through outward show; it is a state of the mind and, though certain outward modes of living may be necessary to express it, they are valued only if they are true signs of inward purity and detachment. Without these, such outward modes are mere forms without life in them.

[From Gujarati]
Navajivan, 28-8-1927

376. LETTER TO MANILAL AND SUSHILA GANDHI

BANGALORE,
August 28, 1927

CHI. MANILAL AND SUSHILA,

I have no time today to write myself. I am dictating this letter while I am having my meal. After I sent the cable to you, I have not missed a single mail. Mr. Andrews is here. I shall write more by the next mail.

Sushila's health must improve.

Blessings from
BAPU

From the photostat of the Gujarati: G.N. 4738

377. SPEECH TO VOLUNTEERS, BANGALORE[1]

August 28, 1927

The prayer over, each came one by one and received at Gandhiji's hands a copy of the *Bhagavad Gita* with his autograph. . . . There was considerable tremor in Gangadharrao's voice as he interpreted the blessings sentence by sentence in Kannada.

It is not by accident that things happen in this world. Why should we have met at this particular hour [4 a.m.], and on this particular day, and why should the *Gita* of all other books have been selected to be presented to you? Why, too, should we have read the third chapter of the *Gita* on this occasion? It was not for you that we selected this chapter; today was the day on which we read the third chapter. But some agency conspired to combine all these things, and we will see that it has been all in the fitness of things. A true servant gets up before sunrise, performs his ablutions and starts the day with prayer. Take it that your life of

[1] From Mahadev Desai's article, "The Leave-taking"

service begins from this auspicious hour. The exclusive devotion that you bestowed on me was only an occasion for the larger life of service that you are entering today. And the *Bhagavad Gita* provides you with a Code of Conduct. Whenever you are in trouble, doubt, depression or despair, you will turn to the Code and the Compendium. And what can be a better inspiration for you than Chapter III that we read this morning? It lays down that God created man, and at the same time imposed on him the duty of *yajna* or sacrifice. Both these words are derived from roots meaning that which purifies, and the Lord also said that "by sacrifice shall you propagate your kind". Sacrifice thus means service, and the *Gita* says that he who works only for himself is a thief. "Sacrifice ye for the gods, and pleased they will give you the reward of your sacrifice", says the *Gita*. To proceed a little further, sacrifice means laying down one's life so that others may live. Let us suffer, so that others may be happy and the highest service and the highest love is wherein man lays down his life for his fellowmen. That highest love is thus ahimsa which is the highest service. There is an eternal struggle between life and death, but the sum-total of life and death does not mean extinction but life. For life persists in spite of death. We have an ocular demonstration, positive proof of the unquestioned sovereignty of ahimsa, and this triumph of ahimsa is possible through sacrifice. There is thus no higher law than the law of *yajna*, the law of service, which is the law for the volunteer. Even for those whom you love most, even for me, you may not hate anyone else. If you do, it will not be love or service, but infatuation. If you have served me out of infatuation, this service will not be of avail. But I know you have not done so. You did not know me except by hearsay. You had never seen me, and you have during these four months never even come near me to receive a word of thanks from me. Yours was genuine selfless service. And let this service be to you an incentive to serve the cause I have been serving—the cause of *Daridranarayana.* And as I read in today's chapter a clear indication that the spinning-wheel affords us in India the highest instrument of universal service, I have placed the spinning-wheel before the country, and whenever your interest in the wheel flags you will turn to the *Gita* and replenish your faith. I know none of you, but I know full well the service you have rendered. It is not for me to reward you for it, it is beyond my power, and it is well that it is so. God alone can give the reward, and it is His covenant that He always rewards service truly and selflessly rendered.

Young India, 8-9-1927

378. SPEECH AT OPENING OF GYMNASIUM, BANGALORE

August 28, 1927

FRIENDS,

I feel grateful for the opportunity you have given me for performing this auspicious ceremony of opening your gymnasium[1]. I am also thankful to the donor of the gift to you. He has chosen the right expression to his desire of keeping alive the memory of his son by giving you this gymnasium. That only shows he is anxious that the youth of the country should become strong and healthy. I know that in a land where engineers like Sir M. Vishveshvarayya had come forth to serve the motherland there would be engineers like Mr. Venkatasubba Rao to come forward to build this gymnasium. You know very well that just as the intellect requires exercise and development the body also requires exercise. But only a few have realized this and many giant intellects go about the country in enfeebled bodies. It does not appear to me that this is the right way of education. It is not right that they should neglect their bodies. It gives me much pleasure that you are alive to this necessity of affording your young men physical exercise. I have known your young men serving in the cause of khadi and I am glad they know of the importance of physical exercise. I am also glad that as you are trying to exercise your intellect outside your schools, you would be trying to give your bodies sufficient exercise in service outside your gymnasium. I hope that every one of you educationalists in your home would pay particular attention to this. I hope also that you would devote attention to physical exercise for your girls. Lastly I should like to remind you that walking daily in the morning hours is one of the good exercises you might adopt.

Before I declare the gymnasium open I should like to remind you also of the necessity of developing your spiritual side as you are going to develop your physical bodies. You know that in this gymnasium you are going to perform your physical exercises where Sri Hanuman is presiding and that under his direction you are going to develop your bodies. But the bodily strength of Sri Hanuman is only a second thing. The first is his spiritual strength, the great strength that he possesses on account of his *brahmacharya*. I hope you will remember this great spiritual

[1] Shri Krishnaswami Vyayama Shala at National High School

strength that comes from *brahmacharya*. Have that *vrata* and may God bless you to develop into strong spiritual and physical sons and daughters of your motherland.

The Hindu, 29-8-1927

379. SPEECH AT TEXTILE LABOUR UNION[1], BANGALORE

August 28, 1927

FRIENDS,

You have given me addresses and a purse and I am thankful. I know of your difficulties, particularly in meeting here today and I am sorry that many of your Union members could not be present. But I know also that though many of you could not be present you have told them all of my work and the purpose for which I am in your midst. You have said in your address that you have given up drinking. That means you have realized the importance of your lives, that you have recognized the value of your relationship with your family, your country and your duty. In expressing my gratification at this I must ask you to leave the other evil habits like gambling, etc. You can do so only if you utilize the time in your improvement, and in educating yourselves. For, you must realize your duties and your rights as mill-workers and you can do so only by educating yourselves. Do not forget this as you will not forget your future or your ambitions, as labourers among your employers. For this you must cultivate good habits. You must rise early and pray to God for strength. You must know that this blessing is necessary and this could not be had by evil habits. You have given me a purse and it means to me that you realize there are many many poorer brethren than you. If so I only ask you to help these poor brothers and sisters of yours, to take the cloth spun and woven by them. If you wear khadi you will be really helping them. You could help them still more if you spin yourselves and make your relatives at home spin more. I can tell you that the workers in our place, Ahmedabad, are doing this and are helping in this great task. You can also understand that in the days of your strikes you cannot do better than spin and earn your living. This is an important thing and I ask you to remember this. Before I take leave of you, workmen,

[1] Of Binny Mills

I have one word to tell you. It is usually said that morals among workers are not very high or strict. I want every one of you to realize and hold every woman other than your wives as your own mothers and sisters. You must be morally very strong for therein lies your destiny. I hope you will not forget this. May God bless you with wisdom and strength.

The Hindu, 29-8-1927

380. SPEECH TO ADI KARNATAKAS, BANGALORE[1]

August 28, 1927

Soon after the function at the Labour Union was over, Mahatmaji and party motored to the *Adi Karnataka* Colony on the New Mysore Road. Many hundreds of *Adi Karnatakas* had assembled to receive Mahatmaji, many of them being women. They entertained the distinguished visitors with a few simple songs after which Mahatmaji said:

"ADI KARNATAKA" FRIENDS,

I am pleased to see you all today and I want to tell you two things. You should not eat flesh and you should not kill cows. This is against your dharma, the Hindu dharma and you are all Hindus. If you tell me you have got to carry on your trade in leather, then I ask you to do that using leather of only dead animals. Do not drink and commit sins. Wear khaddar and save your poor sisters and brothers. Do not forget this.

The Hindu, 29-8-1927

381. SPEECH AT CITIZENS' MEETING, BANGALORE

August 28, 1927

FRIENDS,

I am unable to raise my voice and therefore I request you to keep silent. For the last five months I have been staying here recouping my health but I am still not able to raise my voice sufficiently high. Friends, you have given me several addresses this evening and I thank you all and I thank you for the help you have all given me. I can never forget your manifold kindness and I pray God to bless you all. Friends, you know after all I

[1] At Lal Bagh

am a servant and I have to say very little. What I have to say to you this evening I have written it down for you to know. Of course it is in English, but let me tell you that using this medium of communication is not a thing to be proud of. I would rather you all knew Hindi, and that I had written it in Hindi, but I do not know when that time is going to come to us.

From His Highness the Maharaja of Mysore and his officials down to the people at the lowest rung of the ladder you have by the wonderful and unmerited affection bestowed upon me so closely bound me to you that to say thank you for the addresses and the purse that you have given me today seems to be a cold, almost insulting, formality. Though to the great benefit of my health I have stayed in your midst for over four months, your affection makes it difficult for me to be reconciled to the impending separation from you. The only return that is within my power to make to the Maharaja Saheb and you, his people, for the kind hospitality extended to me when I was so much in need of it is to make you co-sharers of my innermost thoughts about the well-being of this beautiful State.

It has done my soul good to watch the wonderful progress you have made in many directions. I have seen your educational institutions in Bangalore as well as in many other places that I was privileged to visit. I have seen the institutes specially designed for *Adi Karnatakas*. I have understood somewhat the workings of your Municipal administration. I saw with wonder and admiration Krishnarajasagar and the Bhadravati Iron Works, the two great monuments of Sir M. Vishveshvarayya's zeal and skill. (Cheers) I saw by deputy, for want of time, also Sivasamudram. These great undertakings have an undoubted place in your march towards economic progress. Wherever I have gone I have noticed cordial relations between the officials and the people. You have no Hindu-Muslim quarrels. You are unaffected by the misdoings in the North. I tender His Highness the Maharaja and you my hearty congratulations upon all these good things and many others that I could relate. And I consider it to have been my good fortune that I happened to be in this fair land at the time of the celebration of the Silver Jubilee of the beneficent rule of the Maharaja to share your rejoicings and to witness the manifestation of genuine regard shown by the people for His Highness.

But great though this progress is, it would be wrong to be satisfied with it. It seems to me to be confined to the middle class and not to take enough note of the peasantry, the backbone of

Mysore as it is of the rest of India. The purses given to me everywhere for khadi work demonstrate the faith of the citizens of Mysore in the message of the spinning-wheel and khadi. My wanderings in the different parts of Mysore have convinced me that it has a big future if the State and the people work out the spinning-wheel in a scientific spirit. I assure you, it requires a detailed organization and expert knowledge no less than the building and working of the great undertakings like the Bhadravati Iron Works; the difference is only that of degree. And even as the latter must fall to pieces if they do not receive skilled and vigilant attention, so must the spinning movement fall to pieces if it is not backed by expert knowledge and ceaseless effort. Do not let this great movement die for want of skilled and careful nursing. Hand-spinning raises the income of the peasantry by at least 20 per cent with an outlay which would be considered ridiculous compared to what has been required for some of the great enterprises, which are naturally the pride of Mysore. If you universalize the spinning-wheel, the benefit filtrates at a bound down to the poorest peasants. It creates an indissoluble bond between them and you, and it gives an honourable occupation to the peasantry during their leisure time which is estimated to be at least four months during the year. And it is a matter of great joy to me to find that the Department of Industries and the Co-operative Department are putting forth their effort in this direction. For, there is no industry greater than this and no co-operative effort complete without the organization of the spinning-wheel and all it means. And every one of you can extend your co-operation to the villagers if you will but use khadi for your clothing material.

But the spinning-wheel though it is the centre of rural prosperity is *not all*. If our cattle become an economic drag upon us, we cannot live. I do not know whether you have all noted the noble appeal made by His Highness the Maharaja in his reply to the jubilee address on behalf of the dumb creation. Let me reproduce the beautiful words:

> I pray that a similar spirit (of brotherhood) may extend itself to the dumb creation and that we may see animals, and especially those we hold sacred, treated with ever increasing consideration for feelings which they cannot express.

I read in this passage a delicately expressed wish that His Highness's Mussalman, Christian and *Adi Karnataka* subjects should voluntarily protect the cow and her progeny from destruction. But in my humble opinion this question of cattle protection is not to be solved without hard thinking and harder labour. I feel convinced that it is possible to make cow-slaughter an economically unsound proposition. Today it is undoubtedly an economically sound proposition. This is an evil which no private agency can fully cope with. It is pre-eminently a matter for the State. It requires education of the people, in cattle-breeding, dairying and selection of breeding bulls. In my humble opinion, it is the duty of the State to protect the cattle-wealth of the country by a firm and enlightened treatment of the whole subject. I hold it to be one of the primary concerns of a State to see that its children and its people are provided with wholesome, cheap milk. I entirely associate myself with the remark made by Blatchford that the price and quality of milk should be standardized as much as are those of postage stamps. I do not suppose that many of you know what happens to the hide of dead cattle of Mysore. If you study the question as I have done, you will have many a painful revelation. Is it not a matter for shame that our foot-wear should be made of slaughtered hide and our dead-cattle hide should be exported from India to the tune, as I am told, of nine crores per year? Here there is work for an army of trained chemists to give the art of tanning its proper and legitimate status to the profit of themselves and the country. Again, only the State can deal with this very important branch of the cattle question.

But I must hurry forward to the next point to which I want to draw your attention. And here too I fall back upon the Maharaja's utterance. Here are his words:

> I pray that we may all be assisted in years to come to work together in a spirit of brotherhood for the same good end, so that with efficient administration, increased facilities for agriculture, industry and commerce, and equal opportunities for all, we may devote our common energies to raising Mysore to a level with the foremost countries of the world. It is my earnest desire that this spirit of brotherhood should be extended to the continuous improvement of the conditions of those who are less fortunate than ourselves, remembering that all communities alike are members of my people and children of our country.

The State cannot enforce brotherhood if the people don't believe in it. I was pained, as was the revered Pandit Madan Mohan Malaviyaji, to learn that there were in this State erudite Sanskrit Pundits who will not teach the Vedas to *Adi Karnatakas* and who uphold the doctrine of inherent untouchability. If I could be convinced that untouchability, as we believe it today, is an integral part of Hinduism, I should not think twice before renouncing Hinduism. But I venture to state before my Hindu brethren that though I have endeavoured, in my humble way, to understand Hinduism and live up to the letter and the spirit of it, I have found no warrant in it for the curse of untouchability. We sin before God and man to consider a single human being as untouchable because he is born under particular surroundings.

Closely allied with the question of untouchability is that of drink. The curse of drink could be driven out of this fair land if only the so-called higher classes would brother the so-called low classes. But here again, I know to my cost, having worked in the cause of prohibition for years, that without State aid much is not possible. Ignorant poor people will drink if drink is made accessible to them. If there is any spot on earth where total prohibition is easy of accomplishment, it is India, for the simple reason that the drink habit, thank God, has not yet acquired any respectability. It is still considered to be a degrading habit. I have met in my tours thousands of *Adi Karnatakas*. I met a party of Lambanis, I put them straight questions. There was not one hand raised in defence of drink, and the vast majority have undertaken to abjure both beef and drink. May God give them strength to keep their promise. But I urge you and the State to help them. Difficulties there are in the way, but man is made to face, battle with and conquer them.

Lastly, let me plead for child widows and child wives. They are also unhappily for us and to our shame made part of dumb creation. Our enlightenment or education will be counted as dust if this infamy is not removed wherever it may exist. Here is work for your Civic and Social Progress Association.

You will not consider me to be ungrateful for having invited your attention to what I think should be done in order to make Mysore a real model State so as to entitle it to be called *Ramarajya.* It is not as if the shortcomings to which I have drawn attention do not exist in other parts of India. Alas, they do exist and some of them perhaps in an intenser form than here. But it has been my privilege to notice greater progress in Mysore than elsewhere in many things, and it has therefore created a desire for still greater.

More is expected of those who give much. I have found so much good in this State that I almost fancy that if you and the Maharaja together will it, you can make this State *Ramarajya.*

The Hindu, 29-8-1927

382. *FAREWELL SPEECH AT PRAYER MEETING, BANGALORE*[1]

August 28, 1927

After the meeting[2] was the prayer which had become an institution during our stay at Kumara Park. The last day's meeting was a treasurable experience for the presence of Mr. Andrews, and the Bjerrums who sang "When I survey the wondrous Cross", which Gandhiji said transported him to Pretoria where he heard the wonderful hymn sung for the first time, and also for the parting talk that Gandhiji gave to the congregation. "How many of you have been coming here regularly?" asked Gandhiji, and most of them raised their hands.

I am glad you have been coming. For me it has been both a joy, and a privilege, inasmuch as I have felt its elevating influence. I ask you to keep it up. You may not know the verses, you may not know Sanskrit and the hymns, but Ramanama is there for all, the heritage handed down from ages. And I tell you why I ask you to continue this congregational prayer. Man is both an individual and a social being. As an individual he may have his prayer during all the waking hours, but as a member of society he has to join in the congregational prayer. I for one may tell you that when I am alone I do have my prayer, but I do feel very lonely without a congregation to share the prayer with me. I knew and even now know very few of you, but the fact that I had the evening prayers with you was enough for me. Among the many memories that will abide in my heart after I leave Bangalore, not the least will be the prayer meetings. But I shall have my congregation at the next place I reach, and forget the wrench. For one who accepts the brotherhood of man and fatherhood of God should find a congregation wherever he goes, and he may not hug or nurse the feeling of parting or separation. Please therefore keep up the prayer. You can form your own congregation in your own places, and as a last resource one's family can become one's congregation well enough. Do meet every evening at this hour, learn a few hymns, learn the *Gita*, do the best and the most you can for the purpose of self-purification.

Young India, 8-9-1927

[1] From Mahadev Desai's article, "The Leave-taking"

[2] *Vide* the preceding item.

383. TELEGRAM TO NON-BRAHMIN CONFERENCE[1]

BANGALORE,
[On or before *August 29, 1927*]

JUST READ LETTER. NON-BRAHMINS SHOULD CERTAINLY JOIN THE CONGRESS IN A SPIRIT OF SERVICE AND GOODWILL.

The Bombay Chronicle, 30-8-1927

384. LETTER TO MIRABEHN

August 29, 1927

CHI. MIRA,

I have your letters.

I read your message to Andrews. And we had a hearty laugh over his not understanding the word संदेश. To him it meant a Bengali sweet.

You will certainly have the three days all to yourself when you return to Sabarmati and the other times you want. You will confer with Maganlal and arrange your hours as may seem best. Only you must go slow and leave margin between periods especially in the initial stages.

You must have got my dictated letter[2] about segregation. Please do not give me up but tackle me again and again till you fully understand my meaning. And then too do not as I like but as you like.

Are you talking to Krishnadas in Hindi? I have not told you that your Hindi has been comparatively free from errors. The few I detect, I get no time to correct.

Andrews leaves with me tomorrow but he goes to Madras dropping me at Vellore. I wonder if you ever got your beautiful map back!

[1] Released by the Associated Press of India under the date-line "Bombay, August 29". The Secretary of the Special Non-Brahmin Provincial Conference sent on the 29th the following reply: "Thankful for your advice. We join Congress to Non-Brahminize and thus democratize it."

[2] *Vide* "Letter to Mirabehn", 26-8-1927.

With love,

BAPU

From the original: C.W. 5265. Courtesy: Mirabehn

385. LETTER TO ASHRAM WOMEN

Silence Day, Bhadarwa Sud 2 [August 29, 1927][1]

SISTERS,

I have your letter drafted by Ramaniklalbhai.

You have not caught my point. There were several things implied in my letter. It is always so in letters. If they were all made explicit, this is what it would come to:

When we are engaged in a particular task, we should not think of other fields of service so long as they are not urgent. If we do, it must be regarded as *moha*[2]. Here I am doing a necessary piece of service as well as a sick man can do it. If at such a time I thought of Gujarat flood relief or of the Ashram problems and how I would solve them if I were there, it would be *moha*. If you were in such a condition, it would be true of you too. There is no question of one's being great or small. You are engaged there in doing service in your own way. Suppose I fall ill, very ill, or suppose there were floods here, as heavy as those in Gujarat, it would be madness for you to entertain a needless thought (of running down here), even though you are not considered as wise as I. That would not mean that you would have no feeling or sympathy for me or for the sufferers in the Madras floods. Sympathy there will be and must be, in which your feeling for others finds expression. But if you become restless about it, it is *moha*, and should be avoided. It is of course a different question to decide when it becomes one's dharma to rush to the help of another at the sacrifice of one's own duty. To do flood relief work, most of the members left the Ashram. That was clearly our duty. And yet, for those who could not go, there was no need to feel restless. Ask me if you still do not understand what I say.

Blessings from

BAPU

From a photostat of the Gujarati: G.N. 3666

[1] The year is inferred from the reference to Gujarat floods.

[2] Infatuation

386. INTERVIEW TO THE ASSOCIATED PRESS OF INDIA

BANGALORE,
August 29, 1927[1]

Mahatma Gandhi, interviewed by an Associated Press representative regarding the Viceroy's proposal to convene a conference, said that he was not over-enthusiastic about the official initiative in solving the Hindu-Muslim question but welcomed co-operation from any quarter in this matter.

The Tribune, 31-8-1927

387. SPEECH AT VOORHEE'S COLLEGE, VELLORE[2]

August 30, 1927[3]

MR. PRINCIPAL, STUDENTS AND FRIENDS,[4]

At the outset I would like to express my very deep sorrow over the domestic affliction[5] that has befallen your Principal. I heard of it as soon as I reached here. I appreciate, Mr. Principal, the very courteous consideration that you have shown by not merely allowing this function to take place under your roof but also, in spite of your overwhelming grief, gracing this function by your presence and presiding at it. I ask you to regard me as a partner in your grief.

I thank all the students and others for the address that has been presented to me this afternoon and the purse for the Khadi Fund. This demonstration of your personal affection for me and your identification with the poorest of the land does not surprise me now, because it has become a common feature wherever I go throughout the length and breadth of our beautiful country. It has been a matter of the greatest joy to me and consolation in the face of many difficulties to find that the student world throughout India has a warm corner for me in their heart. The students have lightened my burden to a very great extent. But I

[1] Released from Bangalore on this date, which was a Monday

[2] This appeared under the title "What Students Can Do?" and with the introductory words: "The following is a verbatim report of Gandhiji's address to the students of Vellore."

[3] & [4] From *The Hindu*, 2-9-1927

[5] De Boer, the Principal of Voorhee's College, had lost his child.

cannot suppress from me the feeling that in spite of this personal affection that the students have shown to me everywhere and even identification with the poorest of the land, the students have yet to cover a vast amount of ground. For, you are the hope of the future. You will be called upon, when you are discharged from your colleges and schools, to enter upon public life to lead the poor people of this country. I would, therefore, like you, students, to have a sense of your responsibility and show it in a much more tangible manner. It is a remarkable fact and a regrettable fact that in the case of the vast majority of students, whilst they entertain noble impulses during their student days, they disappear when they finish their studies. The vast majority of them look out for loaves and fishes. Surely, there is something wrong in this. There is one reason which is obvious. Every educationist, everyone who has had anything to do with the students has realized that our educational system is faulty. It does not correspond to the requirements of the country, certainly not to the requirements of pauper India. There is no correspondence between the education that is given and the home life and the village life. But that is I fear a larger question than you and I can deal with in a meeting of this character.

Taking things as they are, we have to consider what is possible for the students to do and what more can we do in order to serve the country. The answer that has come to me and to many, who are eager to see that the student world gives a good account of itself, is that the students have to search within and look after their personal character. Purity of personal life is the one indispensable condition for building a sound education. And my meetings with thousands of students and the correspondence which I continuously have with the students in which they pour out their innermost feelings and take me into their confidence show me quite clearly that there is much left to be desired. I am sure that all of you understand thoroughly what I mean. In our languages, there is a beautiful word, equivalent for the word student, that is, *brahmachari. Vidyarthi* is a coined word and a poor equivalent for *brahmachari*. And I hope you know what the word *brahmachari* means. It means searcher after God, one who conducts himself so as to bring himself nearest to God in the least possible time. And all the great religions of the world, however much they may differ, are absolutely one on this fundamental thing that no man or woman with an impure heart can possibly appear before the Great White Throne. All our learning or recitation of the Vedas, correct knowledge of Sanskrit, Latin, Greek and what not will avail us nothing if they do not enable us to cultivate absolute purity of heart. The end of all knowledge must be building up of character.

An English friend in Shimoga, whom I did not know before, came up to me and asked me why it was, if India was really a spiritually advanced country, he did not observe in the students a real yearning after knowledge of God, why was it that the students, many of them, did not even know what the *Bhagavad Gita* was[1]. I gave what appeared to me an honest explanation and excuse for this discovery of his. But I do not propose to give that explanation to you nor seek to excuse this very great and grave defect. The very first and earnest request that I would make to the students before me here is that each one of you should search within and wherever you find that my remarks are justified you will begin to reform and rebuild yourself, and those of you who are Hindus, and the vast majority are Hindus I know, will endeavour to understand the very simple, beautiful, and to me soulful message of the *Gita.* The experience, and I think I can say the experience without a single exception, of those who have really carried on this search after truth to render their hearts pure is that it is an utterly impossible effort, unless it is accompanied by a heart prayer to the Almighty. Whatever, therefore, we do, do not lose faith in God. I cannot reason out the thing for you, because really speaking, it is a fact which transcends reason. But I want you to cultivate a spirit of real humility and not summarily reject the experiences of so many teachers, *rishis* and others of the world and not regard them as so many superstitious men. And if you will but do this, all the rest that I want to say will be as clear as crystal to you. This will be to me the test of your sincerity of profession. If you have real faith in God, you cannot but feel for the humblest of His creation. And whether it is the spinning-wheel and khadi, or untouchability, total prohibition, or social reform in connection with child widows and child wives and many other similar things, you will find that all these activities are derived from the same source. I was therefore glad to find that you sympathize with and approve of the spinning movement, the struggle against untouchability and other things with which I am identified. I accept your assurance that henceforth you will do better in regard to khadi.

It is really the easiest thing in the world for you to make your choice once for all and say to yourself that you shall use

[1] *Vide* "Students and the *Gita*", 25-8-1927.

henceforth nothing but khadi since it puts a few coppers into the pockets of those who need them most. In this one institution alone, I understand, you are more than 1,400. Just think what the 1,400 by giving only half an hour to spinning can add materially to the wealth of the country. Think also what 1,400 can do on behalf of the so-called untouchables, and if all the 1,400 young men were to make a solemn resolve, and they can do so, that they are not going to have anything whatsoever to do with child wives, imagine what a great reform you will make in society around you. If the 1,400 amongst you, or a respectable number even, devote your leisure hours or part of your Sundays to going amidst those who are given to drink and in the kindliest manner possible steal into their hearts, imagine what service you will render to them and to the country. All these things you can do in spite of the existing faulty education. Nor do you require much effort for doing these things except that you have got to change your heart, and to use a current expression in the political world, alter the "angle of vision".

And I want you to turn this occasion to advantage, and you will do so if only you will consider the solemn circumstance under which we have met this evening and by reference to which I started my address. A mere man of the world would be justified, and he will be justified by the world, if he excused himself from attending a function of this character on account of domestic affliction. Surely there is something noble and majestic when a man instead of brooding over such sorrows, transmutes them into service for God and humanity. Every such act enables us to understand the essential oneness of humanity. May God enable you to understand the words that I have spoken to you. I thank you once more for your address and the purse and all that you have said.

Young India, 8-9-1927

388. LETTER TO T. R. MAHADEVA IYER

CAMP VELLORE,
August 31, 1927

DEAR FRIEND,

I have your letter. I can only repeat what I have said, that in my opinion it is better for you to give up possession. You will be morally in the right in giving up possession right, if those who you feel are of your opinion are duly informed before you give up possession. Not to give notice and remain in possession is, in my opinion, indefensible. So far as I have been able to understand the intentions of the Committee, they are averse to going to arbitration on matters about which they have no moral qualms and no legal difficulty.

Yours sincerely,

From a microfilm: S.N. 12941

389. SPEECH AT PUBLIC MEETING, VELLORE[1]

August 31, 1927

MR. CHAIRMAN AND FRIENDS,

I thank you for the addresses and the purse containing Rs. 2,001 and odd. It is really with Vellore that the khadi tour in Tamil Nadu commences. Last week I went to Krishnagiri[2] and Hosur which are also in the Tamil province; but that may pass as part of the Mysore programme. Coming to Vellore, I am reminded of my first visit to this place accompanied by Maulana Shaukat Ali. And when I cast back my memory upon those times and now look at this assembly today, I cannot help feeling sad—sad not because you have in any way misbehaved yourselves but because of what is going on in the North. As a matter of fact my sadness is considerably reduced when I, on enquiry, discover that in your midst at any rate you have no such quarrels as are going on there, to disturb the even tenor of your life. My irrepressible optimism is strengthened by living in your midst

[1] At Gandhi Maidan. C. Rajagopalachari translated the speech into Tamil.

[2] *Vide* "Speech at Krishnagiri", 24-8-1927.

and discovering that you stand untouched and unruffled by the misdoings of our countrymen in the North. For my hope will last as long as my faith in God lasts and even though Hindus and Mussalmans all over India were to fly at one another's throats, which God forbid, I hope that I shall still have the same strength that I possess today to declare in my own person that the day is coming when Hindus and Mussalmans will stand shoulder to shoulder, fight for their country's freedom and remain united for ever as brothers. I want you people of Vellore, men and women, to share that faith with me. I have no doubt that posterity will laugh at our barbarity and ask themselves how foolish and how mad we must have been that in the name of God we should cut each other to pieces. But as you know I hold of equal importance with Hindu-Muslim unity the question of khaddar and the spinning-wheel. To spin for the sake of *Daridranarayana* and to use nothing but khadi for the same reason is as much an act of pleasing God as it is that Hindus and Mussalmans should remain united together. Just as Hindu-Muslim unity binds the two together so does the thread that is spun on the spinning-wheel bind the millions of paupers of India to us, the middle class. At the present moment it is true that we do not cut their throats but it is equally true that in a sense we suck from the villagers their very life-blood. We are both directly and indirectly responsible for sucking the life-blood from the villagers. It is we the middle class people who are responsible for the condition of perpetual starvation to which the villagers have been reduced today. As traders we are directly responsible for that condition because instead of trading in the cloth manufactured by their sacred hands we worshipped Moloch, soiled our fingers with foreign goods and began to sell foreign cloth. I regard this as an act of treachery against those starving voiceless millions. And the rest of the middle classes are indirectly responsible for that starvation because they did not resist their temptation of buying the flimsy cloth that our neighbours offered to them in lieu of our own sacred cloth. And your purse I regard as but a slight token of your desire for repentance for the sins that we have committed. But I assure you that the penance will not be complete till all the traders have retraced their steps, given up trading in foreign cloth and they as well as others have taken to khaddar, however coarse it may be, and however expensive it may be. Real repentance counts no sacrifice too much. And how I wish that while leaving this the first place of my tour in Tamil Nad I could go with the confidence that you have got the same sense of sorrow and grief for our starving countrymen and women and have the same consciousness of our sins towards them that I have. My remarks are as much applicable to the sisters to my right as they are to the men in front of me and my left. You the women of Vellore will not deserve to be daughters of the same land that was hallowed by the sacred feet of Sita. We men and women of India take the sacred name of Sita as among the seven *satis* early in the morning. If we do not follow the simplicity and the purity of Sita, what right have we got to take her name? It should be just as natural to us to wear khaddar produced in our villages as it is, thank God, for us to cook our own food and eat it in preference to the richest dishes that may be cooked in hotels and offered free of charge.

I attach the same importance to the question of untouchability. We Hindus are staking our religion and our reputation so long as we continue to regard a single human being as untouchable by birth. As human beings they have as much right to enter our temples, to send their children to our schools and to help themselves with the same water from the same tanks which we use. I hope that if there is in this audience anyone who still hugs the belief in untouchability, he or she will revise that belief and understand there is no warrant whatsoever for the curse in Hinduism.

Of equal importance, or almost equal importance, is the question of drink. I said almost equal importance not because the question of temperance is by itself of less importance to the man who has got to give it up, but because it affects a smaller number of people than untouchability. Those of us who are not given to the habit of drinking should not be satisfied so long as there is a single neighbour who is prey to that evil. You should devise and adopt all the gentle means that may be at our disposal to wean our falling brethren from their bad habit. If I were you I would not be satisfied till there is total prohibition in the land. If I were you, I would make the position of the Minister intolerable so long as he does not take up this question seriously and in right earnest.

I must not take up more of your time now. We have some work before us. You have given me this beautiful casket. I have received those silver plates presented to me with the addresses of the District Board and Municipality. It is now known all over India that I have nowhere to keep such plates and caskets in and that by my vow I am debarred from owning any possession on this earth. I regard these articles as having been given to me in order to enable me to auction them in your presence and to get what more money I can for *Daridranarayana*. They will therefore be put up before you for auction, and I hope that those of you who can afford it will try to outbid one another. But all may not have come with enough money to take part in the bidding. For them there is another course. I know that all men and women present at this meeting have not contributed to this purse. It is possible that some of you who have contributed have not given to the best of your ability. In order to give you an opportunity to give anything you may wish to, at this meeting, volunteers would presently go in your midst to make collections. I hope that those of you who can and believe in spinning and khaddar will not spare yourselves in giving. Sisters all over India are in the habit of giving their jewellery also. I want all those who can to give for the sake of *Daridranarayana*. A pie given with a willing heart is just as welcome as the gold mohur. I thank you once more for your gift and for your addresses.

The Hindu, 2-9-1927

390. IS IT MARRIAGE?

I give the following from a letter received by me while I was hardly able to attend to any correspondence, that is, during the first days of my recent illness. I have omitted the names of parties though the correspondent gives every detail.

> During this marriage season there has been a heart-breaking marriage ceremony at Sadashivgad, Karwar. The bride is about 12 years and comes from a very poor family from Goa. The bridegroom is 60 years old. His first wife died about three years ago, leaving two children behind her out of eight or nine. The bridegroom is the founder of an English school. Last year he tried to secure a bride of tender age, but owing to the agitation in his community, the transaction was abandoned. This year he succeeded by offering rupees two hundred to the parents of the bride. What is to be done in the matter? Men like—[1] who are social reformers of the place do not raise their little finger against this inhuman act.

There seems to me to be no reason to doubt the accuracy of the statement made in the letter from which I have given the foregoing condensation. I wish it were possible to say that this is only a rare instance. Instances of this character occur often enough to call for a drastic remedy. One remedy is undoubtedly

[1] As in the source

to publish every such case and expose it and create a healthy strong public opinion against repetition of such crimes against womanhood. But local agitation whenever such immoral alliances are impending is no doubt the most effective. According to this correspondent, the first attempt on the part of this old progenitor of eight children was frustrated because of timely agitation. I wonder why such an agitation did not take place in the present instance. Surely many people in the locality must have known about the attempt to secure possession of a girl of tender age for the old widower. I wonder why agitation was not set on foot immediately to save the girl from a life of torture and misery. But in my opinion, if local public opinion can be mobilized it is not too late even now to help the girl wife. I gather from the correspondent's letter that the widower seems to have been a kind of a philanthropist at one time. May he not be persuaded to put the girl away from him at the Seva Sadan or some such institution for education, and then, when she is of full age, be given the choice either of living with him or regarding the marriage bond as a nullity? But whether in the present moribund condition of society such a step is possible or not, there is no reason why young men of undoubted character should not form themselves into bands of mercy pledged by all just and legitimate means to prevent child marriages and to promote wherever possible remarriage of child widows. The two things appear to me to go hand in hand. These bands of mercy to be able to do effective work must localize their activity. They will find then that in the course of a few years, they would become an irresistible force. The majority of our towns have after all a very small population each, and it is not impossible to know when immoral bargains such as the correspondent has drawn attention to are contemplated, or to know the child widows of their respective towns. There is no doubt however that a great deal of tact and exemplary self-restraint will have to be exercised by these bands of mercy. The slightest impatience or violence on their part will cause revulsion against them and frustrate the very object they have in view.

Young India, 1-9-1927

391. LEST WE FORGET

There is some danger of the calamities of Orissa and Sind being forgotten in the midst of the universal attention that the Gujarat floods have attracted. Probably the distress is more felt in Sind than in Gujarat and the most felt in Orissa, for it is the least organized and the poorest of our provinces. Gujarat has produced an army of workers whose numbers are already proving embarrassing to Sjt. Vallabhbhai. After all everywhere it is the merchant class that is the freest with its purse and most able to organize relief in times of distress. Let those Gujaratis, who are not wanted for work in Gujarat, or who can be spared, turn their attention to the places where help may be most needed. The distress of Gujarat must not blind the Gujaratis to the need of the other provinces. The present distress must be utilized to make us less provincial and more national. We must feel one with the least and the remotest of the thirty crores of God's creatures who inhabit this land.

Young India, 1-9-1927

392. TRUE 'SHRADDHA'

A friend sends from Rangoon rupees twenty-five as donation for the propaganda of the spinning-wheel and writes:

> My father died on the 18th April 1927 at Tanjore (South India) while I was there on a short leave. When I was confronted with the question of "Sixteenth Day Ceremony", a slavish, meaningless imitation of *shraddha*, I resolutely refused to abide by the desire of my relatives simply because I have no belief in it as it prevails today. I do not believe in a departed soul waiting in *Pitruloka* or some such other unseen places for water or rice balls. Nor can I see any reason to attach any importance to the rites performed by a mercenary priest and in a language which is Greek both to me and the officiating priest. In short the whole affair seems to be a hoax designed to be practised on the religious susceptibilities of the people. But I can believe in *shraddha* as a thing offered in piety and devotion with a charitable intention. From a commonsense point of view the main principle and the original purpose of this ceremony ought to be charity. As you say in *Young India* dated 24-2-1927, "only two classes of people are entitled to charity and none else—the Brahmin

who possesses nothing and whose business it is to spread holy learning, and the cripple and the blind." Our great immortal sage, Thiruvalluvar has said: "A Brahmin is that sannyasi who has an overflowing love towards all living creatures." Because I could not conceive of a man who has a better claim than you and a more charitable purpose than that of the spinning-wheel, I have sent you this amount. There is also another way of commemorating the memory of one's own parents. The same sage Thiruvalluvar has again said: "The gratitude of a son to his father must consist in the son conducting himself in the world in such a way as to excite from the world the approbation that his father must have performed a great *tapasya* to beget this son." I may add that I have this ideal at my heart.

I have omitted from the letter several personal references. Though I have performed *shraddha* ceremonies myself in my youth, I have not been able to understand their religious usefulness. This letter is not the first of its kind I have received. But not being able to understand the hidden meaning, if any, of the practices which are almost universal in Hinduism, I have hitherto refrained from dealing with them in these pages. The rule that the correspondent has chosen has however appealed to me. We do very often meekly submit to many conventional ceremonies although we may have no faith in them, and although they may have no meaning for us. Submission to convention in trivial matters in which there is no danger of deceiving others or oneself is often desirable and even necessary. But submission in matters of religion, especially where there is a positive repugnance from within and a danger of deceiving our neighbours and ourselves, cannot but be debasing. There are today many religious ceremonies, which, whatever meaning and importance they might have had in ages gone by, have neither importance nor meaning for the rising generation. There can be no doubt that it is necessary for this generation to strike out an original path by giving a new form and even meaning to many old ceremonies. The idea of keeping green and of respecting the memory of one's parents is not to be given up. But it is hardly necessary on that account to retain the old conventions and forms, which have lost their reality and therefore ceased to have any influence on us. I therefore commend the example of the correspondent to those who are anxious to do only that which is right, and free themselves from self-deception.

Young India, 1-9-1927

393. HOW TO KEEP HEALTH

The Polish Professor with whom the reader is now familiar writing on my illness says:

> As I have been reading in *Young India* about your illness and discussion with 'jailors', let me tell you of my own experience how to prevent such breakdowns. Within the last nine months—September to May—I have visited 40 towns all over Poland, and lectured for 100 days at the rate of 3-7 hours a day. At the age of 64, I feel as young as 40 years ago whenever I stand before the public. My rules are:
>
> 1. No *worry* whatever. There is an Almighty God who takes care of all, and nothing happens without His permission. I am not His chief steward, only a very humble servant with a clearly defined task, and have to look at that task, that small part of universal becoming. If there is somewhere on earth an earthquake or a flood or a famine, no real harm can happen to immortal souls, nobody can suffer without some advantage to him designed by God, and everywhere God has His servants who help so far as He permits them. Therefore worry is weakness of faith, and my faith being infinite I cannot worry.
>
> 2. *Much sleep* in every moment when I am not at work, even for a few minutes many times a day. Before falling into sleep always praying: Lord Jesus enlighten me, give me strength and joy. With this prayer a clear image of joy, light, strength flowing into me. Such a sleep is prayer, is intercourse with the Highest and refreshing. When I wake up from such a sleep, I know exactly what I have to do, and I do it gladly.

The professor adds a third rule which is about fasting and diet. As it is incomplete, I have asked for further information before sharing it with reader. But there is no doubt that the two rules above mentioned about absence of worry and necessity for sleep are golden rules. There is nothing that wastes the body like worry, and one who has any faith in God should be ashamed to worry about anything whatsoever. It is a difficult rule no doubt for the simple reason, that faith in God with the majority of mankind is either an intellectual belief or a blind belief, a kind of superstitious fear of something indefinable. But to ensure absolute freedom from worry requires a living utter faith which is a plant of slow, almost unperceived, growth and requires to be constantly watered by tears that accompany genuine prayer. They are the tears of a lover who cannot brook a moment's separation from the loved one, or of the penitent who knows that it is some trace of impurity in him that keeps him away from the loved one.

The ability to sleep during odd moments seems to be a necessity in old age. Whilst the first rule is applicable to all, young and old, the rule about sleep is not to be copied by youngsters. It is the privilege only of babies and old people. And to induce such sweet innocent sleep, it is surely necessary to put oneself in tune with the Infinite at every step. This sleep is not to be mistaken for the sleep of the sluggard or the opium-eater. But it is 'Nature's sweet restorer', a tonic for a brain that gets easily fagged in old age.

Young India, 1-9-1927

394. LETTER TO SATIS CHANDRA DAS GUPTA

GUDIATHAM,
September 1, 1927

DEAR SATIS BABU,

I enclose herewith Jamini Babu's letter which please destroy after perusal. It gave me great joy to find all the good coming out of Jamini Babu. I know you will handle him in the gentlest manner possible.

With love,

Yours,
BAPU

From a photostat: G.N. 1575

395. LETTER TO KAILASNATH KATJU

GUDIATHAM (SOUTH INDIA),
September 1, 1927

DEAR FRIEND,

My weakness of body is my excuse for dictating this letter. But for that weakness I would have gladly written myself. I thank you for your letter and the first instalment of your contribution to khadi. Your letter is so good and is likely to influence others. If you have no objection, I would like to publish that part of it which relates to khadi. But please do not hesitate to refuse permission if you would on any account not like the publication of the letter, whether with or without your name.

As for the black alpaca *chapkan* concerned, give me an order and I can have for you one made of very fine black khadi. It looks as good as alpaca. You may not know that in Madras many advocates and *vakils* wear khaddar *chapkans* even when they do not use khadi for other articles of dress and as it so happens, the khaddar *chapkans*, the poor practitioners find to be suitable because of their comparative cheapness. In your case I may not think of cheapness at all. If you give the order, I am not going to secure for you the cheapest but the most expensive and the most elegant.

Now a word about personal spinning. I quite agree with you that love of khaddar need not include personal spinning. But love of the starving millions does, for two reasons: first, because, personal spinning renews our daily bond with them. Secondly, by personally spinning each known member of society creates a spinning atmosphere which makes it easier for workers to induce the unwilling, because unbelieving, villagers to take to hand-spinning. I would like to add a third reason which I know you would not despise. Every yard of well-spun yarn adds to the wealth of the country, be the addition ever so infinitesimal. You know what the lawyers do so often whilst awaiting their turn in the law courts. They either play with their pencils or with their paper-tape or worse still open out their little pen-knives and fidget with the edges of the desks at which they are sitting. I wonder if I could induce you to take up the little *takli* which could be made of silver, gold or ivory if you like, and put in a delicate little cylinder. *Takli*-spinning is easily learnt. Will you take to it? It will be, I know, laughed at in the beginning; then it will cease to attract notice one way or the other and if you could go through the two stages and persist, it will be copied by others. I hope you do not resent my saying all this to you. You have given me an inch with hearty goodwill and you must not be surprised if I now ask for more.

Yes, indeed, I demanded great sacrifices from lawyers. But looking back to 1920 and '21, I feel that I asked for nothing very extraordinary and I feel that I had a right to demand the largest measure of sacrifice from those to whose profession I once belonged.

The little ones now consider themselves too big to sit in my lap. Please, however, tell them that whenever I meet them again, am going to make them pay for still remembering me.

I am passing your cheque for Rs. 100/- to the Treasurer of the All-India Spinners' Association.

Yours sincerely,

DR. KAILASNATH KATJU
9, EDMUNTON ROAD
ALLAHABAD

From a photostat: S.N. 13275

396. *LETTER TO GULZAR MOHAMAD 'AQUIL'*

VELLORE,
September 1, 1927

DEAR FRIEND,

I have your letter of the 19th ultimo. I enclose herewith copy of the article in *Young India*. The extracts you have sent me do not in any shape or form do* your point: that is to say, they do not show that Justice Dilip Singh was in any way prejudiced against Mussalmans or that he otherwise gave a decision which he did not believe to be absolutely correct. That other judges differed from him as to the interpretation of the law is nothing new in Indian experience or in the experience of the world. So long as the world lasts, there will be honestly different interpretations of the same laws. Indeed, one extract that you have collected clearly bears out my own opinion that Justice Dilip Singh was wholly unprejudiced. I still adhere to the opinion that much of the agitation over *Rangila Rasul* was uncalled for, unfortunate, avoidable. But as I have already intimated to you[1], I do not desire, unless I feel compelled, to take part in the controversy.

From a microfilm: S.N. 12390

* Evidently a slip for "prove your point".
[1] In letter dated August 7

397. LETTER TO S. G. VAZE

VELLORE,
September 1, 1927

MY DEAR VAZE,

It is curious your letter enclosing copy of the *Servant of India* came to me the very day that I read your signed article and the reference myself. The cutting was given to me by Andrews. When I read that cutting I thought of writing to you to tell you that whenever you expect me to deal with any question you should write to me. Much as I should like to, I really do not get much time to read any papers or books except to see a local newspaper for a few minutes daily. I remain somewhat posted with current events only because friends correspond with me on them. Now about the subject-matter of your letter.

Before it came I had discussed the East African among other questions with Andrews. It needs very delicate handling. I do not consider myself to be as competent to pronounce an opinion on the East African situation as I do on the South African. I had been given to write views on the East African question also not because of my being well posted with a knowledge of all the problems and local conditions but a long course of very serious study of the South African question has given me, so I fancy, the capacity for coming to a right decision. My own opinion is that we would be better without any representation in the East African legislature. Any representation that we might have will be exploited by the predominant European element for the purpose of robbing the sons of the soil of their just rights. I would, therefore, resist communal representation. If I can, I would retain for the Indian settlers the franchise on the same rights as the Europeans. But that can only be, if an educational qualification is accepted by the Europeans which they will resist because, they always in the colonies want the principle of "one man, one vote" to be established. What I am anxious for and what I would fight unto death for is our immigration and unrestricted rights to own landed property unlike as in South Africa and Rhodesia. We were the pioneers in South Africa. Our peasants, so far as I know, have done no harm to the Africans. We were, therefore, in large numbers, solely dependent upon their goodwill. In all fairness, therefore, Europeans have to reconvince us that having got the might on their side they may ride roughshod over our rights may be too true [*sic*] but then I should not compromise by a hair's breadth on these two fundamental questions. At the present moment whilst my opinion is an . . .[1] state so far as the political part of the question is concerned, I do not feel inclined to write to say anything in public unless later on it becomes absolutely necessary. I know and it grieves me to know that our people in East Africa are not acting in the correct manner and that their leaders there are not selfless.

Yours sincerely,

S. G. VAZE, ESQ.
SERVANTS OF INDIA SOCIETY
POONA CITY

From a photostat: S.N. 13276

398. LETTER TO BAL KALELKAR

ARNI,
September 2, 1927

CHI. BAL,

I got your letter and liked it very much. I could not reply immediately for want of time. I shall answer two of your questions. A *brahmachari* sacrifices all pleasures merely through faith or in obedience to his parents or a custom. There is obedience in his sacrifice, but not knowledge. And if he cannot bring himself to make for ever that sacrifice, he has freedom to enjoy pleasures within limits after completing his studies. A sannyasi makes the same sacrifice knowingly and willingly. He does not and cannot keep it open for him to return to pleasures after having abjured them. Both types of sacrifice are very essential to individuals as well as to society.

Now the second question. Non-violence means not harming anyone in thought, word or action out of ill will or selfishness. If we wish or do ill to any stranger in the interests of our parents, that is violence. We can see and prove with the help of our knowledge that wishing or doing ill benefits neither the world nor our parents. Hence I had written that it was my belief that we discover non-violence the moment we realize that its root is to be found in wishing well to the world as much as to ourselves. You

[1] The source has a blank here.

will thus see that we can of course prove independently that one should wish well to the world, but if we abide by the dharma of non-violence the responsibility to wish well to the world as well devolves on us even in pursuance of that dharma. If we understand this from our very childhood, our reason would admit it and the heart too would like it. That is to say, if we continue for ever the sacrifice which we have undertaken in good faith during the stage of *brahmacharya* we become sannyasis. Shankaracharya did this in the past. Dayananda did it in our own age. That we all cannot do so is due to our shortcoming and that constitutes an obstacle to doing good to the world. But we cannot do such things merely by exercising our reasoning. But if, with the help of our intellect, we imprint it day after day on our hearts and if it gets so imprinted, the whole world will not, even if it tried, be able to stop us from sacrificing our all. If any special problems arise, do tell me. Read this to all the pupils if you can.

[From Gujarati]

From the manuscript of Mahadev Desai's Diary. Courtesy: Narayan Desai

399. *SPEECH AT ARNI*[1]

September 2, 1927

You love to get a little bit of a rag, or cocoanut, or anything that you can get as *prasadam* from temples from which, alas, all holiness has fled. I would ask you to transfer that spirit of humility and devotion to khaddar which is spun and woven in the living temple of *Daridranarayana*. Our temples have their proper place in our religion and society only in so far as they enable us to reach out the hand of fellowship to the starving millions of India. But these very temples will be the instruments of forging our shackles if they become impassable barriers between the masses and us. If you will wear khaddar in the true spirit you will purify yourselves and the temples. I need not explain to you now, how the removal of untouchability necessarily follows from this proposition.

Young India, 8-9-1927

[1] From Mahadev Desai's "Weekly Letter"

400. SPEECH AT ARCOT

September 2, 1927

I am very thankful for the cordial reception and for the purse you have given me, but I am not satisfied with this amount. I know that there are many in this gathering who have not contributed to the Fund which is intended for our poor brethren. You must encourage spinning by wearing khaddar. I am very glad to find here that the Hindus and the Mussalmans have met together in mutual co-operation unlike in the North where communal hatred is prevailing.

Yesterday when I had been to a Hindu temple on my way I was given the *prasad* by the *gurukkal*[1]. I told him that I am a pariah and asked him whether he would allow a pariah inside the temple. He laughed at me and said that he would do it gradually. I appeal to all men and women who have assembled here to treat the so-called pariah as our equal and move with him freely.

Since I find no place to have this silver plate, I shall have it auctioned. Volunteers will come in your midst for collection and you can give whatever you please. As I have to go to another place I shall conclude my speech, once more thanking you for your gifts and addresses.

The Hindu, 5-9-1927

401. LETTER TO BALWANTRAI MEHTA

[After *September 2, 1927*][2]

I have your letter. You may rest assured that I shall not take a decision hastily. I am now conveying all my doubts to everyone who should know them and am seeking assistance in coming to a decision. I make no distinction between K and Devdas. It is no pleasure to me to entertain any suspicion about K. K and K are in fact related to me as children. Hence it is not at all possible that I shall decide anything in haste.

Your argument does not appeal to me. You may know that I myself am a proof before you that sex does not discriminate bet-

[1] Temple priest

[2] The source has this letter after the entries for September 2.

ween the young and the old. Even today I have to erect all sorts of walls around me for the sake of safety.

Despite this, I was in danger of succumbing a few years ago. Moreover, sexual desire does not bother about time either. Despite our belief that Bhai K's ideas about *brahmacharya*, etc., were pure it is no wonder if ultimately he succumbed to desire. A young man whose case was almost similar confessed to me in Bangalore. He is regarded as a *brahmachari*. He is a darling of his family. No one can suspect him as things stand. He studies in the intermediate class. He has not been able to save himself from a widow who is related to him. He came to me saying, "Save me from this fever." Despite having sworn to a friend, he fell again. Hence he sought refuge in me. What refuge could I provide? But that is a digression.

What I have learnt is this: K had closer relations with K and her family than warranted. Both were reprimanded and both were convinced. Both agreed not to have such intimacy. In spite of this, they were seen secretly meeting each other. So Maganlal went on a fast. Notwithstanding this, they again met secretly. If my information is correct, I cannot get over my doubt. And if K has committed this slip such a man can in no time succumb to temptations of money. But these are all my inferences based on a single premise. I cannot but have all sorts of doubt about a person who acts with deliberate dishonesty. I am still investigating. I am not unaware of Maganlal's opinion which you quote. You are also aware that I have great confidence in his judgment. I shall write to him too.

Now the question that either you or his father should reimburse the amount, if K has embezzled any, does not arise at all. I am considering only the ethical aspect of this question.

Whatever I shall now write for *Navajivan* cannot but reflect my doubt; hence if you let me have some draft I shall consider and publish it, if I can.

I have not made light of suicides. I know of only two occasions when suicide becomes a duty. There are many grounds for that opinion. A man who is helpless against indulgence and cannot control himself but has sense enough to bring about his end ought to do so. That would be his dharma. Likewise, when a beast of a man attempts to criminally assault a woman, it is her duty to save herself by committing suicide. Indeed I have very often quoted these two instances in the Ashram. And I think it is only proper. Even if K has committed all the three faults mentioned above, as far as the tenets of the Ashram are concerned the duty to commit suicide cannot be established nor that of running away. Atonement is the only duty in such a case but I know from the many letters K wrote to me that he has always opposed a number of rules observed in the Ashram.

Blessings from
MOHANDAS

[From Gujarati]

From the manuscript of Mahadev Desai's Diary. Courtesy: Narayan Desai

402. TELEGRAM TO MIRABEHN

MADRAS,
September 3, 1927

MIRABEHN
SATYAGRAHA ASHRAM, WARDHA

YOU MAY GO BOMBAY FOR EXAMINATION APPENDIX AND EYES. WIRE CONDITION.

BAPU

From the original: C.W. 5266. Courtesy: Mirabehn

403. TELEGRAM TO MIRABEHN

MADRAS,
September 3, 1927

TO
MIRABEHN
SATYAGRAHA ASHRAM, WARDHA

WIRE RECEIVED. DISTRESSED. GOD BE WITH YOU. EXPECT DAILY REPORTS. LOVE. ANDREWS JOINS.

BAPU

From the original: C.W. 5267. Courtesy: Mirabehn

404. *SPEECH TO LABOUR, PERAVALLUR*

September 3, 1927

FRIENDS,

I thank you for the address and the two purses. I congratulate you on having the club[1] whose main object is to advance the cause of khadi. The ingenious manner in which you are advocating its cause is worthy of imitation by all of us. For a poor man it is the most convenient form of getting a loan free of interest. But as in most things in this also the honesty on the part of all members is an indispensable condition. As you know, having myself become a labourer and having worked with them in their midst and for them for over 35 years I am deeply interested in everything connected with labour. I do not propose just now to deal with the disabilities that labour is labouring under in India and here in particular. As a matter of fact I know nothing of your special hardship and special conditions. At the present moment what I wish to lay the greatest stress upon is what labour can do for itself.

The one curse with which it is afflicted from within is the terrible drink habit. If labourers do not get rid of it betimes they will be digging their own graves. When the drink habit possesses a man it turns him into a beast. He knows no distinction between the sister and his wife. I therefore advise you all to give up drink. I know what a severe temptation it is for a man who is once given to drink; but God has given man the capacity, if he will only use it, for conquering such defects and temptations. The other defect which I have found amongst the labourers is that they have no consciousness of the strength which is possessed by combination. Labourers must learn to consider that the welfare of all is the welfare of the individual. You must therefore cultivate amongst yourselves a real brotherly spirit. I have known that in many parts of India labourers squander their money in gambling. It is a vicious habit and you should give it up. The morale amongst the labourers in some parts of India is also not all as it should be. If as labourers we want to become a recognized force in the Indian society and in the political world also, it is absolutely necessary for us to recognize the binding tie

[1] Gandhi Club

of marriage and all the obligations that that tie imposes upon us. I have congratulated you upon having this club for the advancement of khadi. But instead of there being a hundred members in that club every one of you should belong to it. Remember that khadi binds us to those who are much poorer than yourselves. To throw away the foreign cloth or even your mill-made cloth costs you nothing but the simple thought on behalf of the starving millions of people who are living in our villages. It has given me great pleasure to lay the foundation-stone[1] which I have just laid over the place there. May God help you to do the things I have suggested to you. If you will but do these things, you will find that the majority of your difficulties will disappear without any further efforts.

The Hindu, 5-9-1927

405. SPEECH TO STUDENTS, MADRAS

September 3, 1927

You have called your purse a small purse, much smaller than you had expected to raise. I also endorse the sentiment that this purse[2] is all too small for the students of Madras to present to me. And for what purpose? Not for buying a few collars or neckties for distribution among the modern students who may be in need—not intended for any small work. It is intended for the starving millions in 7,00,000 villages. And I am positive that you, the students, if you could possibly realize the meaning of the starvation of these millions, you could raise a far larger sum. If you knew the conditions of these starving millions, as I do expect you to know, you would have raised a much larger sum. However, for your comfort, let me tell you that you have done no less than the students elsewhere. Not only does your purse not suffer in comparison with purses received by me from students elsewhere, but it comes to me with the assurance that your Chairman has given, that your purse is a token of your association with the khadi work I am doing. And, coming as it does with that assurance, I hold your purse very precious indeed, and it has given me additional joy to know that the largest amount collected by any single worker was by a lady

[1] Of the building of the Madras and Southern Maharatta Railway Employees' Union at Perambur

[2] Of Rs. 1607

student.[1] I wish indeed that all the young ladies of India will beat all the young men of India in the competition of service of the motherland. Why should not women be the first in the field in matters of service? Your purse should carry with it a lesson to you as it does to me. The lesson that the purse carries to me is, that taking all these moneys from the student world, I should realize more fully my responsibility not only to you but to the starving millions. The lesson that it should carry to you is that having given your mite to this purse, you should study the condition of these millions of villagers, in order to fit you all the better for their service. And if you do so, you will make this painful discovery that your education is paid for out of the life-blood of these millions. I hope that every student here also knows that the fees he pays for his education do not, in any way whatsoever, pay for the cost of his education. I hope that the students also know and realize that the education is paid for out of the drink and drug revenue.

Now, consider for yourselves what you owe to these men who pay for your education. I suggest then that you should render ceaseless service to these starving millions and that you should not be satisfied till this gnawing poverty is banished from our land. And, I have told you that khaddar is the easiest and the only way. I ask you not to allow your minds to be befogged by all kinds of specious reasoning that will be advanced against the spinning-wheel and against khadi in these days of rush for machinery. I do not propose to go into all the arguments for the spinning-wheel and khadi, but I commend to your attention a small book that has been published by the All-India Spinners' Association and which has been written by two students, Professor Puntambekar and Mr. N. S. Varadachari. You will find in that little book most of the arguments carefully marshalled, in order to show that khadi and khadi alone can become the only means of alleviating this universal misery of starving India. I want you to bear in mind the qualifications that I have introduced into the proposition with great care. Do not dismiss from your minds the words "universal" and "alleviation" and then raise an argument, which nobody has ever advanced, and then proceed to demolish it. And if you have understood this message of khadi, then you will not rest until you have discarded every inch of foreign cloth and substituted it by hand-woven and hand-spun cloth.

[1] Miss Ananda Bai of the Law College had collected Rs. 150.

But, I have said that khadi is really the least part of your performance. It is the beginning of the service and the centre round which all other things can be built up. You will have to bring to bear, on this question of removing the awful distress among the villagers of India, an irreproachable character. You will never be able to put together the shattered fragments of society unless you have got this binding cement of character. I am sure that it will do your soul good to hear from me that students in Gujarat are, at the present moment, working wonders in those flood-stricken areas. They could not do so, if they had not love overflowing and outgoing to those people in distress, and character at the back of their service. Some of them have left off their studies and have gone into villages with pick-axes, shovels and baskets and have restored villages which were stinking with dead cattle and rotten grain to a habitable condition. They did not wait for the *Panchama* brethren to go to their assistance to remove these carcasses, but removed them themselves. And, I know, what has been possible for the few Gujarati students to do, is also possible for every one of you, boys and girls, to do, given the occasion. But I must not take up much of your time, nor tax myself unduly the very first day of my coming to Madras. There are many other things of which I should like to talk to you. I wish I had the time to give you that conversation. But I would like to make a little request to you. I gave to students in Vellore a fairly considered address,[1] and I understand that it has been reported almost verbatim in *The Hindu*. Probably some of you have already read it. But even if you have done so, I commend it to you for reading again carefully and I ask those who have not read it to get a loan of the paper or buy it and read it. You are the hope of the future and I should love to think that students all over India should realize their duty to the country to which they owe not only their birth, but also their education, derived as it is from the life-blood of the downtrodden villagers. Whenever the devil presses you and you simply think of yourselves and not of your country, just remember this thing, which I have told you this evening. Remember the debt you are incurring from day to day whilst you are receiving your education, and may the memory of that debt keep you from every temptation.

The Hindu, 5-9-1927

[1] *Vide* "Speech at Voorhee's College, Vellore", 30-8-1927.

406. AFTER THE FLOODS

From the letters which I received regarding the flood-relief work and from the reports in *Navajivan* I observe that volunteers are doing their work conscientiously showing no signs of exhaustion. But I have formed the impression that all of us are not accustomed to doing physical work, that we feel aversion against certain types of work and that certain things are left undone or delayed or done with too much expense because we do not know how to do them. For example, I read the following in reports by some volunteers which are lying with me.

> The wells in this place stink.
>
> The basin at the top of the well in this place is about to crumble.
>
> A buffalo has fallen into the well here and the water stinks with the smell of her rotting body. But the poor Bhangis still use it.
>
> The grain which is rotting in this place gives off foul smell. The people dig up even that and eat it.
>
> We found the Bhangis here lazy. They do not work even when asked.

I have given these statements from different letters and all of them are not in the words of the writers themselves. I have not, however, twisted the writer's meaning in any of them.

I think that in our work we should not have one set of people to do the actual work and another to supervise. Our poor country can progress only if the supervisors and the workers are the same persons. The number of persons who issue orders should be the smallest possible. Of course we cannot do without overseers[1] altogether, but we should bear in mind that their function is largely to keep watch against possible malpractices. Volunteers, too, need supervision. If no supervisor is appointed over a volunteer's work, he should ask for one to be appointed. Even so, our aim should be to get out of this unhappy condition of supervisors having to be appointed. In any case, supervisors and others, all should carry hoes and spades with them. If these are not available, they should use their hands as much as possible.

I would, therefore, expect to receive reports as follows: 'In village 'A', the well emitted a foul smell. A bucket and rope were procured from the villagers and the well was cleaned up with the latter's help. Some potassium permanganate was obtained

[1] Gandhiji uses the English word.

from a hospital nearby and mixed with the well-water. We then tasted the water and satisfied ourselves that it was pure.

'In village 'B' the basin platform round the mouth of the well was unusable, and so a hedge of thorny plants was put up round it with the help of villagers. This notice was put up on the hedge. 'The platform is in bad repair. No one should go near it.' There is another well in the village, and, therefore, there will be no hardship.

'We found only one well in village 'C'. Its basin was quite unusable. The village mason, therefore, was brought along and the basin repaired and made strong enough so that it could be used for the time being. The people have been advised to get it made stronger.

'In village 'D' a buffalo had fallen into the well. We saw that she could not be pulled out even if we tried. There was not much water in the well. With the consent and help of the village people, the well was filled up. As I had never lifted a weight or held a spade, my shoulders are aching and the palms are sore. But the foul smell which could be felt even at a distance of several hundred yards has ceased. When I see now boys playing on the spot where the well stood, I completely forget my pain. And the experience of real appetite is an additional benefit.

'We saw two wells in village 'E', the second being for the use of Bhangi friends. There was hardly any water in it. On inquiry, I was told that it usually contained only a small quantity of water, and that too full of dirt and mud. So I pleaded with the elders of the village. They agreed to let the Bhangis draw water [from the other well], but insisted on these conditions. 'The women in our families will not yet accept your idea of mixing [with Bhangis]. You may, therefore, fix certain hours when they may draw water from the well.' I welcomed even this, little as it was. I thanked them. I got together Bhangi boys and, with their help, filled up the well in a little while and left the place.

'I found the Bhangis in village 'F' very lazy. I saw ankle-deep slush mud round their wells. The refuse-heap was right near their dwellings. I tried hard to explain things to them, but in vain. I then asked for a spade. 'There it is', said one of them, and went away. Another said: 'Why do you waste your labour, dear Sir? We don't mind all this dirt and mud. We have always lived thus.' I said: 'I can't bear the sight of these things. Persons like me work hard for you, plead with people not to treat you as untouchables. But what can we do if this is how you behave?' The man said: 'Yes, that is certainly true. But we cannot help the slowness in our improvement.' I made no reply to this, but removed the mud, covered the ground with dry sand and single-handed cleared out the refuse-heaps from near the dwellings. Occasionally a boy would come along, remove two spadefuls of the refuse and walk away. I called to mind the *Gita* teaching of disinterested service and left the place.'

The reader may think up more such imaginary reports, and should cherish the ambition to act in the manner suggested and demonstrate that these things can be done.

The substance of what one volunteer writes may be stated as follows:

> You were alone so far, but you are two now, for Kakasaheb has joined you. Should we not get some benefit of your being together? Will not one of you write and explain how to create a new world after the *pralaya*?

I have been trying to see that Kakasaheb's pen is active and dancing. Staying here, I cannot think of any suggestions to make about creating a new world. Those which occur to me do not seem worth putting down on paper. My appeal, therefore, to workers who are already active is this:

Instead of expecting us, invalids, to make suggestions from this distance, you who are on the spot should yourselves think out plans and execute them, limiting them to your villages. You should not wait for the whole of Gujarat to undertake reconstruction before you do so, but should effect what reforms you can in your own village if you can carry the local people with you. I give here a miscellaneous list of do's and dont's.

1. Do not build houses which look like slums.
2. Do not use tin-sheets.
3. Do not imitate America or England, for the climate there is different from ours.
4. Use only a minimum of stone and mortar.
5. In our country, we can build fine houses with straw, stalks, reeds and finely powdered, moistened earth.
6. The site must be cleaned and made level before a house is built.
7. There must be proper provision for ventilation.
8. If there is enough space, a separate shed should be provided for cattle. I saw an inexpensive and very hygienic arrangement for them, which consisted of an enclosure in which they were not tied but were left free. A strong fence of sticks or wire could be put up for the purpose. There should be a small shed

in the enclosure where the cattle can rest when they feel inclined to do so.

Miscellaneous

1. Do not give people black, foreign caps, even if received as gifts for them. A thing which is unacceptable in itself should not be received even as a gift. A vegetarian would not accept meat because it was offered to him free.

2. Our aim in life is not to live merely for the sake of living. It should be, rather, to live for a good end, to awaken the soul sleeping in this body which is its house. The difference between dharma and *adharma* is this: One who follows dharma will refuse to live if he has to violate certain restraints for that purpose. One who follows *adharma* accepts no such restraints. He will sell himself, his wife and children and his country in order that he may live.

3. A trader may save and may also destroy. The merchants of Gujarat are doing both without knowing it. I have been observing that there is a shower of foreign and mill cloth. Now that the immediate shock of the heavy floods is over, I caution them and the people. It is Gujaratis and Marwaris who are responsible for the presence of foreign cloth among us. Both these classes of merchants should consider. If I were asked to choose between the destruction caused by foreign cloth and that caused by excessive floods, I know which I should choose. Let the reader know that one kills the body; this can be borne and is inescapable. The other kind of destruction kills the soul and we can always escape it. Who will explain to Gujarat this profound difference between the two kinds of destruction? Man is always helpless in saving his body from destruction, and he is always free concerning the saving of his soul. That is why the various religions proclaim in the most emphatic words: "The *atman* is its own friend and its own foe."[1]

[From Gujarati]

Navajivan, 4-9-1927

[1] *Bhagavad Gita*, VI. 5

407. *SPEECH AT Y.M.C.A., MADRAS*[1]

September 4, 1927[2]

FRIENDS,[3]

The Chairman has asked me to give you a religious discourse. I do not know that I have ever given a religious discourse, or to put it the other way, I do not know a single speech of mine or a talk of mine, within my own recollection, which has not been a religious discourse. I think, if I am not deceived, that at the back of every word that I have uttered since I have known what public life is, and of every act that I have done, there has been a religious consciousness and a downright religious motive. My acts may have appeared to my audiences, or to the readers of the words that I have written, political, economic and many other things. But I ask you to accept my word that the motive behind every one of them has been essentially and predominantly religious. And so is it to be this morning.

When I asked what I was expected to speak about, I was told that I was to speak what I liked. Well, the message came to me this morning as I was on my way to this meeting and I propose now to think before you aloud.

I had very precious moments with a missionary friend in Vellore. I had a heart-to-heart talk[4] with the students of that place, and the next morning I was told something like this: 'Your speech was very nice. You talked of the things of the spirit. But how is it that in the middle of the speech like King Charles' head with the renowned Mr. Dick, khadi came up? Can you explain what connection khadi can possibly have with spirituality?' Then he went on, 'You spoke about temperance; that delighted us and it was certainly spiritual. You spoke about untouchability, a very fine subject for an audience spiritually inclined or for a spiritually inclined man to speak about. But both these came in your speech after your message of khadi. It seemed to jar on some of us.' I have given you the substance of the conversation in my own words but faithfully. I gave the answer that came to me at the time and this morning I want to amplify that answer.

[1] This was published under the caption "Two Speeches".

[2] & [3] From *The Hindu*, 5-9-1927

[4] *Vide* "Speech at Voorhee's College, Vellore", 30-8-1927.

It is quite true that I place khaddar first and then only untouchability and temperance. All these came at the end of the speech I gave to the students of Vellore, in which I made a fervent appeal for purity of life and told them that without purity of life all their learning would be as dust and probably a hindrance to the true progress of the world. Then I took up these three things and a few more by way of illustration. Throughout 35 years' unbroken experience of public service in several parts of the world, I have not yet understood that there is anything like spiritual or moral value apart from work and action. I have often repeated to audiences like this that great verse which has always remained with me ever since I read it: "Not everyone that says unto me Lord, Lord, shall enter the Kingdom of Heaven but he who doeth the will of my Father who is in Heaven."[1] I have not reproduced that verse correctly but you know what that verse is and it is so true. I recall to my mind two brilliant instances of men in English public life who, in their own times, were regarded as very great reformers, and as pillars of spirituality. I am now talking to you of about 1889 and 1890 when many of you were not born. I used to attend temperance meetings in those days. I was interested in that reform. Those two pillars of spirituality were supposed to be great temperance workers, but they were workers with their speeches. They were always in demand when a harangue was required on temperance. I am sorry to have to inform you that I was a witness to their fall. Both of them were found out. They were no workers. The words God, Lord, Jehovah were on their lips always, but they simply adorned their lips, they were not in their hearts. They used the temperance platform for their own base ends. One of them was a speculator and the other was a moral leper. Perhaps you now understand what I want to say. In India also, I am not able to say that the temperance platform is always a spiritual platform or that the platform of untouchability must necessarily be a spiritual platform. I have known, I know now as I am talking to you, that both these platforms are being abused today in this very land by several people. Others are using them aright. The moral I want to submit to you is that every act may be done, conceived and presented from a spiritual standpoint or it may have none of it at all. I want to claim before you today that the message of the spinning-wheel and khadi is supremely a spiritual message; and it is supremely a spiritual message for this land that it has got

[1] *St. Matthew*, vii. 21

tremendous economic consequences as also political consequences.

Only the other day, an American friend, Prof. Sam Higginbottom, writing to me upon a subject in which both he and I are deeply interested, said,—I give you the substance of the letter — "I don't believe in a religion bereft of economics. Religion to be worth anything must be capable of being reduced when necessary to terms of economics." I entirely endorse that remark with a big mental reservation. Not that Mr. Higginbottom also had not that reservation. But I must not claim to speak for him. The mental reservation is this, that whereas religion to be worth anything must be capable of being reduced to terms of economics, economics, to be worth anything, must also be capable of being reduced to terms of religion or spirituality. Therefore in this scheme of religion *cum* economics there is no room for exploitation and for Americanization as the technical term is known. As a distinguished son of India put it—he is no other than Sir M. Vishveshvarayya—whereas an Englishman owns 30 slaves, or is it 36,—I speak subject to correction—an American owns 33 slaves. Personally, I think there is no room in true economics which is convertible with religion for the owning of slaves whether they are human beings, cattle or machinery. There is no room for slavery in economics. Then I suggest to you that you cannot escape khadi and it has the largest limit. Temperance takes in its orbit a certain number of people. It blesses the man who converts the drunkard to teetotalism, and it undoubtedly blesses the drunkard who is so converted by the word of the reformer. Untouchability takes in its orbit at the most seven crores of people of this unhappy land, and not every one of us can do untouchability work. You may certainly give the untouchable education; you may dig wells for him and build temples. But these would not make him touchable unless the so-called touchables will come down from their insolent heights and brother the untouchable. So you will see it is a somewhat complex problem for the man and woman in the street to handle. And as a man whose sole occupation in life is, be it ever so humble, to find out truth, I was searching for something that everyone can do without exception—everybody in this room—that something which would also remedy the most deep-seated disease of India.

And the most deep-seated disease of India is undoubtedly not drunkenness, undoubtedly not untouchability, great as those diseases are and greater perhaps for those who are suffering from them; but when you examine the numerical content of this disease, you will find with me, if you take any census returns, or any authentic book on history, such for instance as Sir William Hunter's history, or take the evidence of Mr. Higginbottom given before a Commission only two years ago—he said that the largest number of people in India were poverty-stricken, and Sir William Hunter says that one-tenth of the population in India is living barely on one meal a day consisting of a stale *roti* and a pinch of dirty salt which perhaps you and I will not touch — that state of things persists in India today. If you were to go into the interior, outside the railway track, you will find as I have found that the villages are being reduced to dungheaps, the villagers are not there, vultures are to be seen because they could not support themselves, and were reduced to carcasses.

India is suffering from meningitis, and if you will perform the necessary operation and make some return to those starving millions today, I say there is nothing but khadi for you. And if, as men spiritually inclined, you will think of those less fortunate than you are and who have not even enough to support themselves or clothe themselves, if you will have an indissoluble bond between them and yourselves, I say once more there is nothing for you but khadi. But it jars, and the reason why it jars is that this is a new thing and is a visionary thing, a day-dream as it appears to many. The missionary friend of Vellore, whom I spoke about, told me at the end of our conversation, "Yes, but can you stem the march of modern progress? Can you put back the hands of the clock, and induce people to take to your khadi and make them work on a mere pittance?" All I would say is that this friend did not know his India. From the Vellore meeting I went to two places, Arcot and Arni. I did not see much of the people there, I assure you, but saw the villagers less well clad than I am. I saw them not in their tens but in their tens of thousands. They were in their rags and their wages were practically nil for four months in the year. They gave me of their substance; I was hungrily looking at the thing they gave me. They gave me not pice; they gave pies.

Come with me to Orissa in November, to Puri, a holy place, and a sanatorium, where you will find soldiers and the Governor's residence during summer months. Within ten miles' radius of Puri you will see skin and bone. With this very hand I have collected soiled pies from them tied tightly in their rags, and their hands were more paralysed than mine were at Kolhapur. Talk to them of modern progress. Insult them by taking the name of God before them in vain. They will call you and me fiends if we talk about God to them. They know, if they know any God at all, a God of terror, vengeance, a pitiless tyrant. They do not know what love is. What can you do for them? You will find it difficult to change these delightful sisters (pointing to the ladies present) from their silk saris to coarse khadi woven by those paralytic and crude hands. Khadi is rough! It is too heavy! Silk is soft to be touched and they can wear nine yards of silk, but they cannot wear 9 yards of khadi. The poor sisters of Orissa have no saris; they are in rags. But they have not lost all sense of decency, but I assure you we have. We are naked in spite of our clothing, and they are clothed in spite of their nakedness. It is because of these that I wander about from place to place, I humour my people, I humour my American friends. I humoured two stripling youths from Harvard. When they wanted my autograph, I said, "No autograph for Americans". We struck a bargain, "I give you my autograph; and you take to khadi". They have promised and I rely on the word of an American gentleman. Many of them are doing this work—make no mistake about it, and they like it also.

But I cannot be satisfied, not till every man and woman in India is working at his or at her wheel. Burn that wheel if you find a better substitute. This is the one and only work which can supply the needs of the millions without disturbing them from their homes. It is a mighty task and I know that I cannot do it. I know also that God can do it. The mightiest and strongest matter is but a tiny affair for Him, when it pleases Him. He can destroy them all in the twinkling of an eye, as He has destroyed now thousands of homes in Gujarat and as He had destroyed thousands of homes a few years ago in South India. I carry this message of khadi and the spinning-wheel with the fullest faith in God, and therefore in His creation, man. You may laugh at me today. You may call this a sordid thing. If you like you may distrust me and say this is some political schemer who has come to place his khaddar before us, but he has got many things up his sleeve. You may misinterpret me and my message. You may say: 'We are too weak to do these things and too poor'. I know it is possible for you to repel me by your arguments and make me speechless. But I shall not lose faith in you so long as I cannot lose faith in God. It is impossible for me to lose that faith, and therefore I cannot lose faith in the message of khadi and the spinning-wheel.

If I have not succeeded in opening out my heart to you, and if I have not succeeded in showing to you the rock-bottom spirituality of the message of khaddar, I don't think I shall ever succeed in doing so. All I can say is I mean to succeed. My lips may not deliver the true message. God will do it all, in whose name I have delivered this message to you. God bless you.

Young India, 15-9-1927

408. SPEECH AT PUBLIC MEETING, MADRAS[1]

September 4, 1927

MR. CHAIRMAN AND FRIENDS,

I thank you for the addresses that you have presented to me and the different purses. The general purse amounts to Rs. 13,235-2-6. Rs. 100 from Purasawalkam labourers, Rs. 52-0-11 from the staff of the Indian Industrial Company, Rs. 13 from Jam Bazaar, and additional collections from students Rs. 18. For all this I thank you. I wish that it was possible for me to speak on the various topics that engage the attention of the servants of the country at the present moment. Though I hold strong views on most of those questions, I do not propose at the present moment to deal with them. But let me reiterate my faith before this vast audience. I believe in non-violent non-co-operation as much as I ever did. So far as I can see, there is nothing but non-violent non-co-operation as an alternative to violence. My faith in the possibility and necessity of Hindu-Muslim unity is as strong as ever. But so far as I am concerned, I have nothing but heart-felt prayer for its early achievement. I ask this vast audience to pray for the success of the deliberations of the Hindu and Mussalman leaders that are to take place on the 6th instant[2] and thereafter at Simla. My faith in the necessity of removing untouchability, which is a blot upon Hinduism, is also as green as ever.

I have been watching with very considerable interest the agitation that is going on in your midst on the part of some of the youths for the removal of the Neill Statue. To me it is like a cloud no bigger than a man's thumb. It is also like every other cloud capable of overspreading the Indian skies. I do hope that those who are owners of this statue will understand the significance of this movement although it appears to be trifling at the present moment. I appeal to the young men who are behind this

[1] At Triplicane Beach

[2] At Delhi

movement, of whom I have no knowledge whatsoever, not to spoil a good case by a single, hasty and inconsiderate step.

You have invited the National Assembly to meet here in this great city during the year. Madras enjoys the unique reputation of having one of its most distinguished sons as President[1] of this great Assembly. I cannot tell you how much I miss his presence this evening. It is up to you and up to every citizen of Madras to make the coming session of the Congress a brilliant success. I know that you have here, unfortunately, dissensions between Brahmins and Non-Brahmins. In view of the great task that lies in front of you, I beseech you, everyone, to see to it that these dissensions are removed so far as it is humanly possible to remove them and that they are not allowed to interfere with the preparations that you must make in order to ensure the success of the national gathering. I look forward to the time when we shall not think of Hindus, Mussalmans, Christians, Jews, Parsis, etc., or Brahmins, Non-Brahmins, untouchables, etc., as warring elements in our midst. But I look forward to the time—so long as these diversities must continue—when we shall all regard ourselves as branches of one great beautiful tree called the undivided and indivisible Indian Nation. And I wish that this so-called benighted city in the so-called benighted presidency should enjoy the honour of having brought about this desirable result.

And now I will come to the business that has brought me to Madras and that will send me to the end of this Southern Presidency. How I wish I could convince every one of you here that khadi is really calculated to become the best cement to bind all of us together. How I wish I could convince you that in all our little quarrels and squabbles we take little or no account of the voiceless millions whom for the time being we misrepresent. How I wish I could convince you that our obstinacy in not seeing the obvious results that must come from the adoption of khadi makes the progress of khadi itself so lamentably slow. And owing to the slowness of the progress of khadi, some of you turn against me and tell me that khadi has no vitality. And ignoring your obstinacy, you make the advance of khadi not only slow but you make the advance of the country itself almost impossible. And in your impatience to reach the common goal you refuse to see that you are yourselves the greatest obstacle in our march. You refuse to see the simple thing that is in front of you and then not finding any other activity you give way to unmanly despair. I ask you,

[1] S. Srinivasa Iyengar

for the sake of the country, for the sake of the toiling millions, for the sake of God, to shake yourselves free from this lethargy.

I wish that I had the courage to keep this great audience waiting to hear more of what is swelling up in my breast. I therefore conclude with the prayer to God who is watching over us all that He may give us the wisdom to see the path that lies in front of us and the courage to tread that path.

The Hindu, 5-9-1927

409. SPEECH ON "GITA", MADRAS[1]

September 4, 1927

I thank you for the address and the purse. The purse is doubly welcome to me as also the address after the knowledge that I have now gained that Mr. Sastri was the Headmaster of this school. I congratulate you on having given to the Servants of India Society, Mr. Gokhale's successor, and to India one of her most brilliant and devoted sons. Your school professes to be a Hindu school, with emphasis on the word "Hindu". I suppose therefore I have a right to expect something characteristic of the Hindu about all of you. If you will live up to your name you would be expected to show Hindu culture at its best in every one of your acts. I wonder if all of you are able to say that you have read the *Bhagavad Gita*. Those who have, will please raise their hands, honestly of course (about 10 persons raised their hands). Now it seems to me that in the very test I have applied the vast majority of you have failed. "If the salt loses its flavour wherewith shall it be salted?" I have given an English proverb, but there is a corresponding one which we know in the North and it is this: "When the ocean is on fire who will be able to quench the fire?" Will you not in all humility ask that question very seriously of every one of you? Will you not make a confession that you have been weighed and found wanting? Imagine a Christian High School and its Old Boys' Association being unaware of the contents of the Bible! Imagine a Mahomedan High School and the Muslim Old Boys' Association of that school not knowing the Koran, and don't you feel with me that every Hindu boy and, for that matter, every Hindu girl, should know the book in the Hindu scriptures which is equal to and should be in the estimation of the Hindu, the Koran and

[1] At Singarachari Hall, Hindu High School, Triplicane

Bible? I hope therefore that now that your eyes have been opened publicly you will immediately set about correcting yourself and understanding the message of the *Gita*. I would like to know how many of you know the elements of Sanskrit. Those of you who do know it, please raise your hands (A number of hands was raised). Thank you.

Half, or perhaps a little more than half of you know Sanskrit. Then let me inform you that the Sanskrit of the *Gita* is incredibly simple. Those of you who know Sanskrit should tomorrow, if possible today, buy the *Gita*—and I understand you can get the book for a very small price—and begin to study the book. Have private *Gita* classes for yourselves. Those of you who do not know Sanskrit should study Sanskrit only for the sake of the *Gita*. If you have not got that much facility, then you should read *Gita* written in English or in Tamil, if there is a Tamil translation of it. I tell you that it contains treasures of knowledge of which you have no conception whatsoever. I suggest to you that at first you may begin to read the third chapter of the *Gita*. You will find there the gospel of selfless work expounded in a most convincing manner. Selfless work there is described characteristically by one beautiful word called *yajna*. If you will read the book with my eyes you will find charkha also described there. There is one passage which says that "He who eats without serving, without *yajna*, is a thief."[1] I want you not to go to the dictionary for finding out the meaning of the word *yajna*. Do not run away with the idea that by purchasing a few faggots of wood and then burning them with ghee to the accompaniment of certain hymns, you have performed *yajna*. That the word has had that meaning at one time, there is no doubt about it; and when it did bear the meaning, it had its use. You will find in another part of the *Gita* an injunction almost that you must bring your intelligence and your reason to bear upon the meaning of the Shastras. Applying my reason to find out the meaning of this beautiful word I come to the conclusion that the *yajna* that you, I and these sisters and the old boys and the little girls can perform—it must be a *yajna* of that character in order to follow the context of the *Gita*—is nothing apart from the spinning-wheel. But I do not want to give you a discourse on the spinning-wheel. What I desire to tell you is that, if you will search that book through and through, you will find there mentioned in such simple words, *brahmacharya*, *satya*, ahimsa, *abhayam* and others which ought to be the primary qualities of every

[1] III. 12

man of God. The last word I leave with you is that you should read that book with a prayerful spirit, not in a carping spirit, and to obey the dictates of that book.

The Hindu, 5-9-1927

410. TELEGRAM TO MIRABEHN

MADRAS,
September 5, 1927

TO
MIRABEHN
SATYAGRAHA ASHRAM
WARDHA

SORRY FEVER PROVING OBSTINATE. PRAY TAKE PRESCRIBED MEDICINE. LOVE.

BAPU

From the original: C.W. 5268. Courtesy: Mirabehn

411. LETTER TO MIRABEHN

September 5, 1927

CHI. MIRA,

I have just got Jamnalalji's wire. The fever seems to be proving obstinate. It is better for you not to object to the medicines that the doctors may prescribe. There are many delicate reasons why you may not object to medicines under the circumstances that face you today.

My fear is that probably your brain is overwrought. You may have brooded much over the segregation matter and your future plans at the Ashram. Our motto is 'Be careful for nothing'. Anxiety is the mother of many diseases. But whatever the cause, let the physical effect be treated by physical remedies such as medicines, etc. Control of the mind and freedom from all care must be cultivated side by side. No anxiety please about speaking in Hindi to everybody there. My advice and expectations are always conditional. The condition being "consistently with capacity". Of your own capacity you must be the final judge. On no account must health be placed in jeopardy. I suppose Krishnadas and Valunjker are nursing you. I assume that you are keeping altogether cheerful in the midst of this pain and trial.

May God be your Rock, Help, Strength and All.
With love,

BAPU

From the original: C.W. 5270. Courtesy: Mirabehn

412. LETTER TO AN INMATE OF THE ASHRAM

September 5, 1927

I have your letter. It was good you gave me all the details. I cannot doubt you.

We should observe a convention which does not run counter to morality. *Brahmacharya* is said to be protected by nine hedges. If you have not read of it, do so in Raichandbhai's book. We neglect some of those hedges. I am responsible for this. Hence such neglect is only tentative. But we do observe the rule of never being alone in the company of even our own sister. I fully see the need for this. That protects both.

A *brahmachari* should be utterly humble and should not trust himself. There are two reasons for such diffidence. One is that he himself may thereby remain pure and the other is that the sister who comes in contact with him may not entertain lustful thoughts even in her dreams.

All the world has a right to suspect a *brahmachari* and it ought to have this right. The world does not observe *brahmacharya*. The world believes that no one can conquer the passions which it cannot itself conquer and that is only right. Hence we should not be offended by the world's suspicion. Know that all who stay there are included in the world.

Others have slipped through the liberty which you have taken innocently. In the beginning they were innocent. Even if you yourself have reached the stage at which you can never succumb to passion, you should still observe the restraints for the sake of others. We come across many who claim to observe *brahmacharya*. Could we allow them all to take such liberties?

I myself have not yet been able to conquer passions. Do you not know this? If I am not able to assure myself or the world about myself, you should be all the more careful about yourself.

Desire is a scorpion. One never knows when it will sting. It is *ananga*[1]. So we cannot see it; we cannot catch it, even if we try.

[1] Without body; in Indian mythology, sexual desire is symbolized by a deity without a body. The body of the God of love perished in the fire from Siva's third eye.

That is why a *brahmachari* has to remain ever vigilant.

What you write about Bhai Chhaganlal Joshi and others is not right. They are all making efforts. We do not live outside the world, nor do we wish to hate the passions in others; we only wish to be free from them ourselves and live on thus free.

You should therefore be vigilant. If you wish to ask me something more, do so.

[From Gujarati]

From the manuscript of Mahadev Desai's Diary. Courtesy: Narayan Desai

413. LETTER TO ASHRAM WOMEN

Silence Day [September 5, 1927][1]

SISTERS,

I have your note.

You must have understood the point of my suggestion that you should develop contacts with the women labourers of the Ashram. Getting a couple of cowries from them for relief work is just an excuse. The chief purpose is that through such occasions you should establish a bond of fellowship with them. You should try to understand each other and should partake of each other's joys and sorrows. I do not mean that you should spend much time over this. It is really a matter of change of heart. It should be your desire that they have the same food as we, and the same clothes, that they too get everything we desire and obtain for ourselves. And we should put this into practice as far as we can.

You will be overwhelmed if you try to give what I am saying a wide meaning. Words have at least two meanings—a narrow one and a broad one. We should try to comprehend the broader meaning, but begin cautiously to put into effect the narrower one, so that we are not crushed by the immensity of the task.

Blessings from
BAPU

From a photostat of the Gujarati: G.N. 3664

[1] From the reference to taking interest in the women labourers at the Ashram

414. LETTER TO SHANTIKUMAR MORARJI

[After *September 5, 1927*][1]

There are of course many types of valour in the world. There should be an Indian type for an Indian Victoria Cross. If a Gango Teli[2] moves with his bullock in endless circles and crushes oil for society and does it selflessly, is it not great valour? The devout Gango became famous obviously because he had courage. Why did not Ghelo[3] the oilman attain fame?

[From Gujarati]

From the manuscript of Mahadev Desai's Diary. Courtesy: Narayan Desai

415. SPEECH ON PROHIBITION, MADRAS[4]

September 6, 1927

FRIENDS,

I am supposed to talk to you this morning about prohibition. I don't remember having talked to a select audience on 'Prohibition' in my life except at one time, although I can claim to be a staunch prohibitionist as I am a staunch khaddarite. My life has been so cast that I get little chance of talking on such matters to a select audience. The one reason for that flaw in me is that I am a crank or I am supposed to be a crank, and therefore very often before a select audience I feel like a fish out of water. All cranks are necessarily extremists and where others feel the necessity for caution and moderation and such like about things that matter in life, I feel as if I am nowhere, as if I have no place. When someone says to me that in this practical world I must go slowly, I become impatient and tell him, "How can you go slowly in the matter of prohibition? You won't talk like that to a woman whose husband is a drunkard." I have lived in a family where the husband happened to be a drunkard. That was in Pretoria in 1893. The lady tried to make both ends meet and was always in dread as to what would happen when her lord and

[1] In the source this letter appears after the entries for September 5.

[2] Oilman

[3] A proper name also meaning 'silly'

[4] At Mani Aiyar Hall, Triplicane

master returned home. If I had told her that "In this practical world we must go slowly", she would not have allowed me to continue as her co-tenant. You may imagine me to be in that plight but not with one husband, not one but thousands of husbands. How can you ask me to wait? I become impatient, angry and, non-violent though I am, you will see fierceness in my eyes. I said the same thing to Mr. Anderson, the Secretary of the Temperance Association. I feel strongly about it. There are more things about which my feelings are strong and speech becomes useless for me. Those are really sacred things which I keep in my bosom and when opportunity offers itself I express my views strongly which the world cannot possibly mistake.

In this matter of prohibition we have some Englishmen with us, because they happen to be Missionaries or Christians. I do not know whether there are other Englishmen with us in this matter. They are all for some purpose too practical. They say we should realize the difficulties of Government. Why should I realize the difficulties of Government in this matter? The difficulties are purely financial and nothing else. There are three acid tests in this connection.

Not one Englishman has yet told me that prohibition is an impossibility in India except for finance. Everybody says: "Oh yes. You want to make India bear the burden of additional taxation by the introduction of prohibition, for the education of your children, etc." I would like India to become a pauper rather than that India should have lakhs and lakhs of drunkards in her midst in order to educate her children, or I would have Indian children illiterate rather than have drunkenness in the land as the price of their education. But when I am called upon to become a party to additional taxation I say "Hands off"; because there are other ways in which you can make up this financial loss. I think Government made the initial blunder of considering *abkari* as a source of revenue. It should never have been considered a source of revenue and it is not to be a source of revenue. And my grievance is definite and tangible that this source of revenue should have been left in charge of the transferred departments to meet the charges of education, sanitation, etc., so that our ministers have to fall back upon this immoral, sinful and hideous source of revenue. There is nothing so sinful as this kind of revenue. It is difficult to contain myself and I have therefore to talk to you in a strained language.

I feel that so far as India is concerned she has a complete case for prohibition and not prohibition piece-meal in one or two districts. I have read the speech of the Madras Excise Minister. I am sorry I have had to write something criticizing that speech in the coming issue of the *Young India*.[1] The method of experimenting in one or two districts does not appeal to me. I shall not be surprised if he makes the experiment in one or two districts and if the experiment fails then it would be said that prohibition can never be tried and it can never be successful. You will try to do the right thing in the wrong manner and then denounce the right thing instead of the wrong manner. The country is in favour of prohibition. If it is a question of lakhs and lakhs of signatures in favour of prohibition it is merely a matter of organization. I have not found a single place where there has been really agitation against prohibition except when it is manufactured and financed also. There are States where territorial prohibition has been declared and where not a single man has come forward to say "we want a shop at least here." In one of the States, Europeans, who consumed whisky and brandy, are exempted. But, we are in this matter terribly handicapped; we have as our rulers or Governors those who do not consider drink as a crime or immorality. I have myself English friends who laugh at me when I talk of prohibition. I have great regard for them. They seem to think that if they drink in moderation they would not lose their sense and would not become brutes. I have myself seen these friends not only losing their sense but becoming brutes. I have seen many friends losing self-control when they drink. They are first-class men. But when they drink they become asses. It may be excusable to have spirituous liquor in countries near the North Pole. There is no need in this country at all for drink. Yet some agitation is going on here against prohibition. I had [from someone] a pile of anti-prohibition pamphlets published anonymously. They constituted a hymn in praise of liquor. Radical, scriptural and all sorts of authorities have been quoted in favour of drinking in moderation and the whole thing has been presented in such an insidiously attractive form that a man who has not his wits about him may easily become a convert to the drink habit.

If you are a fierce prohibitionist like myself and if you will agitate from one end of the country to the other for prohibition, you will certainly succeed. Let us not fall into the financial trap that is laid for us. Our position should be absolutely clear. It is not our purpose to find out finances. Those who committed

[1] *Vide* "Total Prohibition", 8-9-1927.

the initial blunder must retrace their steps. There is also a way out of the financial difficulty. Cut out 25 crores from the crores upon crores you spend upon military expenditure. The military expenditure has been jumping from day to day. If you prepare a chart it would show a staggering growth of that expenditure. You can cut out a heavy slice from that expenditure. I must not go into the political history of the question. Whatever deficit that is found in connection with the *abkari* revenue should be made good out of military expenditure and no other. There should be no additional taxation on this score. The result will be that in 10 years' time the revenue of the Government will increase enormously and that is the experience of countries where prohibition has been tried.

Do not believe the interested writings in newspapers that total prohibition has been a failure in America. Scarcely an American who comes to India goes away without seeing me. These Americans and the literature published by the Prohibition League give the testimony that the sum-total effect of prohibition is to the good of the country although they have not been able to claim all the brilliant results that they had thought they would be able to have. There is no public opinion in America supporting the removal of prohibition. The Government is their own government and people are satisfied with the state of things there. The labourer leads a sober and honest life there. Is not that sufficient consideration for loss of revenue? Such a state of things exists in another part of the world, but not in India unfortunately. The experience of countries which have tried prohibition is that the people have become better and that the country has not been financially ruined. No ruin, no financial crisis will befall India if prohibition is introduced in India. It is the solemn duty of every one of us to see the use of drink wiped out of the land altogether if we possibly can. If I had the power and if I could have my way, I would do so today.

I come to picketing. I confess that some pickets were violent; but the real reason for Government not tolerating picketing was the loss of revenue. People in Bihar all on a sudden became teetotallers and they were faithful to the pickets. In Assam the same thing happened. The opium dens were closed for the time being. It was a thing too terrible for Government to contemplate. There was ample evidence to show that picketing was useful and necessary and it conferred immense benefit upon India. It showed the possibility of prohibition. In America prohibition has created a tremendous spiritual upheaval. But the task of creating that spiritual consciousness was great in America. But we in India have not the hundredth part of the difficulty that the Americans had to surmount. They had to surmount the American nature itself. Here it is not so for the atmosphere is favourable to prohibition. Therefore you need not go here cautiously. Arm-chair politicians who have no knowledge of the conditions of India do not distinguish between American and Indian life. They cannot see that we can attain prohibition if only you have the will and courage.

I make a distinction between opium and drink. Opium acts as an opiate and makes a man an idiot, whereas drink makes a man a beast. A woman would rather have her husband an idiot than a drunkard. I am willing to make an exception for the use of liquor or brandy for medicinal purposes. I make also the distinction between England and India. What is good enough for England is not necessarily good enough for India. If we allow this drink problem to continue, our posterity will curse us.

The Hindu, 6-9-1927

416. SPEECH AT HINDI PRACHAR OFFICE[1]

September 6, 1927

Gandhiji said it was superfluous for him to receive an address from the institution as he regarded it as his own.

Still I understand your view of the matter. This was till now a child being nourished and looked after by the generous people of the North. It has now become a youth who should look after himself and become self-reliant. I meant that henceforward South India should collect enough money from here to make the institution self-supporting.

I appeal to the Marwaris, Gujaratis and other northern settlers here to regard this institution as their own and pay more attention to the work in all possible ways. Marwaris are businessmen by nature and I want them to instil that spirit in the workers of this institution and help to make this a prosperous and successful one. I would like them to go through the accounts which are open to the public and give necessary instructions, if any, for improvement.

[1] In reply to addresses, one by the members of the Hindi Premi Mandal and another by the staff and workers of the Hindi Prachar Press

Lastly I want to tell the *pracharaks* that they can do successful work in this, as in other works of this sort, only if they would lead ideal lives and possess sterling character. For workers of this kind the first essential quality required is firmness and determination to push on the work to a successful end. I am sure the *pracharaks* will all make this their life-mission if they have not already done so.

The Hindu, 6-9-1927

417. LETTER TO MIRABEHN

[*September 7, 1927*]

CHI. MIRA,

I anxiously wait for your wires and they come but not to present me with a clean bill.[1] But we must not grumble. Even illness must be turned to advantage and must be taken cheerfully. Your last wire has come just now to tell me that perhaps fever is under control. Let us hope it is. I often think of wiring to you but say to myself I have no right. But my prayers and my blessings are with you always.

"The same in happiness and misery!" is the teaching of the *Gita*.

With love,

BAPU

From the original: C.W. 5271. Courtesy: Mirabehn

418. DISCUSSION WITH NEILL STATUE VOLUNTEERS, MADRAS

September 6 and 7, 1927

We publish today, with the approval of Mahatma Gandhi, a full report of the Conference which the volunteers of the Neill Statue agitation had with Mahatma Gandhi during his stay in Madras on Tuesday and Wednesday. . . . The notes were taken by *The Hindu* representative and were revised by Mahatma Gandhi.

Some 20 members of the Tamil Nadu Volunteer Corps who are now engaged in the agitation for the removal of the Neill Statue from the City on

[1] Mirabehn explains: "I had been having a severe attack of malaria. My temperature had been up to over 105."

Tuesday afternoon conferred with Mahatma Gandhi on the subject for over an hour. The conversations were not over and they were continued the next day.

Mr. D. Kulandai introduced himself as the leader of these young men and told Mahatmaji how he came into this movement. He said he was horrified at the barbarous sentences which were inflicted upon these youths by the Magistrate and he felt it necessary to give his help and advice as a Congressman and a Secretary of the District Congress Committee. He was not under any pledge and was not courting arrest.

GANDHIJI: Are there one or two who have been sentenced to two years' R.I. in this connection?

The answer was in the affirmative and Mr. Kulandai added that as a result of their intervention the sentences were not too severe.

KULANDAI: So far 27 had gone to prison on this issue, two of whom are ladies. Most of those had taken part in what was called the Sword Satyagraha at Madura and the total strength of the corps was 200 drawn mainly from Madura and Ramnad districts.

Who conceived this plan of attacking Neill Statue ?

And the reply was that Somayajulu and Srinivasavaradan were responsible.

That was after the failure at Madura?

A VOLUNTEER: It was not a failure at all. We went into the streets freely with our swords and we were not arrested. We have thus successfully broken the Arms Act.

Mahatmaji could not contain his laughter and told them not to delude themselves into thinking that it was a success.

When the Government saw what you were carrying were merely tin swords and you had no public backing, they left you alone in order not to give you any advertisement; and it is therefore no use in saying that because you were not arrested it is a success to your credit. When the Government removes the Arms Act and makes it possible for every Indian to carry arms you will have achieved your object. But remember that it is not possible. Not even a Swaraj Government can do without an Arms Act. Some check there ought to be.

Therefore, I would like you to believe that the Madura Satyagraha has failed. It is much better to own our failures, if we are to succeed henceforward.

Mahatmaji next put one or two questions to one or two of other volunteers to test their understanding of the real spirit of satyagraha.

That is why I asked you to define satyagraha. Unless you take up the definition from *Young India* and learn it, you are not going to succeed in a satyagraha campaign. If you are saturated with the true spirit of satyagraha, I will be at your back and the whole of India will be at your back.

One thing of practical value, I must tell you in this connection. You must not expect public associations to guide you or to identify themselves with satyagraha at the present moment. . . .

"Congress Committees included?" eagerly enquired one present.

Yes, at the present moment. I shall tell you why? The Congress has just now a very difficult task before it; and it cannot possibly handle these sectional movements. By sectional is not meant communal. If the Congress is called upon to help such movements, it will cut a sorry figure. The Congress has a status and a reputation to lose. Therefore it is much better for you young men not to expect the Congress or other public bodies to immediately shoulder your movement.

You know the agitation in Cherala-Perala[1]. I sympathized with it. I was keeping myself in touch with that movement. I had even gone to that place because I used to entertain a high regard for it; and addressed a large public meeting. At that time I had influence in the Congress which I do not possess now. Whatever I said then that the Congress should do, it automatically did and hardly any arguments were required. Even in those days I said to Cherala-Perala: "The Congress is not going to shoulder your agitation. The Congress when it is ready will initiate its own civil disobedience. But it cannot take on itself a movement, initiated by others, however great it may be or however ably it may be conducted. It can only look at it from a distance. It can take credit if the movement is successful and can never share the discredit if it becomes unsuccessful."

Mahatmaji then gave a chapter from his life in South Africa.

I was Secretary of the British Indian Association, brought into being by me. And when I embarked on satyagraha campaign there, I did not want to break up that Association, in which were all kinds of men, by making it a party to that agitation and thereby risking its reputation. From the moment I launched on the agitation, the British Indian Association was kept aloof from satyagraha. Therefore a new association was brought into being

[1] *Vide* Vol. XXI, pp. 16-8.

called Passive Resistance Association with a separate fund and separate officers. When the full victory was gained the British Indian Association took the credit. That was why I had been able to carry through the struggle without much difficulty. Difficulties there were. I was hammered almost to death. If I had made the blunder of dragging the British Indian Association into the agitation, I would have cut the Association into pieces and there would have been no South African victory. And I would have missed Mahatmaship.

So, you yourself must say to the Congress: 'You may remain out, let us try our strength in this agitation. You may share the success that we may achieve but not the discredit if we fail.' I met Mr. Satyamurti this morning and told him also that the Congress cannot possibly today adopt the movement. It will have to study the movement and the men. Let us not sully the fair name of the Congress by any hasty or ill-considered act. But I tell you this also: that when you have proved your mettle and your merit the Congress must be at your back. If the Congress is not at your back under these circumstances, I would be the first to denounce the Congress. In the mean time I want you to be absolutely honest to yourselves. Some persons told me, "Oh, oh, you don't know what they are. They are doing this for getting something in order to live, as they cannot live otherwise". Don't try to guess who the informants are and don't get angry. But falsify the accusation by your conduct.

A chit came at this stage giving the information that two of the youths who offered satyagraha had expressed their regret to the Magistrate and were let off with a fine.

"They are bogus volunteers," shouted one present.

I don't expect all of you to be sixteen annas in the rupee. Some wouldn't be a pie and a few not even that. The apology of the two does not therefore disturb me. And if they were bogus men, you have nothing to answer for.

KULANDAI: One difficulty I want to be cleared, Mahatmaji. Suppose the Government and the public know that the Congress is not supporting this movement, it is ten to one possible these boys will get more punishment and less support from the public. I went into this movement because, as I said, I was anxious as the Secretary of the District Congress Committee to save the honour and prestige of the Congress by not leaving these men in the lurch without sympathy or support.

I have already given an illustration of what I did in South Africa as Secretary of the British Indian Association.

KULANDAI: If the Government come to know that the Congress has no sympathy for this movement, all these boys would be clapped in jail.

It does not matter.

KULANDAI: Not only that, they will not get any support from the public.

Therefore my plan is to make you independent and self-supporting. We shall not take the name of the Congress, not until we have succeeded. You may take a leaf out of the book of our conquerors. Take the East India Company. It was not owned by the Crown. The Crown came afterwards. Therefore I say that the movement should not be conducted in the name of the Congress and with the authority of the Congress. As individual Congressmen you may carry on the fight.

A satyagrahi never acts hastily, exhausts all other resources before he resorts to civil disobedience. It is only then that the word 'civil disobedience' can be used and not otherwise. Yours may be civil disobedience, but if you have been hasty and have not exhausted all the other steps, then I say you should suspend your movement. I give you that advice so that public opinion may be consolidated in your favour, and so that you may be real satyagrahis. You should allow the public to take all the steps possible in their own way to remove the statue; and watch the Government whether they would do anything in the matter. If they don't do, then launch on satyagraha.

If you ask my opinion of what you should do, I shall give it. I should say you are right in your agitation, provided you fulfil the conditions I pointed out. I feel very much for you. It was by accident that I learnt of you and your movement in *The Hindu* and I at once wrote what I thought proper in *Young India*.[1] Now that I have seen you and talked to you, I shall try to do more. But before I can do so, I want a guarantee that there is no dishonesty, no self-glorification at least about the leaders of the movement. The leaders may be cobblers or tailors, it does not matter. I want to make sure that your leaders are pure and above board and are not actuated by any expectation of any pecuniary reward. A satyagrahi must stand or fall on his own strength of will.

Don't give me an answer now. I shall give you another opportunity of meeting me. You consider carefully what I have said and tell me when you come back what your plan is. I want you to give me a list of all the volunteers you have, their age, address

[1] *Vide* "Notes", 25-8-1927, sub-title "Insolent Reminders".

and occupation; and I want Mr. Kulandai as Congressman to give his certificate, if necessary, about the honesty of the movement and about the trustworthiness of the men in it. If you do not satisfy me in this simple test, you cannot go forward. You have already done spade work. The Neill Statue has got to go some time or other. The success will depend on our own strength. There is no danger in your slowing down.

Replying to Mr. M. S. Subramania Iyer, Mahatmaji said:

The present method might be a satyagrahic act or a violent act. It all depends on the motive. The motive would decide the character of the act. Damage to or destruction of an inanimate object is not always a violent act.

PAVALAR: Do you advise, Mahatma, to suspend the movement?

Yes, if you have not the real strength. But please consider well and tell me what you think, tomorrow.

When the conversations were resumed on Wednesday afternoon, one of the volunteers read the following statement as representing their opinion as a result of the discussions they had that morning and the previous night in the light of the advice given by Mahatmaji:

We have carefully considered your advice given to us yesterday and we have also had a discussion with Mr. S. Satyamurti last night. We have since reconsidered the whole matter this morning. We realize that the situation is a difficult and complex one. We would therefore prefer your advising us as to what we should do now. We will follow your advice. We only crave leave to place before you our considered views for your favourable consideration. We are very anxious that the enthusiasm roused by this movement should not be allowed to fade. We recognize that in order to carry on this struggle to a successful issue we must exhaust all other means of getting the statue removed, must rouse public enthusiasm and organize ourselves. We are afraid that if the movement be suspended without adequate provision being made for keeping up the enthusiasm of the people for organizing the movement and for trying every available means of getting the statue removed the movement may die of inanition. We are anxious therefore that the enthusiasm now roused by the movement should be kept up by all legitimate and peaceful means and that if the movement is to be suspended it should be done as the result of your advice so stated publicly. Moreover, the suspension should be for the express purpose of resorting to this movement at the proper time on a more efficient scale, if necessary.

With a view to that we respectfully suggest that you should be pleased to give this movement a paragraph in *Young India* each week and speak about it in the course of your tour in Tamil Nadu. Moreover, we should like to have the strength of an assurance from you that at the proper time and if all other means fail you will yourself help us in this movement in all possible ways.

If these things secure your approval we agree for the suspension of the movement for three months as suggested by you. In the mean time we request you to use your influence with the local Congress leaders to give us the necessary help to keep up the agitation for the removal of the statue.

What is the necessary help?

VOLUNTEER: Delivering lectures, enlisting volunteers and strengthening our financial position—these are the ways in which we expect Mahatmaji to help us.

What is the financial assistance for?

The volunteer replied that the volunteers, about a hundred of them, were scattered over Madura and Ramnad Districts. To encamp them, to feed and bring them to Madras money was required.

They are supporting themselves at present?

VOLUNTEER: Yes.

Therefore no money is required for their support at present?

Answer to this question also was in the affirmative.

I should imagine that no money would be required in the future even?

VOLUNTEER: We want money for propaganda work.

What propaganda work?

VOLUNTEER: Convening meetings to get support for the enlistment of volunteers.

Supposing the Congress holds meetings, you wouldn't require money. Your business really arises when you have to go to jail. The question of bringing volunteers to Madras is a small matter. You do not want all the thousand volunteers, even supposing you have that number, to arrive at Madras at the same time. You are going to court arrest only in twos at the most. A true satyagrahi who is courting arrest and who is even prepared to die for his cause would not want any train fare from you. He is sure to find the train fare himself. If he has not the money himself, other people in his place are sure to find it for him. As for propaganda work, you need not do it yourselves; others will do it for you.

You must really leave finance out of your consideration. Money when required will come to you. But you must not insist upon it. And you must do only what is in your capacity to do and no more. I am interested in your cause because it is an appealing one. I do not want that it should get discredited. That is why I gave you an hour yesterday and another today. I repeat that you must erase financial consideration out of your mind. Otherwise, the thing will break down.

If you want to continue this fight with determination, you must do it in the gentlest manner possible. You must be absolutely honest and self-disciplined; there must be no bluster or violence. You must rely on the innate strength of satyagraha. Some day it is sure to gather irresistible strength. If you think you have not the required strength or patience in you, leave it at once. You have done your part. You have laid the foundation. The struggle will go on and the statue will go because it seeks to perpetuate terrorism of the worst type. The best place for it is the sea. Barring that it must go to England or some lumber room.

The second thing I want to tell you is that by a suspension of the movement if you are afraid of getting disorganized and disunited, I do not want you to stop. But if you do not think so and after three months you would still hold together, you issue a manifesto that you have suspended the struggle saying therein we have been so advised and therefore we have done so. We now expect the Congress and all the public associations to take up this thing in hand and do whatever they can, to have this statue removed. When it has become sufficiently demonstrated that this kind of agitation won't move the Government, it will be our turn to suffer. Then let it not be said against us that we have been hasty and that once having drawn attention to it, we did not give a chance for the removal of the statue. For these reasons we suspend satyagraha.

Then comes my part in the struggle. I cannot say I won't lead the struggle; nor am I able to say I shall certainly do so. It will depend on how I feel at the time and how you yourselves have behaved in the mean time. In these matters I am guided by impulse—impulse is not the right word—I wish to say intuition, a sacred word. But all the support the *Young India* can give will be entirely yours. I shall do whatever I can to educate public opinion through its columns.

In answer to a question:

The final decision will rest with you and not with me. I would not absolve you from your own responsibility. You are the originators; I can only direct your energy in proper channel and give you advice. But if you accept my advice and use my name, then you will understand you will do it on my terms. I have given them to you already. I shall reduce them to writing if you want. If there is a departure from those terms by a hair's breadth even, I shall have nothing to do with it. The cause is good. It will be damaged if at the back of it are bad men. The movement must be a *bona fide* movement. If it is found that you speak one thing with your lips and mean another, I would not hesitate to denounce it.

To Satyamurti:

What do you say to this? Do you think that the Congress may or will take up this question in any way?

SATYAMURTI: I see no objection to the Congress taking it up. As far as I can ascertain from friends, the general feeling is that the movement must be supported. What we can do is that in the Corporation we can move resolutions and in the Legislative Council also. And I think we will. Besides that we will use the Press and the platform to create a feeling against the statue as representing terrorism as Mahatmaji put it. For this no financial responsibility need be taken by the young men. The Congress will find money. Is that right, Mr. Kulandai?

KULANDAI: That is one view of the subject.

SATYAMURTI: Even about Congress doing it?

KULANDAI: If this opportunity is lost the South Indian temperament is such that the whole thing will fizzle out. That is my own honest individual opinion. If the majority are for suspending it now and taking it up again after three months and if the Congress Committees will do the propaganda work as efficiently as they have been doing the work . . .

SATYAMURTI: That is for you, the Secretary of the District Congress Committee.

KULANDAI: My own honest impression is that the moment we give it up, the movement is lost for ever. Three months means never. The enthusiasm evoked in this presidency over this matter is genuine and it should not be allowed to die out. It is not North Indian temperament, Mahatmaji.

I don't consider that North India is any better than South India. We are chips of the same block. Absolutely no difference.

A VOLUNTEER: Our only fear is from the incident which took place two days back. Every one of us may not be an absolute satyagrahi. We don't want demoralization to set in. We want to organize ourselves well; and we want to add more to our number by our further agitation and propaganda. We do not know who among us are real satyagrahis. We started the movement all on a sudden.

Therefore this is really a new ground for suspension.

VOLUNTEER: I do not want at the same time that the Government should be given rest. The agitation must go on in other ways to remove the statue. Ours is only a strategic retreat and no surrender. It is meant for us to go forward with redoubled vigour. We do not want to confess our inability because it would have a demoralizing effect.

This is a new situation. You are really now desirous of covering your weakness under my name.

VOLUNTEER: No, we are merely respecting Mahatmaji's opinion and advice; and we follow it, lest Mahatmaji should denounce us and lose real satyagrahis.

You said it may be a strategic move. That means you are not at present a well-organized body of real satyagrahis. You may say that it is a discovery you made after conversation with me, and you want to postpone the movement irrespective of all other considerations in order to make up for this defect. There is room for that honest strategy in satyagraha. In making an announcement of your suspension, you can state that after conversations with me you were ill-prepared to satisfy the test that I laid down and recognizing that unless you could fulfil that test, the movement would not succeed, you proposed to postpone this thing for 3 months, during which time you proposed to equip yourselves well so as to satisfy the test and that you would afterwards reopen satyagraha, if in the mean time the offending statue was not removed. That would be the correct satyagraha state. Or do you say you are now ready?

VOLUNTEER: We want the Neill Statue to be removed. If the hundred volunteers we have with us are exhausted, the movement will automatically stop. But the statue may not be removed. Thus we would have failed in our purpose. We want a continuous stream of volunteers coming up until the statue is removed.

You suspend in order to ensure a continuous stream. Suspension therefore is required on that ground. On the other hand, if you feel that you must finish the one hundred or twenty, do so and let it not be said that your enthusiasm was allowed by suspension to cool down. But I must tell you again that in satyagraha there are occasions for suspension. Did I not suspend the Vykom Satyagraha?

You say there would be demoralization if you suspend satyagraha stating you are not ready now. There is no such thing as demoralization in satyagraha. A satyagrahi relies upon his own internal strength and not outside support. But I would feel shocked if at the end of three months you are not ready and if the statue is still there, as is bound to be there, because you know the Government will not yield easily and without a tremendous effort.

Don't really suspend if you have any fear of its fizzling out. If you want to suspend it, do it on this absolute frank admission that under the circumstances I have mentioned now, you want to suspend.

A VOLUNTEER: Why shall we not go forward?

Yes; I do not want to clamp the zeal of a single man among you. I am anxious to be cautious in this matter.

A VOLUNTEER: We want to ask you one question. That is whether Mahatmaji will give us his support?

Yes, I will support you so long as I find you on the straight road.

Another offer I will make, if you want. I have got complete notes of yesterday; and I believe today also notes are being taken. If you like, I will have them published. It is right for you to let the public know about it. If you don't want the publication, I shall not do so. I tell you there is no harm in publishing what has happened here; and there is no secrecy about it. Shall I publish them?

VOICES: Yes, yes.

A VOLUNTEER: We shall leave it to your choice to continue the struggle or leave it.

If I were in your place I will suspend the movement making this confession that we are not fully equipped and strong. If you make that confession, you must suspend the movement.

PAVALAR: Some are afraid and some are not. They want your advice, Mahatmaji.

I have given the advice that if I were you, I would suspend.

A VOLUNTEER: Do you permit us to proceed with our struggle?

I don't prohibit you; in that sense you have my permission.

A VOLUNTEER; You will bless the movement?

You have had my blessings; I shall bless you again.

ANOTHER VOLUNTEER: As for suspending the movement, if you advise us to suspend, we are prepared to suspend.

I cannot take any responsibility. You must not suspend in deference to anybody else. If you suspend, you will do so in response to your own inner voice.

VOLUNTEER: We don't find our inner voice asking us to suspend.

Then go on.

VOLUNTEER: We shall continue the struggle in the manner in which we are doing at present. Meanwhile we request you to give your support. We will conduct the movement in perfect satyagraha spirit and well-disciplined. But if outsiders of their own accord come in our way and cause disturbance, we request Mahatmaji not to blame us. Further, we want you to write in *Young India*.

In *Young India*, certainly.

VOLUNTEER: We request you to advise some local Congress leaders to do propaganda work.

I shall certainly advise them. I have discussed the whole thing with Mr. Satyamurti. I suppose he will tell them. I shall publicly advise Congressmen; and you will find it in the notes also to which I have referred. You go on fearlessly; only don't have complications. Don't countenance violence or untruth. Either will spoil the cause.

In reply to another volunteer:

You will give me the list of volunteers, with their age, address and occupation. I shall scan the list. You must publish the list also to make the public know who are the authorized satyagrahis. If anyone offers satyagraha he does at his own risk. If more men come into your hand, publish their names also. When you go to the statue don't attract the public. Go there in the night, even dead of night, in order to avoid a crowd. Give, however, intimation to the police about the time you go there. If you come to know that the police give intimation of the time to the public or people whom they want to create mischief, then you would not inform the Police at all. Let not the public interfere with your work. If they want to take part, let them hold demonstration elsewhere, hold meetings, pass resolutions.

This closed the Conference and the volunteers withdrew.

The Hindu, 10-9-1927

419. SPEECH AT PACHAIYAPPA'S COLLEGE, MADRAS[1]

September 7, 1927[2]

MR. PRINCIPAL, STUDENTS AND FRIENDS[3],

I thank you sincerely for all the gifts you have given me for *Daridranarayana.* This is not the first time I enter this Hall. It was in 1896 that I entered this Hall in connection with the struggle in South Africa.[4] Dr. Subramania Aiyar of revered memory presided at the function. The reason why I recall this meeting is that I made the acquaintance of the students of India then for the first time. As you may know I am a matriculate, and therefore never had any college education worth the name in India. But when after the address was finished and the thanksgiving completed I went out to students who were lying in wait for me and took away from me all the copies of the "Green Pamphlet"[5] that I was then circulating throughout India, and it was for the sake of those students that I asked the late Mr. G. Parameshwaran Pillai, who befriended the cause and me as no one else did, to print copies and circulate them. With supreme pleasure he printed 10,000 copies of the Pamphlet. Such was the demand on the part of the students for understanding the situation in South Africa and it pleased me immensely, and I said to myself, "Yes, India may be proud of her children and may base all her hopes upon them." Since that time my acquaintance with students has been growing in volume and intensity. As I said in Bangalore,[6] "more is expected from those who give much, and since you have given me so much you have also given me the right to expect much more. I shall never be satisfied with all that you could give me! You have endorsed some of the work that it has been my privilege to do. You have mentioned with affection and reverence in your address the name of *Daridranarayana* and you, Sir (Principal), have—and I have no doubt with utmost sincerity—endorsed the claim that I have made on behalf of the spinning-wheel. Many of my distinguished and learned countrymen, I know, have rejected

[1] This was published under the caption, "Two Speeches".

[2] & [3] From *The Hindu*, 7-9-1927

[4] *Vide* Vol. II, pp. 94-121.

[5] *Vide* Vol. II, pp. 1-70.

[6] *Vide* "Speech at Citizens' Meeting, Bangalore", 28-8-1927.

that claim, saying that the little bit of a wheel which was happily put away by our sisters and our mothers could never lead to the attainment of swaraj. And yet you have endorsed that claim and pleased me immensely. Though you, students, have not said as much in your address, yet you have said sufficient in it to warrant the belief that you have in your hearts a real corner for the spinning-wheel. Let not therefore this purse be the first and last demonstration of your affection for the spinning-wheel. I tell you it would be an embarrassment for me if it is the last demonstration of your affection; for I shall have no use for the money if the khadi that may be produced through the distribution of that money amongst the starving millions is not used by you. After all a lip profession of faith in the charkha and the throwing of a few rupees at me in a patronizing manner won't bring swaraj and won't solve the problem of the ever-deepening poverty of the toiling and starving millions. I want to correct myself. I have said toiling millions. I wish that it was a true description. Unfortunately, as we have not revised our tastes about clothing, we have made it impossible for these starving millions to toil throughout the year. We have imposed upon them a vacation, which they do not need, for at least four months in the year. This is not a figment of my imagination, but it is a truth repeated by many English administrators, if you reject the testimony of your own countrymen who have moved in the midst of these masses. So then if I take this purse away and distribute it amongst the starving sisters, it does not solve the question. On the contrary it will impoverish their soul. They will become beggars and get into the habit of living upon charity. Heaven help the man, the woman or the nation that learns to live on charity! What you and I want to do is to provide work for those sisters of ours living protected in their own homes, and this is the only work that you can provide them with. It is dignified and honest work, and it is good enough work. One anna may mean nothing to you. You will throw it away in getting into a tram car and lazily passing your time instead of taking exercise for 2, 3, 4 or 5 miles as the case may be. But when it finds its way into the pockets of one poor sister it fructifies. She labours for it and she gives me beautiful yarn spun by her sacred hands, a yarn that has a history behind it. It is a thread worth weaving a garment out of, for princes and potentates. A piece of calico from a mill has no such history behind it. I must not detain you over this one theme, great as it is for me, and though it engrosses practically the whole of my time. *This purse of yours will not be a help but a hindrance to me if it is not an earnest of your determination henceforth, if you have not it already, that you are not going to wear anything else but khadi.*

Let me not be deluded into the belief that you believe in this gospel of khadi, because you give me the purse and because you applaud me. I want you to act up to your profession. I do not want it to be said of you—the salt of India—that you gave this money merely to bamboozle me, that you do not want to wear khadi and that you have no belief in it. Do not fulfil the prophecy that had been made by a distinguished son of Tamil Nadu and a friend of mine. He has said that when I die I will not need any other firewood to reduce my corpse to ashes but the wood that will be collected out of the spinning-wheels that I am now distributing. He has no faith in the charkha and he thinks that those who utter the name of the charkha do so merely out of respect for me. It is an honest opinion. It will be a great national tragedy if the khadi movement turns out to be that and you will have been direct contributors to the tragedy and participators in that crime. It will be a national suicide. If you have no living faith in the charkha, reject it. It would be a truer demonstration of your love; you will open my eyes and I shall go about my way crying hoarse in the wilderness: "You have rejected the charkha and thereby you have rejected *Daridranarayana*." But save me and save yourselves the pain, the degradation and the humiliation that await us if there is any delusion or camouflage about this. This is one thing. But there are many things more in your address.

You have mentioned there child marriage and child widows. A learned Tamilian has written to me to address students on child widows. He has said that the hardships of child widows in this presidency are far greater than those of child widows in other parts of India. I have not been able to test the truth of this statement. You should know that better than I do. But what I would like you, young men around me, to do is that you should have a touch of chivalry about you. If you have that, I have a great suggestion to offer. I hope the majority of you are unmarried, and a fair number of you are also *brahmacharis*. I have to say "a fair number" because I know students; a student who casts his lustful eyes upon his sister is not a *brahmachari*. I want you to make this sacred resolve that you are not going to marry a girl who is not a widow, you will seek out a widow girl and if you cannot get a widow girl you are not going to marry at all. Make that determination, announce it to the world, announce it to your parents if you have them or to your sisters. I call them widow girls by way of correction because I believe that a child ten or fifteen years old, who was no consenting party to the so-called marriage, who having married, having never lived with the so-called husband, is suddenly declared to be a widow, is not a widow. It is an abuse of the term, abuse of language and a sacrilege. The word 'widow' in Hinduism has a sacred odour about it. I am a worshipper of a true widow like the late Mrs. Ramabai Ranade who knew what it was to be a widow. But a child nine years old knows nothing of what a husband should be. If it is not true that there are such child widows in the presidency, then my case falls to the ground. But if there are such child widows, it becomes your sacred duty to make the determination to marry a girl widow if you want to rid ourselves of this curse. I am superstitious enough to believe that all such sins that a nation commits react upon it physically. I believe that all these sins of ours have accumulated together to reduce us to a state of slavery. You may get the finest constitution that is conceivable dropping upon you from the House of Commons. It will be worthless if there are not men and women fit enough to work that constitution. Do you suppose that we can possibly call ourselves men worthy of ruling ourselves or others or shaping the destiny of a nation containing 30 crores so long as there is one single widow who wishes to fulfil her fundamental wants but is violently prevented from doing so? It is not religion, but irreligion. I say that, saturated as I am with the spirit of Hinduism. Do not make the mistake that it is the Western spirit in me that is speaking. I claim to be full to overflowing with the spirit of India undefiled. I have assimilated many things from the West but not this. There is no warrant for this kind of widowhood in Hinduism.

All I have said about child widows necessarily applies to child wives. You must be able surely to control your lust to this extent, that you are not going to marry a girl that is under 16 years of age. If I could do so I would lay down 20 as the minimum. Twenty years is early enough even in India. It is we who are responsible for the precocity of girls, not even the Indian climate, because I know girls of the age of 20 who are pure and undefiled and able to stand the storm that may rage round. Let us not hug that precocity to ourselves. Some Brahmin students tell me that they cannot follow this principle, that they cannot get Brahmin girls sixteen years old, very few Brahmins keep their daughters unmarried till that age, the Brahmin girls are married mostly before 10, 12 and 13 years. Then I say to the Brahmin youth, "Cease to be a Brahmin, if you cannot possibly control yourself." Choose a grown-up girl of 16 who became a widow when she was a child. If you cannot get a Brahmin widow who has reached that age, then go and take any girl you like. And I tell you that the God of the Hindus will pardon that boy who has preferred to marry out of his caste rather than ravish a girl of twelve. When your heart is not pure and you cannot master your passions, you cease to be an educated man. You have called your institution a premier institution. I want you to live up to the name of the premier institution which must produce boys who will occupy the front rank in character. And what is education without character and what is character without elementary personal purity? Brahminism I adore. I have defended Varnashrama Dharma. But Brahminism that can tolerate untouchability, virgin widowhood, spoliation of virgins, stinks in my nostrils. It is a parody of Brahminism. There is no knowledge of Brahman therein. There is no true interpretation of the scriptures. It is undiluted animalism. Brahminism is made of sterner stuff. I want these few remarks of mine to go deep down into your hearts. I am watching the boys whilst I am pouring out my heart. I have not come to appeal to your intellects but to your hearts. You are the hope of the country and what I have said is of primary importance for you.

In response to the request of a Calicut professor I shall now proceed to say something about cigarette smoking and coffee and tea drinking. These are not necessities of life. There are some who manage to take ten cups of coffee a day. Is it necessary for their healthy development and for keeping them awake, for the performance of their duties? If it is necessary to take coffee or tea to keep them awake, let them not drink coffee or tea but go to sleep. We must not become slaves to these things. But the majority of the people who drink coffee or tea are slaves to them. Cigars and cigarettes, whether foreign or indigenous, must be avoided. Cigarette smoking is like an opiate and the cigars that you smoke have a touch of opium about them. They get to your nerves and you cannot leave them afterwards. How can a single student foul his mouth by converting it into a chimney? If you give up these habits of smoking cigars and cigarettes and drinking coffee and tea you will find out for yourselves how much you are able to save. A drunkard in Tolstoy's story is hesitating to execute his design of murder so long as he has not smoked his cigar. But he puffs it, and then gets up smiling and saying, "What a coward am I," takes the dagger and does the deed. Tolstoy spoke from experience. He has written nothing without having had personal experience of it. And he is much more against cigars and cigarettes than against drink. But do not make the mistake that between drink and tobacco, drink is a lesser evil. No. If cigarette is Beelzebub, then drink is Satan.

There is the Hindi Prachar office supported by people in the North. They have spent nearly a lakh of rupees and the Hindi teachers have been doing their work regularly. Some progress has been made but we have yet to make substantial progress. You can all learn Hindi in one year provided you give one hour a day. You can understand simple Hindi in six months. I can't speak to you in Hindi because most of you do not know it. Hindi should be made the universal tongue in India. You should know also Sanskrit, for then you will be able to read *Bhagavad Gita.* As students of a premier Hindu institution, you ought to be taught *Bhagavad Gita.* I would expect Mussalman boys also to read in this institution.

A VOICE: No *Panchama* is admitted.

This is a discovery to me. This institution should be flung open to *Panchamas* and Mussalmans. I would de-Hinduize this institution if a *Panchama* has no entry here. (Hear! hear!) The fact that this is a Hindu institution is no reason why a Mussalman or a *Panchama* could not receive education here. I think it is high time that the trustees revise their constitution. This is a petition from me, an earnest and a very god-fearing Hindu, saturated with the spirit of Hinduism, not from a petty-fogging reformer, but from one who is trying to live the best in Hinduism. Mr. Principal, you will please convey this petition to the proper quarters, and it will be a great joy to me to hear during my sojourn in this presidency that my petition has been heard.[1] I thank you for listening to this message.

Young India, 15-9-1927

[1] The principal of the College in his vote of thanks said that attempts were being made to throw open the College to all classes of Indians.

420. *SPEECH AT ROYAPURAM, MADRAS*[1]

September 7, 1927

FRIENDS,

I thank you for the address and purse for khadi. I am glad to find that you are taking interest in all that pertains to the Congress. And it pleases me to find your assurance that you are determined to do your share of work in making the forthcoming Congress a thorough success. The Reception Committee here has unanimously elected a tried servant of India to preside over the deliberations. He comes to his task with one great mission that he has set before himself. Dr. Ansari, Surgeon, and one of the best surgeons that India has produced, surgeon that he is, is bent upon healing the breach between Hindus and Mussalmans. I know that many Provincial Congress Committees gave their votes in favour of Dr. Ansari's name in the high hope that his chairmanship of the Congress will result in healing the deep wounds. But let us not make the mistake of supposing that because we have elected him our task is fulfilled. A patient's task is never fulfilled simply because he calls in for his assistance the wisest and best surgeon. He is expected to co-operate with his surgeon body and mind. He is expected to be faithful to the directions of the surgeon. We are the patients. Dr. Ansari is the surgeon whom we have invited. And if we do not co-operate with him in the great task that he has undertaken, the fault will not be his but ours. And since the greatest burden will fall upon the shoulders of those Congressmen who are in Madras and delegates that will flock in largest numbers from the South, it is a matter of great pleasure to me that you are determined to make this Congress a success. You have taken upon your shoulders a very great and grave responsibility. I understand that Sjt. S. Srinivasa Iyengar is daily in telegraphic communication with the secretary here betraying his care and anxiety about the forthcoming session of the Congress. It is for the men and women of Madras to lighten his labours and make his task easy. We must not expect our leaders to do everything for us. It is often heard against us as a reproach that we, the rank and file, will not put the shoulders to the wheel. I would like Madras to remove the reproach.

[1] At Kalmandapam Maidan

You have declared your faith in the spinning-wheel and khadi. You tell me in your address that if arrangements are made for supplying you with cotton and for taking all the yarn that may be spun off your shoulders, you will be able to organize spinning and weaving of khadi. If you are serious about this matter you have to go one step further. You must form your own committee and find your own cotton. Every spinner in order to be a good spinner has got to learn carding and make his or her own sliver. You should aim at weaving all the yarn that is produced; that is the best and cheapest method of producing khadi. If you cannot weave khadi for yourselves and if you give good, strong, even and weavable yarn the All-India Spinners' Association will certainly take up all the yarn that you can give.

I understand that this is a labour centre. To the fellow labourers I would say just one word. You must give up drink at any cost. And so must you gambling and vice. It is not a difficult task for the labourers to give up this great curse of drink which is sapping their vitality and morals. Indian labour has a bright future before it if it will only help itself. The best beginning in self-help is self-purification. Let the labourers also remember that there are millions who are, so far as finance is concerned, brothers infinitely worse than they are. And if they will but think of these brothers and sisters who are poorer and worse off than they are, they will at least adopt khadi. I know that all the men and the sisters here have not contributed to this purse. Volunteers will be presently going in your midst and if you desire to contribute something please do so. No one need give a single pie unless she or he believes in khadi. The pies of the poor are just as welcome as the rupees of the rich if either is given with a willing heart.

There is a request made to me just now that I should talk about the Neill Statue Satyagraha. I have said what was in my mind at the meeting in the Beach.[1] I gave more than one hour yesterday and more than one hour today also to those volunteers who could come to discuss the matter with me. I have given them all the advice that I was capable of giving. You will find in a day or two the substance of the conversation in the papers; and the notes of this interview, as soon as I get them, will be revised by me and then there will be an authentic publication.[2] But this much I would like to declare here. The cause appeals

[1] *Vide* "Speech at Public Meeting, Madras", 4-9-1927.

[2] *Vide* "Discussion with Neill Statue Volunteers", 6 & 7-9-1927.

to me most forcibly. I have not a shadow of doubt that that statue must be removed from that site. I have seen the inscription there with its false history.[1] The statue there is a standing insult to the nation, and the volunteers deserve congratulation for having drawn attention to the existence of the statue by their suffering. But every cause or many causes in this world have been ruined by bad management and bad handling. The volunteers, if they continue the fight, will have to take care that no dirt creeps into their movement. If satyagraha is a very fine weapon to handle, it is also a very dangerous weapon. It becomes a dangerous weapon if the slightest uncleanliness touches it. Just as the tiniest drop of poison makes the most wholesome milk unfit for human consumption, so it is the slightest touch of impurity spoils the battle of satyagraha and damages both the cause and those who are connected with it. If there is the slightest violence on the part of the satyagrahi or if there is the slightest departure from truth, they will damage themselves and the cause. Satyagraha abhors secrecy. It is the openest form of warfare I have ever known. Similarly, satyagraha abhors cowardice. And he who preaches satyagraha with any selfishness about him damns himself. Satyagraha is a weapon which can be handled without the slightest financial support—because it is the essence of suffering. The greater the amount of suffering voluntarily undertaken, the quicker and purer is the success. If therefore the satyagrahis approach their task well, understanding these conditions and limitations and if they will fulfil all these conditions, let them rest assured that success is doubtless theirs. If they do not possess these qualifications and if they have no faith in these conditions let them give up satyagraha. I shall count it as bravery on their part, if they give up satyagraha because they cannot fulfil its conditions. It also requires a certain measure of bravery to own up one's mistakes or limitations and retrace one's steps. But if they will fulfil the conditions I have stated just now, they have my blessings and they will deserve the blessings and encouragement of every patriot.

The Hindu, 8-9-1927

[1] *Vide* Vol. XXXV, pp. 53–5.

421. TOTAL PROHIBITION

> I ask you to realize the fact that the alteration of the present Abkari Act with regard to making, manufacture and possession of liquor, etc., must necessarily, to a large extent, lead to harassing of the people. You must be prepared for such a harassment which is an inevitable concomitant of the policy of prohibition. I must count then upon your unstinted support. I do not want your support for picketing shops, to preach about the evils of drink and other kindred work. But I want your help in the matter of putting down illicit manufacture of liquor and kindred crimes.

This is an extract from the speech of the Madras Minister for Public Health and Excise reported in *The Hindu*. There is one more assistance the Minister has asked the people to render, i.e., submit to increased taxation. Of this I do not propose at present to say anything except that where the people are able, they should submit to further taxation on proof of necessity. No monetary cost is too great to pay for achieving total prohibition.

But at the present moment, I would confine myself to the extract quoted by me. I fear that the Minister has taken a wrong view of prohibition. In my opinion, it has not to be taken piecemeal. To be successful it should be taken as a whole. It is not a one-district question but it is an all-India question. I have not hesitated to give my opinion, that it was a wicked thing for the Imperial Government to have transferred this the most immoral source of revenue to the provinces and to have thus made this tainted revenue the one source for defraying the cost of the education of Indian youth.

But what pains me about the Minister's speech is his superficial treatment of a question which affects the well-being of the masses. Surely he is not serious about his scheme if he expects the people to do his police work. And why does he frighten the people by saying that *there must be harassment* if prohibition is tried? Is there harassment of the people because theft or manufacture of gunpowder are classed as crimes? Is not unlicensed distillation even now a crime? What the Minister implies therefore is that the men who today hold licences to manufacture or sell liquor will after the prohibition distil surreptitiously and that therefore they will be harassed. There need be in this no harassment of the people.

But it betrays want of imagination and lack of sympathy with the people, if the Minister believes that as a prohibitionist he has nothing more to do but to declare prohibition and prosecute those who will break his laws. I venture to submit that prosecutions are the smallest and the destructive part of prohibition. I suggest that there is a larger and constructive side to prohibition. People drink because of the conditions to which they are reduced. It is the factory labourers and others that drink. They are forlorn, uncared for, and they take to drink. They are no more vicious by nature than teetotallers are saints by nature. The majority of people are controlled by their environment. Any minister who is sincerely anxious to make prohibition a success will have to develop the zeal and qualities of a reformer. He will then require precisely the help that the Madras Minister is reported to have scorned. In my humble opinion, he does need pickets and men and women who would "preach about the evils of drink" and do "other kindred work." It is just in these very things that he will want an army of volunteers who will be associated with him in reforming the life of the drunkard. He will have to convert every drink shop into a refreshment shop and concert room combined. Poor labourers will want some place where they can congregate and get wholesome, cheap, refreshing, non-intoxicating drinks, and if they can have some good music at the same time it would prove as a tonic to them and draw them. These can, by judicious management and association of the people, become paying concerns for the State. He who will handle the problem of temperance will have to give a more serious study to it than the Minister seems to have done. Let him study the methods adopted in America and tried by the great temperance organizations of the world. This study will give but limited help. For the Western conditions are widely different from the Indian. Our methods too, will have, therefore, to be largely different. Whereas total prohibition in the West is most difficult of accomplishment, I hold that it is the easiest of accomplishment in this country. When an evil like drink in the West attains the status of respectability, it is the most difficult to deal with. With us drink is still, thank God, sufficiently disrespectable and confined not to the general body of the people but to a minority of the poor classes.

Young India, 8-9-1927

422. OUR CULTURE[1]

Gift from a Peasant

I received while on tour the following from a poor peasant of U.P. It bears the date November 4, 1924. I have been all this time hoarding it among my papers. I give it here just as it was received. I do not even hold back the name, for there is not the slightest fear of Ramchandra being flattered. It is most likely that he does not even read *Navajivan*. Even if he does, I am certain that one who has sent me these beautiful verses[2] of Tulsidas will not become swollen with pride.

Gift from Borodada

I received another equally priceless gift from the late Borodada[3], which I always carry with me. He gave me the following verse, written out in his own hands, when I visited Santiniketan the last time[4] before his death.

I shall give the meaning :

> In the company of a saint, one's suffering turns into welcome happiness, death into immortality and a dull person into a man of perfect illumination.[5]

A supposedly uncultured peasant can, on occasion, quote verses from Tulsidas which fill one with the joy of knowledge and devotion, and another, a great poet, forgets his ego though he is a man of profound knowledge and seeks the company of saintly men. If the reader reflects over both these instances in a detached

[1] A Gujarati version of this was published in *Navajivan*, 11-9-1927.

[2] He who gathers up all objects of natural affection—mother, father, brother, son and wife, wealth, home, friends and family—like strands, and makes of them one strong rope to bind his soul to my feet; he who looks on all with an impartial eye and has abandoned all desire, and in whose heart is neither joy nor sorrow nor fear, such a saint abides in my heart like riches in the heart of an avaricious man. Saints like yourself are dear to me; it is only for their sake I am constrained to take on mortal form.

Those who worship the Personal and devote themselves to the good of others, and persevere in the ways of virtue and religious duty, and love the feet of the twice-born, are dear to me as my own life.

[3] Dwijendranath Tagore, elder brother of Rabindranath Tagore

[4] In May 1925; *vide* Vol. XXVII.

[5] "A dull person into a man of perfect illumination" is a paraphrase. The literal meaning is: "Nothingness into fullness."

spirit, leaving out the reference to me, he will realize what our culture is and how we can make ourselves worthy of it.

[From Hindi]

Hindi Navajivan, 8-9-1927

423. SPEECH AT CONJEEVARAM

September 8, 1927

FRIENDS,

I thank you for the several addresses and also the purses. I congratulate the Municipality upon their efforts to reduce to practical shape the message of the spinning-wheel. I hope the boys and girls of the elementary school are learning spinning regularly and in a scientific manner. In many municipalities where this experiment has been tried, the spinning-wheels have practically remained idle because of want of personal interest on the part of councillors. And you will not make it a real success unless at least one or two of the municipal councillors will themselves become expert spinners and keep a vigilant watch over what is being done in these schools. I wish also to draw your attention to the experience of other municipal and non-municipal schools that it is not the wheel which can be successfully worked but it is the *takli*.

You ask me to tell you what more can be done to serve the poorest of the land. You, the parents of the children who go to the schools, can see to it that your children are dressed in khadi. You can successfully induce the municipal employees from the highest to the lowest to wear nothing but khadi. Several municipalities have successfully performed this operation.

One of the addresses asks me to do something to heal the widened breach between Brahmins and Non-Brahmins. I assure you that I should heal the breach today if I had the power. I have told both Brahmin and Non-Brahmin friends that I am prepared during my tour to discuss the thing with you and assist in arriving at a solution, if it is at all possible. It is a spectacle humiliating to both Brahmins and Non-Brahmins. And really our capacity for swaraj can only be tested by your ability successfully to handle such problems. Beyond stating that I am always willing to assist, it is not possible for me to make any concrete suggestions.

Yours is a city renowned for its holiness throughout India. But unfortunately as in other places here also holiness has become but an empty name. Though you do something for khaddar and something more in some other directions, it does not make the city holy. Holiness is made of sterner stuff. It means purity of conduct and purity of heart in the majority of its citizens. I wish to ask you to ask yourselves and answer the question whether you regard a single being as untouchable. Belief in untouchability and holiness are contradictory terms.

I received a letter today in this place asking me to dwell exclusively upon the question of child widows. Whilst it is not possible for me to deal with this great evil to the exclusion of every other, I am painfully conscious of the fact that you are not free from this evil. It is no credit to Hinduism that it has so many child virgin widows. If I had the power I would certainly insist upon every parent getting married his child widow in his home. Child widow, again, is a contradiction in terms. Only a full grown woman who has been a consenting party to her marriage and who has enjoyed the married life can become a widow.

Closely related to the question of child widows is the question of child marriages. It is an inhuman thing to give away in marriage a little girl under sixteen years. We do violence to our Shastras when we wrest from them a meaning which panders to our lust. Now, perhaps, you understand a little of what I mean by holiness. I hope that you, who are naturally and pardonably proud of this city, will bestir yourselves and take early and energetic steps to rid yourselves of the evils to which I have drawn attention. If you really feel for the poorest of the land as you claim to do in your address, you will not rest content until you have brought about total prohibition.

There is a note handed to me asking me to tell you something about the Tilak Swaraj Fund and the present Khaddar Fund for which you have given purses today. I gladly give you the information. So far as the Tilak Swaraj Fund is concerned, I may inform you that the audited accounts have been published and circulated on behalf of the All-India Congress Committee all over India. Anyone who is even now desirous of seeing how much was collected and how the fund was distributed, is entitled to get from the General Secretary a copy of the accounts. The manner of disbursements was in this way. A certain percentage went to the Central Fund in the hands of the All-India Congress Committee and the balance was kept with the respective provinces in which the amounts were collected. And the respective provinces have also, so far as I am aware, except in one or two instances, published audited accounts. You may also know that the largest amounts were collected in Bombay and these remained vested in a number of trustees specially appointed. Furthermore, very large amounts of this fund were earmarked and these earmarked funds were administered by those donors who gave the funds so earmarked. It is my conviction that no fund of that magnitude has been so cleanly administered as the Tilak Swaraj Fund.

But that does not mean there has never been any misappropriation of these funds. Look at every other human institution. The Congress has had its share of faithless servants. But my examination has disclosed the fact that in the Congress there has been less defalcation. This refers to the Tilak Swaraj Fund and you are able to achieve it because of the extraordinary care that was taken in the appointment of responsible officers. You had in Seth Jamnalalji a treasurer who was not only inviolable, but whose vigilance was not surpassed by a single treasurer on the face of the earth. When I say this of Seth Jamnalalji, I assure you that I speak from personal experience.

Now about the Khadi Fund of which also Seth Jamnalalji is the treasurer and Shankerlal Banker is the Secretary. I am entirely satisfied that it is impossible to find two better men than these friends for the administration of this fund. And over and above them is a Board consisting of picked men, who believe in the message of the spinning-wheel. These funds are kept in banks of first-class credit. There is a periodical inspection all over India of provincial accounts; and the accounts also are periodically audited both in the provinces and at the centres. It is open to anyone whether he is a contributor or not to see these accounts. The method of distribution of this bund is to confine the purses that are being collected to the provinces in which they are collected. But the Board does not follow that absolute rule. For instance, we have collected large amounts in Bombay but almost nothing has been spent in Bombay itself. Though very little has been collected in Orissa large amounts were spent in organizing khadi work in Orissa. Similarly more has been spent in Tamil Nadu than has been hitherto collected. This is an absolute rule that wherever there is great distress and there is a chance of working in the distressed area through able and honest workers, funds are always made available.

I always invite enquiries and searching enquiries about the finances of public institutions and it was in appreciation of that fact that I entered into an elaborate explanation of the question that was handed to me. I wish the public take much more and abler interest in the financial administration of all trust funds. I am painfully conscious of the fact that in spite of the care that I am capable of devoting, it is not possible for me to do it unless I get vigilant assistance from the public to ensure absolute purity of the administration of numerous funds which the public have trusted me with. To ensure absolute correctness and purity of administration, without active and intelligent assistance of the public, is beyond the power of one single individual. I will gladly answer any further questions that may arise out of my explanation either now or by writing.

The Hindu, 10-9-1927

424. SPEECH TO ARUNDHATIYAS, PERAMBUR

September 8, 1927

In replying to the address, Mahatmaji exhorted this community of cobblers to carry on their trade with dead cattle hide instead of with hide of slaughtered animals. Mahatmaji said he himself had made shoes and could make fairly good shoes even now. He could not however make such a beautiful pair as the one they had presented him with.[1] Shoemaking was a respectable trade of which no one need be ashamed. He himself had now organized a tannery at Sabarmati where dead cattle hide was tanned.

Mahatmaji then asked the men to give up drink. Drink, he said, made beasts of men and was the enemy of the family. He also asked them to refrain from vices of all kinds. If they only followed his advice in some details of their daily conduct, their status would be raised automatically in society.

Finally, Mahatmaji asked the men to remember that there were millions of people in rural India much poorer than they. They should sympathize with them and help them by wearing khaddar. It was as wrong for them to wear foreign cloth, as it would be for him to buy foreign shoes without encouraging local shoemakers.

The Hindu, 12-9-1927

[1] Sandals made out of the hide of dead cattle were presented to Gandhiji and Kasturba.

425. SPEECH TO GUJARATIS AND MARWARIS, MADRAS

September 9, 1927

I thank you for the purse and the address. I am satisfied with the purse that you have given me because it is a sacred work. There is a special bond between myself and Gujaratis for Gujarat is my birth-place. Ever since I came to India my connection with Gujaratis and Marwaris has been one of increasing affection. Swaraj will have come to India if only the two communities had realized their duties as merchants and had given some place to selfless work in the course of their business. One of the reasons why India is still a slave country is the importation of foreign cloth and in the trade of foreign cloth you have a prime share. Therefore when you give money for the service of *Daridranarayana*, whatever you give will be unsatisfactory because your work has a bearing on India's poverty-stricken millions. You are taking away the money of the poor and the *prayaschitta* after the commission of the sin lies when you discharge your duties to those from whom you took your money. So if you are going to perform the true dharma, I beg of you to take to khadi business. This is your work and not my work. Though I am myself born a Bania I have given up business. Therefore I have got to learn business from you. Moreover, the biggest business in India has now fallen into my hands and so if you take up this work from my hands, there will be no need to beg throughout the country. You have given me a welcome address in Hindi and I thank you for it. There is a Hindi Pracharak Sabha in South India. The money for it comes from North India now and then. In this work Marwaris have given large amounts of money. I beg of you now to make this your own work. You should not depend upon North India for finance and will have to do it actively yourselves. There is another duty still for you, cow-protection. Gujaratis and Marwaris have taken a prominent part. I must tell you that the work cannot be done by money alone. You have got the Shastra knowledge about this and that is more necessary than money. If you do not open dairies and tanneries in the various parts of the country this work can never be done properly. You are traders in all parts of India. You should make friends with all the people of the country. Do not think of them as strangers. Think of them as sons and daughters of the same country. If you think one a Punjabi, another a Bengali, Marwari, Gujarati and so on, no good will result. May God give you wisdom and desire to serve!

The Hindu, 10-9-1927

426. SPEECH TO WOMEN, MADRAS[1]

September 9, 1927

Mahatmaji first thanked the women of Madras for the welcome they had accorded to him and for the purse. Regarding the purse, he said he was not satisfied with the same. He also doubted whether all of them who had assembled there knew for what purpose they had given the purse, for if they had realized it they would have given much more. The money was not intended to be distributed among a hundred poor people for charity but was going to be used for the relief of millions of starving people throughout India. He saw round him a large number of ladies with costly jewellery on their persons. They would not have realized that one bit of such jewellery would amount to a fortune to the starving millions. The toiling millions did not know what gold, diamonds, and silver were. Their jewellery was made of wood, stone and copper. Mahatmaji even doubted whether the women who had gathered around him had ever seen their sisters in the villages. He had a great mind to take some of them round those villages and show them the conditions in which some of their sisters lived. Then only they would realize the true significance of the movement he had set afoot, and the object of his mission. They had given a few hundreds of rupees but until they did some other things, that money would become useless. Millions of starving sisters were toiling all round the year and if more fortunate women had any affection for them they must wear khadi prepared by the poor people. Then they must show their self-sacrifice and spirit by spending at least half an hour a day and giving away the yarn. Mahatmaji said that he had been working for the relief of these poor millions and wherever he went he had received the full sympathy of all women. His work would be in vain if womenfolk of India did not co-operate with him. Referring to the welcome address, Mahatmaji said: It was a long one and he did not know whether all the women in the audience knew all subjects dealt with therein. They were all important ones and related only to the middle class people. He did not say that they must be disregarded on that account. He had no time to discuss all the subjects mentioned therein, but would say they had his entire sympathy. He would say only this thing that women had equal rights with men. Hindu Shastras made no differentiation between the sexes and had even symbolized God as *Ardha-*

[1] At Singrachari Hall in Hindu High School, Triplicane

nareeshwara. The English saying that the wives were the better halves was quite true. India had produced many ideal women and among the seven great *satis* worshipped by Hindu woman every morning to ward off her sins Sita stood foremost. That a better place was given to women was significant in the fact that people don't call "Ram-Sita" but call "Sita-Ram". Sita was an embodiment of self-sacrifice and dharma. Her sacrifices were greater than those of Rama. If the Hindus were the true followers and worshippers of Sita and Rama they would not have allowed such disgraceful customs as were prevalent among their society. They would immediately try to purify their Hinduism. If they were determined to purify their society he would ask them first of all not to marry their daughters before they were 16 years old. The next thing they must do is to remarry young widows. It was a sin not to remarry such girls. Consent was necessary for a life contract and he believed that in early marriages there was no consent. He would then ask them to remove from their midst the custom of *Devadasis.* Such reforms as he had mentioned could effectively and easily be done by women's associations and not by male workers however capable they might be.

Continuing, Mahatmaji said that he was gratified at the fact that Dr. Muthulakshmi Ammal was the Deputy President of the Legislative Council. Though he was himself a non-co-operator, he believed that Dr. Muthulakshmi Ammal would do many things in the Council on behalf of the women of India. He would only request her not to completely adopt Western methods. She must instil the Indian atmosphere in the Council and never forget the interests of women. India's progress would be sure and certain if only the women of India worked for it.

In-conclusion, Mahatmaji said then the greatest problem in India at the present day was the relief of poverty among the millions of toiling masses scattered in thousands of villages in India. If educated and more fortunate women did not realize their duties to their less fortunate sisters and do something for their relief India would never progress. He believed that the spinning-wheel would do much in this direction. It must become the centre of their activities. The khadi movement was a women's movement and he hoped that they would take it up and relieve him of his duties. He prayed to God Almighty that He should give them courage and energy to take up this good work.

The Hindu, 10-9-1927

427. SPEECH ON C. R. DAS, MADRAS

September 9, 1927

FRIENDS,

I congratulate Mr. Satyamurti on having presented this portrait to the Mahajana Sabha and I congratulate the Mahajana Sabha upon having secured this very precious possession. If I may do so, I would like to congratulate myself also upon having received the honour of unveiling this portrait. But whilst I prize this honour, I cannot help confessing to you that I am somewhat embarrassed, embarrassed because I am unveiling the portrait of one who unveiled my own. There is some lack of adjustment in this thing. Not that anybody is responsible for this accident; but it is there. Because Deshbandhu unveiled my portrait it was impossible to avoid me, seeing that I happened to be in Madras when the portrait was presented. So it is quite in the fitness of things considered in that light. But all the same, there are things over which we have no control and yet which mar all our dispositions. The fact that I have brought to your notice really mars my joy, it makes it difficult for me to pour out my heart in connection with Deshbandhu Das but I must struggle through my performance in the best manner I can.

I want to lift myself and yourself out of the political setting that has been given to this function. Deshbandhu's name will always be remembered so long as time lasts and India lasts, as one of the liberators of India. There can be not a shadow of doubt about it. But Deshbandhu himself claimed and was entitled to far higher honour than that of being ranked as one of the liberators—though high that honour is. I came to know this secret of his life myself during his last days, about which you have just now heard as from his very magnificent letter that Mr. Satyamurti read to us.[1] All his strength was really derived from his spirituality and I consider his spirituality even greater than his politics. He considered that his politics were dependent upon and were deri-

[1] The concluding paragraph of this letter of April 19, 1925 read: "No, my dear Satyamurti, I feel a broken man. I feel that my work is over and somebody is constantly calling me from the other side. I should love now to give up all this fight and worry and retire to seclusion. Surely the last few years—may be a very few—should be given to God. The work should be taken up by younger men—yours affectionately, C. R. Das."

ved from his spirituality, as I have said more than once in connection with another liberator of India, now no more, Lokamanya Bala Gangadhara Tilak. I think it was in writing about him or speaking about him, I said it had been a misfortune of some of the greatest sons of India to sacrifice their cherished ambition in order to realize what to them was a lesser ambition for the motherland. Lokamanya Tilak, if he had not been born in these times and in India, would have been considered a literary giant but that would not have been enough. He would have been considered a religious scholar, a man capable of giving *smritis* and giving living interpretations of old faiths. But that which was his highest ambition became subservient to the political work that he saw before him and that greatest work became a matter of leisure hours. All the best his energy could possibly give was given to the political emancipation of India. And so it was with Deshbandhu. When I had the honour of making his acquaintance in Lahore, I remember his having engaged me always whenever we had done with the report on which we were both engaged, in spiritual discussions. We used to talk about and think of things of permanent interest in life. I remember his having said once or twice in my presence that he could not possibly do these things in the thorough manner in which he wanted to.

I confess that I did not know Deshbandhu then as I knew him during his last moments at Darjeeling. I came closest to him there and I look back upon those few days of my association with him among the precious treasures of my memory. But in Lahore I unwittingly did an injustice to him by my thinking for one moment that this spirituality of his was a mere pastime as I have known it to be of so many other distinguished sons of India. But as our friendship, may I say, ripened, I came closer to him and I felt that I occupied a little corner in his heart also. And yet there were some cobwebs. God had designed that those cobwebs should be removed before his eyes were closed. He could not tolerate the idea of a seeker of truth remaining under any illusion whatsoever or any misunderstanding whatsoever in connection with a man so good. I omit the word 'great' deliberately. Greatness without goodness counts for nothing in my estimation as I expect it counted for nothing in Deshbandhu's estimation. So I was privileged to enter his heart, understand him through and and through and understand the depth of his devotion.

Reckless sacrifice he had. Reckless courage also he had. But all this beautiful recklessness of his was really derived from his very deep spirituality. He himself told me when he was in

Darjeeling that he would not be satisfied and consider his work over unless the spiritual treasures he had locked up in his heart had been also delivered to India. That ambition of his was not destined to be fulfilled through no fault of his. Perhaps you do not know his childlike simplicity. I was amazed; his own partner in life was amazed at that incredible simplicity of his heart. In his search for spiritual consolation he placed himself under one who has and had very little education as we understand the word education. But in order to find that real everlasting peace that a spiritual quickening gives, he was reckless and did not mind ridicule of his friends in going forward with that service. I cannot and dare not give you more details. I have given you just enough to share with me the belief that in Deshbandhu if we have lost a great man, one of the greatest of India's patriots, we have lost also in Deshbandhu a very great spiritual teacher.

I have endeavoured to lift ourselves out of the political setting also because I know that if his spirit is brooding over our proceedings then I know that he shares to the fullest extent the ideas that I am expressing to you. It was another patriot of India, again now no more, who expressed this thought that a time comes in the life of every Indian when mere political battle jars on him and that he seeks to base everything on spiritual, livingly moral foundations. There is no distinction between spirituality and morality, if we rightly understand the latter term. Today somehow or other we have come to distinguish between the two and so I have added the adverb 'livingly' moral. This I heard several years ago; but ever since then, I have seen that utterance more and more exemplified in this manner.

I have introduced this thing for a deliberate purpose; and that purpose is: Let us have the political ambition that we live for the freedom of the country. Today it is impossible for an Indian worth the name even to exist without political ambition, because the political domination of India has unfortunately resulted in, if not spiritual subjection, in spiritual *inanity*. And we have simply got the outer husk of spirituality; the kernel of it seems to have been entirely dried up. Let us not delude ourselves into the belief that this political ambition of us is going to serve this *Karmabhumi*, this *Devabhumi* as we flatter ourselves in calling Bharatavarsha. Let us not delude ourselves with the belief that this sacred land can ever be served by or can ever assimilate a political message unless it has got a spiritual foundation. It has got to be broadbased upon that foundation if it is to last and permeate the distant villages of India. That brings me to the appeal which the President of the Sabha made to me. I seemed to have neglected politics, he said. But he corrected himself. "No, he did not". I accept that correction. I have not neglected politics. But having had the privilege of sitting side by side with Deshbandhu Das and having had the privilege of many conversations with Lokamanya and most of our leaders, I have understood the secret of achieving India's freedom, as I fancy. In having done so, I bide my time in endeavouring to translate politics in terms of spirituality. I must restate my doctrine even at the risk of being misunderstood. When I was challenged I had no hesitation in saying that I would sacrifice India herself on the altar not of freedom but of truth. There is a catch about this thing. The catch consists in this, that freedom which is inconsistent with truth is no freedom whatsoever. But catch or no catch, when I wrote that,[1] I know it jarred on some friends and it incensed some. But what could I do? I can only speak what I feel; or else I should be really worthless. So I have got to repeat really the beautiful language that Deshbandhu uttered on that occasion which was reproduced today, namely, that although he had boundless affection for me, he could only do what his soul could ascend to and not what I wished or asked.[2] And no man can do more. I cannot do more—I know that. When my soul ascends to things which you are in the habit of calling political, I shall not wait for an invitation; and I shall lead the cause. But till then, I must be content to contemplate on the treasures that have been left to us by Deshbandhu and his predecessors—spiritual treasures —and must continue to hold the belief that all the politics that may have been handed down to us from the West will be turned to dust in India, good as they might be in the West, if we cannot possibly reduce them to terms of spirituality.

And I consider it a great privilege for me that as my stay in Madras is about to close, I have not only got this privilege of unveiling the portrait of one whose memory I hold dear and near to me, but that I have also in that connection got the privilege of interpreting as I know the mission for which Deshbandhu lived

[1] Presumably the *Young India* passage reproduced in Vol. XXXII, p. 587

[2] While unveiling a portrait of Gandhiji in the same Hall, C. R. Das had said: "I followed Mahatma Gandhi because my soul ascended to his. But I shall refuse to agree to anything which my soul does not ascend to. I have the highest respect, nay veneration, for the Mahatma; but I shall never trample my soul under my foot. The Mahatma knew that and I believe he respected me for that."

and for which he gave his life. I have much pleasure in unveiling the portrait.

The Hindu, 10-9-1927

428. SPEECH AT ST. THOMAS MOUNT, MADRAS

September 9, 1927

SISTERS AND FRIENDS,

I thank you for the addresses[1] that you have given me and the purse. I thank you also for saving my time, when I am pressed for it, by waiving your right to read all the addresses. I congratulate the Sangham and its beneficial public activities. I note that you are conducting some schools, doing sanitation work and even the lighting of your streets. This is undoubtedly public service in the right direction but I hope your work is thorough. Sanitation, until substantially done, has been known sometimes to do more harm than good. It is only things that are well done that produce permanent and beneficial services. I am glad too to find that you have taken up the work of the spinning-wheel. I hope you will keep all the wheels going regularly. I hope too that you will keep them in good shape. There is no reason why everyone living in these parts should not be dressed in khadi.

If there are any here who are given to drink habit, I hope you will urge them to give it up. Those who do not drink I ask them to go to their neighbours who drink and gently wean them from that awful habit. I wish that you would initiate a movement which will not end till total prohibition is carried out in the land.

I was also glad to receive an address from the Jain friends. To them also I would suggest that at the present moment the widest application of the doctrine of ahimsa is possible only through the spinning-wheel. It has been conceived and calculated to benefit the remotest village and the neediest people in the land. What ahimsa, what love can be deeper and faster than that which takes in its sweep millions of starving people!

I am glad that all your addresses make reference to untouchability. I hope you will rid yourselves of that curse in the quickest time possible. No religion can possibly countenance

[1] By the Jain community, the general public and the Podu Jana Oozhiyar Sangham (Social Service League)

the considering of a single human being as an untouchable from birth.

I have been recently drawing attention to child marriages and child widows. It is high time that parents understand their duties by their children. It cannot be a right thing to give away girls of tender years in marriage, nor can it be right to treat the child as a widow when her so-called husband dies. It is the bounden duty of every parent to give in marriage such child widows as may be in his family. We have also in the South the immoral and the inhuman institution of *Devadasis*. If we would respect our womanhood as we are expected to respect them in the name of Sita, we have to get rid of this blot upon our society.

As you are aware I have still to prepare to leave Madras tonight and you will not expect me therefore to say anything further upon the important subjects that will engage your attention. It is usual for me at such large meetings as these to give those who have not contributed to this purse and may be present here an opportunity, if they so desire and if they believe in khadi, of giving their mite.

The Hindu, 10-9-1927

429. INTERVIEW TO "THE HINDU", MADRAS

September 9, 1927

Unless I am deceived, the khadi spirit has come to stay.

Thus Mahatma Gandhi summed up to *The Hindu* representative impressions of his stay in Madras. . . .

Although the main theme of almost all my addresses in Madras has been khadi, if I am not deceiving myself, I have not noticed any weariness of spirit about the audience and everyone who has not appeared in khadi has invariably apologized. The financial response has also been satisfactory and khadi sales have been encouraging.

Of personal affection, I can have nothing to say. Even as long ago as 1896, Madras bestowed on me an affection for which I was wholly unprepared and entirely unworthy. That was my very first visit to Madras; and I knew nobody personally. Madras simply took me on trust.

I hope that the citizens of Madras will not postpone to the last minute the preparations for the coming Congress. They will give a practical demonstration of the wisdom as ascribed to the people of the South by Sir Brijendranath Seal, if before the session is held there is no Brahmin-Non-Brahmin quarrel. Of course, I expect the people here to give a good account of themselves in the matter of khadi during the Congress week.

The *Hindu* representative next enquired about Mahatmaji's views on Miss Mayo's book[1] which is agitating the public mind in India today; and Mahatmaji replied:

Under great stress and difficulty, I have just finished a long review of Miss Mayo's book. I entered upon it with much reluctance; and I did so, as many correspondents pressed me to give my own opinion. I could really ill afford the time to read the book, but when I saw I could not escape having to give the opinion, I read it from page to page; and having read it I am glad that I did so, because I saw that it required a fairly exhaustive reply from me. As my writings have been profusely used by the lady, I owed it to the public and to her to express my frank opinion on her work.

You will not expect me to anticipate the contents of the article[2] in *Young India*.

The Hindu, 10-9-1927

430. *TELEGRAM TO MIRABEHN*

CUDDALORE,
September 10, 1927

MIRABAI
SATYAGRAHA ASHRAM, WARDHA

THANK GOD. DELIVERANCE. LETTER REGARDING POONA NOT RECEIVED. DO[3] WHATEVER JAMNALALJI SAYS AND COMMANDS[4] YOU. LOVE.

BAPU

From the original: C.W. 5273. Courtesy: Mirabehn

[1] *Mother India*
[2] *Vide* "Drain Inspector's Report", 15-9-1927.
[3] The source has "to".
[4] The source has "commends".

431. SPEECH AT Y.M.C.A., CUDDALORE

September 10, 1927

MR. CHAIRMAN AND FRIENDS,

I thank you for the address and also for the purse on behalf of the students for the Khadi Fund. Rev. Mr. Lange has invited me to speak to you on how the individual might grow so as to bring about his own advancement and of his surroundings or her surroundings and in doing so, told me that if I expected to address a meeting of saints, I would be sadly disappointed. As I had no such expectations, there is no occasion for me to be disappointed. But, had you been all saints, I assure you, I would have been deeply embarrassed. Being myself a very imperfect man—and this I say not in the language of courtesy, but in terms of truth—I can only address with any degree of usefulness an assembly of men and women similarly imperfect. But this I do own that I am constantly, minute after minute, striving after perfection and it gives me comfort to find myself in the assembly of imperfect men and women who are similarly striving. It consoles me to find that many of them had succeeded in their striving and that therefore there is no reason why I should not succeed likewise, if my striving is prayerful and honest. And in the course of that striving, I fancy that I have made certain discoveries. And I am now endeavouring to the best of my ability to share the results of those discoveries with all I meet. And the one discovery that I have made is that really speaking, there is no distinction whatsoever between individual growth and corporate growth, that corporate growth is therefore entirely dependent upon individual growth and hence that beautiful proverb in the English language that a chain is no stronger than the weakest link in it. And if we realize in its fullness the truth of this homely saying, we would discover that no single lad in this assembly may hope to isolate himself from others and consider himself above them. When I recall my school days, I have a vivid recollection of boys who put on airs, because they were considered to be clever in their class. And some of them domineered over the rest because they had athletic skill and had physical powers. But I soon discovered also that their pride went before destruction. For the weaker ones, realizing their haughtiness, segregated them and regarded them as untouchables and so they really dug their own graves with their own hands. The first condition therefore of individual growth is utmost humility. And if we see at the present moment in our own land, some people in their insolence calling themselves superior and regarding others as below themselves in rank and regarding yet others as untouchables and unapproachables, those who are standing aloof from this strife are able to watch and see that these in their insolence are also digging their own graves. You will therefore see perfect correspondence between the individual and the corporation, and so I always say to students, young men and women, wanting to serve the country and to do big things: "First of all look after yourselves and make yourselves fairly good instruments of service." I hold it to be utterly impossible for any young man and any young woman to serve society unless they start with a clean slate, that is, a pure heart. But to say that we should have pure hearts is really easily said, but it is not equally easy to achieve and so, we have in the Christian scheme of life what is called new birth. The corresponding term in Hinduism is *dwija*, i.e., twice born. The meaning that the term *dwija* has come to bear at the present moment is a prostitution of language. Even this new birth among the many Christians I have seen, has acquired the significance which, when the word was originally used, it never bore. That new birth does not come from any outward circumstance nor through lip profession. It is an inward change which is unmistakable. It is a change which the person himself notices and so do his neighbours. It is a transformation of the heart and it needs no lip declaration. And that absolute transformation can only come by inward prayer and a definite and living recognition of the presence of the mighty spirit residing within. We call this by the name of Bhakti Yoga and rendered in English it means union with God by means of devotion and that yoga is possible alike for the lad, ten years old, as for an old man on the brink of the grave and when that transformation has come as a matter of fact, there is no falling back. But there is very often a subtle self-deception about the person noticing such a transformation about himself or herself, and so in order to make it easy for ourselves we have accommodated ourselves to a term called backsliding. As a matter of fact, this so-called transformation in such cases never was a transformation but a hallucination and the recognition of this fact keeps a man or woman fresh and humble, when the boy or girl who begins to say I am transformed will be found to be self-deluded. Therefore, whenever we notice any such upward lift or tendency to do better, let us be sanguine but let us not cease to strive. Instead of saying to ourselves in our pride, 'I have done with evil, I can never fall', let us humbly say to ourselves, 'I do not know, I must ever be on the watch.' There is irrevocable promise from God to mankind that no single effort made towards one's upliftment ever goes without its adequate result. But I am painfully conscious of the fact that I am saying these things to the young men before me without making my meaning clear. I am labouring under the load of the knowledge that I am almost speaking to the students in a foreign language, that is to say, not in the English language, but in an idiom which has become foreign to them. The very word God has lost its living touch and its living meaning. I recollect a conversation I had with an extremely intelligent and somewhat learned young man only a few months ago and he said: "You so often talk and write about God but I must confess to you that I find no echo of what you say in my own heart." An English friend connected with one of the most noted dailies of England sent me a message also very recently admiring my work about untouchability, temperance and social reform but detesting, as he calls it, God's touch in the pages of *Young India*. And let me tell you that this English friend is not a mean man but he is a most morally upright man. He is also a philanthropist. Similarly this young Indian who is living at the present moment—because I am in constant touch with him—is ever striving after perfection. But both consider that all that counts in this world and all that is required is self-effort, nothing more, nothing less. As against this, I can only say that at least 40 years' experience of conscious and unbroken striving shows to me that whilst self-effort is an absolute necessity, by itself it is an illusory thing. Without the living grace of the living God, all that effort is reduced to dust. I know instances of very dear friends of mine who were able by self-effort, as it appeared to them, to build themselves up, but they found, and I noticed, that because the effort was not touched by this living grace, they had become in an instant a living sepulchre. Before they knew where they were, subtle temptations surrounded them and they found themselves totally unprepared to resist them. And so, whether you understand my language or whether you do not, whether you understand the significance of the word God or whether you do not, I have really no other message for the young men and the young women of India. Do not be deceived by your own little intellect but do have some faith in the experiences of men living in all the climes of the world, in all the places of the world, proclaiming with one voice there is God. I tell you, I give you my assurance, that if you will be patient and exercise that faith, and believe in the definite presence of God within, in spite of yourselves, in spite of your intellect rebelling against your faith, in spite of your surroundings, believe in the presence of God, if you persist in that faith, you will find that some day it will become a living reality for you and it will be the surest shield of protection for you. If you want to know what faith like that can do for you, hear me. May God help you to understand somewhat of what I have been saying to you.

The Hindu, 12-9-1927

432. SPEECH AT PUBLIC MEETING, CUDDALORE[1]

September 10, 1927

FRIENDS,

I thank you for all these addresses and the purses presented to me including the address I received from the Municipality this morning. Some friends disturbed my night's rest and that of my fellow-passengers and made life itself difficult for my co-workers. To those of them who are present here I should like to say a few words. They besieged the train practically at three stations where the train stopped for some time. They insisted upon my presenting myself at the window. I, on the other hand, insisted on not complying with their demands and so they became angry, terribly angry and the anger was vented upon those who were trying to protect me from all the terrible din and noise that they set up. Tired out, I was stretched on my bed but I was awake all the time at the pain of hearing these din voices. It was at times difficult to say whether the noise was the noise of affection or it was hooliganism, pure and undefiled. I know that these guards of mine would have been glad if I had got up and presented myself at the window. But it was really not possible for me to comply with the demand and I wish that those who were throwing their affection to me will be pleased not to disturb me, at least my night's rest. I do not call that true love. It is blind love which harms those who bestow it and on whom it is bestowed. I would urge those blind lovers of mine to follow the beautiful motto that I saw as I was being brought to this place. "Love

[1] *Young India* published this under the caption, "Three Speeches". The first and the last paragraphs reproduced here are from *The Hindu*, 12-9-1927.

the poor and you will love Gandhi." I give you my assurance that there is no poor man or poor woman in this vast audience than whom there are not millions much poorer in this land. I would like you to appreciate the fact that I am doing this tour under the greatest difficulties, I am doing this in spite of the warnings of some of my medical friends, but I feel I have taken this tour in obedience to the promptings of the inner voice. I have been instrumental in monies being collected in several places in this Presidency. These monies are made for the people about whom I just now talked to you. Every rupee collected means food for 16 poor spinners in villages. I tried to ascertain whether these purses collected in several places could be delivered to me without my going personally to those places to receive them, and found that it was not possible. Believe me as I do, that what I am doing is God's work and I feel that even at the risk of my life I should endeavour to travel to those places to unlock those purses which have been put away in the safe. I would therefore urge you all and the whole of the public to co-operate with me in reserving the little energy that is left in me in order to enable me to fulfil this self-imposed task and it is for that reason that I have strictly prohibited my co-workers from making any appointments whatsoever for interviews in rest time that is given to me and which I so much need at every place visited by me. You will pardon me for my having entered upon what may appear to you to be a personal explanation. As a matter of fact it is nothing of the kind. It is a plea on behalf of the voiceless millions for whom I am collecting this money and that brings me to the taking up of the message, which I left this morning when I was addressing the young boys at the Y.M.C.A. meeting. I was this morning dealing with the growth of the individual and I said then that the growth of the individual, if it is real, must be reflected in the growth of the society of which the individual is a member. And every internal takes an external and outward manifestation. A seed that has a capacity of growth within itself immediately goes underneath the ground, sprouts outward into a beautiful tree in a short time. The seed that has no vitality in it and therefore no capacity for growth dies underneath the earth, and so with individuals and nations. If they have capacity for growth, of real life and character within them, it must be manifested by some definite, visible, outward signs. And speaking along these lines, it was in 1918 that I made a discovery—or call it re-discovery—that is, India was really one compact society or one nation and if the component parts of the society, the individuals, were also actuated with one mind and if they had feelings for the lowest and the humblest among them, they must show some universal sign which could be adopted by every man and woman, girl or boy. Hence you find me tirelessly preaching the message of the spinning-wheel which I have considered the message of *Daridranarayana*, and asking you to give me all your best for the charkha.

But I must hasten to the important part of the Municipal address. You have drawn my attention to the existence of the dissensions between the Brahmins and the Non-Brahmins and asked me to find out a solution. As a Non-Brahmin myself, if I could remove the dissensions by forfeiting my life, I should do so this very moment. But God is a very hard taskmaster. He is never satisfied with fireworks display. His mills, although they grind surely and incessantly, grind excruciatingly slow, and He is never satisfied with hasty forfeitures of life. It is a sacrifice of the purest that He demands and so you and I have prayerfully to plod on, live out the life so long as it is vouchsafed to us to live it. I have said, only very recently in Madras, that whenever you want me to take part in your deliberations, or want me to advise you, you will find me at your disposal. I have no clear-cut solution for this difficult question. I confess to you that I do not even now know the points of differences between the two. I tried to draw out some Non-Brahmins, who came to me on Nandi Hills, and they promised to see me in my tour and place all the points of difference before me. I must confess to you that I am no wiser about the Brahmin side of the question. And wily as the Brahmins are, I admit they have not told me what the differences are, knowing fully well what my opinion would be about all these questions. As you are aware, though a Non-Brahmin myself, I have lived more with them and amongst them than amongst Non-Brahmins, and on that account pardonably some of my Non-Brahmin friends suspect me of having taken all my colourings from Brahmin friends. I have a shrewd suspicion that the Non-Brahmin friends consider that I am not to be accepted as a hope for a proper solution. And so I find myself in the happy position of being isolated by both the parties, a position which in the present state of my health suits me admirably. But all the same I give you my assurance that I for my part hold myself in readiness to be wooed by either party. And I assure you too that I shall not plead physical unfitness.

But I have for both the parties two counsels of perfection which I can lay before you. To the Brahmins I will say: 'Seeing that you are repositories of knowledge and embodiments of sacrifice and that you have chosen the life of mendicancy, give up all that the Non-Brahmins want and be satisfied with what they may leave for you.' But the modern Brahmin would, I know, summarily reject my Non-Brahmin interpretation of his dharma. To the Non-Brahmins, I say: 'Seeing that you have got numbers on your side, seeing that you have got wealth on your side, what is it that you are worrying about? Resisting as you are, and as you must, untouchability, do not be guilty of creating a new untouchability in your midst. In your haste, in your blindness, in your anger against the Brahmins, you are trying to trample underfoot the whole of the culture which you have inherited from ages past. With a stroke of the pen, may be at the point of the sword, you are impatient to wreck Hinduism of its bed-rock. Being dissatisfied and properly dissatisfied with the husk of Hinduism, you are in danger of losing even the kernel, life itself. You, in your impatience, seem to think that there is absolutely nothing to be said about *varnashrama*. Some of you are ready even to think that in defending *varnashrama* I am also labouring under a delusion. Make no mistake about it. They who say this have not even taken the trouble of understanding what I mean by *varnashrama*.'

It is a universal law, stated in so many words by Hinduism. It is a law of spiritual economics. Nations of the West and Islam itself unwittingly are obliged to follow that law. It has nothing to do with superiority or inferiority. The customs about eating, drinking and marriage are no integral part of Varnashrama Dharma. It was a law discovered by your ancestors and my ancestors, the *rishis* who saw that if they were to give the best part of their lives to God and to the world, and not to themselves, they must recognize that it is the law of heredity. It is a law designed to set free man's energy for higher pursuits in life. What true Non-Brahmins should therefore set about doing is not to undermine the very foundations on which they are sitting, but to clean all the sweepings that gathered on the foundation and make it perfectly clean. Fight by all means the monster that passes for *varnashrama* today, and you will find me working side by side with you. My *varnashrama* enables me to dine with anybody who will give me clean food, be he Hindu, Muslim, Christian, Parsi whatever he is. My *varnashrama* accommodates a pariah girl under my own roof as my own daughter. My *varnashrama* accommodates many *Panchama* families with whom I dine with the greatest pleasure —to dine with whom is a privilege. My *varnashrama* refuses to bow the head before the greatest potentate on earth but my *varnashrama* compels me to bow down my head in all humility before knowledge, before purity, before every person where I see God face to face. Do not therefore swear by words that have, at the present moment, become absolutely meaningless and obsolete. Swear all you are worth, if you like, against Brahmins but never against Brahminism, and even at the risk of being understood or being mistaken by you to be a pro-Brahmin, I make bold to declare to you that whilst Brahmins have many sins to atone for and many for which they will receive exemplary punishments, there are today Brahmins living in India who are watching the progress of Hinduism and who are trying to protect it with all the piety and all the austerity of which they are capable. Them you perhaps do not even know. They do not care to be known. They expect no reward; they ask for none. Their work is its own reward. They work in this fashion because they must. It is their nature. You and I may swear against them for all we are worth, but they are untouched. Do not run away with the belief that I am putting in a plea for Brahmins, *Vakils* and Ministers and even Justices of the High Courts in India. I have not thought of them in my mind at all. What, therefore, both Brahmins and Non-Brahmins, and for that matter everybody who wants India to progress has to do, is to sweep his own house clean. I therefore suggest to Non-Brahmins who have not yet lost their heads, to think out clearly what it is that they are grieved over and make up their minds and fight for all they are worth to remove those grievances. I recognize however that I have this evening entered upon an academic discussion. Not knowing the merits of their quarrels, I do nothing else. But in my own humble opinion, I have indicated the lines of action for both and within the limits of your capacity, it is open to you to make use of them in any manner you like.

But in trying to grapple with this great problem do not forget the little things for which I am touring in Tamil Nadu. Little they may appear to you but I assure you, that they are great enough to engage the attention of every one of you. I simply summarize them for you without entering into the discussion.

Khadi I have already mentioned. Total prohibition, you can have today if you will act with one mind. Whilst we are quarrelling among ourselves, thousands upon thousands of our countrymen are selling themselves to the devil, they cannot get rid of the curse of drink. And we who witness all these damnations shall have to answer before God for our great criminal neglect of our neighbours. There was a Non-Brahmin lady only yesterday to ask you and ask all the people whom I shall have to see to rid society of the curse of the *Devadasi* institution. Think of the unmanly, unchivalrous manner in which men act towards their sisters. Do not forget these problems which are eating into the vitals of society in trying to fight out the dissensions between Brahmins and Non-Brahmins. And whether I look at Brahmins or Non-Brahmins and treat untouchables as a class of untouchables, I find this one common weakness and error that we, in our impatience, do not think of self-help and self-purification but simply resort to the process of mutual mud-slinging. Since I have no desire to take part in this mutual mud-slinging process, I simply come forward with the humble little things that I have spoken to you. Whatever you may do or may not do, I plead to you that you will not forget these things. I thank you once more for these addresses and purses and what is more for kindly listening to me. May God help you to understand the spirit in which the message has been delivered to you.

Young India, 22-9-1927

433. TEST FOR STUDENTS

I feel proud to read that students are making a fine contribution to flood relief work through physical labour. Our hopes of building a better future depend on them. If this foundation is weak, our efforts to put up a building will be wasted. I hope that no student, boy or girl, feels that he or she is unnecessarily sacrificing studies for this work. If they feel unhappy with such thoughts, their service will have been rendered out of weakness and unwillingly and it will be, in that measure, imperfect.

True education consists in such service. They will not have in a school or college the experiences which they are having in this kind of work. A student is a soldier. Just as a soldier's duty consists in carrying out sincerely the orders of his superiors, so a student's education consists in sincerely obeying his teacher's instructions. There may be error in these instructions, but the student will not have to suffer punishment for any such error. If he carries out the instructions with a pure mind, he will remain untouched by the error. He will, however, enjoy the fruits, undreamt of by him, of sincere obedience. The injunction to work without thought of the fruit of work does not mean that such work bears no fruit. It always achieves results. In carrying out the teacher's instructions, the student is acting without any desire for the fruit of such obedience. His action has a happy reward in his spiritual progress. Everything done while carrying out the teacher's instructions is done at his instance, and so, if there is error in his instructions, it will be he who will reap the fruit of such error. We need not consider here how and when he may have to do this, or whether he will have to reap such fruit at all.

My only aim just now is to express my happiness at the service rendered by students and to give them encouragement; while doing this, I took the opportunity to discuss in brief what, in my view, is the duty of students.

[From Gujarati]

Navajivan, 11-9-1927

434. "WHAT SHOULD I DO?"

A gentleman asks:

> I am trying to get into a railway compartment; someone inside holds the door fast, though there is room, and does not let me get in. What should I do in this situation?

There are three courses open:

1. To complain to the railway authorities on the station;
2. if one has strength enough and courage, to force open the door and get into the compartment and, if necessary, to fight with that passenger who thought he owned the railway;
3. if one has courage and spiritual strength to plead with the bully and, if he does not respond, to forgo one's right and try to find a seat elsewhere. If one fails in that, one may let the train pass. One should have faith that this is for the good of that bully and of oneself. We have no right to ask when he will become reasonable.

All the three courses are legitimate, but the third one is purely of a spiritual character. The first two are practical, but they are not contrary to dharma.

I can imagine a fourth. Being a coward, one may be afraid of getting beaten up in a fight and may look for a seat elsewhere. This is *adharma*. It has, therefore, no place among the legitimate courses open to one. The second question is this:

> I am travelling in a train. I get down at one station to drink water. In my absence, someone enters the compartment and occupies my seat. He refuses to vacate it. What should I do?

I think the answer to this is contained in the answer to the first question.

Such incidents are common during railway journeys. I have often been in such difficulties. On every occasion, I adopted the third course, and have never regretted having done so. In many cases, I remember, the bully's heart had melted. Let not the reader think that people would recognize me because I was a mahatma and would therefore yield. Most of the experiences of which I have the memory belong to a time before I became a mahatma.

But there is one condition for adopting the third course. The person who adopts it should have a living religious faith and should not merely imitate the behaviour of another. If one feels angry with the bully, one should realize that one is not fit to adopt the third course. Dharma is a matter of the heart. If we try to imitate another, there is every possibility of our falling instead of following dharma. I have often observed Gujarat's non-violence becoming timidity and cowardice. I, therefore, feel reluctant to discuss the third course, and there seems no need to discuss the first two. I do not need to explain that they are even and broad. The third is steep and narrow, and in climbing it we get out of breath, so that we can never discuss it too much. In Gujarat more than elsewhere, but generally in the whole of India, people are usually found to adopt the fourth course which is one of *adharma*, and so it is necessary to mention the first two. Anyone who adopts either of them may one day be taught to adopt the third, but I doubt if one who follows the fourth can learn the third.

[From Gujarati]
Navajivan, 11-9-1927

435. REPLIES TO A STUDENT'S QUESTIONS

September 11, 1927

Q: 1. Which is the best education?

A: Knowledge of the Self.

2. What is the adornment of youth?

Brahmacharya.

3. What is the best characteristic of the people's culture?

Steadfast adherence to truth.

4. Wherein lies the ultimate fulfilment of life?

In Self-knowledge.

5. What is life's highest ideal?

Satyagraha.

6. What is the most praiseworthy quality in a woman?

Purity.

7. What is the most praiseworthy quality in a man?

Purity.

8. Which is your favourite book?

The *Gita.*

9. What is dearest to you?

Truth.

[From Gujarati]

From the manuscript of Mahadev Desai's Diary. Courtesy: Narayan Desai

436. SPEECH TO ADI DRAVIDAS, CHIDAMBARAM[1]

September 11, 1927

SWAMI SAHAJANANDA AND FRIENDS,

As you have given me an advance copy of the address, I know what it contains. As you have rightly remarked in the address, Nandanar[2] was one of the bright stars among the satyagrahis of India. I consider myself highly honoured to have had this privilege of laying the foundation of the doorstep of this temple. I consider it to be a great honour that the first act that I am called upon to perform after entering into Chidambaram is to lay the foundation-stone of the doorstep. I am hoping that this will be really a temple where we will be able to see God face to face as Nandanar himself did and I pray that this may be a temple of freedom for everyone who would visit this. But you should understand that Nandanar was trying to enter, by giving his life-blood, not in a temple built of stone and mortar only. Nandanar saw in the temple, which he was seeking to enter, freedom in his own soul. And so by your own lives, the devotees of the temple will be expected to purify the inward atmosphere of which the visible stone and mortar should merely be the symbol. At the present

[1] At Nandanar School

[2] An "untouchable" devotee who became one of the sixty-three Saivite saints of Tamil Nadu

moment I know many temples, whether they be dedicated to Vishnu or Siva, entered into and visited by thousands of the so-called Brahmins, which are no temples of God. Let this temple not be an addition to those numerous temples which today disfigure this holy land. But if you want to do that, those who will be in charge of this temple will have to purify their hearts of all anger. I am glad therefore to notice that in your address you do not seem to seek to destroy Hinduism itself as I see is being done in many places in the present time. I appreciate your idea not to trample underfoot Hindu traditions whether they be bad or indifferent. But as you have decided to make use of the good faculty of discrimination, and as you seek not to destroy that which is good but only that which is bad, let me congratulate you upon your determination to win status by sheer force of merit. You rightly claim to be the descendants of the original inhabitants of this ancient land and if it belongs to any single individual as a matter of right, that right is certainly yours and yours foremost. You are therefore entitled to every consideration. It seems that you are bent upon gaining strength by reform within. Let me draw your attention to one or two points.

There is that drink evil, common almost to every *Adi Dravida.* You must therefore try your level best to rid the community of this drink evil. If I am not mistaken *Adi Dravidas* are also given to beef-eating. Hinduism is a tolerant religion. But tolerant though it is, it is intolerant of beef-eating on the part of its devotees. You must therefore agitate and agitate till every *Adi Dravida* has given up beef-eating and the slaughter of cows. Make this temple at once a seat of devotion, centre of learning and a centre from which the force should spread to every *Adi Dravida* and subsequently to every Hindu and still more subsequently to every Indian. You have said in your address that khaddar itself cannot be successful without the removal of the curse of untouchability.

Here there is a confusion of ideas. The real untouchability will never vanish from this land until khaddar is worn. Let me inform you that there are even now people in India who are poorer and more downtrodden than many *Adi Dravidas.* Are there not many *Adi Dravidas* that I have seen in the course of my tour suffering for want of food? But in many parts of India I can show you many who are not called *Adi Dravidas* but do not get even a single meal a day. This untouchability, of which you complain, has not to go so much as the untouchabilities of those dying millions. Their untouchability is in one way a far more serious affair than the one with which we are placed. So it pleases me to find mention made in your address to having a weaving institute for *Adi Dravida* boys and I appreciate your invitation to me to help this weaving institute. I shall do so with the greatest pleasure if you will fulfil the conditions that are imposed on every weaving institute which seeks my assistance. The first and the foremost condition I propose to mention to you is that in the weaving institute nothing but hand-spun yarn can be used. If you are serious about this, place yourself in correspondence with the Secretary, Mr. S. Ramanathan, who is in charge of the All-India Spinners' Association in this part of the country. You will find him accessible at all times, ready to render any assistance that is in his power. He and I exist for that purpose. As you are about to make this temple a centre of devotion let me also commend to you the two things which are necessary for our children, i.e., the learning of Sanskrit and Hindi which may be helpful in life.

The Hindu, 12-9-1927

437. SPEECH AT PUBLIC MEETING, CHIDAMBARAM

September 11, 1927

MR. CHAIRMAN AND FRIENDS,

I thank you for all these addresses and the different purses. I thank you also for the delicate consideration with which you have saved the reading of all the addresses, as you are aware that I have to catch the train immediately after 7 o'clock and therefore speak against time. The saving of the time which therefore was caused by the saving of reading of the addresses is all the more appreciable. I tell you that it does not give me satisfaction when I have to go away from you in such a short time. Your fame had preceded my coming here through the beautiful story that Mr. C. Rajagopalachariar wrote through the pages of *Young India.* I know the fame of this place of yours. Ever since that time I know that Chidambaram must be a place of pilgrimage for me. I have never claimed to be the original satyagrahi. What I have claimed is the application of that doctrine on almost a universal scale. And yet it remains to be seen and demonstrated that it is a doctrine which is capable of application by thousands and thousands of people in all ways. I know therefore that mine is an experiment still in the making. And it therefore always keeps me humble and rooted to the soil. In that state of humility I always cling to every example of satyagraha that comes under my notice as a child clings to its mother's breast. And so when I hear or read the story of Nandanar and his lofty satyagraha and his great success, my head bows before his spirit. All the day long I have felt elevated to be able to be in a place hallowed by the holy feet of Nandanar. It will not be without a wrench that I shall be leaving this place in a few minutes' time. But it gave me great joy and I considered it to be a great honour that the very first act I was called upon to perform was to lay the foundation-stone of the gateway of the temple that has been erected in memory of the great saint. How I wish that it could be said about the people of Chidambaram that at least they knew no distinction between Brahmins and *Panchamas*. If the people of Chidambaram would rise to that lofty height they would have done nothing more than what the *Gita* expects every Hindu to do. In the eye of God there are no touchables or untouchables. Brahmins are called Brahmins not for their superiority, not for their ability to lord it over others, but because of their ability to serve mankind by their knowledge and their ability to efface themselves in the act of service. Theirs is the privilege, theirs is the duty of serving their fellow-brethren. They cannot do so in its fullness unless they renounce every earthly reward. By his indomitable spirit and by his overwhelming faith in the infinite presence of God, Nandanar was able to bear down the haughty spirit of the haughty Brahmins and showed that he in spirit was infinitely superior to the persecutors who considered him the curse amongst mankind. But let the *Panchamas*, the *Adi Dravida* brothers and sisters, profiting by the example of Nandanar, live up to the spirit which they have inherited. Nandanar broke down every barrier and won his way to freedom not by freak, not by lustre, but by the purest form of self-suffering and did not swear against his persecutors. He would not even condescend to ask from his persecutors what were his dues. But he shamed them into doing justice by his lofty prayers and by the purity of his character, and, if I may commit it into human language, he compelled God Himself to descend and made Him open the eyes of his persecutors. What Nandanar did in his time and in his own person, it is open to every one of us to do today. I wish that you, my hearers, will catch something of the spirit of Nandanar, and if so many of us could possibly imitate Nandanar and assimilate the spark of his spirit, we can make the land, a land again of holy people. I hope and pray that the temple with which the trustees have identified me today will keep green the memory of this great saint by keeping the atmosphere about the temple always pure. I would very much like to leave the atmosphere about this meeting at this stage filled with the spirit of Nandanar. But it would be wrong perhaps on my part if I do not say a few words showing how we can illustrate the spirit of Nandanar in our daily life.

In my humble opinion we cannot better translate that spirit than by clothing ourselves with khaddar in spirit. I am not saying we can imitate Nandanar by wearing khaddar merely. But I say that we must have the khadi spirit. Even a blackguard, even a prostitute will be expected to wear khaddar since he or she, the blackguard, must wear something as they eat wheat and rice in this country in common with us. But the khadi spirit means that we must know the meaning of what the wearing of khaddar carries with it. Every time that we take our khaddar garment early in the morning to wear for going out we should remember that we are doing so in the name of *Daridranarayana* and for the sake of saving the millions of India. If we have the khadi spirit in us we should serve ourselves with simplicity in every walk of life. Khadi spirit means illimitable patience. For those who know anything of production of khaddar know how patiently those spinners and weavers have to toil. Even so must we have patience while spinning the thread of swaraj. Khadi spirit means also equally illimitable faith. So must we have that illimitable faith in truth and non-violence ultimately conquering every obstacle in our way. Khadi spirit means fellow-feeling with every living being on earth. It means the complete renunciation of everything that is likely to harm our fellow creatures. And if we are to cultivate that spirit amongst the millions of our countrymen, what a land this India of ours would be!

I am well aware that khadi cannot compete with the other articles of commerce on their own platform and on their own terms. Even as satyagraha is a weapon unique by itself and not one of the ordinary weapons wielded by politicians so is khadi a unique article of commerce which will not and cannot succeed on terms common to other articles. If khadi is asked for in the khadi spirit that I have endeavoured to describe to you, khadi has illimitable capacities and it would outstand every other article that you see in India today. You will therefore perhaps understand why I do not appreciate all these khadi purses that you are giving me. I know that if you had a tenth of the faith in the khadi which I have, you will not give a few hundreds or few thousands of your plenty but you will satisfy me till there is no money required for khadi. I was really distressed this morning when I discovered that a friend who is conducting a khaddar store here, not for making money but for the love of khaddar, is incurring a loss of Rs. 200 year after year. Surely it is the A B C of patriotism, it is the A B C of your love for these starving millions, that you should all wear khaddar. I was equally distressed to find Swami Sahajananda just as I came here telling me that the reason why his boys and girls were not clothed in khaddar was because the persons responsible did not patronize khaddar and it is just the reverse of the khaddar spirit which I have just described to you. In the face of these facts, you will pardon me for saying that even the intrinsic value of these purses of yours suffers. Let me pass on to the drink evil.

You must ask those here, who are given to the drink habit, to give up this cursed drink and those who are not given to the drink habit should not remain satisfied, if they have any real love for their less unfortunate brethren, till they have been rid of this curse and total prohibition is established in this land. So must you get rid of this disgraceful and immoral *Devadasi* institution. You should be no party whatsoever to child marriages and harbouring child widows in your homes. It is time that we should make these elementary reforms in our society without the slightest delay. I thank you once more for all these addresses and the purses and the patience with which you have listened to me.

The Hindu, 13-9-1927

438. LETTER TO MIRABEHN

Unrevised *September 12, 1927*

CHI. MIRA,

I could not help sending you a wire of thanksgiving yesterday. These have been somewhat anxious days. Though I have not written much nor telegraphed to you, my spirit has hovered about and watched over you. I knew that if I sent you a wire daily, you would like it but I thought that I must not. Letter-writing has been almost impossible these trying days. They leave me just enough time to attend to the programme before me. I have been pouring my soul out to the various audiences that leaves me little energy for anything else. On the top of that come the reading of Miss Mayo's book and the heavy article[1] on it.

But it has been a matter of the greatest relief to me to know

[1] *Vide* "Drain Inspector's Report", 15-9-1927.

that Jamnalalji was with you. Thank God it all seems to be over now. It has been a good test.

And Ramanama! If that has become a living reality with you it is a great thing indeed. But you shall give me your experiences when you are stronger. I want them all and I want to know also why you have been delirious or hysterical. Of course often we do not know.

Now you will go gently.[1] Take all the rest you need. Watch yourself and if any change in your food is necessary, make it. Find out the cause of the enlarged spleen. Stay in Poona as long as you like. Ask for the convenience you need. What you cannot mention to anybody else, you will mention to me. I am faring all right. Rajagopalachari protects me as much as any human being can. He wears himself out in trying to shield me. And I know that the strain is too much for him, but I do not interfere. If God wants this tour to be finished, He will keep those who must be, from all harm. You are therefore not to worry about me. Unless you think otherwise send this to mother.

With love,

BAPU

SHRI[MATI] MIRABEHN
C/o SETH JAMNALAL BAJAJ
KALBADEVI ROAD
BOMBAY

From the original: C.W. 5274. Courtesy: Mirabehn

439. LETTER TO GANGABEHN VAIDYA

Silence Day [Before *September 12, 1927*][2]

CHI. GANGABEHN (VAIDYA),

I have your letter. Your Sanskrit writing is very good indeed. Your Gujarati writing too has improved.

I do not wish that you should spend more time in acquiring knowledge, but I would not consider such a desire on your part improper and would help you to fulfil it. If, comparing yourself with other women who are educated, you feel your lack and desire education like theirs, you have a right within limits to

[1] Mirabehn explains: "After the severe attack of malaria, I was on my way to Poona for recouping my health."

[2] From the reference to the addressee's going for relief work; *vide* "Letter to Ashram Women", 12-9-1927.

acquire it. If, however, your *atman* has come to be completely at peace with itself, I would wish that you should give yourself wholly to any one activity you like. But this is a matter of the heart. One can do nothing but keep on trying until the heart agrees to give up such efforts.

I see that flood relief work will keep you busy for some time.

Blessings from
BAPU

From the Gujarati original: C.W. 8822. Courtesy: Gangabehn Vaidya

440. LETTER TO JETHALAL JOSHI

Bhadrapad Krishna 1 [September 12, 1927][1]

BHAI JETHALALJI,

Your letter. I would advise you to see the Secretary of the Ashram and there take up some work if you find any. There is little possibility of my coming to the Ashram during this year.

Yours,
MOHANDAS

From a photostat of the Hindi: G.N. 1354

441. LETTER TO PRABHASHANKER PATTANI

Monday, Bhadarva Vad 1 [September 12, 1927][2]

SUJNA BHAISHRI,

I had duly received your letter about the problems of life. I have held my peace not to oblige you but because I must. I have understood what you write to me. If I can avoid it, I do not want to make a mistake. Since I did not want to pat myself on the back, I considered it proper to keep silent; but may I not say that you were the person responsible for that decision? But this is neither here nor there.

What I wanted to write to you was that you should take care of your health, because I expect many things from you. If you

[1] The year is inferred from the reference to Gandhiji's inability to go to the Ashram, as also from the discussion about the work to be taken up by the addressee.

[2] The year is inferred from the reference to Mayavaram.

have not read my last speech concerning Mysore, I can send a copy, the hope being that you may carry out as many as you can of the suggestions made in it.

I am getting along as usual. I am writing this from Mayavaram. I am not sending you my itinerary. It will be all right if you write to me c/o the Ashram.

Do you work on the spinning-wheel?

What progress has Lady Pattani made in accepting *pankora*[1] for her garments?

Vandemataram from
MOHANDAS

From a photostat of the Gujarati: C.W. 3214. Courtesy: Mahesh Pattani

442. LETTER TO ASHRAM WOMEN

Silence Day, Bhadarva Vad 1 [September 12, 1927][2]

DEAR SISTERS,

I should not say I have your letter—it was little more than a note. I learn that you have appointed Gangabehn Jhaveri as your President, since Kashibehn has gone to Rajkot. The fact that you can get as many presidents as you need is some proof of your ability to run your organization. It would be a better proof still when you respect your President with all your heart and when all of you work in perfect unison in running the organization. Menfolk have not as yet been able to manage such things well. When we look at the affairs of our Ashram we find that we are not yet trained well enough to carry on the administration of the Ashram without quarrelling among ourselves. So it is not surprising if you also have not attained that stage. But if you persevere, I am sure you will acquire the necessary capacity. Try your best to get rid of factions and cliques. Only by striving for better things can we make progress.

It is good that Gangabehn senior has gone away on relief work.

My work continues to make progress, though slowly.

Blessings from
BAPU

From a photostat of the Gujarati: G.N. 3667

[1] A variety of coarse cloth

[2] From the reference to Gangabehn Jhaveri becoming President of the Ashram Women

443. LETTER TO GANGABEHN JHAVERI

[About *September 12, 1927*][1]

CHI. GANGABEHN JHAVERI,

Even though I owe you no letter, I am writing this. It is good you have got the presidentship. Show yourself worthy of it. Give all your attention to its duties. If difficulties crop up, overcome them with courage. Don't be baffled by anything.

As I write this, I remember that as a matter of fact I owe you a letter. I did not, could not, reply to your question about Marathi. Take the help you need for learning Sanskrit, wherever available. Actually, since you know grammar, you can do a lot on your own. And the same is true about Hindi.

Improve your knowledge of Gujarati, Hindi and Sanskrit and then go ahead in reading. As for work, all other things come in after you have mastered the science of the spinning-wheel. That science of course includes ginning, carding, spinning, repairing the spinning-wheel, straightening the spindle, making a cord for connecting the wheel with the spindle, mounting the *sadi*[2] on to the spindle, etc. The body, too, should be well developed.

Blessings from
BAPU

From a photostat of the Gujarati: G.N. 3126

444. LETTER TO MIRABEHN

[*September 13, 1927*][3]

CHI. MIRA,

I have just a few moments for writing to you. There is no wire from you since Saturday. I therefore presume that you are quite well now and in Bombay. The Monday letter was sent to Bombay as per your instructions.

Your letter in your own hand after the illness was perfectly

[1] *Vide* the preceding item.

[2] A small piece of fine cloth wound around the spindle to secure the position of the cord or to prevent the disc from moving back

[3] From the reference to the "Monday letter" (which is the one dated 12-9-1927)

written and quite legible. In fact the writing was even better than usual.

Yes, the illness was a blessing. The weakness you will soon get over. If you go to Poona, you will take long walks and visit the dairy there in the company of one of our very best friends there. You will love Prof. Trivedi as you see him. You will befriend his boy Manu and you will see the Seva Sadan and the Society's quarters. But that by and by.

With love,

BAPU

From the original: C.W. 5275. Courtesy: Mirabehn

445. LETTER TO VIJAY SINGH PATHIK

Bhadrapad Krishna 2 [September 13, 1927][1]

BHAI PATHIKJI,

I got your letter today. I had sent a reply to your last letter. I am surprised that you did not get it. There has been no change in my attitude. If there was I would not conceal it. You may come over here whenever you wish to. I shall be touring till the 10th of October, not farther than one day's run from Madras. You will be able to locate me from Madras.

I have written nothing to the Government to save Abdul Rashid from the gallows. I have certainly asked Hindus to forgive him. What do you expect me to do for the Kakori case[2] prisoners? What people should I appeal to?

Yours,

MOHANDAS

[From Hindi]

From *Bapu, maine kya dekha, kya samjha*, p. 125

[1] The year is inferred from the reference to Gandhiji's tour programme and to Abdul Rashid, the assassin of Swami Shraddhanand.

[2] An armed dacoity committed on August 9, 1925 near Kakori railway station when cash and currency were plundered from the guard's van of a train going to Lucknow from Moradabad; one person was killed. The dacoity, it was alleged, had been committed by certain members of the Hindustan Republican Association of United Provinces, the object of which was the establishment of a 'Federated Republic of the United States of India'. Of the 21 accused, two were acquitted, three were sentenced to death, one to transportation for life and the rest to terms of imprisonment varying from five to 14 years.

446. SPEECH AT MAYAVARAM

September 13, 1927

LADIES AND FRIENDS,

I thank you for all these several addresses and the several purses. If you want me to make a fairly detailed reply to all the important points referred to in those addresses, it is necessary that you should keep perfect silence during the time when I am speaking.

At the outset I have to tender you the same apology that I tendered at Cuddalore; and that was to ask you, out of your generosity, to pardon me for my having been not accessible to all and sundry that came to me during my rest hours. If I could have had the strength, I would have loved to talk to the citizens in this town to cross-question them and to understand their several view-points; but in the present weak state of my health, such a thing is not possible.

Some of you may perhaps recall that this is not my first visit to Mayavaram. I have a vivid recollection of 1915, when I had the privilege of talking to some of you on swadeshi.[1] But I must not detain you by recalling to you my pleasant recollections of that time.

I congratulate you on your work towards the uplift of the so-called 'untouchables'. . . .

But I must this evening speak to you on a subject which is very dear to me, but on which I have not as yet spoken during this tour of mine. I would like to speak to you on that subject this evening because it was forced on my attention yesterday morning. I want to speak to you upon the sanitation of this place. Your municipality very kindly presented me an address in which you have mentioned some of my activities in which I am interested as a humanitarian, as a reformer. I reckon sanitation also as one of the important things which a humanitarian or a reformer must tackle. Within three or four minutes' walk of the place where you have kindly housed me, I endeavoured unsuspectingly to go out for a walk thinking that it was a beautiful grove by the side of a lovely pond. A rustic bamboo foot-bridge drew my attention to walk over it. I crossed it, turned to the

[1] *Vide* Vol. XIII, pp. 70-1.

right, and walked with my companion but a few paces when you may imagine what I saw. What I saw was a sight too horrible to talk about; and the stench that was coming out of it was suffocating. I saw the water of that pond was being defiled in a disgusting manner, when, at the same time, a woman was filling her pot with that same water. And, in order to get the morning walk, I was obliged to go out for some distance in a motor-car. I felt deeply hurt; I felt as if I was wounded. It recalled to me the sights that I used to see in the principal streets of the Madras city itself in 1915. Surely there is something that is terribly wrong in this state of affairs. The first condition of any municipal life is decent sanitation and an unfailing supply of pure water. Do not for a moment consider that either of these two things require any great outlay of money. Both these things are capable of being secured without your having to spend any money at all, if only you have the will to secure them to the citizens. But it requires a vivid sense of your municipal duties. Membership of a municipal board must not be treated as a place of privilege. No man dare enter a municipality except in the spirit of a scavenger. But what I see so often in the papers is only wrangling over municipal elections and the fight between the Brahmins and the Non-Brahmins arising out of this wrangling. If you will only remember that you are the servants of the people of Mayavaram and not their masters and that you are entrusted with the solemn duty to keep the town in perfect sanitation for the benefit of the people, you will start with a shovel in your hand and set about keeping the water pure and preserving sanitation on the land given to the poor. You have got in your midst so many schools maintained by you; give them a holiday and ask the students of those schools to go about cleaning the streets and also telling the people themselves to keep the streets clean and the water pure. Surely our learning and all the lessons that we receive on sanitation in schools are useless, unless we reduce them to practice in our daily life; and I urge you not to say to yourselves that our people will not listen to these appeals and will not change their habits. The place where I was myself born had terribly impure dungheaps in the streets about fifty years back. But there came to that place an administrator; and, be it said to his credit, he was an Englishman. He removed the dungheaps in a day and there was no protest to his doing so from any of the people. Nor did he use his official authority to impose his imperious will on an unwilling people. But he reasoned with the people, bore down all opposition and carried out his reforms. I have cited this instance before you because I am a determined opponent of this British administration but we have yet got to learn much from the Britisher in the matter of sanitation. I ask you to shake off your lethargy, to take your courage in your hands; and you can easily carry out this reform.

I must now proceed to the very long and well argued address presented to me on behalf of the 'suppressed' society. That address isolates itself from other addresses of the kind, in that it refers not so much to the social disabilities, as it does to the civil disabilities of that community. It casts very serious reflections upon the landlord class. It charges them with having reduced their class to serfdom. It charges the administration with having closed the door against their holding even menial offices. It complains of want of assistance from everybody, except [for] a few isolated instances. It says that, whereas their average income is never more than Rs. 40 a year, their expenses are never less than Rs. 120 per year. It complains that, being rooted to the soil, they have to remain without any occupation at all for a major portion of the year.

I do not know what truth there is in all these allegations. As it is, I can only give these friends of mine the consolation that I will endeavour to verify these statements in their address. Generally speaking, I may assure them of my fullest sympathy and I certainly associate myself with the remark that I notice in their address that they are the first holders of the land in this country.

But there is no cause for the spirit of despair that runs throughout the address. They, in common with the rest, cannot help profiting by the great awakening that has now come over the country. At the present moment, it is true that that awakening has taken a sad turn. In our blindness, we seem to think that each group, each section, each class, each caste should pull its way by itself without the one co-operating with the other. So we are torn by internal dissensions. But these dissensions are only temporary and are bound to die out; and, when the cloud is really lifted and the day dawns, the 'suppressed' classes are bound to partake in the rejoicings that will come in the wake. And in order to partake in the rejoicings at the time of the advent of that dawn, let them understand that, after all, everyone shall have ultimately to depend upon self-help. They have but to become conscious of their own strength which their numbers and their occupation give them; and they will become an irresistible force. Immediately they realize that they are slaves of nobody, and that, after all, without their labour, the lands they are cultivating will become a horrible wilderness, then the day is theirs.

But I would say to the landlord class, that if the allegations made against them in the address are true to any extent, it reflects the greatest discredit upon them. Let them not crush under their feet the shoulders on which they ride. Let them consider these labouring classes, who alone make their barren fields appear smiling with rich crops, let the landlord class consider these labourers as one of their own family and allow them to share in the happiness to which the labours of these people contribute so much. It is wrong, it is sinful to consider our own labourers as 'untouchables'. Let us wipe out this shame.

But I have yet to talk to you of another shame. I saw some friends this afternoon from whose class the *Devadasis* are drawn. I saw some of these sisters also and I engaged them in a very serious conversation. And, as I was talking to them and understanding the hidden meaning of this thing, my whole soul rose against the system in its entirety. In calling them *Devadasis* we insult God Himself under the sacred name of religion; and we commit a double crime in that we use these sisters of ours to serve our lust and take, in the same breath, foul as it is, the name of God. To think that there should be a class of people given to this kind of immoral service and that there is another class of people in this country who perpetuate the continuance of such a system, makes one despair of life itself. And I assure you that, as I was talking to them, there was no evil in their eyes and that they were capable of as fine perceptions and as pure feelings as any other woman in the world. What difference can there be between them and our own blood-sisters ? And if we will not allow our own blood-sisters for such immoral uses, how dare we then use these women for such purposes? Let the Hindus, who are connected in any way with this evil, purge themselves of it. The existence of such an evil in our society saps its foundations. The majority of these sisters, or all of them, have promised me to retrace their steps on certain conditions; and I promised them that I would make it convenient and possible for them to so retrace their steps. God willing, I shall fulfil my promise and let them also do their part. If they cannot fulfil those conditions, I shall blame not them, but the society in which their lot is cast. It is up to you to extend the hand of fellowship to these sisters. It is up to you to see that they are reclaimed from this life of shame. I know that, when again they have to face temptations, it may become a too irresistible force. But, if man will restrain his lust and if society should disapprove of this practice, it is surely possible that they will not go astray.

I thank you for giving me this very patient hearing. I know that you will excuse my straight talk to you this evening. Though, during the period of my stay here I have had every attention bestowed upon me by so many of the kind friends that were by my side, I must own that the two days of my stay here were sad days for me. This *Devadasi* problem which was brought to my notice yesterday and the state of insanitation that I personally observed, caused me intense grief; and in talking to you in the manner in which I did, I endeavoured to lighten my grief by making you share in it. I shall hope that you will share that grief and lighten my burden by following my suggestions.

As is usual at all these meetings, if you will continue to be silent, volunteers will go round to all of you making collections and you may pay them whatever you are willing to pay.

In answer to a question put to him by a member in the meeting at the time the volunteers were going round, Mahatmaji replied:

A friend has asked me, and very legitimately, how these purses that are being received are to be utilized. The usual custom is to utilize the purse collected in any province in that province itself. But, when it is collected in a very rich place as in Bombay, it is usual to spend it in a place where it is most needed. In the largest part of the country, all over India, all the money that is collected goes into the hands of spinners, carders and weavers. No one is called upon to leave his present occupation, if he has one, and to take to spinning or carding or weaving; so, it is only the poorest classes who are being served by the workers. It has not been as yet found possible to distribute the whole of the purses amongst the spinners, carders and weavers alone. The act of organizing the villages for weaving and spinning takes a portion of this money. It is impossible in a poor country like ours to get an army of workers who can afford to devote themselves to this act of organizing, without any remuneration being paid to them. Though we have in this movement scores of volunteers who not only do not get anything but themselves pay something towards this movement, it is not possible to get the 15,000 people, that we are now employing, for nothing. Roughly speaking, I may tell you that anything between twenty to twenty-five per cent of the total expenses is spent in the work of organization alone. The remaining seventy-five to eighty per cent of the money goes directly into the hands of the really famine-stricken poor as wages for the work that they do. And in this manner, throughout the length and breadth of India, 15,000 villages have been thus organized. Over 50,000 spinners all over India are at present getting each between one rupee and a rupee and a half a month[1], whereas, before hand-spinning came, they were getting nothing at all. And, as ten spinners feed one weaver, at least 5,000 weavers are each getting between Rs. 15 and Rs. 20 a month and, side by side with all this, has been resuscitated the old art of printing which had all but died out. And hundreds of printers, dyers, laundrymen and others are earning now an honest livelihood. The object before the All-India Spinners' Association is to reduce the organizing expenses from 25 per cent to somewhere about 15 per cent at least. Let me also inform you that 1,000 to 1,500 men, who are working to organize the villages, are living honest and useful lives; and I repeat what I have said elsewhere that, if khadi becomes universal in India, it opens out a good source of livelihood to thousands of young men who are in want of employment. If it is possible to have achieved what had been done with but 15 or 20 lakhs of rupees, you may realize what will be possible if we get all the 60 crores[2] of rupees that are now being paid for the cloth imported from outside the country.

The Hindu, 15-9-1927

447. LETTER TO MIRABEHN

[*After September 13, 1927*][3]

CHI. MIRA,

I had four letters together yesterday and one I have today. I have so much confidence in Jamnalalji as a man and in Dr. Dalal as a surgeon and physician that I have no anxiety. Absence of wire from you means that no operation has been necessary as yet. You will buy the glasses that may be necessary.

Yes, the 9 o'clock silence[4] is a great thing. It was Kaka's suggestion. I had no hesitation about its adoption.

[1] The source has "day".

[2] The source has "lakhs".

[3] In Mahadev Desai's letter to Mira dated September 12, 1927, he says that Devdas was attending on Subbiah who was ill.

[4] Explaining this Mahadev Desai in his letter dated September 8, 1927 wrote to Mira: "Bapu has decided to go into silence every evening at 9 p.m., so that there may be no engagements and no interviews after that hour. The vow is tentatively for two months after which he will decide if it is to be continued for life. There are two exceptions, illness of self and others and travelling."

Subbiah is still on sick leave though he is now convalescent. He will take about a fortnight before he can rejoin me. Devdas came only today after leaving Subbiah at his father-in-law's.

With love,

BAPU

From the original: C.W. 5276. Courtesy: Mirabehn

448. LETTER TO O. G. VILLARD

AS AT SABARMATI,
September 14, 1927

DEAR FRIEND,

I thank you for your letter and copy of Miss Mayo's book[1]. A friend of hers had already sent me a copy. I have now read it and written for *Young India* a fairly long review. I have asked the publishers to send you a marked copy of *Young India*. In the circumstances, I hope, you do not consider it necessary for me to write anything special. If, however, on reading my review you consider that there is any point requiring elucidation please let me know. I read your review with a great deal of interest.

Yours sincerely,
M. K. GANDHI

OSWALD GARRISON VILLARD, ESQ.
20, VESSEY STREET
NEW YORK

From a photostat: C.W. 9228

449. LETTER TO N. M. KHARE

Wednesday, Bhadarva Vad 3 [September 14, 1927][2]

BHAI PANDITJI,

I got your letter about prayers. Since Kaka has written already I do not write more. There is but one ideal behind our prayers. But we must act according to the limits of our capacity. We should deceive neither the people nor our own selves. If

[1] *Mother India*

[2] From the similarity between the contents of this and the letter dated "Mayavaram, September 13, 1927" from Mahadev Desai to Khare

many do not arrive at 4 o'clock, let us give up our claim that we hold the prayer at that hour, and keep the time that suits all. But once this hour has been fixed, everyone ought to attend. Those who are devoted to the present hour of 4 o'clock should keep up their practice themselves, get up at four and engage themselves in any activity which they choose.

If all the people do not like the *Ramayana*, by all means discontinue it.

Do not think about what I like, but take people's capacity into consideration and introduce whatever changes you wish. Do nothing in haste.

I see no advantage in extending the time for reading the *Gita*. At the most it takes five minutes to read three long chapters. I very much like the 14-day reading programme. But even in this matter, do what is agreeable to all of you.

Blessings from
BAPU

From the Gujarati original: C.W. 252. Courtesy: Lakshmibehn Khare

450. *SPEECH AT KUMBAKONAM*

September 14, 1927

MR. CHAIRMAN AND FRIENDS,

I thank you for all the addresses and purses. Apart from the usual addresses, I see here an address from the Hindi Prachar Office, Kumbakonam. I congratulate you on having a branch of the Hindi Prachar Office of Madras here. Had Hindi been more popular in this part of the country, you could not have me speak in English and translate it into Tamil but to speak in Hindi and translate it. I understand that though a fair sprinkling of students are learning Hindi, it is still to be supported so far as the finances are concerned, from the central office. I think as a matter of fact, in an important centre like this there should be far greater earnestness for the study of Hindi and that the whole of the financial burden should be borne locally. It is now commonly recognized by all lovers of the country that if we are to establish a closer contact between the North and the South, a knowledge of Hindi has to be cultivated, especially among the leaders of the country.

I was pleased and grateful to receive the purse from the students also. They were anxious that I should address them separately. But they gladly relieved me of that responsibility when they realized that it would be a great strain on me to address two meetings separately. I am conscious you are aware that in many places I am obliged to address more than one meeting. I have to do so whenever it becomes inevitable for a variety of reasons. But wherever I can decently avoid these obligations, I do so. And I do so because I am anxious to go through the appointed tour without any breakdown. But though I have not been able to address students separately, let them understand that my heart is always with them. I would like to impress upon the student world the necessity for having pure character. Without a pure character as a foundation, they would not be able to rise to the expectations that have been raised in the nation about the students. All the world over, whether today or in the distant past, the experience is that it is the rising generation that has been able to battle against the entrenched prejudices and superstitions. They are therefore to be found always in the forefront of reforms and the battle for freedom. For the rest, I would advise the students to study the different addresses that I have been giving to them wherever it has been possible during this tour.

To the Municipal and Taluk Board, I would respectfully commend the reply I made yesterday to the Municipal Council at Mayavaram. It was by accident that I happened to draw the attention of the Municipal Council to the terrible insanitation that I witnessed and as a matter of fact the remarks that I passed there are applicable to almost all the municipal councils in this presidency. Nevertheless my remarks do not lose any of their force, because the evil I draw attention to was almost universal. It is high time that municipal councillors understand the responsibility attached to the office. They must not be used as stepping-stones to fame or renown. In the course of having to advise different friends in different parts of India, it has been my painful duty to study the working of the many municipal councils, and I have discovered that much of their time is wasted in mutual recriminations and wranglings. I have noticed that in many municipalities corruption is rampant during election time, whereas every municipal councillor should consider himself a trustee and custodian of public health and public morals. I wish that the municipal councils take to heart the blemishes that I have drawn their attention to and trust that they would make serious endeavour to remove those blemishes. This place is renowned for its holiness and learning. It is not difficult and it is not too much to expect to make this place a model so far as sanitation is concerned.

The mention of the learning that exists in Kumbakonam brings me to a subject on which I want to occupy a few minutes of your time. Unhappily at the present moment our learning—I mean the Sanskrit learning—has become synonymous with superstition. I understand that the very earnest remarks I made before the students in the Pachaiyappa's Hall have given offence to the pundits of this place. They have written to me asking for an appointment. I have sent them the message—I do not know whether it reached them—that though I can ill afford I shall be glad to receive them at 8 o'clock this night. But I would like to appeal with all the earnestness at my command that whatever I said to the students was said after fullest deliberation and I see nothing to alter a single word in that. As a *Sanatani* Hindu, as I call myself to be one, I say with great deliberation that untouchability as we practise today has no warrant in Hinduism and that it is a blot on Hindu society. I say in all humility but with equal firmness that if we, Hindus, do not take care to rid ourselves of this blot, Hinduism itself is in serious danger of being blotted out. A religion whose two great maxims are "*Satyannasti paro dharmah*"[1], "*Ahimsa paramo dharmah*"[2], a religion that is broadbased on fundamental truth and fundamental love, cannot possibly tolerate untouchability because one is born in particular surroundings. I say also with greatest emphasis that there is no warrant in this Hinduism that I have defined to you for child widowhood. Marriage, it is universally acknowledged, gives a status and a change in life. There can be no such thing as a sacred bond on the part of a girl of tender years who is only fit to sit in her mother's or father's lap. And if fathers, who are blind to all affection springing out of parental love, give away their daughters of tender years in marriage, it is not marriage except a stone being married to a man. Therefore I say that there is no such thing as a child widow because there is no such thing as child marriage.[3]

I have no hesitation to repeat the advice that, if there are students who want to be married, they will be performing an act of charity towards the girls of India to seek out child widows

[1] "There is no religion higher than Truth."

[2] "Ahimsa is the highest dharma."

[3] What follows is from *The Hindu*, 16-9-1927.

when they have outgrown their childhood and they will be doing a service to the country if they make up their minds to end child widowhood by refusing child marriage. When a thing is manifestly immoral and repugnant to all reason and all sense of justice, it is wrong to seek shelter under Sanskrit texts of doubtful validity and doubtful authority. Shastras are given to elevate us and light our path towards perfection. Who can possibly offer a moral defence of the painful system of *Devadasis* and of the parent who would consign his daughter to a life of shame and infamy in the name of religion?

I have been told that I am tender when speaking before Christian audiences or Mussalman audiences, whereas I am not at all tender about Hindu religion and Hindu weaknesses. If it is a crime, I plead willingly guilty. About Christianity and Islam I do not claim to know as well as I claim to know Hinduism. Christians and Mussalmans, no matter how open I may be, are likely to misunderstand me but there is no such possibility in Hinduism and I have no fear of being misunderstood by my Hindu people. Therefore courtesy demands that I should be tender before Christian and Mussalman audiences, but it would be totally wrong on my part to be tender in speaking to Hindu audiences about Hinduism and Hindu blemishes. Even as a skilful surgeon knowing his patient and knowing his defects ruthlessly uses his knife to cure the wound, as a reformer, claiming to be saturated at least as well as the tallest among the Hindus, it would be totally wrong if I out of false courtesy and false tenderness do not put emphasis on the defects and weaknesses which are ruining the Hindu society. And I am thankful to be able to say that during a long course of public life I have not been often misunderstood by Hindus or Hindu audiences; but whether I retain the affection of my countrymen or whether I forfeit their affection, the path of duty is absolutely clear before me. Taking all the care that it would be humanly possible for me to take not to give unnecessary offence and not to cause unnecessary displeasure, I must continue to give out what I feel and speak with absolute truth and absolute fairness and so I suggest as humbly as I can to all the learned pundits in this place and to every thinking Hindu, man or woman, to reconsider their views and understand the bearings of untouchability, child-marriages, child widows and *Devadasis* and ask themselves whether there can be any warrant for all these in a religion inspired by *rishis* who went into endless austerities and based their faith upon the teachings of the *Bhagavad Gita*.

I must now come to the spinning-wheel. I am glad that you are, as much as you can, supporting the spinning-wheel. I am glad that there is no difference of opinion about the necessity of the spinning-wheel. You have got in your midst the Saurashtra weavers. Your capacity for khadi service is limitless. But it is not enough that you give me some money when I appear before you. It is not enough that some of you wear khadi on occasions; but it is necessary if you have real fellow-feeling for these starving millions of India, you all throw away your foreign cloth and take to khadi to ward off suffering and poverty. It is equally your duty to see that this curse of drunkenness is removed from this country. If we would but take personal interest in the welfare of our brethren who are given to drink, you should insist upon total prohibition and, to my mind, the day is not far off when India would become dry.

As is usual in all meetings, volunteers will go in your midst and collect contributions from those who desire to contribute. It is usual also to auction all the jewellery and any costly thing that I might receive in the course of my journey and, I propose to auction the ring which I have got now. There was a silver plate which is from my kind host (Mr. Pantulu Aiyer) but unfortunately I have not brought it here.

The Hindu, 15-9-1927 and 16-9-1927

451. DISCUSSION WITH PUNDITS, KUMBAKONAM

September 14, 1927

Several leading pundits of this place had a Conference with Mahatma Gandhi last night. The pundits, it is understood, protested against the recent remarks of Mr. Gandhi about child widows and their marriage and the question of untouchability. They contended Mr. Gandhi's statement that those customs had no sanction in the Hindu Shastras was incorrect and that they could cite authorities.

Mr. Gandhi explained to them that the proper way of upholding Hinduism was not by quoting isolated texts but by acting through the inner voice of conscience. Nothing that was opposed to truth and love could be dharma according to Hindu Shastras. He appealed to them to co-operate with him in his work of conserving Hinduism against the destroying influences of evil customs and not to help the destruction of Hinduism by putting obstacles in the way of reform.

The Bombay Chronicle, 16-9-1927

452. DRAIN INSPECTOR'S REPORT

On the lips of the good vice becomes virtue,

And even virtue appears as vice in the mouth of the evil-minded: this need not surprise us.

For, do not the mighty clouds drink the salt waters of the ocean and return it as sweet refreshing rain,

And does not the cobra, drinking sweet milk, belch it forth as the deadliest poison?

Rivers drink not of their own waters, the trees do not themselves eat the fruit which they bear.

Nor do the clouds partake of the grains they grow; even so the good devote their powers to the good of others.[1]

Several correspondents have sent me cuttings containing reviews of, or protests against, Miss Mayo's *Mother India*. A few have in addition asked me to give my own opinion on it. An enraged correspondent from London asks me to give him answers to several questions that he has framed upon the authoress's references to me. Miss Mayo has herself favoured me with a copy of her book.

I would certainly not have made time, especially when I have only limited energy, and caution has been enjoined upon me by medical friends against overwork, to read the book during my tour. But these letters made it obligatory on me to read the book at once.

The book is cleverly and powerfully written. The carefully chosen quotations give it the appearance of a truthful book. But the impression it leaves on my mind is, that it is the report of a drain inspector sent out with the one purpose of opening and examining the drains of the country to be reported upon, or to give a graphic description of the stench exuded by the opened drains. If Miss Mayo had confessed that she had gone to India merely to open out and examine the drains of India, there would perhaps be little to complain about her compilation. But

[1] गुणायन्ते दोषाः सुजनवदने दुर्जनमुखे
गुणा दोषायन्ते तदिदमपि नो विस्मयपदम् ।
महा मेघः क्षारं पिबति कुरुते वारि मधुरं
फणी क्षीरं पीत्वा वमति गरलं दुःसहतरम् ॥
पिबन्ति नद्यः स्वयमेव नाम्भः स्वयं न खादन्ति फलानि वृक्षाः ।
नादन्ति सस्यं खलु वारिवाहाः परोपकाराय सतां विभूतयः ॥

she says in effect with a certain amount of triumph, "The drains are India". True, in the concluding chapter there is a caution. But her caution is cleverly made to enforce her sweeping condemnation. I feel that no one who has any knowledge of India can possibly accept her terrible accusations against the thought and the life of the people of this unhappy country.

The book is without doubt untruthful, be the facts stated ever so truthful. If I open out and describe with punctilious care all the stench exuded from the drains of London and say "Behold London", my facts will be incapable of challenge, but my judgement will be rightly condemned as a travesty of truth. Miss Mayo's book is nothing better, nothing else.

The authoress says she was dissatisfied with the literature she read about India, and so she came to India "to see what a volunteer unsubsidized, uncommitted and unattached, could observe of common things in daily human life".

After having read the book with great attention, I regret to say that I find it difficult to accept this claim. Unsubsidized she may be. Uncommitted and unattached she certainly fails to show herself in any page. We in India are accustomed to interested publications patronized—"patronized" is accepted as an elegant synonym for "subsidized"—by the Government. We have become used to understanding from pre-British days, that the art (perfected by the British) of government includes the harnessing of the secret services of men learned, and reported to be honest and honourable for shadowing suspects and for writing up the virtues of the Government of the day as if the certificate had come from disinterested quarters. I hope that Miss Mayo will not take offence if she comes under the shadow of such suspicion. It may be some consolation to her to know that even some of the best English friends of India have been so suspected.

But ruling out of consideration the suspicion, it remains to be seen why she has written this untruthful book. It is doubly untruthful. It is untruthful in that she condemns a whole nation or in her words "the peoples of India" (she will not have us as one nation) practically without any reservation as to their sanitation, morals, religion, etc. It is also untruthful because she claims for the British Government merits which cannot be sustained and which many an honest British officer would blush to see the Government credited with.

If she is not subsidized, Miss Mayo is an avowed Indophobe and Anglophil refusing to see anything good about Indians and anything bad about the British and their rule.

She does not give one an elevated idea of Western standard of judgement. Though she represents a class of sensational writers in the West, it is a class that, I flatter myself with the belief, is on the wane. There is a growing body of Americans who hate anything sensational, smart or crooked. But the pity of it is that there are still thousands in the West who delight in 'shilling shockers'. Nor are all the authoress's quotations or isolated facts truthfully stated. I propose to pick up those I have personal knowledge of. The book bristles with quotations torn from their contexts and with extracts which have been authoritatively challenged.

The authoress has violated all sense of propriety by associating the Poet's[1] name with child marriage. The Poet has indeed referred to early marriage as not an undesirable institution. But there is a world of difference between child marriage and early marriage. If she had taken the trouble of making the acquaintance of the free and freedom-loving girls and women of Santiniketan, she would have known the Poet's meaning of early marriage.

She has done me the honour of quoting me frequently in support of her argument. Any person who collects extracts from a reformer's diary, tears them from their context and proceeds to condemn, on the strength of these, the people in whose midst the reformer has worked, would get no hearing from sane and unbiased readers or hearers. But in her hurry to see everything Indian in a bad light, she has not only taken liberty with my writings, but she had not thought it necessary even to verify through me certain things ascribed by her or others to me. In fact she has combined in her own person what we understand in India the judicial and the executive officer. She is both the prosecutor and the judge. She has described the visit to me, and informed her readers that there are always with me two "secretaries" who write down every word I say. I know that this is not a wilful perversion of facts. Nevertheless the statement is not true. I beg to inform her that I have no one near me who has been appointed or is expected to write down every word that I say. I have by me a co-worker called Mahadev Desai who is striving to out-Boswell Boswell and does, whenever he is near me, take down whatever he considers to be wisdom dropping from my lips. I can't repel his advances, even if I would, for the relationship between us is, like the Hindu marriage, indissoluble. But the real crime committed against me is described

[1] Rabindranath Tagore

by her at pages 387-8. She ascribes to the Poet "a fervent declaration that Ayurvedic science surpasses anything that the West can offer" (She has this time no quotation to back her statement.) Then she quotes my opinion that hospitals are institutions for propagating sin, and then distorts out of all recognition a sacred incident, honourable to the British surgeons and, I hope, to myself. I must ask the reader to excuse me for giving the full quotation from the book:

> As he happened to be in the prison at the time, a British surgeon of the Indian Medical Service came straightaway to see him. "Mr. Gandhi," said the surgeon, as the incident was then reported, "I am sorry to tell you that you have appendicitis. If you were my patient, I should operate at once. But you will probably prefer to call in your Ayurvedic physician."
>
> Mr. Gandhi proved otherwise minded.
>
> "I should prefer not to operate," pursued the surgeon, "because in case the outcome should be unfortunate, all your friends will lay it as a charge of malicious intent against us whose duty is to care for you."
>
> "If you will only consent to operate," pleaded Mr. Gandhi, "I will call in my friends, now, and explain to them that you do so at my request."
>
> So Mr. Gandhi wilfully went to an "institution for propagating sin", was operated upon by one of the "worst of all", an officer of the Indian Medical Service and was attentively nursed through convalescence by an English Sister whom he is understood to have thought after all rather a "useful sort of person."

This is a travesty of truth. I shall confine myself to correcting only what is libellous and not the other inaccuracies. There was no question here of calling in any Ayurvedic physician. Colonel Maddock who performed the operation had the right, if he had so chosen, to perform the operation without a reference to me, and even in spite of me. But he and Surgeon-General Hooton showed a delicate consideration to me, and asked me whether I would wait for my own doctors who were known to them and who were also trained in the Western medical and surgical science. I would not be behind-hand in returning their courtesy and consideration, and I immediately told them that they could perform the operation without waiting for my doctors to whom they had telegraphed, and that I would gladly give them a note for their protection in the event of the operation miscarrying. I endeavoured to show that I had no distrust either in their ability or their good faith. It was to me a happy opportunity of demonstrating my personal goodwill.

So far as my opinion about hospitals and the like is concerned, it stands, in spite of my having subjected myself and my wards to treatment more than once by physicians and surgeons, Indian and European, trained in the Western school of medicine. Similarly I use motor-cars and railways, whilst holding to my condemnation of them as strongly as ever. I hold the body itself to be an evil and an impediment in my progress. But I see no inconsistency in my making use of it while it lasts, and trying in the best manner I know to use it for its own destruction. This is a sample of distortion of which I have a personal knowledge.

But the book is brimful of descriptions of incidents of which an average Indian, at any rate, has no knowledge. Thus she describes an ovation said to have been given to the Prince of Wales, of which Indian India has no knowledge, but which could not possibly escape it if it had happened. A crowd is reported to have fought its way to the Prince's car somewhere in Bombay.

> The police tried vainly to form a hedge round the car moving at a crawl unprotected now through a solid mass of shouting humanity which won through to the railway station at last.

Then at the railway station while there were three minutes for the train to steam out, the Prince is reported by Miss Mayo to have ordered the barriers to be dropped and the "mobs" to be let in. The authoress then proceeds:

> Like the sweep of a river in flood, the interminable multitude rolled in, and shouted and laughed and wept, and when the train started, ran alongside the Royal carriage till they could run no more.

All this is supposed to have happened in 1921 on the evening of November 22nd, whilst the dying embers of the riots were still hot. There is much of this kind of stuff in this romantic chapter which is headed "Behold a Light".

The nineteenth chapter is a collection of authorities in praise of the achievements of the British Government, almost every one of which has been repeatedly challenged both by English and Indian writers of unimpeachable integrity. The seventeenth chapter is written to show that we are a "world-menace". If as a result of Miss Mayo's effort the League of Nations is moved to declare India a segregated country unfit for exploitation, I have no doubt both the West and the East would be the gainers. We may then have our internecine wars. Hindus may be eaten up, as she threatens, by the hordes from the North-West and Central Asia—that were a position infinitely superior to one of ever-growing emasculation. Even as electrocution is a humaner method of killing than the torturous method of roasting alive, so would a sudden overwhelming swoop from Central Asia upon the unresisting, insanitary, superstitious and sexuality-ridden Hindus, as Miss Mayo describes us to be, be a humane deliverance from the living and ignominious death which we are going through at the present moment. Unfortunately, however, such is not Miss Mayo's goal. Her case is to perpetuate white domination in India on the plea of India's unfitness to rule herself.

The picturesque statements that this clever authoress puts into the mouths of the various characters read like so many pages from a sensational novel in which no regard has to be paid to truth. Many of her statements seem to me to be utterly unworthy of belief and do not put the men and women to whom they are ascribed in a favourable light. Take for instance this statement put in the mouth of a prince:

> "Our treaties are with the Crown of England," one of them said to me, with incisive calm. "The princes of India made no treaty with a Government that included Bengali *babus*. We shall never deal with this new lot of Jacks-in-office. While Britain stays, Britain will send us English gentlemen to speak for the King Emperor, and all will be as it should be between friends. If Britain leaves, we, the princes will know how to straighten out India, even as princes should." (Page 316)

However fallen Indian princes may be, I should want unimpeachable evidence before I could believe that there can be in India a prince so degraded as to make such a statement. Needless to say the authoress does not give the name of the prince.

A still more scandalous statement occurs on page 314 and reads as follows:

> "His Highness does not believe," said the Dewan, "that Britain is going to leave India. But still, under this new regime in England, they may be so ill-advised. So His Highness is getting his troops in shape, accumulating munitions and coining silver. And if the English do go, three months afterward, not a rupee or a virgin will be left in all Bengal."

The reader is kept in darkness as to the name of His Highness or of the enlightened Dewan.

There are many statements which Miss Mayo puts into the mouths of Englishmen and Englishwomen living in India. All I can say with reference to these statements is that if some of them were really made by the authors, they are unworthy of the trust reposed in them and they have done an injustice to their wards or patients as well as the race to which they belong. I should be sorry indeed to think that there are many Englishmen and Englishwomen who say one thing to their Indian friends and another to their Western confidants. Those Englishmen and Englishwomen who may chance to read the sweepings gathered together by Miss Mayo with her muck-rake will recognize the statements I have in mind. In seeking to see an India degraded, Miss Mayo has unconsciously degraded the characters whom she has used as her instruments for proving her facts which she boasts cannot be "disproved or shaken". I hope I have given sufficient *prima facie* proof in this article to show that many of her facts stand disproved even in isolation. Put together they give a wholly false picture.

But why am I writing this article? Not for the Indian readers but for the many American and English readers who read these pages from week to week with sympathy and attention. I warn them against believing this book. I do not remember having given the message Miss Mayo imputes to me. The only one present who took any notes at all has no recollection of the message imputed to me. But I do know what message I give every American who comes to see me: "Do not believe newspapers and the catchy literature you get in America. But if you want to know anything about India, go to India as students, study India for yourself. If you cannot go, make a study of all that is written about India for her and against her and then form your own conclusions. The ordinary literature you get is either exaggerated vilification of India or exaggerated praise." I warn Americans and Englishmen against copying Miss Mayo. She came not with an open mind as she claims, but with her preconceived notions and prejudices which she betrays on every page, not excluding even the introductory chapter in which she recites the claim. She came to India not to see things with her own eyes, but to gather material three fourths of which she could as well have gathered in America.

That a book like Miss Mayo's can command a large circulation furnishes a sad commentary on Western literature and culture.

I am writing this article also in the hope, be it ever so distant, that Miss Mayo herself may relent and repent of having done, I hope unconsciously, atrocious injustice to an ancient people and equally atrocious injustice to the Americans by having exploited her undoubted ability to prejudice without warrant their minds against India.

The irony of it all is that she has inscribed this book "To the peoples of India". She has certainly not written it as a reformer, and out of love. If I am mistaken in my estimate let her come back to India. Let her subject herself to cross-examination, and if her statements escape unhurt through the fire of cross-examination, let her live in our midst and reform our lives. So much for Miss Mayo and her readers.

I must now come to the other side of the picture. Whilst I consider the book to be unfit to be placed before Americans and Englishmen (for it can do no good to them), it is a book that every Indian can read with some degree of profit. We may repudiate the charge as it has been framed by her, but we may not repudiate the substance underlying the many allegations she has made. It is a good thing to see ourselves as others see us. We need not even examine the motive with which the book is written. A cautious reformer may make some use of it.

There are statements in it which demand investigation. For instance she says that the Vaishnava mark has an obscene meaning. I am a born Vaishnavite. I have perfect recollection of my visits to Vaishnava temples. Mine were orthodox people. I used to have the mark myself as a child, but neither I nor anyone else in our family ever knew that this harmless and rather elegant-looking mark had any obscene significance at all. I asked a party of Vaishnavites in Madras where this article is being written. They knew nothing about the alleged obscene significance. I do not therefore suggest that it never had such significance. But I do suggest that millions are unaware of the obscenity alleged to be behind it. It has remained for our Western visitors to acquaint us with the obscenity of many practices which we have hitherto innocently indulged in. It was in a missionary book that I first learnt that Shivalingam had any obscene significance at all, and even now when I see a Shivalingam neither the shape nor the association in which I see it suggests any obscenity. It was again in a missionary book that I learnt that the temples in Orissa were disfigured with obscene statues. When I went to Puri it was not without an effort that I was able to see those things. But I do know that the thousands who flock to the temple know nothing about the obscenity surrounding these figures. The people are unprepared and the figures do not obtrude themselves upon your gaze.

But let us not resent being made aware of the dark side of the picture wherever it exists. Overdrawn her pictures of our insanitation, child marriages, etc., undoubtedly are. But let them serve as a spur to much greater effort than we have hitherto put forth in order to rid society of all cause of reproach. Whilst we may be thankful for anything good that foreign visitors may be able honestly to say of us, if we curb our anger, we shall learn, as I have certainly learnt, more from our critics than from our patrons. Our indignation which we are bound to express against the slanderous book must not blind us to our obvious imperfections and our great limitations. Our anger will leave Miss Mayo absolutely unhurt and it will only recoil upon ourselves. We too have our due share of thoughtless readers as the West has, and in seeking to disprove everything Miss Mayo has written, we shall make the reading public believe that we are a race of perfect human beings against whom nothing can be said, no one can dare say one word. The agitation that has been set up against the book is in danger of being overdone. There is no cause for fury. I would here close this review which I have undertaken with the greatest reluctance and under great pressure of work with a paraphrase of a beautiful couplet from Tulsidas:

> Everything created by God, animate or inanimate, has its good and bad side. The wise man, like the fabled bird which separating the cream of milk from its water helps himself to the cream leaving the water alone, will take the good from everything leaving the bad alone.[1]

Young India, 15-9-1927

453. SPEECH AT VALANGAIMAN

September 15, 1927

MR. CHAIRMAN AND FRIENDS,

I thank you for the address and the purse. It is a matter of very great joy to find that this is the birth place of Mr. Srinivasa Sastri. As you very properly say, he is one of the greatest sons of India. I have been asked to announce to you that the library is to be opened very shortly. I have been asked also formally to declare that library open from this place. I do so with the greatest pleasure. And I hope that all the old and young men will contemplate that noble life and try as much as is possible for every one of you to follow him in his lofty patriotism, sense of duty

1 जडचेतन गुणदोषमय विश्व कीन्ह करतार
संत हंस गुण गहहिं पय परिहरि वारि विकार ।

and in his untiring zeal. Service to the cause of the country is his motto. May you also learn to be true servants of the country.

I observe that there is a fair Muslim population here. I hope that you have always peaceful relations amongst yourselves. We Hindus and Mussalmans must learn to love one another, because we are all children of the same mother.

I am glad that you all believe in khadi. You must go a step further and translate it into action. All of you should wear it. You see the old lady (sitting by his righthand side) spinning before you. There are thousands and thousands of old ladies much poorer than the one before you, who can eke out a living if all of us will wear khaddar. I thank you once more for your address.

The Hindu, 16-9-1927

454. SPEECH AT NATIONAL HIGH SCHOOL, MANNARGUDI

September 15, 1927

PRINCIPAL, BOYS AND GIRLS,

I thank you for giving me this address as also this purse. Since you told me that you impart instruction in this school in Hindu religion, I would like all the boys and girls to signify by raising their hands how many know the *Bhagavad Gita*. No hands should be raised deceitfully. How many of those who have raised their hands understand the *Bhagavad Gita* in the original properly. (Only one raised his hand.) Now you have answered me honestly and I congratulate you upon it. The first step to knowledge is an open confession of one's ignorance. Having therefore congratulated you upon your open confession, let me also express my grief to you that so few of you have read the *Bhagavad Gita* and fewer still understand the meaning of it in the original. In my own opinion the Hindu boys and girls must commence with the reading of the *Bhagavad Gita* and therefore in a place where I am told that Hindu religion is taught, I should expect all hands to be raised in answer to the question that I had put. I can only hope that you will soon make up this defect. The South is better known more than any other part of India for the use of abundant *vibhuti* or *chandan*. And I see all of you either profusely smeared with *vibhuti* or having perfect geometrical *tilakam* on your foreheads with *chandan*. Whilst these marks may do much good up to a certain extent, without a proper backing behind these marks they are worthless. So far as I am aware, they do not, as they did when they were originally invented, express the inner life. At the present moment it seems that the mere crust in the shape of these marks remains and the real kernel, the substance, has dried up. If you read the *Bhagavad Gita* and pronounce it with exquisite correctness and answer all the questions of grammar also correctly I should not be satisfied with that performance. When I told you that you should read the *Bhagavad Gita*, I meant also that you should translate its teachings in your own individual lives. The divine author of the *Bhagavad Gita* is said to claim it as the substance, the essence of all the Upanishads and of all knowledge and you will find in the *Gita*, a beautiful verse which really means that a man who simply conforms to the outward form and misses the inner is an impostor, a hypocrite and humbug. I therefore ask the boys, I would urge the Principal and the teachers of this school also, to see to it that the inner secret, the essence of Hinduism is expressed in its fullness in this school and if you will read the *Bhagavad Gita* with the eye of devotion and an eye of faith you will discover as I have discovered that there is no room for Hindu-Muslim dissensions or Brahmin and Non-Brahmin dissensions. You will find also in the *Bhagavad Gita*, no warrant whatsoever for untouchability, child marriages, child widows, prostitution in the name of religion, as is practised by our own sisters and daughters who go by the name of *Devadasis*. If you will carefully read the third chapter of the *Gita* you will find also abundant testimony in favour of the spinning-wheel. If the parents and teachers will only make diligent researches they will not allow so many boys and girls, I see before me, dressed in foreign cloth. If you will take care to study the *Bhagavad Gita* in the manner I have suggested, you will find easy solution for many ills of life. I shall be glad to learn from the Principal in future that you have adopted my suggestion and that every boy and girl not only could read and understand *Bhagavad Gita* but is trying his or her best to live up to its message.

The Hindu, 16-9-1927

455. SPEECH AT FINDLAY COLLEGE, MANNARGUDI[1]

September 15, 1927

You state in your address that you read the Gospels daily even as I do. I cannot say that I read the Gospels daily, but I can say that I have read the Gospels in a humble and prayerful spirit, and it is well with you if you are also reading the Gospels in that spirit. But I expect that the vast majority of you are Hindu boys. I wish that you could have said to me that at least your Hindu boys were reading the *Bhagavad Gita* daily to derive inspiration. For I believe that all the great religions of the world are true more or less. I say "more or less" because I believe that everything that the human hand touches, by reason of the very fact that human beings are imperfect, becomes imperfect. Perfection is the exclusive attribute of God and it is indescribable, untranslatable. I do believe that it is possible for every human being to become perfect even as God is perfect. It is necessary for us all to aspire after perfection, but when that blessed state is attained, it becomes indescribable, indefinable. And I therefore admit, in all humility, that even the Vedas, the Koran and the Bible are the imperfect word of God, and imperfect beings that we are, swayed to and fro by a multitude of passions, it is impossible for us even to understand this word of God in its fullness, and so I say to a Hindu boy, that he must not uproot the traditions in which he has been brought up, as I say to a Mussalman or a Christian boy that he must not uproot his traditions. And so whilst I would welcome your learning the Gospel and your learning the Koran, I would certainly insist on all of you Hindu boys, if I had the power of insistence, learning the *Gita*. It is my belief that the impurity that we see about boys in schools, the carelessness about things that matter in life, the levity with which the student world deals with the greatest and most fundamental questions of life is due to this uprooting of tradition from which boys have hitherto derived their sustenance.

But I must not be misunderstood. I do not hold that everything ancient is good because it is ancient, I do not advocate surrender of God-given reasoning faculty in the face of ancient tradition. Any tradition, however ancient, if inconsistent with

[1] This was published under the caption "Three Speeches".

morality, is fit to be banished from the land. Untouchability may be considered to be an ancient tradition, the institution of child widowhood and child marriage may be considered to be ancient tradition, and even so many an ancient horrible belief and superstitious practice. I would sweep them out of existence if I had the power. When, therefore, I talk of respecting the ancient tradition, you now understand what I mean, and it is because I see the same God in the *Bhagavad Gita* as I see in the Bible and the Koran that I say to the Hindu boys that they will derive greater inspiration from the *Bhagavad Gita* because they will be tuned to the *Gita* more than to any other book.

Young India, 22-9-1927

456. SPEECH AT PUBLIC MEETING, MANNARGUDI

September 15, 1927

MR. CHAIRMAN AND FRIENDS,

I thank you for your several addresses and purses on behalf of the *Daridranarayana*. I congratulate the Taluk Board on having given me an advance copy of the translation of its address in Hindi. I am looking forward to the time when everywhere I should be able to make myself understood through Hindi which is or should be the common language throughout India. At the present moment, as you know, there is almost a barrier between the North and the South. Public workers coming from the South find themselves at sea when they are face to face to speak in the North. I do not by any means suggest that Hindi should take the place of vernaculars but I do suggest that all public workers, leaders of public opinion, should know Hindi and should be able to express themselves wherever they go in the Hindi language. You all know that a committee from the North began its operation some six or seven years ago with a view to popularize Hindi in the South. Nearly one lakh of rupees have been spent by this committee, in order to teach Hindi to those who would learn it. The central office at Madras has received from the head office in Prayag the charter of self-government and it is now open to the leaders of public opinion, in the South, to extend the operation of this committee and make it self-supporting.

You have in all your addresses endorsed the work of the spinning-wheel and khadi that is being done throughout India. I had known long ago that Mannargudi was famous for its weaving and I should hope that in the near future there would be no weaver in Mannargudi who is not weaving hand-spun yarn. But the weavers cannot have enough well hand-spun yarn unless you go out in the villages and give work to so many who have so much idle time at their command from year to year. I saw this afternoon a band of workers living about 10 miles from Mannargudi, in a village called Palayur, where they are trying to introduce the spinning-wheel in the village and places surrounding it. They tell me that if they can secure sufficient workers, there is great scope in these villages for the introduction of the spinning-wheel. The remarkable address that I received at Mayavaram, on behalf of the peasantry in that taluk, told me that the villagers and the peasantry had nearly six months during the year when they had no work to do. The address further gives a startling information that the income of the peasantry in this rich district of Tanjore was no more than forty rupees, whereas the expenses were at 120. Making due allowance for exaggeration in this statement, if there is an exaggeration, there is no doubt whatsoever that the peasantry is living from hand to mouth and is in need of supplementary occupation.

The same address proceeded to inform me that the vast masses of toiling millions were considered to be untouchables. And as such they were unworthy of the attention by the middle class people. In order to prevent this atrocious state of affairs, I ventured to present India with the spinning-wheel and khadi. We, the middle class people, take no interest in them, we do not care what happened to their spinning-wheel and what happened to their industry. And so by our criminal indifference we allowed that industry to die an unnatural death. I ask you to approach the spinning-wheel with a new point of view. I also ask you to utilize khadi in order to form an indissoluble bond between the peasantry and ourselves and I am aware that we shall not succeed in our endeavours so long as we consider these toiling millions as untouchables. I had the pleasure, not unmixed with pain, of listening to some of our learned Pundits, expounding the philosophy of untouchability, but I am happy to be able to say that these Pundits were open to conviction and open to arguments on behalf of these people.[1] Instead of brushing aside my arguments summarily, they were pleased to listen and grant that so far as the well-being of the people was concerned, the argument was all in my favour. If that much is admitted by all the Pundits of India,

[1] *Vide* "Discussion with Pundits, Kumbakonam", 14-9-1927.

I should be indifferent to what interpretation they placed upon the Shastras. As a matter of fact for a layman like myself, it is quite enough for me to know that what is consistent with the highest good is the supreme Shastra and I should have no hesitation whatsoever in rejecting the Shastras which were inconsistent with our goal.

In connection with this I must mention the cause of the child widows. Let us not resort to mere arguments and babbling in the act of doing this simple justice to our little daughters. Let us be manly enough to regard every such child marriage as a nullity. So long as we allow a single child widow to remain unmarried when she reaches her proper age, we fail in our elementary duty to humanity. That really leads us naturally to a consideration of child marriages. . . .

You will see that immediately you begin to think of these toiling millions of India and establish a loving bond between them and yourselves, it would be impossible for you to forget the drinkers. We the middle class people have been indifferent to those who are given to this cursed habit. In my humble opinion it is our duty to go out in the midst of these people and try to redeem them from their ways. But I know how difficult it is for those brethren of ours to resist that temptation so long as there are toddy shops. It is therefore our bounden duty to secure total prohibition.

As is usual at all such meetings at the end of the proceedings volunteers go out with collection bags in order to collect contribution from those who have not contributed for the purses. Pies willingly given are just as welcome. This is essentially a matter of service of the poorest in the land. Every man or woman who is desirous to give should consider it his or her duty and privilege to be able to give to this cause. You may know, in answer to a question at Mayavaram, I explained[1] the full working of the organization under which the spinning-wheel work is being carried on. I wish that you would take a lively interest in the progress of this organization and its administration and understand the disposal of the money that is entrusted to it. But I may inform you that over fifty thousand sisters are being served today in at least fifteen hundred villages, throughout the length and breadth of India. Of this the largest number is being served in the South. Nearly 20 lakhs of rupees have been invested in carrying on this organization and nearly 1,500 workers

[1] *Vide* "Speech at Mayavaram", 13-9-1927.

are carrying on this organization. The whole of the finance part of it is audited at the centre and in the province. I invite all those who are interested in this to study its working in all its many branches. It is for this service that I invite everybody in this land to give the best of his or her subscription.

The Hindu, 17-9-1927

APPENDICES

APPENDIX I

GANDHIJI AT THE IMPERIAL DAIRY, BANGALORE

. . . On being told that there are many dairies in Bangalore, Gandhiji has been visiting one of them, the Imperial Dairy, for some days, trying to understand every little detail of its working, inspecting the cattle, eliciting information about their yield, the expenses of their upkeep, the nutrition given to them, the treatment and annual value of their manure, etc., etc. All this he thinks he must do in order to do justice to his office as President of the All-India Cow Protection Association.[1]

. . . The short course of "lessons" that Gandhiji had in the Imperial Dairy, thanks to the courtesy of Mr. Smith, was made interesting as much by the readiness of those in charge to give Gandhiji the best they could, as by the presence of Pandit Malaviyaji during a couple of visits. After giving a couple of days to the dairy processes, Gandhiji was shown the different cattle which are under the close observation of the expert, who measures every ounce of the nutrition that goes into their bodies, and every ounce of their droppings, to arrive at conclusions about the digestibility of different foods, their milking results, and so on. Mr. Smith himself explained the most important and the most simple method of storing grass and fodder in silos. "It is going to solve the question of fodder for cattle," he said. "It is most important and yet so simple, and because it is simple, people do not see its value." The different concrete and pit silos were shown, Mr. Smith going into minute detail and trying to show how, with a little carefulness, and irrespective of weather, the agriculturist can provide for his cattle against times of scarcity. The interest with which he showed us his cows, and gave the history of some of them, spoke eloquently of his love for the cow. "I was born and bred among them," said the good Scotchman with pardonable pride. "My father was a farmer and for twenty years examiner of students going in for the Dairy Diploma, and my mother attended to our home dairy herself. Let every agriculturist in India realize the value of cattle-breeding and cattle protection. Let us not export a single article of food for the cattle"—he might have added the cattle also—"and let us realize that the increased milking capacity of the cows does not affect the quality of the draught animals. On the contrary, put a number of bullocks before me, and I will show that the best of them are the progeny of the cows which have been your best milkers."

[1] From Mahadev Desai's "Weekly Letter" (23-6-1927); what follows is from his "Weekly Letter" (30-6-1927).

On the last day Mr. Smith expressed his desire to have a photograph[1] of Pandit Malaviyaji and Gandhiji with their best cow "Jill", an Ayrshire and Montgomery crossbreed which has calved sixteen times, and given all these years an average yield of 10,000 lbs. of milk. She is naturally the pet of the Dairy. "She was born here, I was present at her birth," said Mr. Smith, "and have watched her growth all these years. We have all kind of cattle diseases here, but Jill has never had one."

Young India, 23-6-1927 and 30-6-1927

APPENDIX II

TELEGRAM FROM MOTILAL NEHRU

ALLAHABAD,
August 23, 1927

MAHATMA GANDHI
BANGALORE

ANSARI PUBLISHED SLIGHTLY MODIFIED BUT EQUALLY OBJECTIONABLE STATEMENT DESPITE YOUR LETTER MY VERBAL AND WRITTEN ENTREATIES STOP ON ARRIVAL SIMLA FOUND OFFICIALS MODERATES RESPONSIVISTS JUBILANT SRINIVASA CHUCKLING WEAKER MEMBERS PARTY WAVERING STRONGER MEMBERS INDIGNANT BUT ALL THINKING ANSARI'S STATEMENT APPROVED BY YOU AND ME STOP HAVE CONSEQUENTLY ISSUED MILDEST POSSIBLE STATEMENT POINTING OUT SUICIDAL CHARACTER ANSARI'S STATEMENT AND APPEALING HIM FOLLOW YOUR ADVICE STOP RETURNING HERE FOUND SAME MISAPPREHENSION AND FEELING. SOME USEFUL SELFOPINIONATED CONGRESSMEN LIKE SHIVAPRASAD GUPTA THINK RESIGNING CONGRESS STOP ASSEMBLY MEMBERS CONGRESS PARTY REPRESENTING ALL PROVINCES WERE DRAFTING MANIFESTO AGAINST ANSARI'S ELECTION WHEN I LEFT STOP GENERAL DEMAND FOR JAWAHARLAL AS ONLY POSSIBLE ALTERNATIVE DESPITE MY PERSUASIONS TO CONTRARY STOP MY STATEMENT WILL DISPEL MISAPPREHENSION ABOUT OUR APPROVAL AND LIKELY PROVOKE UNDESIRABLE CONTROVERSY STOP CONSIDER BEST POSSIBLE COURSE FOR ANSARI TO RETIRE AND INVITE FRESH ELECTIONS STOP GOING LUCKNOW FOR TWO DAYS ADDRESS CHIEF COURT RETURNING HERE TWENTYFIFTH LEAVING FOR BOMBAY TWENTYEIGHTH SAILING THIRTYFIRST WIRE YOUR OPINION AND ACTION YOU PROPOSE IF ANY.

MOTILAL NEHRU

From a photostat: S.N. 12873

[1] *Vide* frontispiece.

SOURCES

Bapuna Patro—Kusumbehn Desaine (Gujarati): Published by Navajivan Publishing House, Ahmedabad.

Bapu, Maine Kya Dekha, Kya Samjha (Hindi): Ed. by Ram Narayan Choudhary, Navajivan Publishing House, Ahmedabad.

(*The*) *Bombay Chronicle:* English daily published from Bombay.

GANDHI SMARAK SANGRAHALAYA, NEW DELHI: Central Museum and Library of Gandhian literature and documents; *vide* Vol. I, p. 349 (first edition) and p. 341 (second revised edition).

Hindi Navajivan: Hindi weekly edited by Gandhiji and published from Ahmedabad.

(*The*) *Hindu*: English daily published from Madras.

(THE) MANUSCRIPT OF MAHADEV DESAI'S DIARY: Kept in Swarajya Ashram, Bardoli.

Navajivan: Gujarati weekly edited by Gandhiji and published from Ahmedabad.

Sabarmati (Gujarati): Manuscript magazine of the National School at Sabarmati Ashram, Ahmedabad.

SABARMATI SANGRAHALAYA: Library and records containing documents relating to Gandhiji's South African period and Indian period up to 1933, *vide* Vol. I, p. 349 (first edition) and p. 341 (second revised edition).

(*The*) *Tribune*: English daily published from Ambala.

Young India: English weekly edited by Gandhiji and published from Ahmedabad.

CHRONOLOGY

(*June 16, 1927—September 15, 1927*)

June 16: In Bangalore, where Gandhiji continued to stay till the end of August

June 19: In *Navajivan* article, "Quarrelling in the Name of Religion", wrote: "I do not distinguish between Hindus and Jains. I can establish the unity of Hinduism, that is, the Vedic doctrine, with Jainism, with the help of *syadvada* itself."

June 25: In letter to Sarojini Naidu emphasized that there was no other man than Dr. Ansari who could be the Congress President in 1927 to pilot a Hindu-Muslim pact through the Congress.

June 27: The Bills dealing with the Indo-South African Agreement passed the final reading.

July 3: In Bangalore, Gandhiji spoke after opening the Khadi Exhibition.

July 8: Spoke to *Adi Karnataka* boys.
Spoke at a prize-distribution ceremony in the Khadi Exhibition in Bangalore.

July 9: In Mysore, spoke at Amateur Dramatic Association.

July 10: In Bangalore, spoke at All-Karnataka Hindi Conference.

July 12: Spoke at Indian Institute of Science.

July 13: Spoke at Mahila Samaj.

July 14: At Tumkur, spoke in reply to Municipal address; visited the Panchama Boarding School; spoke at Prani Daya Sangha.

July 15: At Maddagiri, spoke at public meeting.

July 17: In Bangalore, spoke in reply to Municipal address; addressed labourers' meeting.

July 19: In Mysore, spoke to students.

July 20: Spoke at Hindi Bhasha Seva Samaj.
Spoke in reply to welcome address by the Mysore City Municipal Council and others.

July 21: Spoke to *Adi Karnatakas*.

July 23: Spoke at farewell meeting.

July 24: In Bangalore, spoke at Civic and Social Progress Association.

July 26: Spoke at United Theological College and at Mythic Society.

July 29: Had a discussion with Christian missionaries.

July 30: Spoke at Chamarajendra Sanskrit Pathashala.

August 2: At Arsikere Junction spoke to Lambanis.

August 3: In Hassan, spoke at Town Hall.

August 4: In Bangalore, issued an appeal for funds for Gujarat flood relief.

August 7: In Bangalore, spoke at the Gubbi Theatre.

August 11: At Davengere addressed a meeting of women; also a public meeting.

August 12: Spoke to *Adi Karnatakas*.

August 13: Arrived at Shimoga, addressed a meeting of women; spoke at Harihar.

August 14: At Shimoga, addressed a public meeting.

August 16: Reached Sagar; in the evening addressed a meeting of women.

August 17: At Tirthahalli, spoke at a public meeting.
Left Shimoga for Bhadravati.

August 18: At Bhadravati, addressed the workmen and officers of the Iron Works.
Left for Chikmagalur in the evening.

August 19: At Chikmagalur, addressed a public meeting.
Issued an appeal to Tamil Nadu regarding orderly arrangement of his tour.

August 20: Reached Belur, addressed a public meeting in front of the Belur Temple.
At Arsikere, addressed a public meeting.

August 21: In Tiptur, addressed a meeting at Veerasaivananda Ashram.

August 23: In Bangalore.

August 24: Commenced the first stage of Tamil Nadu tour. Visited Hosur.
In Krishnagiri, spoke at a meeting.

August 28: In Bangalore; addressed five meetings.

August 29: Interview to the Associated Press.

August 30: At Vellore, spoke at Voorhee's College.

September 1: At Gudiatham.

September 2: Spoke at Arni.
Also spoke at Arcot.

September 3: Arrived in Madras; spoke at Provincial Boy Scouts' Association; laid the foundation-stone for the new premises of the Madras and Southern Maharatta Railway Employees' Union.
At Peravallur, spoke at labourers' meeting.
In Madras, spoke to students.

September 4: Spoke at Y.M.C.A.; addressed a public meeting; spoke on the *Gita*.

September 6: Delivered speech at Hindi Prachar Sabha.
Discussion with Neill Statue volunteers.

September 7: Concluded discussion with Neill Statue volunteers.
Addressed meetings at Pachaiyappa's College and Royapuram.

September 8: At Conjeevaram, spoke at a meeting.
In Madras, spoke to Arundhatiyas at Perambur; spoke to Gujaratis and Marwaris.

September 9: Spoke at a meeting of women; delivered address on C. R. Das; spoke at St. Thomas Mount; interview to *The Hindu*.

September 10: Reached Cuddalore; spoke at Y.M.C.A.; addressed a public meeting.

September 11: At Chidambaram; spoke to *Adi Dravidas*; addressed a public meeting.

September 12: In Mayavaram.

September 13: Spoke at a public meeting.

September 14: Reached Kumbakonam; addressed a meeting.
Had discussion with Pundits.

September 15: At Valangaiman, addressed a meeting.
Reached Mannargudi; spoke at National High School; delivered speech at Findlay College; spoke at a public meeting.
In *Young India* article "Drain Inspector's Report", commented on Catherine Mayo's *Mother India*.

INDEX OF TITLES

INDEX

ADDENDA

I

Page 33, item 28, Letter to Manilal and Sushila Gandhi, add at the end:

[PS.]

I am quite well. By the time this reaches you, I shall have already resumed my tour.

II

Page 435, *item 396, line 3, "do your point", add footnote:

Evidently a slip for "prove your point".

ERRATA

PAGE		FOR	READ
70	* Item 67, date-line	June 28, 1977	June 28, 1927
104	* Line 9	villagers	villages
145	* Item 123, line 13	For	Nor
256	* Item 226, line 1	Tehekov	Tchekov
511	* Lines 14 & 13 from bottom	Non-Brahmin	Non-Brahmins

* Due correction made.